John Dewan's Plus/Minus System is the best statistical system I've ever seen for evaluating the defensive abilities of Major League Baseball players.

—Hal Richman, owner, Strat-O-Matic Game Company

The Fielding Bible

The Fielding Bible

John Dewan

Baseball Info Solutions

www.baseballinfosolutions.com

Published by ACTA Sports

A Division of ACTA Publications

www.actasports.com

Cover by Tom A. Wright

Cover Photo by Scott Jordan Levy

First Edition: February 2006

Published by:
ACTA Sports, a division of ACTA Publications
5559 W. Howard Street, Skokie, IL 60077
(800) 397-2282
www.actasports.com www.actapublications.com

ISBN-10: 0-87946-297-3
ISBN-13: 978-0-87946-297-0

Printed in the United States of America

For my wonderful and patient family:
my wife Sue, my son Jason and my daughter Erica.
And Cassie too.

Acknowledgements

Funny. It wasn't even my idea to do this book. Bill James suggested I do it. I don't know whether to blame him or thank him! The amount of time it took to get this thing done was incredible, more than I ever imagined. It felt like the early days at STATS, Inc. when my wife Sue and I worked every minute that we weren't sleeping or eating, seven days a week.

Bill not only suggested doing the book. He jumped in headfirst himself. You'll see his writing contributions all over the book, but more than that, we worked closely together on every aspect. What a pleasure it was to spend time with Bill on this effort. Bill has been my friend and business partner for years, but he has also provided a ton of inspiration for me and continues to do so, as he does for so many others. The first day I read his *Baseball Abstract*, I couldn't believe it. He was doing analysis of baseball in much the same way I was doing analysis of insurance as an actuary. As much as I loved being an actuary, baseball numbers are much more fun than insurance numbers.

Pat Quinn is sitting here right next to me as I write this. He's wrapping up our last-minute edits on the book. That's how it's been all along. The man does absolutely everything. He programs, he analyzes, he edits, he proofs, he suggests ideas, he typesets, etc. His baseball knowledge was invaluable to me as we worked together. He's been a true partner every step of the way in putting this book together. And a true friend.

Without Steve Moyer, *The Fielding Bible* doesn't exist. Baseball Info Solutions was his brainchild, and I am so glad he approached me to work together with him setting up the company. The data they put together on baseball is absolutely incredible. Only BIS has the precision in its hit location data that makes the analysis in this book possible. Steve's personal touch is all over this book.

The opportunity to get back into the publishing business came from another person who became a business partner, Greg Pierce. Greg runs ACTA Publications with such enthusiasm, expertise, and ethics. His excellence shows through in every book ACTA turns out, including this one.

One of the roots of my interest in baseball traces back to a board game called Strat-O-Matic baseball, invented by Hal Richman. I started playing Strat-O-Matic almost 40 years ago. Over the years I've come to know Hal Richman. How fortunate I am. It's not often that the first words you use to describe a successful businessman is "a good, kind man," but those are the best words to describe Hal. But there's another part of Hal that really helped me with this book and that's his incredible knowledge of the defensive abilities of major league baseball players. Hal and Len Schwartz, also from Strat-O-Matic, were invaluable as a resource in doing this book.

Dave Studenmund from The Hardball Times (www.hardballtimes.com) also provided invaluable editing assistance for this book.

Damon Lichtenwalner, the resident computer genius at Baseball Info Solutions, was awesome throughout the process. Nate Birtwell, also from BIS, provided a ton of tremendous insights. My gratitude to Andy Bausher, Matt Lorenzo, Todd Radcliffe, Jim Swavely, and Jon Vrecsics as well.

Andrew Yankech from ACTA Publications provided excellent assistance on every aspect of publishing a book. Charles Fiore from ACTA came through in the clutch as well. Thanks also to Mary, Tom, Donna and Jamie at ACTA.

David Pinto, Mike Canter, Bob Meyerhoff, Barry Kaplan, Mike Kopf, David Creamer, George Lowe, Stacey Izard—thanks for your help! David Pinto has his own excellent fielding analysis system which can be found at his website/blog, www.baseballmusings.com. Cindy, Chelsea, Yuiko, Susie, Reuben, Isaac, Rachel. Thank you!

Table of Contents

Introduction

Hi; this is John Dewan.

Actually, it isn't; this is Bill James, hiding behind John Dewan's laptop. John is hovering over my left shoulder as I write, albeit figuratively.

Welcome to John Dewan's *Fielding Bible*. John and I have been friends, business partners and co-workers for more than 20 years now, 18 ½ of which we have spent arguing about defensive statistics. Not really; we've had a couple of good arguments on the subject; what I mean is not that we have argued constantly but that we have never really seen things the same way.

Fielding statistics in baseball, as you probably know, are kind of a mess. Batting statistics in baseball, on the most superficial level, point large red arrows at the best hitters, and allow you easily to identify the weakest. "Look at this man," they shout, "He had 200 hits! This guy over here drove in 125 runs! This is the batting *champion,* this fellow here. That guy. . .he's a .240 hitter. Don't worry about him." With a more sophisticated analysis, we are able to pin down with a fair degree of precision a common consensus about who the best hitters really are, about how many runs each hitter produces, and about what the impact of that is on the player's team.

When it comes to fielding statistics, a superficial look is nearly useless, and even a sophisticated analysis is not spectacularly reliable. There is no *real* consensus about any of the following issues:

1) Who is the best defensive shortstop in baseball today?

2) How many plays per year does a good shortstop make that an average shortstop would not make?

3) How many runs per year can a good defensive shortstop save for his team?

4) What is the most important defensive statistic for a shortstop?

5) Combining offense and defense, who is more valuable to his team: Edgar Renteria, Orlando Cabrera, Carlos Guillen, David Eckstein or Julio Lugo?

6) Is Derek Jeter a good defensive shortstop?

Basic questions, and we have methods to answer these questions, but the different methods get different answers, and there is no consensus about which methods work best. Different table games rate fielders dramatically different—exactly as if some table game ranked Michael Tucker as a better hitter than Albert Pujols, and nobody would sneer because nobody knew for sure what the right answer was.

None of this is for lack of effort. In my 30-year career in sabermetrics, I have spent far, far, far more hours studying fielding than I have spent studying hitting or pitching. I just don't have as much to show for it. John Dewan has invested countless work weeks studying fielding; and other professionals have as well. A lot of work has been done. We just don't have as much to show for the work as we would like.

I think I can explain, from a historical and theoretical perspective, why we are in this sorry state, and maybe I'll put more time into that later. But for now, just let me note this: that if you look at the "official" fielding statistics of baseball over the course of 130 years, you will note that they're the same at one end of baseball history as they are at the other. This isn't true of pitching or hitting. With hitting stats, over the course of the years we have added Strikeouts, Walks, Runs Batted In, Stolen Bases, Caught Stealing, Grounded Into Double Play, Sacrifice Flies and On-Base Percentage—to the *official* stats, as well as the hundreds of things which have been done unofficially. With pitching stats, over the years we have added Batters Faced, ERA, Hit Batsmen, Home Runs Allowed, Saves, Wild Pitches and other things.

But with Fielding Stats, we started out in 1876 with Games, Putouts, Assists, Errors and Fielding Percentage, and after 130 years we have Games, Putouts, Assists, Errors and Fielding Percentage. OK, they added Double Plays, and maybe the official stats now are keeping track of Stolen Bases Allowed/Runners Caught Stealing, but essentially, the official defensive records are the same now as they have always been.

Batting stats create a complex and subtle image of a player's skills—a portrait of his skills. When something is missing from the portrait, we tend to say, "Oh, we're not counting Grounding Into Double Plays" in exactly the same way we would say, in looking at a portrait of Aunt Lena and Uncle Charlie, "Oh, you left off his eyebrows," or "Why didn't you paint that big wart on her chin?" But fielding stats fail this entry-level test: they do not create an image of the player's skills. When we look at them we don't "see" anything, instinctively, so no consensus emerges about what needs to be added to make the picture more complete.

Fielding statistics, in short, are a failure—and despite our great efforts, we have done embarrassingly little to correct this. John and I have been in the business of collecting and disseminating information about sports for many years now, and, in all honesty, we could have and should have done much more than we have to improve the fielding record. We have not done so, in part, because we tend to see the issue very differently from one another; John doesn't much like my fielding metrics, and I don't much like his. There are a lot of things that we think alike about, and so it has always been easier to work on those things than to sort out the give and take of our divergent opinions about defensive statistics.

Well, there I lied to you again; it is not *really* true that John doesn't like my defensive stats, and I don't like his; it is only *relatively* true. That lack of consensus again. Fifteen, twenty years ago John invented zone ratings. I spent seven years trying to tell him what was wrong with them. I was right about some things; he was right about some things. We move on.

The purpose of this book—which is basically John's book, but I'm helping out—the purpose of this book is to address this deficiency. What we want to do here is not to look at fielding records in John's way or in my way, not in one way or in two ways, but in a wide variety of different ways. We want to create a book which will give fielding statistics what they have not had for 130 years: momentum.

How do you do that? Well, first, we want to put on record specific facts about defensive performance. Lots of specific facts—as many specific facts as possible. Defensive innings, for example, and the number of balls that go up the middle for a single against the Los Angeles/Disneyland Angels, as opposed to the number that go up the middle against the Atlanta Braves, and how many times Raul Ibanez threw to the wrong base, and how many runners went from first to third on Brian Giles. (We don't have the "wrong base" thing yet. Maybe next year.)

And second, we want to experiment with different ways of analyzing that expanded array of defensive statistics. Let's look at it this way; let's look at it that way. Let's see who *this* tells us are the best shortstops; let's see who *that* tells us are the best shortstops.

We are trying to ask specific questions about the player's defensive skills, so that, in time, we can create enough of an image of the player's defense that we will be able to "see" intuitively what we have left out. How well does this second baseman turn the double play? How well does that third baseman field a bunt? How well does that shortstop go to his left? How well does he go to his right? We want to get to the point, ultimately, where people will look at our data and say, "Oh, you're not measuring those foul popups that drop," or, "Oh, you're not measuring how many plays the shortstop makes on the first base side of the bag."

It is my belief that the simple accumulation of *facts*, in time, will help us to understand more than we now understand. Take the simple issue of defensive innings.

The game's first statisticians, for good reasons I suppose, did not record the number of defensive innings at each position. But this turns out to be a tremendous problem because, without defensive innings, you can't measure defensive range. A guy plays 118 games in the outfield and records 200 putouts, he may have played 500 innings or he may have played 1,000. Neither is unlikely. Without knowing which it is, you don't have a clue what you have.

We have been counting defensive innings now for twenty years, and a great deal of information exists about them, here and there. But what we have not done, up to now, is organize and publish that information, so that it becomes a regular part of everybody's understanding of the issue. Reference sources continue to list Defensive GAMES played, when they probably should be listing defensive innings.

One of the incomprehensible decisions of the game's first statisticians was to consider "outfield" to be one defensive position. That was real useful, guys; thanks a lot. The data to straighten this out has been laboriously compiled by many industrious researchers since 1967, but it is still hard to find the specific information that you need, when you need it. That's the sort of thing we want to do here—just improve the record. Do the things that should have been done in 1876. Create a record that makes sense.

And then, once we have done enough of the hard and simple work that underlies the discussion, we will indulge ourselves in the easy and complicated analysis that tries to herd the data toward conclusions and, eventually, consensus. We want to allow the data itself to point a large red arrow at the best fielders. We want to allow the data itself to identify the weakest. The complicated analysis. . .that's icing on the meatloaf.

Jeter vs. Everett

Bill James

We are well aware that we are not the first statistical analysts to question Derek Jeter's defense at shortstop. Others before us have argued that Jeter was not a good shortstop, and yet he has won the Gold Glove the last couple of years, the Yankees certainly have won several baseball games with Jeter at short, and he is among the biggest stars in baseball.

Asked about Derek Jeter's defense on a radio show in New York one year ago, I answered as honestly as I could: I don't know. I know that there are Yankee fans and network TV analysts who believe that he is a brilliant defensive shortstop; I know that there are statistical analysts who think he's an awful shortstop. I don't know what the truth is. You've seen him more than I have; you know more about it than I do.

I am instinctively skeptical. I don't tend to believe what the experts tell me, just because they are experts; I don't tend to believe what the statistical analysts tell me, just because they are statistical analysts. I take a perverse pride in being the last person to be convinced that Pete Rose bet on baseball, and I fully intend to be the last person to be convinced that Barry Bonds uses Rogaine. I am willing to listen, I am willing to be convinced, but I want to see the evidence.

So John Dewan brought me the printouts from his defensive analysis, and he explained what he had done. John's henchmen at Baseball Info Solutions had watched video from every major league game, and had recorded every ball off the bat by the direction in which it was hit (the vector) the type of hit (groundball, flyball, line-drive, popup, mob hit, etc.) and by how hard the ball was hit (softly hit, medium, hard hit). Given every vector and every type of hit, they assigned a percentage probability that the ball would result in an out, and then they had analyzed the outcomes to determine who was best at turning hit balls into outs. One of their conclusions was that Derek Jeter was probably the least effective defensive player in the major leagues, at any position.

So I said, "Well, maybe, but how do I know? How do I know this isn't just some glitch in the analysis that we don't understand yet?"

"I knew you would say that," said John. "So I brought this DVD." The DVD contained video of 80 defensive plays:

The 20 best defensive plays made by Derek Jeter.

The 20 worst defensive plays of Derek Jeter, not including errors.

The 20 best defensive plays of Adam Everett, who the analysis had concluded was the best shortstop in baseball.

The 20 worst plays of Adam Everett, not including errors.

How do we define "best" and "worst"? It's up to the computer. Every play is entered into the computer at Baseball Info Solutions. The computer then computes the totals, and decides that a softly hit groundball on Vector 17 is converted into an out by the shortstop only 26% of the time. Therefore, if, on this occasion, the shortstop converts a slowly hit ball on Vector 17 into an out, that's a heck of a play, and it scores at +.74. The credit for the play made, 1.00, minus the expectation that it should be made, which is 0.26. If the play isn't made—by anybody—it's -.26 for the shortstop.

The best plays are the plays made by shortstops on balls on which shortstops hardly ever make plays, and the worst plays are No Plays made on balls grounded right at the shortstop at medium speed. Sometimes these actually don't look like bad plays when you watch them. Sometimes the ball takes a little bit of a high hop and Ichiro is running, and he beats the play on something the computer thinks should be a routine out—but it's still a legitimate analysis, because the shortstop didn't *have* to play Ichiro that deep. He could have pulled in two steps; he could have charged the ball. He weighed the risks, he used his best judgment, and he lost. That happens.

Anyway, this business of looking at Derek Jeter's 20 best and 20 worst plays and Adam Everett's. . .logically, this would appear to be an ineffective way to see the difference between the two of them. Suppose that you took the video of A-Rod's 20 best at-bats of the season, and his 20 worst, and then you took the video of Casey Blake's 20 best at-bats of the season, and his worst. The video of A-Rod's 20 best at-bats would show him getting 20 extra-base hits in game situations, and the 20 worst would show him striking out or grounding into double plays 20 times in game situations. The video for Casey Blake would show Casey Blake doing exactly the same things. This isn't designed to reveal the differences between them; this is designed to make them look the same.

That being said, watching Derek Jeter make 40 defensive plays and then watching Adam Everett make 40 defensive plays at the same position is sort of like watching video of Barbara Bush dancing at the White House, and then watching Demi Moore dancing in *Striptease.* The two men could not possibly be more different in the style and manner in which they run the office. Jeter, in 40 plays, had maybe three plays in which he threw with his feet set. He threw on the run about 20-25 times; he jumped and threw about 10-15 times, he threw from his knees once. He threw from a stable position only when the ball, by the way it was hit, pinned him back on his heels.

Everett set his feet with almost unbelievable quickness and reliability, and threw off of his back foot on almost every play, good or bad. Jeter played much, much more shallow than Everett, cheated to his left more, and shifted his position from left to right much, much more than Everett did (with the exception of three plays on which Everett was shifted over behind second in a Ted Williams shift. Jeter had none of those.)

Jeter gambled constantly on forceouts, leading to good plays when he beat the runner, bad plays when he didn't. Everett gambled on a forceout only a couple of times, taking the out at first base unless the forceout was a safe play.

Many or most of the good plays made by Jeter were plays made in the infield grass, slow rollers that could easily have died in the infield, but plays on which Jeter, playing shallow and charging the ball aggressively, was able to get the man at first. These were plays that would have been infield hits with most shortstops, and which almost certainly would have been infield hits with Adam Everett at short.

For Everett, those type of plays were the *bad* plays, the plays he failed to make. The good plays for Everett were mostly hard hit groundballs in the hole or behind second base, on which Everett, playing deep and firing rockets, was able to make an out. These, conversely, were the bad plays for Jeter—hard-hit or not-too-hard-hit groundballs fairly near the shortstop's home base which Jeter, playing shallow and often positioning himself near second, was unable to convert. And there was literally not one play in the collection of his 20 best plays in which Jeter planted his feet in the outfield grass and threw. There were only three plays in the 40 in which Jeter made the play from the outfield grass, two of those

were forceouts at third base, and all three of them occurred just inches into the outfield grass.

Now, I want to stress this: I don't know anything about playing shortstop. I don't have any idea whether the shortstop should play shallow or deep, when he should gamble and when he should play it safe, how he should make a throw or whether it is smart for him to shift left and right in playing the hitters. The professional players know these kind of things; I don't.

That's not what I'm saying. I'm not suggesting that Jeter is a bad shortstop because he plays shallow and throws on the run and gambles on forceouts and shifts his position. What I am saying is this: that watching that video, it was very, very easy to believe that, if Adam Everett was on one end of a spectrum of shortstops, Derek Jeter was going to be on the other end of it. But that video is in no way, shape or form the basis on which we argue that Derek Jeter is not a successful shortstop.

OK then, what is that basis?

First of all, there is the summary of Jeter's plays made and plays not made. Both Jeter and Everett had plays that they made on the types of balls a shortstop does not usually make a play on, and both Jeter and Everett had plays they didn't make on balls a shortstop should make the play on. But, as in the case of A-Rod and Casey Blake at the bat, the numbers are quite a bit different.

Adam Everett had 41 No Plays in 2005 on which, given the vector, velocity and type of play, the expectation that the shortstop would make the play was greater than or equal to 50%. Derek Jeter had 93 such plays. 93 plays you would expect the shortstop to make, Jeter didn't make—52 more than Everett.

On the other side of the ledger, Derek Jeter had 19 plays that he did make that one would NOT expect a shortstop to make (less than 50% probability). Adam Everett had 59. Calling these, colloquially, Plus Plays and Missed Plays:

	Plus Plays	Missed Plays
Derek Jeter	19	93
Adam Everett	59	41

Brief accounting problem. . .Our charts show Adam Everett as being 73 plays better (on groundballs) than Derek Jeter—+34 as opposed to -39. The totals here are 92 plays (40 + 52). Why the difference?

The 93 plays that Jeter missed were not plays on which there was a 100% expectation that the shortstop would make a play. Some of them were plays on which there was a 55% expectation the shortstop would make a play; some of them were 95%. He probably should have made about 75% of them, so the 52-play difference between them on those plays leads to something more like a 40-play separation in the data.

The low defensive rating for Derek Jeter is not based on computers, it is not based on statistics, and it is not based on math. It is based on a specific observation that there are balls going through the shortstop hole against the Yankees that might very well have been fielded. Lots of them—93 of them last year, not counting the ones that might have gone through when somebody else was playing short for the Yankees. Yes, there are computers between the original observation and the conclusion; we use computers to summarize our observations, and we do state the summary as a statistic. But, at its base, it is simply a highly organized and systematic observation based on watching the games very carefully and taking notes about what happens.

Jeter, given the balls he was challenged with, had an expectation of recording 439 groundball outs. He actually recorded 400. He missed by 39. Everett, given the balls hit to him, had an expectation of 340 groundball outs. He actually recorded 374. He over-achieved by 33-point-something.

This is an analysis of groundballs. Shortstops also have to field balls hit in the air—not as many of them, but they still have to field them. That part of the analysis helps Jeter a little bit. Jeter is +5 on balls hit in the air; Everett is -1. That cuts the difference between them from 72 plays to 66.

Could these observations be wrong? It's hard to see how, but. . .I'm a skeptic; I'm always looking for ways we could be wrong.

This is not the only basis for our conclusion; actually, this is one of four. Another way of looking at this problem is to make a count of the number of hits, and where those hits land on the field.

Against the Yankees last year there were 196 hits that went up the middle, over the pitcher's mound, over second base and into center field for a hit (more or less. . .near second, and some of them may have been knocked down behind second base by the second baseman, the shortstop, or a passing streaker). That is the most common place where hits go, and an average team gives up 177 hits to that hole. Against Houston, there were 169—27 fewer than against the Pinstripers.

Against the Yankees in 2005 there were 131 hits in the hole between third and short, as opposed to a major

league average of 115. Against the Astros, there were 83.

Against the Yankees in 2005 there were 110 hits that fell into short left field, over the shortstop but in front of the ugly Asian left fielder. The major league average is 106. Against the Astros, there were 94.

The Yankees did have an advantage vs. the average team in terms of infield hits allowed; they allowed 85, whereas the average team allowed 89. (The Astros, 79.) But taking all four of the holes which are guarded in part by the shortstop, the Yankees allowed 35 hits more than an average major league team, and 97 more than the Astros.

	Yanks	Average	Astros
Infield Hits	85	89	79
Up the Middle	196	177	169
In the SS/3B Hole	131	115	83
In short left	110	106	94
Totals	**522**	**487**	**425**

So there is a separate method, relying on a different set of facts, which gives us essentially the same conclusion: that Everett is an outstanding shortstop, and Jeter not so much.

There is a third method, Relative Range Factor, which is explained in a different article. Relative Range Factor is an entirely different method, relying not on Baseball Info Solutions' careful and systematic original observation of the games, but on a thorough and detailed analysis of the traditional fielding statistics. It's just plays made per nine innings in the field, but with adjustments put in for the strikeout and groundball tendencies of the team, the left/right bias of the pitching staff, and whether the player was surrounded by good fielders who took plays away from him or bad fielders who stretched out the innings and created more opportunities. That method is explained on page 199.

In that article, the Relative Range Factor article, I scrupulously avoided any mention of Derek Jeter, which turned out to be more difficult than you might expect. In 2005, Jeter's Relative Range Factor actually is OK. . .it's middle-of-the-pack, not really noteworthy. But the Relative Range Factor is not a precise method; there is some bounce in it from year to year. I believe it is more than accurate enough in one year to make it highly reliable over a period of three years, but it is probably not highly reliable in one year.

Jeter's "OK" performance in Relative Range Factor in 2005 is an aberration in his career. It was only the second time in his career that his Relative Range Factor hasn't been absolutely horrible. In fact, although I haven't figured enough Relative Range Factors yet to say for certain, I will be absolutely astonished if there is any other shortstop in major league history whose Relative Range Factors are anywhere near as bad as Jeter's. I'll be amazed.

In one part of that article, to illustrate the method, I wanted to contrast Ozzie Smith with some player who would be easily recognized and generally understood by modern readers to be a not-very-good defensive shortstop. I started with a list of team assists by shortstops relative to expectation. . .several of Ozzie's seasons were near the top end of the list, and I chose one, and then I went to the bottom of the list to try to find a "bad example."

I was looking for modern seasons, because I wanted modern readers to recognize the player, and I was looking for teams that had shortstops you might remember. Of course, 80% of the teams at the bottom of the list were 25 years ago or more, and most of the other "classically bad" shortstops were guys who were just regulars for one year, so people wouldn't necessarily remember them.

Eventually I found the player I needed—Wilfredo Cordero in 1995. Everybody remembers Wilfredo; everybody knows he wasn't much of a shortstop. I found him after walking past six separate seasons of Derek Jeter. While virtually no other recognizable name at shortstop had had even one season in which his team had 40 fewer assists by shortstops than expected, Jeter had season after season after season in that category.

We have, then, a third independent method which confirms that Jeter's range, in terms of his ability to get to a groundball, is substantially below average. All three methods suggest essentially the same shortfall. We have one more method.

Our fourth method is zone ratings. The concept of zone ratings was invented by John Dewan—the primary author of this book—in the 1980s. Over the years zone ratings have proliferated, some of them better than others. The zone ratings presented here are not exactly the same as the originals. They're better. . .better thought out, better designed, with access to better accounts of the game.

Zone ratings and the plus/minus system are actually very similar concepts. . .what the zone rating actually is is a simpler and less precise statement of the same original observations that make up the fielding plus/minus. What we do in zone ratings is, we take the data from each of the 262 vectors into which the field is divided, and we identify those at which the shortstop records an out more than 50% of the time. Those are the shortstop's "responsible vectors". . .the vectors for which he is held accountable. The zone rating is a percentage of all the plays the shortstop makes in those vectors for which he is accountable.

Derek Jeter's zone rating is .792, and he made 26 plays outside his zone. Adam Everett's zone rating .860, and he made 78 plays outside his zone.

We can't really count this as a fourth indicator that Derek Jeter's range is limited, because the underlying data is redundant of our first indicator, the +/- system (-39 for Jeter, +33 for Everett). Still, setting that aside, we have three independent systems evaluating Jeter's defense (as well as the defense of every other major league shortstop). One system—Relative Range Factor—looks at traditional fielding stats, which is to say it looks at outs made. One system looks at where hits landed, which is to say it looks at hits. One system looks at balls in play, and evaluates the fielder by the rate at which balls in play are divided between outs and hits.

All three systems agree that Jeter has extremely limited range in terms of getting to groundballs—and all three systems provide essentially the same statement of the cost of that limitation. It is very, very difficult for me to understand how all three systems can be reaching the same conclusion, unless that conclusion is true. It's sort of like if you have a videotape of the suspect holding up a bank and shooting the clerk, and you have his fingerprints on the murder weapon, and you recover items taken in the robbery from his garage. Maybe the videotape is not clear; it could be somebody who looks a lot like him. Maybe there is some other explanation for his fingerprints on the murder weapon. Maybe there is some other explanation for the bags of money in his garage. It is REALLY difficult to accept that there is some other explanation for all three.

Those Yankee fans with a one-switch mind will demand to know, "How come we won 95 games, then? If Derek Jeter is such a lousy shortstop, how is it that we were able to win all of these games?"

But first, no one is saying that Derek Jeter is a lousy *player*. Let's assume that the difference between Derek Jeter and Adam Everett is 72 plays on defense. That's huge, obviously; that's not a little thing that you blow off lightly. But almost all of those 72 plays are singles. What's the value of a single, in runs? It's a little less than half a run. 72 plays have a value of 30, 35 runs.

That's huge—but it is still less than the difference between them as hitters. Derek Jeter is still a better *player* than Adam Everett, even if Everett is 72 plays better than Jeter as a shortstop. (Jeter created about 105 runs in 2005; Everett, 61.)

In one way of looking at it, it makes intuitive sense that Derek Jeter could be the worst defensive shortstop of all time. Unusual weaknesses in sports can only survive in the presence of unusual strengths. I don't know who was the worst free throw shooter in NBA history—but I'll guarantee you, whoever he was, he could play. If he couldn't play, he wouldn't have been given a chance to miss all those free throws. If a player is simply *bad*, he is quickly driven out of the game. To be the worst defensive shortstop ever, the player would have to have unusual strengths in other areas, which Jeter certainly has. It would help if he were surrounded by teammates who also have unusual strengths, which Jeter certainly is. The worst defensive shortstop in baseball history would *have* to be someone like Jeter who is unusually good at other aspects of the game.

Second, we have not exhausted the issue of defense. There are other elements of defense which could still be considered—turning the double play, and helping out other fielders, and defending against base advancement, I suppose. The defensive ratings that we have produced, while they are derived from meticulous research, might still be subject to park illusions, to influences of playing on different types of teams, and from influences by teammates. There is still a vast amount of research that needs to be done about fielding.

But at the same time, I have to say that the case for Jeter as a Gold Glove quality shortstop is a dead argument in my mind. There is a lot we don't know, and Derek Jeter could be a better shortstop than we have measured him as being for any of a dozen reasons. He is *not* a Gold Glove quality shortstop. He isn't an average defensive shortstop. Giving him every possible break on the unknowns, he is still going to emerge as a below-average defensive shortstop.

Overview of the Plus/Minus System

*If they had this book when I was playing,
I would have been the best shortstop who every lived!*

—Ozzie Guillen, manager, World Champion Chicago White Sox

That was Ozzie's reaction (with the every-other-word expletive removed) when Pat Quinn and I were explaining the Plus/Minus System in the team version of *The Fielding Bible* to the Chicago White Sox a couple of years ago. Funny thing, that's probably not too far from the truth. We don't have the Plus/Minus System going back to that era, but we have evaluated past seasons using Bill James' new Relative Range Factor system. Turns out that Guillen has several of the best defensive shortstop seasons of all time based on Bill's system. (For more on Bill's new system, see page 199.)

In this article I'll give you the lowdown on the Plus/Minus System, the backbone of this book. Here's the question that we try to answer with the Plus/Minus System:

How many plays did this player make above or below those an average player at his position would make?

That's what you should think to yourself when you're looking at all those plus and minus numbers. The average is zero. If a player makes one play more than the average, that's +1.

Now let me give you the short version of how the Plus/Minus System has been developed. We'll get into further details later.

Baseball Info Solutions reviews videotape of every game in Major League Baseball. Every play is entered into the computer where we record the exact direction, distance, speed and type of every batted ball. Direction and distance is done on a computer screen by simply clicking the exact location of the ball on a replica of the field shown on the screen. Speed is simply soft, medium and hard while types of batted balls are groundball, liner, fly and bunt. We will be introducing a new category in 2006 called fliner. A fliner is a ball that is hard to categorize because it's somewhere between a fly and a liner, so it becomes a fliner. But that's next year.

The computer totals all softly hit groundballs on Vector 17, for example, and determines that these types of batted balls are converted into outs by the shortstop only 26% of the time. Therefore, if, on this occasion, the shortstop converts a slowly hit ball on Vector 17 into an out, that's a heck of a play, and it scores at +.74. The credit for the play made, 1.00, minus the expectation that it should be made, which is 0.26. If the play isn't made—by anybody—it's -.26 for the shortstop.

The key is if a player makes a play on a specific type of batted ball, hit to a specific location on the field, and hit at a specific speed, he gets credit if at least one other player in MLB that season missed that exact ball sometime during the season. A player who misses a play on a specific type of batted ball, hit to a specific location on the field, and hit at a specific speed, he loses credit if a least one other player made the same play some other time.

Add up all the credits the player gets and loses based on each and every play when he's on the field and you get his plus/minus number (rounded to the nearest integer). Let's continue with the Vector 17 example. Vector 17 is a line extending from home plate towards the hole between the normal shortstop and third base positions, but not the exact hole. It's closer to the normal shortstop position. Shortstops fielded a softly hit groundball there 26% of the time in 2005. Medium hit balls on that vector were fielded 52% of the time, while hard hit balls were only fielded at a 10% rate. Overall there are about 260 vectors we use for the field. One more factor we add for outfielders is the distance of every batted ball.

I'll get into more details a little later, but let's get to the more important question:

How do we figure out if the system works?

First Base:
Mark Teixeira, Doug Mientkiewicz, Darin Erstad
Second Base: Orlando Hudson
Third Base: Adrian Beltre, Scott Rolen, Eric Chavez
Shortstop: Adam Everett, Jack Wilson
Left Field: Carl Crawford, Coco Crisp
Center Field: Torii Hunter, Andruw Jones, Carlos Beltran
Right Field: Ichiro Suzuki, Richard Hidalgo

These are all guys who have great defensive reputations, most with at least one Gold Glove. And they are all guys who rank in the top five players at their position in the Plus/Minus System over the last three years.

First Base: Derrek Lee
Second Base: Bret Boone
Third Base: Mike Lowell
Shortstop: Derek Jeter
Left Field: none
Center Field: none
Right Field: Bobby Abreu

These are all the guys who have great defensive reputations, all with at least one Gold Glove. They are all guys who rank poorly in the Plus/Minus System.

This was the first and most important way of evaluating the new defensive rating system we've developed. As much as there was a lot of detailed, theoretical work that went into the system, there needed to be agreement between the best players in the Plus/Minus System and the best players based on visual and subjective impressions by those who know the game. Looking at the first list we felt there was a success. But the second list concerned us. How is it possible that these guys with great defensive reputations, and Gold Gloves, don't fare well? We needed to understand why the system would rate them poorly before we could believe in the system.

Let's go through each of the players who might be expected to rate well in the system but don't.

Derrek Lee has won a Gold Glove in two of the last three years. How is it that he's fielded 13 fewer balls than could be expected of an average major league first baseman in that time? That's what the Plus/Minus System number of -13 for Derrek Lee means. (Technically, the meaning is slightly different, but I'll explain that later). The American League Gold Glover this year was Mark Teixeira, whose +17 was the best in baseball. Why is it that the National League Gold Glover comes out at -13 over three years? OK, so his 2005 number is +2. That doesn't seem very good for the Gold Glove winner.

Well, this is the weakest position for the Plus/Minus System. Most defensive measures have trouble with first basemen. Putouts simply tell you how many groundouts were hit against the team, more a function of the pitchers and other infielders. First baseman assists might have some meaning, but there is no real consensus about what,

and they are not reliable as an indicator of range due to the discretionary nature of the play on which the great majority of first base assists occur, the 3-1 flip. Some first basemen just prefer to step on the bag themselves. There are no range factors at first base. While we are measuring very meaningful information on first basemen in the Plus/Minus System, we are missing one huge element: the ability to handle throws, especially of the errant variety, made by the other infielders. That's a place where Derrek Lee really excels, perhaps. He saves many an error for his fellow infielders, and it's this ability that takes him a long way towards his Gold Gloves—or at least there is the perception that this is true.

Another defensive element that is not measured by plus/minus, but we are measuring in this book, is the handling of bunts. Over three years, Lee has the second highest score among first basemen in handling bunts. (See Fielding Bunts article on page 211.)

Is D.Lee a deserved Glove Glove winner? I don't think so. Just like Mike Lowell (see below), he excels in some areas but not all, and that's not enough for a Gold Glove in my book. Scooping throws and handling bunts are important, but so is handling regular groundballs. While Lee is not bad at handling grounders, he is not excellent, either. Who did deserve the Gold Glove? Take a look at all my Gold Gloves That Should Have Been in the Player Comments section starting on page 143.

Bret Boone won Gold Gloves in 2003 and 2004. Orlando Hudson (finally) was the Gold Glove winner at second base in 2005. Boone's decline over those three years is dramatic as measured by our numbers. His plus/minus numbers went -9, -20 and -25 in that time, while his rank in double plays went from number four and number three in 2003 and 2004 to 21 in 2005. What seems evident here is that Boone's age (34, 35 and 36 over the three years) caught up with him a lot faster than the award did. He won his first Gold Glove in 1998 in the National League, then was overshadowed by Pokey Reese the next year. After he came over to the American League, he was stuck behind the automatic choice of Roberto Alomar until Alomar moved to the National League in 2002. Boone was then the choice for three years. Here's a quote from former MLB outfielder Doug Glanville that I agree with wholeheartedly: "Most Gold Glove winners are excellent defenders overall, however, they can also gain points by being offensively dominant, acrobatic, popular, or just because they are the incumbent." In the last couple of years some of Boone's points may have come from being the incumbent.

Mike Lowell won his first Gold Glove in 2005 and is the best third baseman in baseball handling bunts. He's the only guy who measures out at a grade "A" on bunts over three years. He's also the best at handling balls hit down the line with a +30 over three years. So far the Gold Glove looks solid. But let's look at the rest of his range. On balls hit more or less at him, he's -45 over three years. To his left he's -15. Both of those figures are the worst in baseball at third base. He looks fantastic making those great plays running in on bunts and throwing off balance, and he looks fantastic snaring those shots down the line, but his poor performance in the rest of the third base area drops him down well below average with a sub par -30 Basic Plus/Minus over three years. Enhanced Plus/Minus factors in the bases saved on balls hit down the line, since some of those would have been doubles. Lowell does improve to -21 on the enhanced system, but all in all he's not a deserved Gold Glover, as I see it.

Take Derek Jeter. Please. Don't miss Bill James' article at the beginning of this book. It will tell you all you need to know. Derek Jeter is a great player to have on any team. A tremendous leader. A real winner. A catalyst to the offense. A great hitter for a shortstop. But far from a great defensive shortstop.

And finally there's Bobby Abreu. He has a great arm. Honestly, that's all you can say that's positive about his defense. His other qualification for the Gold Glove is that he hits well enough to win it. Winning the Home Run Derby at the 2005 All-Star game didn't hurt either. But stardom clearly does help in the Gold Glove voting, and always has. The media as well as many of the fans were stumped by Abreu's Gold Glove in 2005. After the Gold Gloves were announced, Abreu's former outfield teammate, Doug Glanville, posted a very thoughtful essay (partially quoted above) on the Strat-O-Matic web site (www.strat-o-matic.com) arguing that, while he liked and respected Abreu, there was no way on earth that the man is a Gold Glove outfielder.

Further details

The short version of the Plus/Minus System explained above summarizes it well, but each and every position has at least one special adjustment to improve accuracy. Let's go through each position:

First Base – There is a big difference between how a first baseman positions himself, depending on whether he's holding the runner or not. To approximate this, we break down all plays involving first basemen into two categories, Holding Required and Holding Not Required. Holding Required is any situation where there's a man on first with second base open. We may refine this in the future, but we found that since the outcomes are very different with runners being held this adjustment made an important difference in improving the accuracy of the first base plus/minus numbers.

A second adjustment for first basemen was mentioned earlier. That's Enhanced Plus/Minus. Basic Plus/Minus counts the number of plays above or below what could be expected by an average first baseman. Enhanced Plus/Minus takes the "value" of those made plays and hits into account. Here's the question that we try to answer with Enhanced Plus/Minus: *How many bases does the player save for his team above those saved by the average first baseman?*

For example, Eric Chavez has a Basic Plus/Minus of +10 and Enhanced Plus/Minus of +15. Simply said, that means, Eric Chavez made 10 *plays* more than expected in 2005, saving his team 15 *bases*. It can work the other way too. Joe Crede made 11 plays more than expected, but it only saved his team two bases. What likely happened here was that Crede played off the line a lot last year. He saved a lot of singles on balls hit into the shortstop hole, but he missed some doubles on balls to his right that other third basemen get to.

Second Base and **Shortstop** – The key adjustment for these two positions is made on hit-and-run plays. We consider any play where the runner on first is breaking towards second a hit-and-run play. It may have been intended as a straight steal, but if the batter hits the ball, it becomes a hit-and-run in practice, at least from the standpoint of the defense. On these plays, either the second baseman or the shortstop is breaking towards second to cover a possible throw and the dynamics of the defense change completely. For the Plus/Minus System, we use Hit-and-Run as another variable.

We don't use the Enhanced Plus/Minus adjustment for middle infielders, since almost all of the plays they don't make become singles, rather than extra base hits.

Third Base – At third base we make the same Enhanced Plus/Minus adjustment as first base, but not the Holding Required adjustment.

Outfield – A key addition that we made to the system last year was to move from three types of balls hit into the air to six different kinds. Prior to doing the Plus/Minus System for the 2004 season, we had three types of balls hit to the outfield: soft, medium and hard. Initially, we didn't think that a distinction between line drives and flyballs was necessary. If it's hard hit, it's hard hit. However, after doing extensive video analysis for Johnny Damon to see why his plus/minus number was so low in 2004, we discovered that the distinction was necessary. It's pretty obvious, now that we know it. A hard hit flyball simply stays in the air longer than a hard hit liner, giving the fielder more time to make the play. So now we have six types of balls hit to the outfield, with soft, medium and hard hit flyballs and soft, medium and hard hit liners. Next year we move to nine categories as we add in "fliners."

For outfielders, we also use the Enhanced version of the system, since balls not fielded by outfielders frequently wind up as extra-base hits.

Estimating runs and wins

One thing we want to do in the future is translate these plus/minus numbers and all the other defensive metrics we have in this book into one number. That might be a number similar to Runs Created, but for defense not offense. Maybe it's called Runs Prevented. But between you and me, you can use the rule of thumb that Bill James used in his article on Derek Jeter and Adam Everett. That is, use a number a little less than half of the plus/minus number as an estimate of runs prevented. Since the value of a single is a little less than half a run, you can use a "little less than half" of the plus/minus figure to estimate runs prevented. Adam Everett's plus/minus figure of +33 could be estimated as preventing about 15 runs. Then using another rule of thumb that estimates the value of a win at 10 runs, Everett's defense generates an extra 1½ wins for the Astros in 2005. Since the Enhanced Plus/Minus System also factors in the value of extra bases, and each extra base is worth somewhat less than a single, you might use an even lower value (.20 for each plus/minus, perhaps?) for the difference between the Enhanced value and the Basic value. Since defense is not an exact science, however, I would suggest that using half and rounding down for both Basic and Enhanced Plus/Minus is close enough as an estimate. After all, it's not horseshoes or hand grenades.

Doing a Runs Prevented calculation will be much more complicated than this estimate as we try to factor in our bunt rating, double play rating, outfielder throwing arms, errant-throw handling, Defensive Misplays (see page 239), etc. In fact, keep in mind that this estimating technique to translate plus/minus to runs or wins is relative to average. For example, Adrian Beltre's +71 over three years at third base doesn't exactly compare to Adam Everett's +76 at shortstop. Both of these numbers are relative to the average player at their positions. But much more skill is required of the average shortstop than the average third baseman.

One-Year Register

The charts that follow summarize fielding data, by position, for every major league player in 2005, except pitchers and catchers. Starting with the first line of the first chart. . .that would be the data for Marlon Anderson as the New York Mets' first baseman in 2005.

The first eight columns, under the heading "Basic", are simply the player's basic fielding statistics at the position—Games, Games Started, Innings, Putouts, Assists, Errors, Double Plays and Fielding Percentage.

After Fielding Percentage, there is one additional column for outfielders entitled Rng. This is range factor per nine innings, the number of plays that the fielder made per nine innings. For second basemen, third basemen and shortstops, we add the Rng column and two others, Rel Rng and Rel +/-. These are based on Bill James' new Relative Range Factor system. The first number (Rel Rng) is an adjustment that is made to range factor to adjust for things (primarily pitching staff tendencies) that bias the traditional range factor calculation. A relative range above 1.000 means range factor should be increased to account for this bias. Below 1.000 means range factor should be decreased. The second number (+/-) translates range factor and relative range into a +/- number that tells you how many plays above or below average this player has made. See "Relative Range Factors" on page 199 for a complete description of Relative Range Factors.

The next four columns, under the heading "Bunts", are a summary of the player's effectiveness at fielding bunts. These are explained in the article "Fielding Bunts", which begins on page 211.

The next two columns, under the heading "Plays", are counts of the number of expected and actual plays that the player made/was expected to make on groundballs. These do not include groundballs to other fielders. . .a play going 5-3 is not a "play opportunity" for the first baseman in this chart. Given the array of groundballs hit near first base when Marlon Anderson was playing first, given how hard they were hit and where they were hit, there is an expectation that Anderson would turn 23 of these balls into outs. In fact, he turned 29 of them into outs, which is +6, which is very, very good for a guy not playing that many innings, but then, he is a second baseman by trade; you would expect him to cover more ground than your average first baseman.

The next seven columns, under the heading "Plus/Minus" breaks that +6 down into balls hit to Anderson's right—or actually, to the right of the position normally taken by a first baseman—balls hit more or less directly to the first base position, and balls hit to the left of the first baseman. You will notice that all of the numbers for balls hit to the left of the first baseman are near zero, since the foul line is just to the left of the first baseman, and there's not a lot of room for negotiation there.

The categories go right, center, left, with the right on the left and the left on the right and the guy in the middle burning his driver's license. (It's an old Johnny Cash song. You'll get the reference if you're 50 years old or grew up in the South.) Anyway, they are in this order because this is the order in which you see them when you go to the game or watch it on TV, normally. To the first baseman's right is to YOUR left if you're sitting behind home plate, or if you are sitting anywhere from the first base line to the left field foul line. It seems more natural to array them from the batter's point of view.

These first three categories summarize ONLY the groundball outs. Then there is the summary of these three, +6 for Anderson, and then there is the same summary for balls hit into the air.

All the "air ball" numbers for first basemen are between +2 and -2. These include, basically, only line drives. Well, they *include* everything, but only line drives really effect the total. When a ball is popped up high in the infield, it is virtually always caught by *somebody*, which makes it a non-event in terms of evaluating fielders. The evaluations are based on making plays that don't always get made. If you make a play that nobody ever makes, that's +1; if you make a play that everybody always makes, that's +/- zero. If you don't make a play that everybody always makes, that's -1. In the real world there are no +1s or -1s, only large decimals, but. . .you get the point.

Anyway, after the groundball/flyball plus/minus and the total of the two, there is a category called "enhanced". The plus/minus total given before was simply the number of plays made/not made, which would be all we would need to know if all hits were singles. Sometimes that play not made down the first base line, however, is a double. Our computer takes into account not merely whether or not an additional play was made or not made, but the likelihood of a double or a triple occurring on a ball of that type, given where it was hit and how hard it was hit. When it takes that into account, that is the "enhanced" number. Mark Teixeira made 14 *plays* more than expected, saving his team 17 *bases*.

The final column in this chart is where the player ranks among the regulars or near-regulars at his position. Mark Teixeira has a "1" there because he ranks first among the first basemen in 2005; Carlos Delgado has a "34" because he ranks 34th and last. But he ranks last only because Willie Aikens is 50 years old and in jail in Mexico.

The one-year register data for third basemen is the same as that for first basemen.

The data for second basemen and shortstops has no "Bunt" columns. Instead, it has columns for "Ground DP". A second baseman or shortstop has a double play opportunity (GDP Opps) whenever

a) he is involved in a fielding play,

b) on a groundball,

c) in a double play situation.

If a play goes 5-4-3 for a double play, that's a GDP opportunity; if it goes 5-4 in the same situation, no throw to first or the throw to first is too late, it's still an opportunity—but that play is NOT an opportunity for the shortstop, since he is not involved in the play.

Todd Walker of the Cubs last year turned, fed or completed 40 double plays in 101 opportunities—.396—while Mark Grudzielanek of the Cardinals converted 104 of 166 chances, or 62.7%. It's a difference of more than 25 double plays per season. In 2003, when Grudzielanek was the Cubs' second baseman, the team turned 137 groundball double plays. Last year, with many of the same pitchers on the mound, they turned 119. Our data suggests that Walker may have been largely responsible for this difference.

For outfielders, of course, we have something different entirely, since outfielders don't field bunts very often or turn double plays with the frequency even of Todd Walker. For outfielders, we also dispensed with the left/right/straight on breakdowns, which tended to be not too instructive, and used the space to include information about runners advancing on balls hit to the outfielder.

When does a baserunner have an opportunity to advance? If a runner is on first and the batter hits a double, that's an opportunity to advance. If a runner is on second and the batter hits a single, the runner has an opportunity to advance. If a runner is on first and the batter hits a single, the runner from first has an opportunity to advance *unless* there in another runner in front of him who stays on third base.

Alexis Rios of Toronto is a pretty near useless player, but the man does have a cannon. When Rios was in right field last year there were 118 situations in which a runner could have advanced against him, but only 50 did, or 42.4%. By contrast, against Jeromy Burnitz. . .and yes, I *am* picking on the Cubs defense. . .against Jeromy there were 124 situations in which a runner could advance, and 78 of them did. There is a swing of about 25 bases there.

Rios was credited with 4 baserunner kills; Burnitz, with 1. The term "baserunner kills" is sometimes used interchangeably with the wimpy, draggle-armed term "outfield assist", but we credited baserunner kills, in these charts, only for plays that were not "double-assisted" by another fielder. A lot of outfield assists occur 9-3-4 when the first baseman cuts off the throw and throws out the batter trying to take second on the throw. . .or 9-3-5, or 7-6-4. We didn't count those as baserunner kills. We only counted the plays on which an outfielder gunned down a runner on his own—9-2, 9-5, whatever.

The standards for left fielders are very different from the standards for right fielders or center fielders. . .each position has its own standards, since batters from first rarely go to third on balls hit to left. You can't compare right fielders' throwing data to left fielders'.

At the bottom of each position we show a line for 2005 MLB averages. We'll repeat the averages for outfielder throwing arms for you here:

Percentage of Runners Advancing on Plays to Left: .381
Percentage of Runners Advancing on Plays to Center: .581
Percentage of Runners Advancing on Plays to Right: .535

We hope you enjoy the charts, and we hope you get something out of them. We're trying to put specific evidence about fielders on the record, and this is one step in that process.

First Basemen 2005

Name	Team	G	GS	Inn	PO	A	E	DP	Pct	Opps	Score	Grade	Rank	Expected GB Outs	GB Outs Made	To His Right	Straight On	To His Left	GB	Air	Total	Enhanced	Rank
Marlon Anderson	NYM	23	16	155.1	173	16	2	18	.990	2	.800	A+	-	23	29	+4	+2	0	+6	0	+6	+6	-
Carlos Baerga	Was	11	9	86.2	65	2	1	2	.985	1	.600	B-	-	8	6	0	-2	0	-2	0	-2	-2	-
Jeff Bagwell	Hou	24	24	202.2	211	14	0	13	1.000	5	.530	C	-	31	34	+2	0	+1	+3	0	+3	+3	-
Lance Berkman	Hou	96	84	737.2	772	49	5	77	.994	11	.714	A-	3	105	99	-1	-2	-3	-6	-1	-7	-7	29
Casey Blake	Cle	4	4	30.0	28	5	1	4	.971	1	.600	B-	-	4	5	0	0	0	+1	0	+1	+1	-
Tony Blanco	Was	3	1	14.0	11	1	2	2	.857				-	3	2	-1	0	0	-1				
Willie Bloomquist	Sea	1	0	1.2	0	1	0	0	1.000					1	1	0			0				
Geoff Blum	2 tms	14	9	92.0	93	6	0	7	1.000				-	12	10	-1	-2	0	-2	-1	-3	-3	-
Russell Branyan	Mil	5	2	24.0	29	2	0	0	1.000					5	6	0	+1	0	+1	0	+1	+1	-
Ben Broussard	Cle	138	112	1050.2	1082	60	9	112	.992	11	.482	D+	31	137	138	-2	+2	+1	+1	-1	0	+1	19
Miguel Cairo	NYM	8	6	50.2	48	2	1	6	.980					12	11	-1	-1	+1	-1	0	-1	-1	-
Sean Casey	Cin	134	132	1138.2	1153	55	2	91	.998	29	.614	B-	11	160	153	-2	-6	+1	-7	-1	-8	-6	27
Hee Seop Choi	LAD	83	78	664.2	698	62	2	59	.997	12	.546	C	17	117	121	+1	+1	+2	+4	-2	+2	+2	17
Jeff Cirillo	Mil	1	0	0.2	0	0	0	0	-									0			0	0	
Tony Clark	Ari	83	70	642.2	663	45	2	59	.997	7	.500	C-	27	77	77	-5	+6	0	0	+1	+1	+4	13
Jeff Conine	Fla	45	22	231.1	247	17	4	27	.985	2	.425	D-	-	41	36	-3	-2	0	-5	0	-5	-6	-
Wil Cordero	Was	12	7	68.2	66	2	0	5	1.000	1	.250	F	-	13	13	0	0	+1	0	0	0	+1	-
Jacob Cruz	Cin	5	2	20.0	15	1	0	2	1.000					4	4	+1	0	0	-1		-1	-1	
Mike Cuddyer	Min	8	3	33.0	36	1	0	8	1.000					4	4	0	0	0	0	0	0	0	
Brian Daubach	NYM	6	4	43.0	39	3	1	3	.977					7	7	0	+1	0	0	0	0	0	
Carlos Delgado	Fla	141	140	1206.0	1147	83	14	132	.989	25	.506	C-	25	179	161	-5	-5	-8	-18	0	-18	-23	34
Mark DeRosa	Tex	1	0	1.0	2	0	0	1	1.000					0		0	0	0	0			
Einar Diaz	StL	3	0	8.0	9	0	0	2	1.000					-1			-1				
Joe Dillon	Fla	1	0	2.0	2	0	0	0	1.000					0		0	0	0	0			
Greg Dobbs	Sea	5	4	37.0	32	8	0	0	1.000					7	10	+1	+1	+1	+3			
Adam Dunn	Cin	33	27	251.1	244	11	4	31	.985	3	.617	B-	-	29	25	0	-2	-2	-4	0	-4	-4	-
Erubiel Durazo	Oak	1	1	8.0	8	0	0	2	1.000					1	1	0			0				
Jermaine Dye	CWS	1	1	9.0	7	1	0	0	1.000					3	3	0			0				
Brad Eldred	Pit	50	46	406.0	435	15	7	46	.985	9	.533	C	-	39	35	+2	-3	-3	-4	0	-4	-4	-
Darin Erstad	LAA	147	144	1279.1	1218	79	4	109	.997	20	.505	C-	26	182	193	+8	0	+2	+11	0	+11	+12	4
Felix Escalona	NYY	1	0	1.0	2	0	0	0	1.000							0			0		0		
Sal Fasano	Bal	1	0	2.0	0	0	0	0	-													
Pedro Feliz	SF	15	9	89.2	76	7	1	7	.988	1	.600	B-	-	12	13	0	0	+1	+1	0	+1	+1	-
Robert Fick	SD	29	22	199.1	224	12	2	23	.992	3	.733	A	-	36	41	0	+5	0	+5	0	+5	+5	-
Prince Fielder	Mil	7	3	34.0	26	4	0	2	1.000	1	.600	B-	-	5	5	0	0	0	0	0	0	0	-
John Flaherty	NYY	1	0	3.0	0	0	0	0	1.000					1	1	0			0				
Julio Franco	Atl	62	45	423.1	450	37	5	46	.990	4	.700	A-	-	66	64	-2	+2	-1	-2	+1	-1	-4	-
Alejandro Freire	Bal	16	13	103.0	101	5	1	10	.991	2	.625	B-	-	15	14	+1	-2	0	-1	0	-1	-1	-
Jason Giambi	NYY	78	77	559.2	580	19	7	50	.988	7	.614	B-	10	69	61	-7	-3	+2	-8	0	-8	-8	30
Jay Gibbons	Bal	22	19	164.1	171	8	1	10	.994	3	.750	A+	-	21	21	-2	+1	0	0	0	0	0	-
Ross Gload	CWS	24	6	89.0	72	4	1	9	.987				-	10	8	0	-2	0	-2	0	-2	-2	-
Chris Gomez	Bal	42	27	241.0	252	15	2	29	.993	2	.800	A+	-	42	37	-2	-2	-1	-5	0	-5	-6	-
Adrian Gonzalez	Tex	10	7	71.0	85	6	2	7	.978	1	.600	B-	-	10	9	+1	-1	-1	-1	0	-1	-1	-
Luis A Gonzalez	Col	10	3	36.1	37	3	0	4	1.000	1	.250	F	-	5	5	+1	-1	0	0	0	0	0	-
Jason Grabowski	LAD	3	1	8.0	11	0	0	1	1.000					0		0			0				
Tony Graffanino	2 tms	22	14	134.0	137	7	1	19	.993	2	.800	A+	-	18	17	0	-1	+1	-1	0	-1	0	-
Travis Hafner	Cle	1	1	7.0	6	2	0	0	1.000					2	2	0			0				
Toby Hall	TB	2	0	5.0	5	2	0	0	1.000					2	2	0			0				
Dave Hansen	Sea	9	0	27.0	18	2	0	3	1.000					3	4	+1	0	0	+1				
Lenny Harris	Fla	1	0	3.0	3	0	0	2	1.000														
Ken Harvey	KC	5	5	37.0	41	0	0	2	1.000					3	1				-2	0	-2	-2	-
Scott Hatteberg	Oak	53	50	436.2	423	38	7	47	.985	5	.970	A+	-	75	69	-3	-4	+1	-6	0	-6	-5	-
Wes Helms	Mil	16	14	114.1	103	9	1	9	.991	1	.600	B-	-	12	13	+1	0	0	+1	0	+1	+1	-
Todd Helton	Col	144	142	1229.2	1236	118	5	136	.996	21	.602	B-	13	200	199	-3	+2	0	-1	+1	0	-1	21
Jose Hernandez	Cle	45	41	339.0	337	27	2	28	.995	2	1.000	A+	-	47	50	+2	+1	+1	+3	+1	+4	+5	-
Shea Hillenbrand	Tor	67	65	587.1	627	48	6	69	.991	5	.540	C	19	95	95	-4	+1	+3	0	-1	-1	0	20
Eric Hinske	Tor	100	97	859.2	868	69	7	77	.993	4	.700	A-	4	145	144	-4	+1	+2	-1	-2	-3	-1	22
Aaron Holbert	Cin	2	0	5.0	4	0	0	0	1.000					2	1	0			-1	0	-1	-2	-
Ryan Howard	Phi	84	79	706.1	707	40	5	53	.993	7	.500	C-	27	82	101	+15	+6	-2	+19	0	+19	+16	2
Justin Huber	KC	19	17	142.1	123	8	3	16	.978	1	.600	B-	-	23	18	-1	-3	-1	-5	0	-5	-5	-
Aubrey Huff	TB	25	18	161.1	134	5	0	15	1.000	3	.250	F	-	12	10	0	-2	0	-2	0	-2	-2	-
Raul Ibanez	Sea	4	4	34.0	26	3	0	1	1.000	1	.250	F	-	7	6	-1							
Conor Jackson	Ari	20	20	161.0	171	11	5	19	.973	7	.500	C-	-	24	22	0	0	-2	-2	-1	-3	-4	-
Mike Jacobs	NYM	28	28	236.0	237	10	4	24	.984	4	.600	B-	-	31	29	-1	-1	-1	-2	0	-2	-3	-
Dan Johnson	Oak	101	98	883.2	898	57	6	94	.994	6	.483	D+	30	116	116	-1	+1	0	0	+1	+1	+2	18
Nick Johnson	Was	129	126	1098.2	1017	95	5	109	.996	22	.650	B	9	170	175	+4	-2	+3	+5	+1	+6	+6	10
Russ Johnson	NYY	7	2	29.0	30	0	0	5	1.000					2	3	0	0	0	+1				
Jeff Kent	LAD	14	10	81.1	92	6	2	9	.980	2	.425	D-	-	16	17	0	0	+2	+1	0	+1	+2	-
Ryan Klesko	SD	1	0	1.0	2	0	0	0	1.000					1	1	0			0				
Paul Konerko	CWS	146	145	1272.2	1320	82	5	135	.996	19	.574	C+	14	173	172	-1	-1	+1	-1	-1	-2	-2	23
Casey Kotchman	LAA	20	13	131.0	111	7	0	10	1.000					21	19	0	0	-3	-2	0	-2	-5	-
Pete LaForest	TB	1	1	8.0	4	0	0	0	1.000					0		0			0		0		
Mike Lamb	Hou	68	47	428.0	429	28	5	39	.989	4	.525	C-	-	64	63	-1	+2	-2	-1	0	-1	-2	-
Adam LaRoche	Atl	125	117	1019.1	1070	77	7	105	.994	14	.532	C	21	175	157	0	-15	-3	-18	0	-18	-17	33
Matt LeCroy	Min	23	21	179.0	203	8	3	18	.986	5	.460	D	-	24	20	-1	-3	+1	-4	0	-4	-3	-
Derrek Lee	ChC	158	158	1386.0	1323	122	6	116	.996	29	.681	B+	6	177	175	0	-7	+6	-2	+2	0	+2	15
Travis Lee	TB	124	101	918.1	874	67	4	87	.996	9	.489	D+	29	135	131	+1	-4	-4	-4	-1	-5	-5	26
Jeff Liefer	Cle	5	4	26.0	17	2	1	2	.950	1	.600	B-	-	3	2	-1			-1	0	-1	-1	-
Javy Lopez	Bal	1	0	2.0	1	0	0	1	1.000							0			0				
John Mabry	StL	14	5	53.0	55	8	0	8	1.000	1	.600	B-	-	13	13	0	0	0	0	0	0	+1	-
Rob Mackowiak	Pit	3	1	16.0	18	1	0	4	1.000					2	1	0	-1		-1				
Eli Marrero	2 tms	9	8	73.2	72	3	1	7	.987					10	9	0	0	-1	-1	0	-1	-2	-
Ramon Martinez	2 tms	10	9	76.0	75	6	0	8	1.000	1	.600	B-	-	13	12	+1	-2	0	-1	0	-1	0	-
Tino Martinez	NYY	122	78	770.1	797	49	8	73	.991	4	.613	B-	12	115	125	+7	+7	-4	+10	+1	+11	+9	8
Paul McAnulty	SD	1	0	4.0	4	0	0	1	1.000					1	1	0			0		0		
Dave McCarty	Bos	12	0	23.0	19	3	0	3	1.000					2	3	+1	+1	0	+1	0	+1	+1	-
Scott McClain	ChC	4	1	16.0	15	0	0	1	1.000					2	1	-1			-1	0	-1	0	-
Joe McEwing	KC	20	8	97.1	101	11	0	15	1.000					19	19	0	0	0	0	0	0	0	-
Lou Merloni	LAA	1	0	2.0	0	0	0	0	-							-1			-1				
Doug Mientkiewicz	NYM	83	79	675.0	690	42	4	59	.995	16	.656	B	7	80	89	+5	+3	+1	+9	0	+9	+9	9
Kevin Millar	Bos	110	102	796.1	799	85	7	67	.992	8	.475	D+	32	153	154	-2	+3	+1	+1	+1	+2	+5	11

16

		BASIC								BUNTS				PLAYS		PLUS/MINUS							
Name	Team	G	GS	Inn	PO	A	E	DP	Pct	Opps	Score	Grade	Rank	Expected GB Outs	GB Outs Made	To His Right	Straight On	To His Left	GB	Air	Total	Enhanced	Rank
Jose Molina	LAA	4	1	10.0	10	0	0	2	1.000											0		0	-
Justin Morneau	Min	138	128	1166.1	1191	91	8	123	.994	12	.742	A	1	151	162	-2	+7	+6	+11	0	+11	+13	3
Eric Munson	TB	1	0	3.0	3	0	0	0	1.000											0		0	-
Brian Myrow	LAD	5	2	26.2	20	0	0	2	1.000					1	1	0							-
Xavier Nady	SD	44	34	299.1	261	27	4	27	.986	4	.338	F		54	58	0	+2	+2	+4	0	+4	+5	-
Norihiro Nakamura	LAD	4	1	15.0	18	0	1	2	.947					3	2	-1							-
Phil Nevin	2 tms	74	71	620.0	592	38	4	52	.994	12	.550	C	16	100	98	+2	-3	-1	-2	0	-2	-3	25
Lance Niekro	SF	74	57	529.0	543	38	5	56	.991	4	.438	D-	33	75	85	+6	+4	+1	+10	-1	+9	+10	7
Jose Offerman	2 tms	15	9	92.2	96	4	2	10	.980	5	.530	C		10	10	0	0	0	0	0	0	-1	-
John Olerud	Bos	80	38	431.0	416	40	1	41	.998	4	.625	B-		66	71	+2	+2	+1	+5	+1	+6	+5	-
David Ortiz	Bos	10	10	78.0	69	11	2	8	.976					13	13	0	-1	0	0	-1	-1	-1	-
Lyle Overbay	Mil	154	143	1265.0	1134	96	10	104	.992	26	.513	C-	23	152	157	+2	+6	-3	+5	0	+5	+4	12
Pablo Ozuna	CWS	2	0	3.0	2	1	0	0	1.000					1	1	0							-
Rafael Palmeiro	Bal	93	82	748.1	748	58	4	68	.995	4	.525	C-	22	107	96	-5	-6	0	-11	-1	-12	-12	31
Carlos Pena	Det	51	49	429.1	418	35	3	46	.993	8	.431	D-		64	61	-4	+1	-1	-3	0	-3	-5	-
Eduardo Perez	TB	49	42	320.0	264	17	2	22	.993	2	.625	B-		38	37	0	0	-1	-1	-1	-2	-2	-
Timo Perez	CWS	2	1	11.0	13	1	1	1	.933					4	5				+1	0	+1	+1	-
Tomas Perez	Phi	24	15	146.0	148	10	0	17	1.000	4	.600	B-		13	17	+2	0	+1	+4	0	+4	+4	-
Roberto Petagine	Bos	10	7	53.2	51	6	1	4	.983	1	.600	B-		12	11	-1	+1	-1	-1	0	-1	-2	-
Josh Phelps	TB	1	0	6.0	5	0	0	2	1.000											0		0	-
Andy Phillips	NYY	19	5	67.0	75	2	1	7	.987					7	8	0	0	+1	+1	0	+1	+1	-
Jason Phillips	LAD	21	18	156.2	143	12	0	16	1.000	4	.425	D-		16	17	+1	-1	+1	+1	0	+1	+1	-
Albert Pujols	StL	158	155	1358.2	1596	97	14	175	.992	14	.718	A-	2	223	232	+6	0	+3	+9	0	+9	+10	6
Robb Quinlan	LAA	9	4	42.0	38	1	0	5	1.000					3	2	0	-1	0	-1	0	-1	-1	-
Humberto Quintero	Hou	1	0	1.0	0	1	0	0	1.000					1	1				0	0	0	0	-
Olmedo Saenz	LAD	66	52	475.0	460	19	1	36	.998	6	.425	D-		57	56	-4	0	+2	-1	-1	-2	-1	-
Scott Seabol	StL	5	2	23.0	33	3	0	4	1.000					6	7	+1	-1	0	+1	0	+1	+1	-
Richie Sexson	Sea	151	151	1302.0	1147	119	7	121	.995	19	.534	C	20	200	187	-11	+7	-9	-13	0	-13	-15	32
Ryan Shealy	Col	19	17	152.2	155	8	0	8	1.000	1	.250	F		22	22	-2	0	+1	+1	0	+1	+2	-
Chris Shelton	Det	84	83	738.1	778	60	6	88	.993	6	.683	B+	5	111	106	-3	-3	+1	-5	+1	-4	-2	24
Rick Short	Was	1	0	4.2	4	1	0	0	1.000					1	1	0							-
Jason Smith	Det	1	0	8.0	10	1	0	0	1.000					1	1				0	0	0	0	-
J.T. Snow	SF	108	96	825.2	813	56	3	62	.997	15	.540	C	18	121	122	-1	-1	+3	+1	0	+1	+2	16
Scott Spiezio	Sea	4	3	26.0	30	0	0	1	1.000										-1	0	-1	-1	-
Matt Stairs	KC	64	61	509.2	500	37	4	60	.993	4	.513	C-	24	81	77	-5	-1	+1	-4	-1	-5	-6	28
B.J. Surhoff	Bal	18	14	113.0	116	8	1	14	.992	1	1.000	A+		19	18	0	0	-1	-1	+1	0	-1	-
Mark Sweeney	SD	53	36	337.2	314	21	4	26	.988	7	.600	B-		50	52	-3	+4	0	+2	-1	+1	+1	-
Mike Sweeney	KC	49	49	419.1	441	29	1	28	.998	2	.250	F		84	80	-3	0	-1	-4	0	-4	-6	-
Nick Swisher	Oak	21	13	119.0	109	10	0	10	1.000	4	.525	C-		13	14	+1	-1	0	+1	0	+1	+1	-
Mark Teixeira	Tex	155	154	1358.0	1378	101	3	127	.998	16	.569	C+	15	228	241	+8	+2	+3	+13	+1	+14	+17	1
Jim Thome	Phi	52	52	436.0	404	30	0	36	1.000	8	.481	D+		51	55	+3	+2	-1	+4	-1	+3	+4	-
Terry Tiffee	Min	13	10	86.0	92	7	1	6	.990	1	1.000	A+		10	11	+1	0	0	+1	0	+1	+1	-
Chad Tracy	Ari	80	72	652.2	706	47	3	75	.996	9	.656	B	8	88	97	+3	+5	0	+9	+2	+11	+11	5
Chase Utley	Phi	8	6	54.2	45	9	1	7	.982	1	.600	B-		8	12	+2	+1	+1	+4	0	+4	+4	-
Javier Valentin	Cin	2	2	18.0	21	0	0	2	1.000					4	3				-1	0	-1	-2	-
Jose Vizcaino	Hou	13	8	72.2	63	4	2	7	.971					13	14	+1	-1	0	+1	0	+1	+1	-
Todd Walker	ChC	4	3	31.0	26	4	0	4	1.000	1	.600	B-		5	6	0	0	0	+1	0	+1	+1	-
Daryle Ward	Pit	109	101	891.2	863	76	6	114	.994	13	.412	D-	34	113	115	-2	+5	-2	+2	0	+2	+3	14
Ty Wigginton	Pit	3	3	23.0	22	2	0	1	1.000					2	3	+1	0		+1				-
Brad Wilkerson	Was	25	19	185.1	172	14	1	20	.995	4	.713	A-		20	21	+1	0	0	+1	-1	0	0	-
Craig Wilson	Pit	15	11	99.1	86	6	1	10	.989	1	.250	F		15	14	-2	+1	0	-1	0	-1	-1	-
Enrique Wilson	ChC	3	0	6.0	7	0	0	0	1.000					1	1				0				-
Chris Woodward	NYM	34	21	199.0	206	10	2	16	.991	4	.613	B-		24	27	+2	+1	0	+3	0	+3	+3	-
Kevin Youkilis	Bos	9	5	47.0	48	0	0	4	1.000					7	7	0	0	0	0	0	0	0	-
Dmitri Young	Det	30	30	257.0	265	22	3	25	.990	4	.425	D-		40	38	-2	-1	+1	-2	0	-2	-1	-
Walter Young	Bal	10	7	54.0	55	6	0	9	1.000	2	.250	F		11	11	0	0	0	0	0	0	0	-
2005 MLB Averages									.993	601	.571	C+											

Second Basemen 2005

BASIC													GROUND DP				PLAYS				PLUS/MINUS						
Name	Team	G	GS	Inn	PO	A	E	DP	Pct	Rng	Rel Rng	Rel +/-	GDP Opps	GDP	Pct	Rank	Expected Outs GB	Expected Outs Air	Outs Made GB	Outs Made Air	To His Right	Straight On	To His Left	GB	Air	Total	Rank
Brent Abernathy	Min	17	14	124.0	24	37	2	9	.968	4.43	.861	-10	13	8	.615	-	34	12	32	12	-2	0	0	-2	0	-2	-
Manny Alexander	SD	5	1	20.0	1	4	0	0	1.000	2.25	.479	-5	0		-	-	3	1	3	1	0	0		0	0	0	-
Edgardo Alfonzo	SF	2	2	12.1	4	4	0	2	1.000	5.84	1.182	+1	2	2	1.000	-	2	2	2	2	0	0	0	0	0	0	-
Marlon Anderson	NYM	20	16	141.1	35	47	1	9	.988	5.22	1.073	+6	23	9	.391	-	37	12	38	14	-1	0	+2	+1	+2	+3	-
Rich Aurilia	Cin	68	64	547.1	128	175	6	38	.981	4.98	1.000	0	74	38	.514	17	143	58	147	53	+1	+3	0	+4	-5	-1	17
Brad Ausmus	Hou	1	0	1.0	0	0	0	0	-	.00	.000	-1	0		-	-		0		0					0		-
Willy Aybar	LAD	6	2	23.1	2	6	0	1	1.000	3.09	.617	-5	1	1	1.000	-	5	1	5	1	-1	0	+1	0	0	0	-
Carlos Baerga	Was	7	5	46.0	15	19	3	3	.919	6.65	1.403	+10	6	2	.333	-	13	8	16	7	0	0	+2	+3	-1	+2	-
Mark Bellhorn	2 tms	85	84	728.0	152	264	7	56	.983	5.14	1.029	+8	102	55	.539	11	232	62	227	65	-5	+2	-2	-5	+3	-2	18
Ronnie Belliard	Cle	141	139	1243.2	259	413	13	95	.981	4.86	1.028	+19	146	86	.589	5	338	105	353	110	+23	-2	-6	+15	+5	+20	4
William Bergolla	Cin	9	6	62.0	11	29	0	6	1.000	5.81	1.166	+6	9	6	.667	-	24	7	25	7	+1	0	0	+1	0	+1	-
Yuniesky Betancourt	Sea	9	6	63.0	23	21	0	5	1.000	6.29	1.314	+11	8	3	.375	-	16	8	18	9	0	0	+2	+2	+1	+3	-
Wilson Betemit	Atl	1	1	8.0	1	3	0	0	1.000	4.50	.856	-1	1			-	3		3		0	0	0	0			-
Craig Biggio	Hou	141	141	1172.1	249	395	16	81	.976	4.94	1.028	+18	152	73	.480	24	340	94	327	93	-10	-1	-3	-13	-1	-14	33
Andres Blanco	KC	24	22	184.0	57	68	3	23	.977	6.11	1.151	+16	40	22	.550	-	52	24	51	24	+2	-2	0	-1	0	-1	-
Willie Bloomquist	Sea	32	29	254.0	60	83	2	22	.986	5.07	1.059	+8	36	18	.500	-	62	22	67	23	+1	0	+5	+5	+1	+6	-
Geoff Blum	2 tms	21	20	180.0	31	52	0	12	1.000	4.15	.885	-11	17	10	.588	-	50	11	44	11	-2	+1	-6	-6	0	-4	-
Bret Boone	2 tms	88	88	768.2	170	229	9	54	.978	4.67	.968	-15	103	50	.485	21	220	72	197	70	-18	-5	0	-23	-2	-25	35
Eric Bruntlett	Hou	28	5	79.2	10	16	2	3	.929	2.94	.611	-17	7	3	.429	-	14	4	13	5	+1	-1	-1	-1	+1	0	-
Chris Burke	Hou	18	7	80.1	15	24	0	5	1.000	4.37	.908	-4	9	4	.444	-	17	5	20	5	0	0	+3	+3	0	+3	-
Freddie Bynum	Oak	3	0	5.0	0	0	0	0	-	.00	.000	-3	0		-	-					0			-1			-
Miguel Cairo	NYM	82	74	657.1	151	212	6	58	.984	4.97	1.022	+8	88	50	.568	7	187	63	177	65	-9	0	-1	-10	+2	-8	28
Robinson Cano	NYY	131	130	1142.0	258	391	17	77	.974	5.11	1.000	0	152	70	.461	29	365	103	332	109	-16	-2	-15	-33	+6	-27	36
Jorge Cantu	TB	80	76	667.2	119	181	9	39	.971	4.04	.851	-51	78	37	.474	26	161	50	152	52	-4	-2	-4	-9	+2	-7	25
Jamey Carroll	Was	63	44	427.2	96	145	5	33	.980	5.07	1.070	+16	63	27	.429	-	113	33	119	32	-4	-1	+10	+6	-1	+5	-
Jose Castillo	Pit	100	99	840.1	237	279	12	92	.977	5.53	1.044	+22	131	82	.626	2	222	84	211	87	-5	-6	+1	-11	+3	-8	27
Luis Castillo	Fla	120	116	1012.1	245	352	7	87	.988	5.31	1.031	+17	172	79	.459	31	283	95	292	95	+20	+3	-14	+9	0	+9	12
Bernie Castro	Bal	11	11	96.0	17	31	3	7	.941	4.50	.902	-5	12	6	.500	-	30	10	27	10	-3	0	0	-3	0	-3	-
Juan Castro	Min	5	3	23.0	4	9	0	3	1.000	5.09	.990	0	3	3	1.000	-	8	2	6	2	-1	-1	0	-2	0	-2	-
Ronny Cedeno	ChC	1	0	1.0	0	1	0	0	1.000	9.00	1.877	0	0		-	-	1		1		0			0			-
Angel Chavez	SF	5	1	19.2	3	4	0	0	1.000	3.20	.649	-4	0		-	-	4	3	4	3				0	0	0	-
Alex Cintron	Ari	23	15	144.2	31	39	1	12	.986	4.35	.819	-15	23	10	.435	-	37	13	33	12	+1	-2	-3	-4	-1	-5	-
Jeff Cirillo	Mil	3	1	11.2	4	2	0	1	1.000	4.63	1.036	0	2	1	.500	-	0	1	1	1	+1			+1	0	+1	-
Jermaine Clark	Oak	2	0	2.0	0	0	0	0	-	.00	.000	-1	0		-	-		0		0					0		-
Alex Cora	2 tms	50	35	328.1	76	107	2	29	.989	5.02	1.023	+4	39	28	.718	-	78	39	89	36	+2	+1	+8	+11	-3	+8	-
Fernando Cortez	TB	3	3	23.0	0	3	0	0	1.000	1.17	.247	-9	0		-	-	4		3		0	0	0	-1	-1	-2	-
Craig Counsell	Ari	143	140	1244.1	304	458	8	97	.990	5.51	1.037	+27	185	95	.514	16	342	113	369	121	+24	-3	+6	+27	+8	+35	1
Deivi Cruz	2 tms	49	35	338.1	81	101	2	32	.989	4.84	1.008	-2	60	27	.450	-	83	19	82	18	+1	+1	-2	-1	-1	-2	-
Mike Cuddyer	Min	11	6	55.0	12	18	0	7	1.000	4.91	.955	-1	9	7	.778	-	12	4	13	3	0	0	0	+1	-1	0	-
Brian Dallimore	SF	2	1	10.2	0	6	0	3	1.000	5.06	1.025	0	3	3	1.000	-	6		6		0	0		0			-
Mark DeRosa	Tex	17	8	78.0	13	20	1	3	.971	3.81	.724	-12	5	3	.600	-	17	7	18	7	+1	0	0	+1	0	+1	-
Joe Dillon	Fla	4	2	26.0	5	7	1	2	.923	4.15	.807	-3	3	2	.667	-	4	1	4	1	0	0	0	0	0	0	-
Ray Durham	SF	133	131	1143.0	250	341	11	81	.982	4.65	.942	-36	148	66	.446	33	282	100	282	96	-2	-1	+3	0	-4	-4	21
Damion Easley	Fla	46	34	324.0	80	98	4	26	.978	4.94	.960	-7	49	24	.490	-	86	37	85	38	-2	+1	-1	-1	+1	0	-
Mark Ellis	Oak	115	109	972.0	204	333	6	83	.989	4.97	1.045	+24	134	74	.552	10	265	97	274	99	+2	+1	+5	+9	+2	+11	11
Felix Escalona	NYY	1	1	9.0	1	4	0	1	1.000	5.00	.977	0	2	1	.500	-	3		4					+1			-
Chone Figgins	LAA	42	36	322.1	67	101	5	20	.971	4.69	1.061	+10	41	19	.463	-	85	23	85	24	-2	0	+3	0	+1	+1	-
Ryan Freel	Cin	48	48	382.2	91	127	6	24	.973	5.13	1.029	+6	51	23	.451	-	106	42	113	40	+4	-1	+3	+7	-2	+5	-
J.J. Furmaniak	Pit	9	6	53.0	14	10	1	1	.960	4.08	.770	-7	5	1	.200	-	9	5	9	5	+1	-1	0	0	0	0	-
Eddy Garabito	Col	18	16	132.1	33	37	1	12	.986	4.76	.899	-8	24	11	.458	-	33	11	27	10	+1	-5	-2	-6	-1	-7	-
Jesse Garcia	SD	2	0	7.0	2	3	0	1	1.000	6.43	1.370	+1	1	1	1.000	-	2	1	2	1	0	0		0	0	0	-
Esteban German	Tex	1	1	9.0	3	8	1	2	.917	11.00	2.091	+6	2	2	1.000	-	6	1	6	1	0	0	+1	0	0	0	-
Marcus Giles	Atl	149	147	1276.0	266	468	12	96	.984	5.18	.984	-12	190	92	.484	23	398	98	399	96	+12	+1	-12	+1	-2	-1	14
Keith Ginter	Oak	25	24	203.2	49	69	3	17	.975	5.21	1.096	+11	32	17	.531	-	57	17	60	16	+3	+1	-1	+3	-1	+2	-
Chris Gomez	Bal	18	13	123.2	31	40	1	12	.986	5.17	1.036	+2	14	11	.786	-	33	16	31	15	+1	0	-2	-2	-1	-3	-
Luis A Gonzalez	Col	83	66	579.1	121	196	0	40	1.000	4.92	.930	-23	81	38	.469	28	175	36	174	36	0	+1	-2	-1	0	-1	15
Ruben Gotay	KC	81	74	666.0	156	231	8	51	.980	5.23	.984	-6	87	46	.529	14	209	71	200	69	-4	0	-5	-9	-2	-11	31
Tony Graffanino	2 tms	73	71	588.0	121	186	4	37	.987	4.70	.926	-27	63	32	.508	19	160	59	157	57	-7	+3	+1	-3	-2	-5	23
Andy Green	Ari	5	4	39.1	10	11	0	4	1.000	4.81	.904	-2	5	3	.600	-	6	3	7	5	-1	0	+1	+1	+2	+3	-
Nick Green	TB	91	83	731.0	141	195	4	45	.988	4.14	.871	-49	76	39	.513	18	168	66	169	68	-2	-2	+5	+1	+2	+3	13
Mark Grudzielanek	StL	137	132	1158.1	245	442	7	108	.990	5.34	.988	-8	166	104	.627	1	344	67	364	67	+15	+2	+3	+20	0	+20	3
Jerry Hairston Jr.	ChC	44	36	331.2	69	111	5	23	.973	4.88	1.019	+3	40	22	.550	-	99	29	96	31	-1	-2	0	-3	+2	-1	-
Bill Hall	Mil	23	21	185.0	44	53	4	5	.960	4.72	1.056	+5	24	5	.208	-	47	17	49	17	0	+2	+1	+2	0	+2	-
Brendan Harris	Was	2	1	13.1	2	5	0	1	1.000	4.73	.997	0	2	1	.500	-	4		4		0	0	0	0			-
Willie Harris	CWS	32	28	248.1	58	78	2	20	.986	4.93	1.031	+4	35	20	.571	-	69	26	70	26	-4	+1	+4	+1	0	+1	-
Anderson Hernandez	NYM	5	5	45.0	9	18	0	1	1.000	5.40	1.110	+3	4	1	.250	-	16	3	18	3	+1	+1	+1	+2	0	+2	-
Jose Hernandez	Cle	4	3	27.0	6	9	0	6	1.000	5.00	1.057	+1	7	6	.857	-	5	0	5	1	-1			0	+1	+1	-
Aaron Hill	Tor	22	19	177.2	33	77	1	15	.991	5.57	1.094	+10	34	14	.412	-	65	12	68	10	0	+1	+2	+3	-2	+1	-
Bobby Hill	Pit	1	0	0.2	0	0	1	0	.000	.00	.000	0	0		-	-									0		-
Denny Hocking	KC	13	12	119.0	33	48	2	13	.976	6.13	1.153	+10	24	13	.542	-	41	16	39	16	0	-1	-1	-2	0	-2	-
Aaron Holbert	Cin	4	3	28.0	11	8	1	3	.950	6.11	1.226	+3	6	3	.500	-	9	5	7	5	-2	0	-1	-2	0	-2	-
Kevin Hooper	Det	1	1	9.0	2	1	0	0	1.000	3.00	.575	-2	0		-	-	1	2	1	2				0	0	0	-
Orlando Hudson	Tor	130	120	1067.2	302	390	6	80	.991	5.83	1.145	+89	143	77	.538	12	313	154	330	157	-1	+1	+18	+17	+3	+20	5
Tadahito Iguchi	CWS	133	129	1171.1	234	375	14	84	.978	4.68	.979	-14	141	79	.560	8	313	103	311	102	-9	+4	+3	-2	-1	-3	20
Omar Infante	Det	69	65	591.2	153	186	4	51	.988	5.16	.989	-4	88	47	.534	13	156	41	150	40	-5	-2	0	-6	-1	-7	26
Maicer Izturis	LAA	1	1	8.0	4	4	0	0	1.000	9.00	2.036	+4	1			-	4	3	4	2	0			0	-1	-1	-
Damian Jackson	SD	35	28	265.0	53	93	1	21	.993	4.96	1.056	+8	35	20	.571	-	74	23	79	25	+3	+1	+1	+5	+2	+7	-
D'Angelo Jimenez	Cin	27	23	211.2	56	63	2	17	.983	5.06	1.016	+2	29	16	.552	-	53	23	52	24	0	0	-1	-1	+1	0	-
Russ Johnson	NYY	1	0	1.0	0	0	0	0	-	.00	.000	-1	0		-	-		0		0					0		-
Matt Kata	2 tms	10	3	33.0	8	12	0	6	1.000	5.45	1.209	0	9	6	.667	-	6	2	7	2	+1	0	0	+1	0	+1	-
Adam Kennedy	LAA	127	123	1107.2	212	352	5	71	.991	4.58	1.037	+20	110	65	.591	4	284	101	302	99	+11	-1	+8	+18	-2	+16	7
Jeff Kent	LAD	140	138	1209.2	284	424	16	88	.978	5.27	1.054	+36	177	78	.441	35	357	86	351	87	-9	+6	-2	-6	+1	-5	22
Felipe Lopez	Cin	7	5	48.0	15	11	0	4	1.000	4.88	.979	-1	7	4	.571	-	5	6	7	7	+1	0	0	+2	+1	+3	-
Jose Lopez	Sea	51	50	439.0	123	159	6	32	.979	5.78	1.208	+49	61	32	.525	-	134	56	134	53	+1	+3	-3	0	-3	-3	-
Luis M Lopez	Cin	4	2	16.0	3	5	0	0	1.000	4.50	.904	-1	2			-	5	1	5	1	0	0	0	0	0	0	-
Pedro Lopez	CWS	1	1	9.0	3	5	0	2	1.000	8.00	1.673	+3	3	1	.333	-	2	2	2	1	0	0		0	-1	-1	-
Mark Loretta	SD	105	105	910.1	201	261	6	61	.987	4.57	.973	-13	109	57	.523	15	228	90	216	91	-1	+1	-12	-12	+1	-11	30
Mike Lowell	Fla	9	9	67.0	18	13	1	3	.969	4.16	.809	-7	13	3	.231	-	13	5	12	5	+1	0	-2	-1	0	-1	-
Hector Luna	StL	22	15	143.0	41	52	2	14	.979	5.85	1.084	+7	27	14	.519	-	36	7	38	7	+1	+1	0	+2	0	+2	-
Alejandro Machado	Bos	3	0	8.0	0	0	0	0	-	.00	.000	-4	0		-	-					-1			-1			-
Jose Macias	ChC	20	11	112.1	27	34	0	8	1.000	4.89	1.019	+1	25	8	.320	-	28	7	28	7	-1	0	+1	0	0	0	-

		BASIC												GROUND DP				PLAYS				PLUS/MINUS						
											Rel	Rel	GDP				Expected Outs		Outs Made		To His	Straight	To His				
Name	Team	G	GS	Inn	PO	A	E	DP	Pct	Rng	Rng	+/-	Opps	GDP	Pct	Rank	GB	Air	GB	Air	Right	On	Left	GB	Air	Total	Rank
Rob Mackowiak	Pit	20	17	146.1	37	43	2	10	.976	4.92	.929	-6	20	8	.400	-	35	11	34	12	-1	-1	+1	-1	+1	0	-
Ramon Martinez	2 tms	5	5	39.0	11	14	3	3	.893	5.77	1.120	+2	8	3	.375	-	14	1	12	1	0	-2	+1	-2	0	-2	-
Henry Mateo	Was	1	1	6.0	1	2	0	0	1.000	4.50	.949	0	0		-	-	1	1	2	1				+1	0	+1	-
Dave Matranga	LAA	1	0	2.0	2	1	0	0	1.000	13.50	3.054	+2	0		-	-		2		2				-1	0	-1	-
Kazuo Matsui	NYM	71	64	560.0	107	187	9	32	.970	4.73	.971	-9	64	31	.484	22	160	52	159	52	0	+2	-3	-1	0	-1	16
John McDonald	2 tms	13	5	57.1	15	16	0	6	1.000	4.87	.995	-2	8	5	.625	-	10	9	12	10	+1	0	+1	+2	+1	+3	-
Marshall McDougall	Tex	2	0	2.0	0	0	0	0		.00	.000	-1	0												-1		-
Joe McEwing	KC	11	10	76.1	15	25	0	6	1.000	4.72	.888	-5	7	5	.714	-	20	8	17	7	0	0	-3	-3	-1	-4	-
Frank Menechino	Tor	26	21	178.1	37	70	1	18	.991	5.40	1.060	+6	26	18	.692	-	56	13	58	12	+4	-1	-1	+2	-1	+1	-
Aaron Miles	Col	79	69	602.0	154	207	6	48	.984	5.40	1.019	+7	100	45	.450	32	178	59	173	56	-6	0	+1	-5	-3	-8	29
Mike Mordecai	Fla	1	1	6.0	2	2	0	0	1.000	6.00	1.165	+1	4	1	.250	-	2	1	2	1	0	0	0	0	0	0	-
Bill Mueller	Bos	5	5	43.0	10	13	1	1	.958	4.81	.955	-1	4	1	.250	-	14	4	12	5	-1	0	0	-2	+1	-1	-
Donald Murphy	KC	29	23	204.2	42	61	3	14	.972	4.53	.853	-17	19	12	.632	-	58	23	53	22	-3	-3	0	-5	-1	-6	-
Norihiro Nakamura	LAD	1	0	2.0	1	0	0	0	1.000	4.50	.900	0	1		-	-								-1			-
Abraham O Nunez	StL	22	15	132.0	26	38	2	15	.970	4.36	.808	-15	18	15	.833	-	29	9	30	8	0	-1	+2	+1	-1	0	-
Jose Offerman	2 tms	1	0	2.0	0	0	0	0					0		-						-1						-
Ray Olmedo	Cin	31	12	137.1	38	40	2	8	.975	5.11	1.026	+2	23	9	.391	-	36	11	32	10	+2	-1	-4	-4	-1	-5	-
Pete Orr	Atl	25	14	159.2	35	57	5	11	.948	5.19	.986	-1	27	10	.370	-	47	11	47	13	0	-1	+1	0	+2	+2	-
Pablo Ozuna	CWS	6	2	29.0	6	6	1	0	.923	3.72	.779	-4	5		-	-	8	1	6	1	-1	0	-1	-2	0	-2	-
Antonio Perez	LAD	29	21	184.1	40	58	3	10	.970	4.78	.957	-4	23	10	.435	-	56	17	49	15	-4	-1	-1	-7	-2	-9	-
Neifi Perez	ChC	26	18	160.0	32	47	2	10	.975	4.44	.927	-6	17	10	.588	-	41	12	41	13	-4	-1	+5	0	+1	+1	-
Brandon Phillips	Cle	2	2	18.0	5	4	0	2	1.000	4.50	.951	0	2	2	1.000	-	3	3	3	3	0	0	0	0	0	0	-
Placido Polanco	2 tms	113	109	945.2	244	322	3	95	.995	5.39	1.058	+31	158	90	.570	6	241	82	255	81	+3	+7	+4	+14	-1	+13	9
Nick Punto	Min	73	63	564.1	131	193	7	44	.979	5.17	1.005	+2	70	42	.600	3	157	57	169	57	-3	+1	+14	+12	0	+12	10
Omar Quintanilla	Col	6	3	31.1	10	10	0	5	1.000	5.74	1.085	+2	7	5	.714	-	6	1	7	1	+1	0	0	+1	0	+1	-
Desi Relaford	Col	11	8	73.2	10	31	2	4	.953	5.01	.946	-2	11	4	.364	-	27	4	28	3	-2	+1	+2	+1	-1	0	-
Luis Rivas	Min	53	40	360.0	77	112	1	26	.995	4.73	.919	-17	36	22	.611	-	92	37	88	36	-4	+1	-1	-4	-1	-5	-
Brian Roberts	Bal	141	138	1208.0	238	413	8	93	.988	4.85	.972	-18	152	84	.553	9	336	99	352	101	+8	+2	+6	+16	+2	+18	6
Oscar Robles	LAD	1	1	8.0	0	1	1	1	.500	1.13	.225	-3	1	1	1.000	-	2		1		0	0	-1	-1			-
Luis Rodriguez	Min	40	22	216.0	53	73	0	22	1.000	5.25	1.021	+3	30	21	.700	-	55	21	60	21	+1	0	+5	+5	0	+5	-
Freddy Sanchez	Pit	58	39	387.1	108	117	2	40	.991	5.23	.988	-3	65	38	.585	-	87	44	83	42	-1	0	-3	-4	-2	-6	-
Rey Sanchez	NYY	9	7	63.0	18	24	1	5	.977	6.00	1.173	+6	9	4	.444	-	24	5	21	5	-1	0	-1	-3	0	-3	-
Ramon Santiago	Sea	2	2	17.0	0	4	0	1	1.000	2.12	.443	-5	1	1	1.000	-	3		4		+1	0	0	+1	0	+1	-
Marco Scutaro	Oak	30	29	267.2	56	92	1	18	.993	4.98	1.046	+7	35	17	.486	-	68	28	77	27	+3	+2	+4	+9	-1	+8	-
Scott Seabol	StL	8	0	12.1	1	5	0	0	1.000	4.38	.811	-1	0		-	-	5		5		0	0	-1	0			-
Rick Short	Was	6	3	30.0	7	8	1	2	.938	4.50	.949	-1	5	2	.400	-	8	1	6	2	0	-1	-1	-2	+1	-1	-
Jason Smith	Det	6	6	51.0	8	16	1	4	.960	4.24	.812	-6	6	4	.667	-	19	4	16	3	0	0	-3	-3	-1	-4	-
Zach Sorensen	LAA	2	2	24.1	3	5	0	1	1.000	2.96	.669	-4	0		-	-	3	3	4	3				+1	0	+1	-
Alfonso Soriano	Tex	153	153	1351.0	284	447	21	101	.972	4.87	.926	-57	198	93	.470	27	402	94	382	92	+2	+1	-23	-20	-2	-22	34
Scott Spiezio	Sea	1	1	8.0	1	1	0	0	1.000	2.25	.470	-2	1		-	-											-
Junior Spivey	2 tms	70	67	594.0	127	179	7	41	.978	4.64	1.020	+5	73	37	.507	20	142	51	156	51	+6	0	+9	+14	0	+14	8
Ryan Theriot	ChC	3	2	18.2	3	9	0	0	1.000	5.79	1.207	+2	1		-	-	7	2	9	2	+1	0	0	+2	0	+2	-
Chase Utley	Phi	135	135	1195.1	296	376	15	72	.978	5.06	1.073	+46	144	64	.444	34	302	128	325	131	+20	+1	+3	+23	+3	+26	2
Ramon Vazquez	2 tms	12	7	70.0	20	16	2	6	.947	4.63	1.020	-2	12	6	.500	-	14	6	11	6	0	-2	-1	-3	-1	-4	-
Jose Vidro	Was	79	79	665.1	134	191	5	39	.985	4.40	.927	-25	76	35	.461	30	173	57	169	55	-4	0	0	-4	-2	-6	24
Jose Vizcaino	Hou	23	10	109.2	30	39	0	14	1.000	5.66	1.177	+11	20	13	.650	-	28	13	26	14	-1	-1	0	-2	+1	-1	-
Todd Walker	ChC	97	93	797.2	164	242	6	44	.985	4.58	.955	-19	101	40	.396	36	217	56	213	58	-2	+1	-4	-4	+2	-2	19
Rickie Weeks	Mil	95	94	837.1	178	233	21	60	.951	4.42	.989	-5	109	52	.477	25	208	76	200	73	-3	-9	+4	-8	-3	-11	31
Ty Wigginton	Pit	1	1	8.0	3	2	0	1	1.000	5.40	1.020	0	2		-	-	2	1	2	1	0	0	0	0	0	0	-
Enrique Wilson	ChC	5	2	18.2	4	9	1	5	.929	6.27	1.307	+3	7	5	.714	-	7		6		0	-1	0	-1	-1	-2	-
Josh Wilson	Fla	4	0	7.0	1	1	0	0	1.000	2.57	.499	-2	2		-	-	1		1		0			0			-
Tony Womack	NYY	24	22	199.0	42	89	1	22	.992	5.92	1.158	+18	32	20	.625	-	85	13	78	13	-5	0	-2	-7	0	-7	-
Chris Woodward	NYM	5	3	30.0	4	7	2	1	.846	3.30	.678	-5	1	1	1.000	-	7	3	6	3	-1	0	-1	-1	0	-1	-
Kevin Youkilis	Bos	2	1	7.0	0	2	0	0	1.000	2.57	.510	-2	0		-	-	2		2		+1	0	-1	0			-
Eric Young	SD	14	10	91.0	25	26	3	8	.944	5.04	1.075	+4	17	8	.471	-	24	9	18	9	-3	-2	-2	-6	0	-6	-
2005 MLB Averages									.982	4.97			5859	3009	.514												

Third Basemen 2005

BASIC													BUNTS				PLAYS		PLUS/MINUS							
Name	Team	G	GS	Inn	PO	A	E	DP	Pct	Rng	Rel Rng	Rel +/-	Opps	Score	Grade	Rank	Expected GB Outs	GB Outs Made	To His Right	Straight On	To His Left	GB	Air	Total	Enhanced	Rank
Manny Alexander	SD	1	0	1.0	0	0	0	0	-	.00	.000	0				-						0				-
Edgardo Alfonzo	SF	97	92	813.0	76	157	8	10	.967	2.58	.933	-17	18	.467	C	19	157	145	-2	-10	0	-12	0	-12	-10	23
Garrett Atkins	Col	136	136	1161.2	78	262	18	23	.950	2.63	.890	-41	26	.425	C-	23	244	250	+6	+1	-1	+6	0	+6	+10	9
Rich Aurilia	Cin	18	14	129.1	12	33	1	4	.978	3.13	1.116	+5	1	1.000	A+	-	34	31	0	-3	0	-3	0	-3	-4	-
Willy Aybar	LAD	20	20	174.0	16	35	2	3	.962	2.64	.958	-2	2	.800	A+	-	32	33	-2	+1	+3	+1	0	+1	+1	-
Carlos Baerga	Was	20	10	100.2	7	16	2	1	.920	2.06	.813	-5	1	.250	F	-	19	16	-1	-2	0	-3	0	-3	-3	-
Jeff Baker	Col	10	10	79.0	3	20	1	1	.958	2.62	.885	-3	1	.250	F	-	22	20	-1	-1	+1	-2	-1	-3	-3	-
Jose Bautista	Pit	7	7	55.2	4	13	1	2	.944	2.75	.910	-2	3	.483	C+	-	11	12	0	+1	0	+1	0	+1	0	-
David Bell	Phi	150	148	1296.2	105	304	21	22	.951	2.84	1.079	+30	27	.519	C+	11	260	286	-6	+25	+7	+26	0	+26	+24	1
Mark Bellhorn	2 tms	4	1	18.0	1	3	0	0	1.000	2.00	.700	-2				-	2	3				+1	0	+1	+1	-
Adrian Beltre	Sea	155	155	1325.2	140	271	14	25	.967	2.79	1.046	+18	18	.536	B-	9	258	265	+5	-3	+5	+7	+1	+8	+11	8
Wilson Betemit	Atl	63	46	431.0	26	94	6	6	.952	2.51	.857	-20	10	.390	D+	-	84	91	0	+3	+3	+7	0	+7	+7	-
Casey Blake	Cle	6	6	40.0	4	9	1	1	.929	2.93	1.093	+1				-	8	9	+1	0	0	+1	0	+1	+1	-
Hank Blalock	Tex	158	156	1374.0	96	304	11	23	.973	2.62	.900	-43	17	.509	C+	12	305	289	-6	-4	-6	-16	-1	-17	-21	26
Tony Blanco	Was	5	0	13.0	0	3	0	0	1.000	2.08	.821	-1				-	3	3		+1	0	0				-
Willie Bloomquist	Sea	6	1	25.0	1	4	0	0	1.000	1.80	.675	-2				-	4	4	0	0	0	0				-
Geoff Blum	2 tms	46	35	316.2	24	91	6	9	.950	3.27	1.277	+25	9	.489	C+	-	77	85	0	+5	+3	+8	0	+8	+9	-
Hiram Bocachica	Oak	2	2	18.0	2	3	0	1	1.000	2.50	.945	0				-	3	3	0	0		0	0	0	0	-
Aaron Boone	Cle	142	139	1249.2	81	298	18	20	.955	2.73	1.020	+7	21	.633	A-	4	279	278	+1	-3	+1	-1	0	-1	+1	15
Russell Branyan	Mil	59	56	456.2	40	82	7	10	.946	2.40	.948	-7	9	.617	A-	-	87	75	-6	-3	-3	-12	-1	-13	-16	-
Eric Bruntlett	Hou	8	0	13.0	1	1	0	0	1.000	1.38	.510	-2				-	2	1	-1			-1	0	-1	-1	-
Sean Burroughs	SD	78	70	656.2	59	145	8	15	.962	2.80	1.105	+19	7	.407	D+	25	130	142	-2	+7	+7	+12	0	+12	+12	7
Miguel Cabrera	Fla	30	29	238.0	21	46	2	5	.971	2.53	.875	-9	7	.500	C+	-	41	40	0	-2	0	-1	0	-1	-1	-
Miguel Cairo	NYM	3	0	6.0	0	2	0	0	1.000	3.00	1.094	0				-	2	2	0	0		0				-
Jorge Cantu	TB	62	58	496.0	31	93	12	7	.912	2.25	.857	-20	5	.540	B-	-	104	86	-8	-7	-3	-18	+1	-17	-19	-
Jamey Carroll	Was	12	5	54.0	1	8	0	0	1.000	1.50	.593	-6	1	.250	F	-	6	8	+1	0	+1	+2	-1	+1	+1	-
Vinny Castilla	Was	138	135	1171.1	142	209	11	23	.970	2.70	1.066	+22	22	.498	C+	13	202	198	-4	+2	-2	-4	-1	-5	-3	19
Juan Castro	Min	22	13	123.0	14	22	4	1	.900	2.63	.934	-3	2	.250	F	-	23	20	+1	-3	-1	-3	0	-3	-3	-
Eric Chavez	Oak	153	153	1348.1	121	301	15	27	.966	2.82	1.065	+26	14	.671	A+	2	280	290	+16	-5	-1	+10	0	+10	+15	3
Alex Cintron	Ari	32	18	192.1	15	41	2	9	.966	2.62	.876	-8	3	.367	D	-	41	38	-4	+2	-1	-3	0	-3	-4	-
Jeff Cirillo	Mil	53	40	365.1	28	70	5	8	.951	2.41	.952	-5	5	.460	C	-	67	66	-3	+2	0	-1	0	-1	-2	-
Alex Cora	2 tms	5	2	24.2	2	7	3	0	.750	3.28	1.177	+1				-	9	6	-2	-2	0	-3	0	-3	-3	-
Fernando Cortez	TB	1	0	1.0	0	0	0	0	-	.00	.000	0				-						-1				-
Joe Crede	CWS	130	122	1120.1	95	243	10	27	.971	2.72	1.028	+9	22	.484	C+	16	224	236	-14	+16	+11	+12	-1	+11	+2	14
Deivi Cruz	2 tms	5	3	37.2	1	11	0	0	1.000	2.87	1.037	0	1	1.000	A+	-	10	10	+1	0	0	0	0	0	0	-
Mike Cuddyer	Min	95	92	816.0	57	188	15	14	.942	2.70	.958	-11	11	.577	B	6	194	183	+4	-6	-8	-11	-1	-12	-10	22
Mark DeRosa	Tex	5	4	36.0	2	5	1	1	.875	1.75	.601	-5	1	.250	F	-	6	5	0	-1	+1	-1	0	-1	-1	-
Joe Dillon	Fla	2	0	9.0	2	1	0	0	1.000	3.00	1.036	0				-	1	1	0			0	0	0	0	-
Greg Dobbs	Sea	2	1	11.0	4	5	0	1	1.000	7.36	2.760	+6				-	5	5	0	+1	-1	0	0	0	0	-
Trent Durrington	Mil	1	0	2.0	0	0	3	0	.000	.00	.000	-1				-			0	-1	-1	-2				-
Damion Easley	Fla	10	7	66.1	9	16	1	1	.962	3.39	1.171	+4	1	.250	F	-	16	15	0	0	-1	-1	+1	0	+1	-
Mike Edwards	LAD	39	33	294.2	22	56	7	6	.918	2.38	.866	-12	5	.690	A+	-	52	53	-1	+3	-1	+1	0	+1	0	-
Edwin Encarnacion	Cin	56	55	478.0	54	116	10	9	.944	3.20	1.141	+20	10	.405	D+	-	108	110	+4	-1	0	+2	0	+2	+5	-
Morgan Ensberg	Hou	148	147	1286.1	100	295	15	31	.963	2.76	1.018	+7	20	.433	C-	22	269	285	+3	+6	+7	+16	-1	+15	+15	4
Felix Escalona	NYY	3	0	6.0	0	1	0	0	1.000	1.50	.525	-1				-	1	1	0			0				-
Pedro Feliz	SF	79	67	591.2	47	144	6	16	.970	2.91	1.051	+9	13	.731	A+	1	118	132	+2	+7	+5	+14	+2	+16	+16	2
Robert Fick	SD	1	0	2.0	0	0	0	0	-	.00	.000	-1				-						-1	0	-1	-1	-
Chone Figgins	LAA	56	48	437.2	34	95	3	8	.977	2.65	1.098	+12	10	.430	C-	-	86	89	+3	+6	-5	+3	-1	+2	+4	-
Ryan Freel	Cin	10	8	69.0	5	25	2	1	.938	3.91	1.395	+8	1	.600	B+	-	21	24	0	+2	+1	+3	0	+3	+3	-
Nomar Garciaparra	ChC	34	34	295.2	20	65	6	1	.934	2.59	.974	-2	8	.544	B-	-	64	58	+3	-8	-1	-6	0	-6	-5	-
Esteban German	Tex	1	0	3.0	0	0	0	0	-	.00	.000	-1				-			-1	0		-1				-
Marcus Giles	Atl	1	0	6.0	0	6	0	0	1.000	9.00	3.079	+4				-	4	6	+1	0	+1	+2				-
Keith Ginter	Oak	12	5	63.0	12	11	3	0	.885	3.29	1.242	+5	1	.600	B+	-	10	10	-1	0	+1	0	0	0	-1	-
Troy Glaus	Ari	145	144	1264.0	113	310	24	25	.946	3.01	1.007	+3	27	.467	C	18	311	297	-2	-1	-11	-14	+2	-12	-12	24
Chris Gomez	Bal	17	13	120.0	11	23	1	1	.971	2.55	.919	-3	4	.338	D-	-	22	22	0	0	+1	0	0	0	0	-
Alex S Gonzalez	TB	98	90	779.2	65	173	14	10	.944	2.75	1.047	+10	15	.437	C-	21	167	162	+4	-4	-5	-5	-1	-6	0	17
Luis A Gonzalez	Col	12	4	51.0	6	7	0	1	1.000	2.29	.775	-4	2	.250	F	-	7	7	0	0		0	0	0	0	-
Tony Graffanino	2 tms	17	14	134.1	7	31	5	3	.884	2.55	.877	-5	2	.425	C-	-	38	30	-4	-5	0	-8	0	-8	-8	-
Nick Green	TB	13	11	104.0	4	21	3	2	.893	2.16	.824	-5	3	.367	D	-	25	21	-3	0	-1	-4	0	-4	-4	-
Bill Hall	Mil	59	49	435.1	39	84	6	11	.953	2.54	1.003	0	11	.618	A-	-	82	82	-2	0	+3	0	+1	+1	0	-
Dave Hansen	Sea	7	4	43.0	5	7	0	0	1.000	2.51	.941	-1	2	.625	A-	-	5	6	0	0		+1	0	+1	+1	-
Brendan Harris	Was	1	1	8.0	1	4	0	0	1.000	5.63	2.223	+3				-	4	4	0			0	0	0	0	-
Lenny Harris	Fla	2	0	2.1	0	0	0	0	-	.00	.000	-1				-			0			0				-
Wes Helms	Mil	35	17	178.2	12	41	2	4	.964	2.67	1.053	+3	3	.483	C+	-	38	39	0	-1	+2	+1	-1	0	0	-
Jose Hernandez	Cle	21	17	163.0	16	35	0	2	1.000	2.82	1.052	+3	1	.600	B+	-	31	33	+1	+1	0	+2	0	+2	+1	-
Aaron Hill	Tor	35	32	286.2	21	73	5	8	.949	2.95	1.009	+1	4	.338	D-	-	69	71	+1	0	+1	+2	0	+2	+2	-
Bobby Hill	Pit	24	14	147.2	10	32	1	4	.977	2.56	.847	-8	6	.375	D	-	32	30	-1	0	-1	-2	0	-2	-3	-
Shea Hillenbrand	Tor	54	52	451.0	31	94	6	8	.954	2.49	.853	-22	6	.308	F	-	100	94	-3	-3	0	-6	0	-6	-7	-
Aaron Holbert	Cin	2	1	10.0	0	5	0	0	1.000	4.50	1.604	+2				-	5	5	0	-2	+2	0				-
Aubrey Huff	TB	4	2	21.0	2	2	0	1	1.000	1.71	.653	-2				-	3	2	0	-1	0	-1	0	-1	-1	-
Brandon Inge	Det	160	159	1399.2	128	378	23	41	.957	3.25	1.104	+48	22	.477	C	17	357	364	+16	-6	-3	+7	-2	+5	+12	5
Maicer Izturis	LAA	45	26	275.2	20	62	8	5	.911	2.68	1.108	+8	9	.450	C	-	53	56	-4	+1	+6	+3	0	+3	+3	-
Damian Jackson	SD	8	7	53.0	2	6	1	1	.889	1.36	.537	-7	1	.250	F	-	6	5	0	-1	0	-1	0	-1	-1	-
Russ Johnson	NYY	8	0	18.0	1	2	0	0	1.000	1.50	.525	-3				-	4	2	0	-1	-1	-2	0	-2	-2	-
Chipper Jones	Atl	101	100	830.1	80	169	5	18	.980	2.70	.923	-21	21	.538	B-	8	154	153	+1	+1	-3	-1	0	-1	-2	18
Corey Koskie	Tor	76	74	674.1	52	158	7	19	.968	2.80	.958	-9	13	.446	C-	20	140	154	-3	+12	+6	+14	-2	+12	+12	6
Mike Lamb	Hou	15	12	103.1	16	34	1	0	.980	4.35	1.604	+19	3	.600	B+	-	27	31	0	+2	+2	+4	0	+4	+5	-
Felipe Lopez	Cin	1	0	1.0	0	1	0	0	1.000	9.00	3.208	+1				-	0	1	+1			+1				-
Jose Lopez	Sea	1	1	9.0	2	2	1	0	.800	4.00	1.499	+1				-	2	2	+1			0	0	0	+1	-
Luis M Lopez	Cin	6	2	29.0	5	4	1	0	.900	2.79	.996	0	1	.250	F	-	6	4	0	-1	0	-2	0	-2	-2	-
Mark Loretta	SD	1	0	1.0	0	0	0	0	-	.00	.000	0				-							0		0	-
Mike Lowell	Fla	135	126	1126.2	107	243	6	34	.983	2.80	.965	-12	24	.656	A	3	234	224	+16	-19	-7	-10	-3	-13	-8	21
Hector Luna	StL	7	4	29.1	4	7	0	2	1.000	3.38	1.109	+1	2	.425	C-	-	6	6	0	0	0	0	0	0	0	-
John Mabry	StL	18	12	106.2	12	19	1	2	.969	2.62	.860	-5	2	.500	C+	-	19	19	0	0	-1	0	0	0	0	-
Jose Macias	ChC	23	7	98.2	6	15	2	1	.913	1.92	.721	-8	3	.483	C+	-	11	13	+2	0	+1	+2	0	+2	+2	-
Rob Mackowiak	Pit	65	50	447.0	38	123	8	15	.953	3.24	1.073	+11	7	.457	C	-	110	114	0	+5	-1	+4	0	+4	+4	-
Andy Marte	Atl	17	13	130.2	4	14	3	1	.857	1.24	.424	-24	2	.625	A-	-	18	12	-2	-2	-2	-6	0	-6	-8	-
Ramon Martinez	2 tms	3	2	17.0	1	3	0	0	1.000	2.12	.805	-1	1	.250	F	-	4	3	-1	-1	+1	-1	0	-1	-1	-
Scott McClain	ChC	3	1	10.1	1	1	0	0	1.000	1.74	.656	-1				-	2	1	0			-1	0	-1	-1	-
John McDonald	2 tms	1	1	9.0	2	0	0	0	1.000	2.00	.679	-1				-						-1	0	-1	-1	-
Marshall McDougall	Tex	5	2	26.0	3	4	0	0	1.000	2.42	.833	-1	2	.425	C-	-	3	3	0	0	0	0	0	0	0	-

		BASIC											BUNTS				PLAYS		PLUS/MINUS							
Name	Team	G	GS	Inn	PO	A	E	DP	Pct	Rng	Rel Rng	Rel +/-	Opps	Score	Grade	Rank	Expected GB Outs	GB Outs Made	To His Right	Straight On	To His Left	GB	Air	Total	Enhanced	Rank
Joe McEwing	KC	29	26	208.2	18	57	3	2	.962	3.23	1.115	+7	3	.250	F		59	59	+4	-2	-2	0	0	0	+1	-
Dallas McPherson	LAA	60	55	483.1	32	86	7	14	.944	2.20	.910	-12	13	.500	C+		73	76	0	+4	-1	+3	0	+3	+2	-
Frank Menechino	Tor	9	4	35.0	2	9	0	2	1.000	2.83	.967	0					9	9	0	0	0	0				-
Lou Merloni	LAA	4	2	16.2	1	8	0	0	1.000	4.86	2.012	+5					7	8	+1	-1	+1	+1	0	+1	+2	-
Melvin Mora	Bal	148	148	1289.2	96	301	18	23	.957	2.77	.998	-1	17	.356	D-	26	291	295	+2	+4	-2	+4	+1	+5	+6	11
Bill Mueller	Bos	142	140	1209.1	87	265	10	20	.972	2.62	.939	-23	9	.578	B	5	258	261	+7	0	-3	+3	+1	+4	+6	12
Eric Munson	TB	2	1	13.0	1	1	0	0	1.000	1.38	.528	-2					2	1	0	-1	0	-1	0	-1	-1	-
Xavier Nady	SD	3	2	18.0	0	6	0	0	1.000	3.00	1.186	+1	1	.250	F		8	6	-1	-1	+1	-2				-
Norihiro Nakamura	LAD	10	6	57.0	3	16	0	2	1.000	3.00	1.090	+2					13	15	+1	+1	+1	+2	0	+2	+2	-
Phil Nevin	2 tms	1	0	1.0	1	1	0	1	1.000	9.00	3.092	+1					0	1				+1				-
David Newhan	Bal	8	1	18.0	1	3	0	1	1.000	2.00	.720	-2					3	3	0	0	0	0	0	0	0	-
Abraham O Nunez	StL	98	77	720.2	54	203	10	19	.963	3.21	1.055	+14	12	.492	C+	15	188	194	+6	+1	-2	+6	+1	+7	+9	10
Pete Orr	Atl	12	3	45.2	2	14	1	2	.941	3.15	1.079	+1	1	1.000	A+		14	13	-1	-1	+1	-1	0	-1	-1	-
Pablo Ozuna	CWS	32	30	261.0	29	67	6	4	.941	3.31	1.253	+20	4	.425	C-		65	65	+3	-2	0	0	0	0	+1	-
Antonio Perez	LAD	35	33	273.0	18	70	5	5	.946	2.90	1.054	+5	6	.433	C-		60	69	+4	+3	+2	+9	-2	+7	+8	-
Eduardo Perez	TB	3	0	7.0	2	0	0	0	1.000	2.57	.980	0										0		0		-
Neifi Perez	ChC	4	0	6.0	0	1	0	0	1.000	1.50	.565	-1					1	1				0				-
Tomas Perez	Phi	15	7	73.0	11	17	0	2	1.000	3.45	1.313	+7	2	.250	F		15	16	0	+2	-1	+1	0	+1	+2	-
Placido Polanco	2 tms	9	6	57.1	7	20	0	2	1.000	4.24	1.589	+10					15	20	+3	+1	+1	+5	0	+5	+5	-
Nick Punto	Min	12	7	69.0	6	22	0	3	1.000	3.65	1.294	+6	3	.367	D		18	20	+1	0	+1	+2	0	+2	+2	-
Robb Quinlan	LAA	33	30	243.0	22	51	7	4	.913	2.70	1.119	+8	5	.390	D+		43	47	-2	+1	+5	+4	+1	+5	+5	-
Aramis Ramirez	ChC	119	119	1020.1	70	218	16	13	.947	2.54	.956	-13	21	.417	D+	24	204	205	-2	0	+3	+1	0	+1	0	16
Joe Randa	2 tms	142	140	1209.2	126	225	12	21	.967	2.61	.971	-10	24	.494	C+	14	228	222	+1	-6	-1	-6	+1	-5	-6	20
Desi Relaford	Col	21	12	124.0	9	22	2	2	.939	2.25	.760	-9	2	.250	F		24	22	0	-2	0	-2	0	-2	-2	-
Oscar Robles	LAD	40	31	292.1	24	70	2	5	.979	2.89	1.051	+5	6	.483	C+		64	63	-2	0	+2	-1	0	-1	-2	-
Alex Rodriguez	NYY	161	161	1384.0	115	288	12	26	.971	2.62	.917	-36	17	.312	F	27	284	286	-7	+13	-3	+2	+4	+6	+2	13
Luis Rodriguez	Min	27	21	198.0	14	43	3	4	.950	2.59	.918	-5	2	.600	B+		42	40	-1	+1	-2	-2	0	-2	-1	-
Scott Rolen	StL	56	55	486.0	22	151	6	17	.966	3.20	1.053	+9	6	.550	B		125	140	+3	+3	+9	+15	0	+15	+16	-
Olmedo Saenz	LAD	17	15	120.0	17	22	2	3	.951	2.93	1.063	+2	3	.733	A+		23	20	-1	-2	0	-3	0	-3	-3	-
Freddy Sanchez	Pit	65	55	477.2	39	130	4	19	.977	3.18	1.054	+9	12	.608	B+		112	124	+7	+3	+2	+12	0	+12	+14	-
Marco Scutaro	Oak	5	2	21.0	4	6	0	1	1.000	4.29	1.620	+4					5	5	0	0	0	0	0	0	0	-
Scott Seabol	StL	20	14	103.0	9	30	3	5	.929	3.41	1.120	+4	3	.950	A+		29	26	-2	+1	-2	-3	-1	-4	-4	-
Jason Smith	Det	3	1	17.0	5	6	0	2	1.000	5.82	1.977	+5					7	7	+1	0	-1	0	0	0	0	-
Zach Sorensen	LAA	1	1	8.0	2	3	1	0	.833	5.63	2.329	+3					3	3	0	-1		0	0	0	0	-
Scott Spiezio	Sea	6	0	14.0	1	1	0	1	1.000	1.29	.482	-2					2	1		-1	0	-1	0	-1	-1	-
Mark Teahen	KC	128	122	1068.1	113	244	20	22	.947	3.01	1.036	+12	19	.521	B-	10	253	228	-9	-6	-11	-25	+1	-24	-30	27
Terry Tiffee	Min	24	20	176.1	18	34	5	6	.912	2.65	.941	-3	3	.367	D		36	32	-1	-2	-2	-4	0	-4	-3	-
Jose Valentin	LAD	29	24	216.1	19	54	7	4	.913	3.04	1.103	+7	5	.470	C		51	53	-1	+1	+2	+2	0	+2	+1	-
Ramon Vazquez	2 tms	8	6	56.0	6	11	0	3	1.000	2.73	.979	0	2	.250	F		12	10	0	-1	-1	-2	0	-2	-2	-
Jose Vizcaino	Hou	8	4	40.1	2	9	3	2	.786	2.45	.904	-1	3	.283	F		8	8	+1	-1	0	0	0	0	0	-
Chris Widger	CWS	1	1	8.1	1	0	0	0	1.000	2.16	.818	0					1	1	-1	0		0	0	0	0	-
Ty Wigginton	Pit	40	36	305.0	19	57	9	5	.894	2.24	.742	-26	6	.367	D		67	52	-11	-5	+1	-15	0	-15	-18	-
Glenn Williams	Min	12	9	81.0	7	19	2	2	.929	2.89	1.024	+1	2	.425	C-		21	18	0	-2	-1	-3	-1	-4	-4	-
Enrique Wilson	ChC	1	1	9.0	0	0	0	0	-	.00	.000	-3										0				-
Chris Woodward	NYM	6	2	25.1	1	11	0	0	1.000	4.26	1.555	+4					8	11	+2	+1	0	+3	0	+3	+4	-
David Wright	NYM	160	160	1404.1	101	337	24	23	.948	2.81	1.024	+10	32	.542	B-	7	327	315	-14	+2	0	-12	-2	-14	-17	25
Kevin Youkilis	Bos	24	14	139.0	10	29	0	3	1.000	2.53	.905	-4	1	.600	B+		31	28	-1	0	-1	-3	0	-3	-5	-
Ryan Zimmerman	Was	14	11	111.0	6	26	0	5	1.000	2.59	1.025	+1	4	.613	A-		22	22	+1	-1	0	0	0	0	+1	-
2005 MLB Averages									.957	2.76			781	.494	C+											

Shortstops 2005

BASIC													GROUND DP				PLAYS				PLUS/MINUS						
																	Expected Outs		Outs Made								
Name	Team	G	GS	Inn	PO	A	E	DP	Pct	Rng	Rel Rng	Rel +/-	GDP Opps	GDP	Pct	Rank	GB	Air	GB	Air	To His Right	Straight On	To His Left	GB	Air	Total	Rank
Russ Adams	Tor	132	122	1100.0	194	326	26	69	.952	4.25	.879	-73	111	65	.586	20	292	98	281	92	+2	-11	-2	-11	-6	-17	29
Manny Alexander	SD	4	3	31.0	4	10	1	1	.933	4.06	.966	0	5	1	.200	-	9	2	9	2	-1	-1	+1	0	0	0	-
Alfredo Amezaga	2 tms	1	0	4.0	1	2	0	1	1.000	6.75	1.416	+1	1	1	1.000	-	1		1		0			0			-
Robert Andino	Fla	17	13	120.0	19	25	2	7	.957	3.30	.705	-18	14	7	.500	-	26	9	21	9	-2	-1	-2	-5	0	-5	-
Rich Aurilia	Cin	30	29	237.2	29	86	3	14	.975	4.35	.961	-5	29	14	.483	-	73	19	74	18	+5	0	-3	+1	-1	0	-
Brad Ausmus	Hou	1	0	1.0	1	1	0	1	1.000	18.00	4.108	+2	1	1	1.000	-		0		0					0		-
Clint Barmes	Col	80	78	681.2	139	247	17	62	.958	5.10	1.060	+21	105	59	.562	22	195	65	212	65	+12	-5	+10	+17	0	+17	6
Jason Bartlett	Min	68	65	585.2	95	227	7	45	.979	4.95	1.056	+17	62	42	.677	3	193	50	205	52	+1	+3	+9	+12	+2	+14	7
Mark Bellhorn	2 tms	3	1	14.0	3	5	1	0	.889	5.14	1.179	0	2			-	5	1	4	1	0	-1		-1	0	-1	-
William Bergolla	Cin	1	0	1.0	0	1	0	0	1.000	9.00	1.985	0	0		-	-	1		1					0			-
Angel Berroa	KC	159	159	1360.1	254	442	25	107	.965	4.60	.938	-44	161	102	.634	10	403	128	379	126	-23	-5	+4	-24	-2	-26	30
Yuniesky Betancourt	Sea	53	52	454.0	82	136	5	34	.978	4.32	.966	-8	50	32	.640	-	115	47	114	47	-2	0	+1	-1	0	-1	-
Wilson Betemit	Atl	25	10	136.1	24	40	1	10	.985	4.22	.889	-8	12	9	.750	-	38	12	33	12	-2	-1	-2	-5	0	-5	-
Andres Blanco	KC	7	2	24.0	7	7	0	2	1.000	5.25	1.070	+1	3	2	.667	-	9	5	7	5	-1	0	0	-2	0	-2	-
Willie Bloomquist	Sea	24	21	180.0	34	49	3	6	.965	4.15	.927	-7	13	7	.538	-	46	26	46	27	+5	-1	-4	0	+1	+1	-
Geoff Blum	2 tms	20	13	122.1	18	35	0	8	1.000	3.90	.918	-5	11	7	.636	-	29	12	31	11	0	+1	+1	+2	-1	+1	-
Eric Bruntlett	Hou	10	4	49.0	9	21	0	4	1.000	5.51	1.258	+6	5	4	.800	-	16	3	18	3	+1	0	+1	+2	0	+2	-
Sean Burroughs	SD	1	0	2.0	0	0	0	0	-	.00	.000	-1	0		-	-											-
Orlando Cabrera	LAA	141	140	1240.2	229	347	7	81	.988	4.18	1.014	+8	128	75	.586	19	307	111	314	111	-8	0	+16	+7	0	+7	12
Jamey Carroll	Was	41	23	241.0	53	65	0	18	1.000	4.41	1.034	+4	23	16	.696	-	56	26	52	26	-1	0	-3	-4	0	-4	-
Juan Castro	Min	73	66	568.2	98	231	5	49	.985	5.21	1.111	+33	64	44	.688	2	196	41	204	42	0	+3	+5	+8	+1	+9	10
Ronny Cedeno	ChC	29	18	158.2	30	39	1	8	.986	3.91	.906	-7	14	6	.429	-	35	12	34	13	-2	+1	0	-1	+1	0	-
Angel Chavez	SF	4	3	27.1	6	5	1	2	.917	3.62	.816	-2	4	2	.500	-	8	2	5	2	0	-1	-1	-3	0	-3	-
Alex Cintron	Ari	39	31	271.0	44	99	5	19	.966	4.75	.979	-3	30	17	.567	-	88	23	89	24	+3	+1	-3	+1	+1	+2	-
Royce Clayton	Ari	141	131	1177.1	180	404	11	90	.982	4.46	.920	-50	153	90	.588	17	357	77	353	75	-13	0	+9	-4	-2	-6	22
Alex Cora	2 tms	35	27	245.2	37	107	3	16	.980	5.28	1.187	+23	21	16	.762	-	91	23	100	22	+6	-1	+5	+9	-1	+8	-
Fernando Cortez	TB	2	0	3.0	1	2	0	0	1.000	9.00	2.076	+2	0		-	-	2	1	2	1	+1			0	0	0	-
Craig Counsell	Ari	1	0	1.0	0	0	0	0	-	.00	.000	-1	0		-	-								0			-
Joe Crede	CWS	1	1	8.0	1	3	0	2	1.000	4.50	1.019	0	2	2	1.000	-	1		2					+1			-
Bobby Crosby	Oak	84	84	743.1	117	251	7	59	.981	4.46	1.007	+3	85	57	.671	4	214	56	222	56	+3	+4	0	+8	0	+8	11
Deivi Cruz	2 tms	24	20	170.2	27	61	2	15	.978	4.64	1.086	+5	20	13	.650	-	55	10	56	10	0	0	+1	+1	0	+1	-
Brian Dallimore	SF	1	0	1.0	0	0	0	0	-	.00	.000	0	0		-	-											-
Mark DeRosa	Tex	16	7	83.0	17	38	1	5	.982	5.96	1.224	+10	7	5	.714	-	35	12	37	12	0	+2	0	+2	0	+2	-
Jermaine Dye	CWS	1	0	0.1	0	0	0	0	-	.00	.000	0	0		-	-											-
Damion Easley	Fla	30	24	215.2	43	77	4	13	.968	5.01	1.070	+8	27	13	.481	-	71	25	69	24	-3	+1	0	-2	-1	-3	-
David Eckstein	StL	156	154	1340.2	244	516	15	122	.981	5.10	1.038	+28	188	118	.628	11	454	99	454	97	-6	+7	-1	0	-2	-2	20
Mike Edwards	LAD	1	0	2.0	0	2	0	0	1.000	9.00	1.992	+1	1			-	1		2		+2			+1			-
Mark Ellis	Oak	7	5	44.0	6	15	0	4	1.000	4.30	.971	-1	7	4	.571	-	12	3	11	3	-2	+1	0	-1	0	-1	-
Felix Escalona	NYY	5	2	29.0	8	8	0	3	1.000	4.97	1.038	+1	3	3	1.000	-	5	3	7	3	0	0	+1	+2	0	+2	-
Adam Everett	Hou	150	147	1291.2	209	420	14	96	.978	4.38	1.000	0	150	88	.587	18	340	97	374	96	+15	+4	+14	+34	-1	+33	1
Chone Figgins	LAA	4	1	11.0	2	4	0	1	1.000	4.91	1.191	+1	1			-	3	1	4	1	0	0	0	+1	0	+1	-
Rafael Furcal	Atl	152	152	1306.1	255	504	15	118	.981	5.23	1.100	+69	172	110	.640	9	415	98	437	102	+14	0	+8	+22	+4	+26	3
J.J. Furmaniak	Pit	2	1	8.0	1	4	0	0	1.000	5.63	1.180	+1	1			-	3		4		+1	0		+1			-
Eddy Garabito	Col	2	2	18.0	3	5	0	0	1.000	4.00	.832	-2	1			-	5	1	5	1	-1	0		0	0	0	-
Jesse Garcia	SD	13	7	82.0	15	19	0	4	1.000	3.73	.887	-4	6	3	.500	-	16	8	15	9	0	0	0	-1	+1	0	-
Nomar Garciaparra	ChC	26	25	206.0	41	51	6	16	.939	4.02	.930	-7	24	15	.625	-	45	13	42	14	-4	+1	0	-3	+1	-2	-
Tony Giarratano	Det	13	12	110.0	16	40	3	5	.949	4.58	.954	-3	8	4	.500	-	37	10	36	10	+1	-3	+2	-1	0	-1	-
Chris Gomez	Bal	10	2	31.0	5	8	1	3	.929	3.77	.817	-3	5	3	.600	-	9	3	8	3	-1	0	0	-1	0	-1	-
Alex Gonzalez	Fla	124	124	1087.1	221	367	16	102	.974	4.87	1.040	+22	138	90	.652	7	316	91	317	89	+2	0	-1	+1	-2	-1	19
Alex S Gonzalez	TB	12	7	80.0	12	18	2	0	.938	3.38	.778	-8	6	1	.167	-	18	7	18	8	+1	0	-1	0	+1	+1	-
Luis A Gonzalez	Col	17	16	132.0	28	34	4	13	.939	4.23	.879	-8	16	12	.750	-	31	12	25	12	-2	-2	-2	-6	0	-6	-
Tony Graffanino	2 tms	1	0	1.0	1	0	0	0	1.000	9.00	1.834	0	0		-	-		1		1					0		-
Andy Green	Ari	2	0	7.0	1	4	0	0	1.000	6.43	1.325	+1	1			-	3	2	4	1	-1	0	+1	+1	-1	0	-
Khalil Greene	SD	121	120	1028.2	161	312	14	64	.971	4.14	.984	-8	111	60	.541	27	294	87	280	85	-7	-2	-5	-14	-2	-16	28
Carlos Guillen	Det	75	74	625.0	85	227	7	44	.978	4.49	.936	-21	76	42	.553	25	197	39	202	37	+9	-1	-2	+5	-2	+3	17
Cristian Guzman	Was	142	133	1161.0	217	327	15	85	.973	4.22	.990	-6	120	78	.650	8	281	107	279	103	-8	+2	+4	-2	-4	-6	23
Jerry Hairston Jr.	ChC	1	0	2.0	1	1	0	1	1.000	9.00	2.083	+1	1	1	1.000	-									-1		-
Bill Hall	Mil	66	58	500.1	87	158	6	31	.976	4.41	1.085	+19	53	28	.528	31	133	46	138	45	0	+1	+4	+5	-1	+4	16
J.J. Hardy	Mil	119	104	937.2	133	259	10	52	.975	3.76	.926	-31	78	46	.590	16	231	75	240	76	+13	0	-4	+9	+1	+10	8
Willie Harris	CWS	5	2	25.0	1	9	0	1	1.000	3.60	.816	-2	2	1	.500	-	7	1	7	1	-1	0	+1	0	0	0	-
Anderson Hernandez	NYM	2	0	4.0	0	0	1	0	.000	.00	.000	-2	0		-	-					-1			-1			-
Jose Hernandez	Cle	1	0	3.0	1	1	0	0	1.000	6.00	1.365	+1	0		-	-	1	0	1	1				0	+1	+1	-
Aaron Hill	Tor	16	15	121.0	18	48	0	9	1.000	4.91	1.014	+1	15	8	.533	-	40	5	39	5	0	-1	0	-1	0	-1	-
Denny Hocking	KC	1	0	2.0	1	3	0	2	1.000	18.00	3.668	+3	3	2	.667	-	2		2					0			-
Kevin Hooper	Det	2	0	5.0	2	3	1	0	.833	9.00	1.875	+2	0		-	-	3	2	3	2	-1	0	0	0	0	0	-
Omar Infante	Det	50	43	389.1	82	149	6	35	.975	5.34	1.112	+23	50	31	.620	-	124	40	132	40	+7	+2	-1	+8	0	+8	-
Cesar Izturis	LAD	106	105	918.0	146	325	11	62	.977	4.62	1.022	+10	106	59	.557	24	277	58	282	57	+5	+3	-2	+5	-1	+4	15
Maicer Izturis	LAA	29	21	212.2	44	55	2	8	.980	4.19	1.017	+2	15	8	.533	-	49	24	49	24	-4	-2	+6	0	0	0	-
Damian Jackson	SD	26	18	189.1	34	52	7	14	.925	4.09	.972	-2	21	13	.619	-	57	18	45	20	-7	-4	-1	-12	+2	-10	-
Derek Jeter	NYY	157	157	1352.0	262	453	15	96	.979	4.76	.995	-3	156	84	.538	29	439	121	400	126	-18	+3	-25	-39	+5	-34	31
Matt Kata	2 tms	1	0	1.0	0	0	0	0	-	.00	.000	0	0		-	-		0		0					0		-
Felipe Lopez	Cin	140	133	1175.1	186	357	17	71	.970	4.16	.917	-48	127	69	.543	26	319	99	322	96	-6	+4	+6	+3	-3	0	18
Pedro Lopez	CWS	1	1	9.0	0	2	0	0	1.000	2.00	.453	-2	0		-	-	1		2		+1			+1			-
Julio Lugo	TB	156	155	1338.2	311	424	24	94	.968	4.94	1.140	+88	154	83	.539	28	374	150	371	151	-4	-5	+6	-3	+1	-2	21
Hector Luna	StL	6	0	14.0	3	3	1	0	.857	3.86	.784	-2	0		-	-	4	2	3	2	-1	0	0	-1	0	-1	-
Alejandro Machado	Bos	1	0	2.2	1	1	0	0	1.000	6.75	1.438	+1	0		-	-	0	1	1	1				+1	0	+1	-
Andy Machado	2 tms	4	4	34.0	7	6	1	1	.929	3.44	.716	-5	2	1	.500	-	6	6	4	5	-1	0	-1	-2	-1	-3	-
Ramon Martinez	2 tms	15	11	100.1	15	29	2	4	.957	3.95	.838	-9	15	4	.267	-	30	6	26	6	0	-2	-2	-4	0	-4	-
John McDonald	2 tms	54	42	375.1	67	157	8	35	.966	5.37	1.119	+23	49	32	.653	-	128	29	135	28	+3	+3	+1	+7	-1	+6	-
Marshall McDougall	Tex	1	0	1.0	1	1	0	1	1.000	18.00	3.693	+1	1	1	1.000	-	1		1					0			-
Joe McEwing	KC	6	1	24.0	7	10	1	4	.944	6.38	1.299	+4	5	4	.800	-	11	3	8	3	-2	+1	-1	-3	0	-3	-
Frank Menechino	Tor	1	0	2.0	1	1	0	1	1.000	9.00	1.859	+1	1	1	1.000	-		0		0					0		-
Aaron Miles	Col	1	0	3.0	0	0	1	0	.000	.00	.000	-2	1			-								-1			-
Mike Mordecai	Fla	1	0	1.1	0	0	0	0	-	.00	.000	-1	0		-	-					0			0			-
Mike Morse	Sea	55	50	450.0	91	120	12	33	.946	4.22	.943	-13	54	29	.537	-	115	43	100	44	-2	-7	-6	-15	+1	-14	-
Donald Murphy	KC	2	0	2.0	0	0	1	0	.000	.00	.000	-1	0		-	-		0		0	0	-1		-1	0	-1	-
Norihiro Nakamura	LAD	2	0	3.0	0	1	0	1	1.000	3.00	.664	-1	1	1	1.000	-	1	0	1	0				0	0	0	-
Abraham O Nunez	StL	21	8	91.0	14	30	2	9	.957	4.35	.885	-6	11	7	.636	-	26	9	24	8	+1	-1	-3	-2	-1	-3	-
Ray Olmedo	Cin	5	1	19.0	4	6	0	2	1.000	4.74	1.045	0	2	2	1.000	-	4	2	5	2	0	0	+1	+1	0	+1	-
Pete Orr	Atl	1	0	1.0	0	0	0	0	-	.00	.000	-1	0		-	-		0		0					0		-
Pablo Ozuna	CWS	15	11	99.0	19	35	2	12	.964	4.91	1.112	+6	16	12	.750	-	28	7	29	8	0	+1	0	+1	+1	+2	-

		BASIC										Rel	Rel	GROUND DP				PLAYS				PLUS/MINUS						
											Rel	Rel		GDP				Expected Outs		Outs Made		To His	Straight	To His				
Name	Team	G	GS	Inn	PO	A	E	DP	Pct	Rng	Rng	+/-	Opps	GDP	Pct	Rank	GB	Air	GB	Air	Right	On	Left	GB	Air	Total	Rank
Jhonny Peralta	Cle	141	138	1232.1	207	412	19	104	.970	4.52	1.029	+18	132	94	.712	1	364	115	352	113	-5	+3	-10	-12	-2	-14	27
Antonio Perez	LAD	9	8	65.0	10	25	1	6	.972	4.85	1.073	+2	12	6	.500	-	22	3	22	3	-1	+1	+1	0	0	0	-
Neifi Perez	ChC	130	118	1063.1	175	385	10	81	.982	4.74	1.097	+50	121	73	.603	13	319	71	339	71	+10	+8	+2	+20	0	+20	5
Tomas Perez	Phi	14	5	61.0	8	12	0	2	1.000	2.95	.687	-9	4	2	.500	-	12	4	12	4	0	0	0	0	0	0	-
Brandon Phillips	Cle	1	0	3.0	1	2	1	1	.750	9.00	2.048	+2	1	1	1.000	-	1	0	1	0	0			0	0	0	-
Placido Polanco	2 tms	1	1	8.0	3	2	0	1	1.000	5.63	1.309	+1	2	1	.500	-	1	1	1	1	0			0	0	0	-
Nick Punto	Min	34	26	244.0	47	76	2	16	.984	4.54	.968	-4	25	14	.560	-	67	25	66	27	-2	0	+1	-1	+2	+1	-
Omar Quintanilla	Col	31	30	268.2	41	89	1	16	.992	4.35	.906	-13	31	15	.484	-	73	19	80	20	0	+1	+6	+7	+1	+8	-
Hanley Ramirez	Bos	2	0	6.0	0	1	0	0	1.000	1.50	.320	-2	0		-	-	1		1		0			0			-
Desi Relaford	Col	37	32	281.1	45	100	6	16	.960	4.64	.965	-5	32	16	.500	-	98	24	94	23	+3	-3	-4	-4	-1	-5	-
Edgar Renteria	Bos	153	150	1293.0	227	398	30	90	.954	4.35	.927	-49	154	82	.532	30	352	110	343	108	+3	-14	+2	-9	-2	-11	26
Jose Reyes	NYM	161	159	1398.1	237	427	18	105	.974	4.27	.959	-29	148	97	.655	5	372	119	359	122	-14	-1	+3	-13	+3	-10	25
Luis Rivas	Min	6	2	22.0	3	5	1	1	.889	3.27	.698	-3	1			-	6	1	5	1	-1	-1	+1	-1	0	-1	-
Oscar Robles	LAD	54	49	437.1	76	132	4	28	.981	4.28	.947	-12	48	26	.542	-	116	42	115	41	-3	0	+2	-1	-1	-2	-
Alex Rodriguez	NYY	3	0	6.0	1	2	0	0	1.000	4.50	.941	0	0		-	-	2	1	2	1	-1	0	0	0	0	0	-
Luis Rodriguez	Min	10	3	44.0	8	14	0	4	1.000	4.50	.960	-1	5	3	.600	-	14	6	14	5	-1	-1	+2	0	-1	-1	-
Eddie Rogers	Bal	1	0	2.0	0	0	0	0	-	.00	.000	-1	0		-	-		0		0					0		-
Jimmy Rollins	Phi	157	156	1356.0	208	411	12	80	.981	4.11	.956	-29	127	76	.598	14	346	104	365	108	+3	-2	+17	+19	+4	+23	4
Freddy Sanchez	Pit	11	6	64.0	11	25	0	3	1.000	5.06	1.062	+2	5	3	.600	-	20	6	22	6	-1	+1	+2	+2	0	+2	-
Rey Sanchez	NYY	10	3	38.0	7	14	1	4	.955	4.97	1.040	+1	7	4	.571	-	14	5	13	4	0	0	0	-1	-1	-2	-
Danny Sandoval	Phi	1	0	1.0	0	1	0	0	1.000	9.00	2.095	+1	1			-	1		1		0	0		0			-
Ramon Santiago	Sea	2	0	2.0	0	1	1	0	.500	4.50	1.005	0	1			-	2		1				-1				-
Marco Scutaro	Oak	81	73	663.0	115	213	8	50	.976	4.45	1.006	+2	76	46	.605	12	198	49	190	49	-7	+2	-2	-8	0	-8	24
Jason Smith	Det	15	5	62.2	14	27	0	6	1.000	5.89	1.227	+8	11	6	.545	-	20	5	23	5	+3	+1	-1	+3	0	+3	-
Miguel Tejada	Bal	160	160	1394.2	252	480	22	105	.971	4.72	1.022	+16	166	95	.572	21	413	108	417	109	+25	-4	-17	+4	+1	+5	13
Juan Uribe	CWS	146	143	1293.1	250	422	16	99	.977	4.68	1.059	+39	149	89	.597	15	361	125	364	131	+12	-2	-7	+3	+6	+9	9
Wilson Valdez	2 tms	50	44	382.2	76	119	6	24	.970	4.59	1.034	+6	44	23	.523	-	103	42	105	43	-4	+3	+2	+2	+1	+3	-
Jose Valentin	LAD	1	0	2.0	0	2	0	1	1.000	9.00	1.992	+1	1	1	1.000	-	2		2		0	0		0			-
Ramon Vazquez	2 tms	14	8	87.0	18	20	1	4	.974	3.93	.848	-6	9	4	.444	-	22	10	18	10	-1	+1	-3	-4	0	-4	-
Jose Vizcaino	Hou	17	12	101.1	9	34	0	1	1.000	3.82	.872	-6	4	1	.250	-	33	9	33	8	+4	-1	-2	0	-1	-1	-
Omar Vizquel	SF	150	144	1292.1	234	426	8	80	.988	4.60	1.035	+22	142	75	.528	32	379	118	383	118	-7	+16	-5	+4	0	+4	14
Enrique Wilson	ChC	3	1	10.0	2	6	0	1	1.000	7.20	1.667	+3	1	1	1.000	-	4	2	5	2	0	0	0	+1	0	+1	-
Jack Wilson	Pit	157	155	1360.0	246	522	14	126	.982	5.08	1.066	+48	184	120	.652	6	414	99	440	104	+27	+8	-9	+26	+5	+31	2
Josh Wilson	Fla	6	1	18.0	3	6	0	2	1.000	4.50	.962	0	2	2	1.000	-	4	1	4	1	0	0	0	0	0	0	-
Chris Woodward	NYM	7	3	33.1	5	7	1	1	.923	3.24	.727	-5	1	1	1.000	-	6	4	6	4	-1	-1	+2	0	0	0	-
Michael Young	Tex	155	155	1356.0	239	426	18	95	.974	4.41	.906	-68	157	88	.561	23	407	121	371	118	-15	-2	-19	-36	-3	-39	32
Ryan Zimmerman	Was	1	1	9.0	3	4	2	0	.778	7.00	1.643	+3	5			-	6	1	4	1	0	-2	0	-2	0	-2	-
2005 MLB Averages									.974	4.55			4946	2932	.593												

Left Fielders 2005

Name	Team	G	GS	Inn	PO	A	E	DP	Pct	Rng	Opps To Advance	Extra Bases	Kills	Pct	Rank	Expected Outs	Outs Made	Total	Enhanced	Rank
Brent Abernathy	Min	5	3	31.1	5	0	0	0	1.000	1.44	3	1	0	.333	-	4	5	+1	+1	-
Chris Aguila	Fla	27	2	53.1	13	0	0	0	1.000	2.19						14	13	-1	-2	-
Chad Allen	Tex	1	0	3.0	0	0	0	0	-	.00					-			0		-
Moises Alou	SF	74	66	576.0	132	1	4	0	.971	2.08	63	21	1	.333	8	131	132	+1	+2	12
Chip Ambres	KC	23	18	170.0	36	0	1	0	.973	1.91	29	12	0	.414	-	39	36	-3	-5	-
Brian Anderson	CWS	9	3	42.0	10	1	0	1	1.000	2.36	6	2	0	.333	-	9	10	+1	+2	-
Garret Anderson	LAA	106	106	920.0	201	4	5	1	.976	2.01	80	32	3	.400	21	207	201	-6	-7	27
Marlon Anderson	NYM	9	4	45.0	9	1	0	1	1.000	2.00	4	2	1	.500	-	7	9	+2	+3	-
Jason Bay	Pit	146	133	1185.2	264	3	1	1	.996	2.03	121	53	3	.438	28	269	266	-3	-4	24
Lance Berkman	Hou	39	35	284.2	50	2	3	1	.945	1.64	24	9	1	.375	-	50	50	0	+2	-
Larry Bigbie	2 tms	57	54	480.1	98	3	0	1	1.000	1.89	48	14	2	.292	-	102	98	-4	-5	-
Tony Blanco	Was	9	4	42.0	9	1	0	1	1.000	2.14	5	3	1	.600	-	9	9	0	-1	-
Willie Bloomquist	Sea	1	0	2.0	0	0	0	0	-	.00	3	3	0	1.000	-			0		-
Barry Bonds	SF	13	13	95.0	18	0	0	0	1.000	1.71	8	2	0	.250	-	17	18	+1	+3	-
Jason Botts	Tex	7	5	40.0	8	1	1	1	.900	2.03	6	2	1	.333	-	8	8	0	-1	-
Russell Branyan	Mil	3	0	7.0	1	0	0	0	1.000	1.29					-	1	1	0	0	-
Emil Brown	KC	11	9	82.1	21	2	1	0	.958	2.51	11	4	1	.364	-	20	21	+1	0	-
Eric Bruntlett	Hou	11	2	28.2	11	0	0	0	1.000	3.45					-	9	11	+2	+2	-
Jaime Bubela	Sea	1	0	1.1	0	0	0	0	-	.00					-			0		-
Chris Burke	Hou	83	74	634.0	120	3	1	1	.992	1.75	45	15	2	.333	7	114	120	+6	+8	7
Pat Burrell	Phi	153	153	1296.2	236	10	7	2	.972	1.71	147	52	9	.354	13	232	236	+4	+3	10
Freddie Bynum	Oak	1	0	2.0	1	0	0	0	1.000	4.50					-	1	1	0	0	-
Marlon Byrd	2 tms	54	41	386.0	100	5	2	2	.981	2.45	40	20	3	.500	-	100	100	0	+1	-
Eric Byrnes	3 tms	106	90	803.0	209	5	4	1	.982	2.40	74	34	4	.459	30	207	209	+2	+6	9
Miguel Cabrera	Fla	134	128	1105.2	188	12	5	3	.976	1.63	106	36	10	.340	9	204	188	-16	-28	29
Miguel Cairo	NYM	2	0	3.0	0	0	0	0	-	.00					-			0		-
Napoleon Calzado	Bal	1	1	8.0	2	0	0	0	1.000	2.25					-	2	2	0	0	-
Bernie Castro	Bal	1	1	7.0	1	0	1	0	.500	1.29	2	2	0	1.000	-	1	1	0	0	-
Frank Catalanotto	Tor	111	99	761.0	163	4	0	0	1.000	1.98	54	13	3	.241	1	164	163	-1	-5	25
Roger Cedeno	StL	6	4	33.1	2	0	0	0	1.000	.54	3	1	0	.333	-	3	2	-1	-1	-
Matt Cepicky	Was	5	5	35.2	13	0	0	0	1.000	3.28	3	2	0	.667	-	11	13	+2	+3	-
Endy Chavez	2 tms	20	3	59.0	15	1	0	0	1.000	2.44	3	1	1	.333	-	14	15	+1	+1	-
Chin-Feng Chen	LAD	3	1	11.0	2	0	0	0	1.000	1.64					-	1	2	+1	+1	-
Ryan Church	Was	51	37	334.2	77	2	0	0	1.000	2.12	32	14	1	.438	-	77	77	0	0	-
Jeff Conine	Fla	37	30	257.2	54	2	0	0	1.000	1.96	32	15	0	.469	-	55	54	-1	0	-
Alex Cora	2 tms	1	0	1.0	0	0	0	0	-	.00					-			0		-
Shane Costa	KC	20	18	162.0	30	1	0	0	1.000	1.72	19	5	0	.263	-	33	30	-3	-3	-
Carl Crawford	TB	147	142	1246.2	341	4	1	2	.994	2.48	155	40	3	.258	2	325	341	+16	+20	2
Coco Crisp	Cle	138	133	1200.0	294	3	4	0	.987	2.23	110	41	2	.373	19	279	294	+15	+26	1
Bubba Crosby	NYY	4	2	20.0	2	0	0	0	1.000	.90	4	1	0	.250	-	3	2	-1	-2	-
Jacob Cruz	Cin	8	5	48.0	5	1	0	1	1.000	1.13					-	6	5	-1	-2	-
Jose Cruz	3 tms	4	2	18.2	3	0	0	0	1.000	1.45					-	3	3	0	0	-
Midre Cummings	Bal	1	0	2.0	0	0	0	0	-	.00					-			0		-
Jeff DaVanon	LAA	17	9	88.2	30	1	0	0	1.000	3.15	5	2	1	.400	-	28	30	+2	+4	-
J.J. Davis	Was	9	7	54.0	15	1	0	0	1.000	2.67	8	2	1	.250	-	16	15	-1	-2	-
David Dellucci	Tex	47	44	378.2	84	4	2	1	.978	2.09	38	16	1	.421	-	86	84	-2	-4	-
Chris Denorfia	Cin	2	1	9.1	3	0	0	0	1.000	2.89	4	1	0	.250	-	3	3	0	+1	-
Matt Diaz	KC	19	16	136.0	34	0	2	0	.944	2.25	14	8	0	.571	-	36	34	-2	-3	-
Victor Diaz	NYM	3	3	26.0	3	1	0	0	1.000	1.38	5	2	1	.400	-	4	3	-1	-1	-
Joe Dillon	Fla	3	0	6.0	2	0	0	0	1.000	3.00					-	2	2	0	+1	-
Greg Dobbs	Sea	4	2	26.0	4	0	0	0	1.000	1.38	3	1	0	.333	-	3	4	+1	+1	-
Jason Dubois	2 tms	41	38	311.1	53	2	1	0	.982	1.59	34	13	2	.382	-	57	53	-4	-6	-
Adam Dunn	Cin	133	126	1090.2	246	6	5	0	.981	2.08	113	41	2	.363	15	250	246	-4	-16	28
Mike Edwards	LAD	32	27	223.1	51	0	0	0	1.000	2.06	17	7	0	.412	-	49	51	+2	+4	-
Jason Ellison	SF	15	0	23.1	3	0	1	0	.750	1.16	4	2	0	.500	-	3	3	0	0	-
Carl Everett	CWS	14	14	117.1	16	1	0	1	1.000	1.30	8	3	1	.375	-	15	16	+1	+3	-
Pedro Feliz	SF	75	70	615.2	138	0	3	0	.979	2.02	66	20	0	.303	3	136	138	+2	-2	17
Robert Fick	SD	4	2	18.0	1	0	0	0	1.000	.50					-	1	1	0	-1	-
Chone Figgins	LAA	15	13	130.0	27	1	0	1	1.000	1.94	9	3	1	.333	-	28	27	-1	-3	-
Cliff Floyd	NYM	150	147	1263.2	283	15	2	0	.993	2.12	147	52	14	.354	12	286	283	-3	+1	13
Lew Ford	Min	18	14	134.0	32	2	1	0	.971	2.28	17	6	2	.353	-	35	32	-3	-3	-
Ryan Freel	Cin	25	17	164.1	45	6	0	0	1.000	2.79	18	6	4	.333	-	48	45	-3	-9	-
John Gall	StL	10	6	48.2	7	1	0	0	1.000	1.48	4	2	1	.500	-	7	7	0	0	-
Jody Gerut	3 tms	21	16	156.0	30	1	0	0	1.000	1.79	22	10	0	.455	-	30	30	0	+1	-
Brian Giles	SD	1	0	1.0	2	0	0	0	1.000	18.00					-	2	2	0	0	-
Keith Ginter	Oak	2	0	6.0	0	0	0	0	-	.00					-			-1	-2	-
Charles Gipson	Hou	7	2	23.0	3	0	0	0	1.000	1.17					-	3	3	0	0	-
Ross Gload	CWS	2	2	14.0	3	0	0	0	1.000	1.93	1	1	0	1.000	-	2	3	+1	+1	-
Jonny Gomes	TB	14	14	110.0	30	1	0	0	1.000	2.54	12	2	1	.167	-	34	30	-4	-9	-
Alexis Gomez	Det	6	3	28.0	7	0	0	0	1.000	2.25					-	9	7	-2	-3	-
Luis Gonzalez	Ari	152	149	1318.1	270	7	3	1	.989	1.89	153	62	0	.405	24	266	270	+4	+7	8
Luis A Gonzalez	Col	1	1	8.0	2	0	0	0	1.000	2.25					-	2	2	0	0	-
Jason Grabowski	LAD	28	20	170.0	31	1	1	0	.970	1.69	20	8	1	.400	-	30	31	+1	+2	-
Curtis Granderson	Det	20	3	54.2	10	0	0	0	1.000	1.65					-	10	10	0	+1	-
Andy Green	Ari	2	2	17.0	3	0	0	0	1.000	1.59	1	1	0	1.000	-	3	3	0	0	-
Ben Grieve	ChC	1	1	7.0	0	0	0	0	-	.00					-			0		-
Marquis Grissom	SF	1	1	9.0	1	0	0	0	1.000	1.00					-	1	1	0	-1	-
Gabe Gross	Tor	19	8	95.1	19	1	0	1	1.000	1.89	8	3	1	.375	-	21	19	-2	-2	-
Jose Guillen	Was	2	2	17.0	2	0	0	0	1.000	1.06	1	1	0	1.000	-	1	2	+1	+1	-
Scott Hairston	Ari	4	1	13.1	3	0	0	0	1.000	2.03					-	3	3	0	0	-
Jerry Hairston Jr.	ChC	20	10	92.2	22	1	0	0	1.000	2.23					-	20	22	+2	+3	-
Jeffrey Hammonds	Was	10	8	58.0	16	0	0	0	1.000	2.48					-	17	16	-1	-3	-
Lenny Harris	Fla	1	0	1.2	0	0	0	0	-	.00					-			0		-
Corey Hart	Mil	2	0	6.0	1	0	0	0	1.000	1.50					-	2	1	-1	-2	-
Jeremy Hermida	Fla	4	2	17.0	3	0	0	0	1.000	1.59	1	1	0	1.000	-	3	3	0	+1	-
Jose Hernandez	Cle	3	3	23.0	3	0	0	0	1.000	1.17					-	3	3	0	-1	-
Bobby Higginson	Det	1	1	9.0	2	1	0	0	1.000	3.00	3	1	0	.333	-	2	2	0	0	-
Todd Hollandsworth	2 tms	98	63	599.0	103	2	1	0	.991	1.58	77	34	2	.442	29	105	103	-2	-2	19
Matt Holliday	Col	123	121	1049.2	236	5	7	2	.972	2.07	117	47	3	.402	22	229	236	+7	+9	6
Damon Hollins	TB	8	3	38.0	14	1	2	1	.882	3.55	2	1	1	.500	-	14	14	0	0	-
Kevin Hooper	Det	3	0	4.1	1	0	0	0	1.000	2.08					-	1	1	0	0	-

BASIC											THROWING					PLAYS		PLUS/MINUS		
Name	Team	G	GS	Inn	PO	A	E	DP	Pct	Rng	Opps To Advance	Extra Bases	Kills	Pct	Rank	Expected Outs	Outs Made	Total	Enhanced	Rank
Adam Hyzdu	2 tms	14	1	34.0	11	1	1	1	.923	3.18	3	2	0	.667	-	11	11	0	0	-
Raul Ibanez	Sea	55	54	463.2	105	6	2	3	.982	2.15	60	20	5	.333	-	104	106	+2	+6	-
Brandon Inge	Det	1	0	6.0	2	0	0	0	1.000	3.00					-	2	2	0	0	-
Conor Jackson	Ari	1	1	9.0	0	0	0	0	-	.00	2	2	0	1.000		0	0	0	0	-
Damian Jackson	SD	37	2	97.0	25	2	0	0	1.000	2.51	16	7	1	.438	-	22	26	+4	+6	-
Ben Johnson	SD	13	6	56.0	10	0	0	0	1.000	1.61	5	3	0	.600	-	10	10	0	0	-
Kelly Johnson	Atl	79	73	648.1	166	6	0	1	1.000	2.39	71	22	5	.310	5	161	166	+5	+10	5
Reed Johnson	Tor	118	55	590.2	134	4	1	1	.993	2.10	46	15	2	.326	6	124	134	+10	+17	4
Brian Jordan	Atl	45	42	358.1	74	5	0	1	1.000	1.98	28	13	3	.464	-	76	75	-1	-	-
Gabe Kapler	Bos	8	0	15.0	1	0	0	0	1.000	.60					-	1	1	0	0	-
Kenny Kelly	2 tms	1	1	8.0	2	0	0	0	1.000	2.25	1	1	0	1.000	-	3	2	-1	-1	-
Bobby Kielty	Oak	58	52	457.0	99	3	1	0	.990	2.01	40	15	1	.375	-	98	99	+1	+6	-
Ryan Klesko	SD	121	120	927.0	204	7	4	1	.981	2.05	93	39	2	.419	26	205	204	-1	-3	21
Mike Lamb	Hou	12	11	90.0	11	0	0	0	1.000	1.10	7	4	0	.571	-	14	11	-3	-4	-
Jason Lane	Hou	4	3	24.0	3	0	0	0	1.000	1.13	4	2	0	.500	-	3	3	0	0	-
Ryan Langerhans	Atl	54	41	379.1	91	0	0	0	1.000	2.16	37	11	0	.297	-	85	91	+6	+10	-
Matt Lawton	3 tms	26	22	184.1	40	0	1	0	.976	1.95	15	10	0	.667	-	37	40	+3	+4	-
Ricky Ledee	LAD	57	46	390.1	57	1	2	1	.967	1.34	33	14	1	.424	-	58	57	-1	0	-
Carlos Lee	Mil	162	161	1404.0	307	8	6	3	.981	2.02	134	49	5	.366	17	312	307	-5	-4	23
Todd Linden	SF	18	7	77.0	22	0	1	0	.957	2.57	5	2	0	.400	-	23	22	-1	0	-
Terrence Long	KC	103	94	794.0	166	9	2	1	.989	1.98	129	52	6	.403	23	166	166	0	-3	22
Ryan Ludwick	Cle	9	8	59.0	16	0	1	0	.941	2.44	10	4	0	.400	-	18	16	-2	-2	-
Hector Luna	StL	3	1	13.0	3	1	0	0	1.000	2.77					-	4	3	-1	-2	-
John Mabry	StL	23	12	117.2	19	0	2	0	.905	1.45	6	4	0	.667	-	21	19	-2	-2	-
Alejandro Machado	Bos	2	0	4.0	1	0	0	0	1.000	2.25					-	1	1	0	+1	-
Jose Macias	ChC	5	0	7.1	3	0	1	0	.750	3.68					-	1	3	+2	+2	-
Chris Magruder	Mil	5	1	19.0	3	0	0	0	1.000	1.42					-	3	3	0	0	-
Eli Marrero	2 tms	15	13	107.0	25	1	1	0	.963	2.19	13	5	0	.385	-	29	25	-4	-6	-
Hideki Matsui	NYY	115	110	976.2	218	7	3	1	.987	2.07	113	41	4	.363	14	221	219	-2	+3	11
Gary Matthews Jr.	Tex	5	5	40.0	8	0	0	0	1.000	1.80					-	8	8	0	-1	-
Paul McAnulty	SD	6	2	29.0	5	0	0	0	1.000	1.55					-	5	5	0	+1	-
Dave McCarty	Bos	1	0	2.0	0	0	0	0	-	.00						0	0		0	-
Quinton McCracken	Ari	11	3	38.1	8	0	0	0	1.000	1.88	3	2	0	.667	-	8	8	0	0	-
Joe McEwing	KC	3	0	4.0	1	0	0	0	1.000	2.25					-	1	1	0	0	-
Kevin Mench	Tex	119	108	978.1	230	8	2	3	.992	2.19	122	52	7	.426	27	227	231	+4	0	15
Jason Michaels	Phi	22	2	46.1	11	1	0	1	1.000	2.33					-	11	11	0	0	-
Kevin Millar	Bos	20	12	119.0	19	0	0	1	1.000	1.44	14	7	0	.500	-	22	19	-3	-5	-
Dustan Mohr	Col	17	13	122.1	25	3	0	1	1.000	2.06	15	5	2	.333	-	27	25	-2	-2	-
Craig Monroe	Det	69	56	501.2	99	6	1	4	.991	1.88	54	22	3	.407	25	99	99	0	0	14
Mike Morse	Sea	8	7	55.0	10	1	0	1	1.000	1.80	6	2	0	.333	-	10	10	0	0	-
Eric Munson	TB	1	0	1.0	1	0	0	0	1.000	9.00					-	1	1	0	0	-
Matt Murton	ChC	43	38	329.0	62	1	2	1	.969	1.72	31	10	0	.323	-	56	62	+6	+8	-
Xavier Nady	SD	26	6	100.0	18	0	1	0	.947	1.62	6	5	0	.833	-	17	18	+1	+1	-
David Newhan	Bal	20	16	132.0	18	1	0	0	1.000	1.30	12	3	1	.250	-	19	18	-1	0	-
Miguel Ojeda	2 tms	3	3	24.0	6	0	0	0	1.000	2.25					-	6	6	0	-1	-
Pete Orr	Atl	3	3	25.0	5	0	0	0	1.000	1.80					-	6	5	-1	-1	-
Pablo Ozuna	CWS	9	8	65.0	10	0	0	0	1.000	1.38	7	2	0	.286	-	9	10	+1	0	-
Orlando Palmeiro	Hou	47	16	187.1	27	0	0	0	1.000	1.30	15	5	0	.333	-	28	27	-1	0	-
Josh Paul	LAA	2	0	3.0	0	0	0	0	-	.00					-				0	-
Jay Payton	2 tms	60	50	465.1	107	1	0	0	1.000	2.09	35	10	1	.286	-	105	107	+2	+1	-
Wily Mo Pena	Cin	10	9	73.2	12	0	2	0	.857	1.47	11	5	0	.455	-	15	12	-3	-5	-
Antonio Perez	LAD	1	0	1.0	0	0	0	0	-	.00					-				0	-
Eduardo Perez	TB	3	2	16.0	2	0	0	0	1.000	1.13	5	3	0	.600	-	4	2	-2	-5	-
Timo Perez	CWS	27	17	175.2	33	3	1	0	.973	1.84	13	7	2	.538	-	34	33	-1	-1	-
Roberto Petagine	Bos	2	0	5.2	0	0	0	0	-	.00					-				0	-
Jorge Piedra	Col	9	6	47.1	5	1	0	0	1.000	1.14	8	3	0	.375	-	6	5	-1	-3	-
Scott Podsednik	CWS	124	118	1061.2	260	3	3	1	.989	2.23	96	35	3	.365	16	248	260	+12	+20	3
Placido Polanco	2 tms	5	4	29.0	10	0	0	0	1.000	3.10					-	10	10	0	+1	-
Curtis Pride	LAA	4	0	5.0	2	0	0	0	1.000	3.60					-	2	2	0	+1	-
Robb Quinlan	LAA	6	2	20.0	3	0	0	0	1.000	1.35					-	3	3	0	0	-
Manny Ramirez	Bos	149	147	1225.0	243	17	7	0	.974	1.91	147	56	13	.381	20	257	243	-14	-31	30
Tike Redman	Pit	2	0	9.0	4	0	0	0	1.000	4.00					-	3	4	+1	+2	-
Kevin Reese	NYY	1	1	7.0	1	0	0	0	1.000	1.29					-	1	1	0	0	-
Jason Repko	LAD	24	13	127.0	26	0	1	0	.963	1.84	17	8	0	.471	-	30	26	-4	-5	-
Mike Restovich	2 tms	15	9	89.0	26	1	1	0	.964	2.73	10	6	0	.600	-	25	26	+1	0	-
Juan Rivera	LAA	33	32	297.2	72	3	0	0	1.000	2.27	31	14	3	.452	-	67	72	+5	+10	-
John Rodriguez	StL	40	32	283.1	60	2	1	0	.984	1.97	41	18	1	.439	-	62	60	-2	-1	-
Jason Romano	Cin	7	4	39.0	5	1	0	0	1.000	1.38					-	7	5	-2	-4	-
Mike Ryan	Min	16	9	99.0	13	1	0	0	1.000	1.27	5	2	0	.400	-	14	13	-1	-1	-
Ray Sadler	Pit	3	3	21.0	4	0	0	0	1.000	1.71	2	1	0	.500	-	5	4	-1	-1	-
Reggie Sanders	StL	80	78	636.0	108	5	2	0	.983	1.60	52	16	2	.308	4	111	108	-3	-2	18
Jared Schumaker	StL	14	0	22.1	6	0	0	0	1.000	2.42	4	2	0	.500	-	7	6	-1	-1	-
Luke Scott	Hou	21	18	151.1	22	2	1	0	.960	1.43	13	3	2	.231	-	21	22	+1	+3	-
Marco Scutaro	Oak	2	1	16.0	5	0	0	0	1.000	2.81					-	5	5	0	0	-
Scott Seabol	StL	2	2	11.0	5	0	0	0	1.000	4.09	1	1	0	1.000	-	5	5	0	+1	-
Todd Self	Hou	5	2	20.0	3	0	0	0	1.000	1.35	3	2	0	.667	-	4	3	-1	-1	-
Adam Shabala	SF	4	3	27.1	5	0	1	0	.833	1.65	4	1	0	.250	-	6	5	-1	0	-
Ruben Sierra	NYY	8	6	54.0	10	0	0	0	1.000	1.67	4	1	0	.250	-	13	10	-3	-3	-
Chris Singleton	TB	2	1	10.0	0	0	0	0	-	.90					-	1	1	-1	-2	-
Terrmel Sledge	Was	12	9	79.1	21	1	0	0	1.000	2.50	8	4	0	.500	-	24	21	-3	-5	-
Chris Snelling	Sea	7	7	66.0	17	2	0	1	1.000	2.59	9	6	1	.667	-	16	17	+1	+2	-
Matt Stairs	KC	2	0	6.0	1	0	0	0	1.000	1.50					-	1	1	0	0	-
Adam Stern	Bos	2	0	4.0	0	0	0	0	-	.00	2	1	0	.500	-			-1	-1	-
Shannon Stewart	Min	125	125	1107.0	249	7	4	2	.985	2.08	104	36	3	.346	11	249	249	0	-1	16
Jamal Strong	Sea	7	2	18.0	4	1	0	0	1.000	2.50	4	2	1	.500	-	4	4	0	+1	-
Cory Sullivan	Col	24	16	149.1	32	2	1	0	.971	2.05	15	8	2	.533	-	31	32	+1	0	-
B.J. Surhoff	Bal	46	42	367.1	76	3	0	0	1.000	1.94	25	6	2	.240	-	72	76	+4	+5	-
Mark Sweeney	SD	1	1	5.0	0	0	0	0	-	.00	1	1	0	1.000	-			0	0	-
So Taguchi	StL	52	27	280.1	50	2	0	1	1.000	1.67	18	7	1	.389	-	49	50	+1	+1	-
Luis Terrero	Ari	1	0	2.0	0	0	0	0	-	.00					-	0	0	0	0	-
Marcus Thames	Det	21	16	153.0	31	0	0	0	1.000	1.82	17	9	0	.529	-	33	31	-2	-4	-
Charles Thomas	Oak	13	8	77.2	17	1	1	0	.947	2.09	3	2	1	.667	-	16	18	+2	+3	-

BASIC											THROWING					PLAYS		PLUS/MINUS		
Name	Team	G	GS	Inn	PO	A	E	DP	Pct	Rng	Opps To Advance	Extra Bases	Kills	Pct	Rank	Expected Outs	Outs Made	Total	Enhanced	Rank
Chad Tracy	Ari	6	4	40.2	7	0	0	0	1.000	1.55	5	1	0	.200	-	8	7	-1	-2	-
Michael Tucker	2 tms	4	2	21.0	6	0	0	0	1.000	2.57					-	6	6	0	-1	-
Jason Tyner	Min	12	11	93.0	19	0	0	0	1.000	1.84	8	4	0	.500	-	17	19	+2	+2	-
Eric Valent	NYM	2	1	12.0	6	0	0	0	1.000	4.50					-	6	6	0	-1	-
Jose Valentin	LAD	22	19	158.1	35	0	1	0	.972	1.99	14	8	0	.571	-	31	35	+4	+7	-
Shane Victorino	Phi	4	0	4.0	0	0	0	0	-	.00					-			0	0	-
Brandon Watson	Was	12	7	69.0	11	1	1	0	.923	1.57	5	1	1	.200	-	11	11	0	0	-
Matt Watson	Oak	14	10	88.1	26	0	0	0	1.000	2.65	7	2	0	.286	-	26	26	0	0	-
Jayson Werth	LAD	64	36	345.1	84	3	0	0	1.000	2.27	27	10	3	.370	-	79	84	+5	+8	-
Rondell White	Det	65	65	534.2	119	0	0	0	1.000	2.00	41	15	0	.366	18	123	119	-4	-5	26
Brad Wilkerson	Was	38	31	288.1	67	0	1	0	.985	2.09	27	8	0	.296	-	63	67	+4	+7	-
Gerald Williams	NYM	10	0	17.0	3	0	0	0	1.000	1.59	6	1	0	.167	-	3	3	0	0	-
Craig Wilson	Pit	19	18	138.1	27	3	0	1	1.000	1.95	18	9	1	.500	-	32	27	-5	-7	-
Preston Wilson	2 tms	11	11	94.0	20	0	0	0	1.000	1.91	6	2	0	.333	-	20	20	0	0	-
Randy Winn	2 tms	92	90	795.2	226	2	0	0	1.000	2.58	84	29	2	.345	10	226	226	0	-3	20
Tony Womack	NYY	40	38	326.0	72	2	2	0	.974	2.04	41	19	1	.463	-	77	72	-5	-5	-
Chris Woodward	NYM	13	7	69.0	17	2	1	1	.950	2.48	9	4	2	.444	-	18	18	0	0	-
Dmitri Young	Det	19	18	142.1	35	1	0	0	1.000	2.28	20	7	1	.350	-	36	35	-1	+1	-
Eric Young	SD	21	19	167.2	47	0	0	0	1.000	2.52	19	8	0	.421	-	43	47	+4	+6	-
2005 MLB Averages									.986	2.02	4373	1667	189	.381	-					

Center Fielders 2005

Name	Team	G	GS	Inn	PO	A	E	DP	Pct	Rng	Opps To Advance	Extra Bases	Kills	Pct	Rank	Expected Outs	Outs Made	Total	Enhanced	Rank
Chris Aguila	Fla	2	1	7.0	3	0	0	0	1.000	3.86						3	3	0	-1	-
Chip Ambres	KC	24	16	157.0	47	2	0	0	1.000	2.81	18	11	2	.611	-	48	47	-1	-2	-
Brian Anderson	CWS	5	3	36.0	7	0	0	0	1.000	1.75	2	1	0	.500	-	6	7	+1	+2	-
Jason Bay	Pit	30	29	217.0	57	1	3	0	.951	2.41	18	13	0	.722	-	58	57	-1	-2	-
Carlos Beltran	NYM	150	149	1289.1	378	5	4	1	.990	2.67	138	91	4	.659	32	377	378	+1	+7	8
Larry Bigbie	2 tms	17	17	136.0	38	1	0	1	1.000	2.58	17	11	0	.647	-	36	38	+2	+3	-
Willie Bloomquist	Sea	15	13	117.0	25	1	1	1	.963	2.00	13	7	1	.538	-	25	25	0	-1	-
Hiram Bocachica	Oak	1	0	3.0	3	0	0	0	1.000	9.00						2	3	+1	+1	-
Milton Bradley	LAD	73	73	628.0	181	6	2	0	.989	2.68	65	37	4	.569	17	182	181	-1	-6	26
Eric Bruntlett	Hou	14	10	95.0	34	2	0	1	1.000	3.41	11	7	1	.636	-	35	34	-1	0	-
Jaime Bubela	Sea	6	5	45.0	17	0	0	0	1.000	3.40	6	4	0	.667	-	17	17	0	+1	-
Chris Burke	Hou	6	1	13.0	1	0	0	0	1.000	.69	1	1	0	1.000	-	1	1	0	0	-
Jeromy Burnitz	ChC	3	2	19.2	8	1	0	0	1.000	4.12	2	1	0	.500	-	8	8	0	+1	-
Freddie Bynum	Oak	1	1	9.0	4	0	0	0	1.000	4.00						4	4	0	0	-
Marlon Byrd	2 tms	16	10	95.0	20	0	0	0	1.000	1.89	1	1	0	1.000	-	21	20	-1	-2	-
Eric Byrnes	3 tms	7	5	42.0	14	1	0	1	1.000	3.21	1	1	0	1.000	-	14	14	0	+2	-
Melky Cabrera	NYY	6	6	49.0	9	0	0	0	1.000	1.65	7	5	0	.714	-	11	9	-2	-6	-
Napoleon Calzado	Bal	1	0	1.0	0	0	0	0	-	.00								0	0	-
Mike Cameron	NYM	10	9	79.0	15	1	0	0	1.000	1.82	8	6	0	.750	-	16	15	-1	-1	-
Endy Chavez	2 tms	34	10	137.0	32	3	1	1	.972	2.30	7	3	1	.429	-	31	32	+1	+1	-
Shin-soo Choo	Sea	5	5	39.0	16	0	0	0	1.000	3.69	6	5	0	.833	-	16	16	0	0	-
Ryan Church	Was	20	12	125.2	49	0	0	0	1.000	3.51	13	7	0	.538	-	46	49	+3	+7	-
Brady Clark	Mil	145	145	1275.1	399	5	2	4	.995	2.85	131	79	5	.603	21	398	399	+1	+1	18
Carl Crawford	TB	8	8	65.0	20	0	0	0	1.000	2.77	8	3	0	.375	-	18	20	+2	+3	-
Coco Crisp	Cle	10	10	79.2	21	0	1	0	.955	2.37	6	4	0	.667	-	22	21	-1	-2	-
Bubba Crosby	NYY	41	12	144.2	57	1	0	1	1.000	3.61	11	7	1	.636	-	58	57	-1	-2	-
Jose Cruz	3 tms	53	50	415.0	87	1	2	0	.978	1.91	51	32	1	.627	-	99	87	-12	-22	-
Johnny Damon	Bos	147	144	1225.0	394	5	6	0	.985	2.93	120	69	4	.575	18	398	396	-2	-2	23
Jeff DaVanon	LAA	24	12	130.2	45	0	1	0	.978	3.10	15	8	0	.533	-	44	45	+1	+2	-
David DeJesus	KC	119	118	1005.1	306	7	4	3	.987	2.80	122	67	7	.549	15	301	306	+5	+1	19
David Dellucci	Tex	3	2	19.0	3	0	0	0	1.000	1.42	4	3	0	.750	-	4	3	-1	-2	-
Chris Denorfia	Cin	10	4	43.0	13	0	1	0	.929	2.72	20	9	0	.450	-	13	13	0	-2	-
J.D. Drew	LAD	30	28	241.2	64	0	0	0	1.000	2.38	25	15	0	.600	-	62	64	+2	+1	-
Chris Duffy	Pit	33	27	248.0	80	1	1	0	.988	2.94	29	19	1	.655	-	75	80	+5	+8	-
Ray Durham	SF	1	0	1.0	0	0	0	0	-	.00					-			0	0	-
Jim Edmonds	StL	139	132	1153.1	318	5	2	1	.994	2.52	117	48	2	.410	1	319	319	0	-6	25
Jason Ellison	SF	78	64	591.2	196	4	6	0	.971	3.04	70	49	3	.700	35	193	197	+4	+3	15
Juan Encarnacion	Fla	11	6	52.1	10	0	0	0	1.000	1.72	6	3	0	.500	-	11	10	-1	-2	-
Chone Figgins	LAA	50	45	398.1	131	1	2	0	.985	2.98	29	16	1	.552	-	132	131	-1	-1	-
Steve Finley	LAA	104	100	895.2	266	5	4	2	.985	2.72	88	44	3	.500	5	273	266	-7	-7	27
Jeff Fiorentino	Bal	12	10	96.0	29	0	0	0	1.000	2.72	12	7	0	.583	-	24	29	+5	+9	-
Lew Ford	Min	63	60	548.0	140	7	4	1	.974	2.41	76	40	1	.526	9	134	140	+6	+11	5
Ryan Freel	Cin	18	10	101.1	41	1	0	0	1.000	3.73	16	11	1	.688	-	40	41	+1	+1	-
Choo Freeman	Col	6	5	41.0	12	2	0	1	1.000	3.07	3	2	2	.667	-	12	12	0	0	-
Joey Gathright	TB	70	56	505.2	180	3	3	2	.984	3.26	54	33	3	.611	25	170	181	+11	+23	3
Brian Giles	SD	17	15	133.0	32	0	0	0	1.000	2.17	12	8	0	.667	-	34	32	-2	-4	-
Charles Gipson	Hou	5	0	12.0	3	0	0	0	1.000	2.25					-	3	3	0	+1	-
Alexis Gomez	Det	3	1	11.0	2	0	0	0	1.000	1.64	3	2	0	.667	-	3	2	-1	-1	-
Curtis Granderson	Det	41	39	320.0	119	2	0	0	1.000	3.40	36	19	1	.528	-	112	119	+7	+13	-
Shawn Green	Ari	41	40	315.0	80	2	0	1	1.000	2.34	31	16	1	.516	-	82	80	-2	-5	-
Ken Griffey Jr.	Cin	124	124	1065.2	285	6	3	1	.990	2.46	136	74	4	.544	12	299	286	-13	-27	33
Marquis Grissom	SF	34	34	284.2	68	0	1	0	.986	2.15	33	22	0	.667	-	76	68	-8	-14	-
Aaron Guiel	KC	24	21	185.0	54	1	1	0	.982	2.68	17	10	0	.588	-	49	54	+5	+9	-
Franklin Gutierrez	Cle	2	0	3.0	1	0	0	0	1.000	3.00						1	1	0	0	-
Scott Hairston	Ari	1	0	0.2	0	0	0	0	-	.00					-			0	-1	-
Jerry Hairston Jr.	ChC	48	44	386.0	90	2	2	0	.979	2.15	25	14	1	.560	-	88	90	+2	+2	-
Corey Hart	Mil	11	11	96.0	19	0	0	0	1.000	1.78	10	7	0	.700	-	18	19	+1	+2	-
Richard Hidalgo	Tex	3	2	18.0	5	0	0	0	1.000	2.50					-	5	5	0	0	-
Damon Hollins	TB	80	72	619.0	199	4	3	2	.985	2.95	91	62	3	.681	34	206	198	-8	-13	32
Torii Hunter	Min	93	92	813.1	218	9	3	4	.987	2.51	94	58	7	.617	26	217	218	+1	+5	11
Adam Hyzdu	2 tms	8	2	34.2	11	0	0	0	1.000	2.86	2	2	0	1.000	-	10	11	+1	+3	-
Brandon Inge	Det	1	0	0	0	0	0	0	-	.00								0	0	-
Damian Jackson	SD	15	8	79.2	23	0	0	0	1.000	2.60	6	5	0	.833	-	21	23	+2	+2	-
Ben Johnson	SD	9	6	60.0	14	0	1	0	.933	2.10	11	7	0	.636	-	14	14	0	+1	-
Reed Johnson	Tor	9	5	53.0	11	0	0	0	1.000	1.87	7	4	0	.571	-	12	11	-1	-3	-
Andruw Jones	Atl	159	158	1366.1	365	11	2	1	.995	2.48	138	73	6	.529	10	361	365	+4	+7	9
Jacque Jones	Min	10	9	86.0	17	1	0	0	1.000	1.88	11	6	1	.545	-	18	17	-1	-2	-
Gabe Kapler	Bos	12	9	80.0	19	0	0	0	1.000	2.14	7	4	0	.571	-	20	19	-1	-2	-
Austin Kearns	Cin	2	0	2.0	1	0	0	0	1.000	4.50						1	1	0	0	-
Kenny Kelly	2 tms	2	0	2.1	2	0	0	0	1.000	7.71						2	2	0	0	-
Mark Kotsay	Oak	137	137	1184.1	298	7	4	3	.987	2.32	103	50	6	.485	3	300	300	0	+1	20
Dave Krynzel	Mil	1	1	8.1	2	0	0	0	1.000	2.16						2	2	0	0	-
Jason Lane	Hou	6	4	37.0	11	0	0	0	1.000	2.68	1	1	0	1.000	-	11	11	0	0	-
Ryan Langerhans	Atl	19	4	77.1	28	0	0	0	1.000	3.26	8	5	0	.625	-	26	28	+2	+3	-
Kenny Lofton	Phi	97	88	741.0	201	7	4	1	.981	2.53	51	26	6	.510	7	199	201	+2	+1	21
Nook Logan	Det	123	93	874.1	282	3	6	2	.979	2.93	87	51	1	.586	19	274	282	+8	+19	4
Terrence Long	KC	6	4	35.0	5	0	0	0	1.000	1.29	6	3	0	.500	-	6	5	-1	-4	-
Hector Luna	StL	1	0	1.0	1	0	0	0	1.000	9.00						1	1	0	0	-
Alejandro Machado	Bos	3	0	7.1	2	0	0	0	1.000	2.45	1	1	0	1.000	-	2	2	0	+1	-
Jose Macias	ChC	7	5	47.2	20	1	1	0	.955	3.97	9	5	1	.556	-	18	20	+2	+3	-
Rob Mackowiak	Pit	41	31	281.2	68	2	1	0	.986	2.24	26	16	1	.615	-	68	68	0	+1	-
Chris Magruder	Mil	9	5	58.1	19	0	2	0	.905	2.93	4	2	0	.500	-	18	19	+1	+3	-
Eli Marrero	2 tms	8	6	56.0	15	0	0	0	1.000	2.41	8	5	0	.625	-	14	15	+1	+2	-
Luis Matos	Bal	120	110	990.0	298	7	5	2	.984	2.77	105	64	3	.610	23	298	299	+1	+4	13
Hideki Matsui	NYY	28	28	222.1	54	0	0	0	1.000	2.19	21	13	0	.619	-	57	54	-3	-5	-
Gary Matthews Jr.	Tex	97	95	846.0	257	5	5	2	.981	2.79	134	79	3	.590	20	257	258	+1	+5	10
Quinton McCracken	Ari	46	30	306.0	66	2	2	0	.971	2.00	31	16	0	.516	-	64	66	+2	+3	-
Nate McLouth	Pit	21	19	166.0	36	0	0	0	1.000	1.95	15	8	0	.533	-	37	36	-1	-3	-
Jason Michaels	Phi	75	62	536.0	161	5	2	1	.988	2.79	43	19	1	.442	2	156	161	+5	+4	14
Dustan Mohr	Col	10	8	63.0	19	1	0	0	1.000	2.86	11	8	0	.727	-	19	19	0	0	-
Craig Monroe	Det	33	29	229.1	63	0	1	0	.984	2.47	18	9	0	.500	-	62	63	+1	+3	-

		BASIC										THROWING					PLAYS		PLUS/MINUS		
Name	Team	G	GS	Inn	PO	A	E	DP	Pct	Rng	Opps To Advance	Extra Bases	Kills	Pct	Rank	Expected Outs	Outs Made	Total	Enhanced	Rank
Xavier Nady	SD	30	28	244.1	54	0	1	0	.982	1.99	20	12	0	.600	-	55	54	-1	-4	-
David Newhan	Bal	32	29	234.2	61	0	0	0	1.000	2.34	33	23	0	.697	-	64	61	-3	-5	-
Ramon Nivar	Bal	4	3	25.0	10	0	0	0	1.000	3.60					-	8	10	+2	+3	-
Laynce Nix	Tex	61	60	526.0	160	3	2	1	.988	2.79	60	31	2	.517	8	159	160	+1	+2	17
Orlando Palmeiro	Hou	5	4	30.0	6	0	0	0	1.000	1.80	3	2	0	.667	-	6	6	0	-1	-
Corey Patterson	ChC	122	111	986.2	239	6	5	2	.980	2.23	97	59	5	.608	22	243	240	-3	-2	24
Jay Payton	2 tms	41	28	290.0	74	2	0	0	1.000	2.36	27	11	1	.407	-	71	73	+2	+4	-
Wily Mo Pena	Cin	25	22	192.2	57	0	1	0	.983	2.66	18	13	0	.722	-	61	57	-4	-8	-
Timo Perez	CWS	2	2	17.0	7	0	0	0	1.000	3.71	1	1	0	1.000	-	7	7	0	0	-
Juan Pierre	Fla	160	155	1383.0	332	7	4	3	.988	2.21	148	94	5	.635	30	334	332	-2	-9	28
Scott Podsednik	CWS	7	6	55.0	14	0	0	0	1.000	2.29	2	1	0	.500	-	12	14	+2	+2	-
Chris Prieto	LAA	2	1	9.0	5	0	0	0	1.000	5.00	1	1	0	1.000	-	6	5	-1	0	-
Nick Punto	Min	2	1	11.0	0	0	0	0		.00					-			0	0	-
Julio Ramirez	SF	2	0	5.1	3	0	0	0	1.000	5.06					-	3	3	0	0	-
Tike Redman	Pit	75	56	523.1	158	5	7	0	.959	2.80	50	31	0	.620	28	155	158	+3	+3	16
Jeremy Reed	Sea	137	129	1149.2	383	7	3	1	.992	3.05	128	79	4	.617	27	371	384	+13	+28	2
Keith Reed	Bal	1	1	8.0	0	0	0	0		.00	3	3	0	1.000	-	1	1	0	0	-
Kevin Reese	NYY	1	0	2.0	1	0	0	0	1.000	4.50					-	1	1	0	0	-
Jason Repko	LAD	58	38	363.0	97	5	1	1	.990	2.53	38	16	4	.421	-	100	97	-3	-5	-
Alexis Rios	Tor	5	4	36.0	12	0	0	0	1.000	3.00					-	11	12	+1	+1	-
Juan Rivera	LAA	4	4	30.0	10	0	0	0	1.000	3.00					-	10	10	0	0	-
Dave Roberts	SD	109	101	900.2	235	4	2	1	.992	2.39	81	51	2	.630	29	239	234	-5	-10	30
Jason Romano	Cin	5	3	26.0	10	0	1	0	.909	3.46	4	2	0	.500	-	10	10	0	0	-
Aaron Rowand	CWS	157	151	1367.2	388	3	3	1	.992	2.57	117	58	1	.496	4	373	388	+15	+30	1
Alex Sanchez	2 tms	22	21	175.0	59	1	4	0	.938	3.09	26	15	0	.577	-	62	59	-3	-4	-
Jared Schumaker	StL	4	1	12.1	4	0	0	0	1.000	2.92					-	4	4	0	-1	-
Luke Scott	Hou	1	0	1.0	0	0	0	0		.00					-			0	0	-
Chris Singleton	TB	6	4	39.1	15	0	0	0	1.000	3.43	6	2	0	.333	-	15	15	0	0	-
Grady Sizemore	Cle	155	152	1370.0	373	3	3	1	.992	2.47	118	60	2	.508	6	370	373	+3	+10	6
Adam Stern	Bos	6	1	18.0	3	0	0	0	1.000	1.50	2	2	0	1.000	-	3	3	0	0	-
Jamal Strong	Sea	4	4	30.0	8	0	0	0	1.000	2.40	1	1	0	1.000	-	8	8	0	+1	-
Cory Sullivan	Col	83	67	617.2	172	4	2	2	.989	2.56	64	35	3	.547	14	172	172	0	+1	22
So Taguchi	StL	50	28	274.0	58	0	0	0	1.000	1.91	26	19	0	.731	-	57	58	+1	+3	-
Willy Taveras	Hou	148	144	1254.0	332	10	3	2	.991	2.45	100	56	8	.560	16	329	332	+3	+9	7
Reggie Taylor	TB	9	5	48.2	17	0	0	0	1.000	3.14	8	5	0	.625	-	17	17	0	-1	-
Luis Terrero	Ari	74	42	419.2	121	1	2	0	.984	2.62	35	19	1	.543	-	121	121	0	-1	-
Charles Thomas	Oak	9	1	29.0	14	0	0	0	1.000	4.34	8	5	0	.625	-	14	14	0	0	-
Andres Torres	Tex	4	3	30.0	11	0	0	0	1.000	3.30	4	4	0	1.000	-	10	11	+1	+2	-
Michael Tucker	2 tms	7	5	45.0	13	1	1	0	.933	2.80	7	5	0	.714	-	14	13	-1	-2	-
Jason Tyner	Min	2	0	6.0	3	0	0	0	1.000	4.50					-	2	3	+1	+1	-
Eric Valent	NYM	2	0	4.0	2	0	0	0	1.000	4.50	1	1	0	1.000	-	2	2	0	0	-
Shane Victorino	Phi	5	0	7.0	0	0	0	0		.00					-			0	0	-
Larry Walker	StL	1	1	5.0	1	0	0	0	1.000	1.80					-	2	1	-1	-1	-
Brandon Watson	Was	1	0	3.0	2	0	0	0	1.000	6.00					-	2	2	0	0	-
Vernon Wells	Tor	155	153	1358.0	351	12	0	4	1.000	2.41	149	91	7	.611	24	350	351	+1	+4	12
Jayson Werth	LAD	30	23	194.2	63	1	3	0	.955	2.96	21	14	1	.667	-	59	63	+4	+7	-
Brad Wilkerson	Was	92	88	758.2	233	6	3	1	.988	2.84	75	41	4	.547	13	239	234	-5	-9	29
Bernie Williams	NYY	112	99	862.1	226	6	2	1	.991	2.42	93	63	1	.677	33	247	226	-21	-37	35
Gerald Williams	NYM	10	4	51.0	12	0	0	0	1.000	2.12	8	4	0	.500	-	12	12	0	-2	-
Preston Wilson	2 tms	124	122	1068.2	265	5	3	0	.989	2.27	122	79	3	.648	31	281	266	-15	-28	34
Randy Winn	2 tms	61	61	532.2	184	2	1	1	.995	3.14	49	26	1	.531	11	185	184	-1	-10	31
Tony Womack	NYY	22	17	149.2	36	0	0	0	1.000	2.16	12	6	0	.500	-	39	36	-3	-4	-
Chris Woodward	NYM	5	0	12.1	4	0	0	0	1.000	2.92					-	4	4	0	0	-
Eric Young	SD	4	3	20.0	6	0	0	0	1.000	2.70					-	7	6	-1	-4	-
2005 MLB Averages									.988	2.59	4465	2595	149	.581	-					

Right Fielders 2005

Name	Team	G	GS	Inn	PO	A	E	DP	Pct	Rng	Opps To Advance	Extra Bases	Kills	Pct	Rank	Expected Outs	Outs Made	Total	Enhanced	Rank
Bobby Abreu	Phi	158	158	1364.0	266	7	4	0	.986	1.80	118	58	4	.492	11	272	267	-5	-13	28
Chris Aguila	Fla	14	9	84.0	24	1	0	0	1.000	2.68	9	5	1	.556	-	27	24	-3	-3	-
Chad Allen	Tex	1	1	6.0	1	0	0	0	1.000	1.50					-	1	1	0	0	-
Moises Alou	SF	53	51	412.2	90	4	4	3	.959	2.05	47	35	3	.745	-	90	90	0	-1	-
Brian Anderson	CWS	1	1	7.0	2	0	0	0	1.000	2.57					-	2	2	0	+1	-
Marlon Anderson	NYM	14	9	73.0	13	1	0	0	1.000	1.73	5	2	0	.400	-	14	13	-1	-3	-
Lance Berkman	Hou	11	10	78.0	16	0	0	0	1.000	1.85	5	3	0	.600	-	16	16	0	-1	-
Larry Bigbie	2 tms	5	4	38.0	8	0	0	0	1.000	1.89	5	2	0	.400	-	10	8	-2	-5	-
Casey Blake	Cle	138	132	1188.2	287	3	8	0	.973	2.20	128	76	2	.594	29	284	287	+3	+14	2
Tony Blanco	Was	2	1	9.0	1	0	0	0	1.000	1.00	4	4	0	1.000	-	1	1	0	0	-
Hiram Bocachica	Oak	5	3	25.0	3	0	0	0	1.000	1.08	1	1	0	1.000	-	3	3	0	0	-
Joe Borchard	CWS	2	0	7.0	3	0	0	0	1.000	3.86					-	3	3	0	0	-
Emil Brown	KC	129	126	1097.1	243	7	11	0	.958	2.05	154	95	1	.617	30	248	243	-5	-9	26
Eric Bruntlett	Hou	1	0	2.0	1	1	0	1	1.000	9.00					-	1	1	0	0	-
Jeromy Burnitz	ChC	158	153	1359.2	303	5	5	1	.984	2.04	124	78	1	.629	31	311	303	-8	-4	16
Marlon Byrd	2 tms	4	3	34.0	10	0	0	0	1.000	2.65	2	1	0	.500	-	9	10	+1	+2	-
Eric Byrnes	3 tms	12	9	86.0	24	1	2	1	.926	2.62	16	11	1	.688	-	22	24	+2	+2	-
Miguel Cairo	NYM	1	1	7.0	1	0	0	0	1.000	1.29	3	2	0	.667	-	1	1	0	0	-
Mike Cameron	NYM	68	67	593.0	136	2	6	1	.958	2.09	55	27	2	.491	10	137	137	0	+2	12
Roger Cedeno	StL	10	5	42.0	7	0	2	0	.778	1.50	5	2	0	.400	-	8	7	-1	-1	-
Matt Cepicky	Was	1	1	9.0	5	0	0	0	1.000	5.00					-	5	5	0	0	-
Endy Chavez	2 tms	5	0	10.0	2	0	0	0	1.000	1.80					-	3	2	-1	-1	-
Ryan Church	Was	21	14	135.2	43	0	0	0	1.000	2.85	13	6	0	.462	-	44	43	-1	0	-
Jeff Conine	Fla	28	21	186.2	51	0	3	0	.944	2.46	23	14	0	.609	-	53	51	-2	-6	-
Bubba Crosby	NYY	23	9	100.0	24	1	0	0	1.000	2.25	9	6	0	.667	-	26	24	-2	-2	-
Jacob Cruz	Cin	12	5	48.1	7	0	0	0	1.000	1.30					-	6	7	+1	0	-
Jose Cruz	3 tms	55	51	433.0	110	4	5	0	.958	2.37	45	25	4	.556	-	105	110	+5	+9	-
Nelson Cruz	Mil	6	1	16.0	4	0	0	0	1.000	2.25	3	1	0	.333	-	4	4	0	0	-
Mike Cuddyer	Min	20	18	159.0	35	0	0	0	1.000	1.98	7	3	0	.429	-	32	35	+3	+6	-
Jeff DaVanon	LAA	26	12	133.2	30	0	0	0	1.000	2.02	12	6	0	.500	-	30	30	0	+2	-
J.J. Davis	Was	1	0	3.0	1	0	0	0	1.000	3.00					-	1	1	0	0	-
David Dellucci	Tex	3	3	26.0	6	0	1	0	.857	2.08					-	5	6	+1	+1	-
Chris Denorfia	Cin	2	2	16.1	9	0	0	0	1.000	4.96	1	1	0	1.000	-	9	9	0	0	-
Mark DeRosa	Tex	25	21	185.0	46	1	0	0	1.000	2.29	17	7	1	.412	-	42	46	+4	+4	-
Matt Diaz	KC	2	1	11.0	4	0	0	0	1.000	3.27					-	4	4	0	0	-
Victor Diaz	NYM	78	74	651.2	153	2	3	1	.981	2.14	66	25	2	.379	1	159	153	-6	-8	23
Ryan Doumit	Pit	3	3	23.0	0	0	0	0	-	.00	5	3	0	.600	-	1	1	-1	-2	-
J.D. Drew	LAD	44	44	382.0	83	3	2	0	.977	2.03	54	27	2	.500	-	84	83	-1	+1	-
Jason Dubois	2 tms	4	4	30.0	8	0	0	0	1.000	2.40					-	8	8	0	0	-
Chris Duncan	StL	1	0	1.0	0	0	0	0	-	.00					-		0	0	0	-
Jermaine Dye	CWS	140	137	1235.1	259	9	8	2	.971	1.95	119	61	5	.513	15	265	259	-6	-6	21
Mike Edwards	LAD	3	1	11.0	2	0	0	0	1.000	1.64					-	2	2	0	0	-
Jason Ellison	SF	32	18	166.1	36	1	1	1	.974	2.00	19	11	1	.579	-	37	36	-1	-1	-
Juan Encarnacion	Fla	135	126	1112.2	216	4	4	0	.982	1.78	126	66	2	.524	16	220	216	-4	-12	27
Carl Everett	CWS	8	8	70.0	18	0	0	0	1.000	2.31	9	5	0	.556	-	20	18	-2	-3	-
Robert Fick	SD	9	6	57.0	16	1	0	0	1.000	2.68	7	4	0	.571	-	17	16	-1	-1	-
Chone Figgins	LAA	8	7	53.0	12	1	0	0	1.000	2.21	3	2	1	.667	-	14	12	-2	-2	-
Lew Ford	Min	16	14	133.0	26	0	1	0	.963	1.76	10	5	0	.500	-	25	26	+1	+1	-
Jeff Francoeur	Atl	67	65	589.0	131	13	5	3	.966	2.20	69	34	10	.493	12	126	131	+5	+10	7
Ryan Freel	Cin	13	6	69.2	23	0	0	0	1.000	2.97	9	4	0	.444	-	25	23	-2	-2	-
Jody Gerut	3 tms	26	25	217.1	40	0	0	0	1.000	1.66	24	14	0	.583	-	42	40	-2	-4	-
Jay Gibbons	Bal	71	69	558.2	133	6	2	1	.986	2.24	77	42	1	.545	21	128	133	+5	+10	6
Brian Giles	SD	143	140	1220.0	295	6	4	1	.987	2.22	143	78	4	.545	20	297	295	-2	-5	20
Ross Gload	CWS	1	0	2.0	2	0	0	0	1.000	9.00					-	2	2	0	0	-
Jonny Gomes	TB	36	34	291.0	68	6	4	1	.949	2.29	30	20	4	.667	-	70	68	-2	-1	-
Adrian Gonzalez	Tex	1	1	8.0	3	0	1	0	.750	3.38	2	2	0	1.000	-	3	3	0	0	-
Luis A Gonzalez	Col	7	5	43.1	14	0	0	0	1.000	2.91	3	2	0	.667	-	13	14	+1	+3	-
Jason Grabowski	LAD	4	2	23.1	5	0	0	0	1.000	1.93	3	3	0	1.000	-	5	5	0	0	-
Shawn Green	Ari	135	109	1031.1	232	2	0	0	1.000	2.04	103	56	0	.544	19	232	232	0	-4	17
Marquis Grissom	SF	1	1	8.0	0	0	0	0	-	.00					-		0	0	0	-
Gabe Gross	Tor	20	16	143.1	32	1	1	0	.971	2.07	16	12	0	.750	-	31	32	+1	+2	-
Vladimir Guerrero	LAA	120	120	1040.0	242	8	3	2	.988	2.16	83	38	6	.458	6	238	245	+7	+10	5
Aaron Guiel	KC	7	5	47.2	10	0	0	0	1.000	1.89	6	2	0	.333	-	10	10	0	0	-
Jose Guillen	Was	140	135	1189.2	299	10	7	0	.978	2.34	136	73	7	.537	18	297	299	+2	+10	4
Jerry Hairston Jr.	ChC	1	1	7.0	2	0	0	0	1.000	2.57					-	2	2	0	0	-
Jeffrey Hammonds	Was	1	1	9.0	2	0	0	0	1.000	2.00					-	2	2	0	0	-
Corey Hart	Mil	3	3	27.0	8	1	1	0	.900	3.00	4	2	1	.500	-	8	8	0	0	-
Brad Hawpe	Col	89	79	693.0	148	10	3	2	.981	2.05	107	59	6	.551	22	150	148	-2	-3	15
Jeremy Hermida	Fla	10	6	58.2	17	0	0	0	1.000	2.61	5	3	0	.600	-	16	17	+1	+2	-
Jose Hernandez	Cle	3	1	8.0	1	0	0	0	1.000	1.13					-	2	1	-1	-1	-
Richard Hidalgo	Tex	83	78	699.2	174	3	2	0	.989	2.28	87	43	2	.494	13	168	174	+6	+8	8
Bobby Higginson	Det	6	5	48.0	6	0	0	0	1.000	1.13	4	1	0	.250	-	6	6	0	+1	-
Todd Hollandsworth	2 tms	9	4	37.1	3	0	1	0	.750	.72	1	1	0	1.000	-	3	3	0	+1	-
Damon Hollins	TB	48	15	170.0	38	3	1	2	.976	2.17	15	10	1	.667	-	39	38	-1	0	-
Aubrey Huff	TB	97	95	786.2	204	6	3	2	.986	2.40	96	49	4	.510	14	205	204	-1	-4	19
Adam Hyzdu	2 tms	5	2	22.0	2	0	0	0	1.000	.82					-	2	2	0	0	-
Raul Ibanez	Sea	3	3	24.1	0	0	0	0	-	.00	4	4	0	1.000	-	0	0	0	0	-
Damian Jackson	SD	1	0	1.0	0	0	0	0	-	.00					-		0	0	0	-
Geoff Jenkins	Mil	144	144	1241.1	307	10	5	7	.984	2.30	127	72	10	.567	25	300	307	+7	+13	3
Ben Johnson	SD	11	8	73.1	27	0	1	0	.964	3.31	8	4	0	.500	-	26	27	+1	+1	-
Reed Johnson	Tor	35	30	247.0	51	1	1	0	.981	1.89	18	9	1	.500	-	52	51	-1	-3	-
Russ Johnson	NYY	3	0	6.1	1	0	0	0	1.000	1.42					-	1	1	0	0	-
Jacque Jones	Min	123	121	1080.1	261	9	4	2	.985	2.25	101	48	7	.475	8	266	262	-4	-8	22
Brian Jordan	Atl	17	17	141.2	38	1	0	0	1.000	2.48	17	7	1	.412	-	38	38	0	-1	-
Gabe Kapler	Bos	22	16	144.2	45	0	0	0	1.000	2.80	7	3	0	.429	-	41	45	+4	+8	-
Matt Kata	2 tms	1	0	3.0	0	0	0	0	-	.00					-		0	0	0	-
Austin Kearns	Cin	107	103	890.0	237	8	3	3	.988	2.48	97	47	8	.485	9	232	238	+6	+7	10
Kenny Kelly	2 tms	3	0	7.0	0	0	0	0	-	.00	1	1	0	1.000	-		0	0	-1	-
Bobby Kielty	Oak	42	37	324.0	67	2	2	1	.972	1.92	38	23	2	.605	-	69	67	-2	-4	-
Gerald Laird	Tex	1	0	1.0	0	0	0	0	-	.00					-		0	0	0	-
Mike Lamb	Hou	1	1	7.0	1	0	0	0	1.000	1.29					-	1	1	0	0	-

30

		BASIC										THROWING					PLAYS		PLUS/MINUS		
Name	Team	G	GS	Inn	PO	A	E	DP	Pct	Rng	Opps To Advance	Extra Bases	Kills	Pct	Rank	Expected Outs	Outs Made	Total	Enhanced	Rank
Jason Lane	Hou	137	126	1115.2	225	4	6	0	.974	1.85	111	48	3	.432	3	226	225	-1	-4	18
Ryan Langerhans	Atl	48	39	356.0	75	3	1	1	.987	1.97	46	24	1	.522	-	69	75	+6	+11	-
Jason LaRue	Cin	1	0	1.0	1	0	0	0	1.000	9.00					-	1	1	0	+1	-
Matt Lawton	3 tms	113	109	953.0	230	4	2	1	.992	2.21	94	42	3	.447	4	233	230	-3	-17	29
Ricky Ledee	LAD	17	9	87.2	19	1	0	0	1.000	2.05	9	2	1	.222	-	19	19	0	+1	-
Jeff Liefer	Cle	3	1	16.0	4	0	0	0	1.000	2.25					-	4	4	0	0	-
Todd Linden	SF	40	36	318.2	92	0	1	0	.989	2.60	23	12	0	.522	-	89	92	+3	+8	-
Terrence Long	KC	17	15	128.0	32	3	1	0	.972	2.46	29	19	2	.655	-	32	32	0	-1	-
Ryan Ludwick	Cle	6	3	34.0	6	0	0	0	1.000	1.59	3	2	0	.667	-	6	6	0	+1	-
Hector Luna	StL	21	12	113.2	29	2	2	0	.939	2.45	10	6	1	.600	-	29	29	0	-1	-
John Mabry	StL	49	25	252.0	35	1	0	0	1.000	1.29	25	10	0	.400	-	36	35	-1	0	-
Alejandro Machado	Bos	1	0	1.0	0	0	0	0	-	.00					-			0	0	-
Jose Macias	ChC	8	3	27.1	3	1	0	0	1.000	1.32	5	3	1	.600	-	4	3	-1	-1	-
Rob Mackowiak	Pit	23	13	127.1	34	2	1	2	.973	2.54	14	6	2	.429	-	32	34	+2	+3	-
Chris Magruder	Mil	31	14	153.2	32	0	0	0	1.000	1.87	13	4	0	.308	-	33	32	-1	-4	-
Eli Marrero	2 tms	13	9	80.0	15	1	1	0	.941	1.80	8	5	0	.625	-	17	15	-2	-2	-
Hideki Matsui	NYY	4	4	29.2	6	0	0	0	1.000	1.82	5	4	0	.800	-	7	6	-1	0	-
Gary Matthews Jr.	Tex	22	21	189.2	51	2	1	2	.981	2.51	19	11	2	.579	-	46	51	+5	+8	-
Quinton McCracken	Ari	2	0	3.0	1	0	0	0	1.000	3.00					-	1	1	0	+1	-
Marshall McDougall	Tex	3	1	10.0	0	0	0	0	-	.00					-			0		-
Joe McEwing	KC	1	0	1.0	0	0	0	0	-	.00					-			0	0	-
Nate McLouth	Pit	8	5	52.2	10	0	2	0	.833	1.71	5	3	0	.600	-	9	10	+1	+2	-
Kevin Mench	Tex	41	36	311.1	60	0	2	0	.968	1.73	39	15	0	.385	-	57	60	+3	+9	-
Jason Michaels	Phi	13	4	53.0	13	2	0	0	1.000	2.55	7	4	1	.571	-	12	14	+2	+3	-
Kevin Millar	Bos	14	12	87.0	22	1	0	0	1.000	2.38	11	7	0	.636	-	19	22	+3	+4	-
Dustan Mohr	Col	55	43	382.2	103	0	2	0	.981	2.42	46	23	0	.500	-	99	103	+4	+5	-
Raul Mondesi	Atl	40	39	339.0	67	2	1	0	.986	1.83	37	20	2	.541	-	67	67	0	0	-
Craig Monroe	Det	85	69	632.1	132	4	4	0	.971	1.94	49	26	2	.531	17	141	132	-9	-18	30
Xavier Nady	SD	13	7	82.0	11	0	0	0	1.000	1.21	12	6	0	.500	-	11	11	0	0	-
David Newhan	Bal	30	9	116.0	20	0	1	0	.952	1.55	13	8	0	.615	-	18	20	+2	+3	-
Trot Nixon	Bos	118	107	935.1	240	8	1	3	.996	2.39	110	62	5	.564	24	228	240	+12	+18	1
Miguel Ojeda	2 tms	2	1	10.0	4	0	0	0	1.000	3.60					-	5	4	-1	-1	-
Magglio Ordonez	Det	81	79	672.1	139	5	1	0	.993	1.93	82	47	2	.573	27	138	139	+1	+3	11
Dan Ortmeier	SF	7	5	46.2	13	0	0	0	1.000	2.51	3	2	0	.667	-	13	13	0	+1	-
Orlando Palmeiro	Hou	26	15	149.1	35	2	1	2	.974	2.23	19	14	0	.737	-	35	35	0	+2	-
Jay Payton	2 tms	31	20	181.0	54	2	0	0	1.000	2.78	25	15	1	.600	-	52	54	+2	+1	-
Wily Mo Pena	Cin	50	47	401.2	92	2	1	0	.989	2.11	54	25	1	.463	-	96	92	-4	-10	-
Eduardo Perez	TB	1	0	5.0	3	0	0	0	1.000	5.40	1	1	0	1.000	-	3	3	0	0	-
Timo Perez	CWS	21	16	152.1	35	2	2	1	.949	2.19	13	8	1	.615	-	38	35	-3	-5	-
Jorge Piedra	Col	17	16	121.2	22	0	0	0	1.000	1.63	18	11	0	.611	-	23	22	-1	-2	-
Nick Punto	Min	1	0	2.0	1	0	0	0	1.000	4.50					-	1	1	0	0	-
Julio Ramirez	SF	4	0	5.1	0	0	0	0	-	.00					-			-1	-1	-
Tike Redman	Pit	8	3	37.1	8	0	0	0	1.000	1.93	8	5	0	.625	-	11	8	-3	-4	-
Keith Reed	Bal	5	0	11.0	3	0	0	0	1.000	2.45					-	3	3	0	-1	-
Desi Relaford	Col	3	0	4.0	0	1	0	0	1.000	2.25	3	1	0	.333	-			0		-
Jason Repko	LAD	42	22	213.2	50	2	4	2	.929	2.19	18	14	2	.778	-	47	50	+3	+4	-
Mike Restovich	2 tms	27	16	136.2	31	0	0	0	1.000	2.04	26	18	0	.692	-	29	31	+2	+5	-
Alexis Rios	Tor	138	116	1056.2	245	7	2	1	.992	2.15	118	50	4	.424	2	244	246	+2	+1	13
Juan Rivera	LAA	38	23	237.2	45	2	1	1	.979	1.78	17	12	2	.706	-	44	45	+1	+2	-
John Rodriguez	StL	9	4	38.1	9	1	1	0	.909	2.35					-	10	9	-1	-1	-
Jason Romano	Cin	2	0	3.0	0	0	0	0	-	.00					-			0	0	-
Cody Ross	LAD	9	5	52.1	12	2	1	0	.933	2.41	7	5	1	.714	-	11	12	+1	+1	-
Mike Ryan	Min	10	7	76.0	17	1	0	1	1.000	2.13	7	5	0	.714	-	17	17	0	+1	-
Alex Sanchez	2 tms	20	17	145.1	25	1	2	0	.929	1.61	12	7	1	.583	-	29	25	-4	-8	-
Reggie Sanders	StL	1	1	6.0	0	0	0	0	-	.00					-			0	0	-
Jared Schumaker	StL	7	0	11.1	3	0	0	0	1.000	2.38					-	3	3	0	+1	-
Luke Scott	Hou	4	2	18.0	2	0	0	0	1.000	1.00					-	2	2	0	0	-
Scott Seabol	StL	2	2	14.0	1	0	0	0	1.000	.64	3	2	0	.667	-	1	1	0	0	-
Todd Self	Hou	10	9	72.0	20	0	0	0	1.000	2.50	5	3	0	.600	-	21	20	-1	-1	-
Adam Shabala	SF	1	0	3.0	2	0	0	0	1.000	6.00	1	1	0	1.000	-	2	2	0	+1	-
Gary Sheffield	NYY	131	130	1099.0	239	5	3	0	.988	2.00	118	53	3	.449	5	260	240	-20	-25	31
Ruben Sierra	NYY	10	7	63.2	13	0	1	0	.929	1.84	11	9	0	.818	-	15	13	-2	-2	-
Chris Singleton	TB	11	6	62.0	20	0	1	0	.952	2.90	10	5	0	.500	-	21	20	-1	-2	-
Terrmel Sledge	Was	1	0	2.0	0	0	0	0	-	.00					-			0	0	-
Chris Snelling	Sea	3	1	12.0	3	0	0	0	1.000	2.25					-	2	3	+1	+1	-
Sammy Sosa	Bal	66	66	577.0	121	3	3	1	.976	1.93	47	27	1	.574	28	126	121	-5	-8	24
Ryan Spilborghs	Col	1	1	8.0	6	1	0	1	1.000	7.88	1	1	1	1.000	-	6	6	0	0	-
Matt Stairs	KC	13	12	94.1	17	0	0	0	1.000	1.62	11	7	0	.636	-	19	17	-2	-2	-
Adam Stern	Bos	13	1	27.0	7	0	0	0	1.000	2.33	3	2	0	.667	-	7	7	0	0	-
Cory Sullivan	Col	8	0	16.0	7	0	0	0	1.000	3.94					-	6	7	+1	+1	-
B.J. Surhoff	Bal	16	12	118.0	33	0	1	0	.971	2.52	11	7	0	.636	-	31	33	+2	+2	-
Ichiro Suzuki	Sea	158	158	1388.1	381	9	2	2	.995	2.53	180	103	6	.572	26	377	383	+6	+7	9
Mark Sweeney	SD	4	0	12.0	5	0	1	0	.833	3.75					-	5	5	0	+1	-
Nick Swisher	Oak	121	115	1027.1	196	6	2	2	.990	1.77	82	46	4	.561	23	192	197	+5	-1	14
So Taguchi	StL	57	35	318.2	75	3	2	0	.975	2.20	30	14	3	.467	-	72	76	+4	+7	-
Luis Terrero	Ari	2	1	10.1	3	0	0	0	1.000	2.61					-	2	3	+1	+1	-
Marcus Thames	Det	10	9	82.0	14	0	1	0	.933	1.54	6	2	0	.333	-	15	14	-1	-2	-
Charles Thomas	Oak	8	3	30.0	7	0	1	0	.875	2.10	5	2	0	.400	-	7	7	0	0	-
Tony Torcato	SF	1	0	3.0	1	0	0	0	1.000	3.00					-	1	1	0	0	-
Andres Torres	Tex	2	0	3.1	1	0	0	0	1.000	2.70	2	2	0	1.000	-	1	1	0	0	-
Chad Tracy	Ari	47	47	376.0	86	2	2	0	.978	2.11	32	16	1	.500	-	84	86	+2	+2	-
Michael Tucker	2 tms	64	46	439.2	90	5	1	1	.990	1.94	45	20	3	.444	-	94	91	-3	-3	-
Jason Tyner	Min	2	2	14.0	8	0	0	0	1.000	5.14	1	1	0	1.000	-	7	8	+1	+1	-
Eric Valent	NYM	8	7	63.0	13	0	1	0	.929	1.86	4	4	0	1.000	-	13	13	0	-1	-
Mike Vento	NYY	2	0	7.0	2	1	0	1	1.000	3.86	1	1	1	1.000	-	2	2	0	0	-
Shane Victorino	Phi	3	0	5.0	0	0	0	0	-	.00					-			0	0	-
Larry Walker	StL	83	78	648.2	107	5	2	0	.982	1.55	56	26	1	.464	7	112	107	-5	-8	25
Matt Watson	Oak	3	2	17.0	4	0	0	0	1.000	2.12					-	3	4	+1	+1	-
Jayson Werth	LAD	43	37	291.0	71	3	0	2	1.000	2.29	23	11	3	.478	-	68	71	+3	+2	-
Brad Wilkerson	Was	6	5	45.2	12	0	1	0	.923	2.36	3	1	0	.333	-	12	12	0	+1	-
Gerald Williams	NYM	7	0	10.0	1	1	0	0	1.000	1.80	1	1	0	1.000	-	1	1	0	-1	-
Craig Wilson	Pit	30	27	236.0	50	0	1	0	.980	1.91	22	12	0	.545	-	48	50	+2	+4	-

		BASIC										THROWING					PLAYS		PLUS/MINUS		
Name	Team	G	GS	Inn	PO	A	E	DP	Pct	Rng	Opps To Advance	Extra Bases	Kills	Pct	Rank	Expected Outs	Outs Made	Total	Enhanced	Rank
Preston Wilson	2 tms	2	2	17.0	4	0	0	0	1.000	2.12	2	1	0	.500	-	5	4	-1	-2	-
Tony Womack	NYY	4	3	31.2	5	0	0	0	1.000	1.42	1	1	0	1.000	-	5	5	0	0	-
Chris Woodward	NYM	6	4	38.0	6	1	0	0	1.000	1.66	3	3	0	1.000	-	6	6	0	0	-
Dmitri Young	Det	1	0	1.0	0	0	0	0	-	.00					-				0	-
2005 MLB Averages									.981	2.11	4564	2442	176	.535	-					

Team Totals

When the Phillies acquired Gold Glover That Should Have Been Aaron Rowand from the White Sox, I'm sure it was a move planned to make their defense stronger. But I'm also sure they didn't know that based on last year's Plus/Minus System, it was the absolute perfect move.

The team totals on the following pages are based on the new statistics in this book. Explanations for the numbers under the four main column headings (Plus/Minus, Ground DP, Bunts and Throwing) can each be found in their own separate section. In the columns under the heading Plus/Minus, we've broken down the data into three groupings: Middle Infield (second base and shortstop), Corner Infield (first and third base) and Outfield (left, center and right). This helps answer questions such as "Who had the best outfield in 2005?" Answer: The Atlanta Braves, with their foursome of Andruw Jones, Jeff Francoeur, Kelly Johnson and Ryan Langerhans sharing the duties. Their Outfield plus/minus figure of +50 was the best in baseball. They also ranked number three in Outfield Advance percentage (.462) and had the most baserunner kills (28) in baseball.

The next three main column headings each are associated with one of those same position groupings. Ground DP tells you how often the team turned double plays given their opportunites (groundball with a man on first and less than two outs) and primarily applies to the middle infielders, though all GDPs are included in these team totals. Bunts apply primarily to the corner infielders, though all bunts are included in the team totals regardless who fielded them. Throwing only applies to outfielders.

Let's get back to the Phillies outfield. The Phillies had the best Middle Infield in baseball according to the Plus/Minus System. Their +50 tops all teams in 2005. They also had the best Corner Infield with a mark of +57.

But their +1 in the Outfield was average. What did the Phillies do? They went out and traded for the top plus/minus outfielder in all of baseball. Aaron Rowand made 15 more plays in center field than you would expect from the average center fielder last year. Those 15 plays led to 30 bases saved for the White Sox. That's +30 in the Enhanced Plus/Minus System and the highest figure for any outfielder last year.

Pity the poor Yankees. OK, don't. But you gotta wonder how they do it with that pitifully poor defense. Their -164 figure in 2005 almost doubles their major league worst -83 in 2004. And that -83 was almost double the next worst team that year! Misery loves company and the Kansas City Royals attempted to explore the depths of the Plus/Minus System along with the Yanks with their own -143 in 2005. The Bronx Bombers were also last in handling bunts last year, thanks in large part to the grade "F" earned by Alex Rodriguez.

By the way, the Phillies did have the number one throwing outfield in 2005 and Rowand won't hurt that with his excellent arm.

The St. Louis Cardinal infield at +49 fell well short of the Phillies' +107, but it was excellent nonetheless, especially when you factor in their #1 ranking in double plays and #2 ranking in handling bunts. Mix in the #2 ranked outfield throwing arms and you have an awesome defense supporting the team with the best record in baseball last year.

The World Champion White Sox were outstanding as well, with #4 rankings in overall team plus/minus, double plays and outfield throwing. In fact, excluding the Yankees and the Red Sox, *the eight teams with the best records in baseball were in the top nine teams defensively* based on the Plus/Minus System. The only exception was the good-field, no-hit Dodgers.

Team Totals and Rankings - 2005

Team	PLUS/MINUS Middle Infield	Corner Infield	Outfield	Total	Rank	GROUND DP GDP Opps	GDP	Pct	Rank	BUNTS Opps	Score	Grade	Rank	THROWING Opps To Advance	Extra Bases	Kills	Pct	Rank
Philadelphia Phillies	+50	+57	+1	+108	1	287	111	.387	19	51	.504	C+	19	377	164	23	.435	1
Cleveland Indians	+16	+9	+44	+69	2	300	137	.457	3	37	.605	B+	3	420	210	5	.500	14
Los Angeles Angels	+24	+22	+11	+57	3	272	115	.423	7	57	.472	C	24	373	178	21	.477	7
Chicago White Sox	+7	-1	+46	+52	4	319	143	.448	4	46	.518	C+	18	394	185	13	.470	4
Houston Astros	+22	+14	+14	+50	5	316	123	.389	18	46	.520	C+	17	367	175	17	.477	6
Atlanta Braves	+22	-25	+50	+47	6	355	144	.406	13	52	.533	C+	12	455	210	28	.462	3
Oakland Athletics	+20	+12	+8	+40	7	309	137	.443	5	30	.662	A	1	385	184	17	.478	8
Los Angeles Dodgers	-12	+11	+37	+36	8	335	118	.352	30	51	.525	C+	16	426	218	26	.512	19
St Louis Cardinals	+16	+33	-15	+34	9	375	180	.480	1	40	.614	B+	2	401	178	12	.444	2
Toronto Blue Jays	+13	+6	+12	+31	10	319	134	.420	8	32	.453	C-	28	416	197	18	.474	5
Minnesota Twins	+25	-8	+14	+31	10	300	140	.467	2	41	.568	B-	6	444	215	21	.484	10
Baltimore Orioles	+16	-14	+28	+30	12	319	126	.395	16	35	.460	C-	27	436	227	12	.521	24
Chicago Cubs	+17	-1	+5	+21	13	331	119	.360	28	62	.563	B-	8	410	224	13	.546	30
Detroit Tigers	+8	+4	+8	+20	14	356	149	.419	9	40	.494	C	21	420	211	10	.502	16
Seattle Mariners	-25	-4	+45	+16	15	301	120	.399	15	40	.533	C+	13	510	267	21	.524	26
Milwaukee Brewers	+16	-12	+9	+13	16	286	108	.378	21	56	.547	B-	11	426	216	21	.507	18
Pittsburgh Pirates	+19	-5	-10	+4	17	369	163	.442	6	57	.470	C	26	445	238	11	.535	27
Arizona Diamondbacks	+30	-5	-24	+1	18	360	142	.394	17	53	.502	C+	20	454	227	5	.500	14
Washington Nationals	-7	+1	+2	-4	19	342	125	.365	25	56	.570	B-	5	431	221	20	.513	20
Colorado Rockies	-4	+6	-9	-7	20	365	133	.364	26	54	.471	C	25	525	281	21	.535	28
San Francisco Giants	-4	+19	-24	-9	21	319	117	.367	24	52	.564	B-	7	454	235	12	.518	22
Boston Red Sox	-15	+4	-9	-20	22	296	121	.409	11	25	.528	C+	14	466	239	24	.513	21
New York Mets	-15	0	-5	-20	22	353	126	.357	29	63	.587	B	4	463	227	26	.490	12
San Diego Padres	-39	+28	-16	-27	24	313	118	.377	22	49	.484	C	23	443	240	9	.542	29
Texas Rangers	-58	-6	+31	-33	25	335	125	.373	23	37	.526	C+	15	534	267	19	.500	13
Tampa Bay Devil Rays	-7	-34	+2	-39	26	283	102	.360	27	37	.453	C-	29	521	253	20	.486	11
Cincinnati Reds	+2	-22	-76	-96	27	318	121	.381	20	63	.559	B-	10	503	241	20	.479	9
Florida Marlins	-1	-37	-59	-97	28	371	149	.402	14	59	.559	B-	9	456	237	18	.520	23
Kansas City Royals	-59	-58	-26	-143	29	336	140	.417	10	33	.492	C	22	580	303	20	.522	25
New York Yankees	-72	+3	-95	-164	30	314	128	.408	12	28	.430	D+	30	467	236	11	.505	17

Team Totals and Rankings - 2004

Team	PLUS/MINUS Middle Infield	Corner Infield	Outfield	Total	Rank	GROUND DP GDP Opps	GDP	Pct	Rank	BUNTS Opps	Score	Grade	Rank	THROWING Opps To Advance	Extra Bases	Kills	Pct	Rank
Los Angeles Dodgers	+10	+21	+37	+68	1	335	130	.388	13	64	.564	B-	7	371	195	11	.526	18
Atlanta Braves	+7	+13	+33	+53	2	386	149	.386	14	47	.495	C	23	468	225	22	.481	5
Toronto Blue Jays	+25	-12	+34	+47	3	310	122	.394	12	39	.488	C	25	490	245	25	.500	12
Arizona Diamondbacks	+1	+7	+36	+44	4	377	121	.321	30	50	.558	B-	8	439	235	17	.535	21
St Louis Cardinals	+26	+34	-22	+38	5	359	131	.365	19	41	.546	B-	13	399	180	18	.451	1
Houston Astros	+43	-4	-4	+35	6	344	117	.340	24	63	.554	B-	10	407	200	21	.491	10
Seattle Mariners	-31	-3	+55	+21	7	295	117	.397	11	33	.573	B	6	451	209	16	.463	3
Philadelphia Phillies	+10	+30	-22	+18	8	330	120	.364	21	48	.556	B-	9	407	203	21	.499	11
Florida Marlins	+17	-4	+1	+14	9	296	120	.405	8	62	.638	A-	1	387	217	15	.561	28
Boston Red Sox	+19	+19	-25	+13	10	327	107	.327	29	27	.626	B+	3	431	233	12	.541	23
Chicago White Sox	+15	-22	+17	+10	11	315	136	.432	2	47	.474	C	26	422	217	25	.514	15
Milwaukee Brewers	+32	-42	+16	+6	12	299	110	.368	18	59	.626	B+	2	418	236	15	.565	29
Minnesota Twins	-9	-13	+28	+6	12	320	133	.416	5	49	.456	C-	28	460	224	11	.487	7
Colorado Rockies	+25	+19	-40	+4	14	412	136	.330	27	68	.585	B	4	513	279	12	.544	24
Chicago Cubs	+3	-10	+10	+3	15	317	105	.331	26	66	.520	C+	18	362	200	14	.552	26
Montreal Expos	-38	+6	+27	-5	16	340	135	.397	10	52	.584	B	5	442	208	32	.471	4
Tampa Bay Devil Rays	+1	+4	-10	-5	16	307	124	.404	9	30	.433	D+	29	459	224	20	.488	8
San Diego Padres	-6	+17	-18	-7	18	307	126	.410	7	49	.500	C+	22	415	218	15	.525	17
San Francisco Giants	-4	0	-6	-10	19	385	130	.338	25	55	.526	C+	15	449	259	12	.577	30
Detroit Tigers	-24	-13	+26	-11	20	336	144	.429	3	51	.492	C	24	479	264	23	.551	25
Cleveland Indians	+6	-4	-16	-14	21	312	116	.372	17	29	.526	C+	16	484	251	15	.519	16
Oakland Athletics	-24	-6	+15	-15	22	354	146	.412	6	41	.522	C+	17	446	216	15	.484	6
Baltimore Orioles	+10	-35	+9	-16	23	366	137	.374	16	36	.514	C+	21	506	266	17	.526	19
Kansas City Royals	-27	-12	+20	-19	24	311	143	.460	1	53	.518	C+	20	511	284	20	.556	27
Cincinnati Reds	+3	+1	-27	-23	25	309	102	.330	28	63	.464	C-	27	470	215	24	.457	2
Texas Rangers	-55	+12	+10	-33	26	365	133	.364	20	38	.549	B-	12	453	240	13	.530	20
New York Mets	-4	-6	-29	-39	27	359	124	.345	23	60	.551	B-	11	469	230	15	.490	9
Anaheim Angels	+12	-8	-43	-39	27	273	99	.363	22	48	.520	C+	19	449	229	21	.510	13
Pittsburgh Pirates	+6	-2	-48	-44	29	372	158	.425	4	43	.542	B-	14	453	232	13	.512	14
New York Yankees	-42	+16	-57	-83	30	315	118	.375	15	34	.409	D	30	460	248	19	.539	22

Team Totals and Rankings - 2003

Team	PLUS/MINUS Middle Infield	Corner Infield	Outfield	Total	Rank	GROUND DP GDP Opps	GDP	Pct	Rank	BUNTS Opps	Score	Grade	Rank	THROWING Opps To Advance	Extra Bases	Kills	Pct	Rank
Texas Rangers	-1	+80	+16	+95	1	330	138	.418	7	38	.458	C-	28	548	297	18	.542	23
Los Angeles Dodgers	+14	+28	+18	+60	2	355	136	.383	19	47	.699	A+	1	350	185	11	.529	19
Atlanta Braves	+40	0	+2	+42	3	370	147	.397	12	40	.505	C+	20	460	240	14	.522	15
Chicago White Sox	-5	+21	+24	+40	4	327	135	.413	9	56	.498	C	23	407	213	17	.523	16
San Francisco Giants	+13	+6	+20	+39	5	329	138	.419	6	61	.558	B-	14	390	192	20	.492	8
Seattle Mariners	-12	+8	+41	+37	6	282	132	.468	1	38	.538	C+	16	411	199	13	.484	5
Houston Astros	+11	+31	-7	+35	7	333	126	.378	21	50	.563	B-	13	402	184	33	.458	3
Cleveland Indians	+10	+9	+15	+34	8	374	150	.401	10	65	.481	C	27	448	245	20	.547	26
Anaheim Angels	+17	-4	+20	+33	9	276	114	.413	8	48	.564	B-	12	475	235	17	.495	10
Philadelphia Phillies	+35	-13	+9	+31	10	323	137	.424	4	55	.567	B-	10	396	174	14	.439	2
Tampa Bay Devil Rays	+1	+6	+7	+14	11	312	125	.401	11	32	.613	B+	4	448	220	15	.491	7
Oakland Athletics	+17	+7	-11	+13	12	344	128	.372	23	50	.509	C+	19	394	204	7	.518	13
Cincinnati Reds	+7	+6	-1	+12	13	328	128	.390	15	55	.564	B-	11	454	239	21	.526	17
Baltimore Orioles	+18	-8	-5	+5	14	330	139	.421	5	44	.500	C+	22	454	243	19	.535	22
Minnesota Twins	-45	+11	+36	+2	15	264	93	.352	27	54	.531	C+	18	435	220	13	.506	11
San Diego Padres	+5	-25	+21	+1	16	332	113	.340	28	54	.604	B+	6	472	233	26	.494	9
St Louis Cardinals	-5	-5	+3	-7	17	306	112	.366	24	37	.538	C+	17	451	254	26	.563	28
Boston Red Sox	-10	+14	-12	-8	18	320	108	.338	29	36	.442	C-	29	480	245	17	.510	12
Pittsburgh Pirates	+13	-5	-17	-9	19	361	140	.388	17	59	.581	B	9	503	274	13	.545	24
Toronto Blue Jays	+23	-15	-25	-17	20	359	142	.396	13	35	.431	D+	30	435	237	15	.545	25
Colorado Rockies	+3	-5	-16	-18	21	365	136	.373	22	51	.610	B+	5	507	216	16	.426	1
Detroit Tigers	-9	-1	-9	-19	22	382	165	.432	3	42	.493	C	24	522	316	17	.605	30
Arizona Diamondbacks	-10	+6	-17	-21	23	355	108	.304	30	72	.613	B+	3	426	242	12	.568	29
Montreal Expos	0	-20	-12	-32	24	327	119	.364	25	42	.481	C	26	424	198	26	.467	4
Chicago Cubs	-12	-17	-5	-34	25	349	137	.393	14	57	.551	B-	15	414	233	11	.563	27
Florida Marlins	-5	-34	-4	-43	26	306	138	.451	2	56	.629	B+	2	443	237	22	.535	21
New York Yankees	-26	-5	-17	-48	27	294	105	.357	26	42	.592	B	7	444	234	15	.527	18
New York Mets	-1	-45	-13	-59	28	340	132	.388	16	54	.581	B	8	436	226	21	.518	14
Kansas City Royals	-43	0	-39	-82	29	308	119	.386	18	58	.503	C+	21	516	273	26	.529	20
Milwaukee Brewers	-37	-35	-20	-92	30	318	121	.381	20	78	.490	C	25	471	229	20	.486	6

Team Charts

As beautiful as they may be, the charts which follow are not here just to make the book look pretty.

The point of defense is to prevent balls in play from becoming hits. One way to look at defense, then, is to study where hits land. The places where hits land can be summarized into 19 groups:

1) In the infield.
2) Down the first base line, between the first baseman and the bag.
3) In the hole between first and second.
4) Up the middle.
5) In the hole between shortstop and third.
6) Down the third base line.
7) Down the left field line (between the left fielder and the line.)
8) In front of the left fielder.
9) Over the left fielder's head.
10) Off the left field wall.
11) In the gap in left/center.
12) In front of the center fielder.
13) Over the center fielder's head or off the CF fence.
14) In the gap in right/center.
15) In front of the right fielder.
16) Over the right fielder's head.
17) Off the right field wall.
18) Down the right field line.
19) Out of play, home run, long gone, Holy Cow, It's Outta Here, touch 'em all.

The charts which follow detail this information versus each of the 30 major league teams—how many hits landed in each of these slots. The World Champion Chicago White Sox, for example, were playing two center fielders—one in center and one in left. They allowed only 123 hits in the gap in left/center, against a major league average of 149. Big deal. . . .26 doubles that aren't there.

The Cleveland Indians double-play combination is Rafael Belliard, who looks way too much like Manny Ramirez to be considered a good second baseman, and Jhonny Peralta, about whom Indians fans like to observe that he is not Omar Vizquel. But the fact is, only 147 hits went through the middle against the Indians last year—30 fewer than the major league average, 67 fewer than the Minnesota Twins, who have artificial turf, no second baseman and no shortstop. These things matter.

The Royals last year would tell you that Terrence Long was a Gold Glove left fielder, but there were 194 hits in the left field gap against the Royals—71 more than against the White Sox.

The charts which follow present this information in two forms—all of it, against every team—in two forms. The "field diagram" style charts are color-coded so that you can appraise the team's defense at a glance. Red is bad; blue is good. No smoking.

Where Hits Landed -- Arizona Diamondbacks

Through The Infield

	Infield	1B Line	1B/2B Hole	Up Middle	SS/3B Hole	3B Line
vs Dbacks	99	19	78	148	153	51
vs Opponents	84	27	116	175	87	42
ML Average	89	22	94	177	115	41

Through The Outfielders

	LF Line	Front of LF	LF Gap	Front of CF	RF Gap	Front of RF	RF Line
vs Dbacks	56	120	145	110	148	118	62
vs Opponents	41	85	128	80	141	101	63
ML Average	52	106	149	89	144	109	49

Over the Outfielders

	LF Wall	Over LF	Over CF	RF Wall	Over RF	Gone
vs Dbacks	10	8	40	8	14	193
vs Opponents	2	6	33	6	11	191
ML Average	10	14	20	9	10	167

The Diamondbacks outperformed their opponents by at least 5 hits in the following places:
Hits down First Base Line (19 to 27)
Hits between First and Second (78 to 116)
Hits Up the Middle (148 to 175)

They were outperformed by 5 or more hits in the following places:
Infield Hits (99 to 84)
Hits between Shortstop and Third (153 to 87)
Hits down Third Base Line (51 to 42)
Hits down Left Field Line (56 to 41)
Hits in front of the Left Fielder (120 to 85)
Hits in the Left Field Gap (145 to 128)
Hits in front of the Center Fielder (110 to 80)
Hits in the Right Field Gap (148 to 141)
Hits in front of the Right Fielder (118 to 101)
Hits off the Left Field Wall (10 to 2)
Hits over the Center Fielder (40 to 33)

Where Hits Landed Against the Arizona Diamondbacks
2005 - Home and Road

Look for patterns of red and blue. A box outlined in red means the team allowed significantly more hits than the Major League average. The blue outline means the team allowed significantly fewer hits than average.

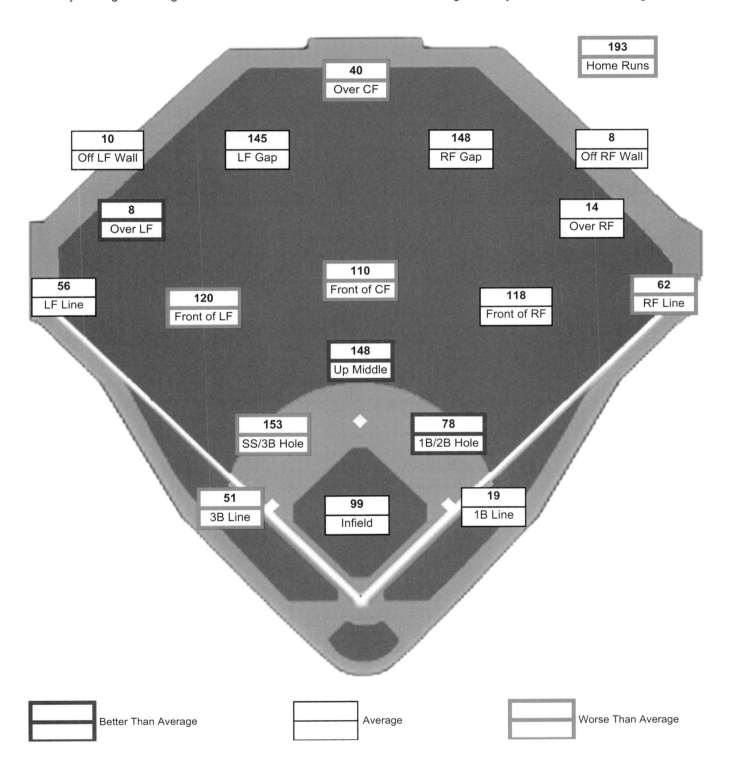

193
Home Runs

40
Over CF

10
Off LF Wall

145
LF Gap

148
RF Gap

8
Off RF Wall

8
Over LF

14
Over RF

110
Front of CF

56
LF Line

120
Front of LF

118
Front of RF

62
RF Line

148
Up Middle

153
SS/3B Hole

78
1B/2B Hole

51
3B Line

99
Infield

19
1B Line

Better Than Average   Average   Worse Than Average

Where Hits Landed -- Atlanta Braves

Through The Infield						
	Infield	**1B Line**	**1B/2B Hole**	**Up Middle**	**SS/3B Hole**	**3B Line**
vs Braves	103	30	127	183	107	31
vs Opponents	87	18	90	177	100	52
ML Average	89	22	94	177	115	41

Through The Outfielders							
	LF Line	**Front of LF**	**LF Gap**	**Front of CF**	**RF Gap**	**Front of RF**	**RF Line**
vs Braves	39	110	156	83	160	118	49
vs Opponents	43	96	148	73	140	120	58
ML Average	52	106	149	89	144	109	49

Over the Outfielders						
	LF Wall	**Over LF**	**Over CF**	**RF Wall**	**Over RF**	**Gone**
vs Braves	6	13	13	4	10	145
vs Opponents	2	11	27	10	17	184
ML Average	10	14	20	9	10	167

The Braves outperformed their opponents by at least 5 hits in the following places:
  Hits down Third Base Line (31 to 52)
  Hits down Right Field Line (49 to 58)
  Hits over the Center Fielder (13 to 27)
  Hits off the Right Field Wall (4 to 10)
  Hits over the Right Fielder (10 to 17)
  Home Runs (145 to 184)

They were outperformed by 5 or more hits in the following places:
  Infield Hits (103 to 87)
  Hits down First Base Line (30 to 18)
  Hits between First and Second (127 to 90)
  Hits Up the Middle (183 to 177)
  Hits between Shortstop and Third (107 to 100)
  Hits in front of the Left Fielder (110 to 96)
  Hits in the Left Field Gap (156 to 148)
  Hits in front of the Center Fielder (83 to 73)
  Hits in the Right Field Gap (160 to 140)

Where Hits Landed Against the Atlanta Braves
2005 - Home and Road

Look for patterns of red and blue. A box outlined in red means the team allowed significantly more hits than the Major League average. The blue outline means the team allowed significantly fewer hits than average.

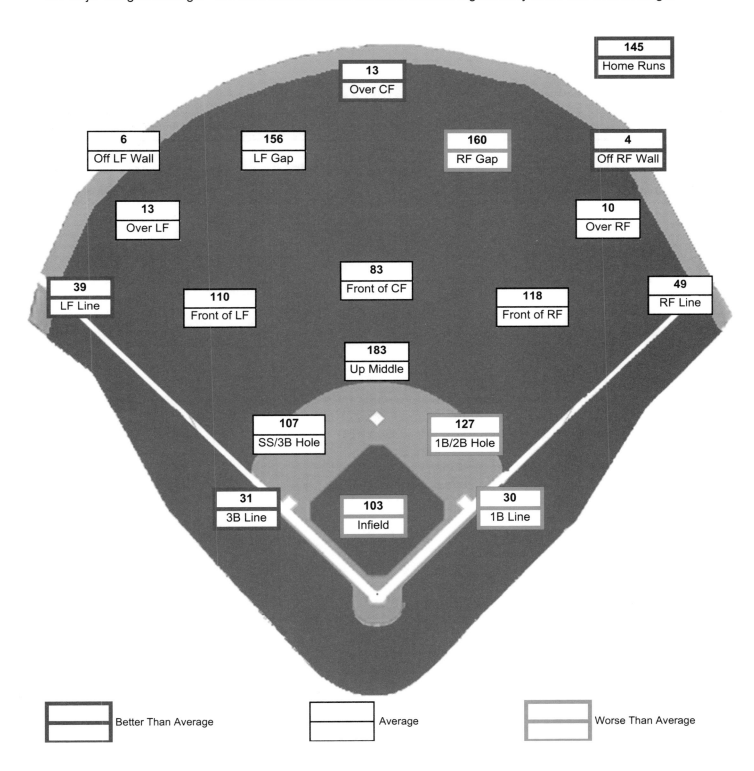

Where Hits Landed -- Baltimore Orioles

Through The Infield

	Infield	1B Line	1B/2B Hole	Up Middle	SS/3B Hole	3B Line
vs Orioles	103	28	111	212	91	26
vs Opponents	104	19	102	173	119	47
ML Average	89	22	94	177	115	41

Through The Outfielders

	LF Line	Front of LF	LF Gap	Front of CF	RF Gap	Front of RF	RF Line
vs Orioles	51	99	140	94	127	98	46
vs Opponents	57	113	154	66	146	104	49
ML Average	52	106	149	89	144	109	49

Over the Outfielders

	LF Wall	Over LF	Over CF	RF Wall	Over RF	Gone
vs Orioles	4	9	17	12	10	180
vs Opponents	10	13	10	11	6	189
ML Average	10	14	20	9	10	167

The Orioles outperformed their opponents by at least 5 hits in the following places:
>Hits between Shortstop and Third (91 to 119)
>Hits down Third Base Line (26 to 47)
>Hits down Left Field Line (51 to 57)
>Hits in front of the Left Fielder (99 to 113)
>Hits in the Left Field Gap (140 to 154)
>Hits in the Right Field Gap (127 to 146)
>Hits in front of the Right Fielder (98 to 104)
>Hits off the Left Field Wall (4 to 10)
>Home Runs (180 to 189)

They were outperformed by 5 or more hits in the following places:
>Hits down First Base Line (28 to 19)
>Hits between First and Second (111 to 102)
>Hits Up the Middle (212 to 173)
>Hits in front of the Center Fielder (94 to 66)
>Hits over the Center Fielder (17 to 10)

Where Hits Landed Against the Baltimore Orioles
2005 - Home and Road

Look for patterns of red and blue. A box outlined in red means the team allowed significantly more hits than the Major League average. The blue outline means the team allowed significantly fewer hits than average.

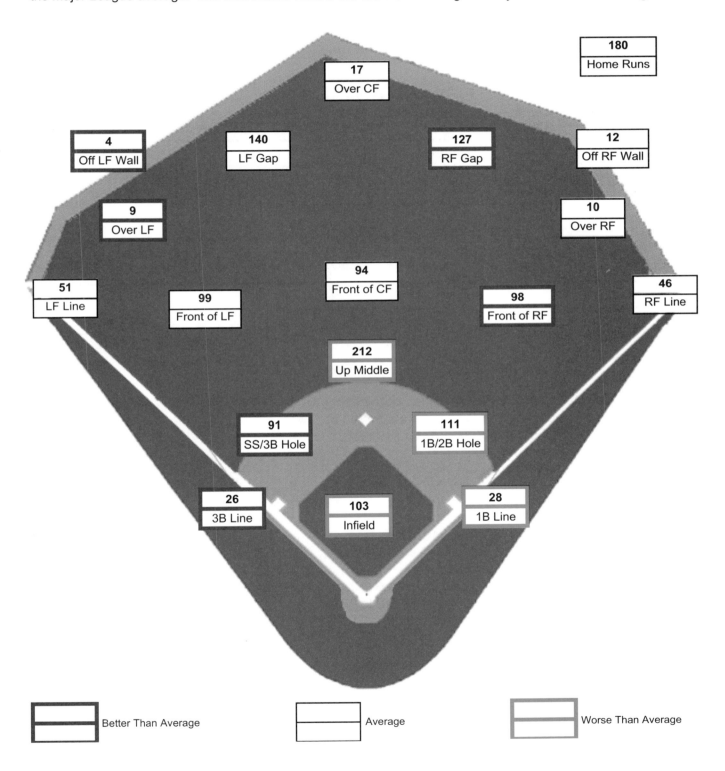

Better Than Average

Average

Worse Than Average

Where Hits Landed -- Boston Red Sox

Through The Infield

	Infield	1B Line	1B/2B Hole	Up Middle	SS/3B Hole	3B Line
vs Red Sox	90	19	85	181	111	50
vs Opponents	76	22	113	164	112	43
ML Average	89	22	94	177	115	41

Through The Outfielders

	LF Line	Front of LF	LF Gap	Front of CF	RF Gap	Front of RF	RF Line
vs Red Sox	78	103	172	93	134	111	68
vs Opponents	70	93	170	99	161	115	64
ML Average	52	106	149	89	144	109	49

Over the Outfielders

	LF Wall	Over LF	Over CF	RF Wall	Over RF	Gone
vs Red Sox	42	12	27	5	5	164
vs Opponents	30	13	22	7	7	198
ML Average	10	14	20	9	10	167

The Red Sox outperformed their opponents by at least 5 hits in the following places:
Hits between First and Second (85 to 113)
Hits in front of the Center Fielder (93 to 99)
Hits in the Right Field Gap (134 to 161)
Home Runs (164 to 198)

They were outperformed by 5 or more hits in the following places:
Infield Hits (90 to 76)
Hits Up the Middle (181 to 164)
Hits down Third Base Line (50 to 43)
Hits down Left Field Line (78 to 70)
Hits in front of the Left Fielder (103 to 93)
Hits off the Left Field Wall (42 to 30)
Hits over the Center Fielder (27 to 22)

Where Hits Landed Against the Boston Red Sox
2005 - Home and Road

Look for patterns of red and blue. A box outlined in red means the team allowed significantly more hits than the Major League average. The blue outline means the team allowed significantly fewer hits than average.

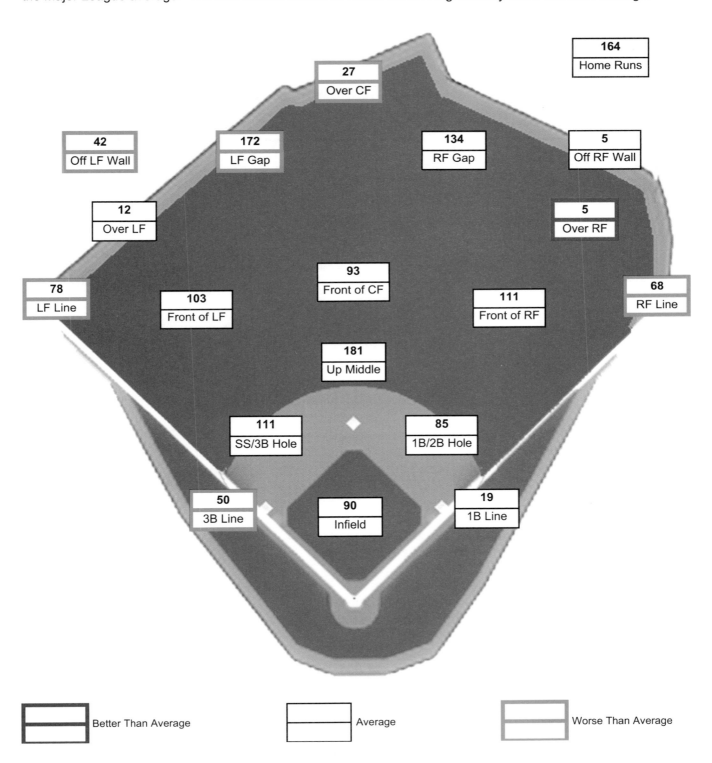

164
Home Runs

27
Over CF

42
Off LF Wall

172
LF Gap

134
RF Gap

5
Off RF Wall

12
Over LF

5
Over RF

93
Front of CF

78
LF Line

103
Front of LF

111
Front of RF

68
RF Line

181
Up Middle

111
SS/3B Hole

85
1B/2B Hole

50
3B Line

90
Infield

19
1B Line

Better Than Average   Average   Worse Than Average

Where Hits Landed -- Chicago Cubs

Through The Infield

	Infield	1B Line	1B/2B Hole	Up Middle	SS/3B Hole	3B Line
vs Cubs	84	23	85	157	111	34
vs Opponents	107	30	88	165	109	47
ML Average	89	22	94	177	115	41

Through The Outfielders

	LF Line	Front of LF	LF Gap	Front of CF	RF Gap	Front of RF	RF Line
vs Cubs	53	100	115	71	125	125	49
vs Opponents	63	100	141	68	148	140	59
ML Average	52	106	149	89	144	109	49

Over the Outfielders

	LF Wall	Over LF	Over CF	RF Wall	Over RF	Gone
vs Cubs	5	7	14	7	6	186
vs Opponents	10	10	12	6	9	194
ML Average	10	14	20	9	10	167

The Cubs outperformed their opponents by at least 5 hits in the following places:
Infield Hits (84 to 107)
Hits down First Base Line (23 to 30)
Hits Up the Middle (157 to 165)
Hits down Third Base Line (34 to 47)
Hits down Left Field Line (53 to 63)
Hits in the Left Field Gap (115 to 141)
Hits in the Right Field Gap (125 to 148)
Hits in front of the Right Fielder (125 to 140)
Hits down Right Field Line (49 to 59)
Hits off the Left Field Wall (5 to 10)
Home Runs (186 to 194)

They were outperformed by 5 or more hits in the following places:
None

Where Hits Landed Against the Chicago Cubs
2005 - Home and Road

Look for patterns of red and blue. A box outlined in red means the team allowed significantly more hits than the Major League average. The blue outline means the team allowed significantly fewer hits than average.

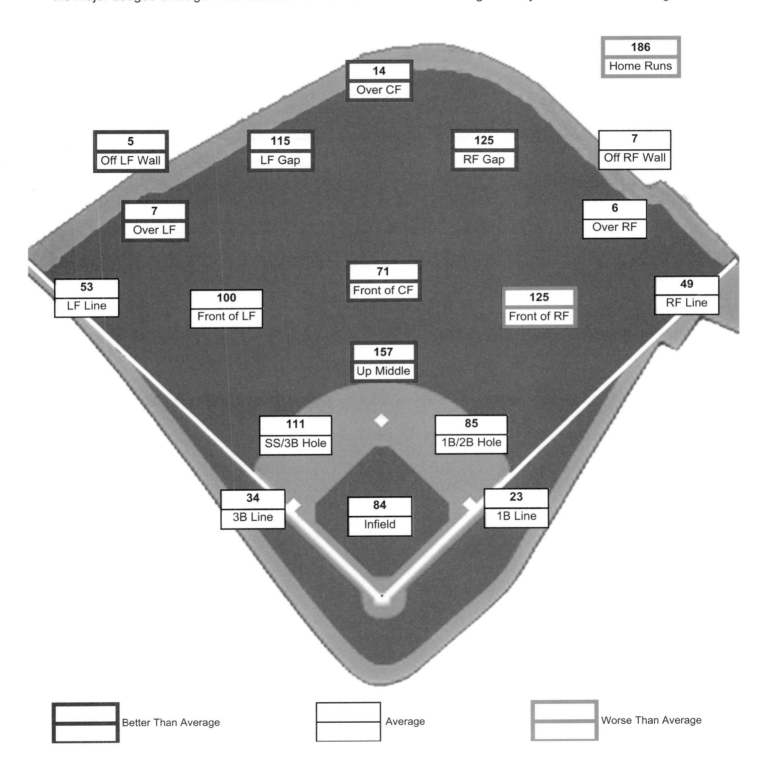

186
Home Runs

14
Over CF

5	**115**	**125**	**7**
Off LF Wall	LF Gap	RF Gap	Off RF Wall

7	**6**
Over LF	Over RF

71
Front of CF

53	**100**	**125**	**49**
LF Line	Front of LF	Front of RF	RF Line

157
Up Middle

111	**85**
SS/3B Hole	1B/2B Hole

34	**84**	**23**
3B Line	Infield	1B Line

	Better Than Average		Average		Worse Than Average

Where Hits Landed -- Chicago White Sox

Through The Infield

	Infield	1B Line	1B/2B Hole	Up Middle	SS/3B Hole	3B Line
vs White Sox	80	22	92	176	77	53
vs Opponents	110	20	83	171	135	33
ML Average	89	22	94	177	115	41

Through The Outfielders

	LF Line	Front of LF	LF Gap	Front of CF	RF Gap	Front of RF	RF Line
vs White Sox	47	101	123	81	144	116	54
vs Opponents	51	120	132	84	140	78	36
ML Average	52	106	149	89	144	109	49

Over the Outfielders

	LF Wall	Over LF	Over CF	RF Wall	Over RF	Gone
vs White Sox	15	10	13	14	7	167
vs Opponents	12	14	13	11	7	200
ML Average	10	14	20	9	10	167

The White Sox outperformed their opponents by at least 5 hits in the following places:
>   Infield Hits (80 to 110)
>   Hits between Shortstop and Third (77 to 135)
>   Hits in front of the Left Fielder (101 to 120)
>   Hits in the Left Field Gap (123 to 132)
>   Home Runs (167 to 200)

They were outperformed by 5 or more hits in the following places:
>   Hits between First and Second (92 to 83)
>   Hits Up the Middle (176 to 171)
>   Hits down Third Base Line (53 to 33)
>   Hits in front of the Right Fielder (116 to 78)
>   Hits down Right Field Line (54 to 36)

Where Hits Landed Against the Chicago White Sox
2005 - Home and Road

Look for patterns of red and blue. A box outlined in red means the team allowed significantly more hits than the Major League average. The blue outline means the team allowed significantly fewer hits than average.

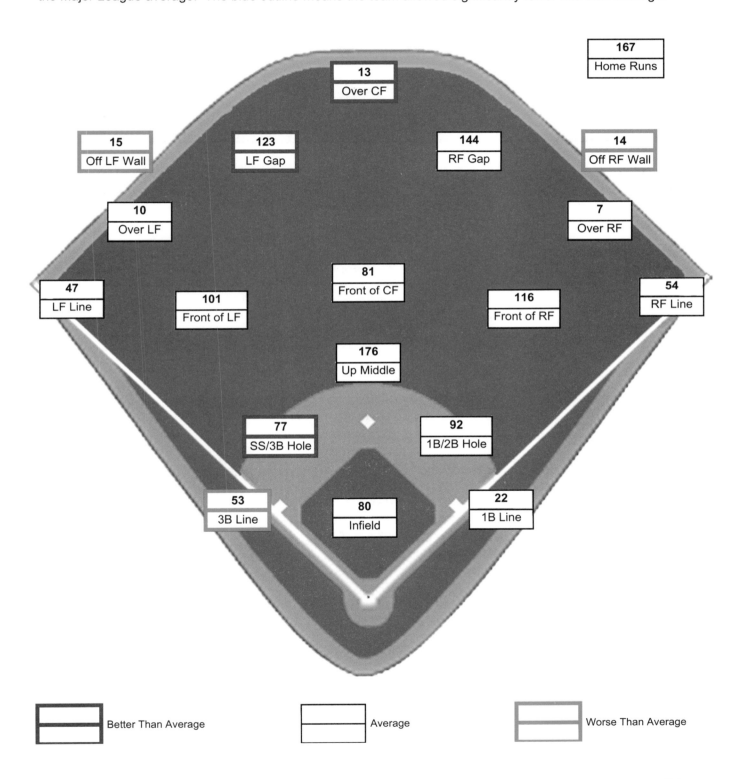

167	Home Runs

13	Over CF

15	Off LF Wall

123	LF Gap

144	RF Gap

14	Off RF Wall

10	Over LF

7	Over RF

81	Front of CF

47	LF Line

101	Front of LF

116	Front of RF

54	RF Line

176	Up Middle

77	SS/3B Hole

92	1B/2B Hole

53	3B Line

80	Infield

22	1B Line

Better Than Average   Average   Worse Than Average

Where Hits Landed -- Cincinnati Reds

Through The Infield

	Infield	1B Line	1B/2B Hole	Up Middle	SS/3B Hole	3B Line
vs Reds	90	23	90	171	139	49
vs Opponents	68	24	89	163	99	40
ML Average	89	22	94	177	115	41

Through The Outfielders

	LF Line	Front of LF	LF Gap	Front of CF	RF Gap	Front of RF	RF Line
vs Reds	71	114	179	95	162	112	47
vs Opponents	62	92	137	64	137	122	65
ML Average	52	106	149	89	144	109	49

Over the Outfielders

	LF Wall	Over LF	Over CF	RF Wall	Over RF	Gone
vs Reds	17	20	34	15	11	218
vs Opponents	11	13	20	12	13	222
ML Average	10	14	20	9	10	167

The Reds outperformed their opponents by at least 5 hits in the following places:
Hits in front of the Right Fielder (112 to 122)
Hits down Right Field Line (47 to 65)

They were outperformed by 5 or more hits in the following places:
Infield Hits (90 to 68)
Hits Up the Middle (171 to 163)
Hits between Shortstop and Third (139 to 99)
Hits down Third Base Line (49 to 40)
Hits down Left Field Line (71 to 62)
Hits in front of the Left Fielder (114 to 92)
Hits in the Left Field Gap (179 to 137)
Hits in front of the Center Fielder (95 to 64)
Hits in the Right Field Gap (162 to 137)
Hits off the Left Field Wall (17 to 11)
Hits over the Left Fielder (20 to 13)
Hits over the Center Fielder (34 to 20)

Where Hits Landed Against the Cincinnati Reds
2005 - Home and Road

Look for patterns of red and blue. A box outlined in red means the team allowed significantly more hits than the Major League average. The blue outline means the team allowed significantly fewer hits than average.

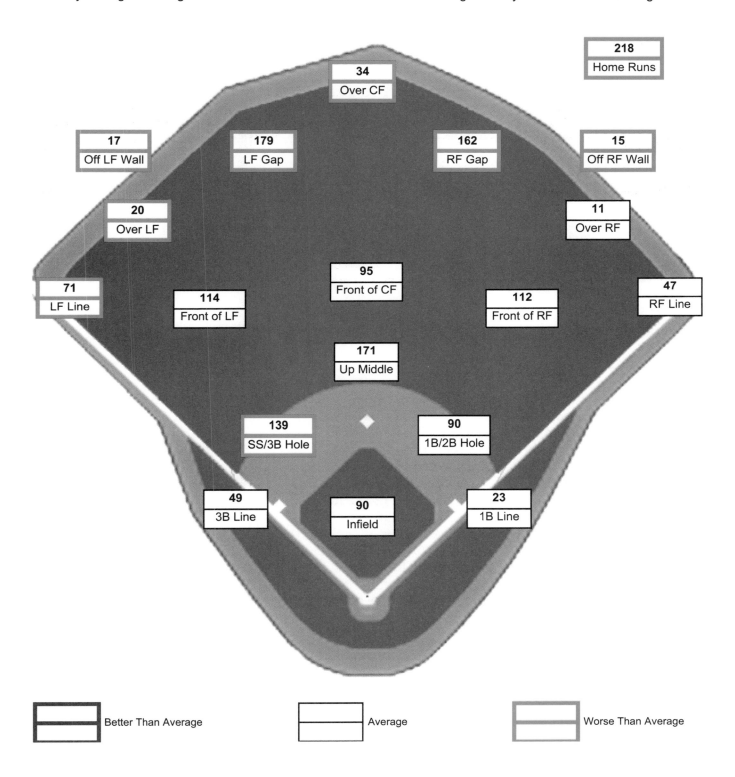

218
Home Runs

34
Over CF

17
Off LF Wall

179
LF Gap

162
RF Gap

15
Off RF Wall

20
Over LF

11
Over RF

95
Front of CF

71
LF Line

114
Front of LF

112
Front of RF

47
RF Line

171
Up Middle

139
SS/3B Hole

90
1B/2B Hole

49
3B Line

90
Infield

23
1B Line

Better Than Average

Average

Worse Than Average

Where Hits Landed -- Cleveland Indians

Through The Infield

	Infield	1B Line	1B/2B Hole	Up Middle	SS/3B Hole	3B Line
vs Indians	94	25	88	147	125	33
vs Opponents	74	24	112	172	126	38
ML Average	89	22	94	177	115	41

Through The Outfielders

	LF Line	Front of LF	LF Gap	Front of CF	RF Gap	Front of RF	RF Line
vs Indians	55	117	114	65	120	110	45
vs Opponents	52	113	154	71	157	102	63
ML Average	52	106	149	89	144	109	49

Over the Outfielders

	LF Wall	Over LF	Over CF	RF Wall	Over RF	Gone
vs Indians	17	14	21	8	8	157
vs Opponents	16	13	14	8	7	206
ML Average	10	14	20	9	10	167

The Indians outperformed their opponents by at least 5 hits in the following places:
>Hits between First and Second (88 to 112)
>Hits Up the Middle (147 to 172)
>Hits down Third Base Line (33 to 38)
>Hits in the Left Field Gap (114 to 154)
>Hits in front of the Center Fielder (65 to 71)
>Hits in the Right Field Gap (120 to 157)
>Hits down Right Field Line (45 to 63)
>Home Runs (157 to 206)

They were outperformed by 5 or more hits in the following places:
>Infield Hits (94 to 74)
>Hits in front of the Right Fielder (110 to 102)
>Hits over the Center Fielder (21 to 14)

Where Hits Landed Against the Cleveland Indians
2005 - Home and Road

Look for patterns of red and blue. A box outlined in red means the team allowed significantly more hits than the Major League average. The blue outline means the team allowed significantly fewer hits than average.

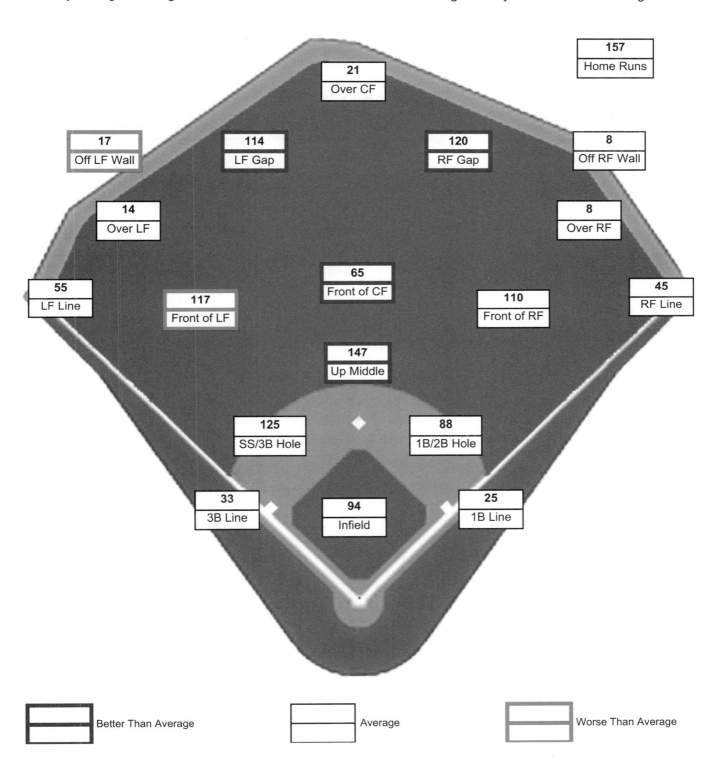

| **157** |
| Home Runs |

| **21** |
| Over CF |

| **17** | | **114** | | **120** | | **8** |
| Off LF Wall | | LF Gap | | RF Gap | | Off RF Wall |

| **14** | | | **8** |
| Over LF | | | Over RF |

| **65** |
| Front of CF |

| **55** | **117** | | **110** | **45** |
| LF Line | Front of LF | | Front of RF | RF Line |

| **147** |
| Up Middle |

| **125** | **88** |
| SS/3B Hole | 1B/2B Hole |

| **33** | **94** | **25** |
| 3B Line | Infield | 1B Line |

| | Better Than Average | | | Average | | | Worse Than Average |

Where Hits Landed -- Colorado Rockies

Through The Infield

	Infield	1B Line	1B/2B Hole	Up Middle	SS/3B Hole	3B Line
vs Rockies	92	26	103	197	98	41
vs Opponents	80	18	77	185	118	40
ML Average	89	22	94	177	115	41

Through The Outfielders

	LF Line	Front of LF	LF Gap	Front of CF	RF Gap	Front of RF	RF Line
vs Rockies	53	112	143	122	175	129	54
vs Opponents	52	124	165	111	134	111	49
ML Average	52	106	149	89	144	109	49

Over the Outfielders

	LF Wall	Over LF	Over CF	RF Wall	Over RF	Gone
vs Rockies	12	12	31	11	14	175
vs Opponents	9	9	25	10	12	148
ML Average	10	14	20	9	10	167

The Rockies outperformed their opponents by at least 5 hits in the following places:
    Hits between Shortstop and Third (98 to 118)
    Hits in front of the Left Fielder (112 to 124)
    Hits in the Left Field Gap (143 to 165)

They were outperformed by 5 or more hits in the following places:
    Infield Hits (92 to 80)
    Hits down First Base Line (26 to 18)
    Hits between First and Second (103 to 77)
    Hits Up the Middle (197 to 185)
    Hits in front of the Center Fielder (122 to 111)
    Hits in the Right Field Gap (175 to 134)
    Hits in front of the Right Fielder (129 to 111)
    Hits down Right Field Line (54 to 49)
    Hits over the Center Fielder (31 to 25)
    Home Runs (175 to 148)

Where Hits Landed Against the Colorado Rockies
2005 - Home and Road

Look for patterns of red and blue. A box outlined in red means the team allowed significantly more hits than the Major League average. The blue outline means the team allowed significantly fewer hits than average.

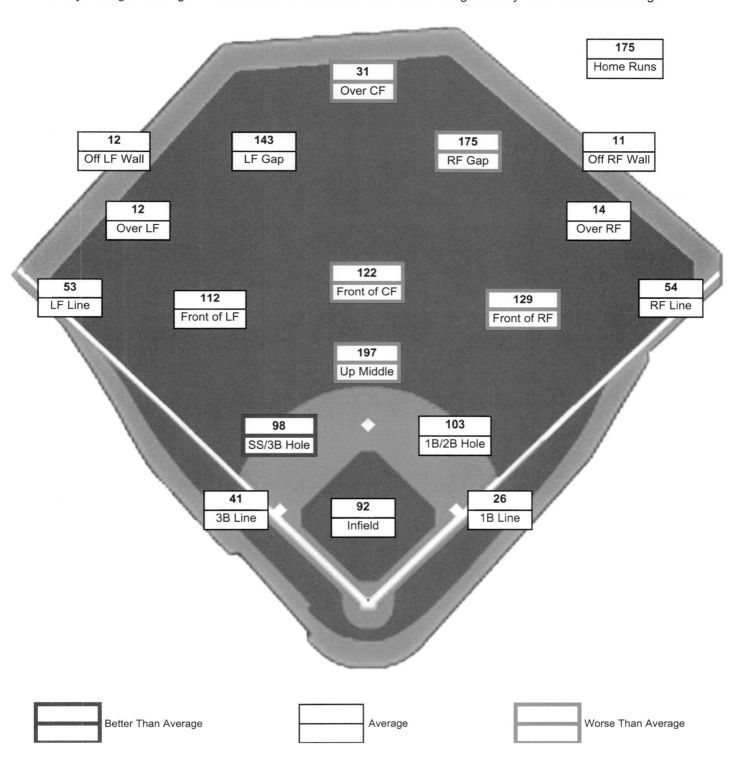

175		
Home Runs		

31
Over CF

12	143	175	11
Off LF Wall	LF Gap	RF Gap	Off RF Wall

12	14
Over LF	Over RF

53	112	122	129	54
LF Line	Front of LF	Front of CF	Front of RF	RF Line

197
Up Middle

98	103
SS/3B Hole	1B/2B Hole

41	92	26
3B Line	Infield	1B Line

Better Than Average	Average	Worse Than Average

Where Hits Landed -- Detroit Tigers

Through The Infield

	Infield	1B Line	1B/2B Hole	Up Middle	SS/3B Hole	3B Line
vs Tigers	85	25	93	188	155	28
vs Opponents	112	15	66	210	137	46
ML Average	89	22	94	177	115	41

Through The Outfielders

	LF Line	Front of LF	LF Gap	Front of CF	RF Gap	Front of RF	RF Line
vs Tigers	48	114	141	90	143	91	53
vs Opponents	52	109	143	89	148	103	45
ML Average	52	106	149	89	144	109	49

Over the Outfielders

	LF Wall	Over LF	Over CF	RF Wall	Over RF	Gone
vs Tigers	11	13	16	11	8	191
vs Opponents	12	24	22	12	9	167
ML Average	10	14	20	9	10	167

The Tigers outperformed their opponents by at least 5 hits in the following places:
   Infield Hits (85 to 112)
   Hits Up the Middle (188 to 210)
   Hits down Third Base Line (28 to 46)
   Hits in the Right Field Gap (143 to 148)
   Hits in front of the Right Fielder (91 to 103)
   Hits over the Left Fielder (13 to 24)
   Hits over the Center Fielder (16 to 22)

They were outperformed by 5 or more hits in the following places:
   Hits down First Base Line (25 to 15)
   Hits between First and Second (93 to 66)
   Hits between Shortstop and Third (155 to 137)
   Hits in front of the Left Fielder (114 to 109)
   Hits down Right Field Line (53 to 45)
   Home Runs (191 to 167)

Where Hits Landed Against the Detroit Tigers
2005 - Home and Road

Look for patterns of red and blue. A box outlined in red means the team allowed significantly more hits than the Major League average. The blue outline means the team allowed significantly fewer hits than average.

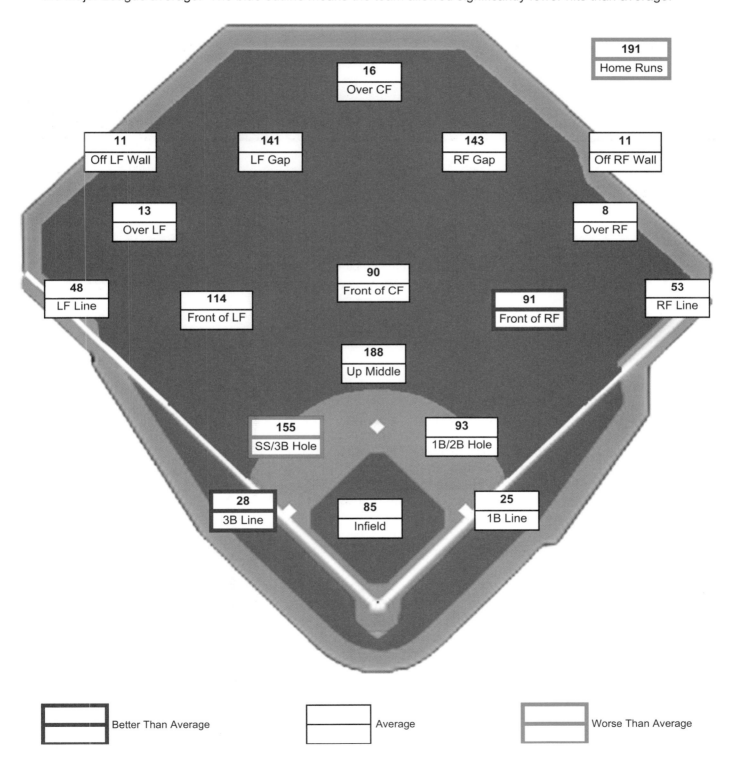

| **191** |
| Home Runs |

16 — Over CF

11 — Off LF Wall   **141** — LF Gap   **143** — RF Gap   **11** — Off RF Wall

13 — Over LF   **8** — Over RF

90 — Front of CF

48 — LF Line   **114** — Front of LF   **91** — Front of RF   **53** — RF Line

188 — Up Middle

155 — SS/3B Hole   **93** — 1B/2B Hole

28 — 3B Line   **85** — Infield   **25** — 1B Line

Better Than Average   Average   Worse Than Average

Where Hits Landed -- Florida Marlins

Through The Infield

	Infield	1B Line	1B/2B Hole	Up Middle	SS/3B Hole	3B Line
vs Marlins	86	31	118	164	133	30
vs Opponents	131	19	76	164	139	45
ML Average	89	22	94	177	115	41

Through The Outfielders

	LF Line	Front of LF	LF Gap	Front of CF	RF Gap	Front of RF	RF Line
vs Marlins	52	115	146	87	150	106	51
vs Opponents	65	144	156	97	114	93	49
ML Average	52	106	149	89	144	109	49

Over the Outfielders

	LF Wall	Over LF	Over CF	RF Wall	Over RF	Gone
vs Marlins	16	19	20	7	13	115
vs Opponents	21	27	19	5	7	128
ML Average	10	14	20	9	10	167

The Marlins outperformed their opponents by at least 5 hits in the following places:
Infield Hits (86 to 131)
Hits between Shortstop and Third (133 to 139)
Hits down Third Base Line (30 to 45)
Hits down Left Field Line (52 to 65)
Hits in front of the Left Fielder (115 to 144)
Hits in the Left Field Gap (146 to 156)
Hits in front of the Center Fielder (87 to 97)
Hits off the Left Field Wall (16 to 21)
Hits over the Left Fielder (19 to 27)
Home Runs (115 to 128)

They were outperformed by 5 or more hits in the following places:
Hits down First Base Line (31 to 19)
Hits between First and Second (116 to 78)
Hits in the Right Field Gap (150 to 114)
Hits in front of the Right Fielder (106 to 93)
Hits over the Right Fielder (13 to 7)

Where Hits Landed Against the Florida Marlins
2005 - Home and Road

Look for patterns of red and blue. A box outlined in red means the team allowed significantly more hits than the Major League average. The blue outline means the team allowed significantly fewer hits than average.

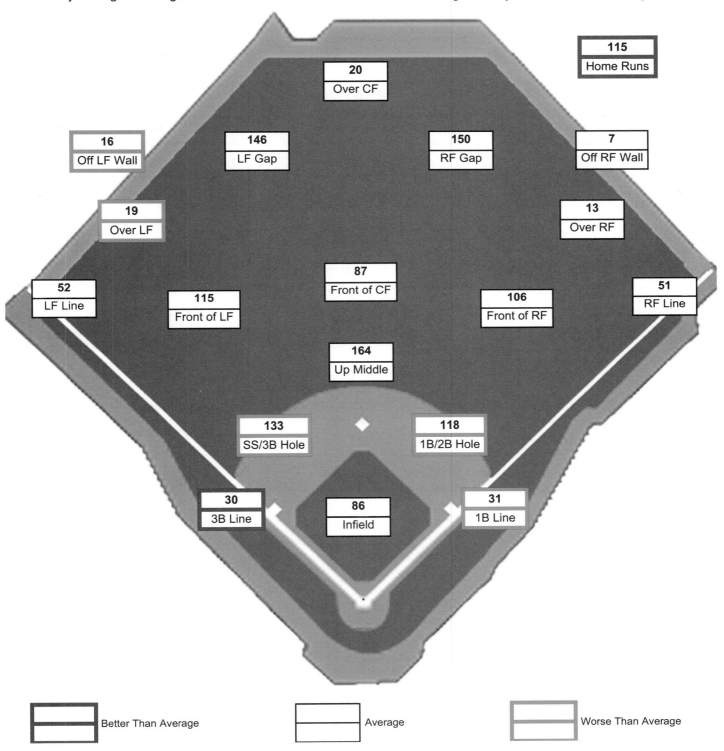

Where Hits Landed -- Houston Astros

Through The Infield

	Infield	1B Line	1B/2B Hole	Up Middle	SS/3B Hole	3B Line
vs Astros	79	20	95	169	83	43
vs Opponents	138	13	65	137	139	47
ML Average	89	22	94	177	115	41

Through The Outfielders

	LF Line	Front of LF	LF Gap	Front of CF	RF Gap	Front of RF	RF Line
vs Astros	49	94	129	81	122	108	46
vs Opponents	66	98	148	75	125	100	32
ML Average	52	106	149	89	144	109	49

Over the Outfielders

	LF Wall	Over LF	Over CF	RF Wall	Over RF	Gone
vs Astros	8	15	17	6	17	155
vs Opponents	13	15	16	7	5	161
ML Average	10	14	20	9	10	167

The Astros outperformed their opponents by at least 5 hits in the following places:
  Infield Hits (79 to 138)
  Hits between Shortstop and Third (83 to 139)
  Hits down Left Field Line (49 to 66)
  Hits in the Left Field Gap (129 to 148)
  Hits off the Left Field Wall (8 to 13)
  Home Runs (155 to 161)

They were outperformed by 5 or more hits in the following places:
  Hits down First Base Line (20 to 13)
  Hits between First and Second (95 to 65)
  Hits Up the Middle (169 to 137)
  Hits in front of the Center Fielder (81 to 75)
  Hits in front of the Right Fielder (108 to 100)
  Hits down Right Field Line (46 to 32)
  Hits over the Right Fielder (17 to 5)

Where Hits Landed Against the Houston Astros
2005 - Home and Road

Look for patterns of red and blue. A box outlined in red means the team allowed significantly more hits than the Major League average. The blue outline means the team allowed significantly fewer hits than average.

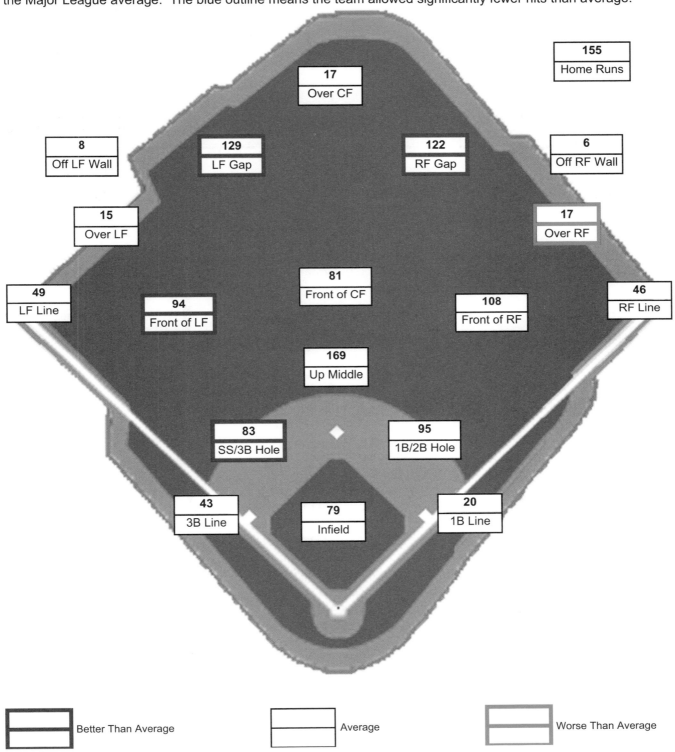

155
Home Runs

17
Over CF

8
Off LF Wall

129
LF Gap

122
RF Gap

6
Off RF Wall

15
Over LF

17
Over RF

49
LF Line

94
Front of LF

81
Front of CF

108
Front of RF

46
RF Line

169
Up Middle

83
SS/3B Hole

95
1B/2B Hole

43
3B Line

79
Infield

20
1B Line

Better Than Average   Average   Worse Than Average

Where Hits Landed -- Kansas City Royals

Through The Infield

	Infield	1B Line	1B/2B Hole	Up Middle	SS/3B Hole	3B Line
vs Royals	85	29	120	182	155	57
vs Opponents	77	21	106	206	116	51
ML Average	89	22	94	177	115	41

Through The Outfielders

	LF Line	Front of LF	LF Gap	Front of CF	RF Gap	Front of RF	RF Line
vs Royals	59	118	194	82	160	109	56
vs Opponents	47	114	134	89	148	93	53
ML Average	52	106	149	89	144	109	49

Over the Outfielders

	LF Wall	Over LF	Over CF	RF Wall	Over RF	Gone
vs Royals	8	19	16	10	3	178
vs Opponents	9	17	23	9	8	124
ML Average	10	14	20	9	10	167

The Royals outperformed their opponents by at least 5 hits in the following places:
  Hits Up the Middle (182 to 206)
  Hits in front of the Center Fielder (82 to 89)
  Hits over the Center Fielder (16 to 23)
  Hits over the Right Fielder (3 to 8)

They were outperformed by 5 or more hits in the following places:
  Infield Hits (85 to 77)
  Hits down First Base Line (29 to 21)
  Hits between First and Second (120 to 106)
  Hits between Shortstop and Third (155 to 116)
  Hits down Third Base Line (57 to 51)
  Hits down Left Field Line (59 to 47)
  Hits in the Left Field Gap (194 to 134)
  Hits in the Right Field Gap (160 to 148)
  Hits in front of the Right Fielder (109 to 93)
  Home Runs (178 to 124)

Where Hits Landed Against the Kansas City Royals
2005 - Home and Road

Look for patterns of red and blue. A box outlined in red means the team allowed significantly more hits than the Major League average. The blue outline means the team allowed significantly fewer hits than average.

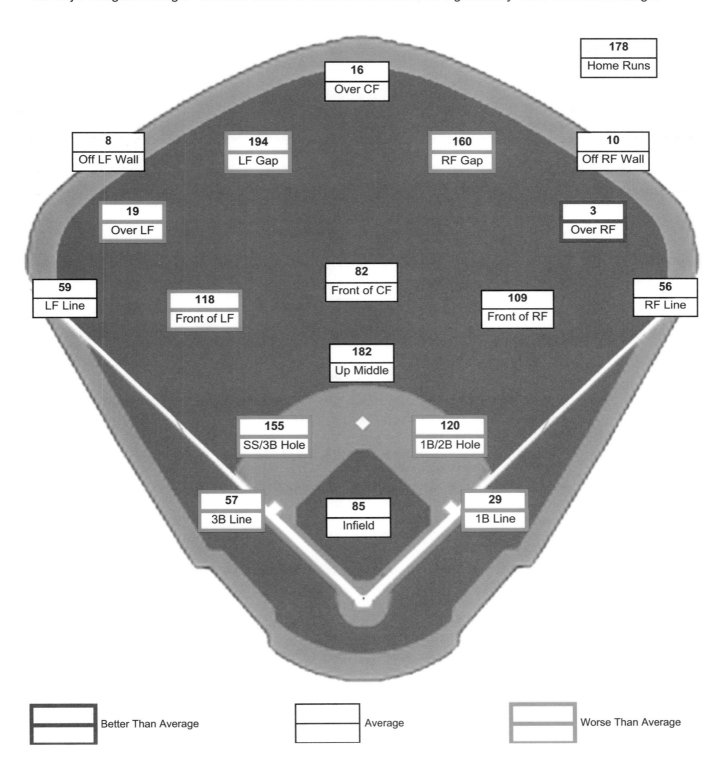

178
Home Runs

16
Over CF

8
Off LF Wall

194
LF Gap

160
RF Gap

10
Off RF Wall

19
Over LF

3
Over RF

82
Front of CF

59
LF Line

118
Front of LF

109
Front of RF

56
RF Line

182
Up Middle

155
SS/3B Hole

120
1B/2B Hole

57
3B Line

85
Infield

29
1B Line

Better Than Average

Average

Worse Than Average

Where Hits Landed -- Los Angeles Angels

Through The Infield

	Infield	1B Line	1B/2B Hole	Up Middle	SS/3B Hole	3B Line
vs Angels	97	27	91	168	91	34
vs Opponents	78	31	111	193	97	42
ML Average	89	22	94	177	115	41

Through The Outfielders

	LF Line	Front of LF	LF Gap	Front of CF	RF Gap	Front of RF	RF Line
vs Angels	44	96	178	74	171	100	39
vs Opponents	60	107	153	114	164	104	59
ML Average	52	106	149	89	144	109	49

Over the Outfielders

	LF Wall	Over LF	Over CF	RF Wall	Over RF	Gone
vs Angels	9	9	16	9	10	156
vs Opponents	10	11	13	12	14	147
ML Average	10	14	20	9	10	167

The Angels outperformed their opponents by at least 5 hits in the following places:
Hits between First and Second (91 to 111)
Hits Up the Middle (168 to 193)
Hits between Shortstop and Third (91 to 97)
Hits down Third Base Line (34 to 42)
Hits down Left Field Line (44 to 60)
Hits in front of the Left Fielder (96 to 107)
Hits in front of the Center Fielder (74 to 114)
Hits down Right Field Line (39 to 59)

They were outperformed by 5 or more hits in the following places:
Infield Hits (97 to 78)
Hits in the Left Field Gap (178 to 153)
Hits in the Right Field Gap (171 to 164)
Home Runs (156 to 147)

Where Hits Landed Against the Los Angeles Angels
2005 - Home and Road

Look for patterns of red and blue. A box outlined in red means the team allowed significantly more hits than the Major League average. The blue outline means the team allowed significantly fewer hits than average.

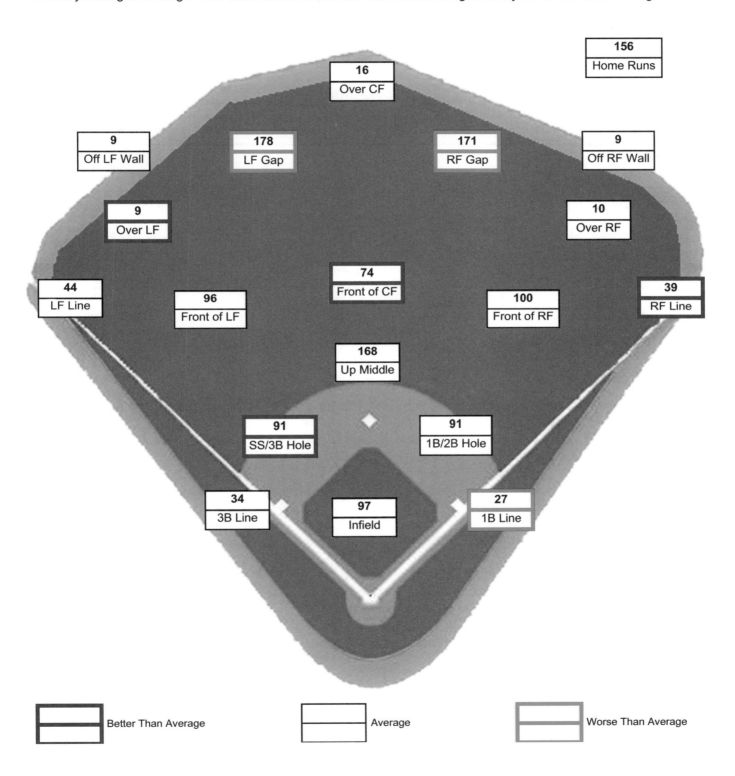

156
Home Runs

16
Over CF

9		178		171		9
Off LF Wall		LF Gap		RF Gap		Off RF Wall

9		10
Over LF		Over RF

74
Front of CF

44		96		100		39
LF Line		Front of LF		Front of RF		RF Line

168
Up Middle

91		91
SS/3B Hole		1B/2B Hole

34		97		27
3B Line		Infield		1B Line

Better Than Average	Average	Worse Than Average

67

Where Hits Landed -- Los Angeles Dodgers

Through The Infield

	Infield	1B Line	1B/2B Hole	Up Middle	SS/3B Hole	3B Line
vs Dodgers	85	29	104	193	105	41
vs Opponents	74	25	90	159	101	26
ML Average	89	22	94	177	115	41

Through The Outfielders

	LF Line	Front of LF	LF Gap	Front of CF	RF Gap	Front of RF	RF Line
vs Dodgers	52	83	144	87	115	113	50
vs Opponents	45	107	129	111	152	111	44
ML Average	52	106	149	89	144	109	49

Over the Outfielders

	LF Wall	Over LF	Over CF	RF Wall	Over RF	Gone
vs Dodgers	4	14	23	8	2	182
vs Opponents	4	11	25	5	6	149
ML Average	10	14	20	9	10	167

The Dodgers outperformed their opponents by at least 5 hits in the following places:
   Hits in front of the Left Fielder (83 to 107)
   Hits in front of the Center Fielder (87 to 111)
   Hits in the Right Field Gap (115 to 152)

They were outperformed by 5 or more hits in the following places:
   Infield Hits (85 to 74)
   Hits between First and Second (104 to 90)
   Hits Up the Middle (193 to 159)
   Hits down Third Base Line (41 to 26)
   Hits down Left Field Line (52 to 45)
   Hits in the Left Field Gap (144 to 129)
   Hits down Right Field Line (50 to 44)
   Home Runs (182 to 149)

Where Hits Landed Against the Los Angeles Dodgers
2005 - Home and Road

Look for patterns of red and blue. A box outlined in red means the team allowed significantly more hits than the Major League average. The blue outline means the team allowed significantly fewer hits than average.

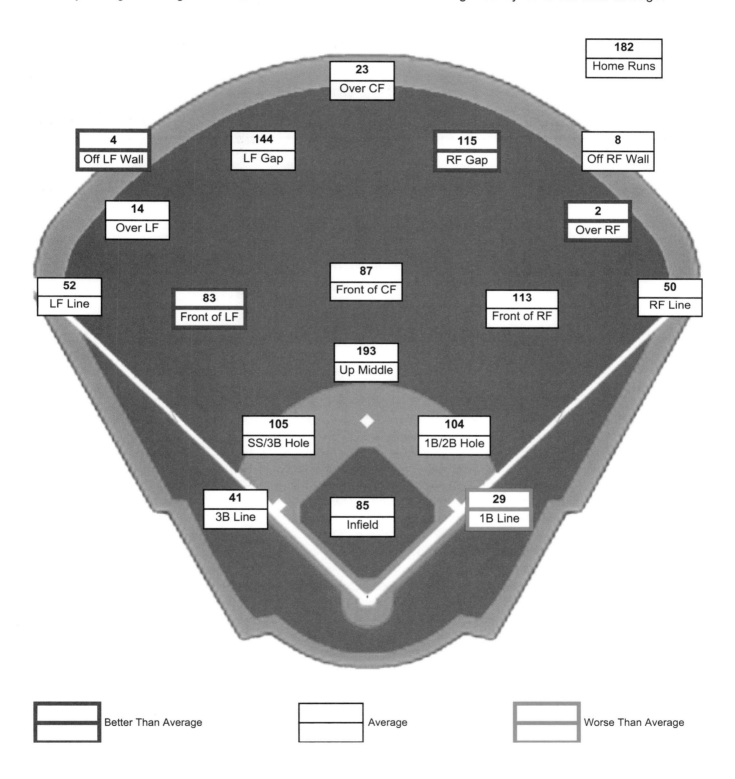

| Better Than Average | Average | Worse Than Average |

Where Hits Landed -- Milwaukee Brewers

Through The Infield

	Infield	1B Line	1B/2B Hole	Up Middle	SS/3B Hole	3B Line
vs Brewers	107	18	72	155	82	53
vs Opponents	54	13	62	172	121	44
ML Average	89	22	94	177	115	41

Through The Outfielders

	LF Line	Front of LF	LF Gap	Front of CF	RF Gap	Front of RF	RF Line
vs Brewers	49	94	172	71	134	100	44
vs Opponents	56	107	140	82	138	126	52
ML Average	52	106	149	89	144	109	49

Over the Outfielders

	LF Wall	Over LF	Over CF	RF Wall	Over RF	Gone
vs Brewers	7	14	25	8	8	169
vs Opponents	5	18	31	6	11	175
ML Average	10	14	20	9	10	167

The Brewers outperformed their opponents by at least 5 hits in the following places:
> Hits Up the Middle (155 to 172)
> Hits between Shortstop and Third (82 to 121)
> Hits down Left Field Line (49 to 56)
> Hits in front of the Left Fielder (94 to 107)
> Hits in front of the Center Fielder (71 to 82)
> Hits in front of the Right Fielder (100 to 126)
> Hits down Right Field Line (44 to 52)
> Hits over the Center Fielder (25 to 31)
> Home Runs (169 to 175)

They were outperformed by 5 or more hits in the following places:
> Infield Hits (107 to 54)
> Hits down First Base Line (18 to 13)
> Hits between First and Second (72 to 62)
> Hits down Third Base Line (53 to 44)
> Hits in the Left Field Gap (172 to 140)

Where Hits Landed Against the Milwaukee Brewers
2005 - Home and Road

Look for patterns of red and blue. A box outlined in red means the team allowed significantly more hits than the Major League average. The blue outline means the team allowed significantly fewer hits than average.

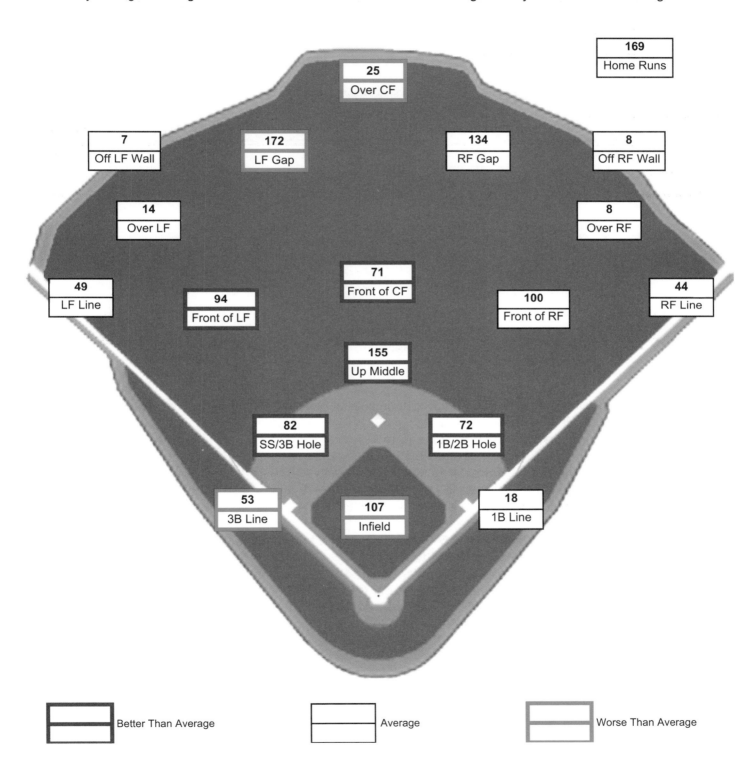

| **169** |
| Home Runs |

25 / Over CF

7 / Off LF Wall

172 / LF Gap

134 / RF Gap

8 / Off RF Wall

14 / Over LF

8 / Over RF

71 / Front of CF

49 / LF Line

94 / Front of LF

100 / Front of RF

44 / RF Line

155 / Up Middle

82 / SS/3B Hole

72 / 1B/2B Hole

53 / 3B Line

107 / Infield

18 / 1B Line

Better Than Average   Average   Worse Than Average

Where Hits Landed -- Minnesota Twins

Through The Infield						
	Infield	1B Line	1B/2B Hole	Up Middle	SS/3B Hole	3B Line
vs Twins	84	6	82	214	131	29
vs Opponents	110	19	101	206	138	47
ML Average	89	22	94	177	115	41

Through The Outfielders							
	LF Line	Front of LF	LF Gap	Front of CF	RF Gap	Front of RF	RF Line
vs Twins	49	106	140	102	142	102	35
vs Opponents	48	111	124	86	118	102	36
ML Average	52	106	149	89	144	109	49

Over the Outfielders						
	LF Wall	Over LF	Over CF	RF Wall	Over RF	Gone
vs Twins	6	12	18	18	13	169
vs Opponents	10	14	15	17	5	134
ML Average	10	14	20	9	10	167

The Twins outperformed their opponents by at least 5 hits in the following places:
 Infield Hits (84 to 110)
 Hits down First Base Line (6 to 19)
 Hits between First and Second (82 to 101)
 Hits between Shortstop and Third (131 to 138)
 Hits down Third Base Line (29 to 47)
 Hits in front of the Left Fielder (106 to 111)

They were outperformed by 5 or more hits in the following places:
 Hits Up the Middle (214 to 206)
 Hits in the Left Field Gap (140 to 124)
 Hits in front of the Center Fielder (102 to 86)
 Hits in the Right Field Gap (142 to 118)
 Hits over the Right Fielder (13 to 5)
 Home Runs (169 to 134)

Where Hits Landed Against the Minnesota Twins
2005 - Home and Road

Look for patterns of red and blue. A box outlined in red means the team allowed significantly more hits than the Major League average. The blue outline means the team allowed significantly fewer hits than average.

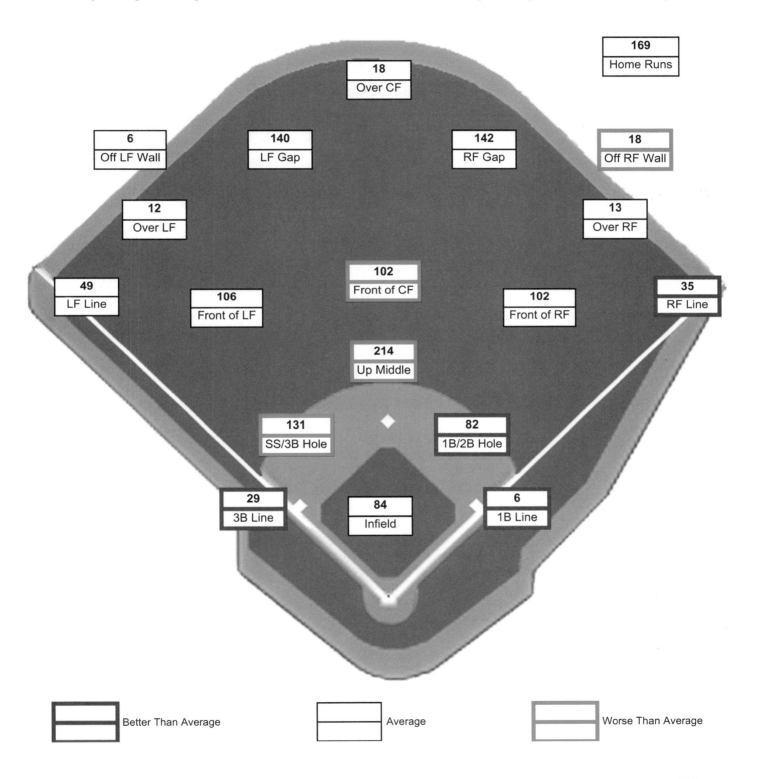

169
Home Runs

18
Over CF

6
Off LF Wall

140
LF Gap

142
RF Gap

18
Off RF Wall

12
Over LF

13
Over RF

102
Front of CF

49
LF Line

106
Front of LF

102
Front of RF

35
RF Line

214
Up Middle

131
SS/3B Hole

82
1B/2B Hole

29
3B Line

84
Infield

6
1B Line

Better Than Average   Average   Worse Than Average

Where Hits Landed -- New York Mets

Through The Infield

	Infield	1B Line	1B/2B Hole	Up Middle	SS/3B Hole	3B Line
vs Mets	94	13	79	141	111	59
vs Opponents	104	25	112	164	109	38
ML Average	89	22	94	177	115	41

Through The Outfielders

	LF Line	Front of LF	LF Gap	Front of CF	RF Gap	Front of RF	RF Line
vs Mets	50	101	159	83	151	121	40
vs Opponents	48	106	135	85	150	88	35
ML Average	52	106	149	89	144	109	49

Over the Outfielders

	LF Wall	Over LF	Over CF	RF Wall	Over RF	Gone
vs Mets	5	16	14	10	8	135
vs Opponents	2	11	17	6	12	174
ML Average	10	14	20	9	10	167

The Mets outperformed their opponents by at least 5 hits in the following places:
> Infield Hits (94 to 104)
> Hits down First Base Line (13 to 25)
> Hits between First and Second (79 to 112)
> Hits Up the Middle (141 to 164)
> Hits in front of the Left Fielder (101 to 106)
> Home Runs (135 to 174)

They were outperformed by 5 or more hits in the following places:
> Hits down Third Base Line (59 to 38)
> Hits in the Left Field Gap (159 to 135)
> Hits in front of the Right Fielder (121 to 88)
> Hits down Right Field Line (40 to 35)
> Hits over the Left Fielder (16 to 11)

Where Hits Landed Against the New York Mets
2005 - Home and Road

Look for patterns of red and blue. A box outlined in red means the team allowed significantly more hits than the Major League average. The blue outline means the team allowed significantly fewer hits than average.

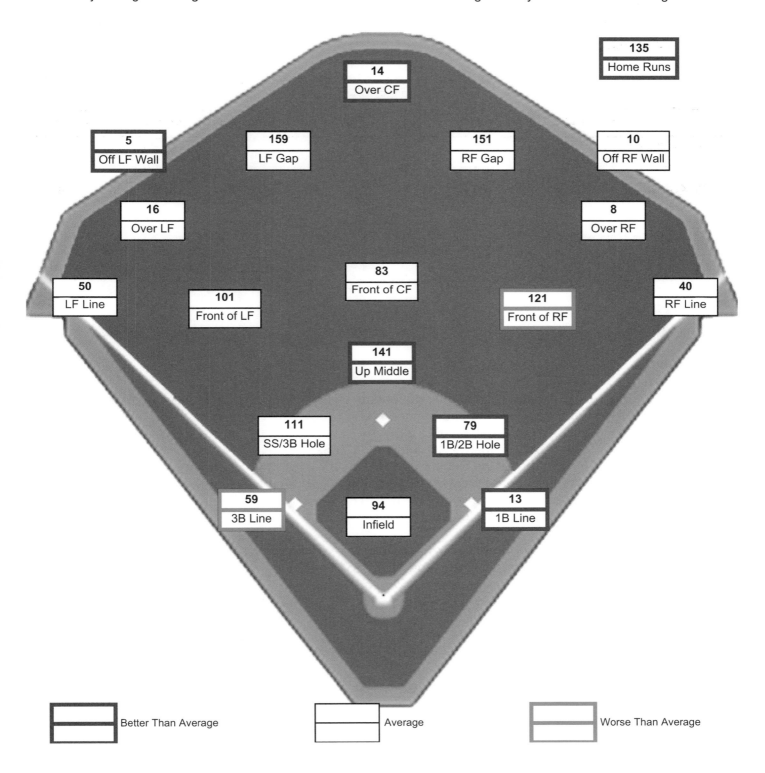

135		
Home Runs		

14
Over CF

5	**159**	**151**	**10**
Off LF Wall	LF Gap	RF Gap	Off RF Wall

16	**8**
Over LF	Over RF

83
Front of CF

50	**101**	**121**	**40**
LF Line	Front of LF	Front of RF	RF Line

141
Up Middle

111	**79**
SS/3B Hole	1B/2B Hole

59	**94**	**13**
3B Line	Infield	1B Line

	Better Than Average		Average		Worse Than Average

75

Where Hits Landed -- New York Yankees

Through The Infield

	Infield	1B Line	1B/2B Hole	Up Middle	SS/3B Hole	3B Line
vs Yankees	85	21	106	196	131	51
vs Opponents	85	24	126	223	124	32
ML Average	89	22	94	177	115	41

Through The Outfielders

	LF Line	Front of LF	LF Gap	Front of CF	RF Gap	Front of RF	RF Line
vs Yankees	46	110	150	71	162	92	43
vs Opponents	36	76	144	82	144	107	53
ML Average	52	106	149	89	144	109	49

Over the Outfielders

	LF Wall	Over LF	Over CF	RF Wall	Over RF	Gone
vs Yankees	7	22	15	10	14	163
vs Opponents	10	11	17	17	12	229
ML Average	10	14	20	9	10	167

The Yankees outperformed their opponents by at least 5 hits in the following places:
Hits between First and Second (106 to 126)
Hits Up the Middle (196 to 223)
Hits in front of the Center Fielder (71 to 82)
Hits in front of the Right Fielder (92 to 107)
Hits down Right Field Line (43 to 53)
Hits off the Right Field Wall (10 to 17)
Home Runs (163 to 229)

They were outperformed by 5 or more hits in the following places:
Hits between Shortstop and Third (131 to 124)
Hits down Third Base Line (51 to 32)
Hits down Left Field Line (46 to 36)
Hits in front of the Left Fielder (110 to 76)
Hits in the Left Field Gap (150 to 144)
Hits in the Right Field Gap (162 to 144)
Hits over the Left Fielder (22 to 11)

Where Hits Landed Against the New York Yankees
2005 - Home and Road

Look for patterns of red and blue. A box outlined in red means the team allowed significantly more hits than the Major League average. The blue outline means the team allowed significantly fewer hits than average.

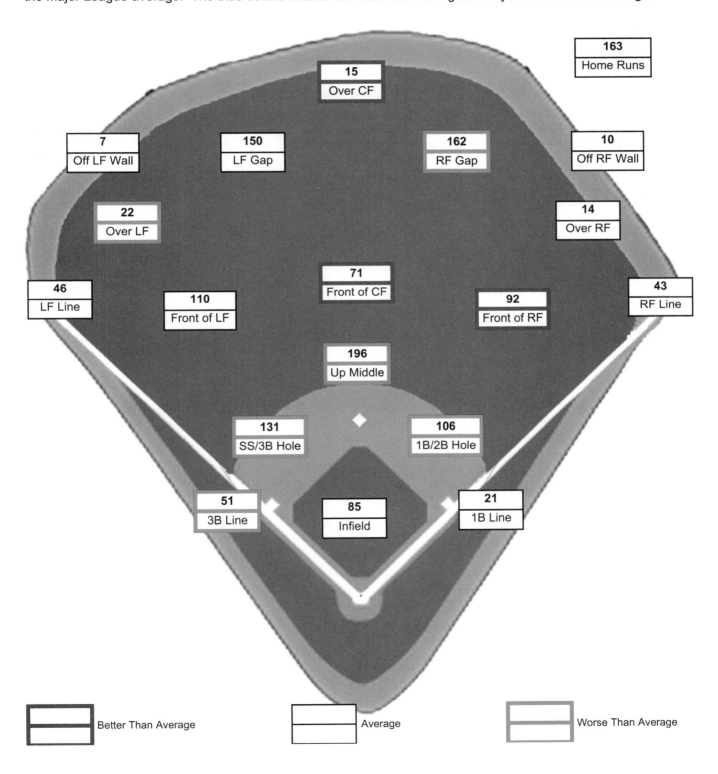

163 Home Runs

15 Over CF

7 Off LF Wall

150 LF Gap

162 RF Gap

10 Off RF Wall

22 Over LF

14 Over RF

46 LF Line

110 Front of LF

71 Front of CF

92 Front of RF

43 RF Line

196 Up Middle

131 SS/3B Hole

106 1B/2B Hole

51 3B Line

85 Infield

21 1B Line

Better Than Average

Average

Worse Than Average

Where Hits Landed -- Oakland Athletics

Through The Infield

	Infield	1B Line	1B/2B Hole	Up Middle	SS/3B Hole	3B Line
vs Athletics	55	18	94	136	121	27
vs Opponents	80	28	90	180	121	40
ML Average	89	22	94	177	115	41

Through The Outfielders

	LF Line	Front of LF	LF Gap	Front of CF	RF Gap	Front of RF	RF Line
vs Athletics	54	101	129	84	148	95	39
vs Opponents	41	94	142	89	171	138	50
ML Average	52	106	149	89	144	109	49

Over the Outfielders

	LF Wall	Over LF	Over CF	RF Wall	Over RF	Gone
vs Athletics	10	20	15	3	12	154
vs Opponents	13	17	8	5	15	154
ML Average	10	14	20	9	10	167

The Athletics outperformed their opponents by at least 5 hits in the following places:
Infield Hits (55 to 80)
Hits down First Base Line (18 to 28)
Hits Up the Middle (136 to 180)
Hits down Third Base Line (27 to 40)
Hits in the Left Field Gap (129 to 142)
Hits in front of the Center Fielder (84 to 89)
Hits in the Right Field Gap (148 to 171)
Hits in front of the Right Fielder (95 to 138)
Hits down Right Field Line (39 to 50)

They were outperformed by 5 or more hits in the following places:
Hits down Left Field Line (54 to 41)
Hits in front of the Left Fielder (101 to 94)
Hits over the Center Fielder (15 to 8)

Where Hits Landed Against the Oakland Athletics
2005 - Home and Road

Look for patterns of red and blue. A box outlined in red means the team allowed significantly more hits than the Major League average. The blue outline means the team allowed significantly fewer hits than average.

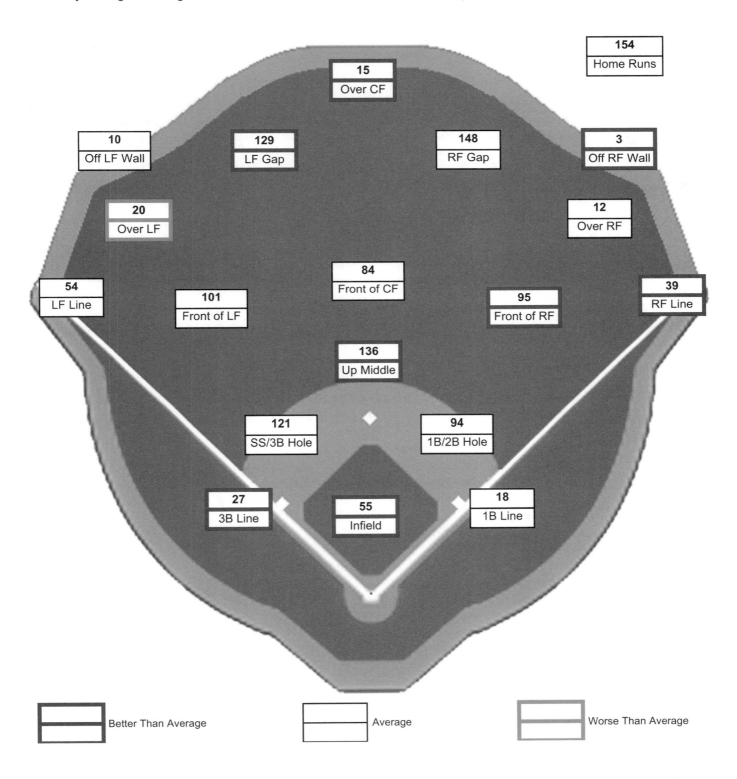

154
Home Runs

15
Over CF

10
Off LF Wall

129
LF Gap

148
RF Gap

3
Off RF Wall

20
Over LF

12
Over RF

84
Front of CF

54
LF Line

101
Front of LF

95
Front of RF

39
RF Line

136
Up Middle

121
SS/3B Hole

94
1B/2B Hole

27
3B Line

55
Infield

18
1B Line

Better Than Average   Average   Worse Than Average

79

Where Hits Landed -- Philadelphia Phillies

Through The Infield

	Infield	1B Line	1B/2B Hole	Up Middle	SS/3B Hole	3B Line
vs Phillies	82	17	67	147	99	46
vs Opponents	59	17	130	171	119	32
ML Average	89	22	94	177	115	41

Through The Outfielders

	LF Line	Front of LF	LF Gap	Front of CF	RF Gap	Front of RF	RF Line
vs Phillies	51	113	140	80	125	113	51
vs Opponents	37	106	165	110	165	102	36
ML Average	52	106	149	89	144	109	49

Over the Outfielders

	LF Wall	Over LF	Over CF	RF Wall	Over RF	Gone
vs Phillies	5	18	17	9	10	189
vs Opponents	9	17	29	14	10	166
ML Average	10	14	20	9	10	167

The Phillies outperformed their opponents by at least 5 hits in the following places:
> Hits between First and Second (67 to 130)
> Hits Up the Middle (147 to 171)
> Hits between Shortstop and Third (99 to 119)
> Hits in the Left Field Gap (140 to 165)
> Hits in front of the Center Fielder (80 to 110)
> Hits in the Right Field Gap (125 to 165)
> Hits over the Center Fielder (17 to 29)
> Hits off the Right Field Wall (9 to 14)

They were outperformed by 5 or more hits in the following places:
> Infield Hits (82 to 59)
> Hits down Third Base Line (46 to 32)
> Hits down Left Field Line (51 to 37)
> Hits in front of the Left Fielder (113 to 106)
> Hits in front of the Right Fielder (113 to 102)
> Hits down Right Field Line (51 to 36)
> Home Runs (189 to 166)

Where Hits Landed Against the Philadelphia Phillies
2005 - Home and Road

Look for patterns of red and blue. A box outlined in red means the team allowed significantly more hits than the Major League average. The blue outline means the team allowed significantly fewer hits than average.

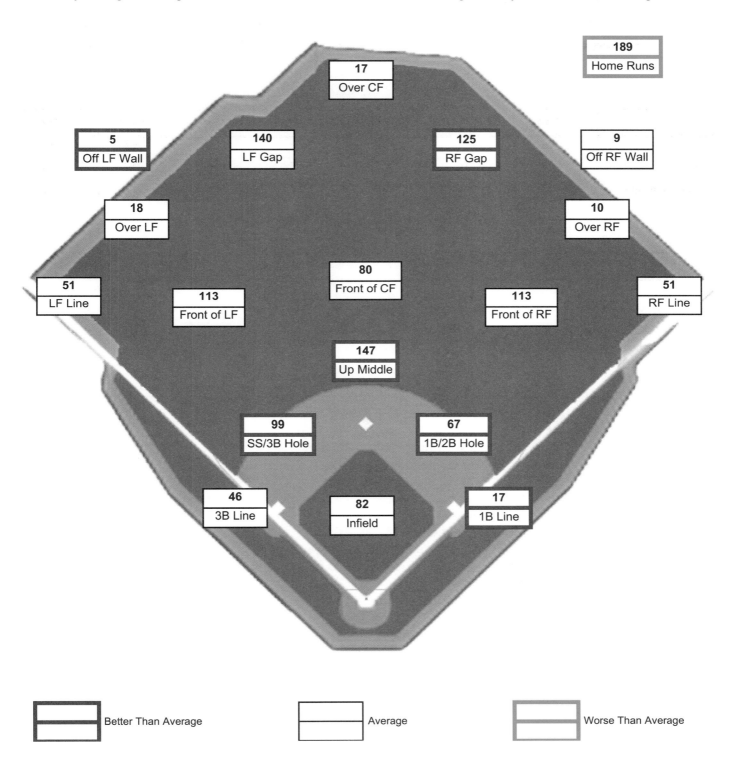

189
Home Runs

17
Over CF

5
Off LF Wall

140
LF Gap

125
RF Gap

9
Off RF Wall

18
Over LF

10
Over RF

51
LF Line

113
Front of LF

80
Front of CF

113
Front of RF

51
RF Line

147
Up Middle

99
SS/3B Hole

67
1B/2B Hole

46
3B Line

82
Infield

17
1B Line

Better Than Average

Average

Worse Than Average

Where Hits Landed -- Pittsburgh Pirates

Through The Infield

	Infield	1B Line	1B/2B Hole	Up Middle	SS/3B Hole	3B Line
vs Pirates	98	16	84	180	94	38
vs Opponents	94	20	83	170	115	39
ML Average	89	22	94	177	115	41

Through The Outfielders

	LF Line	Front of LF	LF Gap	Front of CF	RF Gap	Front of RF	RF Line
vs Pirates	62	116	162	78	176	92	44
vs Opponents	59	126	157	87	154	86	39
ML Average	52	106	149	89	144	109	49

Over the Outfielders

	LF Wall	Over LF	Over CF	RF Wall	Over RF	Gone
vs Pirates	7	15	12	11	9	162
vs Opponents	10	17	22	15	13	139
ML Average	10	14	20	9	10	167

The Pirates outperformed their opponents by at least 5 hits in the following places:
    Hits between Shortstop and Third (94 to 115)
    Hits in front of the Left Fielder (116 to 126)
    Hits in front of the Center Fielder (78 to 87)
    Hits over the Center Fielder (12 to 22)

They were outperformed by 5 or more hits in the following places:
    Hits Up the Middle (180 to 170)
    Hits in the Left Field Gap (162 to 157)
    Hits in the Right Field Gap (176 to 154)
    Hits in front of the Right Fielder (92 to 86)
    Hits down Right Field Line (44 to 39)
    Home Runs (162 to 139)

Where Hits Landed Against the Pittsburgh Pirates
2005 - Home and Road

Look for patterns of red and blue. A box outlined in red means the team allowed significantly more hits than the Major League average. The blue outline means the team allowed significantly fewer hits than average.

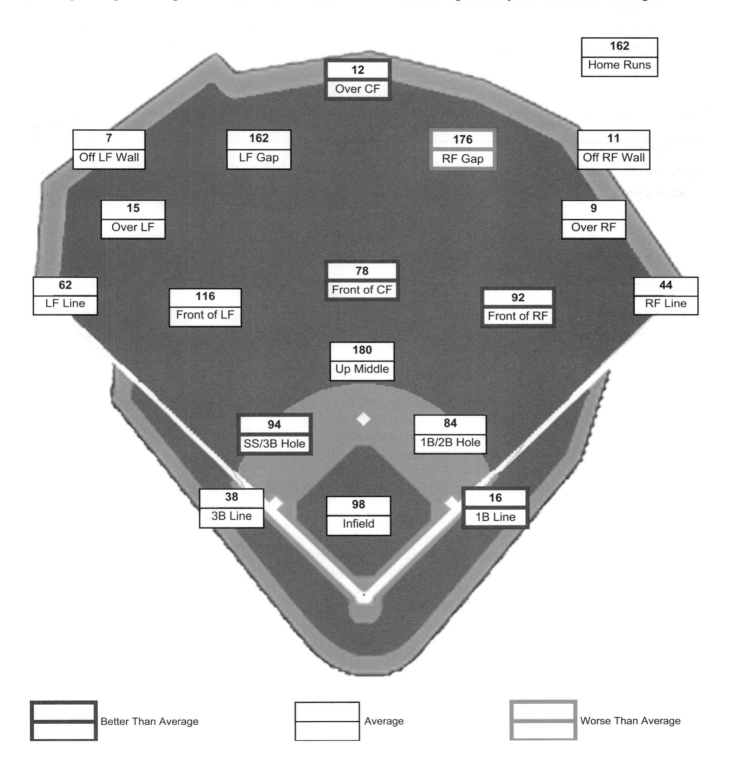

Where Hits Landed -- San Diego Padres

Through The Infield

	Infield	1B Line	1B/2B Hole	Up Middle	SS/3B Hole	3B Line
vs Padres	93	16	94	158	109	30
vs Opponents	88	16	93	148	113	35
ML Average	89	22	94	177	115	41

Through The Outfielders

	LF Line	Front of LF	LF Gap	Front of CF	RF Gap	Front of RF	RF Line
vs Padres	46	108	163	101	158	115	55
vs Opponents	53	90	165	100	185	110	46
ML Average	52	106	149	89	144	109	49

Over the Outfielders

	LF Wall	Over LF	Over CF	RF Wall	Over RF	Gone
vs Padres	4	14	24	8	11	145
vs Opponents	2	11	13	7	11	130
ML Average	10	14	20	9	10	167

The Padres outperformed their opponents by at least 5 hits in the following places:
 Hits down Third Base Line (30 to 35)
 Hits down Left Field Line (46 to 53)
 Hits in the Right Field Gap (158 to 185)

They were outperformed by 5 or more hits in the following places:
 Infield Hits (93 to 88)
 Hits Up the Middle (158 to 148)
 Hits in front of the Left Fielder (108 to 90)
 Hits in front of the Right Fielder (115 to 110)
 Hits down Right Field Line (55 to 46)
 Hits over the Center Fielder (24 to 13)
 Home Runs (145 to 130)

Where Hits Landed Against the San Diego Padres
2005 - Home and Road

Look for patterns of red and blue. A box outlined in red means the team allowed significantly more hits than the Major League average. The blue outline means the team allowed significantly fewer hits than average.

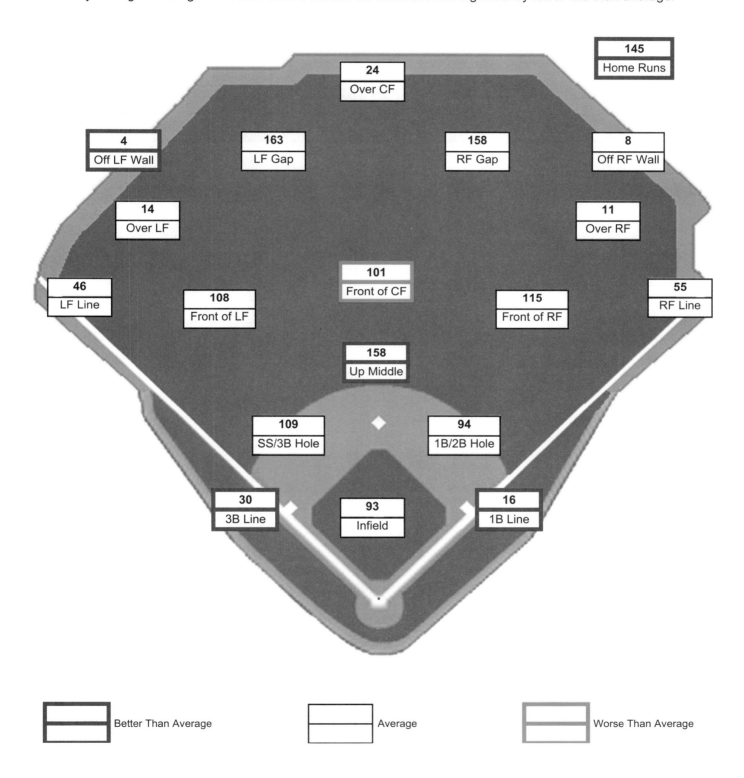

145		
Home Runs		

24
Over CF

4	**163**	**158**	**8**
Off LF Wall	LF Gap	RF Gap	Off RF Wall

14	**11**
Over LF	Over RF

101
Front of CF

46	**108**	**115**	**55**
LF Line	Front of LF	Front of RF	RF Line

158
Up Middle

109	**94**
SS/3B Hole	1B/2B Hole

30	**93**	**16**
3B Line	Infield	1B Line

Better Than Average	Average	Worse Than Average

Where Hits Landed -- San Francisco Giants

Through The Infield

	Infield	1B Line	1B/2B Hole	Up Middle	SS/3B Hole	3B Line
vs Giants	83	20	86	164	126	39
vs Opponents	88	17	78	172	112	38
ML Average	89	22	94	177	115	41

Through The Outfielders

	LF Line	Front of LF	LF Gap	Front of CF	RF Gap	Front of RF	RF Line
vs Giants	51	106	143	107	150	107	52
vs Opponents	57	118	149	107	113	126	58
ML Average	52	106	149	89	144	109	49

Over the Outfielders

	LF Wall	Over LF	Over CF	RF Wall	Over RF	Gone
vs Giants	8	9	27	12	15	151
vs Opponents	10	17	22	8	9	128
ML Average	10	14	20	9	10	167

The Giants outperformed their opponents by at least 5 hits in the following places:
 Infield Hits (83 to 88)
 Hits Up the Middle (164 to 172)
 Hits down Left Field Line (51 to 57)
 Hits in front of the Left Fielder (106 to 118)
 Hits in the Left Field Gap (143 to 149)
 Hits in front of the Right Fielder (107 to 126)
 Hits down Right Field Line (52 to 58)
 Hits over the Left Fielder (9 to 17)

They were outperformed by 5 or more hits in the following places:
 Hits between First and Second (86 to 78)
 Hits between Shortstop and Third (126 to 112)
 Hits in the Right Field Gap (150 to 113)
 Hits over the Center Fielder (27 to 22)
 Hits over the Right Fielder (15 to 9)
 Home Runs (151 to 128)

Where Hits Landed Against the San Francisco Giants
2005 - Home and Road

Look for patterns of red and blue. A box outlined in red means the team allowed significantly more hits than the Major League average. The blue outline means the team allowed significantly fewer hits than average.

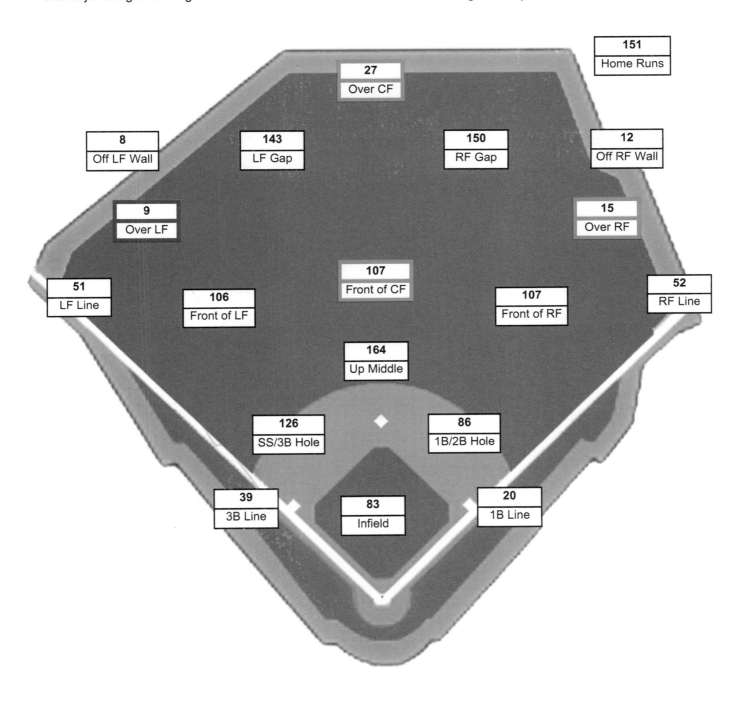

Where Hits Landed -- Seattle Mariners

Through The Infield

	Infield	1B Line	1B/2B Hole	Up Middle	SS/3B Hole	3B Line
vs Mariners	71	35	104	214	104	39
vs Opponents	89	28	99	181	107	40
ML Average	89	22	94	177	115	41

Through The Outfielders

	LF Line	Front of LF	LF Gap	Front of CF	RF Gap	Front of RF	RF Line
vs Mariners	55	115	143	81	138	99	48
vs Opponents	50	94	164	103	137	88	43
ML Average	52	106	149	89	144	109	49

Over the Outfielders

	LF Wall	Over LF	Over CF	RF Wall	Over RF	Gone
vs Mariners	13	9	18	9	9	179
vs Opponents	7	14	20	8	6	130
ML Average	10	14	20	9	10	167

The Mariners outperformed their opponents by at least 5 hits in the following places:
- Infield Hits (71 to 89)
- Hits in the Left Field Gap (143 to 164)
- Hits in front of the Center Fielder (81 to 103)
- Hits over the Left Fielder (9 to 14)

They were outperformed by 5 or more hits in the following places:
- Hits down First Base Line (35 to 28)
- Hits between First and Second (104 to 99)
- Hits Up the Middle (214 to 181)
- Hits down Left Field Line (55 to 50)
- Hits in front of the Left Fielder (115 to 94)
- Hits in front of the Right Fielder (99 to 88)
- Hits down Right Field Line (48 to 43)
- Hits off the Left Field Wall (13 to 7)
- Home Runs(179 to 130)

Where Hits Landed Against the Seattle Mariners
2005 - Home and Road

Look for patterns of red and blue. A box outlined in red means the team allowed significantly more hits than the Major League average. The blue outline means the team allowed significantly fewer hits than average.

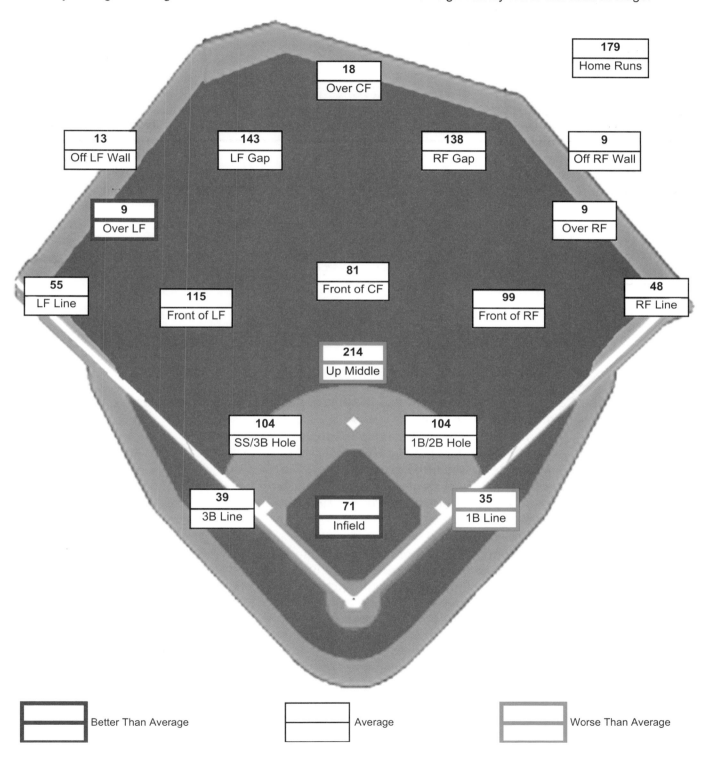

179
Home Runs

18
Over CF

13	143	138	9
Off LF Wall	LF Gap	RF Gap	Off RF Wall

9	9
Over LF	Over RF

55	115	81	99	48
LF Line	Front of LF	Front of CF	Front of RF	RF Line

214
Up Middle

104	104
SS/3B Hole	1B/2B Hole

39	71	35
3B Line	Infield	1B Line

Better Than Average   Average   Worse Than Average

Where Hits Landed -- St Louis Cardinals

Through The Infield						
	Infield	1B Line	1B/2B Hole	Up Middle	SS/3B Hole	3B Line
vs Cardinals	80	22	81	175	129	46
vs Opponents	106	25	94	187	114	44
ML Average	89	22	94	177	115	41

Through The Outfielders							
	LF Line	Front of LF	LF Gap	Front of CF	RF Gap	Front of RF	RF Line
vs Cardinals	45	107	142	81	102	117	49
vs Opponents	46	117	139	104	122	115	47
ML Average	52	106	149	89	144	109	49

Over the Outfielders						
	LF Wall	Over LF	Over CF	RF Wall	Over RF	Gone
vs Cardinals	10	15	28	5	12	153
vs Opponents	14	14	20	5	11	170
ML Average	10	14	20	9	10	167

The Cardinals outperformed their opponents by at least 5 hits in the following places:
    Infield Hits (80 to 106)
    Hits between First and Second (81 to 94)
    Hits Up the Middle (175 to 187)
    Hits in front of the Left Fielder (107 to 117)
    Hits in front of the Center Fielder (81 to 104)
    Hits in the Right Field Gap (102 to 122)
    Home Runs (153 to 170)

They were outperformed by 5 or more hits in the following places:
    Hits between Shortstop and Third (129 to 114)
    Hits over the Center Fielder (28 to 20)

Where Hits Landed Against the St Louis Cardinals
2005 - Home and Road

Look for patterns of red and blue. A box outlined in red means the team allowed significantly more hits than the Major League average. The blue outline means the team allowed significantly fewer hits than average.

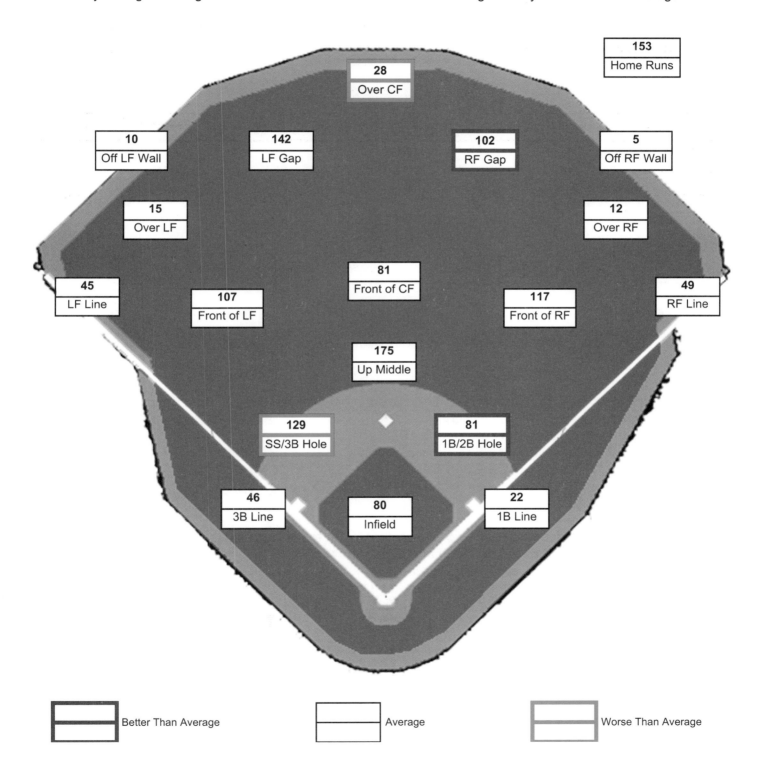

91

Where Hits Landed -- Tampa Bay Devil Rays

Through The Infield

	Infield	1B Line	1B/2B Hole	Up Middle	SS/3B Hole	3B Line
vs Devil Rays	92	26	95	179	141	38
vs Opponents	103	23	97	197	117	46
ML Average	89	22	94	177	115	41

Through The Outfielders

	LF Line	Front of LF	LF Gap	Front of CF	RF Gap	Front of RF	RF Line
vs Devil Rays	64	94	159	122	145	99	69
vs Opponents	48	109	159	101	137	117	48
ML Average	52	106	149	89	144	109	49

Over the Outfielders

	LF Wall	Over LF	Over CF	RF Wall	Over RF	Gone
vs Devil Rays	14	14	12	8	6	193
vs Opponents	13	12	20	7	9	156
ML Average	10	14	20	9	10	167

The Devil Rays outperformed their opponents by at least 5 hits in the following places:
>Infield Hits (92 to 103)
>Hits Up the Middle (179 to 197)
>Hits down Third Base Line (38 to 46)
>Hits in front of the Left Fielder (94 to 109)
>Hits in front of the Right Fielder (99 to 117)
>Hits over the Center Fielder (12 to 20)

They were outperformed by 5 or more hits in the following places:
>Hits between Shortstop and Third (141 to 117)
>Hits down Left Field Line (64 to 48)
>Hits in front of the Center Fielder (122 to 101)
>Hits in the Right Field Gap (145 to 137)
>Hits down Right Field Line (69 to 48)
>Home Runs (193 to 156)

Where Hits Landed Against the Tampa Bay Devil Rays
2005 - Home and Road

Look for patterns of red and blue. A box outlined in red means the team allowed significantly more hits than the Major League average. The blue outline means the team allowed significantly fewer hits than average.

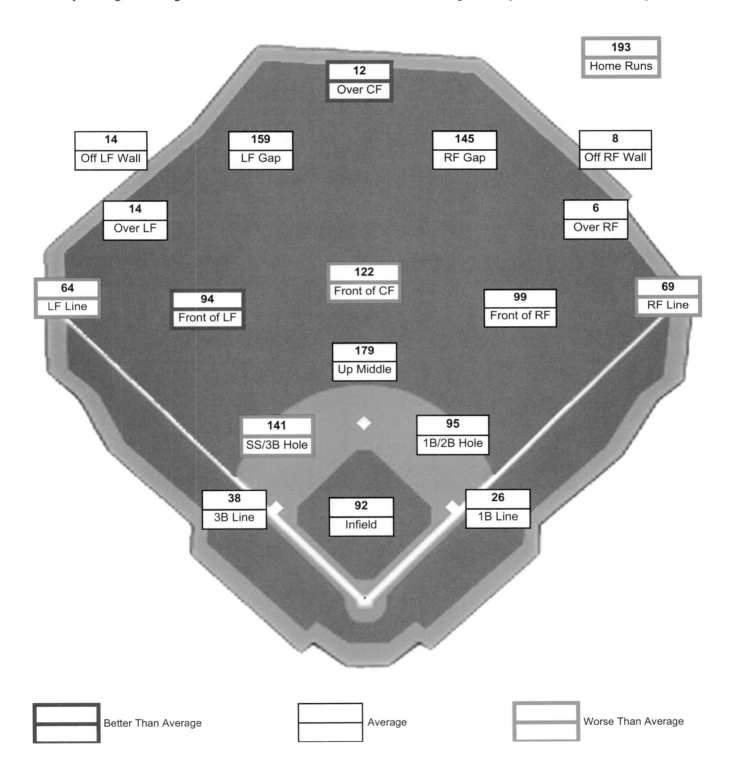

193
Home Runs

12
Over CF

14
Off LF Wall

159
LF Gap

145
RF Gap

8
Off RF Wall

14
Over LF

6
Over RF

64
LF Line

94
Front of LF

122
Front of CF

99
Front of RF

69
RF Line

179
Up Middle

141
SS/3B Hole

95
1B/2B Hole

38
3B Line

92
Infield

26
1B Line

Better Than Average   Average   Worse Than Average

Where Hits Landed -- Texas Rangers

Through The Infield

	Infield	1B Line	1B/2B Hole	Up Middle	SS/3B Hole	3B Line
vs Rangers	105	21	114	223	151	42
vs Opponents	57	24	83	170	94	34
ML Average	89	22	94	177	115	41

Through The Outfielders

	LF Line	Front of LF	LF Gap	Front of CF	RF Gap	Front of RF	RF Line
vs Rangers	52	94	139	120	141	117	48
vs Opponents	65	134	160	80	154	111	48
ML Average	52	106	149	89	144	109	49

Over the Outfielders

	LF Wall	Over LF	Over CF	RF Wall	Over RF	Gone
vs Rangers	10	19	13	16	5	159
vs Opponents	12	11	14	9	8	260
ML Average	10	14	20	9	10	167

The Rangers outperformed their opponents by at least 5 hits in the following places:
Hits down Left Field Line (52 to 65)
Hits in front of the Left Fielder (94 to 134)
Hits in the Left Field Gap (139 to 160)
Hits in the Right Field Gap (141 to 154)
Home Runs (159 to 260)

They were outperformed by 5 or more hits in the following places:
Infield Hits (105 to 57)
Hits between First and Second (114 to 83)
Hits Up the Middle (223 to 170)
Hits between Shortstop and Third (151 to 94)
Hits down Third Base Line (42 to 34)
Hits in front of the Center Fielder (120 to 80)
Hits in front of the Right Fielder (117 to 111)
Hits over the Left Fielder (19 to 11)
Hits off the Right Field Wall (16 to 9)

Where Hits Landed Against the Texas Rangers
2005 - Home and Road

Look for patterns of red and blue. A box outlined in red means the team allowed significantly more hits than the Major League average. The blue outline means the team allowed significantly fewer hits than average.

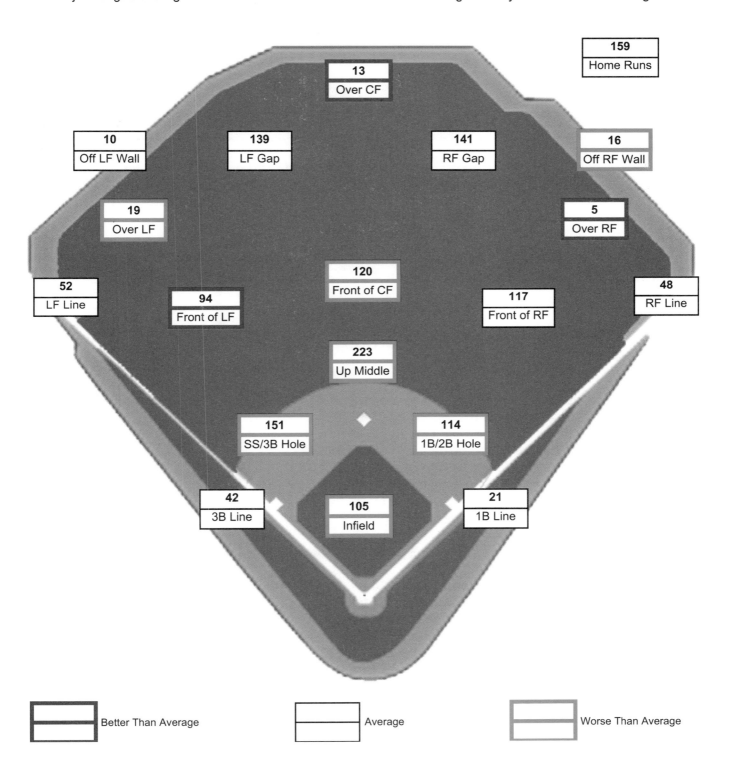

	159	
	Home Runs	

13
Over CF

10	**139**	**141**	**16**
Off LF Wall	LF Gap	RF Gap	Off RF Wall

19			**5**
Over LF			Over RF

120
Front of CF

52	**94**	**117**	**48**
LF Line	Front of LF	Front of RF	RF Line

223
Up Middle

151	**114**
SS/3B Hole	1B/2B Hole

42	**105**	**21**
3B Line	Infield	1B Line

Better Than Average	Average	Worse Than Average

Where Hits Landed -- Toronto Blue Jays

Through The Infield

	Infield	1B Line	1B/2B Hole	Up Middle	SS/3B Hole	3B Line
vs Blue Jays	107	20	93	199	83	51
vs Opponents	82	24	96	184	115	40
ML Average	89	22	94	177	115	41

Through The Outfielders

	LF Line	Front of LF	LF Gap	Front of CF	RF Gap	Front of RF	RF Line
vs Blue Jays	50	103	144	94	140	119	37
vs Opponents	61	92	181	85	130	135	55
ML Average	52	106	149	89	144	109	49

Over the Outfielders

	LF Wall	Over LF	Over CF	RF Wall	Over RF	Gone
vs Blue Jays	7	16	15	5	9	183
vs Opponents	8	13	24	12	7	136
ML Average	10	14	20	9	10	167

The Blue Jays outperformed their opponents by at least 5 hits in the following places:
Hits between Shortstop and Third (83 to 115)
Hits down Left Field Line (50 to 61)
Hits in the Left Field Gap (144 to 181)
Hits in front of the Right Fielder (119 to 135)
Hits down Right Field Line (37 to 55)
Hits over the Center Fielder (15 to 24)
Hits off the Right Field Wall (5 to 12)

They were outperformed by 5 or more hits in the following places:
Infield Hits (107 to 82)
Hits Up the Middle (199 to 184)
Hits down Third Base Line (51 to 40)
Hits in front of the Left Fielder (103 to 92)
Hits in front of the Center Fielder (94 to 85)
Hits in the Right Field Gap (140 to 130)
Home Runs (183 to 136)

Where Hits Landed Against the Toronto Blue Jays
2005 - Home and Road

Look for patterns of red and blue. A box outlined in red means the team allowed significantly more hits than the Major League average. The blue outline means the team allowed significantly fewer hits than average.

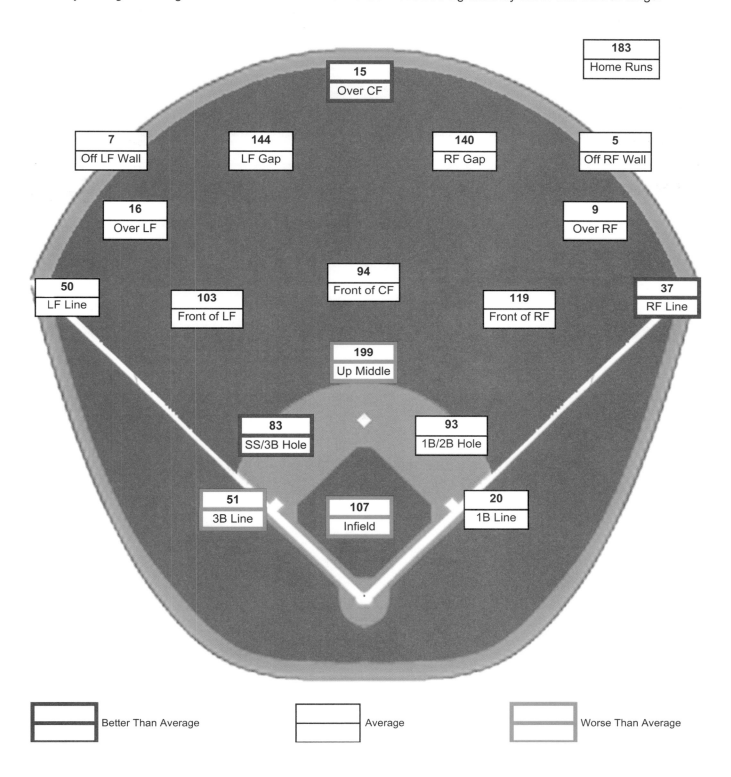

	183
	Home Runs

15
Over CF

7	**144**	**140**	**5**
Off LF Wall	LF Gap	RF Gap	Off RF Wall

16	**9**
Over LF	Over RF

94
Front of CF

50	**103**	**119**	**37**
LF Line	Front of LF	Front of RF	RF Line

199
Up Middle

83	**93**
SS/3B Hole	1B/2B Hole

51	**107**	**20**
3B Line	Infield	1B Line

Better Than Average Average Worse Than Average

97

Where Hits Landed -- Washington Nationals

Through The Infield

	Infield	1B Line	1B/2B Hole	Up Middle	SS/3B Hole	3B Line
vs Nationals	86	21	85	184	105	36
vs Opponents	75	37	88	162	98	37
ML Average	89	22	94	177	115	41

Through The Outfielders

	LF Line	Front of LF	LF Gap	Front of CF	RF Gap	Front of RF	RF Line
vs Nationals	38	104	169	87	161	126	54
vs Opponents	38	73	157	85	156	130	43
ML Average	52	106	149	89	144	109	49

Over the Outfielders

	LF Wall	Over LF	Over CF	RF Wall	Over RF	Gone
vs Nationals	3	20	21	5	11	140
vs Opponents	4	23	26	5	13	117
ML Average	10	14	20	9	10	167

The Nationals outperformed their opponents by at least 5 hits in the following places:
   Hits down First Base Line (21 to 37)
   Hits over the Center Fielder (21 to 26)

They were outperformed by 5 or more hits in the following places:
   Infield Hits (86 to 75)
   Hits Up the Middle (184 to 162)
   Hits between Shortstop and Third (105 to 98)
   Hits in front of the Left Fielder (104 to 73)
   Hits in the Left Field Gap (169 to 157)
   Hits in the Right Field Gap (161 to 156)
   Hits down Right Field Line (54 to 43)
   Home Runs (140 to 117)

Where Hits Landed Against the Washington Nationals
2005 - Home and Road

Look for patterns of red and blue. A box outlined in red means the team allowed significantly more hits than the Major League average. The blue outline means the team allowed significantly fewer hits than average.

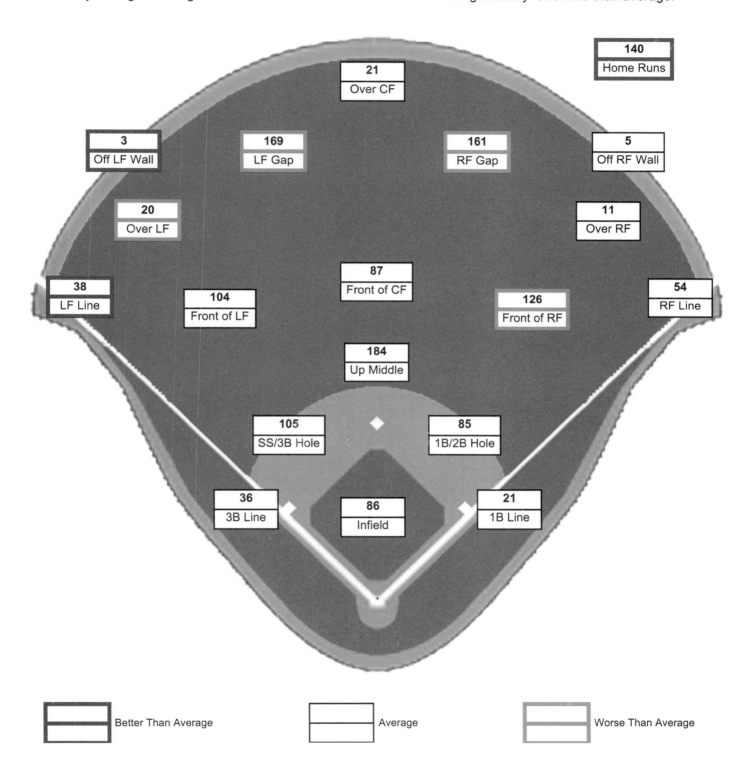

Three-Year Register

A few pages ago, I wrote an introduction to the one-year fielding registers. Now we have the Three-Year Register. If you want to know what we have here, just go back and read the other essay three times. ;-)

Multi-year records are an essential part of building a true and deep understanding of data. Multi-year data gives you a feel for the extent to which data is shaped by flukes, by park effects, and by talent. Derek Lowe moved from Boston to Los Angeles a year ago, and his won-lost record was worse but his ERA dropped by almost two runs. Nobody was at all surprised by this, because everybody pretty much knows that you're likely to post a better ERA in Los Angeles than you are in Boston, but you're likely to win more games with Boston. Same thing here; if a player plays in Houston one year and Detroit the next and has the same statistics in both parks, you tend to figure it's him, and if he has totally different statistics one place than he does the other, you tend to figure it's the park or the team context or something.

Eric Milton had a .700 winning percentage in 2004 (14-6), but .348 in 2005 (8-15). Glendon Rusch had a .077 winning percentage (1-12) in 2003, but a .750 winning percentage the next year (6-2). Nobody was too surprised at this, because everybody knows that winning percentages are pretty flukey, and guys like Glendon Rusch don't have .750 winning percentages every year. On the other hand, Eric Milton allowed 43 homers in 2004, leading the National League, and 40 again in 2005, leading the majors. Again, nobody was too surprised by this, because pitchers who allow home runs tend to continue allowing home runs. Every man is entitled to his hobby.

Same thing here; some numbers are stable; some are kind of flukey and we take them with a grain of salt. Except that we don't, yet, because we don't really understand fielding that well. . .we don't understand it well enough to make intuitive adjustments. That's the point of multi-year records, sort of. . .to build up the reader's intuitive understanding of the data.

We are trying to use the data to create a portrait of each fielder, so that you can truly "see" his fielding skills the way you can see his pitching skills or his hitting skills. We did multi-year records only for the regular players, and only for the last three years. We did only the regular players because we don't like printing charts full of zeroes, and we did only the last three years because we only have perfect data for the last three years. Thanks.

First Basemen

Lance Berkman

Year	Team	G	GS	Inn	PO	A	E	DP	Pct	Opps	Score	Grade	Rank	Expected GB Outs	GB Outs Made	To His Right	Straight On	To His Left	GB	Air	Total	Enhanced	Rank
2004	Hou	4	0	4.0	5	1	0	2	1.000				-	1	1	0			0				-
2005	Hou	96	84	737.2	772	49	5	77	.994	11	.714	A-	3	105	99	-1	-2	-3	-6	-1	-7	-7	29
		100	84	741.2	777	50	5	79	.994	11	.714	A-	-	106	100	-1	-2	-3	-6	-1	-7	-7	-

Ben Broussard

Year	Team	G	GS	Inn	PO	A	E	DP	Pct	Opps	Score	Grade	Rank	Expected GB Outs	GB Outs Made	To His Right	Straight On	To His Left	GB	Air	Total	Enhanced	Rank
2003	Cle	114	101	925.0	957	63	9	87	.991	26	.600	B-	17	126	121	-2	0	-3	-5	+1	-4	-7	26
2004	Cle	133	107	1019.1	991	77	6	106	.994	6	.617	B-	10	133	138	-1	+9	-3	+5	0	+5	+3	15
2005	Cle	138	112	1050.2	1082	60	9	112	.992	11	.482	D+	31	137	138	-2	+2	+1	+1	-1	0	+1	19
		385	320	2995.0	3030	200	24	305	.993	43	.572	C+	19	396	397	-5	+11	-5	+1	0	+1	-3	18

Sean Casey

Year	Team	G	GS	Inn	PO	A	E	DP	Pct	Opps	Score	Grade	Rank	Expected GB Outs	GB Outs Made	To His Right	Straight On	To His Left	GB	Air	Total	Enhanced	Rank
2003	Cin	144	144	1251.2	1257	75	6	115	.996	19	.674	B+	7	165	169	0	0	+4	+4	-1	+3	+3	12
2004	Cin	145	142	1245.2	1233	56	8	86	.994	23	.487	D+	28	149	149	-1	-3	+4	0	+2	+2	+5	12
2005	Cin	134	132	1138.2	1153	55	2	91	.998	29	.614	B-	11	160	153	-2	-6	+1	-7	-1	-8	-6	27
		423	418	3636.0	3643	186	16	292	.996	71	.589	C+	13	474	471	-3	-9	+9	-3	0	-3	+2	12

Hee Seop Choi

Year	Team	G	GS	Inn	PO	A	E	DP	Pct	Opps	Score	Grade	Rank	Expected GB Outs	GB Outs Made	To His Right	Straight On	To His Left	GB	Air	Total	Enhanced	Rank
2003	ChC	69	55	504.2	523	40	5	46	.991	8	.650	B	11	67	69	-1	+3	0	+2	+1	+3	+3	13
2004	2 tms	112	98	867.2	881	51	9	78	.990	16	.653	B	5	100	92	0	-6	-2	-8	-1	-9	-10	29
2005	LAD	83	78	664.2	698	62	2	59	.997	12	.546	C	17	117	121	+1	+1	+2	+4	-2	+2	+2	17
		264	231	2037.0	2102	153	16	183	.993	36	.617	B-	7	284	282	0	-2	0	-2	-2	-4	-5	20

Tony Clark

Year	Team	G	GS	Inn	PO	A	E	DP	Pct	Opps	Score	Grade	Rank	Expected GB Outs	GB Outs Made	To His Right	Straight On	To His Left	GB	Air	Total	Enhanced	Rank
2003	NYM	80	50	499.2	465	25	4	44	.992	12	.550	C	-	54	45	-2	-5	-2	-9	-3	-12	-13	-
2004	NYY	99	64	623.2	602	49	4	64	.994	3	.600	B-	14	97	93	-8	+5	-1	-4	+1	-3	-4	24
2005	Ari	83	70	642.2	663	45	2	59	.997	7	.500	C-	27	77	77	-5	+6	0	0	+1	+1	+4	13
		262	184	1766.0	1730	119	10	167	.995	22	.541	C	23	228	215	-15	+6	-3	-13	-1	-14	-13	27

Carlos Delgado

Year	Team	G	GS	Inn	PO	A	E	DP	Pct	Opps	Score	Grade	Rank	Expected GB Outs	GB Outs Made	To His Right	Straight On	To His Left	GB	Air	Total	Enhanced	Rank
2003	Tor	147	147	1278.0	1355	103	10	136	.993	10	.470	D	31	219	214	-5	+8	-8	-5	-1	-6	-8	28
2004	Tor	120	120	1038.2	1041	89	5	97	.996	9	.489	D+	26	180	185	+5	-3	+3	+5	0	+5	+9	2
2005	Fla	141	140	1206.0	1147	83	14	132	.989	25	.506	C-	25	179	161	-5	-5	-8	-18	0	-18	-23	34
		408	407	3522.2	3543	275	29	365	.992	44	.494	D+	30	578	560	-5	0	-13	-18	-1	-19	-22	31

Darin Erstad

Year	Team	G	GS	Inn	PO	A	E	DP	Pct	Opps	Score	Grade	Rank	Expected GB Outs	GB Outs Made	To His Right	Straight On	To His Left	GB	Air	Total	Enhanced	Rank
2004	Ana	124	124	1065.1	986	65	4	82	.996	10	.505	C-	25	152	161	+6	+2	+1	+9	0	+9	+9	3
2005	LAA	147	144	1279.1	1218	79	4	109	.997	20	.505	C-	26	182	193	+8	0	+2	+11	0	+11	+12	4
		271	268	2344.2	2204	144	8	191	.997	30	.505	C-	28	334	354	+14	+2	+3	+20	0	+20	+21	5

Jason Giambi

Year	Team	G	GS	Inn	PO	A	E	DP	Pct	Opps	Score	Grade	Rank	Expected GB Outs	GB Outs Made	To His Right	Straight On	To His Left	GB	Air	Total	Enhanced	Rank
2003	NYY	85	85	742.2	747	19	4	62	.995	5	.690	A-	5	99	93	0	-8	+2	-6	0	-6	-6	24
2004	NYY	47	47	375.0	372	14	4	30	.990	6	.617	B-	-	49	48	-2	+3	-2	-1	0	-1	-1	-
2005	NYY	78	77	559.2	580	19	7	50	.988	7	.614	B-	10	69	61	-7	-3	+2	-8	0	-8	-8	30
		210	209	1677.1	1699	52	15	142	.992	18	.636	B	5	217	202	-9	-8	+2	-15	0	-15	-15	29

First Basemen

Todd Helton

Year Team	G	GS	Inn	PO	A	E	DP	Pct	Opps	Score	Grade	Rank	Expected GB Outs	GB Outs Made	To His Right	Straight On	To His Left	GB	Air	Total	Enhanced	Rank
2003 Col	159	159	1369.0	1419	156	11	152	.993	30	.652	B	10	223	219	+1	-3	-2	-4	-5	-9	-11	31
2004 Col	153	151	1320.2	1356	143	4	131	.997	39	.640	B	7	182	191	+10	+1	-2	+9	0	+9	+11	1
2005 Col	144	142	1229.2	1236	118	5	136	.996	21	.602	B-	13	200	199	-3	+2	0	-1	+1	0	-1	21
	456	452	3919.1	4011	417	20	419	.996	90	.635	B	6	605	609	+8	0	-4	+4	-4	0	-1	15

Shea Hillenbrand

Year Team	G	GS	Inn	PO	A	E	DP	Pct	Opps	Score	Grade	Rank	Expected GB Outs	GB Outs Made	To His Right	Straight On	To His Left	GB	Air	Total	Enhanced	Rank
2003 2 tms	84	69	624.2	633	40	5	46	.993	13	.496	D+	24	90	84	+1	-5	-2	-6	0	-6	-7	27
2004 Ari	131	129	1113.2	1126	72	13	103	.989	21	.607	B-	13	149	143	-4	-1	-1	-6	0	-6	-7	26
2005 Tor	67	65	587.1	627	48	6	69	.991	5	.540	C	19	95	95	-4	+1	+3	0	-1	-1	0	20
	282	263	2325.2	2386	160	24	218	.991	39	.562	C+	21	334	322	-7	-5	0	-12	-1	-13	-14	28

Eric Hinske

Year Team	G	GS	Inn	PO	A	E	DP	Pct	Opps	Score	Grade	Rank	Expected GB Outs	GB Outs Made	To His Right	Straight On	To His Left	GB	Air	Total	Enhanced	Rank
2005 Tor	100	97	859.2	868	69	7	77	.993	4	.700	A-	4	145	144	-4	+1	+2	-1	-2	-3	-1	22

Ryan Howard

Year Team	G	GS	Inn	PO	A	E	DP	Pct	Opps	Score	Grade	Rank	Expected GB Outs	GB Outs Made	To His Right	Straight On	To His Left	GB	Air	Total	Enhanced	Rank
2004 Phi	8	5	60.2	59	6	0	9	1.000				-	5	7	+1	+1	0	+2	0	+2	+2	-
2005 Phi	84	79	706.1	707	40	5	53	.993	7	.500	C-	27	82	101	+15	+6	-2	+19	0	+19	+16	2
	92	84	767.0	766	46	5	62	.994	7	.500	C-		87	108	+16	+7	-2	+21	0	+21	+18	-

Dan Johnson

Year Team	G	GS	Inn	PO	A	E	DP	Pct	Opps	Score	Grade	Rank	Expected GB Outs	GB Outs Made	To His Right	Straight On	To His Left	GB	Air	Total	Enhanced	Rank
2005 Oak	101	98	883.2	898	57	6	94	.994	6	.483	D+	30	116	116	-1	+1	0	0	+1	+1	+2	18

Nick Johnson

Year Team	G	GS	Inn	PO	A	E	DP	Pct	Opps	Score	Grade	Rank	Expected GB Outs	GB Outs Made	To His Right	Straight On	To His Left	GB	Air	Total	Enhanced	Rank
2003 NYY	60	60	529.0	512	34	5	45	.991	8	.475	D+	30	71	67	0	0	-4	-4	+1	-3	-6	25
2004 Mon	73	70	610.0	618	43	4	69	.994	5	.460	D	32	75	76	-1	+1	+2	+1	+1	+2	+2	16
2005 Was	129	126	1098.2	1017	95	5	109	.996	22	.650	B	9	170	175	+4	-2	+3	+5	+1	+6	+6	10
	262	256	2237.2	2147	172	14	223	.994	35	.583	C+	16	316	318	+3	-1	+1	+2	+3	+5	+2	13

Paul Konerko

Year Team	G	GS	Inn	PO	A	E	DP	Pct	Opps	Score	Grade	Rank	Expected GB Outs	GB Outs Made	To His Right	Straight On	To His Left	GB	Air	Total	Enhanced	Rank
2003 CWS	119	105	938.2	890	79	2	109	.998	17	.615	B-	14	147	145	-1	-3	+2	-2	+2	0	+4	11
2004 CWS	139	137	1177.2	1151	78	6	135	.995	18	.536	C	23	141	130	-8	-6	+3	-11	-2	-13	-12	32
2005 CWS	146	145	1272.2	1320	82	5	135	.996	19	.574	C+	14	173	172	-1	-1	+1	-1	-1	-2	-2	23
	404	387	3389.0	3361	239	13	379	.996	54	.574	C+	18	461	447	-10	-10	+6	-14	-1	-15	-10	22

Adam LaRoche

Year Team	G	GS	Inn	PO	A	E	DP	Pct	Opps	Score	Grade	Rank	Expected GB Outs	GB Outs Made	To His Right	Straight On	To His Left	GB	Air	Total	Enhanced	Rank
2004 Atl	98	82	720.0	739	40	5	86	.994	9	.528	C-	24	86	87	+2	-2	+1	+1	0	+1	+1	17
2005 Atl	125	117	1019.1	1070	77	7	105	.994	14	.532	C	21	175	157	0	-15	-3	-18	0	-18	-17	33
	223	199	1739.1	1809	117	12	191	.994	23	.530	C	24	261	244	+2	-17	-2	-17	0	-17	-16	30

Derrek Lee

Year Team	G	GS	Inn	PO	A	E	DP	Pct	Opps	Score	Grade	Rank	Expected GB Outs	GB Outs Made	To His Right	Straight On	To His Left	GB	Air	Total	Enhanced	Rank
2003 Fla	155	153	1353.2	1279	98	5	144	.996	22	.609	B-	16	165	150	-4	-8	-3	-15	+2	-13	-13	34
2004 ChC	161	159	1432.0	1259	128	6	112	.996	32	.628	B-	8	188	185	0	-4	+1	-3	0	-3	-2	21
2005 ChC	158	158	1386.0	1323	122	6	118	.996	29	.681	B+	6	177	175	0	-7	+6	-2	+2	0	+2	15
	474	470	4171.2	3861	348	17	374	.996	83	.642	B	2	530	510	-4	-19	+4	-20	+4	-16	-13	24

First Basemen

Travis Lee

		BASIC								BUNTS				PLAYS		PLUS/MINUS							
Year	Team	G	GS	Inn	PO	A	E	DP	Pct	Opps	Score	Grade	Rank	Expected GB Outs	GB Outs Made	To His Right	Straight On	To His Left	GB	Air	Total	Enhanced	Rank
2003	TB	142	141	1244.1	1223	100	3	123	.998	13	.700	A-	4	185	195	0	+8	+2	+10	0	+10	+12	5
2004	NYY	6	4	42.0	44	4	0	2	1.000					7	9	+1	0	+1	+2	0	+2	+2	
2005	TB	124	101	918.1	874	67	4	87	.996	9	.489	D+	29	135	131	+1	-4	-1	-4	-1	-5	-5	26
		272	246	2204.2	2141	171	7	212	.997	22	.614	B-	8	327	335	+2	+4	+2	+8	-1	+7	+9	10

Tino Martinez

		BASIC								BUNTS				PLAYS		PLUS/MINUS							
Year	Team	G	GS	Inn	PO	A	E	DP	Pct	Opps	Score	Grade	Rank	Expected GB Outs	GB Outs Made	To His Right	Straight On	To His Left	GB	Air	Total	Enhanced	Rank
2003	StL	126	126	1065.0	1026	85	3	91	.997	18	.586	C+	18	136	135	0	0	-1	-1	0	-1	0	17
2004	TB	114	110	959.2	876	67	3	85	.997	6	.367	F	33	138	142	-1	+1	+5	+4	-1	+3	+6	9
2005	NYY	122	78	770.1	797	49	8	73	.991	4	.613	B-	12	115	125	+7	+7	-4	+10	+1	+11	+9	8
		362	314	2795.0	2699	201	14	249	.995	28	.543	C	22	389	402	+6	+8	0	+13	0	+13	+15	7

Doug Mientkiewicz

		BASIC								BUNTS				PLAYS		PLUS/MINUS							
Year	Team	G	GS	Inn	PO	A	E	DP	Pct	Opps	Score	Grade	Rank	Expected GB Outs	GB Outs Made	To His Right	Straight On	To His Left	GB	Air	Total	Enhanced	Rank
2003	Min	139	133	1159.1	1091	68	4	86	.997	10	.610	B-	15	144	160	+4	+7	+5	+16	+1	+17	+17	2
2004	2 tms	125	100	940.2	923	62	5	77	.995	13	.646	B	6	137	140	-3	+4	+2	+3	+1	+4	+6	10
2005	NYM	83	79	675.0	690	42	4	59	.995	16	.656	B	7	80	89	+5	+3	+1	+9	0	+9	+9	9
		347	312	2775.0	2704	172	13	222	.996	39	.641	B	3	361	389	+6	+14	+8	+28	+2	+30	+32	2

Kevin Millar

		BASIC								BUNTS				PLAYS		PLUS/MINUS							
Year	Team	G	GS	Inn	PO	A	E	DP	Pct	Opps	Score	Grade	Rank	Expected GB Outs	GB Outs Made	To His Right	Straight On	To His Left	GB	Air	Total	Enhanced	Rank
2003	Bos	101	96	853.0	858	81	4	82	.996	14	.482	D+	29	153	149	-1	-8	+5	-4	+2	-2	+1	16
2004	Bos	69	66	512.0	466	57	6	45	.989	4	.800	A+	1	79	86	+3	+3	+2	+7	0	+7	+8	5
2005	Bos	110	102	796.1	799	85	7	67	.992	8	.475	D+	32	153	154	-2	+3	+1	+1	+1	+2	+5	11
		280	264	2161.1	2123	223	17	194	.993	26	.529	C-	25	385	389	0	-2	+8	+4	+3	+7	+14	8

Justin Morneau

		BASIC								BUNTS				PLAYS		PLUS/MINUS							
Year	Team	G	GS	Inn	PO	A	E	DP	Pct	Opps	Score	Grade	Rank	Expected GB Outs	GB Outs Made	To His Right	Straight On	To His Left	GB	Air	Total	Enhanced	Rank
2003	Min	7	2	34.2	29	4	1	1	.971	1	1.000	A+	-	8	6	-1	-1	0	-2	0	-2	-3	-
2004	Min	61	61	538.1	523	41	3	54	.995	5	.320	F	34	68	66	-2	+1	-2	-2	-1	-3	-3	22
2005	Min	138	128	1166.1	1191	91	8	123	.994	12	.742	A	1	151	162	-2	+7	+6	+11	0	+11	+13	3
		206	191	1739.1	1743	136	12	178	.994	18	.639	B	4	227	234	-5	+7	+4	+7	-1	+6	+7	11

Phil Nevin

		BASIC								BUNTS				PLAYS		PLUS/MINUS							
Year	Team	G	GS	Inn	PO	A	E	DP	Pct	Opps	Score	Grade	Rank	Expected GB Outs	GB Outs Made	To His Right	Straight On	To His Left	GB	Air	Total	Enhanced	Rank
2003	SD	31	30	261.0	238	21	1	25	.996	5	.620	B-	-	45	45	+1	-1	0	0	0	0	0	-
2004	SD	144	142	1207.1	1131	91	13	108	.989	30	.488	D+	27	165	163	+1	-4	+1	-2	+1	-1	-1	20
2005	2 tms	74	71	620.0	592	38	4	52	.994	12	.550	C	16	100	98	+2	-3	-1	-2	0	-2	-3	25
		249	243	2088.1	1961	150	18	185	.992	47	.518	C-	27	310	306	+4	-8	0	-4	+1	-3	-4	19

Lance Niekro

		BASIC								BUNTS				PLAYS		PLUS/MINUS							
Year	Team	G	GS	Inn	PO	A	E	DP	Pct	Opps	Score	Grade	Rank	Expected GB Outs	GB Outs Made	To His Right	Straight On	To His Left	GB	Air	Total	Enhanced	Rank
2003	SF	3	0	7.0	4	0	0	1	1.000														-
2005	SF	74	57	529.0	543	38	5	56	.991	4	.438	D-	33	75	85	+6	+4	+1	+10	-1	+9	+10	7
		77	57	536.0	547	38	5	57	.992	4	.438	D-		75	85	+6	+4	+1	+10	-1	+9	+10	-

Lyle Overbay

		BASIC								BUNTS				PLAYS		PLUS/MINUS							
Year	Team	G	GS	Inn	PO	A	E	DP	Pct	Opps	Score	Grade	Rank	Expected GB Outs	GB Outs Made	To His Right	Straight On	To His Left	GB	Air	Total	Enhanced	Rank
2003	Ari	75	69	604.0	643	58	2	51	.997	10	.675	B+	6	118	126	0	+4	+4	+8	-1	+7	+9	6
2004	Mil	158	150	1360.1	1311	113	11	109	.992	25	.628	B-	9	171	162	+2	-2	-9	-9	0	-9	-14	33
2005	Mil	154	143	1265.0	1134	96	10	104	.992	26	.513	C-	23	152	157	+2	+6	-3	+5	0	+5	+4	12
		387	362	3229.1	3088	267	23	264	.993	61	.587	C+	14	441	445	+4	+8	-8	+4	-1	+3	-1	16

First Basemen

Rafael Palmeiro

		BASIC								BUNTS				PLAYS		PLUS/MINUS							
Year	Team	G	GS	Inn	PO	A	E	DP	Pct	Opps	Score	Grade	Rank	Expected GB Outs	GB Outs Made	To His Right	Straight On	To His Left	GB	Air	Total	Enhanced	Rank
2003	Tex	55	55	462.0	445	49	2	57	.996	2	.425	D-	-	66	79	+6	+6	+1	+13	+1	+14	+15	-
2004	Bal	130	128	1137.2	1089	94	8	114	.993	8	.700	A-	3	171	156	-7	-3	-5	-15	0	-15	-16	34
2005	Bal	93	82	748.1	748	58	4	68	.995	4	.525	C-	22	107	96	-5	-6	0	-11	-1	-12	-12	31
		278	265	2348.2	2282	201	14	239	.994	14	.611	B-	10	344	331	-6	-3	-4	-13	0	-13	-13	26

Albert Pujols

		BASIC								BUNTS				PLAYS		PLUS/MINUS							
Year	Team	G	GS	Inn	PO	A	E	DP	Pct	Opps	Score	Grade	Rank	Expected GB Outs	GB Outs Made	To His Right	Straight On	To His Left	GB	Air	Total	Enhanced	Rank
2003	StL	62	36	369.2	340	33	1	36	.997	3	.483	D+	-	50	55	+3	-1	+3	+5	+1	+6	+7	-
2004	StL	150	150	1338.2	1458	114	10	135	.994	13	.612	B-	11	221	227	-1	+1	+6	+6	-1	+5	+8	4
2005	StL	158	155	1358.2	1596	97	14	175	.992	14	.718	A-	2	223	232	+6	0	+3	+9	0	+9	+10	6
		370	341	3067.0	3394	244	25	346	.993	30	.648	B	1	494	514	+8	0	+12	+20	0	+20	+25	3

Richie Sexson

		BASIC								BUNTS				PLAYS		PLUS/MINUS							
Year	Team	G	GS	Inn	PO	A	E	DP	Pct	Opps	Score	Grade	Rank	Expected GB Outs	GB Outs Made	To His Right	Straight On	To His Left	GB	Air	Total	Enhanced	Rank
2003	Mil	162	162	1452.0	1363	130	11	134	.993	35	.506	C-	22	172	165	+4	-3	-8	-7	+3	-4	-11	32
2004	Ari	23	23	204.1	198	26	1	19	.996	7	.607	B-	2	31	33	0	+3	-2	+2	0	+2	-2	-
2005	Sea	151	151	1302.0	1147	119	7	121	.995	19	.534	C	20	200	187	-11	+7	-9	-13	0	-13	-15	32
		336	336	2958.1	2708	275	19	274	.994	61	.526	C-	26	403	385	-7	+7	-19	-18	+3	-15	-28	32

Chris Shelton

		BASIC								BUNTS				PLAYS		PLUS/MINUS							
Year	Team	G	GS	Inn	PO	A	E	DP	Pct	Opps	Score	Grade	Rank	Expected GB Outs	GB Outs Made	To His Right	Straight On	To His Left	GB	Air	Total	Enhanced	Rank
2004	Det	8	2	26.0	22	4	0	3	1.000				-	5	5	-1	0	0	0	0	0	0	-
2005	Det	84	83	738.1	778	60	6	88	.993	6	.683	B+	5	111	106	-3	-3	+1	-5	+1	-4	-2	24
		92	85	764.1	800	64	6	91	.993	6	.683	B+	-	116	111	-4	-3	+1	-5	+1	-4	-2	-

J.T. Snow

		BASIC								BUNTS				PLAYS		PLUS/MINUS							
Year	Team	G	GS	Inn	PO	A	E	DP	Pct	Opps	Score	Grade	Rank	Expected GB Outs	GB Outs Made	To His Right	Straight On	To His Left	GB	Air	Total	Enhanced	Rank
2003	SF	98	94	812.1	814	74	5	81	.994	17	.671	B+	8	102	111	+4	+5	0	+9	-1	+8	+9	7
2004	SF	100	88	793.0	801	56	4	69	.995	11	.477	D+	30	99	103	+4	+3	-2	+4	0	+4	0	18
2005	SF	108	96	825.2	813	56	3	62	.997	15	.540	C	18	121	122	-1	-1	+3	+1	0	+1	+2	16
		306	278	2431.0	2428	186	12	212	.995	43	.576	C+	17	322	336	+7	+7	+1	+14	-1	+13	+11	9

Matt Stairs

		BASIC								BUNTS				PLAYS		PLUS/MINUS							
Year	Team	G	GS	Inn	PO	A	E	DP	Pct	Opps	Score	Grade	Rank	Expected GB Outs	GB Outs Made	To His Right	Straight On	To His Left	GB	Air	Total	Enhanced	Rank
2003	A	31	27	214.0	212	10	2	16	.991	3	.733	A	-	23	18	-1	-3	-2	-5	0	-5	-6	-
2004	KC	30	25	229.0	207	11	3	25	.986	4	.338	F	-	23	18	-3	-3	+1	-5	0	-5	-4	-
2005	KC	64	61	509.2	500	37	4	60	.993	4	.513	C-	24	81	77	-5	-1	+1	-4	-1	-5	-6	28
		125	113	952.2	919	58	9	101	.991	11	.509	C-	-	127	113	-9	-7	0	-14	-1	-15	-16	-

Mark Teixeira

		BASIC								BUNTS				PLAYS		PLUS/MINUS							
Year	Team	G	GS	Inn	PO	A	E	DP	Pct	Opps	Score	Grade	Rank	Expected GB Outs	GB Outs Made	To His Right	Straight On	To His Left	GB	Air	Total	Enhanced	Rank
2003	Tex	116	104	932.2	931	71	4	99	.996	17	.397	F	34	120	149	+11	+16	+2	+29	+2	+31	+29	1
2004	Tex	142	138	1223.1	1210	98	10	114	.992	15	.487	D+	29	220	224	0	-1	+5	+4	-1	+3	+7	6
2005	Tex	155	154	1358.0	1378	101	3	127	.998	16	.569	C+	15	228	241	+8	+2	+3	+13	+1	+14	+17	1
		413	396	3514.0	3519	270	17	340	.996	48	.482	D+	31	568	614	+19	+17	+10	+46	+2	+48	+53	1

Jim Thome

		BASIC								BUNTS				PLAYS		PLUS/MINUS							
Year	Team	G	GS	Inn	PO	A	E	DP	Pct	Opps	Score	Grade	Rank	Expected GB Outs	GB Outs Made	To His Right	Straight On	To His Left	GB	Air	Total	Enhanced	Rank
2003	Phi	156	155	1361.2	1372	86	5	135	.997	27	.628	B-	13	184	172	-1	-8	-3	-12	-1	-13	-12	33
2004	Phi	134	134	1179.2	1090	84	7	103	.994	16	.566	C+	18	142	148	+12	+3	-9	+6	-4	+2	-5	25
2005	Phi	52	52	436.0	404	30	0	36	1.000	8	.481	D+	-	51	55	+3	+2	-1	+4	-1	+3	+4	-
		342	341	2977.1	2866	200	12	274	.996	51	.585	C+	15	377	375	+14	-3	-13	-2	-6	-8	-13	25

First Basemen

Chad Tracy

Year	Team	G	GS	Inn	PO	A	E	DP	Pct	Opps	Score	Grade	Rank	Expected GB Outs	GB Outs Made	To His Right	Straight On	To His Left	GB	Air	Total	Enhanced	Rank
						BASIC					**BUNTS**			**PLAYS**						**PLUS/MINUS**			
2004	Ari	11	2	33.0	29	3	1	2	.970	1	.600	B-	-	4	5	-1	+2	0	+1	0	+1	+1	-
2005	Ari	80	72	652.2	706	47	3	75	.996	9	.656	B	8	88	97	+3	+5	0	+9	+2	+11	+11	5
		91	74	685.2	735	50	4	77	.995	10	.650	B	-	92	102	+2	+7	0	+10	+2	+12	+12	-

Daryle Ward

Year	Team	G	GS	Inn	PO	A	E	DP	Pct	Opps	Score	Grade	Rank	Expected GB Outs	GB Outs Made	To His Right	Straight On	To His Left	GB	Air	Total	Enhanced	Rank
						BASIC					**BUNTS**			**PLAYS**						**PLUS/MINUS**			
2003	LA	13	11	95.1	108	10	1	14	.992	2	.425	D-	-	16	14	+1	-1	-1	-2	0	-2	-2	-
2004	Pit	71	63	559.0	547	34	5	73	.991	10	.460	D	31	63	60	-3	+1	-1	-3	0	-3	-3	23
2005	Pit	109	101	891.2	863	76	6	114	.994	13	.412	D-	34	113	115	-2	+5	-2	+2	0	+2	+3	14
		193	175	1546.0	1518	120	12	201	.993	25	.432	D-	32	192	189	-4	+5	-4	-3	0	-3	-2	17

Second Basemen

Rich Aurilia

Year	Team	G	GS	Inn	PO	A	E	DP	Pct	Rng	Rel Rng	Rel +/-	GDP Opps	GDP	Pct	Rank	Exp Outs GB	Air	Outs Made GB	Air	To His Right	Straight On	To His Left	GB	Air	Total	Rank
2004	2 tms	7	1	25.0	6	9	1	3	.938	5.40	1.123	+2	4	3	.750	-	7	2	5	2				-2	0	-2	-
2005	Cin	68	64	547.1	128	175	6	38	.981	4.98	1.000	0	74	38	.514	17	143	58	147	53	+1	+3	0	+4	-5	-1	17
		75	65	572.1	134	184	7	41	.978	5.00	1.006	+2	78	41	.526	-	150	60	152	55	+1	+3	0	+2	-5	-3	-

Mark Bellhorn

Year	Team	G	GS	Inn	PO	A	E	DP	Pct	Rng	Rel Rng	Rel +/-	GDP Opps	GDP	Pct	Rank	Exp Outs GB	Air	Outs Made GB	Air	To His Right	Straight On	To His Left	GB	Air	Total	Rank
2003	2 tms	12	12	118.1	31	41	2	6	.973	5.48	.950	-4	14	6	.429	-	34	11	35	13	0	0	+2	+1	+2	+3	-
2004	Bos	124	118	1044.2	189	348	11	61	.980	4.63	.942	-34	117	56	.479	21	298	68	298	67	-5	-4	+9	0	-1	-1	18
2005	2 tms	85	84	728.0	152	264	7	56	.983	5.14	1.029	+8	102	55	.539	11	232	62	227	65	-5	+2	-2	-5	+3	-2	18
		229	214	1891.0	372	653	20	123	.981	4.88	.977	-30	233	117	.502	14	564	141	560	145	-10	-2	+9	-4	+4	0	17

Ronnie Belliard

Year	Team	G	GS	Inn	PO	A	E	DP	Pct	Rng	Rel Rng	Rel +/-	GDP Opps	GDP	Pct	Rank	Exp Outs GB	Air	Outs Made GB	Air	To His Right	Straight On	To His Left	GB	Air	Total	Rank
2003	Col	113	105	909.1	224	311	15	78	.973	5.30	.919	-46	143	72	.503	18	261	65	257	66	+8	-3	-9	-4	+1	-3	20
2004	Cle	151	148	1320.2	278	426	14	87	.981	4.80	.975	-18	144	72	.500	17	335	108	340	104	+15	-1	-10	+5	-4	+1	12
2005	Cle	141	139	1243.2	259	413	13	95	.981	4.86	1.028	+19	146	86	.589	5	338	105	353	110	+23	-2	-6	+15	+5	+20	4
		405	392	3473.2	761	1150	42	260	.978	4.95	.979	-45	433	230	.531	7	934	278	950	280	+46	-6	-25	+16	+2	+18	10

Craig Biggio

Year	Team	G	GS	Inn	PO	A	E	DP	Pct	Rng	Rel Rng	Rel +/-	GDP Opps	GDP	Pct	Rank	Exp Outs GB	Air	Outs Made GB	Air	To His Right	Straight On	To His Left	GB	Air	Total	Rank
2005	Hou	141	141	1172.1	249	395	16	81	.976	4.94	1.028	+18	152	73	.480	24	340	94	327	93	-10	-1	-3	-13	-1	-14	33

Bret Boone

Year	Team	G	GS	Inn	PO	A	E	DP	Pct	Rng	Rel Rng	Rel +/-	GDP Opps	GDP	Pct	Rank	Exp Outs GB	Air	Outs Made GB	Air	To His Right	Straight On	To His Left	GB	Air	Total	Rank
2003	Sea	159	159	1375.0	268	426	7	106	.990	4.54	1.044	+30	177	100	.565	4	367	92	358	92	-9	0	0	-9	0	-9	23
2004	Sea	148	148	1308.2	280	349	14	90	.978	4.33	.956	-29	148	81	.547	3	308	123	287	124	-17	+4	-8	-21	+1	-20	33
2005	2 tms	88	88	768.2	170	229	9	54	.978	4.67	.968	-15	103	50	.485	21	220	72	197	70	-18	-5	0	-23	-2	-25	35
		395	395	3452.1	718	1004	30	250	.983	4.49	.995	-14	428	231	.540	5	895	287	842	286	-44	-1	-8	-53	-1	-54	25

Miguel Cairo

Year	Team	G	GS	Inn	PO	A	E	DP	Pct	Rng	Rel Rng	Rel +/-	GDP Opps	GDP	Pct	Rank	Exp Outs GB	Air	Outs Made GB	Air	To His Right	Straight On	To His Left	GB	Air	Total	Rank
2003	StL	40	33	294.2	58	88	2	17	.986	4.46	.899	-17	29	17	.586	-	77	28	79	27	0	+1	+1	+2	-1	+1	-
2004	NYY	113	96	856.0	195	274	6	58	.987	4.93	1.001	+1	104	55	.529	8	242	82	220	90	-10	-1	-11	-22	+8	-14	30
2005	NYM	82	74	657.1	151	212	6	58	.984	4.97	1.022	+8	88	50	.568	7	187	63	177	65	-9	0	-1	-10	+2	-8	28
		235	203	1808.0	404	574	14	133	.986	4.87	.994	-8	221	122	.552	3	506	173	476	182	-19	0	-11	-30	+9	-21	21

Robinson Cano

Year	Team	G	GS	Inn	PO	A	E	DP	Pct	Rng	Rel Rng	Rel +/-	GDP Opps	GDP	Pct	Rank	Exp Outs GB	Air	Outs Made GB	Air	To His Right	Straight On	To His Left	GB	Air	Total	Rank
2005	NYY	131	130	1142.0	258	391	17	77	.974	5.11	1.000	0	152	70	.461	29	365	103	332	109	-16	-2	-15	-33	+6	-27	36

Jorge Cantu

Year	Team	G	GS	Inn	PO	A	E	DP	Pct	Rng	Rel Rng	Rel +/-	GDP Opps	GDP	Pct	Rank	Exp Outs GB	Air	Outs Made GB	Air	To His Right	Straight On	To His Left	GB	Air	Total	Rank
2004	TB	33	31	274.0	48	85	5	19	.964	4.37	.906	-14	42	19	.452	-	68	19	63	18	-1	-1	-2	-5	-1	-6	-
2005	TB	80	76	667.2	119	181	9	39	.971	4.04	.851	-51	78	37	.474	26	161	50	152	52	-4	-2	-4	-9	+2	-7	25
		113	107	941.2	167	266	14	58	.969	4.14	.868	-65	120	56	.467	-	229	69	215	70	-5	-3	-6	-14	+1	-13	-

Jose Castillo

Year	Team	G	GS	Inn	PO	A	E	DP	Pct	Rng	Rel Rng	Rel +/-	GDP Opps	GDP	Pct	Rank	Exp Outs GB	Air	Outs Made GB	Air	To His Right	Straight On	To His Left	GB	Air	Total	Rank
2004	Pit	123	105	951.0	230	301	11	81	.980	5.03	.965	-19	146	74	.507	14	216	78	212	76	-2	-2	0	-4	-2	-6	24
2005	Pit	100	99	840.1	237	279	12	92	.977	5.53	1.044	+22	131	82	.626	2	222	84	211	87	-5	-6	+1	-11	+3	-8	27
		223	204	1791.1	467	580	23	173	.979	5.26	1.004	+3	277	156	.563	1	438	162	423	163	-7	-8	+1	-15	+1	-14	19

Second Basemen

Luis Castillo

Year	Team	G	GS	Inn	PO	A	E	DP	Pct	Rng	Rel Rng	Rel +/-	GDP Opps	GDP	Pct	Rank	Exp Outs GB	Air	Outs Made GB	Air	To His Right	Straight On	To His Left	GB	Air	Total	Rank
2003	Fla	152	151	1312.1	286	434	10	99	.986	4.94	1.024	+17	184	94	.511	14	349	112	356	116	+4	+6	-2	+7	+4	+11	7
2004	Fla	148	147	1274.1	275	405	6	97	.991	4.80	1.002	+2	164	86	.524	10	312	103	319	104	+15	0	-8	+7	+1	+8	8
2005	Fla	120	116	1012.1	245	352	7	87	.988	5.31	1.031	+17	172	79	.459	31	283	95	292	95	+20	+3	-14	+9	0	+9	12
		420	414	3599.0	806	1191	23	283	.989	4.99	1.018	+36	520	259	.498	15	944	310	967	315	+39	+9	-24	+23	+5	+28	7

Craig Counsell

Year	Team	G	GS	Inn	PO	A	E	DP	Pct	Rng	Rel Rng	Rel +/-	GDP Opps	GDP	Pct	Rank	Exp Outs GB	Air	Outs Made GB	Air	To His Right	Straight On	To His Left	GB	Air	Total	Rank
2003	Ari	10	7	67.2	9	22	0	4	1.000	4.12	.831	-6	10	4	.400	-	21	4	20	3	0	0	-1	-1	-1	-2	-
2005	Ari	143	140	1244.1	304	458	8	97	.990	5.51	1.037	+27	185	95	.514	16	342	113	369	121	+24	-3	+6	+27	+8	+35	1
		153	147	1312.0	313	480	8	101	.990	5.44	1.029	+21	195	99	.508	-	363	117	389	124	+24	-3	+5	+26	+7	+33	-

Ray Durham

Year	Team	G	GS	Inn	PO	A	E	DP	Pct	Rng	Rel Rng	Rel +/-	GDP Opps	GDP	Pct	Rank	Exp Outs GB	Air	Outs Made GB	Air	To His Right	Straight On	To His Left	GB	Air	Total	Rank
2003	SF	105	101	867.2	185	309	5	65	.990	5.12	1.053	+25	116	60	.517	11	264	67	268	70	-3	+4	+4	+4	+3	+7	10
2004	SF	118	115	990.1	243	314	16	75	.972	5.06	.991	-5	158	64	.405	27	260	77	258	79	-5	-1	+3	-2	+2	0	13
2005	SF	133	131	1143.0	250	341	11	81	.982	4.65	.942	-36	148	66	.446	33	282	100	282	96	-2	-1	+3	0	-4	-4	21
		356	347	3001.0	678	964	32	221	.981	4.92	.992	-16	422	190	.450	22	806	244	808	245	-10	+2	+10	+2	+1	+3	14

Mark Ellis

Year	Team	G	GS	Inn	PO	A	E	DP	Pct	Rng	Rel Rng	Rel +/-	GDP Opps	GDP	Pct	Rank	Exp Outs GB	Air	Outs Made GB	Air	To His Right	Straight On	To His Left	GB	Air	Total	Rank
2003	Oak	153	147	1297.2	324	455	14	94	.982	5.40	1.045	+34	174	87	.500	20	377	135	394	141	-1	+1	+16	+17	+6	+23	2
2005	Oak	115	109	972.0	204	333	6	83	.989	4.97	1.045	+24	134	74	.552	10	265	97	274	99	+2	+1	+9	+9	+2	+11	11
		268	256	2269.2	528	788	20	177	.985	5.22	1.045	+58	308	161	.523	10	642	232	668	240	+1	+2	+21	+26	+8	+34	4

Marcus Giles

Year	Team	G	GS	Inn	PO	A	E	DP	Pct	Rng	Rel Rng	Rel +/-	GDP Opps	GDP	Pct	Rank	Exp Outs GB	Air	Outs Made GB	Air	To His Right	Straight On	To His Left	GB	Air	Total	Rank
2003	Atl	140	137	1213.2	278	471	14	86	.982	5.55	1.026	+19	168	79	.470	27	386	101	412	102	+18	-1	+10	+26	+1	+27	1
2004	Atl	97	94	789.0	186	289	12	69	.975	5.42	1.053	+24	136	66	.485	20	223	50	237	48	+5	+5	+4	+14	-2	+12	7
2005	Atl	149	147	1276.0	266	468	12	96	.984	5.18	.984	-12	190	92	.484	23	398	98	399	96	+12	+1	-12	+1	-2	-1	14
		386	378	3278.2	730	1228	38	251	.981	5.37	1.017	+31	494	237	.480	19	1007	249	1048	246	+35	+5	+2	+41	-3	+38	2

Luis A Gonzalez

Year	Team	G	GS	Inn	PO	A	E	DP	Pct	Rng	Rel Rng	Rel +/-	GDP Opps	GDP	Pct	Rank	Exp Outs GB	Air	Outs Made GB	Air	To His Right	Straight On	To His Left	GB	Air	Total	Rank
2004	Col	40	33	293.0	84	96	1	27	.994	5.53	.983	-3	53	25	.472	-	69	24	67	24	+1	-4	+1	-2	0	-2	-
2005	Col	83	66	579.1	121	196	0	40	1.000	4.92	.930	-23	81	38	.469	28	175	36	174	36	0	+1	-2	-1	0	-1	15
		123	99	872.1	205	292	1	67	.998	5.13	.949	-26	134	63	.470	-	244	60	241	60	+1	-3	-1	-3	0	-3	-

Ruben Gotay

Year	Team	G	GS	Inn	PO	A	E	DP	Pct	Rng	Rel Rng	Rel +/-	GDP Opps	GDP	Pct	Rank	Exp Outs GB	Air	Outs Made GB	Air	To His Right	Straight On	To His Left	GB	Air	Total	Rank
2004	KC	42	41	368.1	78	97	3	30	.983	4.28	.828	-36	38	28	.737	-	69	33	61	34	-1	0	-7	-8	+1	-7	-
2005	KC	81	74	666.0	156	231	8	51	.980	5.23	.984	-6	87	46	.529	14	209	71	200	69	-4	0	-5	-9	-2	-11	31
		123	115	1034.1	234	328	11	81	.981	4.89	.935	-42	125	74	.592	-	278	104	261	103	-5	0	-12	-17	-1	-18	-

Tony Graffanino

Year	Team	G	GS	Inn	PO	A	E	DP	Pct	Rng	Rel Rng	Rel +/-	GDP Opps	GDP	Pct	Rank	Exp Outs GB	Air	Outs Made GB	Air	To His Right	Straight On	To His Left	GB	Air	Total	Rank
2003	CWS	29	22	202.0	53	77	3	22	.977	5.79	1.221	+24	34	20	.588	-	58	19	61	20	+1	+2	0	+3	+1	+4	-
2004	KC	75	72	630.1	185	219	5	69	.988	5.77	1.118	+42	109	62	.569	2	137	68	137	68	0	+2	-3	0	0	0	17
2005	2 tms	73	71	588.0	121	186	4	37	.987	4.70	.926	-27	63	32	.508	19	160	59	157	57	-7	+3	+1	-3	-2	-5	23
		177	165	1420.1	359	482	12	128	.986	5.33	1.065	+39	206	114	.553	-	355	146	355	145	-6	+7	-2	0	-1	-1	-

Second Basemen

Nick Green

Year	Team	G	GS	Inn	PO	A	E	DP	Pct	Rng	Rel Rng	Rel +/-	GDP Opps	GDP	Pct	Rank	Exp GB	Exp Air	Made GB	Made Air	To His Right	Straight On	To His Left	GB	Air	Total	Rank
2004	Atl	75	61	572.0	137	203	8	43	.977	5.35	1.039	+13	99	41	.414	25	167	55	168	53	-1	-1	+4	+1	-2	-1	19
2005	TB	91	83	731.0	141	195	4	45	.988	4.14	.871	-49	76	39	.513	18	168	66	169	68	-2	-2	+5	+1	+2	+3	13
		166	144	1303.0	278	398	12	88	.983	4.67	.956	-36	175	80	.457	-	335	121	337	121	-3	-3	+9	+2	0	+2	-

Mark Grudzielanek

Year	Team	G	GS	Inn	PO	A	E	DP	Pct	Rng	Rel Rng	Rel +/-	GDP Opps	GDP	Pct	Rank	Exp GB	Exp Air	Made GB	Made Air	To His Right	Straight On	To His Left	GB	Air	Total	Rank
2003	ChC	121	115	1011.2	231	331	8	92	.986	5.00	1.020	+11	158	88	.557	5	275	72	274	68	+4	-1	-5	-1	-4	-5	21
2004	ChC	76	61	568.0	136	186	5	30	.985	5.10	1.100	+29	78	28	.359	31	153	55	155	53	-5	+1	+5	+2	-2	0	16
2005	StL	137	132	1158.1	245	442	7	108	.990	5.34	.988	-8	166	104	.627	1	344	67	364	67	+15	+2	+3	+20	0	+20	3
		334	308	2738.0	612	959	20	230	.987	5.16	1.022	+32	402	220	.547	4	772	194	793	188	+14	+2	+3	+21	-6	+15	11

Orlando Hudson

Year	Team	G	GS	Inn	PO	A	E	DP	Pct	Rng	Rel Rng	Rel +/-	GDP Opps	GDP	Pct	Rank	Exp GB	Exp Air	Made GB	Made Air	To His Right	Straight On	To His Left	GB	Air	Total	Rank
2003	Tor	139	129	1146.2	267	477	12	98	.984	5.84	1.096	+64	180	93	.517	12	393	98	410	103	-7	0	+24	+17	+5	+22	3
2004	Tor	133	128	1124.2	275	449	12	90	.984	5.79	1.153	+96	162	79	.488	18	344	107	370	116	+4	+7	+16	+26	+9	+35	1
2005	Tor	130	120	1067.2	302	390	6	80	.991	5.83	1.145	+89	143	77	.538	12	313	154	330	157	-1	+1	+18	+17	+3	+20	5
		402	377	3339.0	844	1316	30	268	.986	5.82	1.131	+249	485	249	.513	12	1050	359	1110	376	-4	+8	+58	+60	+17	+77	1

Tadahito Iguchi

Year	Team	G	GS	Inn	PO	A	E	DP	Pct	Rng	Rel Rng	Rel +/-	GDP Opps	GDP	Pct	Rank	Exp GB	Exp Air	Made GB	Made Air	To His Right	Straight On	To His Left	GB	Air	Total	Rank
2005	CWS	133	129	1171.1	234	375	14	84	.978	4.68	.979	-14	141	79	.560	8	313	103	311	102	-9	+4	+3	-2	-1	-3	20

Omar Infante

Year	Team	G	GS	Inn	PO	A	E	DP	Pct	Rng	Rel Rng	Rel +/-	GDP Opps	GDP	Pct	Rank	Exp GB	Exp Air	Made GB	Made Air	To His Right	Straight On	To His Left	GB	Air	Total	Rank
2003	Det	2	1	13.0	3	3	0	2	1.000	4.15	.757	-2	2	2	1.000	-	2	1	2	1				0	0	0	-
2004	Det	105	97	871.2	204	280	12	73	.976	5.00	.982	-9	124	71	.573	1	204	75	196	74	-6	-5	+3	-8	-1	-9	27
2005	Det	69	65	591.2	153	186	4	51	.988	5.16	.989	-4	88	47	.534	13	156	41	150	40	-5	-2	0	-6	-1	-7	26
		176	163	1476.1	360	469	16	126	.981	5.05	.983	-15	214	120	.561	-	362	117	348	115	-11	-7	+3	-14	-2	-16	-

Adam Kennedy

Year	Team	G	GS	Inn	PO	A	E	DP	Pct	Rng	Rel Rng	Rel +/-	GDP Opps	GDP	Pct	Rank	Exp GB	Exp Air	Made GB	Made Air	To His Right	Straight On	To His Left	GB	Air	Total	Rank
2003	Ana	140	125	1119.2	235	371	6	77	.990	4.87	1.070	+40	131	70	.534	8	311	119	326	119	+6	0	+8	+15	0	+15	6
2004	Ana	144	138	1225.0	255	387	12	71	.982	4.72	1.055	+33	133	62	.466	22	321	110	320	118	+2	0	-3	-1	+8	+7	10
2005	LAA	127	123	1107.2	212	352	5	71	.991	4.58	1.037	+20	110	65	.591	4	284	101	302	99	+11	-1	+8	+18	-2	+16	7
		411	386	3452.1	702	1110	23	219	.987	4.72	1.054	+93	374	197	.527	8	916	330	948	336	+19	-1	+13	+32	+6	+38	3

Jeff Kent

Year	Team	G	GS	Inn	PO	A	E	DP	Pct	Rng	Rel Rng	Rel +/-	GDP Opps	GDP	Pct	Rank	Exp GB	Exp Air	Made GB	Made Air	To His Right	Straight On	To His Left	GB	Air	Total	Rank
2003	Hou	128	127	1113.0	278	354	11	81	.983	5.11	1.026	+16	174	81	.466	29	296	92	291	89	+1	-2	-4	-5	-3	-8	22
2004	Hou	139	138	1189.1	276	374	7	73	.989	4.92	1.019	+12	185	71	.384	28	272	86	291	82	-3	+3	+19	+19	-4	+15	5
2005	LAD	140	138	1209.2	284	424	16	88	.978	5.27	1.054	+36	177	78	.441	35	357	86	351	87	-9	+6	-2	-6	+1	-5	22
		407	403	3512.0	838	1152	34	242	.983	5.10	1.034	+64	536	230	.429	23	925	264	933	258	-11	+7	+13	+8	-6	+2	15

Mark Loretta

Year	Team	G	GS	Inn	PO	A	E	DP	Pct	Rng	Rel Rng	Rel +/-	GDP Opps	GDP	Pct	Rank	Exp GB	Exp Air	Made GB	Made Air	To His Right	Straight On	To His Left	GB	Air	Total	Rank
2003	SD	150	144	1247.1	273	412	7	84	.990	4.94	.989	-7	160	77	.481	24	343	98	352	98	+4	+4	+1	+9	0	+9	8
2004	SD	154	154	1339.0	289	451	10	101	.987	4.97	1.035	+25	178	93	.522	12	372	112	365	112	-2	-2	-3	-7	0	-7	25
2005	SD	105	105	910.1	201	261	6	61	.987	4.57	.973	-13	109	57	.523	15	228	90	216	91	-1	+1	-12	-12	+1	-11	30
		409	403	3496.2	763	1124	23	246	.988	4.86	1.003	+5	447	227	.508	13	943	300	933	301	+1	+3	-14	-10	+1	-9	18

Second Basemen

Kazuo Matsui

		BASIC											GROUND DP				PLAYS				PLUS/MINUS						
										Rel	Rel		GDP				Expected Outs		Outs Made		To His	Straight	To His				
Year	Team	G	GS	Inn	PO	A	E	DP	Pct	Rng	Rng	+/-	Opps	GDP	Pct	Rank	GB	Air	GB	Air	Right	On	Left	GB	Air	Total	Rank
2004	NYM	3	3	24.0	4	8	1	3	.923	4.50	.864	-2	4	3	.750	-	8	2	7	2	0	0	0	-1	0	-1	-
2005	NYM	71	64	560.0	107	187	9	32	.970	4.73	.971	-9	64	31	.484	22	160	52	159	52	0	+2	-3	-1	0	-1	16
		74	67	584.0	111	195	10	35	.968	4.72	.967	-11	68	34	.500	-	168	54	166	54	0	+2	-3	-2	0	-2	-

Aaron Miles

		BASIC											GROUND DP				PLAYS				PLUS/MINUS						
										Rel	Rel		GDP				Expected Outs		Outs Made		To His	Straight	To His				
Year	Team	G	GS	Inn	PO	A	E	DP	Pct	Rng	Rng	+/-	Opps	GDP	Pct	Rank	GB	Air	GB	Air	Right	On	Left	GB	Air	Total	Rank
2003	CWS	3	1	14.0	1	6	0	0	1.000	4.50	.949	0	0		-	-	6		6		0	+1	0	0			-
2004	Col	128	116	1029.0	273	353	10	70	.984	5.48	.974	-17	169	63	.373	30	254	96	272	99	-1	+5	+14	+18	+3	+21	2
2005	Col	79	69	602.0	154	207	6	48	.984	5.40	1.019	+7	100	45	.450	32	178	59	173	56	-6	0	+1	-5	-3	-8	29
		210	186	1645.0	428	566	16	118	.984	5.44	.990	-10	269	108	.401	25	438	155	451	155	-7	+6	+15	+13	0	+13	12

Placido Polanco

		BASIC											GROUND DP				PLAYS				PLUS/MINUS						
										Rel	Rel		GDP				Expected Outs		Outs Made		To His	Straight	To His				
Year	Team	G	GS	Inn	PO	A	E	DP	Pct	Rng	Rng	+/-	Opps	GDP	Pct	Rank	GB	Air	GB	Air	Right	On	Left	GB	Air	Total	Rank
2003	Phi	99	99	873.2	213	301	4	69	.992	5.29	1.038	+19	130	67	.515	13	233	83	252	82	+8	+5	+5	+19	-1	+18	4
2004	Phi	109	105	944.0	264	304	3	76	.995	5.42	1.134	+68	138	67	.486	19	231	90	224	93	+11	-6	-12	-7	+3	-4	21
2005	2 tms	113	109	945.2	244	322	3	95	.995	5.39	1.058	+31	158	90	.570	6	241	82	255	81	+3	+7	+4	+14	-1	+13	9
		321	313	2763.1	721	927	10	240	.994	5.37	1.078	+118	426	224	.526	9	705	255	731	256	+22	+6	-3	+26	+1	+27	8

Nick Punto

		BASIC											GROUND DP				PLAYS				PLUS/MINUS						
										Rel	Rel		GDP				Expected Outs		Outs Made		To His	Straight	To His				
Year	Team	G	GS	Inn	PO	A	E	DP	Pct	Rng	Rng	+/-	Opps	GDP	Pct	Rank	GB	Air	GB	Air	Right	On	Left	GB	Air	Total	Rank
2003	Phi	16	7	83.0	36	6	1	6	.985	6.94	1.360	+17	17	5	.294	-	23	13	24	14	-1	0	+2	+1	+1	+2	-
2004	Min	19	11	111.1	20	34	1	10	.982	4.37	.897	-6	19	10	.526	-	26	7	28	7	+2	+2	-2	+2	0	+2	-
2005	Min	73	63	564.1	131	193	7	44	.979	5.17	1.005	+2	70	42	.600	3	157	57	169	57	-3	+1	+14	+12	0	+12	10
		108	81	758.2	187	255	9	60	.980	5.24	1.043	+13	106	57	.538	-	206	77	221	78	-2	+3	+14	+15	+1	+16	

Brian Roberts

		BASIC											GROUND DP				PLAYS				PLUS/MINUS						
										Rel	Rel		GDP				Expected Outs		Outs Made		To His	Straight	To His				
Year	Team	G	GS	Inn	PO	A	E	DP	Pct	Rng	Rng	+/-	Opps	GDP	Pct	Rank	GB	Air	GB	Air	Right	On	Left	GB	Air	Total	Rank
2003	Bal	107	105	925.0	198	324	7	67	.987	5.08	1.004	+2	120	63	.525	9	260	77	272	81	-3	+3	+13	+12	+4	+16	5
2004	Bal	150	148	1322.1	235	426	8	92	.988	4.50	.889	-82	167	89	.533	5	357	93	355	93	-1	-4	+3	-2	0	-2	20
2005	Bal	141	138	1208.0	238	413	8	93	.988	4.85	.972	-18	152	84	.553	9	336	99	352	101	+8	+2	+6	+16	+2	+18	6
		398	391	3455.1	671	1163	23	252	.988	4.78	.951	-98	439	236	.538	6	953	269	979	275	+4	+1	+22	+26	+6	+32	5

Alfonso Soriano

		BASIC											GROUND DP				PLAYS				PLUS/MINUS						
										Rel	Rel		GDP				Expected Outs		Outs Made		To His	Straight	To His				
Year	Team	G	GS	Inn	PO	A	E	DP	Pct	Rng	Rng	+/-	Opps	GDP	Pct	Rank	GB	Air	GB	Air	Right	On	Left	GB	Air	Total	Rank
2003	NYY	155	154	1376.0	293	444	19	87	.975	4.82	1.032	+23	162	82	.506	17	384	121	379	123	-6	-6	+6	-5	+2	-3	19
2004	Tex	142	142	1248.1	308	418	23	104	.969	5.23	1.028	+20	198	100	.505	15	350	118	334	119	-7	-2	-6	-16	+1	-15	31
2005	Tex	153	153	1351.0	284	447	21	101	.972	4.87	.926	-57	198	93	.470	27	402	94	382	92	+2	+1	-23	-20	-2	-22	34
		450	449	3975.1	885	1309	63	292	.972	4.97	.996	-14	558	275	.493	16	1136	333	1095	334	-11	-7	-23	-41	+1	-40	24

Junior Spivey

		BASIC											GROUND DP				PLAYS				PLUS/MINUS						
										Rel	Rel		GDP				Expected Outs		Outs Made		To His	Straight	To His				
Year	Team	G	GS	Inn	PO	A	E	DP	Pct	Rng	Rng	+/-	Opps	GDP	Pct	Rank	GB	Air	GB	Air	Right	On	Left	GB	Air	Total	Rank
2003	Ari	98	90	808.2	169	269	8	55	.982	4.87	.983	-7	111	49	.441	31	234	54	238	52	0	+3	+1	+4	-2	+2	15
2004	Mil	58	58	517.2	111	177	11	41	.963	5.01	1.045	+12	70	36	.514	13	134	44	141	45	+7	-1	+1	+7	+1	+8	9
2005	2 tms	70	67	594.0	127	179	7	41	.978	4.64	1.020	+5	73	37	.507	20	142	51	156	51	+6	0	+9	+14	0	+14	8
		226	215	1920.1	407	625	26	137	.975	4.84	1.011	+10	254	122	.480	18	510	149	535	148	+13	+2	+11	+25	-1	+24	9

Chase Utley

		BASIC											GROUND DP				PLAYS				PLUS/MINUS						
										Rel	Rel		GDP				Expected Outs		Outs Made		To His	Straight	To His				
Year	Team	G	GS	Inn	PO	A	E	DP	Pct	Rng	Rng	+/-	Opps	GDP	Pct	Rank	GB	Air	GB	Air	Right	On	Left	GB	Air	Total	Rank
2003	Phi	37	36	302.0	65	107	3	30	.983	5.13	1.005	+1	47	29	.617	-	86	20	86	19	+6	0	-6	0	-1	-1	-
2004	Phi	50	46	410.1	100	123	4	29	.982	4.89	1.024	+5	54	26	.481	-	93	36	97	39	+6	-3	+2	+4	+3	+7	-
2005	Phi	135	135	1195.1	296	376	15	72	.978	5.06	1.073	+46	144	64	.444	34	302	128	325	131	+20	+1	+3	+23	+3	+26	2
		222	217	1907.2	461	606	22	131	.980	5.03	1.052	+52	245	119	.486	17	481	184	508	189	+32	-2	-1	+27	+5	+32	6

Second Basemen

Jose Vidro

Year	Team	G	GS	Inn	PO	A	E	DP	Pct	Rng	Rel Rng	Rel +/-	GDP Opps	GDP	Pct	Rank	Exp Outs GB	Air	Outs Made GB	Air	To His Right	Straight On	To His Left	GB	Air	Total	Rank
2003	Mon	137	137	1158.1	199	396	10	76	.983	4.62	.900	-66	141	66	.468	28	342	55	346	52	-5	0	+9	+4	-3	+1	16
2004	Mon	105	104	879.1	175	269	6	70	.987	4.54	.906	-47	119	60	.504	16	197	43	185	40	-4	-4	-4	-12	-3	-15	32
2005	Was	79	79	665.1	134	191	5	39	.985	4.40	.927	-25	76	35	.461	30	173	57	169	55	-4	0	0	-4	-2	-6	24
		321	320	2703.0	508	856	21	185	.985	4.54	.908	-138	336	161	.479	20	712	155	700	147	-13	-4	+5	-12	-8	-20	20

Todd Walker

Year	Team	G	GS	Inn	PO	A	E	DP	Pct	Rng	Rel Rng	Rel +/-	GDP Opps	GDP	Pct	Rank	Exp Outs GB	Air	Outs Made GB	Air	To His Right	Straight On	To His Left	GB	Air	Total	Rank
2003	Bos	139	134	1187.1	235	391	16	79	.975	4.75	.943	-37	145	71	.490	21	354	99	340	97	-3	-6	-5	-14	-2	-16	29
2004	ChC	89	88	749.1	150	213	7	32	.981	4.36	.940	-23	93	30	.323	33	200	56	197	55	-2	0	0	-3	-1	-4	22
2005	ChC	97	93	797.2	164	242	6	44	.985	4.58	.955	-19	101	40	.396	36	217	56	213	58	-2	+1	-4	-4	+2	-2	19
		325	315	2734.1	549	846	29	155	.980	4.59	.946	-79	339	141	.416	24	771	211	750	210	-7	-5	-9	-21	-1	-22	22

Rickie Weeks

Year	Team	G	GS	Inn	PO	A	E	DP	Pct	Rng	Rel Rng	Rel +/-	GDP Opps	GDP	Pct	Rank	Exp Outs GB	Air	Outs Made GB	Air	To His Right	Straight On	To His Left	GB	Air	Total	Rank
2003	Mil	4	2	21.0	1	1	1	0	.667	.86	.169	-10	1			-	1		1		-1			0			-
2005	Mil	95	94	837.1	178	233	21	60	.951	4.42	.989	-5	109	52	.477	25	208	76	200	73	-3	-9	+4	-8	-3	-11	31
		99	96	858.1	179	234	22	60	.949	4.33	.985	-15	110	52	.473	-	209	76	201	73	-4	-9	+4	-8	-3	-11	-

Tony Womack

Year	Team	G	GS	Inn	PO	A	E	DP	Pct	Rng	Rel Rng	Rel +/-	GDP Opps	GDP	Pct	Rank	Exp Outs GB	Air	Outs Made GB	Air	To His Right	Straight On	To His Left	GB	Air	Total	Rank
2003	3 tms	21	15	137.1	32	39	0	8	1.000	4.65	.897	-9	18	8	.444	-	30	12	33	12	0	+1	+1	+3	0	+3	-
2004	StL	133	125	1113.0	225	391	15	81	.976	4.98	.966	-22	160	72	.450	24	315	87	329	89	+5	+4	+5	+14	+2	+16	4
2005	NYY	24	22	199.0	42	89	1	22	.992	5.92	1.158	+18	32	20	.625	-	85	13	78	13	-5	0	-2	-7	0	-7	-
		178	162	1449.1	299	519	16	111	.981	5.08	.990	-13	210	100	.476	-	430	112	440	114	0	+5	+4	+10	+2	+12	-

Third Basemen

Edgardo Alfonzo

						BASIC				BUNTS				PLAYS		PLUS/MINUS							
Year	Team	G GS Inn	PO A E	DP	Pct	Rng	Rel Rng	Rel +/-	Opps	Score	Grade	Rank	Expected GB Outs	GB Outs Made	To His Right	Straight On	To His Left	GB	Air	Total	Enhanced	Rank		
2003	SF	133 133 1143.0	79 233 11	18	.966	2.46	.920	-28	26	.600	B+	7	205	195	-10	0	-1	-10	-1	-11	-13	29
2004	SF	129 122 1081.1	87 246 12	20	.965	2.77	.974	-9	25	.568	B	5	232	220	-3	0	-8	-12	0	-12	-17	30
2005	SF	97 92 813.0	76 157 8	10	.967	2.58	.933	-17	18	.467	C	19	157	145	-2	-10	0	-12	0	-12	-10	23
		359 347 3037.1	242 636 31	48	.966	2.60	.944	-54	69	.554	B	6	594	560	-15	-10	-9	-34	-1	-35	-40	27

Garrett Atkins

Year	Team	G GS Inn	PO A E	DP	Pct	Rng	Rel Rng	Rel +/-	Opps	Score	Grade	Rank	Expected GB Outs	GB Outs Made	To His Right	Straight On	To His Left	GB	Air	Total	Enhanced	Rank
2003	Col	19 16 134.0	9 25 6	0	.850	2.28	.742	-12	2	.625	A-	-	23	18	-1	-3	0	-5	+1	-4	-3	-
2004	Col	4 3 27.0	2 4 0	1	1.000	2.00	.626	-4					4	4	+1	-1	0	0	0	0	0	-
2005	Col	136 136 1161.0	78 262 18	23	.950	2.63	.890	-41	26	.425	C-	23	244	250	+6	+1	-1	+6	0	+6	+10	9
		159 155 1322.2	89 291 24	24	.941	2.59	.872	-57	28	.439	C-	-	271	272	+6	-3	-1	+1	+1	+2	+7	-

Tony Batista

Year	Team	G GS Inn	PO A E	DP	Pct	Rng	Rel Rng	Rel +/-	Opps	Score	Grade	Rank	Expected GB Outs	GB Outs Made	To His Right	Straight On	To His Left	GB	Air	Total	Enhanced	Rank
2003	Bal	154 154 1364.1	92 292 20	32	.950	2.53	.931	-28	22	.473	C	22	262	259	+8	-8	-3	-3	+2	-1	-2	18
2004	Mon	155 149 1326.0	83 308 19	35	.954	2.65	.993	-3	22	.430	C-	26	244	238	+7	+1	-14	-6	0	-6	-3	19
		309 303 2690.1	175 600 39	67	.952	2.59	.963	-31	44	.451	C	25	506	497	+15	-7	-17	-9	+2	-7	-5	18

David Bell

Year	Team	G GS Inn	PO A E	DP	Pct	Rng	Rel Rng	Rel +/-	Opps	Score	Grade	Rank	Expected GB Outs	GB Outs Made	To His Right	Straight On	To His Left	GB	Air	Total	Enhanced	Rank
2003	Phi	85 81 703.2	62 168 8	17	.966	2.94	1.075	+16	12	.588	B+	8	151	156	0	+5	0	+5	0	+5	+6	9
2004	Phi	142 141 1239.2	89 307 24	22	.943	2.87	1.065	+24	25	.534	B-	11	245	268	-1	+15	+9	+23	+1	+24	+22	3
2005	Phi	150 148 1296.2	105 304 21	22	.951	2.84	1.079	+30	27	.519	C+	11	260	286	-6	+25	+7	+26	0	+26	+24	1
		377 370 3240.0	256 779 53	61	.951	2.88	1.073	+70	64	.538	B-	9	656	710	-7	+45	+16	+54	+1	+55	+52	2

Adrian Beltre

Year	Team	G GS Inn	PO A E	DP	Pct	Rng	Rel Rng	Rel +/-	Opps	Score	Grade	Rank	Expected GB Outs	GB Outs Made	To His Right	Straight On	To His Left	GB	Air	Total	Enhanced	Rank
2003	LA	157 150 1346.0	112 309 19	32	.957	2.82	1.017	+7	19	.734	A+	1	244	270	+13	+11	+2	+26	-1	+25	+30	2
2004	LA	155 154 1340.1	120 322 10	32	.978	2.97	1.090	+37	34	.496	C+	20	252	282	+10	+18	+1	+30	-1	+29	+30	2
2005	Sea	155 155 1325.2	140 271 14	25	.967	2.79	1.046	+18	18	.536	B-	9	258	265	+5	-3	+5	+7	+1	+8	+11	8
		467 459 4012.0	372 902 43	89	.967	2.86	1.052	+62	71	.570	B	2	754	817	+28	+26	+8	+63	-1	+62	+71	1

Hank Blalock

Year	Team	G GS Inn	PO A E	DP	Pct	Rng	Rel Rng	Rel +/-	Opps	Score	Grade	Rank	Expected GB Outs	GB Outs Made	To His Right	Straight On	To His Left	GB	Air	Total	Enhanced	Rank
2003	Tex	141 131 1167.0	110 238 15	31	.959	2.68	1.000	0	17	.526	B-	17	182	216	+4	+29	+1	+34	+3	+37	+34	1
2004	Tex	159 154 1378.0	103 279 17	33	.957	2.49	.921	-33	19	.563	B	6	252	262	-5	+14	0	+10	-2	+8	+5	13
2005	Tex	158 156 1374.0	96 304 11	23	.973	2.62	.900	-43	17	.509	C+	12	305	289	-6	-4	-6	-16	-1	-17	-21	26
		458 441 3919.0	309 821 43	87	.963	2.60	.938	-76	53	.534	B-	11	739	767	-7	+39	-5	+28	0	+28	+18	8

Aaron Boone

Year	Team	G GS Inn	PO A E	DP	Pct	Rng	Rel Rng	Rel +/-	Opps	Score	Grade	Rank	Expected GB Outs	GB Outs Made	To His Right	Straight On	To His Left	GB	Air	Total	Enhanced	Rank
2003	2 tms	137 133 1178.0	98 291 20	26	.951	2.97	1.107	+37	21	.488	C+	21	248	255	-2	+5	+5	+7	+1	+8	+9	7
2005	Cle	142 139 1249.2	81 298 18	20	.955	2.73	1.020	+7	21	.633	A-	4	279	278	+1	-3	+1	-1	0	-1	+1	15
		279 272 2427.2	179 589 38	46	.953	2.85	1.063	+44	42	.561	B	3	527	533	-1	+2	+6	+6	+1	+7	+10	11

Sean Burroughs

Year	Team	G GS Inn	PO A E	DP	Pct	Rng	Rel Rng	Rel +/-	Opps	Score	Grade	Rank	Expected GB Outs	GB Outs Made	To His Right	Straight On	To His Left	GB	Air	Total	Enhanced	Rank
2003	SD	137 132 1144.2	105 239 12	22	.966	2.70	1.023	+8	24	.633	A-	4	222	219	-5	-2	+3	-3	0	-3	-4	21
2004	SD	125 119 1060.0	100 209 14	25	.957	2.62	.996	-1	13	.504	C+	16	174	194	-5	+10	+14	+20	+1	+21	+14	6
2005	SD	78 70 656.2	59 145 8	15	.962	2.80	1.105	+19	7	.407	D+	25	130	142	-2	+7	+7	+12	0	+12	+12	7
		340 321 2861.1	264 593 34	62	.962	2.70	1.033	+26	44	.559	B	4	526	555	-12	+15	+24	+29	+1	+30	+22	6

Third Basemen

Vinny Castilla

Year	Team	G	GS	Inn	PO	A	E	DP	Pct	Rng	Rel Rng	Rel +/-	Opps	Score	Grade	Rank	Expected GB Outs	GB Outs Made	To His Right	Straight On	To His Left	GB	Air	Total	Enhanced	Rank
2003	Atl	147	144	1266.1	98	307	19	25	.955	2.88	.958	-18	22	.470	C	23	284	288	+8	-1	-3	+4	+1	+5	+3	13
2004	Col	148	147	1286.2	124	315	6	30	.987	3.07	.962	-17	25	.496	C+	18	265	274	+8	-3	+4	+9	-3	+6	+7	10
2005	Was	138	135	1171.1	142	209	11	23	.970	2.70	1.066	+22	22	.498	C+	13	202	198	-4	+2	-2	-4	-1	-5	-3	19
		433	426	3724.1	364	831	36	78	.971	2.89	.991	-13	69	.488	C+	19	751	760	+12	-2	-1	+9	-3	+6	+7	12

Eric Chavez

Year	Team	G	GS	Inn	PO	A	E	DP	Pct	Rng	Rel Rng	Rel +/-	Opps	Score	Grade	Rank	Expected GB Outs	GB Outs Made	To His Right	Straight On	To His Left	GB	Air	Total	Enhanced	Rank
2003	Oak	154	153	1333.1	125	343	14	33	.971	3.16	1.077	+34	23	.528	B-	15	287	292	+3	-1	+3	+5	0	+5	+9	6
2004	Oak	125	125	1129.0	113	276	13	31	.968	3.10	1.070	+26	22	.511	C+	13	233	243	+8	0	+2	+10	-1	+9	+13	7
2005	Oak	153	153	1348.1	121	301	15	27	.966	2.82	1.065	+26	14	.671	A+	2	280	290	+16	-5	-1	+10	0	+10	+15	3
		432	431	3810.2	359	920	42	91	.968	3.02	1.071	+86	59	.556	B	5	800	825	+27	-6	+4	+25	-1	+24	+37	4

Joe Crede

Year	Team	G	GS	Inn	PO	A	E	DP	Pct	Rng	Rel Rng	Rel +/-	Opps	Score	Grade	Rank	Expected GB Outs	GB Outs Made	To His Right	Straight On	To His Left	GB	Air	Total	Enhanced	Rank
2003	CWS	151	149	1306.0	107	264	14	28	.964	2.56	1.001	0	24	.433	C-	27	238	250	+10	-3	+5	+12	+2	+14	+16	5
2004	CWS	144	142	1235.0	90	243	12	22	.965	2.43	.894	-40	23	.470	C	22	228	219	-3	-5	-2	-9	-1	-10	-11	27
2005	CWS	130	122	1120.1	95	243	10	27	.971	2.72	1.028	+9	22	.484	C+	16	224	236	-14	+16	+11	+12	-1	+11	+2	14
		425	413	3661.1	292	750	36	77	.967	2.56	.976	-31	69	.462	C	24	690	705	-7	+8	+14	+15	0	+15	+7	13

Mike Cuddyer

Year	Team	G	GS	Inn	PO	A	E	DP	Pct	Rng	Rel Rng	Rel +/-	Opps	Score	Grade	Rank	Expected GB Outs	GB Outs Made	To His Right	Straight On	To His Left	GB	Air	Total	Enhanced	Rank
2003	Min	7	5	52.0	2	7	0	0	1.000	1.56	.634	-5	5	.400	D+	-	4	3	+1	-1		-1	0	-1	0	-
2004	Min	43	36	338.0	33	51	7	7	.923	2.24	.844	-15	6	.308	F	-	60	45	-1	-9	-5	-15	0	-15	-14	-
2005	Min	95	92	816.0	57	188	15	14	.942	2.70	.958	-11	11	.577	B	6	194	183	+4	-6	-8	-11	-1	-12	-10	22
		145	133	1206.0	92	246	22	21	.939	2.52	.921	-31	22	.464	C	-	258	231	+4	-16	-13	-27	-1	-28	-24	-

Morgan Ensberg

Year	Team	G	GS	Inn	PO	A	E	DP	Pct	Rng	Rel Rng	Rel +/-	Opps	Score	Grade	Rank	Expected GB Outs	GB Outs Made	To His Right	Straight On	To His Left	GB	Air	Total	Enhanced	Rank
2003	Hou	111	89	818.0	77	184	9	16	.967	2.87	1.077	+19	18	.553	B	11	148	167	+10	+9	0	+19	-1	+18	+19	3
2004	Hou	118	103	920.2	80	163	13	23	.949	2.38	.911	-23	15	.510	C+	15	154	148	-3	-7	+4	-6	0	-6	-8	25
2005	Hou	148	147	1286.1	100	295	15	31	.963	2.76	1.018	+7	20	.433	C-	22	269	285	+3	+6	+7	+16	-1	+15	+15	4
		377	339	3025.0	257	642	37	70	.960	2.67	1.007	+3	53	.495	C+	17	571	600	+10	+8	+11	+29	-2	+27	+26	5

Pedro Feliz

Year	Team	G	GS	Inn	PO	A	E	DP	Pct	Rng	Rel Rng	Rel +/-	Opps	Score	Grade	Rank	Expected GB Outs	GB Outs Made	To His Right	Straight On	To His Left	GB	Air	Total	Enhanced	Rank
2003	SF	49	28	293.0	24	82	3	8	.972	3.26	1.219	+19	5	.320	F	-	63	69	+2	+1	+4	+6	+1	+7	+7	-
2004	SF	51	37	339.1	32	85	3	7	.975	3.10	1.090	+10	4	.513	C+	-	72	83	+7	+4	0	+11	0	+11	+13	-
2005	SF	79	67	591.2	47	144	6	16	.970	2.91	1.051	+9	13	.731	A+	1	118	132	+2	+7	+5	+14	+2	+16	+16	2
		179	132	1224.0	103	311	12	31	.972	3.04	1.106	+38	22	.598	B+	-	253	284	+11	+12	+9	+31	+3	+34	+36	-

Chone Figgins

Year	Team	G	GS	Inn	PO	A	E	DP	Pct	Rng	Rel Rng	Rel +/-	Opps	Score	Grade	Rank	Expected GB Outs	GB Outs Made	To His Right	Straight On	To His Left	GB	Air	Total	Enhanced	Rank
2004	Ana	92	80	705.1	57	129	11	9	.944	2.37	1.029	+5	13	.615	A-	3	110	114	-3	+1	+6	+4	-1	+3	+1	16
2005	LAA	56	48	437.2	34	95	3	8	.977	2.65	1.098	+12	10	.430	C-	-	86	89	+3	+6	-5	+3	-1	+2	+4	-
		148	128	1143.0	91	224	14	17	.957	2.48	1.057	+17	23	.535	B-	-	196	203	0	+7	+1	+7	-2	+5	+5	-

Troy Glaus

Year	Team	G	GS	Inn	PO	A	E	DP	Pct	Rng	Rel Rng	Rel +/-	Opps	Score	Grade	Rank	Expected GB Outs	GB Outs Made	To His Right	Straight On	To His Left	GB	Air	Total	Enhanced	Rank
2003	Ana	87	86	732.1	56	136	16	10	.923	2.36	.981	-4	16	.528	B-	16	122	108	-9	-5	-1	-14	+2	-12	-12	28
2004	Ana	19	19	165.0	11	27	2	2	.950	2.07	.899	-4	2	.250	F	-	26	26	-1	+1	0	0	-1	-1	-1	-
2005	Ari	145	144	1264.0	113	310	24	25	.946	3.01	1.007	+3	27	.467	C	18	311	297	-2	-1	-11	-14	+2	-12	-12	24
		251	249	2161.1	180	473	42	37	.940	2.72	.993	-5	45	.479	C	22	459	431	-12	-5	-12	-28	+3	-25	-25	24

Third Basemen

Alex S Gonzalez

				BASIC									BUNTS				PLAYS		PLUS/MINUS							
Year	Team	G	GS	Inn	PO	A	E	DP	Pct	Rng	Rel Rng	Rel +/-	Opps	Score	Grade	Rank	Expected GB Outs	GB Outs Made	To His Right	Straight On	To His Left	GB	Air	Total	Enhanced	Rank
2005	TB	98	90	779.2	65	173	14	10	.944	2.75	1.047	+10	15	.437	C-	21	167	162	+4	-4	-5	-5	-1	-6	0	17

Brandon Inge

				BASIC									BUNTS				PLAYS		PLUS/MINUS							
Year	Team	G	GS	Inn	PO	A	E	DP	Pct	Rng	Rel Rng	Rel +/-	Opps	Score	Grade	Rank	Expected GB Outs	GB Outs Made	To His Right	Straight On	To His Left	GB	Air	Total	Enhanced	Rank
2004	Det	73	58	524.2	42	131	12	12	.935	2.97	1.079	+13	14	.539	B-	10	119	114	-4	-7	+6	-5	-1	-6	-8	26
2005	Det	160	159	1399.2	128	378	23	41	.957	3.25	1.104	+48	22	.477	C	17	357	364	+16	-6	-3	+7	-2	+5	+12	5
		233	217	1924.1	170	509	35	53	.951	3.18	1.098	+61	36	.501	C+	16	476	478	+12	-13	+3	+2	-3	-1	+4	15

Chipper Jones

				BASIC									BUNTS				PLAYS		PLUS/MINUS							
Year	Team	G	GS	Inn	PO	A	E	DP	Pct	Rng	Rel Rng	Rel +/-	Opps	Score	Grade	Rank	Expected GB Outs	GB Outs Made	To His Right	Straight On	To His Left	GB	Air	Total	Enhanced	Rank
2004	Atl	96	93	802.0	58	177	6	13	.975	2.64	.922	-20	18	.511	C+	14	157	165	+2	-4	+10	+8	0	+8	+8	9
2005	Atl	101	100	830.1	80	169	5	18	.980	2.70	.923	-21	21	.538	B-	8	154	153	+1	+1	-3	-1	0	-1	-2	18
		197	193	1632.1	138	346	11	31	.978	2.67	.923	-41	39	.526	B-	13	311	318	+3	-3	+7	+7	0	+7	+6	14

Corey Koskie

				BASIC									BUNTS				PLAYS		PLUS/MINUS							
Year	Team	G	GS	Inn	PO	A	E	DP	Pct	Rng	Rel Rng	Rel +/-	Opps	Score	Grade	Rank	Expected GB Outs	GB Outs Made	To His Right	Straight On	To His Left	GB	Air	Total	Enhanced	Rank
2003	Min	131	130	1128.0	91	234	9	15	.973	2.59	1.055	+17	21	.560	B	10	197	196	+6	-5	-2	-1	-1	-2	+1	16
2004	Min	115	112	1004.0	79	207	11	14	.963	2.56	.968	-9	22	.443	C-	25	172	172	+2	-7	+5	0	+1	+1	+3	14
2005	Tor	76	74	674.1	52	158	7	19	.968	2.80	.958	-9	13	.446	C-	20	140	154	-3	+12	+6	+14	-2	+12	+12	6
		322	316	2806.1	222	599	27	48	.968	2.63	1.000	-1	56	.488	C+	20	509	522	+5	0	+9	+13	-2	+11	+16	9

Mike Lowell

				BASIC									BUNTS				PLAYS		PLUS/MINUS							
Year	Team	G	GS	Inn	PO	A	E	DP	Pct	Rng	Rel Rng	Rel +/-	Opps	Score	Grade	Rank	Expected GB Outs	GB Outs Made	To His Right	Straight On	To His Left	GB	Air	Total	Enhanced	Rank
2003	Fla	128	128	1109.2	84	243	9	27	.973	2.65	.997	-1	30	.670	A+	3	231	218	+2	-13	-2	-13	-1	-14	-12	27
2004	Fla	154	153	1326.0	117	272	7	30	.982	2.64	.999	0	32	.619	A-	2	235	228	+12	-13	-6	-7	+4	-3	-1	18
2005	Fla	135	126	1126.2	107	243	6	34	.983	2.80	.965	-12	24	.656	A	3	234	224	+16	-19	-7	-10	-3	-13	-8	21
		417	407	3562.1	308	758	22	91	.980	2.69	.987	-13	86	.647	A	1	700	670	+30	-45	-15	-30	0	-30	-21	23

Melvin Mora

				BASIC									BUNTS				PLAYS		PLUS/MINUS							
Year	Team	G	GS	Inn	PO	A	E	DP	Pct	Rng	Rel Rng	Rel +/-	Opps	Score	Grade	Rank	Expected GB Outs	GB Outs Made	To His Right	Straight On	To His Left	GB	Air	Total	Enhanced	Rank
2004	Bal	138	138	1210.1	122	258	21	21	.948	2.83	1.051	+18	20	.450	C	24	256	240	-4	-12	-1	-16	+2	-14	-15	29
2005	Bal	148	148	1289.2	96	301	18	23	.957	2.77	.998	-1	17	.356	D-	26	291	295	+2	+4	-2	+4	+1	+5	+6	11
		286	286	2500.0	218	559	39	44	.952	2.80	1.024	+17	37	.407	D+	26	547	535	-2	-8	-3	-12	+3	-9	-9	19

Bill Mueller

				BASIC									BUNTS				PLAYS		PLUS/MINUS							
Year	Team	G	GS	Inn	PO	A	E	DP	Pct	Rng	Rel Rng	Rel +/-	Opps	Score	Grade	Rank	Expected GB Outs	GB Outs Made	To His Right	Straight On	To His Left	GB	Air	Total	Enhanced	Rank
2003	Bos	135	124	1118.1	76	235	16	22	.951	2.50	.958	-13	12	.463	C	25	231	232	-6	+5	+1	+1	+1	+2	+3	14
2004	Bos	96	94	827.2	71	162	14	15	.943	2.53	.996	-1	8	.613	A-	4	154	151	-11	+7	+2	-3	-1	-4	-6	21
2005	Bos	142	140	1209.1	87	265	10	20	.972	2.62	.939	-23	9	.578	B	5	258	261	+7	0	-3	+3	+1	+4	+6	12
		373	358	3155.1	234	662	40	57	.957	2.56	.961	-37	29	.540	B-	7	643	644	-10	+12	0	+1	+1	+2	+3	16

Abraham O Nunez

				BASIC									BUNTS				PLAYS		PLUS/MINUS							
Year	Team	G	GS	Inn	PO	A	E	DP	Pct	Rng	Rel Rng	Rel +/-	Opps	Score	Grade	Rank	Expected GB Outs	GB Outs Made	To His Right	Straight On	To His Left	GB	Air	Total	Enhanced	Rank
2003	Pit	1	0	1.0	0	1	0	0	1.000	9.00	3.108	+1				-	0	1	+1			+1				-
2004	Pit	6	2	21.1	0	5	1	0	.833	2.11	.730	-2	1	.600	B+	-	4	4	+1	-1	0	0	-1	-1	-1	-
2005	StL	98	77	720.2	54	203	10	19	.963	3.21	1.055	+14	12	.492	C+	15	188	194	+6	+1	-2	+6	+1	+7	+9	10
		105	79	743.0	54	209	11	19	.960	3.19	1.057	+13	13	.500	C+	-	192	199	+8	0	-2	+7	0	+7	+8	-

Aramis Ramirez

				BASIC									BUNTS				PLAYS		PLUS/MINUS							
Year	Team	G	GS	Inn	PO	A	E	DP	Pct	Rng	Rel Rng	Rel +/-	Opps	Score	Grade	Rank	Expected GB Outs	GB Outs Made	To His Right	Straight On	To His Left	GB	Air	Total	Enhanced	Rank
2003	2 tms	159	156	1397.2	97	284	33	24	.929	2.79	1.008	+3	24	.490	C+	20	310	306	+1	-1	-4	-4	-3	-7	-4	20
2004	ChC	144	141	1245.1	92	221	10	15	.969	2.26	.894	-37	25	.496	C+	18	215	205	+2	-9	-3	-10	-1	-11	-8	24
2005	ChC	119	119	1020.1	70	218	16	13	.947	2.54	.956	-13	21	.417	D+	24	204	205	-2	0	+3	+1	0	+1	0	16
		422	416	3663.1	259	775	59	52	.946	2.54	.959	-47	70	.470	C	23	729	716	+1	-10	-4	-13	-4	-17	-12	21

Third Basemen

Joe Randa

Year	Team	G	GS	Inn	PO	A	E	DP	Pct	Rng	Rel Rng	Rel +/-	Opps	Score	Grade	Rank	Expected GB Outs	GB Outs Made	To His Right	Straight On	To His Left	GB	Air	Total	Enhanced	Rank
2003	KC	129	127	1073.1	102	238	7	12	.980	2.85	1.019	+6	20	.505	C+	18	217	218	-1	+4	-2	+1	-1	0	-2	19
2004	KC	119	118	1021.2	85	241	11	23	.967	2.87	1.003	+1	21	.560	B	7	187	197	+8	+10	-8	+10	-1	+9	+10	8
2005	2 tms	142	140	1209.2	126	225	12	21	.967	2.61	.971	-10	24	.494	C+	14	228	222	+1	-6	-1	-6	+1	-5	-6	20
		390	385	3304.2	313	704	30	56	.971	2.77	.997	-3	65	.518	C+	14	632	637	+8	+8	-11	+5	-1	+4	+2	17

Alex Rodriguez

Year	Team	G	GS	Inn	PO	A	E	DP	Pct	Rng	Rel Rng	Rel +/-	Opps	Score	Grade	Rank	Expected GB Outs	GB Outs Made	To His Right	Straight On	To His Left	GB	Air	Total	Enhanced	Rank
2004	NYY	155	155	1364.1	101	261	13	25	.965	2.39	.950	-19	21	.336	D-	31	223	244	-1	+19	+2	+21	+1	+22	+17	4
2005	NYY	161	161	1384.0	115	288	12	26	.971	2.62	.917	-36	17	.312	F	27	284	286	-7	+13	-3	+2	+4	+6	+2	13
		316	316	2748.1	216	549	25	51	.968	2.51	.933	-55	38	.325	F	28	507	530	-8	+32	-1	+23	+5	+28	+19	7

Scott Rolen

Year	Team	G	GS	Inn	PO	A	E	DP	Pct	Rng	Rel Rng	Rel +/-	Opps	Score	Grade	Rank	Expected GB Outs	GB Outs Made	To His Right	Straight On	To His Left	GB	Air	Total	Enhanced	Rank
2003	StL	153	152	1339.0	109	298	13	23	.969	2.74	1.066	+25	14	.529	B-	14	251	249	-2	+4	-4	-2	0	-2	-7	25
2004	StL	142	140	1228.0	93	325	10	23	.977	3.06	1.084	+33	18	.544	B	9	270	302	+6	+13	+13	+32	+2	+34	+37	1
2005	StL	56	55	486.0	22	151	6	17	.966	3.20	1.053	+9	6	.550	B	-	125	140	+3	+3	+9	+15	0	+15	+16	-
		351	347	3053.0	224	774	29	63	.972	2.94	1.071	+67	38	.539	B-	8	646	691	+7	+20	+18	+45	+2	+47	+46	3

Mark Teahen

Year	Team	G	GS	Inn	PO	A	E	DP	Pct	Rng	Rel Rng	Rel +/-	Opps	Score	Grade	Rank	Expected GB Outs	GB Outs Made	To His Right	Straight On	To His Left	GB	Air	Total	Enhanced	Rank
2005	KC	128	122	1068.1	113	244	20	22	.947	3.01	1.036	+12	19	.521	B-	10	253	228	-9	-6	-11	-25	+1	-24	-30	27

Chad Tracy

Year	Team	G	GS	Inn	PO	A	E	DP	Pct	Rng	Rel Rng	Rel +/-	Opps	Score	Grade	Rank	Expected GB Outs	GB Outs Made	To His Right	Straight On	To His Left	GB	Air	Total	Enhanced	Rank
2004	Ari	135	120	1061.2	104	258	25	27	.935	3.07	1.058	+19	15	.467	C	23	225	237	+12	+3	-3	+12	+1	+13	+17	5

David Wright

Year	Team	G	GS	Inn	PO	A	E	DP	Pct	Rng	Rel Rng	Rel +/-	Opps	Score	Grade	Rank	Expected GB Outs	GB Outs Made	To His Right	Straight On	To His Left	GB	Air	Total	Enhanced	Rank
2004	NYM	69	68	603.2	39	139	11	10	.942	2.65	.909	-18	8	.481	C+	21	122	132	-2	+14	-2	+10	-3	+7	+6	12
2005	NYM	160	160	1404.1	101	337	24	23	.948	2.81	1.024	+10	32	.542	B-	7	327	315	-14	+2	0	-12	-2	-14	-17	25
		229	228	2008.0	140	476	35	33	.946	2.76	.991	-8	40	.530	B-	12	449	447	-16	+16	-2	-2	-5	-7	-11	20

Shortstops

Russ Adams

	BASIC											GROUND DP				PLAYS				PLUS/MINUS						
										Rel	Rel	GDP				Expected Outs		Outs Made		To His	Straight	To His				
Year Team	G	GS	Inn	PO	A	E	DP	Pct	Rng	Rng	+/-	Opps	GDP	Pct	Rank	GB	Air	GB	Air	Right	On	Left	GB	Air	Total	Rank
2004 Tor	21	18	159.1	26	47	5	9	.936	4.12	.881	-10	16	8	.500	-	49	14	45	16	-4	-3	+2	-4	+2	-2	-
2005 Tor	132	122	1100.0	194	326	26	69	.952	4.25	.879	-73	111	65	.586	20	292	98	281	92	+2	-11	-2	-11	-6	-17	29
	153	140	1259.1	220	373	31	78	.950	4.24	.879	-83	127	73	.575	-	341	112	326	108	-2	-14	0	-15	-4	-19	-

Clint Barmes

	BASIC											GROUND DP				PLAYS				PLUS/MINUS						
										Rel	Rel	GDP				Expected Outs		Outs Made		To His	Straight	To His				
Year Team	G	GS	Inn	PO	A	E	DP	Pct	Rng	Rng	+/-	Opps	GDP	Pct	Rank	GB	Air	GB	Air	Right	On	Left	GB	Air	Total	Rank
2003 Col	12	8	75.0	19	27	2	7	.958	5.52	1.088	+4	6	4	.667	-	23	5	19	5	-1	-1	-2	-4	0	-4	-
2004 Col	9	9	76.0	17	36	1	7	.981	6.28	1.240	+10	9	6	.667	-	12	6	15	5	+1	0	+2	+3	-1	+2	-
2005 Col	80	78	681.2	139	247	17	62	.958	5.10	1.060	+21	105	59	.562	22	195	65	212	65	+12	-5	+10	+17	0	+17	6
	101	95	832.2	175	310	20	76	.960	5.24	1.083	+35	120	69	.575	-	230	76	246	75	+12	-6	+10	+16	-1	+15	-

Jason Bartlett

	BASIC											GROUND DP				PLAYS				PLUS/MINUS						
										Rel	Rel	GDP				Expected Outs		Outs Made		To His	Straight	To His				
Year Team	G	GS	Inn	PO	A	E	DP	Pct	Rng	Rng	+/-	Opps	GDP	Pct	Rank	GB	Air	GB	Air	Right	On	Left	GB	Air	Total	Rank
2004 Min	5	2	22.0	5	11	2	3	.889	6.55	1.437	+5	5	3	.600	-	8	2	8	3	+1	0	-1	0	+1	+1	-
2005 Min	68	65	585.2	95	227	7	45	.979	4.95	1.056	+17	62	42	.677	3	193	50	205	52	+1	+3	+9	+12	+2	+14	7
	73	67	607.2	100	238	9	48	.974	5.01	1.074	+22	67	45	.672	-	201	52	213	55	+2	+3	+8	+12	+3	+15	-

Angel Berroa

	BASIC											GROUND DP				PLAYS				PLUS/MINUS						
										Rel	Rel	GDP				Expected Outs		Outs Made		To His	Straight	To His				
Year Team	G	GS	Inn	PO	A	E	DP	Pct	Rng	Rng	+/-	Opps	GDP	Pct	Rank	GB	Air	GB	Air	Right	On	Left	GB	Air	Total	Rank
2003 KC	158	158	1381.2	264	473	24	106	.968	4.80	1.021	+15	158	97	.614	9	394	128	384	125	-13	0	+2	-10	-3	-13	33
2004 KC	133	132	1143.0	207	388	28	95	.955	4.69	.977	-14	133	84	.632	3	310	94	294	90	-4	-10	-2	-16	-4	-20	33
2005 KC	159	159	1360.1	254	442	25	107	.965	4.60	.938	-44	161	102	.634	10	403	128	379	126	-23	-5	+4	-24	-2	-26	30
	450	449	3885.0	725	1303	77	308	.963	4.70	.980	-43	452	283	.626	4	1107	350	1057	341	-40	-15	+4	-50	-9	-59	29

Orlando Cabrera

	BASIC											GROUND DP				PLAYS				PLUS/MINUS						
										Rel	Rel	GDP				Expected Outs		Outs Made		To His	Straight	To His				
Year Team	G	GS	Inn	PO	A	E	DP	Pct	Rng	Rng	+/-	Opps	GDP	Pct	Rank	GB	Air	GB	Air	Right	On	Left	GB	Air	Total	Rank
2003 Mon	162	160	1385.2	258	456	18	100	.975	4.64	1.024	+17	157	90	.573	22	310	99	317	97	-1	+1	+7	+7	-2	+5	13
2004 2 tms	159	158	1358.2	226	437	15	93	.978	4.39	.994	-7	152	83	.546	27	315	99	325	102	+2	+3	+4	+10	+3	+13	5
2005 LAA	141	140	1240.2	229	347	7	81	.988	4.18	1.014	+8	128	75	.586	19	307	111	314	111	-8	0	+16	+7	0	+7	12
	462	458	3985.0	713	1240	40	274	.980	4.41	1.011	+18	437	248	.568	22	932	309	956	310	-7	+4	+27	+24	+1	+25	7

Juan Castro

	BASIC											GROUND DP				PLAYS				PLUS/MINUS						
										Rel	Rel	GDP				Expected Outs		Outs Made		To His	Straight	To His				
Year Team	G	GS	Inn	PO	A	E	DP	Pct	Rng	Rng	+/-	Opps	GDP	Pct	Rank	GB	Air	GB	Air	Right	On	Left	GB	Air	Total	Rank
2003 Cin	24	18	154.0	28	43	0	14	1.000	4.15	.917	-6	15	11	.733	-	27	11	31	11	+2	0	+2	+4	0	+4	-
2004 Cin	31	21	190.1	32	72	2	16	.981	4.92	1.120	+11	23	13	.565	-	57	10	57	12	-2	+1	0	0	+2	+2	-
2005 Min	73	66	568.2	98	231	5	49	.985	5.21	1.111	+33	64	44	.688	2	196	41	204	42	0	+3	+5	+8	+1	+9	10
	128	105	913.0	158	346	7	79	.986	4.97	1.086	+38	102	68	.667	-	280	62	292	65	0	+4	+7	+12	+3	+15	-

Royce Clayton

	BASIC											GROUND DP				PLAYS				PLUS/MINUS						
										Rel	Rel	GDP				Expected Outs		Outs Made		To His	Straight	To His				
Year Team	G	GS	Inn	PO	A	E	DP	Pct	Rng	Rng	+/-	Opps	GDP	Pct	Rank	GB	Air	GB	Air	Right	On	Left	GB	Air	Total	Rank
2003 Mil	141	137	1217.2	193	396	14	76	.977	4.35	.978	-13	126	72	.571	23	323	93	315	93	-14	+2	+5	-8	0	-8	30
2004 Col	144	140	1241.0	213	417	9	89	.986	4.57	.902	-67	150	82	.547	25	341	84	345	80	-7	+3	+8	+4	-4	0	22
2005 Ari	141	131	1177.1	180	404	11	90	.982	4.46	.920	-50	153	90	.588	17	357	77	353	75	-13	0	+9	-4	-2	-6	22
	426	408	3636.0	586	1217	34	255	.981	4.46	.933	-130	429	244	.569	20	1021	254	1013	248	-34	+5	+22	-8	-6	-14	24

Bobby Crosby

	BASIC											GROUND DP				PLAYS				PLUS/MINUS						
										Rel	Rel	GDP				Expected Outs		Outs Made		To His	Straight	To His				
Year Team	G	GS	Inn	PO	A	E	DP	Pct	Rng	Rng	+/-	Opps	GDP	Pct	Rank	GB	Air	GB	Air	Right	On	Left	GB	Air	Total	Rank
2003 Oak	9	0	20.0	5	11	2	2	.889	7.20	1.493	+5	9	2	.222	-	12	1	10	1	-2	0	0	-2	0	-2	-
2004 Oak	151	151	1356.0	242	505	19	107	.975	4.96	1.021	+15	169	100	.592	15	417	103	420	105	+9	+6	-11	+3	+2	+5	12
2005 Oak	84	84	743.1	117	251	7	59	.981	4.46	1.007	+3	85	57	.671	4	214	56	222	56	+3	+4	0	+8	0	+8	11
	244	235	2119.1	364	767	28	168	.976	4.80	1.023	+23	263	159	.605	12	643	160	652	162	+10	+10	-11	+9	+2	+11	12

Shortstops

David Eckstein

		BASIC												GROUND DP				PLAYS				PLUS/MINUS						
Year	Team	G	GS	Inn	PO	A	E	DP	Pct	Rng	Rel Rng	Rel +/-	GDP Opps	GDP	Pct	Rank	Exp Outs GB	Air	Outs Made GB	Air	To His Right	Straight On	To His Left	GB	Air	Total	Rank
2003	Ana	116	114	985.0	193	293	8	64	.984	4.44	1.061	+28	101	59	.584	17	243	83	245	85	-4	+2	+4	+2	+2	+4	14
2004	Ana	139	137	1191.2	198	309	6	75	.988	3.83	.927	-40	125	68	.544	28	269	79	270	79	+3	0	-2	+1	0	+1	20
2005	StL	156	154	1340.2	244	516	15	122	.981	5.10	1.038	+28	188	118	.628	11	454	99	454	97	-6	+7	-1	0	-2	-2	20
		411	405	3517.1	635	1118	29	261	.984	4.49	1.013	+16	414	245	.592	14	966	261	969	261	-7	+9	+1	+3	0	+3	15

Adam Everett

		BASIC												GROUND DP				PLAYS				PLUS/MINUS						
Year	Team	G	GS	Inn	PO	A	E	DP	Pct	Rng	Rel Rng	Rel +/-	GDP Opps	GDP	Pct	Rank	Exp Outs GB	Air	Outs Made GB	Air	To His Right	Straight On	To His Left	GB	Air	Total	Rank
2003	Hou	128	116	1000.2	207	344	17	74	.970	4.96	1.133	+65	109	63	.578	20	285	104	305	105	+13	+2	+5	+20	+1	+21	1
2004	Hou	99	97	842.0	137	278	10	56	.976	4.44	1.040	+16	83	51	.614	8	223	61	242	64	+10	+5	+4	+19	+3	+22	1
2005	Hou	150	147	1291.2	209	420	14	96	.978	4.38	1.000	0	150	88	.587	18	340	97	374	96	+15	+4	+14	+34	-1	+33	1
		377	360	3134.1	553	1042	41	226	.975	4.58	1.056	+81	342	202	.591	17	848	262	921	265	+38	+11	+23	+73	+3	+76	1

Rafael Furcal

		BASIC												GROUND DP				PLAYS				PLUS/MINUS						
Year	Team	G	GS	Inn	PO	A	E	DP	Pct	Rng	Rel Rng	Rel +/-	GDP Opps	GDP	Pct	Rank	Exp Outs GB	Air	Outs Made GB	Air	To His Right	Straight On	To His Left	GB	Air	Total	Rank
2003	Atl	155	154	1350.0	237	481	31	107	.959	4.79	.983	-12	174	103	.592	14	409	91	419	91	+6	-8	+12	+10	0	+10	6
2004	Atl	131	130	1134.0	191	412	24	100	.962	4.79	1.039	+22	160	95	.594	13	342	69	343	70	-1	-2	+5	+1	+1	+2	18
2005	Atl	152	152	1306.1	255	504	15	118	.981	5.23	1.100	+69	172	110	.640	9	415	98	437	102	+14	0	+8	+22	+4	+26	3
		438	436	3790.1	683	1397	70	325	.967	4.94	1.042	+79	506	308	.609	10	1166	258	1199	263	+19	-10	+25	+33	+5	+38	4

Nomar Garciaparra

		BASIC												GROUND DP				PLAYS				PLUS/MINUS						
Year	Team	G	GS	Inn	PO	A	E	DP	Pct	Rng	Rel Rng	Rel +/-	GDP Opps	GDP	Pct	Rank	Exp Outs GB	Air	Outs Made GB	Air	To His Right	Straight On	To His Left	GB	Air	Total	Rank
2003	Bos	156	155	1364.2	216	455	20	82	.971	4.43	.975	-17	155	78	.503	34	393	86	407	85	-4	+3	+15	+14	-1	+13	2
2004	2 tms	79	78	676.0	121	176	9	34	.971	3.95	.922	-27	75	31	.413	34	163	53	155	49	-2	-6	+1	-8	-4	-12	29
2005	ChC	26	25	206.0	41	51	6	16	.939	4.02	.930	-7	24	15	.625	-	45	13	42	14	-4	+1	0	-3	+1	-2	-
		261	258	2246.2	378	682	35	132	.968	4.25	.956	-51	254	124	.488	31	601	152	604	148	-10	-2	+16	+3	-4	-1	17

Alex Gonzalez

		BASIC												GROUND DP				PLAYS				PLUS/MINUS						
Year	Team	G	GS	Inn	PO	A	E	DP	Pct	Rng	Rel Rng	Rel +/-	GDP Opps	GDP	Pct	Rank	Exp Outs GB	Air	Outs Made GB	Air	To His Right	Straight On	To His Left	GB	Air	Total	Rank
2003	Fla	150	150	1315.2	237	427	16	106	.976	4.54	1.056	+35	143	99	.692	4	366	109	358	108	-6	0	-3	-8	-1	-9	31
2004	Fla	158	155	1351.2	225	425	16	99	.976	4.33	1.015	+10	144	88	.611	10	347	103	357	102	+8	-1	+3	+10	-1	+9	7
2005	Fla	124	124	1087.1	221	367	16	102	.974	4.87	1.040	+22	138	90	.652	7	316	91	317	89	+2	0	-1	+1	-2	-1	19
		432	429	3754.2	683	1219	48	307	.975	4.56	1.037	+67	425	277	.652	2	1029	303	1032	299	+4	-1	-1	+3	-4	-1	16

Khalil Greene

		BASIC												GROUND DP				PLAYS				PLUS/MINUS						
Year	Team	G	GS	Inn	PO	A	E	DP	Pct	Rng	Rel Rng	Rel +/-	GDP Opps	GDP	Pct	Rank	Exp Outs GB	Air	Outs Made GB	Air	To His Right	Straight On	To His Left	GB	Air	Total	Rank
2003	SD	20	18	155.0	27	51	3	11	.963	4.53	1.028	+2	17	10	.588	-	40	13	40	13	0	-1	+1	0	0	0	-
2004	SD	136	134	1189.2	177	380	20	81	.965	4.21	.981	-11	123	76	.618	7	312	88	316	88	-4	-3	+12	+4	0	+4	16
2005	SD	121	120	1028.2	161	312	14	64	.971	4.14	.984	-8	111	60	.541	27	294	87	280	85	-7	-2	-5	-14	-2	-16	28
		277	272	2373.1	365	743	37	156	.968	4.20	.986	-17	251	146	.582	19	646	188	636	186	-11	-6	+8	-10	-2	-12	23

Carlos Guillen

		BASIC												GROUND DP				PLAYS				PLUS/MINUS						
Year	Team	G	GS	Inn	PO	A	E	DP	Pct	Rng	Rel Rng	Rel +/-	GDP Opps	GDP	Pct	Rank	Exp Outs GB	Air	Outs Made GB	Air	To His Right	Straight On	To His Left	GB	Air	Total	Rank
2003	Sea	76	70	620.0	122	162	11	57	.963	4.12	1.032	+9	66	45	.682	3	138	66	132	68	-8	-4	+6	-6	+2	-4	27
2004	Det	135	133	1151.0	220	416	17	90	.974	4.97	1.061	+36	138	84	.609	11	330	109	309	112	-21	+1	0	-21	+3	-18	32
2005	Det	75	74	625.0	85	227	7	44	.978	4.49	.936	-21	76	42	.553	25	197	39	202	37	+9	-1	-2	+5	-2	+3	17
		286	277	2396.0	427	805	35	191	.972	4.63	1.022	+24	280	171	.611	8	665	214	643	217	-20	-4	+4	-22	+3	-19	27

Cristian Guzman

		BASIC												GROUND DP				PLAYS				PLUS/MINUS						
Year	Team	G	GS	Inn	PO	A	E	DP	Pct	Rng	Rel Rng	Rel +/-	GDP Opps	GDP	Pct	Rank	Exp Outs GB	Air	Outs Made GB	Air	To His Right	Straight On	To His Left	GB	Air	Total	Rank
2003	Min	141	137	1232.1	195	352	11	68	.980	3.99	.960	-23	109	61	.560	28	312	99	297	98	-6	+3	-12	-15	-1	-16	35
2004	Min	145	143	1304.2	234	440	12	103	.983	4.65	1.021	+14	158	97	.614	9	341	115	341	115	+3	+2	-6	0	0	0	23
2005	Was	142	133	1161.0	217	327	15	85	.973	4.22	.990	-6	120	78	.650	8	281	107	279	103	-8	+2	+4	-2	-4	-6	23
		428	413	3698.0	646	1119	38	256	.979	4.30	.992	-15	387	236	.610	9	934	321	917	316	-11	+7	-14	-17	-5	-22	28

Shortstops

Bill Hall

Year	Team	G	GS	Inn	PO	A	E	DP	Pct	Rng	Rel Rng	Rel +/-	GDP Opps	GDP	Pct	Rank	Exp Outs GB	Exp Outs Air	Outs Made GB	Outs Made Air	To His Right	Straight On	To His Left	GB	Air	Total	Rank
2003	Mil	18	18	153.0	30	48	4	10	.951	4.59	1.031	+2	15	11	.733	-	44	14	40	13	+1	-3	-2	-4	-1	-5	-
2004	Mil	37	33	303.2	59	116	8	23	.956	5.19	1.232	+33	38	20	.526	-	90	27	96	27	+4	+2	+1	+6	0	+6	-
2005	Mil	66	58	500.1	87	158	6	31	.976	4.41	1.085	+19	53	28	.528	31	133	46	138	45	0	+1	+4	+5	-1	+4	16
		121	109	957.0	176	322	18	64	.965	4.68	1.129	+54	106	59	.557	-	267	87	274	85	+5	0	+3	+7	-2	+5	-

J.J. Hardy

Year	Team	G	GS	Inn	PO	A	E	DP	Pct	Rng	Rel Rng	Rel +/-	GDP Opps	GDP	Pct	Rank	Exp Outs GB	Exp Outs Air	Outs Made GB	Outs Made Air	To His Right	Straight On	To His Left	GB	Air	Total	Rank
2005	Mil	119	104	937.2	133	259	10	52	.975	3.76	.926	-31	78	46	.590	16	231	75	240	76	+13	0	-4	+9	+1	+10	8

Cesar Izturis

Year	Team	G	GS	Inn	PO	A	E	DP	Pct	Rng	Rel Rng	Rel +/-	GDP Opps	GDP	Pct	Rank	Exp Outs GB	Exp Outs Air	Outs Made GB	Outs Made Air	To His Right	Straight On	To His Left	GB	Air	Total	Rank
2003	LA	158	154	1365.1	197	481	16	94	.977	4.47	1.002	+2	149	87	.584	18	384	77	393	78	+19	+1	-11	+9	+1	+10	7
2004	LA	159	156	1386.0	234	430	10	96	.985	4.31	1.001	+1	144	89	.618	6	361	111	376	115	+11	0	+4	+15	+4	+19	2
2005	LAD	106	105	918.0	146	325	11	62	.977	4.62	1.022	+10	106	59	.557	24	277	58	282	57	+5	+3	-2	+5	-1	+4	15
		423	415	3669.1	577	1236	37	252	.980	4.45	1.007	+13	399	235	.589	18	1022	246	1051	250	+35	+4	-9	+29	+4	+33	6

Derek Jeter

Year	Team	G	GS	Inn	PO	A	E	DP	Pct	Rng	Rel Rng	Rel +/-	GDP Opps	GDP	Pct	Rank	Exp Outs GB	Exp Outs Air	Outs Made GB	Outs Made Air	To His Right	Straight On	To His Left	GB	Air	Total	Rank
2003	NYY	118	118	1033.2	159	271	14	51	.968	3.74	.849	-75	88	46	.523	33	250	100	235	101	-12	+3	-6	-15	+1	-14	34
2004	NYY	154	154	1341.2	273	392	14	96	.979	4.46	.990	-6	146	85	.582	17	352	120	327	129	-24	+5	-5	-25	+9	-16	31
2005	NYY	157	157	1352.0	262	453	15	96	.979	4.76	.995	-3	156	84	.538	29	439	121	400	126	-18	+3	-25	-39	+5	-34	31
		429	429	3727.1	694	1116	42	242	.977	4.37	.959	-84	390	215	.551	28	1041	341	962	356	-54	+11	-36	-79	+15	-64	30

Felipe Lopez

Year	Team	G	GS	Inn	PO	A	E	DP	Pct	Rng	Rel Rng	Rel +/-	GDP Opps	GDP	Pct	Rank	Exp Outs GB	Exp Outs Air	Outs Made GB	Outs Made Air	To His Right	Straight On	To His Left	GB	Air	Total	Rank
2003	Cin	50	42	397.1	60	132	15	20	.928	4.35	.961	-	41	19	.463	-	109	31	102	30	-4	-1	-2	-7	-1	-8	-
2004	Cin	51	41	391.0	65	137	9	25	.957	4.65	1.059	+11	51	24	.471	-	110	23	105	21	-9	+2	+2	-5	-2	-7	-
2005	Cin	140	133	1175.1	186	357	17	71	.970	4.16	.917	-48	127	69	.543	26	319	99	322	96	-6	+4	+6	+3	-3	0	18
		241	216	1963.2	311	626	41	116	.958	4.29	.957	-45	219	112	.511	29	538	153	529	147	-19	+5	+6	-9	-6	-15	26

Julio Lugo

Year	Team	G	GS	Inn	PO	A	E	DP	Pct	Rng	Rel Rng	Rel +/-	GDP Opps	GDP	Pct	Rank	Exp Outs GB	Exp Outs Air	Outs Made GB	Outs Made Air	To His Right	Straight On	To His Left	GB	Air	Total	Rank
2003	2 tms	139	137	1198.0	241	391	20	83	.969	4.75	1.097	+57	132	72	.545	30	331	117	331	119	+1	-4	+2	0	+2	+2	17
2004	TB	143	142	1238.0	237	422	25	91	.963	4.79	1.093	+57	138	86	.623	4	352	122	360	119	+2	-1	+6	+8	-3	+5	13
2005	TB	156	155	1338.2	311	424	24	94	.968	4.94	1.140	+88	154	83	.539	28	374	150	371	151	-4	-5	+6	-3	+1	-2	21
		438	434	3774.2	789	1237	69	268	.967	4.83	1.111	+202	424	241	.568	21	1057	389	1062	389	-1	-10	+14	+5	0	+5	13

Jhonny Peralta

Year	Team	G	GS	Inn	PO	A	E	DP	Pct	Rng	Rel Rng	Rel +/-	GDP Opps	GDP	Pct	Rank	Exp Outs GB	Exp Outs Air	Outs Made GB	Outs Made Air	To His Right	Straight On	To His Left	GB	Air	Total	Rank
2003	Cle	72	69	624.0	104	222	8	41	.976	4.70	.996	-1	67	38	.567	24	177	45	176	46	+4	+2	-8	-1	+1	0	20
2004	Cle	7	6	55.0	7	17	3	2	.889	3.93	.862	-4	4	2	.500	-	14	2	12	3	0	-2	0	-2	+1	-1	-
2005	Cle	141	138	1232.1	207	412	19	104	.970	4.52	1.029	+18	132	94	.712	1	364	115	352	113	-5	+3	-10	-12	-2	-14	27
		220	213	1911.1	318	651	30	147	.970	4.56	1.014	+13	203	134	.660	1	555	162	540	162	-1	+3	-18	-15	0	-15	25

Neifi Perez

Year	Team	G	GS	Inn	PO	A	E	DP	Pct	Rng	Rel Rng	Rel +/-	GDP Opps	GDP	Pct	Rank	Exp Outs GB	Exp Outs Air	Outs Made GB	Outs Made Air	To His Right	Straight On	To His Left	GB	Air	Total	Rank
2003	SF	45	33	311.0	71	129	2	33	.990	5.79	1.323	+50	48	32	.667	-	92	27	100	29	+8	+1	-1	+8	+2	+10	-
2004	2 tms	76	60	560.1	87	198	7	39	.976	4.58	1.028	+7	66	34	.515	31	157	38	166	35	+4	+1	+4	+9	-3	+6	11
2005	ChC	130	118	1063.1	175	385	10	81	.982	4.74	1.097	+50	121	73	.603	13	319	71	339	71	+10	+8	+2	+20	0	+20	5
		251	211	1934.2	333	712	19	153	.982	4.86	1.122	+107	235	139	.591	16	568	136	605	135	+22	+10	+5	+37	-1	+36	5

Shortstops

Edgar Renteria

Year	Team	G	GS	Inn	PO	A	E	DP	Pct	Rng	Rel Rng	Rel +/-	GDP Opps	GDP	GDP Pct	Rank	Exp GB	Exp Air	Made GB	Made Air	To His Right	Straight On	To His Left	GB	Air	Total	Rank
2003	StL	156	154	1367.1	191	439	16	83	.975	4.15	.963	-24	124	76	.613	10	346	91	347	88	-6	+3	+5	+1	-3	-2	23
2004	StL	149	148	1307.1	222	418	11	92	.983	4.41	.955	-31	147	83	.565	20	338	89	347	89	-2	-1	+12	+9	0	+9	8
2005	Bos	153	150	1293.0	227	398	30	90	.954	4.35	.927	-49	154	82	.532	30	352	110	343	108	+3	-14	+2	-9	-2	-11	26
		458	452	3967.2	640	1255	57	265	.971	4.30	.949	-104	425	241	.567	23	1036	290	1037	285	-5	-12	+19	+1	-5	-4	21

Jose Reyes

Year	Team	G	GS	Inn	PO	A	E	DP	Pct	Rng	Rel Rng	Rel +/-	GDP Opps	GDP	GDP Pct	Rank	Exp GB	Exp Air	Made GB	Made Air	To His Right	Straight On	To His Left	GB	Air	Total	Rank
2003	NYM	69	69	596.1	107	214	9	42	.973	4.84	1.068	+20	73	39	.534	31	180	58	189	59	+9	+3	-2	+9	+1	+10	8
2004	NYM	10	7	72.2	18	26	2	5	.957	5.45	1.176	+7	9	5	.556	-	22	14	23	11	0	0	+1	+1	-3	-2	-
2005	NYM	161	159	1398.1	237	427	18	105	.974	4.27	.959	-29	148	97	.655	5	372	119	359	122	-14	-1	+3	-13	+3	-10	25
		240	235	2067.1	362	667	29	152	.973	4.48	1.002	-2	230	141	.613	7	574	191	571	192	-5	+2	+2	-3	+1	-2	18

Alex Rodriguez

Year	Team	G	GS	Inn	PO	A	E	DP	Pct	Rng	Rel Rng	Rel +/-	GDP Opps	GDP	GDP Pct	Rank	Exp GB	Exp Air	Made GB	Made Air	To His Right	Straight On	To His Left	GB	Air	Total	Rank
2003	Tex	158	158	1369.2	227	464	8	110	.989	4.54	.983	-12	169	99	.586	16	377	79	385	82	-9	+1	+16	+8	+3	+11	5
2004	NYY	2	0	2.0	1	1	0	0	1.000	9.00	2.000	+1	1	1	1.000	-	0		0			0				0	
2005	NYY	3	0	6.0	1	2	0	0	1.000	4.50	.941	0	0				2	1	2	1	-1	0	0	0	0	0	-
		163	158	1377.2	229	467	8	111	.989	4.55	.986	-11	170	100	.588	-	379	80	387	83	-10	+1	+16	+8	+3	+11	-

Jimmy Rollins

Year	Team	G	GS	Inn	PO	A	E	DP	Pct	Rng	Rel Rng	Rel +/-	GDP Opps	GDP	GDP Pct	Rank	Exp GB	Exp Air	Made GB	Made Air	To His Right	Straight On	To His Left	GB	Air	Total	Rank
2003	Phi	154	153	1357.2	203	463	14	92	.979	4.41	.978	-15	140	89	.636	5	392	107	403	108	+6	+5	0	+11	+1	+12	3
2004	Phi	154	153	1376.2	214	398	9	88	.986	4.00	.927	-48	130	82	.631	3	317	120	322	120	+2	+4	-1	+5	0	+5	14
2005	Phi	157	156	1356.0	208	411	12	80	.981	4.11	.956	-29	127	76	.598	14	346	104	365	108	+3	-2	+17	+19	+4	+23	4
		465	462	4090.1	625	1272	35	260	.982	4.17	.954	-92	397	247	.622	5	1055	331	1090	336	+11	+7	+16	+35	+5	+40	3

Marco Scutaro

Year	Team	G	GS	Inn	PO	A	E	DP	Pct	Rng	Rel Rng	Rel +/-	GDP Opps	GDP	GDP Pct	Rank	Exp GB	Exp Air	Made GB	Made Air	To His Right	Straight On	To His Left	GB	Air	Total	Rank
2003	NYM	1	0	2.0	1	1	0	0	1.000	9.00	1.984	+1	0			-	1	1	1	1				0	0	0	-
2004	Oak	16	11	113.1	25	42	2	9	.971	5.32	1.095	+6	16	8	.500	-	41	8	38	8	-1	0	-1	-3	0	-3	-
2005	Oak	81	73	663.0	115	213	8	50	.976	4.45	1.006	+2	76	46	.605	12	198	49	190	49	-7	+2	-2	-8	0	-8	24
		98	84	778.1	141	256	10	59	.975	4.59	1.026	+9	92	54	.587	-	240	58	229	58	-8	+2	-3	-11	0	-11	-

Miguel Tejada

Year	Team	G	GS	Inn	PO	A	E	DP	Pct	Rng	Rel Rng	Rel +/-	GDP Opps	GDP	GDP Pct	Rank	Exp GB	Exp Air	Made GB	Made Air	To His Right	Straight On	To His Left	GB	Air	Total	Rank
2003	Oak	162	162	1417.2	240	490	21	94	.972	4.63	.961	-30	151	85	.563	27	379	106	372	109	-5	+2	-4	-7	+3	-4	25
2004	Bal	162	162	1421.2	263	526	24	118	.970	4.99	1.082	+60	191	105	.550	24	433	114	448	113	+6	+7	+2	+15	-1	+14	4
2005	Bal	160	160	1394.2	252	480	22	105	.971	4.72	1.022	+16	166	95	.572	21	413	108	417	109	+25	-4	-17	+4	+1	+5	13
		484	484	4234.0	755	1496	67	317	.971	4.78	1.023	+46	508	285	.561	25	1225	328	1237	331	+26	+5	-19	+12	+3	+15	11

Juan Uribe

Year	Team	G	GS	Inn	PO	A	E	DP	Pct	Rng	Rel Rng	Rel +/-	GDP Opps	GDP	GDP Pct	Rank	Exp GB	Exp Air	Made GB	Made Air	To His Right	Straight On	To His Left	GB	Air	Total	Rank
2003	Col	74	69	598.1	143	242	11	57	.972	5.79	1.141	+46	90	53	.589	15	183	67	191	66	+17	+1	-10	+8	-1	+7	11
2004	CWS	38	32	287.1	54	115	3	31	.983	5.29	1.139	+21	44	30	.682	-	88	24	98	23	+11	-2	+1	+10	-1	+9	-
2005	CWS	146	143	1293.1	250	422	16	99	.977	4.68	1.059	+39	149	89	.597	15	361	125	364	131	+12	-2	-7	+3	+6	+9	9
		258	244	2179.0	447	779	30	187	.976	5.06	1.095	+106	283	172	.608	11	632	216	653	220	+40	-3	-16	+21	+4	+25	8

Omar Vizquel

Year	Team	G	GS	Inn	PO	A	E	DP	Pct	Rng	Rel Rng	Rel +/-	GDP Opps	GDP	GDP Pct	Rank	Exp GB	Exp Air	Made GB	Made Air	To His Right	Straight On	To His Left	GB	Air	Total	Rank
2003	Cle	64	63	551.1	114	203	7	58	.978	5.17	1.097	+28	79	54	.684	2	165	58	174	59	+7	+2	-1	+9	+1	+10	9
2004	Cle	147	141	1245.0	200	395	11	90	.982	4.30	.945	-35	140	74	.529	30	330	85	336	85	+5	+4	-4	+6	0	+6	9
2005	SF	150	144	1292.1	234	426	8	80	.988	4.60	1.035	+22	142	75	.528	32	379	118	383	118	-7	+16	-5	+4	0	+4	14
		361	348	3088.2	548	1024	26	228	.984	4.58	1.014	+15	361	203	.562	24	874	261	893	262	+5	+22	-10	+19	+1	+20	9

Shortstops

Jack Wilson

		BASIC									GROUND DP				PLAYS				PLUS/MINUS						
										Rel	Rel	GDP				Expected Outs		Outs Made		To His	Straight	To His				
Year	Team	G	GS	Inn	PO	A	E	DP	Pct	Rng	Rng	+/-	Opps	GDP	Pct	Rank	GB	Air	GB	Air	Right	On	Left	GB	Air	Total	Rank
2003	Pit	149	148	1294.2	218	454	17	104	.975	4.67	.969	-21	161	96	.596	13	346	80	351	83	+3	0	+2	+5	+3	+8	10
2004	Pit	156	155	1355.2	235	492	17	129	.977	4.83	1.046	+32	177	118	.667	1	379	101	388	103	+14	0	-6	+9	+2	+11	6
2005	Pit	157	155	1360.0	246	522	14	126	.982	5.08	1.066	+48	184	120	.652	6	414	99	440	104	+27	+8	-9	+26	+5	+31	2
		462	458	4010.1	699	1468	48	359	.978	4.86	1.029	+59	522	334	.640	3	1139	280	1179	290	+44	+8	-13	+40	+10	+50	2

Michael Young

		BASIC									GROUND DP				PLAYS				PLUS/MINUS						
										Rel	Rel	GDP				Expected Outs		Outs Made		To His	Straight	To His				
Year	Team	G	GS	Inn	PO	A	E	DP	Pct	Rng	Rng	+/-	Opps	GDP	Pct	Rank	GB	Air	GB	Air	Right	On	Left	GB	Air	Total	Rank
2003	Tex	7	1	17.0	4	5	0	1	1.000	4.76	1.031	0	2	1	.500	-	6	2	6	2				0	0	0	-
2004	Tex	158	158	1387.0	225	422	19	98	.971	4.20	.888	-82	167	92	.551	23	389	123	359	119	+1	-3	-27	-30	-4	-34	34
2005	Tex	155	155	1356.0	239	426	18	95	.974	4.41	.906	-68	157	88	.561	23	407	121	371	118	-15	-2	-19	-36	-3	-39	32
		320	314	2760.0	468	853	37	194	.973	4.31	.898	-150	326	181	.555	26	802	246	736	239	-14	-5	-46	-66	-7	-73	31

Left Fielders

Moises Alou

	BASIC									THROWING					PLAYS		PLUS/MINUS		
Year Team	G	GS	Inn	PO	A	E	DP	Pct	Rng	Opps To Advance	Extra Bases	Kills	Pct	Rank	Expected Outs	Outs Made	Total	Enhanced	Rank
2003 ChC	142	140	1219.0	203	4	6	1	.972	1.53	106	52	4	.491	27	199	199	0	-2	16
2004 ChC	154	152	1338.1	240	7	8	2	.969	1.66	91	36	4	.396	15	234	236	+2	+3	11
2005 SF	74	66	576.0	132	1	4	0	.971	2.08	63	21	1	.333	8	131	132	+1	+2	12
	370	358	3133.1	575	12	18	3	.970	1.69	260	109	9	.419	25	564	567	+3	+3	14

Garret Anderson

	BASIC									THROWING					PLAYS		PLUS/MINUS		
Year Team	G	GS	Inn	PO	A	E	DP	Pct	Rng	Opps To Advance	Extra Bases	Kills	Pct	Rank	Expected Outs	Outs Made	Total	Enhanced	Rank
2003 Ana	144	144	1241.1	326	14	1	2	.997	2.47	135	58	7	.430	19	305	302	-3	+2	8
2005 LAA	106	106	920.0	201	4	5	1	.976	2.01	80	32	3	.400	21	207	201	-6	-7	27
	250	250	2161.1	527	18	6	3	.989	2.27	215	90	10	.419	24	512	503	-9	-5	24

Jason Bay

	BASIC									THROWING					PLAYS		PLUS/MINUS		
Year Team	G	GS	Inn	PO	A	E	DP	Pct	Rng	Opps To Advance	Extra Bases	Kills	Pct	Rank	Expected Outs	Outs Made	Total	Enhanced	Rank
2003 2 tms	24	20	180.1	34	0	1	0	.971	1.70	16	7	0	.438	-	29	29	0	0	-
2004 Pit	117	107	963.0	208	3	2	0	.991	1.97	94	42	2	.447	23	179	179	0	+1	14
2005 Pit	146	133	1185.2	264	3	1	1	.996	2.03	121	53	3	.438	28	269	266	-3	-4	24
	287	260	2329.0	506	6	4	1	.992	1.98	231	102	5	.442	30	477	474	-3	-3	21

Larry Bigbie

	BASIC									THROWING					PLAYS		PLUS/MINUS		
Year Team	G	GS	Inn	PO	A	E	DP	Pct	Rng	Opps To Advance	Extra Bases	Kills	Pct	Rank	Expected Outs	Outs Made	Total	Enhanced	Rank
2003 Bal	76	74	648.1	153	4	1	0	.994	2.18	67	27	2	.403	16	159	150	-9	-10	25
2004 Bal	114	102	915.0	215	2	2	0	.991	2.13	116	53	1	.457	24	200	207	+7	+17	1
2005 2 tms	57	54	480.1	98	3	0	0	1.000	1.89	48	14	2	.292	-	102	98	-4	-5	-
	247	230	2043.2	466	9	3	0	.994	2.09	231	94	5	.407	18	461	455	-6	+2	15

Barry Bonds

	BASIC									THROWING					PLAYS		PLUS/MINUS		
Year Team	G	GS	Inn	PO	A	E	DP	Pct	Rng	Opps To Advance	Extra Bases	Kills	Pct	Rank	Expected Outs	Outs Made	Total	Enhanced	Rank
2003 SF	123	122	1044.0	236	5	2	2	.992	2.08	82	28	3	.341	3	203	209	+6	+6	7
2004 SF	133	132	1130.2	214	11	4	0	.983	1.79	111	54	5	.486	27	208	208	0	-2	18
2005 SF	13	13	95.0	18	0	0	0	1.000	1.71	8	2	0	.250	-	17	18	+1	+3	-
	269	267	2269.2	468	16	6	2	.988	1.92	201	84	8	.418	23	428	435	+7	+7	11

Chris Burke

	BASIC									THROWING					PLAYS		PLUS/MINUS		
Year Team	G	GS	Inn	PO	A	E	DP	Pct	Rng	Opps To Advance	Extra Bases	Kills	Pct	Rank	Expected Outs	Outs Made	Total	Enhanced	Rank
2005 Hou	83	74	634.0	120	3	1	1	.992	1.75	45	15	2	.333	7	114	120	+6	+8	7

Pat Burrell

	BASIC									THROWING					PLAYS		PLUS/MINUS		
Year Team	G	GS	Inn	PO	A	E	DP	Pct	Rng	Opps To Advance	Extra Bases	Kills	Pct	Rank	Expected Outs	Outs Made	Total	Enhanced	Rank
2003 Phi	140	138	1186.2	234	7	6	0	.976	1.83	110	40	4	.364	6	219	229	+10	+11	3
2004 Phi	122	121	1060.0	217	9	4	1	.983	1.92	98	28	7	.286	4	206	207	+1	-2	19
2005 Phi	153	153	1296.2	236	10	7	2	.972	1.71	147	52	9	.354	13	232	236	+4	+3	10
	415	412	3543.1	687	26	17	3	.977	1.81	355	120	20	.338	5	657	672	+15	+12	4

Eric Byrnes

	BASIC									THROWING					PLAYS		PLUS/MINUS		
Year Team	G	GS	Inn	PO	A	E	DP	Pct	Rng	Opps To Advance	Extra Bases	Kills	Pct	Rank	Expected Outs	Outs Made	Total	Enhanced	Rank
2003 Oak	44	31	283.1	49	3	0	0	1.000	1.65	29	8	1	.276	-	40	40	0	+1	-
2004 Oak	109	98	871.1	172	7	2	2	.989	1.85	89	28	3	.315	9	162	165	+3	+1	15
2005 3 tms	106	90	803.0	209	5	4	1	.982	2.40	74	34	4	.459	30	207	209	+2	+6	9
	259	219	1957.2	430	15	6	3	.987	2.05	192	70	8	.365	10	409	414	+5	+8	8

Left Fielders

Miguel Cabrera

		BASIC									THROWING					PLAYS		PLUS/MINUS		
Year	Team	G	GS	Inn	PO	A	E	DP	Pct	Rng	Opps To Advance	Extra Bases	Kills	Pct	Rank	Expected Outs	Outs Made	Total	Enhanced	Rank
2003	Fla	55	55	481.0	99	5	3	1	.972	1.95	52	17	5	.327	-	102	99	-3	-5	-
2004	Fla	59	58	504.0	92	6	2	0	.980	1.75	40	12	5	.300	6	84	87	+3	+6	9
2005	Fla	134	128	1105.2	188	12	5	3	.976	1.63	106	36	10	.340	9	204	188	-16	-28	29
		248	241	2090.2	379	23	10	4	.976	1.73	198	65	20	.328	4	390	374	-16	-27	28

Frank Catalanotto

		BASIC									THROWING					PLAYS		PLUS/MINUS		
Year	Team	G	GS	Inn	PO	A	E	DP	Pct	Rng	Opps To Advance	Extra Bases	Kills	Pct	Rank	Expected Outs	Outs Made	Total	Enhanced	Rank
2003	Tor	61	55	460.1	91	4	1	0	.990	1.86	49	16	3	.327	-	81	84	+3	+1	-
2004	Tor	41	34	309.2	66	1	2	1	.971	1.95	33	13	1	.394	-	60	62	+2	+1	-
2005	Tor	111	99	761.0	163	4	0	0	1.000	1.98	54	13	3	.241	1	164	163	-1	-5	25
		213	188	1531.0	320	9	3	1	.991	1.93	136	42	7	.309	2	305	309	+4	-3	22

Carl Crawford

		BASIC									THROWING					PLAYS		PLUS/MINUS		
Year	Team	G	GS	Inn	PO	A	E	DP	Pct	Rng	Opps To Advance	Extra Bases	Kills	Pct	Rank	Expected Outs	Outs Made	Total	Enhanced	Rank
2003	TB	137	131	1159.1	317	10	3	1	.991	2.54	136	52	5	.382	10	287	294	+7	+11	2
2004	TB	123	116	1010.0	274	5	1	1	.996	2.49	100	30	3	.300	7	259	270	+11	+14	2
2005	TB	147	142	1246.2	341	3	2	1	.994	2.48	155	40	3	.258	2	325	341	+16	+20	2
		407	389	3416.0	932	18	6	3	.994	2.50	391	122	11	.312	3	871	905	+34	+45	1

Coco Crisp

		BASIC									THROWING					PLAYS		PLUS/MINUS		
Year	Team	G	GS	Inn	PO	A	E	DP	Pct	Rng	Opps To Advance	Extra Bases	Kills	Pct	Rank	Expected Outs	Outs Made	Total	Enhanced	Rank
2003	Cle	39	38	347.0	88	4	1	0	.989	2.39	33	12	2	.364	-	76	80	+4	+4	-
2004	Cle	37	31	293.1	81	2	0	1	1.000	2.55	23	10	0	.435	-	73	77	+4	+9	-
2005	Cle	138	133	1200.0	294	3	4	0	.987	2.23	110	41	1	.373	19	279	294	+15	+26	1
		214	202	1840.1	463	9	5	1	.990	2.31	166	63	3	.380	12	428	451	+23	+39	2

David Dellucci

		BASIC									THROWING					PLAYS		PLUS/MINUS		
Year	Team	G	GS	Inn	PO	A	E	DP	Pct	Rng	Opps To Advance	Extra Bases	Kills	Pct	Rank	Expected Outs	Outs Made	Total	Enhanced	Rank
2003	2 tms	6	2	21.1	2	0	0	0	1.000	.84	1	1	0	1.000	-	1	2	+1	+1	-
2004	Tex	84	77	648.2	152	0	2	0	.987	2.11	61	31	0	.508	28	148	147	-1	-6	23
2005	Tex	47	44	378.2	84	4	2	1	.978	2.09	38	16	1	.421	-	86	84	-2	-4	-
		137	123	1048.2	238	4	4	1	.984	2.08	100	48	1	.480	-	235	233	-2	-9	-

Adam Dunn

		BASIC									THROWING					PLAYS		PLUS/MINUS		
Year	Team	G	GS	Inn	PO	A	E	DP	Pct	Rng	Opps To Advance	Extra Bases	Kills	Pct	Rank	Expected Outs	Outs Made	Total	Enhanced	Rank
2003	Cin	99	98	828.2	205	5	9	2	.959	2.28	99	39	3	.394	14	187	184	-3	-4	18
2004	Cin	156	146	1327.1	250	10	8	1	.970	1.76	128	38	7	.297	5	231	225	-6	-18	26
2005	Cin	133	126	1090.2	246	6	5	0	.981	2.08	113	41	2	.363	15	250	246	-4	-16	28
		388	370	3246.2	701	21	22	3	.970	2.00	340	118	12	.347	6	668	655	-13	-38	30

Pedro Feliz

		BASIC									THROWING					PLAYS		PLUS/MINUS		
Year	Team	G	GS	Inn	PO	A	E	DP	Pct	Rng	Opps To Advance	Extra Bases	Kills	Pct	Rank	Expected Outs	Outs Made	Total	Enhanced	Rank
2003	SF	14	11	92.2	22	0	1	0	.957	2.14	11	4	0	.364	-	19	20	+1	+2	-
2004	SF	2	0	2.0	1	0	0	0	1.000	4.50					-	1	1	0	0	-
2005	SF	75	70	615.2	138	0	3	0	.979	2.02	66	20	0	.303	3	136	138	+2	-2	17
		91	81	710.1	161	0	4	0	.976	2.04	77	24	0	.312	-	156	159	+3	0	-

Cliff Floyd

		BASIC									THROWING					PLAYS		PLUS/MINUS		
Year	Team	G	GS	Inn	PO	A	E	DP	Pct	Rng	Opps To Advance	Extra Bases	Kills	Pct	Rank	Expected Outs	Outs Made	Total	Enhanced	Rank
2003	NYM	95	94	728.2	159	8	5	4	.971	2.06	74	29	6	.392	13	163	159	-4	0	13
2004	NYM	107	106	863.2	164	5	2	1	.988	1.76	93	48	3	.516	29	163	162	-1	-4	21
2005	NYM	150	147	1263.2	283	15	2	0	.993	2.12	147	52	14	.354	12	286	283	-3	+1	13
		352	347	2856.0	606	28	9	5	.986	2.00	314	129	23	.411	20	612	604	-8	-3	20

Left Fielders

Luis Gonzalez

Year Team	G	GS	Inn	PO	A	E	DP	Pct	Rng	Opps To Advance	Extra Bases	Kills	Pct	Rank	Expected Outs	Outs Made	Total	Enhanced	Rank
				BASIC								**THROWING**			**PLAYS**			**PLUS/MINUS**	
2003 Ari	154	154	1359.1	249	9	3	0	.989	1.71	114	51	2	.447	23	238	235	-3	-3	17
2004 Ari	104	103	900.2	162	2	6	0	.965	1.64	83	35	2	.422	21	156	157	+1	+3	12
2005 Ari	152	149	1318.1	270	7	3	1	.989	1.89	153	62	0	.405	24	266	270	+4	+7	8
	410	406	3578.1	681	18	12	1	.983	1.76	350	148	4	.423	27	660	662	+2	+7	10

Todd Hollandsworth

Year Team	G	GS	Inn	PO	A	E	DP	Pct	Rng	Opps To Advance	Extra Bases	Kills	Pct	Rank	Expected Outs	Outs Made	Total	Enhanced	Rank
2003 Fla	61	56	491.1	106	5	2	0	.982	2.03	68	25	3	.368	-	102	99	-3	-8	-
2004 ChC	4	3	29.0	5	0	0	0	1.000	1.55	2	2	0	1.000	-	5	5	0	0	-
2005 2 tms	98	63	599.0	103	2	1	0	.991	1.58	77	34	2	.442	29	105	103	-2	-2	19
	163	122	1119.1	214	7	3	0	.987	1.78	147	61	5	.415	-	212	207	-5	-10	-

Matt Holliday

Year Team	G	GS	Inn	PO	A	E	DP	Pct	Rng	Opps To Advance	Extra Bases	Kills	Pct	Rank	Expected Outs	Outs Made	Total	Enhanced	Rank
2004 Col	115	109	917.0	177	4	7	1	.963	1.78	111	46	1	.414	18	168	168	0	0	16
2005 Col	123	121	1049.2	236	5	7	2	.972	2.07	117	47	3	.402	22	229	236	+7	+9	6
	238	230	1966.2	413	9	14	3	.968	1.93	228	93	4	.408	19	397	404	+7	+9	6

Raul Ibanez

Year Team	G	GS	Inn	PO	A	E	DP	Pct	Rng	Opps To Advance	Extra Bases	Kills	Pct	Rank	Expected Outs	Outs Made	Total	Enhanced	Rank
2003 KC	128	119	1042.0	231	8	3	1	.988	2.06	102	36	6	.353	5	222	215	-7	-5	21
2004 Sea	110	106	949.1	227	10	4	3	.983	2.25	94	34	6	.362	12	212	216	+4	+7	7
2005 Sea	55	54	463.2	105	6	2	3	.982	2.15	60	20	5	.333	-	104	106	+2	+6	-
	293	279	2455.0	563	24	9	7	.985	2.15	256	90	17	.352	8	538	537	-1	+8	7

Kelly Johnson

Year Team	G	GS	Inn	PO	A	E	DP	Pct	Rng	Opps To Advance	Extra Bases	Kills	Pct	Rank	Expected Outs	Outs Made	Total	Enhanced	Rank
2005 Atl	79	73	648.1	166	6	0	1	1.000	2.39	71	22	5	.310	5	161	166	+5	+10	5

Reed Johnson

Year Team	G	GS	Inn	PO	A	E	DP	Pct	Rng	Opps To Advance	Extra Bases	Kills	Pct	Rank	Expected Outs	Outs Made	Total	Enhanced	Rank
2003 Tor	53	33	326.2	74	2	1	0	.987	2.09	27	13	2	.481	-	59	61	+2	+4	
2004 Tor	57	53	461.1	96	5	2	1	.981	1.97	46	15	4	.326	-	91	94	+3	+8	
2005 Tor	118	55	590.2	134	4	1	1	.993	2.10	46	15	2	.326	6	124	134	+10	+17	4
	228	141	1378.2	304	11	4	2	.987	2.06	119	43	8	.361	-	274	289	+15	+29	

Ryan Klesko

Year Team	G	GS	Inn	PO	A	E	DP	Pct	Rng	Opps To Advance	Extra Bases	Kills	Pct	Rank	Expected Outs	Outs Made	Total	Enhanced	Rank
2004 SD	104	102	723.2	135	2	2	0	.986	1.70	68	42	0	.618	30	138	128	-10	-18	28
2005 SD	121	120	927.0	204	7	4	1	.981	2.05	93	39	2	.419	26	205	204	-1	-3	21
	225	222	1650.2	339	9	6	1	.983	1.90	161	81	2	.503	31	343	332	-11	-21	26

Ryan Langerhans

Year Team	G	GS	Inn	PO	A	E	DP	Pct	Rng	Opps To Advance	Extra Bases	Kills	Pct	Rank	Expected Outs	Outs Made	Total	Enhanced	Rank
2003 Atl	3	0	5.0	1	0	0	0	1.000	1.80					-	1	1	0	0	-
2005 Atl	54	41	379.1	91	0	0	0	1.000	2.16	37	11	0	.297	-	85	91	+6	+10	-
	57	41	384.1	92	0	0	0	1.000	2.15	37	11	0	.297	-	86	92	+6	+10	-

Carlos Lee

Year Team	G	GS	Inn	PO	A	E	DP	Pct	Rng	Opps To Advance	Extra Bases	Kills	Pct	Rank	Expected Outs	Outs Made	Total	Enhanced	Rank
2003 CWS	156	155	1328.2	307	8	7	1	.978	2.13	134	64	4	.478	26	297	303	+6	+14	1
2004 CWS	148	148	1277.2	282	11	0	2	1.000	2.06	113	46	8	.407	17	276	277	+1	+8	5
2005 Mil	162	161	1404.0	307	8	6	3	.981	2.02	134	49	5	.366	17	312	307	-5	-4	23
	466	464	4010.1	896	27	13	6	.986	2.07	381	159	17	.417	22	885	887	+2	+18	3

Left Fielders

Terrence Long

Year	Team	G	GS	Inn	PO	A	E	DP	Pct	Rng	Opps To Advance	Extra Bases	Kills	Pct	Rank	Expected Outs	Outs Made	Total	Enhanced	Rank
											THROWING					**PLAYS**		**PLUS/MINUS**		
2003	Oak	75	62	567.2	105	1	0	0	1.000	1.68	46	18	1	.391	12	90	92	+2	+1	11
2004	SD	61	30	330.2	85	1	2	0	.977	2.34	30	11	1	.367	-	73	80	+7	+10	-
2005	KC	103	94	794.0	166	9	2	1	.989	1.98	129	52	6	.403	23	166	166	0	-3	22
		239	186	1692.1	356	11	4	1	.989	1.95	205	81	8	.395	16	329	338	+9	+8	9

Hideki Matsui

Year	Team	G	GS	Inn	PO	A	E	DP	Pct	Rng	Opps To Advance	Extra Bases	Kills	Pct	Rank	Expected Outs	Outs Made	Total	Enhanced	Rank
2003	NYY	118	110	997.1	210	11	7	1	.969	1.99	120	51	4	.425	26	220	210	-10	-12	26
2004	NYY	162	160	1388.0	303	8	7	2	.978	2.02	131	37	5	.282	2	306	289	-17	-24	30
2005	NYY	115	110	976.2	218	7	3	1	.987	2.07	113	41	4	.363	14	221	219	-2	+3	11
		395	380	3362.0	731	26	17	6	.978	2.03	364	129	13	.354	9	747	718	-29	-33	29

Kevin Mench

Year	Team	G	GS	Inn	PO	A	E	DP	Pct	Rng	Opps To Advance	Extra Bases	Kills	Pct	Rank	Expected Outs	Outs Made	Total	Enhanced	Rank
2003	Tex	34	30	267.0	56	1	1	0	.983	1.92	38	15	0	.395	-	57	54	-3	-3	-
2004	Tex	53	37	362.2	73	1	1	1	.987	1.84	28	8	0	.286	-	73	73	0	-2	-
2005	Tex	119	108	978.1	230	8	2	3	.992	2.19	122	52	7	.426	27	227	231	+4	0	15
		206	175	1608.0	359	10	4	4	.989	2.07	188	75	7	.399	17	357	358	+1	-5	25

Craig Monroe

Year	Team	G	GS	Inn	PO	A	E	DP	Pct	Rng	Opps To Advance	Extra Bases	Kills	Pct	Rank	Expected Outs	Outs Made	Total	Enhanced	Rank
2003	Det	75	70	602.2	148	6	4	1	.975	2.30	73	32	5	.438	21	141	138	-3	-4	19
2004	Det	65	50	446.0	102	1	8	0	.928	2.08	48	21	0	.438	-	78	80	+2	+3	-
2005	Det	69	56	501.2	99	6	1	4	.991	1.88	54	22	3	.407	25	99	99	0	0	14
		209	176	1550.1	349	13	13	5	.965	2.10	175	75	8	.429	28	318	317	-1	-1	17

Jay Payton

Year	Team	G	GS	Inn	PO	A	E	DP	Pct	Rng	Opps To Advance	Extra Bases	Kills	Pct	Rank	Expected Outs	Outs Made	Total	Enhanced	Rank
2003	Col	149	143	1230.0	298	6	3	1	.990	2.22	147	40	3	.272	1	276	273	-3	-5	20
2004	SD	9	4	48.0	9	0	0	0	1.000	1.69	3	1	0	.333	-	7	8	+1	+2	-
2005	2 tms	60	50	465.1	107	1	0	0	1.000	2.09	35	10	1	.286	-	105	107	+2	+1	-
		218	197	1743.1	414	7	3	1	.993	2.17	185	51	4	.276	1	388	388	0	-2	18

Scott Podsednik

Year	Team	G	GS	Inn	PO	A	E	DP	Pct	Rng	Opps To Advance	Extra Bases	Kills	Pct	Rank	Expected Outs	Outs Made	Total	Enhanced	Rank
2003	Mil	3	0	8.1	0	0	0	0	-	.00					-				0	
2005	CWS	124	118	1061.2	260	3	3	1	.989	2.23	96	35	3	.365	16	248	260	+12	+20	3
		127	118	1070.0	260	3	3	1	.989	2.21	96	35	3	.365	-	248	260	+12	+20	-

Manny Ramirez

Year	Team	G	GS	Inn	PO	A	E	DP	Pct	Rng	Opps To Advance	Extra Bases	Kills	Pct	Rank	Expected Outs	Outs Made	Total	Enhanced	Rank
2003	Bos	128	126	1073.0	207	11	4	1	.982	1.83	118	41	5	.347	4	214	207	-7	-20	28
2004	Bos	132	132	1087.2	198	4	7	0	.967	1.67	123	52	2	.423	22	207	197	-10	-18	27
2005	Bos	149	147	1225.0	243	17	7	0	.974	1.91	147	56	13	.381	20	257	243	-14	-31	30
		409	405	3385.2	648	32	18	1	.974	1.81	388	149	20	.384	14	678	647	-31	-69	31

Reggie Sanders

Year	Team	G	GS	Inn	PO	A	E	DP	Pct	Rng	Opps To Advance	Extra Bases	Kills	Pct	Rank	Expected Outs	Outs Made	Total	Enhanced	Rank
2003	Pit	39	36	311.2	67	1	2	1	.971	1.96	29	10	1	.345	-	42	46	+4	+5	-
2004	StL	38	36	297.1	65	2	1	1	.985	2.03	22	10	2	.455	-	56	60	+4	+7	-
2005	StL	80	78	636.0	108	5	2	0	.983	1.60	52	16	2	.308	4	111	108	-3	-2	18
		157	150	1245.0	240	8	5	2	.980	1.79	103	36	5	.350	-	209	214	+5	+10	-

Left Fielders

Shannon Stewart

		BASIC									THROWING						PLAYS			PLUS/MINUS		
										Opps To	Extra					Expected	Outs					
Year	Team	G	GS	Inn	PO	A	E	DP	Pct	Rng	Advance	Bases	Kills	Pct	Rank	Outs	Made	Total	Enhanced	Rank
2003	2 tms	115	113	986.1	247	7	4	0	.984	2.32	96	38	5	.396	15	231	233	+2	+2	9
2004	Min	71	71	639.1	103	2	3	0	.972	1.48	57	24	0	.421	20	97	96	-1	0	17
2005	Min	125	125	1107.0	249	7	4	2	.985	2.08	104	36	3	.346	11	249	249	0	-1	16
		311	309	2732.2	599	16	11	2	.982	2.03	257	98	8	.381	13	577	578	+1	+1	16

Rondell White

		BASIC									THROWING						PLAYS			PLUS/MINUS		
										Opps To	Extra					Expected	Outs					
Year	Team	G	GS	Inn	PO	A	E	DP	Pct	Rng	Advance	Bases	Kills	Pct	Rank	Outs	Made	Total	Enhanced	Rank
2003	2 tms	121	119	969.1	218	6	5	2	.978	2.08	110	43	5	.391	11	204	209	+5	+8	5
2004	Det	74	73	614.2	127	2	3	0	.977	1.89	84	40	1	.476	25	108	110	+2	+7	8
2005	Det	65	65	534.2	119	0	0	0	1.000	2.00	41	15	0	.366	18	123	119	-4	-5	26
		260	257	2118.2	464	8	8	2	.983	2.01	235	98	6	.417	21	435	438	+3	+10	5

Randy Winn

		BASIC									THROWING						PLAYS			PLUS/MINUS		
										Opps To	Extra					Expected	Outs					
Year	Team	G	GS	Inn	PO	A	E	DP	Pct	Rng	Advance	Bases	Kills	Pct	Rank	Outs	Made	Total	Enhanced	Rank
2003	Sea	139	134	1188.0	299	3	3	1	.990	2.29	98	40	1	.408	17	284	290	+6	+10	4
2004	Sea	40	32	288.0	74	0	0	0	1.000	2.31	37	13	0	.351	-	70	70	0	-2	-
2005	2 tms	92	90	795.2	226	2	0	0	1.000	2.58	84	29	2	.345	10	226	226	0	-3	20
		271	256	2271.2	599	5	3	1	.995	2.39	219	82	3	.374	11	580	586	+6	+5	12

Center Fielders

Carlos Beltran

	BASIC									THROWING					PLAYS		PLUS/MINUS		
										Opps To Advance	Extra Bases	Kills	Pct	Rank	Expected Outs	Outs Made	Total	Enhanced	Rank
Year	Team	G	GS	Inn	PO	A	E	DP	Pct	Rng									
2003	KC	130	129	1123.0	371	10	5	1	.987	3.05	120	72	6	.600	17	341	338	-3	-2	18
2004	2 tms	158	157	1369.1	397	13	8	4	.981	2.69	154	91	7	.591	16	331	332	+1	+9	6
2005	NYM	150	149	1289.1	378	5	4	1	.990	2.67	138	91	4	.659	32	377	378	+1	+7	8
		438	435	3781.2	1146	28	17	6	.986	2.79	412	254	17	.617	24	1049	1048	-1	+14	5

Milton Bradley

	BASIC									THROWING					PLAYS		PLUS/MINUS		
										Opps To Advance	Extra Bases	Kills	Pct	Rank	Expected Outs	Outs Made	Total	Enhanced	Rank
Year	Team	G	GS	Inn	PO	A	E	DP	Pct	Rng									
2003	Cle	93	93	838.2	245	6	2	2	.992	2.69	96	59	3	.615	20	233	235	+2	+1	16
2004	LA	93	91	792.2	231	2	4	1	.983	2.65	69	42	1	.609	21	232	230	-2	0	14
2005	LAD	73	73	628.0	181	6	2	0	.989	2.68	65	37	4	.569	17	182	181	-1	-6	26
		259	257	2259.1	657	14	8	3	.988	2.67	230	138	8	.600	17	647	646	-1	-5	22

Brady Clark

	BASIC									THROWING					PLAYS		PLUS/MINUS		
										Opps To Advance	Extra Bases	Kills	Pct	Rank	Expected Outs	Outs Made	Total	Enhanced	Rank
Year	Team	G	GS	Inn	PO	A	E	DP	Pct	Rng									
2003	Mil	6	4	49.0	17	3	0	2	1.000	3.67	10	5	2	.500	-	17	17	0	-1	-
2004	Mil	9	7	63.0	22	1	0	1	1.000	3.29	6	4	0	.667	-	11	13	+2	+2	-
2005	Mil	145	145	1275.1	399	5	2	4	.995	2.85	131	79	5	.603	21	398	399	+1	+1	18
		160	156	1387.1	438	9	2	7	.996	2.90	147	88	7	.599	-	426	429	+3	+2	-

Johnny Damon

	BASIC									THROWING					PLAYS		PLUS/MINUS		
										Opps To Advance	Extra Bases	Kills	Pct	Rank	Expected Outs	Outs Made	Total	Enhanced	Rank
Year	Team	G	GS	Inn	PO	A	E	DP	Pct	Rng									
2003	Bos	144	141	1265.0	362	7	1	1	.997	2.63	132	85	3	.644	23	355	363	+8	+15	3
2004	Bos	148	145	1256.1	349	5	5	2	.986	2.54	121	72	4	.595	18	354	346	-8	-16	30
2005	Bos	147	144	1225.0	394	5	6	0	.985	2.93	120	69	4	.575	18	398	396	-2	-2	23
		439	430	3746.1	1105	17	12	3	.989	2.70	373	226	11	.606	20	1107	1105	-2	-3	21

David DeJesus

	BASIC									THROWING					PLAYS		PLUS/MINUS		
										Opps To Advance	Extra Bases	Kills	Pct	Rank	Expected Outs	Outs Made	Total	Enhanced	Rank
Year	Team	G	GS	Inn	PO	A	E	DP	Pct	Rng									
2003	KC	8	0	21.0	2	0	0	0	1.000	.86	5	5	0	1.000	-	2	2	0	0	-
2004	KC	85	85	732.1	231	3	4	0	.983	2.88	95	62	3	.653	26	201	206	+5	+10	5
2005	KC	119	118	1005.1	306	7	4	3	.987	2.80	122	67	7	.549	15	301	306	+5	+1	19
		212	203	1758.2	539	10	8	3	.986	2.81	222	134	10	.604	18	504	514	+10	+11	10

Jim Edmonds

	BASIC									THROWING					PLAYS		PLUS/MINUS		
										Opps To Advance	Extra Bases	Kills	Pct	Rank	Expected Outs	Outs Made	Total	Enhanced	Rank
Year	Team	G	GS	Inn	PO	A	E	DP	Pct	Rng									
2003	StL	128	118	1017.1	334	12	5	4	.986	3.06	113	61	8	.540	6	302	305	+3	+3	13
2004	StL	146	141	1241.2	314	11	4	2	.988	2.36	117	52	9	.444	1	306	305	-1	-12	27
2005	StL	139	132	1153.1	318	5	2	1	.994	2.52	117	48	2	.410	1	319	319	0	-6	25
		413	391	3412.1	966	28	11	7	.989	2.62	347	161	19	.464	1	927	929	+2	-15	28

Jason Ellison

	BASIC									THROWING					PLAYS		PLUS/MINUS		
										Opps To Advance	Extra Bases	Kills	Pct	Rank	Expected Outs	Outs Made	Total	Enhanced	Rank
Year	Team	G	GS	Inn	PO	A	E	DP	Pct	Rng									
2003	SF	1	0	1.0	1	0	0	0	1.000	9.00					-	1	1	0	0	-
2004	SF	4	0	10.0	5	0	0	0	1.000	4.50					-	5	5	0	+1	-
2005	SF	78	64	591.2	196	4	6	0	.971	3.04	70	49	3	.700	35	193	197	+4	+3	15
		83	64	602.2	202	4	6	0	.972	3.08	70	49	3	.700	-	199	203	+4	+4	-

Steve Finley

	BASIC									THROWING					PLAYS		PLUS/MINUS		
										Opps To Advance	Extra Bases	Kills	Pct	Rank	Expected Outs	Outs Made	Total	Enhanced	Rank
Year	Team	G	GS	Inn	PO	A	E	DP	Pct	Rng									
2003	Ari	140	130	1168.1	258	9	5	1	.982	2.06	120	60	8	.500	2	253	245	-8	-4	20
2004	2 tms	158	157	1381.1	359	5	3	3	.992	2.37	153	90	2	.588	14	340	351	+11	+22	1
2005	LAA	104	100	895.2	266	5	4	2	.985	2.72	88	44	3	.500	5	273	266	-7	-7	27
		402	387	3445.1	883	19	12	6	.987	2.36	361	194	13	.537	6	866	862	-4	+11	9

Center Fielders

Lew Ford

Year	Team	G	GS	Inn	PO	A	E	DP	Pct	Rng	Opps To Advance	Extra Bases	Kills	Pct	Rank	Expected Outs	Outs Made	Total	Enhanced	Rank
2003	Min	13	5	74.1	18	1	2	1	.905	2.30	16	11	0	.688	-	18	18	0	+1	-
2004	Min	46	35	341.0	101	1	3	0	.971	2.69	41	29	0	.707	-	78	82	+4	+8	-
2005	Min	63	60	548.0	140	7	4	1	.974	2.41	76	40	1	.526	9	134	140	+6	+11	5
		122	100	963.1	259	9	9	2	.968	2.50	133	80	1	.602	-	230	240	+10	+20	-

Joey Gathright

Year	Team	G	GS	Inn	PO	A	E	DP	Pct	Rng	Opps To Advance	Extra Bases	Kills	Pct	Rank	Expected Outs	Outs Made	Total	Enhanced	Rank
2004	TB	11	11	96.0	27	0	0	0	1.000	2.53	14	8	0	.571	-	27	27	0	-1	-
2005	TB	70	56	505.2	180	3	3	2	.984	3.26	54	33	3	.611	25	170	181	+11	+23	3
		81	67	601.2	207	3	3	2	.986	3.14	68	41	3	.603	-	197	208	+11	+22	-

Ken Griffey Jr.

Year	Team	G	GS	Inn	PO	A	E	DP	Pct	Rng	Opps To Advance	Extra Bases	Kills	Pct	Rank	Expected Outs	Outs Made	Total	Enhanced	Rank
2003	Cin	43	43	355.2	89	3	1	0	.989	2.33	39	26	2	.667	-	90	87	-3	-6	-
2004	Cin	76	76	656.1	173	4	1	1	.994	2.43	74	41	1	.554	7	178	168	-10	-25	32
2005	Cin	124	124	1065.2	285	6	3	1	.990	2.46	136	74	4	.544	12	299	286	-13	-27	33
		243	243	2077.2	547	13	5	2	.991	2.43	249	141	7	.566	13	567	541	-26	-58	31

Damon Hollins

Year	Team	G	GS	Inn	PO	A	E	DP	Pct	Rng	Opps To Advance	Extra Bases	Kills	Pct	Rank	Expected Outs	Outs Made	Total	Enhanced	Rank
2005	TB	80	72	619.0	199	4	3	2	.985	2.95	91	62	3	.681	34	206	198	-8	-13	32

Torii Hunter

Year	Team	G	GS	Inn	PO	A	E	DP	Pct	Rng	Opps To Advance	Extra Bases	Kills	Pct	Rank	Expected Outs	Outs Made	Total	Enhanced	Rank
2003	Min	151	149	1299.1	425	5	4	1	.991	2.98	154	89	4	.578	14	383	390	+7	+22	1
2004	Min	126	124	1100.0	311	5	4	0	.988	2.59	136	70	5	.515	3	296	301	+5	+17	2
2005	Min	93	92	813.1	218	9	3	4	.987	2.51	94	58	7	.617	26	217	218	+1	+5	11
		370	365	3212.2	954	19	11	5	.989	2.73	384	217	16	.565	12	896	909	+13	+44	1

Andruw Jones

Year	Team	G	GS	Inn	PO	A	E	DP	Pct	Rng	Opps To Advance	Extra Bases	Kills	Pct	Rank	Expected Outs	Outs Made	Total	Enhanced	Rank
2003	Atl	155	153	1329.0	390	8	3	1	.993	2.70	156	85	3	.545	7	373	387	+14	+13	4
2004	Atl	154	153	1347.0	389	10	3	3	.993	2.67	163	88	6	.540	6	376	382	+6	+6	9
2005	Atl	159	158	1366.1	365	11	2	1	.995	2.48	138	73	6	.529	10	361	365	+4	+7	9
		468	464	4042.1	1144	29	8	5	.993	2.61	457	246	15	.538	7	1110	1134	+24	+26	3

Mark Kotsay

Year	Team	G	GS	Inn	PO	A	E	DP	Pct	Rng	Opps To Advance	Extra Bases	Kills	Pct	Rank	Expected Outs	Outs Made	Total	Enhanced	Rank
2003	SD	127	121	1055.1	324	13	3	3	.991	2.87	142	82	6	.577	13	312	315	+3	+4	12
2004	Oak	145	140	1255.0	347	11	6	3	.984	2.57	129	72	6	.558	9	324	331	+7	+7	8
2005	Oak	137	137	1184.1	298	7	4	3	.987	2.32	103	50	6	.485	3	300	300	0	+1	20
		409	398	3494.2	969	31	13	9	.987	2.58	374	204	18	.545	8	936	946	+10	+12	7

Kenny Lofton

Year	Team	G	GS	Inn	PO	A	E	DP	Pct	Rng	Opps To Advance	Extra Bases	Kills	Pct	Rank	Expected Outs	Outs Made	Total	Enhanced	Rank
2003	2 tms	137	133	1170.0	314	8	3	2	.991	2.48	107	64	6	.598	16	300	303	+3	+2	15
2004	NYY	65	62	539.1	162	3	1	3	.994	2.75	52	38	3	.731	31	161	155	-6	-3	21
2005	Phi	97	88	741.0	201	7	4	1	.981	2.53	51	26	6	.510	7	199	201	+2	+1	21
		299	283	2450.1	677	18	8	6	.989	2.55	210	128	15	.610	21	660	659	-1	0	17

Center Fielders

Nook Logan

	BASIC									THROWING					PLAYS		PLUS/MINUS		
Year Team	G	GS	Inn	PO	A	E	DP	Pct	Rng	Opps To Advance	Extra Bases	Kills	Pct	Rank	Expected Outs	Outs Made	Total	Enhanced	Rank
2004 Det	46	41	359.2	117	3	2	1	.984	3.00	44	28	2	.636	-	98	97	-1	+1	-
2005 Det	123	93	874.1	282	3	6	2	.979	2.93	87	51	1	.586	19	274	282	+8	+19	4
	169	134	1234.0	399	6	8	3	.981	2.95	131	79	3	.603	-	372	379	+7	+20	

Luis Matos

	BASIC									THROWING					PLAYS		PLUS/MINUS		
Year Team	G	GS	Inn	PO	A	E	DP	Pct	Rng	Opps To Advance	Extra Bases	Kills	Pct	Rank	Expected Outs	Outs Made	Total	Enhanced	Rank
2003 Bal	106	105	920.0	299	5	4	1	.987	2.97	123	71	4	.577	12	281	285	+4	+12	11
2004 Bal	89	85	781.1	219	3	1	1	.996	2.56	85	65	2	.765	32	220	219	-1	-3	20
2005 Bal	120	110	990.0	298	7	5	2	.984	2.77	105	64	3	.610	23	298	299	+1	+4	13
	315	300	2691.1	816	15	10	4	.988	2.78	313	200	9	.639	28	799	803	+4	+13	6

Gary Matthews Jr.

	BASIC									THROWING					PLAYS		PLUS/MINUS		
Year Team	G	GS	Inn	PO	A	E	DP	Pct	Rng	Opps To Advance	Extra Bases	Kills	Pct	Rank	Expected Outs	Outs Made	Total	Enhanced	Rank
2003 2 tms	75	65	593.2	165	3	0	0	1.000	2.55	68	40	1	.588	15	154	158	+4	+6	11
2004 Tex	30	25	221.2	69	3	0	0	1.000	2.92	25	16	3	.640	-	65	69	+4	+8	-
2005 Tex	97	95	846.0	257	5	5	2	.981	2.79	134	79	3	.590	20	257	258	+1	+5	10
	202	185	1661.1	491	11	5	2	.990	2.72	227	135	7	.595	16	476	485	+9	+19	4

Jason Michaels

	BASIC									THROWING					PLAYS		PLUS/MINUS		
Year Team	G	GS	Inn	PO	A	E	DP	Pct	Rng	Opps To Advance	Extra Bases	Kills	Pct	Rank	Expected Outs	Outs Made	Total	Enhanced	Rank
2003 Phi	5	3	29.0	8	0	0	0	1.000	2.48						8	8	0	-1	-
2004 Phi	44	40	323.0	95	1	3	0	.970	2.67	30	17	0	.567	-	90	92	+2	-1	-
2005 Phi	75	62	536.0	161	5	2	1	.988	2.79	43	19	1	.442	2	156	161	+5	+4	14
	124	105	888.0	264	6	5	1	.982	2.74	73	36	1	.493	-	254	261	+7	+2	-

Laynce Nix

	BASIC									THROWING					PLAYS		PLUS/MINUS		
Year Team	G	GS	Inn	PO	A	E	DP	Pct	Rng	Opps To Advance	Extra Bases	Kills	Pct	Rank	Expected Outs	Outs Made	Total	Enhanced	Rank
2003 Tex	21	18	145.0	55	0	0	0	1.000	3.41	12	6	0	.500	-	49	52	+3	+4	-
2004 Tex	111	99	875.2	222	4	1	1	.996	2.32	97	57	1	.588	13	226	218	-8	-6	23
2005 Tex	61	60	526.0	160	3	2	1	.988	2.79	60	31	2	.517	8	159	160	+1	+2	17
	193	177	1546.2	437	7	3	2	.993	2.58	169	94	3	.556	11	434	430	-4	0	18

Corey Patterson

	BASIC									THROWING					PLAYS		PLUS/MINUS		
Year Team	G	GS	Inn	PO	A	E	DP	Pct	Rng	Opps To Advance	Extra Bases	Kills	Pct	Rank	Expected Outs	Outs Made	Total	Enhanced	Rank
2003 ChC	82	79	710.1	152	3	4	1	.975	1.96	73	53	1	.726	29	150	150	0	+1	17
2004 ChC	157	152	1367.2	324	8	1	5	.997	2.18	111	58	6	.523	4	319	321	+2	+3	12
2005 ChC	122	111	986.2	239	6	5	2	.980	2.23	97	59	5	.608	22	243	240	-3	-2	24
	361	342	3064.2	715	17	10	8	.987	2.15	281	170	12	.605	19	712	711	-1	+2	14

Juan Pierre

	BASIC									THROWING					PLAYS		PLUS/MINUS		
Year Team	G	GS	Inn	PO	A	E	DP	Pct	Rng	Opps To Advance	Extra Bases	Kills	Pct	Rank	Expected Outs	Outs Made	Total	Enhanced	Rank
2003 Fla	161	161	1433.1	402	6	3	5	.993	2.56	150	95	5	.633	22	387	391	+4	+12	5
2004 Fla	162	162	1439.0	364	3	2	1	.995	2.30	123	87	1	.707	28	343	345	+2	-3	19
2005 Fla	160	155	1383.0	332	7	4	3	.988	2.21	148	94	5	.635	30	334	332	-2	-9	28
	483	478	4255.1	1098	16	9	9	.992	2.36	421	276	11	.656	30	1064	1068	+4	0	16

Tike Redman

	BASIC									THROWING					PLAYS		PLUS/MINUS		
Year Team	G	GS	Inn	PO	A	E	DP	Pct	Rng	Opps To Advance	Extra Bases	Kills	Pct	Rank	Expected Outs	Outs Made	Total	Enhanced	Rank
2003 Pit	54	51	449.1	127	1	2	0	.985	2.56	66	49	0	.742	-	105	108	+3	+3	-
2004 Pit	147	134	1207.2	338	2	5	1	.986	2.53	127	77	2	.606	19	310	305	-5	-8	24
2005 Pit	75	56	523.1	158	5	7	0	.959	2.80	50	31	0	.620	28	155	158	+3	+3	16
	276	241	2180.1	623	8	14	1	.978	2.60	243	157	2	.646	29	570	571	+1	-2	20

Center Fielders

Jeremy Reed

	BASIC									THROWING					PLAYS		PLUS/MINUS		
Year Team	G	GS	Inn	PO	A	E	DP	Pct	Rng	Opps To Advance	Extra Bases	Kills	Pct	Rank	Expected Outs	Outs Made	Total	Enhanced	Rank
2004 Sea	16	14	123.1	50	0	1	0	.980	3.65	7	4	0	.571	-	47	50	+3	+3	-
2005 Sea	137	129	1149.2	383	7	3	1	.992	3.05	128	79	4	.617	27	371	384	+13	+28	2
	153	143	1273.0	433	7	4	1	.991	3.11	135	83	4	.615	-	418	434	+16	+31	-

Dave Roberts

	BASIC									THROWING					PLAYS		PLUS/MINUS		
Year Team	G	GS	Inn	PO	A	E	DP	Pct	Rng	Opps To Advance	Extra Bases	Kills	Pct	Rank	Expected Outs	Outs Made	Total	Enhanced	Rank
2003 LA	105	98	870.1	202	4	5	1	.976	2.13	70	42	1	.600	18	188	191	+3	+3	14
2004 2 tms	35	18	206.0	59	2	1	1	.984	2.67	10	6	1	.600	-	56	56	0	-3	-
2005 SD	109	101	900.2	235	4	2	1	.992	2.39	81	51	2	.630	29	239	234	-5	-10	30
	249	217	1977.0	496	10	8	3	.984	2.30	161	99	4	.615	23	483	481	-2	-10	26

Aaron Rowand

	BASIC									THROWING					PLAYS		PLUS/MINUS		
Year Team	G	GS	Inn	PO	A	E	DP	Pct	Rng	Opps To Advance	Extra Bases	Kills	Pct	Rank	Expected Outs	Outs Made	Total	Enhanced	Rank
2003 CWS	65	39	378.2	101	6	0	0	1.000	2.54	35	21	3	.600	-	99	98	-1	-1	-
2004 CWS	126	114	1018.2	290	8	6	1	.980	2.63	104	58	6	.558	8	288	289	+1	+5	11
2005 CWS	157	151	1367.2	388	3	3	1	.992	2.57	117	58	1	.496	4	373	388	+15	+30	1
	348	304	2765.0	779	17	9	2	.989	2.59	256	137	10	.535	5	760	775	+15	+34	2

Grady Sizemore

	BASIC									THROWING					PLAYS		PLUS/MINUS		
Year Team	G	GS	Inn	PO	A	E	DP	Pct	Rng	Opps To Advance	Extra Bases	Kills	Pct	Rank	Expected Outs	Outs Made	Total	Enhanced	Rank
2004 Cle	42	38	348.1	105	0	1	1	.991	2.71	37	16	0	.432	-	94	95	+1	+2	-
2005 Cle	155	152	1370.0	373	3	3	1	.992	2.47	118	60	2	.508	6	370	373	+3	+10	6
	197	190	1718.1	478	3	4	1	.992	2.52	155	76	2	.490	2	464	468	+4	+12	8

Cory Sullivan

	BASIC									THROWING					PLAYS		PLUS/MINUS		
Year Team	G	GS	Inn	PO	A	E	DP	Pct	Rng	Opps To Advance	Extra Bases	Kills	Pct	Rank	Expected Outs	Outs Made	Total	Enhanced	Rank
2005 Col	83	67	617.2	172	4	2	2	.989	2.56	64	35	3	.547	14	172	172	0	+1	22

Willy Taveras

	BASIC									THROWING					PLAYS		PLUS/MINUS		
Year Team	G	GS	Inn	PO	A	E	DP	Pct	Rng	Opps To Advance	Extra Bases	Kills	Pct	Rank	Expected Outs	Outs Made	Total	Enhanced	Rank
2004 Hou	4	0	6.0	1	0	0	0	1.000	1.50					-	2	1	-1	-2	-
2005 Hou	148	144	1254.0	332	10	3	2	.991	2.45	100	56	8	.560	16	329	332	+3	+9	7
	152	144	1260.0	333	10	3	2	.991	2.45	100	56	8	.560	-	331	333	+2	+7	-

Vernon Wells

	BASIC									THROWING					PLAYS		PLUS/MINUS		
Year Team	G	GS	Inn	PO	A	E	DP	Pct	Rng	Opps To Advance	Extra Bases	Kills	Pct	Rank	Expected Outs	Outs Made	Total	Enhanced	Rank
2003 Tor	161	161	1416.0	383	3	4	0	.990	2.45	147	98	3	.667	26	356	351	-5	-10	24
2004 Tor	131	130	1135.0	327	5	1	0	.997	2.63	116	71	4	.612	23	310	313	+3	+12	3
2005 Tor	155	153	1358.0	351	12	0	4	1.000	2.41	149	91	7	.611	24	350	351	+1	+4	12
	447	444	3909.0	1061	20	5	4	.995	2.49	412	260	14	.631	26	1016	1015	-1	+6	12

Brad Wilkerson

	BASIC									THROWING					PLAYS		PLUS/MINUS		
Year Team	G	GS	Inn	PO	A	E	DP	Pct	Rng	Opps To Advance	Extra Bases	Kills	Pct	Rank	Expected Outs	Outs Made	Total	Enhanced	Rank
2003 Mon	42	40	303.1	71	2	1	0	.986	2.17	38	19	0	.500	-	53	54	+1	-1	-
2004 Mon	18	16	140.0	46	3	1	0	.980	3.15	33	24	2	.727	-	41	42	+1	+3	-
2005 Was	92	88	758.2	233	6	3	1	.988	2.84	75	41	4	.547	13	239	234	-5	-9	29
	152	144	1202.0	350	11	5	1	.986	2.70	146	84	6	.575	-	333	330	-3	-7	-

Bernie Williams

	BASIC									THROWING					PLAYS		PLUS/MINUS		
Year Team	G	GS	Inn	PO	A	E	DP	Pct	Rng	Opps To Advance	Extra Bases	Kills	Pct	Rank	Expected Outs	Outs Made	Total	Enhanced	Rank
2003 NYY	115	113	1001.1	290	3	1	1	.997	2.63	119	85	1	.714	28	301	291	-10	-20	29
2004 NYY	97	93	830.1	214	2	1	1	.995	2.34	88	63	2	.716	29	226	207	-19	-21	31
2005 NYY	112	99	862.1	226	6	2	1	.991	2.42	93	63	1	.677	33	247	226	-21	-37	35
	324	305	2694.0	730	11	4	3	.995	2.48	300	211	4	.703	32	774	724	-50	-78	32

Center Fielders

Preston Wilson

	BASIC									THROWING					PLAYS		PLUS/MINUS		
Year Team	G	GS	Inn	PO	A	E	DP	Pct	Rng	Opps To Advance	Extra Bases	Kills	Pct	Rank	Expected Outs	Outs Made	Total	Enhanced	Rank
2003 Col	155	153	1307.1	331	8	7	0	.980	2.33	163	94	4	.577	11	309	297	-12	-15	28
2004 Col	52	51	436.0	118	3	6	1	.953	2.50	52	33	0	.635	-	117	114	-3	-4	-
2005 2 tms	124	122	1068.2	265	5	3	0	.989	2.27	122	79	3	.648	31	281	266	-15	-28	34
	331	326	2812.0	714	16	16	1	.979	2.34	337	206	7	.611	22	707	677	-30	-47	30

Randy Winn

	BASIC									THROWING					PLAYS		PLUS/MINUS		
Year Team	G	GS	Inn	PO	A	E	DP	Pct	Rng	Opps To Advance	Extra Bases	Kills	Pct	Rank	Expected Outs	Outs Made	Total	Enhanced	Rank
2003 Sea	20	17	154.0	60	0	0	0	1.000	3.51	20	10	0	.500	-	57	60	+3	+6	-
2004 Sea	128	119	1070.1	342	5	4	1	.989	2.92	121	69	2	.570	11	326	330	+4	+11	4
2005 2 tms	61	61	532.2	184	2	1	1	.995	3.14	49	26	1	.531	11	185	184	-1	-10	31
	209	197	1757.0	586	7	5	2	.992	3.04	190	105	3	.553	10	568	574	+6	+7	11

Right Fielders

Bobby Abreu

Year	Team	G	GS	Inn	PO	A	E	DP	Pct	Rng	Opps To Advance	Extra Bases	Kills	Pct	Rank	Expected Outs	Outs Made	Total	Enhanced	Rank
2003	Phi	158	156	1373.1	304	6	6	0	.981	2.03	126	53	3	.421	5	297	302	+5	+7	5
2004	Phi	158	157	1394.2	311	13	6	4	.982	2.09	139	83	9	.597	22	297	295	-2	-6	21
2005	Phi	158	158	1364.0	266	7	4	0	.986	1.80	118	58	4	.492	11	272	267	-5	-13	28
		474	471	4132.0	881	26	16	4	.983	1.98	383	194	16	.507	8	866	864	-2	-12	20

Casey Blake

Year	Team	G	GS	Inn	PO	A	E	DP	Pct	Rng	Opps To Advance	Extra Bases	Kills	Pct	Rank	Expected Outs	Outs Made	Total	Enhanced	Rank
2005	Cle	138	132	1188.2	287	3	8	0	.973	2.20	128	76	2	.594	29	284	287	+3	+14	2

Emil Brown

Year	Team	G	GS	Inn	PO	A	E	DP	Pct	Rng	Opps To Advance	Extra Bases	Kills	Pct	Rank	Expected Outs	Outs Made	Total	Enhanced	Rank
2005	KC	129	126	1097.1	243	7	11	0	.958	2.05	154	95	1	.617	30	248	243	-5	-9	26

Jeromy Burnitz

Year	Team	G	GS	Inn	PO	A	E	DP	Pct	Rng	Opps To Advance	Extra Bases	Kills	Pct	Rank	Expected Outs	Outs Made	Total	Enhanced	Rank
2003	2 tms	50	37	342.0	81	1	1	0	.988	2.16	34	16	1	.471	12	80	81	+1	0	-
2004	Col	79	56	527.1	105	6	3	1	.974	1.89	64	33	2	.516	12	93	94	+1	-3	18
2005	ChC	158	153	1359.2	303	5	5	1	.984	2.04	124	78	1	.629	31	311	303	-8	-4	16
		287	246	2229.0	489	12	9	2	.982	2.02	222	127	4	.572	19	484	478	-6	-7	18

Mike Cameron

Year	Team	G	GS	Inn	PO	A	E	DP	Pct	Rng	Opps To Advance	Extra Bases	Kills	Pct	Rank	Expected Outs	Outs Made	Total	Enhanced	Rank
2005	NYM	68	67	593.0	136	2	6	1	.958	2.09	55	27	2	.491	10	137	137	0	+2	12

Victor Diaz

Year	Team	G	GS	Inn	PO	A	E	DP	Pct	Rng	Opps To Advance	Extra Bases	Kills	Pct	Rank	Expected Outs	Outs Made	Total	Enhanced	Rank
2004	NYM	14	12	108.0	29	0	2	0	.935	2.42	9	4	0	.444	-	31	27	-4	-6	-
2005	NYM	78	74	651.2	153	2	3	1	.981	2.14	66	25	2	.379	1	159	153	-6	-8	23
		92	86	759.2	182	2	5	1	.974	2.18	75	29	2	.387	-	190	180	-10	-14	-

J.D. Drew

Year	Team	G	GS	Inn	PO	A	E	DP	Pct	Rng	Opps To Advance	Extra Bases	Kills	Pct	Rank	Expected Outs	Outs Made	Total	Enhanced	Rank
2003	StL	53	47	391.0	101	5	1	1	.991	2.44	40	27	3	.675	-	89	90	+1	+3	-
2004	Atl	138	137	1193.0	277	11	3	0	.990	2.17	133	79	5	.594	20	262	272	+10	+21	2
2005	LAD	44	44	382.0	83	3	2	0	.977	2.03	54	27	2	.500	-	84	83	-1	+1	-
		235	228	1966.0	461	19	6	1	.988	2.20	227	133	10	.586	23	435	445	+10	+25	3

Jermaine Dye

Year	Team	G	GS	Inn	PO	A	E	DP	Pct	Rng	Opps To Advance	Extra Bases	Kills	Pct	Rank	Expected Outs	Outs Made	Total	Enhanced	Rank
2003	Oak	60	59	500.1	102	1	0	0	1.000	1.85	57	34	0	.596	23	91	91	0	0	14
2004	Oak	134	132	1178.0	257	3	2	1	.992	1.99	119	71	3	.597	21	231	234	+3	-1	16
2005	CWS	140	137	1235.1	259	9	8	2	.971	1.95	119	61	5	.513	15	265	259	-6	-6	21
		334	328	2913.2	618	13	10	4	.984	1.95	295	166	8	.563	17	587	584	-3	-7	17

Juan Encarnacion

Year	Team	G	GS	Inn	PO	A	E	DP	Pct	Rng	Opps To Advance	Extra Bases	Kills	Pct	Rank	Expected Outs	Outs Made	Total	Enhanced	Rank
2003	Fla	155	155	1355.1	329	7	0	2	1.000	2.23	126	79	5	.627	28	319	318	-1	-9	29
2004	2 tms	125	123	1072.0	247	5	6	0	.977	2.12	82	47	2	.573	17	246	245	-1	+1	14
2005	Fla	135	126	1112.2	216	4	4	0	.982	1.78	126	66	2	.524	16	220	216	-4	-12	27
		415	404	3540.0	792	16	10	2	.988	2.05	334	192	9	.575	21	785	779	-6	-20	25

Right Fielders

Jeff Francoeur

Year	Team	G	GS	Inn	PO	A	E	DP	Pct	Rng	Opps To Advance	Extra Bases	Kills	Pct	Rank	Expected Outs	Outs Made	Total	Enhanced	Rank
2005	Atl	67	65	589.0	131	13	5	3	.966	2.20	69	34	10	.493	12	126	131	+5	+10	7

Jay Gibbons

Year	Team	G	GS	Inn	PO	A	E	DP	Pct	Rng	Opps To Advance	Extra Bases	Kills	Pct	Rank	Expected Outs	Outs Made	Total	Enhanced	Rank
2003	Bal	144	144	1274.2	283	8	5	0	.983	2.05	125	73	6	.584	22	275	270	-5	-9	30
2004	Bal	66	63	556.1	116	6	2	1	.984	1.97	65	30	6	.462	5	113	114	+1	+2	13
2005	Bal	71	69	558.2	133	6	2	1	.986	2.24	77	42	1	.545	21	128	133	+5	+10	6
		281	276	2389.2	532	20	9	2	.984	2.08	267	145	13	.543	13	516	517	+1	+3	10

Brian Giles

Year	Team	G	GS	Inn	PO	A	E	DP	Pct	Rng	Opps To Advance	Extra Bases	Kills	Pct	Rank	Expected Outs	Outs Made	Total	Enhanced	Rank
2004	SD	159	158	1383.0	323	8	7	3	.979	2.15	162	94	5	.580	18	315	314	-1	+3	12
2005	SD	143	140	1220.0	295	6	4	1	.987	2.22	143	78	4	.545	20	297	295	-2	-5	20
		302	298	2603.0	618	14	11	4	.983	2.19	305	172	9	.564	18	612	609	-3	-2	14

Shawn Green

Year	Team	G	GS	Inn	PO	A	E	DP	Pct	Rng	Opps To Advance	Extra Bases	Kills	Pct	Rank	Expected Outs	Outs Made	Total	Enhanced	Rank
2003	LA	157	157	1397.2	261	9	5	0	.982	1.74	105	64	3	.610	26	240	239	-1	-2	19
2004	LA	52	46	427.1	81	2	2	1	.976	1.75	36	20	2	.556	-	79	81	+2	+7	-
2005	Ari	135	109	1031.1	232	2	0	0	1.000	2.04	103	56	0	.544	19	232	232	0	-4	17
		344	312	2856.1	574	13	7	1	.988	1.85	244	140	5	.574	20	551	552	+1	+1	13

Vladimir Guerrero

Year	Team	G	GS	Inn	PO	A	E	DP	Pct	Rng	Opps To Advance	Extra Bases	Kills	Pct	Rank	Expected Outs	Outs Made	Total	Enhanced	Rank
2003	Mon	112	112	949.2	217	10	7	0	.970	2.15	99	57	7	.576	19	175	170	-5	-6	26
2004	Ana	143	143	1234.0	308	13	9	2	.973	2.34	128	70	8	.547	15	315	299	-16	-18	30
2005	LAA	120	120	1040.0	242	8	3	2	.988	2.16	83	38	6	.458	6	238	245	+7	+10	5
		375	375	3223.2	767	31	19	4	.977	2.23	310	165	21	.532	12	728	714	-14	-14	21

Jose Guillen

Year	Team	G	GS	Inn	PO	A	E	DP	Pct	Rng	Opps To Advance	Extra Bases	Kills	Pct	Rank	Expected Outs	Outs Made	Total	Enhanced	Rank
2003	2 tms	96	92	802.2	183	9	8	0	.960	2.15	72	42	7	.583	21	154	161	+7	+11	2
2004	Ana	4	1	22.0	4	0	0	0	1.000	1.64	1	1	0	1.000	-	3	4	+1	0	-
2005	Was	140	135	1189.2	299	10	7	4	.978	2.34	136	73	7	.537	18	297	299	+2	+10	4
		240	228	2014.1	486	19	15	4	.971	2.26	209	116	14	.555	15	454	464	+10	+21	5

Brad Hawpe

Year	Team	G	GS	Inn	PO	A	E	DP	Pct	Rng	Opps To Advance	Extra Bases	Kills	Pct	Rank	Expected Outs	Outs Made	Total	Enhanced	Rank
2004	Col	32	29	233.0	52	1	1	1	.981	2.05	27	17	1	.630	-	48	48	0	-2	-
2005	Col	89	79	693.0	148	10	3	2	.981	2.05	107	59	6	.551	22	150	148	-2	-3	15
		121	108	926.0	200	11	4	3	.981	2.05	134	76	7	.567	-	198	196	-2	-5	-

Richard Hidalgo

Year	Team	G	GS	Inn	PO	A	E	DP	Pct	Rng	Opps To Advance	Extra Bases	Kills	Pct	Rank	Expected Outs	Outs Made	Total	Enhanced	Rank
2003	Hou	137	136	1200.0	277	22	4	3	.987	2.24	115	44	19	.383	1	264	267	+3	+4	9
2004	2 tms	139	132	1160.2	259	14	6	3	.978	2.12	114	48	13	.421	1	252	259	+7	+9	5
2005	Tex	83	78	699.2	174	3	2	0	.989	2.28	87	43	2	.494	13	168	174	+6	+8	8
		359	346	3060.1	710	39	12	6	.984	2.20	316	135	34	.427	1	684	700	+16	+21	4

Right Fielders

Aubrey Huff

	BASIC									THROWING					PLAYS		PLUS/MINUS		
Year Team	G	GS	Inn	PO	A	E	DP	Pct	Rng	Opps To Advance	Extra Bases	Kills	Pct	Rank	Expected Outs	Outs Made	Total	Enhanced	Rank
2003 TB	102	102	850.1	190	5	6	1	.970	2.06	85	45	4	.529	12	169	169	0	-2	20
2004 TB	1	1	1.0	0	0	0	0	-	.00								0		
2005 TB	97	95	786.2	204	6	3	2	.986	2.40	96	49	4	.510	14	205	204	-1	-4	19
	200	198	1638.0	394	11	9	3	.978	2.23	181	94	8	.519	10	374	373	-1	-6	16

Geoff Jenkins

	BASIC									THROWING					PLAYS		PLUS/MINUS		
Year Team	G	GS	Inn	PO	A	E	DP	Pct	Rng	Opps To Advance	Extra Bases	Kills	Pct	Rank	Expected Outs	Outs Made	Total	Enhanced	Rank
2005 Mil	144	144	1241.1	307	10	5	7	.984	2.30	127	72	10	.567	25	300	307	+7	+13	3

Jacque Jones

	BASIC									THROWING					PLAYS		PLUS/MINUS		
Year Team	G	GS	Inn	PO	A	E	DP	Pct	Rng	Opps To Advance	Extra Bases	Kills	Pct	Rank	Expected Outs	Outs Made	Total	Enhanced	Rank
2003 Min	11	10	81.0	23	0	0	0	1.000	2.56	7	4	0	.571	-	19	18	-1	-1	-
2004 Min	141	138	1237.0	314	5	2	2	.994	2.32	132	61	1	.462	6	291	285	-6	-7	22
2005 Min	123	121	1080.1	261	9	4	2	.985	2.25	101	48	7	.475	8	266	262	-4	-8	22
	275	269	2398.1	598	14	6	4	.990	2.30	240	113	8	.471	3	576	565	-11	-16	24

Austin Kearns

	BASIC									THROWING					PLAYS		PLUS/MINUS		
Year Team	G	GS	Inn	PO	A	E	DP	Pct	Rng	Opps To Advance	Extra Bases	Kills	Pct	Rank	Expected Outs	Outs Made	Total	Enhanced	Rank
2003 Cin	50	40	365.0	96	2	1	0	.990	2.42	39	21	2	.538	-	92	93	+1	+1	-
2004 Cin	60	59	508.1	118	1	3	0	.975	2.11	50	27	1	.540	14	102	106	+4	+5	9
2005 Cin	107	103	890.0	237	8	3	3	.988	2.48	97	47	8	.485	9	232	238	+6	+7	10
	217	202	1763.1	451	11	7	3	.985	2.36	186	95	11	.511	9	426	437	+11	+13	6

Jason Lane

	BASIC									THROWING					PLAYS		PLUS/MINUS		
Year Team	G	GS	Inn	PO	A	E	DP	Pct	Rng	Opps To Advance	Extra Bases	Kills	Pct	Rank	Expected Outs	Outs Made	Total	Enhanced	Rank
2003 Hou	2	2	6.0	2	0	0	0	1.000	3.00						2	2		-1	-
2004 Hou	24	13	140.2	28	0	0	0	1.000	1.79	15	5	0	.333	-	27	28	+1	0	-
2005 Hou	137	126	1115.2	225	4	6	0	.974	1.85	111	48	3	.432	3	226	225	-1	-4	18
	163	139	1262.1	255	4	6	0	.977	1.85	126	53	3	.421	-	255	255	0	-5	-

Matt Lawton

	BASIC									THROWING					PLAYS		PLUS/MINUS		
Year Team	G	GS	Inn	PO	A	E	DP	Pct	Rng	Opps To Advance	Extra Bases	Kills	Pct	Rank	Expected Outs	Outs Made	Total	Enhanced	Rank
2003 Cle	13	12	110.1	17	1	0	0	1.000	1.47	11	6	1	.545	-	16	17	+1	+2	-
2004 Cle	19	18	167.2	35	2	1	1	.974	1.99	16	9	0	.563	-	35	35	0	0	-
2005 3 tms	113	109	953.0	230	4	2	2	.992	2.21	94	42	3	.447	4	233	230	-3	-17	29
	145	139	1231.0	282	7	3	2	.990	2.11	121	57	4	.471	-	284	282	-2	-15	-

Craig Monroe

	BASIC									THROWING					PLAYS		PLUS/MINUS		
Year Team	G	GS	Inn	PO	A	E	DP	Pct	Rng	Opps To Advance	Extra Bases	Kills	Pct	Rank	Expected Outs	Outs Made	Total	Enhanced	Rank
2003 Det	38	30	280.0	72	2	3	0	.961	2.38	24	14	1	.583	-	61	65	+4	+4	-
2004 Det	51	45	386.0	110	3	3	1	.974	2.63	49	23	3	.469	-	94	87	-7	-8	-
2005 Det	85	69	632.1	132	4	4	0	.971	1.94	49	26	2	.531	17	141	132	-9	-18	30
	174	144	1298.1	314	9	10	1	.970	2.24	122	63	6	.516	-	296	284	-12	-22	-

Xavier Nady

	BASIC									THROWING					PLAYS		PLUS/MINUS		
Year Team	G	GS	Inn	PO	A	E	DP	Pct	Rng	Opps To Advance	Extra Bases	Kills	Pct	Rank	Expected Outs	Outs Made	Total	Enhanced	Rank
2003 SD	105	98	846.2	170	12	6	2	.968	1.93	79	45	8	.570	16	152	159	+7	+6	7
2004 SD	2	2	14.0	2	0	0	0	1.000	1.29						2	2	0	-1	-
2005 SD	13	7	82.0	11	0	0	0	1.000	1.21	12	6	0	.500		11	11	0	0	-
	120	107	942.2	183	12	6	2	.970	1.86	91	51	8	.560	-	165	172	+7	+5	-

Right Fielders

Trot Nixon

		BASIC									THROWING					PLAYS		PLUS/MINUS		
Year	Team	G	GS	Inn	PO	A	E	DP	Pct	Rng	Opps To Advance	Extra Bases	Kills	Pct	Rank	Expected Outs	Outs Made	Total	Enhanced	Rank
2003	Bos	129	119	1078.2	230	4	4	0	.983	1.95	120	59	2	.492	8	228	231	+3	+7	6
2004	Bos	40	36	306.0	63	1	1	0	.985	1.88	34	26	0	.765	-	61	63	+2	+1	-
2005	Bos	118	107	935.1	240	8	1	3	.996	2.39	110	62	5	.564	24	228	240	+12	+18	1
		287	262	2320.0	533	13	6	3	.989	2.12	264	147	7	.557	16	517	534	+17	+26	2

Magglio Ordonez

		BASIC									THROWING					PLAYS		PLUS/MINUS		
Year	Team	G	GS	Inn	PO	A	E	DP	Pct	Rng	Opps To Advance	Extra Bases	Kills	Pct	Rank	Expected Outs	Outs Made	Total	Enhanced	Rank
2003	CWS	154	154	1324.2	316	7	2	1	.994	2.19	130	65	7	.500	10	311	311	0	+10	4
2004	CWS	43	43	364.0	95	0	1	0	.990	2.35	40	25	0	.625	-	100	94	-6	-3	-
2005	Det	81	79	672.1	139	5	1	0	.993	1.93	82	47	2	.573	27	138	139	+1	+3	11
		278	276	2361.0	550	12	4	1	.993	2.14	252	137	9	.544	14	549	544	-5	+10	9

Alexis Rios

		BASIC									THROWING					PLAYS		PLUS/MINUS		
Year	Team	G	GS	Inn	PO	A	E	DP	Pct	Rng	Opps To Advance	Extra Bases	Kills	Pct	Rank	Expected Outs	Outs Made	Total	Enhanced	Rank
2004	Tor	108	107	943.2	217	11	2	4	.991	2.17	111	49	8	.441	3	201	209	+8	+11	4
2005	Tor	138	116	1056.2	245	7	2	1	.992	2.15	118	50	4	.424	2	244	246	+2	+1	13
		246	223	2000.1	462	18	4	5	.992	2.16	229	99	12	.432	2	445	455	+10	+12	7

Gary Sheffield

		BASIC									THROWING					PLAYS		PLUS/MINUS		
Year	Team	G	GS	Inn	PO	A	E	DP	Pct	Rng	Opps To Advance	Extra Bases	Kills	Pct	Rank	Expected Outs	Outs Made	Total	Enhanced	Rank
2003	Atl	154	154	1288.1	283	7	4	2	.986	2.03	115	66	5	.574	18	280	280	0	-2	18
2004	NYY	136	136	1178.2	270	11	5	3	.983	2.15	140	78	8	.557	16	274	261	-13	-11	27
2005	NYY	131	130	1099.0	239	5	3	0	.988	2.00	118	53	3	.449	5	260	240	-20	-25	31
		421	420	3566.0	792	23	12	5	.985	2.06	373	197	16	.528	11	814	781	-33	-38	27

Sammy Sosa

		BASIC									THROWING					PLAYS		PLUS/MINUS		
Year	Team	G	GS	Inn	PO	A	E	DP	Pct	Rng	Opps To Advance	Extra Bases	Kills	Pct	Rank	Expected Outs	Outs Made	Total	Enhanced	Rank
2003	ChC	137	136	1178.2	212	2	5	1	.977	1.63	115	61	1	.530	13	214	211	-3	-4	23
2004	ChC	124	124	1097.2	238	5	4	2	.984	1.99	96	63	3	.656	29	234	233	-1	-2	17
2005	Bal	66	66	577.0	121	3	3	1	.976	1.93	47	27	1	.574	28	126	121	-5	-8	24
		327	326	2853.1	571	10	12	4	.980	1.83	258	151	5	.585	22	574	565	-9	-14	22

Ichiro Suzuki

		BASIC									THROWING					PLAYS		PLUS/MINUS		
Year	Team	G	GS	Inn	PO	A	E	DP	Pct	Rng	Opps To Advance	Extra Bases	Kills	Pct	Rank	Expected Outs	Outs Made	Total	Enhanced	Rank
2003	Sea	159	156	1367.0	337	12	2	3	.994	2.30	140	56	8	.400	4	328	333	+5	+11	1
2004	Sea	158	158	1405.1	372	12	3	2	.992	2.46	145	63	7	.434	2	346	367	+21	+30	1
2005	Sea	158	158	1388.1	381	9	2	2	.995	2.53	180	103	6	.572	26	377	383	+6	+7	9
		475	472	4160.2	1090	33	7	7	.994	2.43	465	222	21	.477	5	1051	1083	+32	+48	1

Nick Swisher

		BASIC									THROWING					PLAYS		PLUS/MINUS		
Year	Team	G	GS	Inn	PO	A	E	DP	Pct	Rng	Opps To Advance	Extra Bases	Kills	Pct	Rank	Expected Outs	Outs Made	Total	Enhanced	Rank
2004	Oak	4	3	28.0	5	0	2	0	.714	1.61	5	2	0	.400	-	5	5	0	-1	-
2005	Oak	121	115	1027.1	196	6	2	2	.990	1.77	82	46	4	.561	23	192	197	+5	-1	14
		125	118	1055.1	201	6	4	2	.981	1.77	87	48	4	.552	-	197	202	+5	-2	-

Larry Walker

		BASIC									THROWING					PLAYS		PLUS/MINUS		
Year	Team	G	GS	Inn	PO	A	E	DP	Pct	Rng	Opps To Advance	Extra Bases	Kills	Pct	Rank	Expected Outs	Outs Made	Total	Enhanced	Rank
2003	Col	132	128	1102.2	229	8	4	1	.983	1.93	128	51	6	.398	3	221	222	+1	+3	12
2004	2 tms	75	69	604.0	121	5	1	1	.992	1.88	64	40	2	.625	27	120	121	+1	0	15
2005	StL	83	78	648.2	107	5	2	0	.982	1.55	56	26	1	.464	7	112	107	-5	-8	25
		290	275	2355.1	457	18	7	2	.985	1.82	248	117	9	.472	4	453	450	-3	-5	15

Player Rankings and Comments

Gold Gloves That Should Have Been

The first thing you'll see at the beginning of each position in the following section are my Gold Gloves That Should Have Been. Just as in batting and pitching, doesn't it make sense that players can have up-and-down seasons defensively? For example, Ichiro Suzuki won five straight Gold Gloves prior to 2005 and our plus/minus and throwing numbers reflect his superb performance. He ranked #1 in plus/minus in both 2003 and 2004 while ranking #4 and #2 in throwing. But in 2005, he had a down season by his standards. While he had +7 enhanced plays in 2005, he only ranked #9 in right field, his throwing ranking dropped to #26 and he had a three-year low in baserunner kills. Should he have won a Gold Glove in 2005? Check out the right field section for my answer. Maybe if the voters had a better idea of these numbers they might have been able to better understand Ichiro's down season. And maybe those numbers might have made for a tougher decision about the best Gold Glove winner in 2005. So shame on us for not getting better fielding numbers out there.

After having compared our plus/minus figures and other metrics to the actual winners of the Gold Glove awards, I have to say that I believe that the voters have really done a pretty good job. When trying to decide on Gold Glove winners, I found myself agreeing with the choices most of the time. There may have been a couple of downright gaffes (Bobby Abreu in 2005, Rafael Palmeiro in 1999), but for the most part we have good Gold Glove winners. I was especially amazed as I was going through the outfield Gold Gloves. I was expecting to change the award for our book pretty regularly. But I only made a few changes.

As much as we disagree with Derek Jeter as a Gold Glover, he does look good at shortstop. Until you look closer. And you look at the numbers. Pick a number, any number!

I'm sorry. I digressed. Let me summarize by year the number of Gold Glove winners that I changed. There are 18 winners each season, but this book doesn't cover pitchers and catchers, so we're down to 14, seven in each league each season.

Year	Gold Glove Winners Reviewed	Unchanged	Changed
2003	14	9	5
2004	14	11	3
2005	14	6	8

For outfielders, out of the 18 Gold Gloves given out over the three years, I only changed five. Overall, I changed 16 out of 42 Gold Gloves, keeping 26 the same. I especially liked the selections in 2004.

My Personal Ratings

After the Gold Glove section, I give you my personal ratings for the top ten and bottom five defensive players at each position. It's based on every aspect I could think of. That includes both the numbers and the visual observations. A good part of a player's defensive evaluation is based on visual observation and, as much as I like to use numbers to support my arguments, these observations still carry a great deal of weight in evaluating players. Our player commentaries provide a lot of the background for those observations. To get my evaluations, I mix in the subjective evaluations, my own personal observations, and all the numbers in this book that I can assimilate in my brain at one time when thinking about a player.

Rankings

Each position has two pages of rankings. The first page ranks players on the Plus/Minus System over the three years that this book covers. The first chart on the page has the three-year aggregate numbers and the three charts that follow are for each of the three years individually.

The second page of rankings is customized for each position. Corner infielders have rankings based on evaluating their ability to handle bunts. Middle infielders are ranked based on their double play skills. Outfielders are ranked based on the intimidation factor of their arms.

We chose 500 innings in one year and 1,500 innings over three years as qualification levels for the rankings.

These numbers gave us about 30 players in each chart, sometimes more, sometimes a little less. That's about one per team, which works well.

Player Data Blocks

Each player has a short data block of information so that you can compare the commentary to the numbers. For the most part the numbers are explained elsewhere in this book, but let me give you a few notes.

Players in the comments section are arranged in order of their three-year plus/minus rank, just like the first table on the first ranking page. We've included all players who played at least 500 innings in 2005, as well as a dozen or so bonus players who played less than 500 innings but are likely to have full-time jobs in 2006.

This is the only section that has the home/road and righty/lefty splits to look at. They are for the 2005 season only, based on the Basic version of plus/minus.

The breakdown of Plus/Minus by Plays to his right, Straight on, To his left and Plays in the air is for infielders only during the 2005 season. These breakdowns are for the Basic version of plus/minus.

Player Commentaries

If I had to write all the player commentaries in this book, you'd be getting it in 2021. Instead I was smart enough to know that I didn't know enough and enlisted the help of really intelligent people. The insights, writing and editing for the player commentaries come from many people including: Nate Birtwell, John Dewan, Bill James, Steve Moyer, Greg Pierce, Pat Quinn, Hal Richman, Len Schwartz, Dave Studenmund, and the staff of Baseball Info Solutions (BIS). BIS has reviewed thousands of plays in preparation for this book, and I can't tell you how much I respect the opinions of all the guys there. Their visual observations, used in conjunction with the numbers in this book, have been vital to me.

Let me also emphasize the contribution by Hal Richman and Len Schwartz from the Strat-O-Matic Game Company. Hal Richman is a man who studies and rates the defensive abilities of Major League Baseball players more than anyone else on the planet. He and Len Schwartz research players each year by doing a ton a reading and by getting the input of many people who closely follow teams and players. We had the good fortune of being able to tap into their internal brain trust. That work forms the basis for a good many of our player commentaries.

First Basemen Evaluations

Year	League	Gold Glove Winners	Should Have Been
2003	AL	John Olerud	John Olerud
	NL	Derrek Lee	J.T. Snow
2004	AL	Darin Erstad	Darin Erstad
	NL	Todd Helton	Todd Helton
2005	AL	Mark Teixeira	Mark Teixeira
	NL	Derrek Lee	Albert Pujols

My Personal Ratings

Top Ten

1 Mark Teixeira, Tex
2 Doug Mientkiewicz, KC
3 Albert Pujols, StL
4 Darin Erstad, LAA
5 Tino Martinez, FA
6 J.T. Snow, Bos
7 Justin Morneau, Min
8 Derrek Lee, ChC
9 Todd Helton, Col
10 Ryan Howard, Phi

Bottom Five

26 Matt Stairs, KC
27 Shea Hillenbrand, Tor
28 Jason Giambi, NYY
29 Carlos Delgado, NYM
30 Richie Sexson, Sea

Player teams based on transactions through February 5, 2006

First Basemen Rankings

3-Year Plus/Minus Rankings

1	Mark Teixeira	+53	11	Justin Morneau	+7	22	Paul Konerko	-10
2	Doug Mientkiewicz	+32	12	Sean Casey	+2	23	Scott Hatteberg	-11
3	Albert Pujols	+25	13	Nick Johnson	+2	24	Derrek Lee	-13
4	John Olerud	+22	14	Jeff Conine	0	25	Jim Thome	-13
5	Darin Erstad	+21	15	Todd Helton	-1	26	Rafael Palmeiro	-13
6	Jeff Bagwell	+17	16	Lyle Overbay	-1	27	Tony Clark	-13
7	Tino Martinez	+15	17	Daryle Ward	-2	28	Shea Hillenbrand	-14
8	Kevin Millar	+14	18	Ben Broussard	-3	29	Jason Giambi	-15
9	J.T. Snow	+11	19	Phil Nevin	-4	30	Adam LaRoche	-16
10	Travis Lee	+9	20	Hee Seop Choi	-5	31	Carlos Delgado	-22
			21	Carlos Pena	-6	32	Richie Sexson	-28

2005 Plus/Minus Rankings

1	Mark Teixeira	+17	11	Kevin Millar	+5	23	Paul Konerko	-2
2	Ryan Howard	+16	12	Lyle Overbay	+4	24	Chris Shelton	-2
3	Justin Morneau	+13	13	Tony Clark	+4	25	Phil Nevin	-3
4	Darin Erstad	+12	14	Daryle Ward	+3	26	Travis Lee	-5
5	Chad Tracy	+11	15	Derrek Lee	+2	27	Sean Casey	-6
6	Albert Pujols	+10	16	J.T. Snow	+2	28	Matt Stairs	-6
7	Lance Niekro	+10	17	Hee Seop Choi	+2	29	Lance Berkman	-7
8	Tino Martinez	+9	18	Dan Johnson	+2	30	Jason Giambi	-8
9	Doug Mientkiewicz	+9	19	Ben Broussard	+1	31	Rafael Palmeiro	-12
10	Nick Johnson	+6	20	Shea Hillenbrand	0	32	Richie Sexson	-15
			21	Todd Helton	-1	33	Adam LaRoche	-17
			22	Eric Hinske	-1	34	Carlos Delgado	-23

2004 Plus/Minus Rankings

1	Todd Helton	+11	11	Pedro Feliz	+6	23	Daryle Ward	-3
2	Carlos Delgado	+9	12	Sean Casey	+5	24	Tony Clark	-4
3	Darin Erstad	+9	13	Carlos Pena	+4	25	Jim Thome	-5
4	Albert Pujols	+8	14	John Olerud	+3	26	Shea Hillenbrand	-7
5	Kevin Millar	+8	15	Ben Broussard	+3	27	Scott Hatteberg	-8
6	Mark Teixeira	+7	16	Nick Johnson	+2	28	Mike Piazza	-8
7	Jeff Bagwell	+7	17	Adam LaRoche	+1	29	Hee Seop Choi	-10
8	Brad Wilkerson	+7	18	J.T. Snow	0	30	Shawn Green	-10
9	Tino Martinez	+6	19	Julio Franco	0	31	Ken Harvey	-11
10	Doug Mientkiewicz	+6	20	Phil Nevin	-1	32	Paul Konerko	-12
			21	Derrek Lee	-2	33	Lyle Overbay	-14
			22	Justin Morneau	-3	34	Rafael Palmeiro	-16

2003 Plus/Minus Rankings

1	Mark Teixeira	+29	11	Paul Konerko	+4	23	Carlos Pena	-5
2	Doug Mientkiewicz	+17	12	Sean Casey	+3	24	Jason Giambi	-6
3	John Olerud	+14	13	Hee Seop Choi	+3	25	Nick Johnson	-6
4	Scott Spiezio	+13	14	Scott Hatteberg	+2	26	Ben Broussard	-7
5	Travis Lee	+12	15	Andres Galarraga	+2	27	Shea Hillenbrand	-7
6	Lyle Overbay	+9	16	Kevin Millar	+1	28	Carlos Delgado	-8
7	J.T. Snow	+9	17	Tino Martinez	0	29	Eric Karros	-9
8	Jeff Bagwell	+7	18	Randall Simon	0	30	Ryan Klesko	-10
9	Robert Fick	+5	19	Jason Phillips	-1	31	Todd Helton	-11
10	Ken Harvey	+5	20	Wil Cordero	-3	32	Richie Sexson	-11
			21	Fred McGriff	-3	33	Jim Thome	-12
			22	Jeff Conine	-5	34	Derrek Lee	-13

3-Year Bunt Rankings

1	Albert Pujols	.648	11	Jeff Conine	.598	22	Tino Martinez	.543
2	Derrek Lee	.642	12	Jeff Bagwell	.592	23	Tony Clark	.541

1 Albert Pujols .648   11 Jeff Conine .598   22 Tino Martinez .543
2 Derrek Lee .642   12 Jeff Bagwell .592   23 Tony Clark .541
3 Doug Mientkiewicz .641   13 Sean Casey .589   24 Adam LaRoche .530
4 Justin Morneau .639   14 Lyle Overbay .587   25 Kevin Millar .529
5 Jason Giambi .636   15 Jim Thome .585   26 Richie Sexson .526
6 Todd Helton .635   16 Nick Johnson .583   27 Phil Nevin .518
7 Hee Seop Choi .617   17 J.T. Snow .576   28 Darin Erstad .505
8 Travis Lee .614   18 Paul Konerko .574   29 Carlos Pena .497
9 John Olerud .612   19 Ben Broussard .572   30 Carlos Delgado .494
10 Rafael Palmeiro .611   20 Scott Hatteberg .564   31 Mark Teixeira .482
                       21 Shea Hillenbrand .562   32 Daryle Ward .432

2005 Bunt Rankings

1 Justin Morneau .742   11 Sean Casey .614   23 Lyle Overbay .513
2 Albert Pujols .718   12 Tino Martinez .613   24 Matt Stairs .513
3 Lance Berkman .714   13 Todd Helton .602   25 Carlos Delgado .506
4 Eric Hinske .700   14 Paul Konerko .574   26 Darin Erstad .505
5 Chris Shelton .683   15 Mark Teixeira .569   27 Tony Clark .500
6 Derrek Lee .681   16 Phil Nevin .550   28 Ryan Howard .500
7 Doug Mientkiewicz .656   17 Hee Seop Choi .546   29 Travis Lee .489
8 Chad Tracy .656   18 J.T. Snow .540   30 Dan Johnson .483
9 Nick Johnson .650   19 Shea Hillenbrand .540   31 Ben Broussard .482
10 Jason Giambi .614   20 Richie Sexson .534   32 Kevin Millar .475
                       21 Adam LaRoche .532   33 Lance Niekro .438
                       22 Rafael Palmeiro .525   34 Daryle Ward .412

2004 Bunt Rankings

1 Kevin Millar .800   11 Albert Pujols .612   23 Paul Konerko .536
2 Brad Wilkerson .738   12 Julio Franco .610   24 Adam LaRoche .528
3 Rafael Palmeiro .700   13 Shea Hillenbrand .607   25 Darin Erstad .505
4 Shawn Green .662   14 Tony Clark .600   26 Carlos Delgado .489
5 Hee Seop Choi .653   15 Ken Harvey .585   27 Phil Nevin .488
6 Doug Mientkiewicz .646   16 Scott Hatteberg .575   28 Sean Casey .487
7 Todd Helton .640   17 Jeff Bagwell .574   29 Mark Teixeira .487
8 Derrek Lee .628   18 Jim Thome .566   30 J.T. Snow .477
9 Lyle Overbay .628   19 John Olerud .562   31 Daryle Ward .460
10 Ben Broussard .617   20 Carlos Pena .554   32 Nick Johnson .460
                       21 Pedro Feliz .550   33 Tino Martinez .367
                       22 Mike Piazza .541   34 Justin Morneau .320

2003 Bunt Rankings

1 Fred McGriff .811   11 Hee Seop Choi .650   23 Robert Fick .505
2 Ryan Klesko .708   12 Jeff Bagwell .632   24 Shea Hillenbrand .496
3 Scott Spiezio .706   13 Jim Thome .628   25 Andres Galarraga .494
4 Travis Lee .700   14 Paul Konerko .615   26 Eric Karros .490
5 Jason Giambi .690   15 Doug Mientkiewicz .610   27 Ken Harvey .488
6 Lyle Overbay .675   16 Derrek Lee .609   28 Carlos Pena .486
7 Sean Casey .674   17 Ben Broussard .600   29 Kevin Millar .482
8 J.T. Snow .671   18 Tino Martinez .586   30 Nick Johnson .475
9 John Olerud .663   19 Jeff Conine .585   31 Carlos Delgado .470
10 Todd Helton .652   20 Jason Phillips .578   32 Scott Hatteberg .466
                       21 Randall Simon .544   33 Wil Cordero .412
                       22 Richie Sexson .506   34 Mark Teixeira .397

First Basemen

Mark Teixeira

	3-Yr Plus/Minus: +53 in 3514 inn.	
Plays to his right: +8	**2005 Enhanced P/M: +17 in 1358 inn.**	
Straight on: +2	**2005 Basic P/M: +14**	
To his left: +3	Home: +10 in 681 inn.	RHP: +10 in 1010 inn.
Plays in the air: +1	Road: +4 in 681 inn.	LHP: +4 in 348 inn.

A few seasons ago there was some question regarding where Teixeira would play, but the converted third baseman has not only settled in at first base, he ranks number one in enhanced plays made (+53) over the past three years. In fact, in 2003 he had the best season of any first baseman by far (+29), while he also had the best enhanced plus/minus total for 2005 (+17). He has worked hard to learn the position, especially improving his ability to scoop low throws out of the dirt. His third baseman instincts and reactions serve him well on difficult plays.

With that great plus/minus score in 2003, we were tempted to give Teixeira the Gold Glove That Should Have Been. But he earned an "F" in bunt coverage that year, while John Olerud, the actual American League Gold Glove winner, received a grade of "B-" in bunt coverage along with his +14 enhanced plays.

Doug Mientkiewicz

	3-Yr Plus/Minus: +32 in 2775 inn.	
Plays to his right: +5	**2005 Enhanced P/M: +9 in 675 inn.**	
Straight on: +3	**2005 Basic P/M: +9**	
To his left: +1	Home: 0 in 325 inn.	RHP: +9 in 497 inn.
Plays in the air: 0	Road: +9 in 325 inn.	LHP: 0 in 178 inn.

Mientkiewicz is an excellent defender and a former Gold Glover. He has range and agility and is like a vacuum sucking up all throws, good and bad. He really helped the young Mets infield in 2005, but his poor year at bat made him a burden in the lineup.

Albert Pujols

	3-Yr Plus/Minus: +25 in 3068 inn.	
Plays to his right: +6	**2005 Enhanced P/M: +10 in 1359 inn.**	
Straight on: 0	**2005 Basic P/M: +9**	
To his left: +3	Home: +9 in 690 inn.	RHP: +8 in 1069 inn.
Plays in the air: 0	Road: 0 in 690 inn.	LHP: +1 in 290 inn.

Ah, to be one of the greatest young hitters in baseball history and to be a fine fielder to boot. Albert Pujols' bat is so good that his contribution in the field tends to be overlooked. But his range ranks third among all first basemen (+25 enhanced plays made) and he even received an A- for handling bunts in 2005.

With his impressive defensive performance in 2005, Pujols wins the Gold Glove That Should Have Been over Derrek Lee. He had +10 enhanced plays to Lee's +2 and edged out Lee on fielding bunts ranking 2nd in the majors with a grade of "A-" to Lee's 6th (B+). While Lee also has a great reputation for handling errant throws by his infielders, Pujols does well in that department too.

Darin Erstad

	3-Yr Plus/Minus: +21 in 2344 inn.	
Plays to his right: +8	**2005 Enhanced P/M: +12 in 1279 inn.**	
Straight on: 0	**2005 Basic P/M: +11**	
To his left: +2	Home: +13 in 669 inn.	RHP: +8 in 1089 inn.
Plays in the air: 0	Road: -2 in 669 inn.	LHP: +3 in 190 inn.

Erstad is the only player to win Gold Gloves at two different positions, first base and outfield. His range at first is among the best in the game, and he has saved the Angels' infield many errors with his ability to scoop balls. Erstad still plays with that reckless abandon that he had in the outfield; he has no fear of diving for a popup or crashing into the stands to make a play.

Ryan Howard

	3-Yr Plus/Minus: +18 in 767 inn.	
Plays to his right: +15	**2005 Enhanced P/M: +16 in 706 inn.**	
Straight on: +6	**2005 Basic P/M: +19**	
To his left: -2	Home: +9 in 343 inn.	RHP: +15 in 579 inn.
Plays in the air: 0	Road: +10 in 343 inn.	LHP: +4 in 127 inn.

In his first full major league season, Ryan Howard ranked second among all first basemen in enhanced plays made. He's particularly strong moving to his right. His agility and footwork are surprising for a man his size (6'4", 230) and it looks like he will be the Phillies' first baseman for a long time to come. . .or until he's a free agent.

Tino Martinez

	3-Yr Plus/Minus: +15 in 2795 inn.	
Plays to his right: +7	**2005 Enhanced P/M: +9 in 770 inn.**	
Straight on: +7	**2005 Basic P/M: +11**	
To his left: -4	Home: +5 in 385 inn.	RHP: +7 in 560 inn.
Plays in the air: +1	Road: +6 in 385 inn.	LHP: +4 in 210 inn.

Martinez's range and skills have diminished over the years, yet he has managed to consistently rank near the top in enhanced plays made (seventh overall). He has good hands and uses his experience to make up for lost range. He lost the starting job in 2005 to Jason Giambi when Giambi's bat caught fire in the second half of the season. But he did replace Giambi as a late-inning defensive replacement 15 times.

Kevin Millar

	3-Yr Plus/Minus: +14 in 2161 inn.	
Plays to his right: -2	**2005 Enhanced P/M: +5 in 796 inn.**	
Straight on: +3	**2005 Basic P/M: +2**	
To his left: +1	Home: +4 in 411 inn.	RHP: +4 in 613 inn.
Plays in the air: +1	Road: -2 in 411 inn.	LHP: -2 in 183 inn.

Millar ranks high in enhanced plays made (+14, good for eighth place), but he's not a good first baseman. The problem is that, despite his veteran status, he does not have a lot of experience at first base, and it shows. He is very aggressive and sometimes makes plays a long way from first base, but he won't stay at home on plays on which he should cover first. He loses several plays a year by being 30 feet away from first base when the second baseman fields the ball, or by cutting in front of

First Basemen

the second baseman to knock the ball down when he should be covering first to take the throw.

Chad Tracy
3-Yr Plus/Minus: +12 in 686 inn.

Plays to his right:	+3	2005 Enhanced P/M: +11 in 653 inn.		
Straight on:	+5	2005 Basic P/M: +11		
To his left:	0	Home: +5 in 317 inn.	RHP: +10 in 473 inn.
Plays in the air:	+2	Road: +6 in 317 inn.	LHP: +1 in 180 inn.

Despite playing only 80 games at first base in 2005, Tracy ranked fifth in the majors in enhanced plays made (+11). His reactions look a bit slow, but he gets the job done. He also played right field last year and is a work in progress there. Tracy will find a position, most likely returning to third base in 2006, because his bat (.308, 27 homers) definitely belongs in the majors. He fared well at third in 2004, with 17 enhanced plays above average.

J.T. Snow
3-Yr Plus/Minus: +11 in 2431 inn.

Plays to his right:	-1	2005 Enhanced P/M: +2 in 826 inn.		
Straight on:	-1	2005 Basic P/M: +1		
To his left:	+3	Home: +8 in 409 inn.	RHP: +3 in 521 inn.
Plays in the air:	0	Road: -7 in 409 inn.	LHP: -2 in 305 inn.

Age is catching up to J.T. Snow, who won six consecutive Gold Glove awards from 1995 to 2000. Over the last two years, he's only been in the middle, of the pack (18th and 16th) in enhanced plays made and his home/road split hints that he felt more comfortable at Pac Bell in 2005. But Snow is still a joy to watch, very acrobatic and smooth around the bag. He makes difficult plays look routine.

We would have liked to have seen a seventh Gold Glove for Snow. We give him our National League Gold Glove That Should Have Been for his 2003 season. He outperformed Derrek Lee in enhanced plus/minus +9 to -13. He also received a solid B+ in bunt coverage, compared to Lee's B-.

Lance Niekro
3-Yr Plus/Minus: +10 in 536 inn.

Plays to his right:	+6	2005 Enhanced P/M: +10 in 529 inn.		
Straight on:	+4	2005 Basic P/M: +9		
To his left:	+1	Home: +5 in 297 inn.	RHP: +6 in 327 inn.
Plays in the air:	-1	Road: +4 in 297 inn.	LHP: +3 in 202 inn.

Niekro (son of Joe, nephew of Phil) played third and first in the minors, but he has only played first base for the Giants in the majors. Like many players converted from third, he has shown good range at the first base bag (+10 enhanced plays made last year). He offers a big target and is improving his ability to pick up hard grounders and dig balls out of the dirt. J.T. Snow will be a hard act to follow, but Niekro is ready for the challenge.

Travis Lee
3-Yr Plus/Minus: +9 in 2204 inn.

Plays to his right:	+1	2005 Enhanced P/M: -5 in 918 inn.		
Straight on:	-4	2005 Basic P/M: -5		
To his left:	-1	Home: -3 in 482 inn.	RHP: -4 in 541 inn.
Plays in the air:	-1	Road: -2 in 482 inn.	LHP: -1 in 377 inn.

Travis Lee is a fine defensive first baseman. He is smooth, with very good range and excellent ability to dig balls. Lee has great anticipation and instincts, and can start a double play as well as any first baseman.

Having said that, Lee missed almost all of 2004 with a shoulder injury and ranked near the bottom in enhanced plays made in 2005 (-5, 26th place). Look for Lee to bounce back in 2006.

Justin Morneau
3-Yr Plus/Minus: +7 in 1739 inn.

Plays to his right:	-2	2005 Enhanced P/M: +13 in 1166 inn.		
Straight on:	+7	2005 Basic P/M: +11		
To his left:	+6	Home: +1 in 556 inn.	RHP: +6 in 860 inn.
Plays in the air:	0	Road: +10 in 556 inn.	LHP: +5 in 306 inn.

In 2005, his first full year in the majors, Justin Morneau was third in enhanced plays made (+13). Originally a catcher, he has improved dramatically over the last few seasons to become a good first baseman. He initially struggled with his glove and footwork, but he's worked very hard to improve his defense. His biggest improvement has been in digging throws out of the dirt, and he has helped keep a young, inexperienced Twins infield from falling apart. He did a great job handling bunts on his side of the field last year, ranking first among first basemen in all of baseball earning a grade of "A".

Nick Johnson
3-Yr Plus/Minus: +2 in 2238 inn.

Plays to his right:	+4	2005 Enhanced P/M: +6 in 1099 inn.		
Straight on:	-2	2005 Basic P/M: +6		
To his left:	+3	Home: +5 in 500 inn.	RHP: +7 in 1022 inn.
Plays in the air:	+1	Road: +1 in 500 inn.	LHP: -1 in 77 inn.

Johnson is a good defender but all those years playing on the same team as Jason Giambi made him seem better than he really is. While he's got all the tools (good footwork, range, hands and a strong arm), he is not as good as some of the top defensive first basemen. His ranking in enhanced plays made (13th, +2) is about right.

Dan Johnson
3-Yr Plus/Minus: +2 in 884 inn.

Plays to his right:	-1	2005 Enhanced P/M: +2 in 884 inn.		
Straight on:	+1	2005 Basic P/M: +1		
To his left:	0	Home: +2 in 457 inn.	RHP: -1 in 668 inn.
Plays in the air:	+1	Road: -1 in 457 inn.	LHP: +2 in 216 inn.

Dan Johnson is no more than adequate at first. The A's tried him in the outfield but he has below-average speed and the only place on the field he really fits is at first base.

First Basemen

Sean Casey

3-Yr Plus/Minus: +2 in 3637 inn.			
Plays to his right:	-2	2005 Enhanced P/M: -6 in 1139 inn.	
Straight on:	-6	2005 Basic P/M: -8	
To his left:	+1	Home: -8 in 571 inn.	RHP: -3 in 750 inn.
Plays in the air:	-1	Road: 0 in 571 inn.	LHP: -5 in 389 inn.

Casey makes plays on everything he gets to. He doesn't have the range of some of the elite first basemen, but he positions himself well and gets a good read on the ball off the bat.

Lyle Overbay

3-Yr Plus/Minus: -1 in 3229 inn.			
Plays to his right:	+2	2005 Enhanced P/M: +4 in 1265 inn.	
Straight on:	+6	2005 Basic P/M: +5	
To his left:	-3	Home: -4 in 614 inn.	RHP: -1 in 783 inn.
Plays in the air:	0	Road: +9 in 614 inn.	LHP: +6 in 482 inn.

Overbay is a decent defender with a good glove but his range is just average. He was exposed in the second half of the year when Junior Spivey wasn't at second base. He makes all the routine plays but doesn't have great mobility or footwork.

Todd Helton

3-Yr Plus/Minus: -1 in 3920 inn.			
Plays to his right:	-3	2005 Enhanced P/M: -1 in 1230 inn.	
Straight on:	+2	2005 Basic P/M: 0	
To his left:	0	Home: -3 in 623 inn.	RHP: +2 in 894 inn.
Plays in the air:	+1	Road: +3 in 623 inn.	LHP: -2 in 336 inn.

Helton's ranking in enhanced plays made over the last three years has been 31st, 1st, and 21st. Those were huge swings. Helton has fine range, a strong arm (he was a starting college QB at Tennessee), charges balls well (a consistent "B" for handling bunts), and saves the infield with scoops and digs out of the dirt. With his great bat, it's sometimes easy to forget that he is a three-time Gold Glove winner.

Eric Hinske

3-Yr Plus/Minus: -1 in 860 inn.			
Plays to his right:	-4	2005 Enhanced P/M: -1 in 860 inn.	
Straight on:	+1	2005 Basic P/M: -3	
To his left:	+2	Home: -3 in 436 inn.	RHP: -4 in 581 inn.
Plays in the air:	-2	Road: 0 in 436 inn.	LHP: +1 in 279 inn.

The 2005 season was Hinske's first real year at first base, and it showed. When the Blue Jays obtained Corey Koskie to play third, Hinske had to move elsewhere. Unfortunately his basic skills—hands, footwork and range—didn't change when he moved across the diamond. He is actually pretty agile for a big guy (6-2, 235) and he's a good athlete, but he's a below-average defender. He was very poor at third base in 2003 and 2004 and turned in a combined total plus/minus score of -25.

Daryle Ward

3-Yr Plus/Minus: -2 in 1546 inn.			
Plays to his right:	-2	2005 Enhanced P/M: +3 in 892 inn.	
Straight on:	+5	2005 Basic P/M: +2	
To his left:	-2	Home: +1 in 456 inn.	RHP: +6 in 493 inn.
Plays in the air:	0	Road: +1 in 456 inn.	LHP: -4 in 399 inn.

Ward has trouble with his weight which limits his range and mobility at first. He ranked 14th in enhanced plays made in 2005, but even then his range was limited (-2 to either side). He also ranks poorly on bunts. He does have good hands and scoops up bad throws well to save infield errors.

Chris Shelton

3-Yr Plus/Minus: -2 in 764 inn.			
Plays to his right:	-3	2005 Enhanced P/M: -2 in 738 inn.	
Straight on:	-3	2005 Basic P/M: -4	
To his left:	+1	Home: 0 in 407 inn.	RHP: +1 in 468 inn.
Plays in the air:	+1	Road: -4 in 407 inn.	LHP: -5 in 270 inn.

Shelton is limited defensively; his only tool is his bat. Shelton is a former catcher who may still be used there in an emergency. Tigers manager Alan Trammell said, "First seems to be his best position, but if he hits we'll find a place for him."

Ben Broussard

3-Yr Plus/Minus: -3 in 2995 inn.			
Plays to his right:	-2	2005 Enhanced P/M: +1 in 1051 inn.	
Straight on:	+2	2005 Basic P/M: 0	
To his left:	+1	Home: +4 in 497 inn.	RHP: +5 in 678 inn.
Plays in the air:	-1	Road: -4 in 497 inn.	LHP: -5 in 373 inn.

Experience at first base has helped improve Broussard's overall defense. Once thought to be just adequate at first, he has shown good range, improved his ability to dig balls out of the dirt and shown that he can turn a double play well.

Phil Nevin

3-Yr Plus/Minus: -4 in 2088 inn.			
Plays to his right:	+2	2005 Enhanced P/M: -3 in 620 inn.	
Straight on:	-3	2005 Basic P/M: -2	
To his left:	-1	Home: +2 in 309 inn.	RHP: 0 in 511 inn.
Plays in the air:	0	Road: -4 in 309 inn.	LHP: -2 in 109 inn.

Nevin is a converted third baseman who has a strong arm, good reactions and adequate range over at first. However, he doesn't have great footwork, has trouble with his positioning and is still learning the nuances of playing first. He also has some trouble on throws that he needs to react to, and doesn't dig the ball out of the dirt well.

Hee Seop Choi

3-Yr Plus/Minus: -5 in 2038 inn.			
Plays to his right:	+1	2005 Enhanced P/M: +2 in 665 inn.	
Straight on:	+1	2005 Basic P/M: +2	
To his left:	+2	Home: 0 in 330 inn.	RHP: +2 in 593 inn.
Plays in the air:	-2	Road: +2 in 330 inn.	LHP: 0 in 72 inn.

Choi has soft hands and displays good footwork around first. He has almost no range or reactions.

First Basemen

Lance Berkman
3-Yr Plus/Minus: -7 in 742 inn.

Plays to his right:	-1	2005 Enhanced P/M: -7 in 738 inn.
Straight on:	-2	2005 Basic P/M: -7
To his left:	-3	Home: -8 in 405 inn. RHP: -2 in 491 inn.
Plays in the air:	-1	Road: +1 in 405 inn. LHP: -5 in 247 inn.

Berkman is a good athlete but he only had limited experience at first base before 2005. Really, he's a better fit at first base than in the outfield. His knee injuries and some added body weight have made him less mobile. Playing first will put less strain on his body.

Paul Konerko
3-Yr Plus/Minus: -10 in 3390 inn.

Plays to his right:	-1	2005 Enhanced P/M: -2 in 1273 inn.
Straight on:	-1	2005 Basic P/M: -2
To his left:	+1	Home: -2 in 631 inn. RHP: +3 in 965 inn.
Plays in the air:	-1	Road: 0 in 631 inn. LHP: -5 in 308 inn.

Konerko is an archetypal first baseman: a big home run hitter with limited range. Still, he's improved his overall defense the past few seasons, and his ability to scoop or dig balls out of the dirt is a defensive strength.

Jim Thome
3-Yr Plus/Minus: -13 in 2978 inn.

Plays to his right:	+3	2005 Enhanced P/M: +4 in 436 inn.
Straight on:	+2	2005 Basic P/M: +3
To his left:	-1	Home: +5 in 256 inn. RHP: 0 in 331 inn.
Plays in the air:	-1	Road: -2 in 256 inn. LHP: +3 in 105 inn.

Thome is adequate defensively at first base. He does not have great range but he catches what he can get to. He has good size which helps him get high and wild throws. He was traded to the White Sox where he will DH and get some occasional time at first base backing up Paul Konerko.

Tony Clark
3-Yr Plus/Minus: -13 in 1767 inn.

Plays to his right:	-5	2005 Enhanced P/M: +4 in 643 inn.
Straight on:	+6	2005 Basic P/M: +1
To his left:	0	Home: +1 in 362 inn. RHP: 0 in 501 inn.
Plays in the air:	+1	Road: 0 in 362 inn. LHP: +1 in 142 inn.

Clark is a veteran first baseman who is above average defensively. He has good hands and decent range at first.

Derrek Lee
3-Yr Plus/Minus: -13 in 4172 inn.

Plays to his right:	0	2005 Enhanced P/M: +2 in 1386 inn.
Straight on:	-7	2005 Basic P/M: 0
To his left:	+6	Home: -2 in 734 inn. RHP: -2 in 1114 inn.
Plays in the air:	+2	Road: +2 in 734 inn. LHP: +2 in 272 inn.

Lee is generally recognized as the new benchmark for defensive excellent at first base; some scouts say he may be the best defensive first baseman since Keith Hernandez. He is agile, offers a huge 6'5" target for his infielders, and is great at digging bad throws out of the dirt. As a result, he's won two Gold Glove awards.

Our rankings paint a different picture. Overall, Lee is rated the 24th best first baseman in enhanced plays made (-13) and he's dead last in handling balls hit directly to his position (-19). That makes no sense, right? The numbers have got to be wrong, right?

Well, maybe. Our rankings only capture part of what makes a first baseman a good fielding first baseman. Yet when a player's numbers are this low for three straight seasons, you've got to question what you assume to be true. Lee is obviously a tremendously skilled athlete but, like the other Gold Glove Derek (Jeter), the numbers may be picking up something the eyes aren't.

Rafael Palmeiro
3-Yr Plus/Minus: -13 in 2349 inn.

Plays to his right:	-5	2005 Enhanced P/M: -12 in 748 inn.
Straight on:	-6	2005 Basic P/M: -12
To his left:	0	Home: -6 in 415 inn. RHP: -7 in 510 inn.
Plays in the air:	-1	Road: -6 in 415 inn. LHP: -5 in 238 inn.

When Rafael Palmeiro won the Gold Glove in 1999, the voters who voted for him overlooked a key statistic: games played. Palmeiro spent a mere 28 games in the field that year. So the next time someone tells you that statistics aren't useful for comparing fielders, remind them that Games Played is a statistic too. Got to start somewhere.

Palmeiro no longer has the first base skills he once had. His -28 enhanced plus/minus figure over the last two years demonstrates it.

Shea Hillenbrand
3-Yr Plus/Minus: -14 in 2326 inn.

Plays to his right:	-4	2005 Enhanced P/M: 0 in 587 inn.
Straight on:	+1	2005 Basic P/M: -1
To his left:	+3	Home: -3 in 310 inn. RHP: +3 in 386 inn.
Plays in the air:	-1	Road: +2 in 310 inn. LHP: -4 in 201 inn.

Having experience at third base is no guarantee that a player will be a good first baseman. For every Mark Teixeira, there's a Shea Hillenbrand. Actually, Hillenbrand is probably just passing through first base territory on his way to designated-hitter land, where his skills will fit best.

Jason Giambi
3-Yr Plus/Minus: -15 in 1678 inn.

Plays to his right:	-7	2005 Enhanced P/M: -8 in 560 inn.
Straight on:	-3	2005 Basic P/M: -8
To his left:	+2	Home: -7 in 294 inn. RHP: -6 in 414 inn.
Plays in the air:	0	Road: -1 in 294 inn. LHP: -2 in 146 inn.

Giambi splits his time between first base and designated hitter, which tells you all you need to know about his glove. He catches balls and makes plays when they are hit right at him, but leg and knee injuries have taken away whatever little mobility he had in the past.

First Basemen

Matt Stairs **3-Yr Plus/Minus: -16 in 953 inn.**

Plays to his right: -5	2005 Enhanced P/M: -6 in 510 inn.
Straight on: -1	2005 Basic P/M: -5
To his left: +1	Home: -5 in 266 inn. RHP: -3 in 396 inn.
Plays in the air: -1	Road: 0 in 266 inn. LHP: -2 in 114 inn.

Stairs is an outfielder/DH who was used at first base by the Royals because Ken Harvey was in the minors and Mike Sweeney kept hurting himself and losing ballgames trying to play first base. Stairs is very short for a first baseman, built like a fire hydrant, is not quick and lacks experience at first base. However, he does catch the ball if it is thrown to him or hit near him, which makes him a vastly better first baseman than Sweeney or Harvey.

Adam LaRoche **3-Yr Plus/Minus: -16 in 1739 inn.**

Plays to his right: 0	2005 Enhanced P/M: -17 in 1019 inn.
Straight on: -15	2005 Basic P/M: -18
To his left: -3	Home: -8 in 524 inn. RHP: -10 in 778 inn.
Plays in the air: 0	Road: -10 in 524 inn. LHP: -8 in 241 inn.

In his first full major league season at first base, Adam LaRoche ranked next-to-last in enhanced plays made (-17 overall, -15 on balls hit in his area). This is odd, because LaRoche has a fine fielding reputation and draws comparisons to J.T. Snow. He reportedly has excellent range and great hands, and is a slick defender. As a former pitcher (and the son of former major league pitcher Dave LaRoche), his strong throwing arm is also a plus. We'll see in future years if he starts making plays to match his reputation.

Carlos Delgado **3-Yr Plus/Minus: -22 in 3523 inn.**

Plays to his right: -5	2005 Enhanced P/M: -23 in 1206 inn.
Straight on: -5	2005 Basic P/M: -18
To his left: -8	Home: -10 in 610 inn. RHP: -14 in 808 inn.
Plays in the air: 0	Road: -8 in 610 inn. LHP: -4 in 398 inn.

Delgado's limited range and poor instincts seemed to be particularly prominent in 2005, when he ranked last in enhanced plays made (-23). But he makes up for his lack of tools with heads-up plays in the field and great swings at the plate.

(This is Bill James, breaking in. I know that Delgado does not have a good defensive reputation, and I am sure that there are many people who know more about this than I do, but. . .for whatever it may be worth. A few years ago, we videotaped every Red Sox game and counted "Good Fielding Plays", a good fielding play being essentially defined as any fielding play which is made to the advantage of the defense when/after it is unclear, at the time the ball is hit, whether or not the play can be made. Delgado had more good fielding plays against the Red Sox than any other player at any position. . .I think the total was 14 in 19 games, and I think he had more GFP in 19 games than the Red Sox

first basemen did in 162 games. About half of those were throws from Hudson, Hinske or a pitcher that could easily have gotten away from him, but which he was able to save. One was a play at first where he faked a throw to second, forcing the runner to dive back into the base, and then recorded the out, without the runner advancing from second to third. Two, I think, were plays on which he was able to create an angle for the throw to second and thus get an out at second base when it appeared more likely he would have to take the out at first. One was a play on which he deked the runner into holding first on what should have been a double. I will note that none of these are plays which John Dewan's range studies would pick up. I'm not saying that he's a good first baseman or a good defensive player, but against the Red Sox in that season, when we were studying these types of plays very closely, he was a great defensive player. This may have been atypical, I don't know.)

Richie Sexson **3-Yr Plus/Minus: -28 in 2958 inn.**

Plays to his right: -11	2005 Enhanced P/M: -15 in 1302 inn.
Straight on: +7	2005 Basic P/M: -13
To his left: -9	Home: -11 in 701 inn. RHP: -8 in 969 inn.
Plays in the air: 0	Road: -2 in 701 inn. LHP: -5 in 333 inn.

Sexson has come in 32nd in enhanced plays in each of his two full seasons, and he's 32nd overall. That's last. He's a tall guy with a long reach, which helps him handle his infielder's throws and offsets his limited range, but that's probably the most you can say for his fielding.

Second Basemen Evaluations

Year	League	Gold Glove Winners	Should Have Been
2003	AL	Bret Boone	Orlando Hudson
	NL	Luis Castillo	Luis Castillo
2004	AL	Bret Boone	Orlando Hudson
	NL	Luis Castillo	Luis Castillo
2005	AL	Orlando Hudson	Orlando Hudson
	NL	Luis Castillo	Craig Counsell

My Personal Ratings

Top Ten

1 Orlando Hudson, Ari
2 Luis Castillo, Min
3 Mark Ellis, Oak
4 Craig Counsell, Ari
5 Adam Kennedy, LAA
6 Brian Roberts, Bal
7 Placido Polanco, Det
8 Marcus Giles, Atl
9 Mark Grudzielanek, KC
10 Chase Utley, Phi

Bottom Five

26 Jose Vidro, Was
27 Bret Boone, NYM
28 Todd Walker, ChC
29 Alfonso Soriano, Was
30 Robinson Cano, NYY

Player teams based on transactions through February 5, 2006

Second Basemen Rankings

3-Year Plus/Minus Rankings

1	Orlando Hudson	+77	11	Mark Grudzielanek	+15	21	Miguel Cairo	-21
2	Marcus Giles	+38	12	Aaron Miles	+13	22	Todd Walker	-22
3	Adam Kennedy	+38	13	D'Angelo Jimenez	+9	23	Luis Rivas	-35
4	Mark Ellis	+34	14	Ray Durham	+3	24	Alfonso Soriano	-40
5	Brian Roberts	+32	15	Jeff Kent	+2	25	Bret Boone	-54
6	Chase Utley	+32	16	Alex Cora	0			
7	Luis Castillo	+28	17	Mark Bellhorn	0			
8	Placido Polanco	+27	18	Mark Loretta	-9			
9	Junior Spivey	+24	19	Jose Castillo	-14			
10	Ronnie Belliard	+18	20	Jose Vidro	-20			

2005 Plus/Minus Rankings

1	Craig Counsell	+35	11	Mark Ellis	+11	24	Jose Vidro	-6
2	Chase Utley	+26	12	Luis Castillo	+9	25	Jorge Cantu	-7
3	Mark Grudzielanek	+20	13	Nick Green	+3	26	Omar Infante	-7
4	Ronnie Belliard	+20	14	Marcus Giles	-1	27	Jose Castillo	-8
5	Orlando Hudson	+20	15	Luis A. Gonzalez	-1	28	Miguel Cairo	-8
6	Brian Roberts	+18	16	Kazuo Matsui	-1	29	Aaron Miles	-8
7	Adam Kennedy	+16	17	Rich Aurilia	-1	30	Mark Loretta	-11
8	Junior Spivey	+14	18	Mark Bellhorn	-2	31	Ruben Gotay	-11
9	Placido Polanco	+13	19	Todd Walker	-2	32	Rickie Weeks	-11
10	Nick Punto	+12	20	Tadahito Iguchi	-3	33	Craig Biggio	-14
			21	Ray Durham	-4	34	Alfonso Soriano	-22
			22	Jeff Kent	-5	35	Bret Boone	-25
			23	Tony Graffanino	-5	36	Robinson Cano	-27

2004 Plus/Minus Rankings

1	Orlando Hudson	+35	11	Willie Harris	+3	22	Todd Walker	-4
2	Aaron Miles	+21	12	Ronnie Belliard	+1	23	Luis Rivas	-5
3	D'Angelo Jimenez	+18	13	Ray Durham	0	24	Jose Castillo	-6
4	Tony Womack	+16	14	Scott Hairston	0	25	Mark Loretta	-7
5	Jeff Kent	+15	15	Juan Uribe	0	26	Alex Cora	-8
6	Rey Sanchez	+14	16	Mark Grudzielanek	0	27	Omar Infante	-9
7	Marcus Giles	+12	17	Tony Graffanino	0	28	Marco Scutaro	-12
8	Luis Castillo	+8	18	Mark Bellhorn	-1	29	Enrique Wilson	-12
9	Junior Spivey	+8	19	Nick Green	-1	30	Miguel Cairo	-14
10	Adam Kennedy	+7	20	Brian Roberts	-2	31	Alfonso Soriano	-15
			21	Placido Polanco	-4	32	Jose Vidro	-15
						33	Bret Boone	-20

2003 Plus/Minus Rankings

1	Marcus Giles	+27	11	Brandon Phillips	+6	22	Jeff Kent	-8
2	Mark Ellis	+23	12	Bo Hart	+6	23	Bret Boone	-9
3	Orlando Hudson	+22	13	Marlon Anderson	+4	24	D'Angelo Jimenez	-9
4	Placido Polanco	+18	14	Warren Morris	+3	25	Michael Young	-10
5	Brian Roberts	+16	15	Junior Spivey	+2	26	Fernando Vina	-10
6	Adam Kennedy	+15	16	Jose Vidro	+1	27	Desi Relaford	-11
7	Luis Castillo	+11	17	Abraham Nunez	+1	28	Eric Young	-13
8	Mark Loretta	+9	18	Alex Cora	0	29	Todd Walker	-16
9	Jeff Reboulet	+9	19	Alfonso Soriano	-3	30	Carlos Febles	-16
10	Ray Durham	+7	20	Ronnie Belliard	-3	31	Roberto Alomar	-17
			21	Mark Grudzielanek	-5	32	Luis Rivas	-25

3-Year GDP Rankings

1 Jose Castillo	.563	11 Luis Rivas	.522	21 D'Angelo Jimenez	.468
2 Alex Cora	.561	12 Orlando Hudson	.513	22 Ray Durham	.450
3 Miguel Cairo	.552	13 Mark Loretta	.508	23 Jeff Kent	.429
4 Mark Grudzielanek	.547	14 Mark Bellhorn	.502	24 Todd Walker	.416
5 Bret Boone	.540	15 Luis Castillo	.498	25 Aaron Miles	.401
6 Brian Roberts	.538	16 Alfonso Soriano	.493		
7 Ronnie Belliard	.531	17 Chase Utley	.486		
8 Adam Kennedy	.527	18 Junior Spivey	.480		
9 Placido Polanco	.526	19 Marcus Giles	.480		
10 Mark Ellis	.523	20 Jose Vidro	.479		

2005 GDP Rankings

1 Mark Grudzielanek	.627	11 Mark Bellhorn	.539	24 Craig Biggio	.480
2 Jose Castillo	.626	12 Orlando Hudson	.538	25 Rickie Weeks	.477
3 Nick Punto	.600	13 Omar Infante	.534	26 Jorge Cantu	.474
4 Adam Kennedy	.591	14 Ruben Gotay	.529	27 Alfonso Soriano	.470
5 Ronnie Belliard	.589	15 Mark Loretta	.523	28 Luis A. Gonzalez	.469
6 Placido Polanco	.570	16 Craig Counsell	.514	29 Robinson Cano	.461
7 Miguel Cairo	.568	17 Rich Aurilia	.514	30 Jose Vidro	.461
8 Tadahito Iguchi	.560	18 Nick Green	.513	31 Luis Castillo	.459
9 Brian Roberts	.553	19 Tony Graffanino	.508	32 Aaron Miles	.450
10 Mark Ellis	.552	20 Junior Spivey	.507	33 Ray Durham	.446
		21 Bret Boone	.485	34 Chase Utley	.444
		22 Kazuo Matsui	.484	35 Jeff Kent	.441
		23 Marcus Giles	.484	36 Todd Walker	.396

2004 GDP Rankings

1 Omar Infante	.573	11 Juan Uribe	.523	22 Adam Kennedy	.466
2 Tony Graffanino	.569	12 Mark Loretta	.522	23 Willie Harris	.457
3 Bret Boone	.547	13 Junior Spivey	.514	24 Tony Womack	.450
4 Luis Rivas	.537	14 Jose Castillo	.507	25 Nick Green	.414
5 Brian Roberts	.533	15 Alfonso Soriano	.505	26 D'Angelo Jimenez	.414
6 Alex Cora	.530	16 Jose Vidro	.504	27 Ray Durham	.405
7 Marco Scutaro	.529	17 Ronnie Belliard	.500	28 Jeff Kent	.384
8 Miguel Cairo	.529	18 Orlando Hudson	.488	29 Scott Hairston	.376
9 Rey Sanchez	.527	19 Placido Polanco	.486	30 Aaron Miles	.373
10 Luis Castillo	.524	20 Marcus Giles	.485	31 Mark Grudzielanek	.359
		21 Mark Bellhorn	.479	32 Enrique Wilson	.328
				33 Todd Walker	.323

2003 GDP Rankings

1 Warren Morris	.610	11 Ray Durham	.517	22 Roberto Alomar	.488
2 Jeff Reboulet	.573	12 Orlando Hudson	.517	23 Abraham Nunez	.482
3 Marlon Anderson	.566	13 Placido Polanco	.515	24 Mark Loretta	.481
4 Bret Boone	.565	14 Luis Castillo	.511	25 Luis Rivas	.479
5 Mark Grudzielanek	.557	15 Brandon Phillips	.507	26 Desi Relaford	.473
6 Alex Cora	.556	16 Fernando Vina	.507	27 Marcus Giles	.470
7 Michael Young	.556	17 Alfonso Soriano	.506	28 Jose Vidro	.468
8 Adam Kennedy	.534	18 Ronnie Belliard	.503	29 Jeff Kent	.466
9 Brian Roberts	.525	19 D'Angelo Jimenez	.503	30 Bo Hart	.458
10 Carlos Febles	.525	20 Mark Ellis	.500	31 Junior Spivey	.441
		21 Todd Walker	.490	32 Eric Young	.429

Second Basemen

Orlando Hudson

3-Yr Plus/Minus: +77 in 3340 inn.

Plays to his right:	-1	2005 Plus/Minus: +20 in 1068 inn.	
Straight on:	+1		
To his left:	+18	Home: +17 in 560 inn.	RHP: +16 in 743 inn.
Plays in the air:	+3	Road: +3 in 560 inn.	LHP: +4 in 325 inn.

Hudson is the best defensive second baseman in the game. He has great range, especially into the second base hole to his left, and is particularly adept at going back on popups. He is very tough and will stay in on the double play and take contact. His arm is a definite plus but he may occasionally rely on it too much, not using the lower half of his body. Oftentimes he will spin a double play standing flat-footed and throw an absolute laser to first. His -4 plays to his right over three years suggests he may cheat somewhat to his glove side, but the +58 on his glove side more than makes up for the -4.

Hudson finally won his first Gold Glove in 2005 and is likely in line for more. Bret Boone won the American League Gold Glove in 2003 and 2004 but Hudson should have. Hudson's +22 and +35 plays in 2003 and 2004 far exceeded Boone's -9 and -20. Using Bill James' new relative range system, Hudson is off the charts with totals of +64, +96 and +89 over the last three years compared to Boone's +30, -29, and -15.

Adam Kennedy

3-Yr Plus/Minus: +38 in 3453 inn.

Plays to his right:	+11	2005 Plus/Minus: +16 in 1108 inn.	
Straight on:	-1		
To his left:	+8	Home: +9 in 573 inn.	RHP: +13 in 957 inn.
Plays in the air:	-2	Road: +7 in 573 inn.	LHP: +3 in 151 inn.

Kennedy was once considered average at best defensively but has improved greatly over the past few seasons. Not that long ago, the Angels thought about dumping Kennedy and moving David Eckstein to second. They stuck with Kennedy, however, and it has paid dividends. Kennedy now displays great range, especially to his right and has worked hard to become a top tier defender.

Marcus Giles

3-Yr Plus/Minus: +38 in 3279 inn.

Plays to his right:	+12	2005 Plus/Minus: -1 in 1276 inn.	
Straight on:	+1		
To his left:	-12	Home: +4 in 646 inn.	RHP: -4 in 988 inn.
Plays in the air:	-2	Road: -5 in 646 inn.	LHP: +3 in 288 inn.

For a player whom many scouts doubted would ever be any good defensively, Giles' defense is actually very good indeed. Giles has good range and hands. His style is more one of consistency than flash. In contrast to Hudson, he excels on plays to his right (+35) compared to his left (+2) over three years.

We considered Marcus Giles for a retroactive Gold Glove over Luis Castillo in 2003. He had a +27 compared to Castillo's +11, but his weak ranking in double plays that continues to plague him forced us to stay with Castillo.

Mark Ellis

3-Yr Plus/Minus: +34 in 2270 inn.

Plays to his right:	+2	2005 Plus/Minus: +11 in 972 inn.	
Straight on:	+1		
To his left:	+5	Home: +7 in 486 inn.	RHP: +5 in 743 inn.
Plays in the air:	+2	Road: +4 in 486 inn.	LHP: +6 in 229 inn.

Ellis is a converted shortstop whose arm is a bit weak for that position and was moved to second base. He has very good range at second and is not necessarily a flashy player, but is very fundamentally sound. Prior to his surprising 2005 outburst with the bat, Ellis' defense kept him in the lineup as an Oakland regular even with other more offensively-minded candidates available. His +34 plays over the last two years is not an anomaly.

Craig Counsell

3-Yr Plus/Minus: +33 in 1312 inn.

Plays to his right:	+24	2005 Plus/Minus: +35 in 1244 inn.	
Straight on:	-3		
To his left:	+6	Home: +23 in 626 inn.	RHP: +29 in 947 inn.
Plays in the air:	+8	Road: +12 in 626 inn.	LHP: +6 in 297 inn.

Counsell was a better than average shortstop in 2004 and that translated to somewhat surprising excellence at second base, Counsell's best defensive position, in 2005. Counsell's arm is his greatest weakness and that obviously hurts him less at second than it does at short.

The Gold Glove winner for 2005 at second base was Luis Castillo for the third straight year, but we're going to go with Counsell. Injuries limited Castillo to 116 games started and he managed only +9 plays for the year while Counsell led all second basemen in baseball with +35 including a +8 on balls hit in the air. Mark Grudzielanek's great defensive year with St. Louis and his #1 ranking in GDP percentage gained him points, but Counsell squeaks by both Grudzielanek and the incumbent Castillo based on the simple fact that he made more plays beyond what was expected of an average second basemen.

With their acquisition of Orlando Hudson, Arizona now has two of the best second basemen in baseball. They'll move Counsell back to shortstop where his plus/minus was +5 in 2004.

Chase Utley

3-Yr Plus/Minus: +32 in 1907 inn.

Plays to his right:	+20	2005 Plus/Minus: +26 in 1195 inn.	
Straight on:	+1		
To his left:	+3	Home: +10 in 625 inn.	RHP: +21 in 966 inn.
Plays in the air:	+3	Road: +16 in 625 inn.	LHP: +5 in 229 inn.

Utley has made great strides defensively in recent seasons. He has worked hard to make himself an above-average second baseman. He is not always smooth and pretty on defense, but he makes up for that with his quickness. He is big for a second baseman, but has

Second Basemen

shown improved agility and plays in control.

It will be interesting to see if Utley can maintain the excellence he achieved in 2005 when his +26 plus/minus number was second best in baseball. One area where he didn't excel was on the double play, where his double play percentage of .444 ranked him 34th out of 36 players with 500 or more innings at second base in 2005. He finished ahead of Jeff Kent and Todd Walker in this category, which isn't saying much.

Brian Roberts
3-Yr Plus/Minus: +32 in 3455 inn.

Plays to his right: +8		2005 Plus/Minus: +18 in 1208 inn.	
Straight on: +2			
To his left: +6		Home: +9 in 649 inn.	RHP: +10 in 731 inn.
Plays in the air: +2		Road: +9 in 649 inn.	LHP: +8 in 477 inn.

Roberts is very solid in the field. A converted shortstop who did not quite have the arm for the position, he fits in nicely at second base. He is a smooth fielder who turns the double play pivot well. Roberts has had a defensive reputation back to his days in college but now his bat has caught up.

Luis Castillo
3-Yr Plus/Minus: +28 in 3598 inn.

Plays to his right: +20		2005 Plus/Minus: +9 in 1012 inn.	
Straight on: +3			
To his left: -14		Home: +4 in 481 inn.	RHP: +6 in 667 inn.
Plays in the air: 0		Road: +5 in 481 inn.	LHP: +3 in 345 inn.

Castillo consistently garners votes in polls and for awards from writers, managers and his peers attesting to his outstanding defense. Recent hip and leg injuries have hampered his speed at times but when healthy, his speed and quickness allow him to get to balls others cannot reach. A great first step and a very strong arm (maybe the best among second baseman) have helped him win three consecutive National League Gold Gloves.

Due to his injuries in 2005, he played fewer games and his performance dropped as well. While we're allowing him to keep his Gold Gloves in 2003 and 2004, our Gold Glove that should have been for 2005 goes to Craig Counsell.

Placido Polanco
3-Yr Plus/Minus: +27 in 2764 inn.

Plays to his right: +3		2005 Plus/Minus: +13 in 946 inn.	
Straight on: +7			
To his left: +4		Home: +9 in 469 inn.	RHP: +8 in 619 inn.
Plays in the air: -1		Road: +4 in 469 inn.	LHP: +5 in 327 inn.

Polanco is known mostly for his great fundamentals at the plate but is a steady defender with an average arm. He is the prototypical two-hole hitter and can play anywhere in the infield, although second base suits him best. Polanco is rarely out of position defensively.

Junior Spivey
3-Yr Plus/Minus: +24 in 1921 inn.

Plays to his right: +6		2005 Plus/Minus: +14 in 594 inn.	
Straight on: 0			
To his left: +9		Home: +5 in 263 inn.	RHP: +3 in 442 inn.
Plays in the air: 0		Road: +9 in 263 inn.	LHP: +7 in 152 inn.

Spivey has proven to be slightly above average both offensively and defensively. He has shown good athleticism, leading to some consideration of moving him to CF. His outstanding range at second base allows him to get to any kind of ball, including ranging back on popups. Any hiccups in his defense have to do with throws; he does not have an accurate arm. Turns the double play well. Despite the obvious advantages he brings to a team, his injury history raises durability questions. He has not been healthy for a full season since 2002, and until he shakes the injury bug teams should approach him cautiously as an everyday player.

Ronnie Belliard
3-Yr Plus/Minus: +18 in 3474 inn.

Plays to his right: +23		2005 Plus/Minus: +20 in 1244 inn.	
Straight on: -2			
To his left: -6		Home: +15 in 622 inn.	RHP: +17 in 842 inn.
Plays in the air: +5		Road: +5 in 622 inn.	LHP: +3 in 402 inn.

Belliard is short and stocky, but possesses good range for his body type. A strong throwing arm allows him to play deeper than most second basemen and as a result, he'll steal hits, especially up the middle. He displays good footwork, has sure hands, and is adept at turning the double play.

Nick Punto
3-Yr Plus/Minus: +16 in 758 inn.

Plays to his right: -3		2005 Plus/Minus: +12 in 564 inn.	
Straight on: +1			
To his left: +14		Home: +5 in 303 inn.	RHP: +10 in 437 inn.
Plays in the air: 0		Road: +7 in 303 inn.	LHP: +2 in 127 inn.

Punto is a high-energy player who has good range and a strong throwing arm. He formed a slick double play combo with Juan Castro when both were in the Twins' lineup last season. Punto plays aggressively, with little regard for his body, which leads to high injury risk.

Mark Grudzielanek
3-Yr Plus/Minus: +15 in 2738 inn.

Plays to his right: +15		2005 Plus/Minus: +20 in 1158 inn.	
Straight on: +2			
To his left: +3		Home: +12 in 585 inn.	RHP: +23 in 903 inn.
Plays in the air: 0		Road: +8 in 585 inn.	LHP: -3 in 255 inn.

Grudzielanek made impressive strides defensively in 2005. Never more than an average defender, he was much better than average with the Cardinals last season. He showed improved range and has a cannon arm that helps him turn the double play as well as any second baseman in the game. In his 166 double play opportunities he converted 104 for 62.7%, the highest rate among all second basement in 2005. David Eckstein

Second Basemen

and Grudzielanek's excellence on the pivot greatly contributed to the Cardinals' success in 2005.

Aaron Miles — 3-Yr Plus/Minus: +13 in 1645 inn.

Plays to his right:	-6	2005 Plus/Minus: -8 in 602 inn.	
Straight on:	0		
To his left:	+1	Home: -4 in 309 inn.	RHP: -6 in 455 inn.
Plays in the air:	-3	Road: -4 in 309 inn.	LHP: -2 in 147 inn.

Miles is a grinder, who makes up for his lack of quickness and range with hard-nosed effort. He has a strong arm, which will ready him for the utility role he's likely destined for in the future. Miles has been working out at short and third, positions at which he's not seen much time since the minor leagues.

Tony Womack — 3-Yr Plus/Minus: +12 in 1449 inn.

Plays to his right:	-5	2005 Plus/Minus: -7 in 199 inn.	
Straight on:	0		
To his left:	-2	Home: -4 in 146 inn.	RHP: -10 in 150 inn.
Plays in the air:	0	Road: -3 in 146 inn.	LHP: +3 in 49 inn.

Womack was a complete disaster for the Yankees in 2005, and they would have been happy to receive a bucket of balls for him, never mind two minor leaguers. The Reds will give him a shot to win the second base job this year, but he may wind up being only a role player. His days in the outfield are certainly over. Not only are the Reds loaded there, Womack showed that he has trouble in the outfield by his performance last season (-9 enhanced plays in the outfield in less than half a season of play). At second base he still has decent enough speed to have above-average range, but his hands aren't the most reliable and his arm is well below average.

Ray Durham — 3-Yr Plus/Minus: +3 in 3001 inn.

Plays to his right:	-2	2005 Plus/Minus: -4 in 1143 inn.	
Straight on:	-1		
To his left:	+3	Home: 0 in 591 inn.	RHP: -8 in 722 inn.
Plays in the air:	-4	Road: -4 in 591 inn.	LHP: +4 in 421 inn.

Injuries over the years have slowed Durham and his range in the field is now limited. He had particular trouble ranging back on popups this past year and does not turn the double play well. His defensive numbers have dropped progressively over the last three years. His rankings among regulars have gone 10th, 13th, 21st in plus/minus and 11th, 27th, 33rd in double play percentage from 2003 to 2005.

Nick Green — 3-Yr Plus/Minus: +2 in 1303 inn.

Plays to his right:	-2	2005 Plus/Minus: +3 in 731 inn.	
Straight on:	-2		
To his left:	+5	Home: +4 in 381 inn.	RHP: +2 in 448 inn.
Plays in the air:	+2	Road: -1 in 381 inn.	LHP: +1 in 283 inn.

Green is a steady defender in the field with good range and a strong arm. His defensive versatility as well as a weak stick make him most useful as a utility infielder.

Jeff Kent — 3-Yr Plus/Minus: +2 in 3512 inn.

Plays to his right:	-9	2005 Plus/Minus: -5 in 1210 inn.	
Straight on:	+6		
To his left:	-2	Home: -2 in 667 inn.	RHP: -1 in 1054 inn.
Plays in the air:	+1	Road: -3 in 667 inn.	LHP: -4 in 156 inn.

Kent's defense has been maligned for many years but he is not as bad as his reputation. Kent's best weapon is excellent positioning and anticipation, which compensates somewhat for poor range. On the double play pivot and on double plays overall, Kent is consistently below average. His rating on double plays was the second worst in baseball in 2005. Todd Walker bottomed the list.

Mark Bellhorn — 3-Yr Plus/Minus: 0 in 1891 inn.

Plays to his right:	-5	2005 Plus/Minus: -2 in 728 inn.	
Straight on:	+2		
To his left:	-2	Home: +4 in 345 inn.	RHP: -1 in 549 inn.
Plays in the air:	+3	Road: -6 in 345 inn.	LHP: -1 in 179 inn.

Mark Bellhorn is the walking definition of an ugly player, which covers his fielding as well as his unique and emotionally draining performance at the plate. He actually played very well in the field in 2005, especially on the double play. He was much better than in 2004, and he was OK in 2004, but his habit of throwing darts to first base kind of gives you the heebie-jeebies if you are counting on him to hit the bulls-eye.

Tony Graffanino — 3-Yr Plus/Minus: -1 in 1420 inn.

Plays to his right:	-7	2005 Plus/Minus: -5 in 588 inn.	
Straight on:	+3		
To his left:	+1	Home: -7 in 291 inn.	RHP: -2 in 453 inn.
Plays in the air:	-2	Road: +2 in 291 inn.	LHP: -3 in 135 inn.

Essentially Graffanino is the definition of an average ballplayer. He played well after being dealt to Boston last season, but his reputation was tarnished after his Buckner-esque blunder in the ALDS. He has limited range and won't wow the crowd with his glove work, but he won't cost the team many runs either. His ability to play multiple positions makes him an above-average role player on a good team, and an adequate starter for a bad ball club.

Kazuo Matsui — 3-Yr Plus/Minus: -2 in 584 inn.

Plays to his right:	0	2005 Plus/Minus: -1 in 560 inn.	
Straight on:	+2		
To his left:	-3	Home: +3 in 297 inn.	RHP: -1 in 410 inn.
Plays in the air:	0	Road: -4 in 297 inn.	LHP: 0 in 150 inn.

Matsui is another Japanese import who came to the States with a reputation as a top-notch defensive player, not to mention that of an offensive force. He flopped in 2004 at shortstop and was converted to second base in 2005, coinciding with the emergence of Jose Reyes.

Second Basemen

Matsui has shown flashes of good speed and range but overall has been a below-average defender. After returning from injuries late in the year he appeared more comfortable at second base and was improving. He still needs to work at turning the pivot on double plays, which gave him difficulty last year. His pivot percentage of 51.6% in 2005 was the worst among all second basemen in baseball. In 31 pivot opportunities he turned 16 double plays while he could only manage the force play on the other 15.

Rich Aurilia   3-Yr Plus/Minus: -3 in 572 inn.

Plays to his right:	+1	2005 Plus/Minus: -1 in 547 inn.	
Straight on:	+3		
To his left:	0	Home: -2 in 268 inn.	RHP: +1 in 332 inn.
Plays in the air:	-5	Road: +1 in 268 inn.	LHP: -2 in 215 inn.

Aurilia probably fits best at second base now because he no longer has the range to play shortstop and, although his arm is still average, it is more exposed at third base. His performance at second base was average in 2005, which is better than expected given that he's hardly played the position in the last 10 years.

Luis A. Gonzalez   3-Yr Plus/Minus: -3 in 872 inn.

Plays to his right:	0	2005 Plus/Minus: -1 in 579 inn.	
Straight on:	+1		
To his left:	-2	Home: +5 in 293 inn.	RHP: 0 in 434 inn.
Plays in the air:	0	Road: -6 in 293 inn.	LHP: -1 in 145 inn.

Gonzalez is the classic utility player—average defensively all over the field. His range decreases a bit in the middle of the infield and he may be best suited to play third base, although he'll likely continue to see the majority of his time at second.

Tadahito Iguchi   3-Yr Plus/Minus: -3 in 1171 inn.

Plays to his right:	-9	2005 Plus/Minus: -3 in 1171 inn.	
Straight on:	+4		
To his left:	+3	Home: +4 in 651 inn.	RHP: +2 in 890 inn.
Plays in the air:	-1	Road: -7 in 651 inn.	LHP: -5 in 281 inn.

Iguchi is a very fundamentally sound player, which includes his defense. Manager Ozzie Guillen called him his most valuable player in 2005. High praise indeed. Despite an above average arm, his plus/minus figure of -9 on plays to his right suggests he had trouble ranging in that direction. Another year of experience in the United States after several years playing both shortstop and second base in Japan will surely help this key ChiSox middle infielder become even more valuable defensively.

Mark Loretta   3-Yr Plus/Minus: -9 in 3496 inn.

Plays to his right:	-1	2005 Plus/Minus: -11 in 910 inn.	
Straight on:	+1		
To his left:	-12	Home: -6 in 451 inn.	RHP: -13 in 830 inn.
Plays in the air:	+1	Road: -5 in 451 inn.	LHP: +2 in 80 inn.

Loretta does not have much speed or range and has to rely almost entirely on good middle infield instincts and positioning. Loretta is quite adept at making the pivot on the double play.

Rickie Weeks   3-Yr Plus/Minus: -11 in 858 inn.

Plays to his right:	-3	2005 Plus/Minus: -11 in 837 inn.	
Straight on:	-9		
To his left:	+4	Home: -2 in 440 inn.	RHP: -18 in 542 inn.
Plays in the air:	-3	Road: -9 in 440 inn.	LHP: +7 in 295 inn.

Weeks' offense is far ahead of his defense, which has been shaky. He has great athleticism, quickness, good hands and a strong arm but he needs to work on his footwork and throwing mechanics. Weeks has the potential and tools to be a good defender but he has a lot of work to do. His defense may not come around like you'd like, but his offense may more than make up for it if he can be just adequate at second base. Think of him as an agile Jeff Kent; you won't care much about his defense if he puts up great offensive numbers.

Jorge Cantu   3-Yr Plus/Minus: -13 in 942 inn.

Plays to his right:	-4	2005 Plus/Minus: -7 in 668 inn.	
Straight on:	-2		
To his left:	-4	Home: -3 in 348 inn.	RHP: -5 in 369 inn.
Plays in the air:	+2	Road: -4 in 348 inn.	LHP: -2 in 299 inn.

Cantu is a versatile player who can play any position in the infield. He split most of his time between second and third in 2005 and is equal defensively at both positions. Cantu is an average defender at best, but is quick enough to play in the middle infield. His positional future is uncertain, but a move to first base is a possibility.

Jose Castillo   3-Yr Plus/Minus: -14 in 1791 inn.

Plays to his right:	-5	2005 Plus/Minus: -8 in 840 inn.	
Straight on:	-6		
To his left:	+1	Home: -8 in 408 inn.	RHP: -12 in 458 inn.
Plays in the air:	+3	Road: 0 in 408 inn.	LHP: +4 in 382 inn.

Castillo has the skills to eventually become an excellent defender. He has great range and an outstanding arm. His upside may compare to that of Pokey Reese in his prime. Jack Wilson and Castillo are one of the best young double play combos in the majors. Castillo has the best pivot percentage and the best overall double play percentage among second basemen in baseball over the last three years.

Craig Biggio   3-Yr Plus/Minus: -14 in 1172 inn.

Plays to his right:	-10	2005 Plus/Minus: -14 in 1172 inn.	
Straight on:	-1		
To his left:	-3	Home: -17 in 676 inn.	RHP: -9 in 849 inn.
Plays in the air:	-1	Road: +3 in 676 inn.	LHP: -5 in 323 inn.

After a few seasons in the outfield Biggio returned to his old haunt at second base. They say if you don't use it, you lose it, and that certainly seems to be the case with

Second Basemen

Biggio. The Astros can only hope a year of re-experience in the middle infield leads Biggio back toward his prior defensive abilities. In 2005 he was pulled for a defensive replacement, usually Eric Bruntlett, 10 times, the most for any second baseman in baseball.

Omar Infante
3-Yr Plus/Minus: -16 in 1477 inn.

Plays to his right:	-5	2005 Plus/Minus: -7 in 592 inn.	
Straight on:	-2		
To his left:	0	Home: -11 in 342 inn.	RHP: -1 in 365 inn.
Plays in the air:	-1	Road: +4 in 342 inn.	LHP: -6 in 227 inn.

Infante has good range at second, but poor throwing, brought on by shoulder injuries, knocks him down a peg. His erratic throwing needs to be improved if he wants to play everyday. He can turn the double play well and has good hands, but exhibits a lack of concentration at times.

Ruben Gotay
3-Yr Plus/Minus: -18 in 1034 inn.

Plays to his right:	-4	2005 Plus/Minus: -11 in 666 inn.	
Straight on:	0		
To his left:	-5	Home: -5 in 367 inn.	RHP: -9 in 522 inn.
Plays in the air:	-2	Road: -6 in 367 inn.	LHP: -2 in 144 inn.

A weak arm forced former third baseman Gotay to second base. Gotay's defense is a concern. His range is limited and he often is out of position—cheating to anticipate making a play. Gotay needs to expand his range and learn better positioning.

Jose Vidro
3-Yr Plus/Minus: -20 in 2702 inn.

Plays to his right:	-4	2005 Plus/Minus: -6 in 665 inn.	
Straight on:	0		
To his left:	0	Home: -1 in 314 inn.	RHP: -4 in 619 inn.
Plays in the air:	-2	Road: -5 in 314 inn.	LHP: -2 in 46 inn.

Vidro was once a good defender, but has lost a lot the past couple of years, likely due to injury problems. He does not have great speed or range like some other middle infielders but he does have a very strong arm. Vidro's arm allows him to play deeper than most second baseman and that combined with good positioning makes up for his lesser lateral range.

Miguel Cairo
3-Yr Plus/Minus: -21 in 1808 inn.

Plays to his right:	-9	2005 Plus/Minus: -8 in 657 inn.	
Straight on:	0		
To his left:	-1	Home: -4 in 345 inn.	RHP: -7 in 534 inn.
Plays in the air:	+2	Road: -4 in 345 inn.	LHP: -1 in 123 inn.

Cairo is a decent fundamental defender with good hands. He turns the double play well. Cairo has lost some of his range recently, preventing him from being a defensive asset.

Todd Walker
3-Yr Plus/Minus: -22 in 2734 inn.

Plays to his right:	-2	2005 Plus/Minus: -2 in 798 inn.	
Straight on:	+1		
To his left:	-4	Home: +7 in 422 inn.	RHP: +1 in 642 inn.
Plays in the air:	+2	Road: -9 in 422 inn.	LHP: -3 in 156 inn.

Walker has historically been categorized as a defensive liability at second. He has improved a bit in recent years but is still a below-average defender. Walker has limited range and is as poor as they come at turning the double play. His pivot percentage of 52.3% over the last three years is the worst in baseball.

Robinson Cano
3-Yr Plus/Minus: -27 in 1142 inn.

Plays to his right:	-16	2005 Plus/Minus: -27 in 1142 inn.	
Straight on:	-2		
To his left:	-15	Home: -11 in 548 inn.	RHP: -15 in 827 inn.
Plays in the air:	+6	Road: -16 in 548 inn.	LHP: -12 in 315 inn.

Cano is Alfonso Soriano light. His bat is ready for prime time, but his defense is lacking. Cano has some raw defensive skills, but didn't make good use of them in his rookie season. His arm is particularly strong. The Yankees brought in third base coach Larry Bowa, in some part, to try to turn Cano into at least an average second baseman.

Alfonso Soriano
3-Yr Plus/Minus: -40 in 3975 inn.

Plays to his right:	+2	2005 Plus/Minus: -22 in 1351 inn.	
Straight on:	+1		
To his left:	-23	Home: -6 in 694 inn.	RHP: -21 in 996 inn.
Plays in the air:	-2	Road: -16 in 694 inn.	LHP: -1 in 355 inn.

Soriano is a former shortstop who wasn't a very good shortstop and hasn't been much better since converting to second base years ago. He does have good speed and quickness but his hands, footwork and poor instincts are problems. Soriano balks at the thought of a conversion to the outfield, which might be best, but there's no guarantee a third full-time defensive position would be the answer.

Bret Boone
3-Yr Plus/Minus: -54 in 3453 inn.

Plays to his right:	-18	2005 Plus/Minus: -25 in 769 inn.	
Straight on:	-5		
To his left:	0	Home: -11 in 394 inn.	RHP: -16 in 562 inn.
Plays in the air:	-2	Road: -14 in 394 inn.	LHP: -9 in 207 inn.

Unfortunately for Boone, his defense went south about the same time his offense also took a dive. Once considered among the best defensive second baseman, the former Gold Glover's range has suffered and he has displayed concentration problems in the field. At age 37, this decline in defense is not all that puzzling. Barring a surprising rebound, Boone's days are numbered.

See page 10 in the Overview of the Plus/Minus System for more comments on Boone.

Third Basemen Evaluations

Year	League	Gold Glove Winners	Should Have Been
2003	AL	Eric Chavez	Eric Chavez
	NL	Scott Rolen	Adrian Beltre
2004	AL	Eric Chavez	Eric Chavez
	NL	Scott Rolen	Scott Rolen
2005	AL	Eric Chavez	Eric Chavez
	NL	Mike Lowell	David Bell

My Personal Ratings

Top Ten

1 Scott Rolen, StL
2 Eric Chavez, Oak
3 Adrian Beltre, Sea
4 David Bell, Phi
5 Pedro Feliz, SF
6 Sean Burroughs, TB
7 Morgan Ensberg, Hou
8 Corey Koskie, Mil
9 Joe Crede, CWS
10 Alex Rodriguez, NYY

Bottom Five

26 Aramis Ramirez, ChC
27 Mike Cuddyer, Min
28 Troy Glaus, Tor
29 Edgardo Alfonzo, LAA
30 Mark Teahen, KC

Player teams based on transactions through February 5, 2006

Third Basemen Rankings

3-Year Plus/Minus Rankings

1	Adrian Beltre	+71	11	Aaron Boone	+10	21	Aramis Ramirez	-12
2	David Bell	+52	12	Vinny Castilla	+7	22	Eric Munson	-18
3	Scott Rolen	+46	13	Joe Crede	+7	23	Mike Lowell	-21
4	Eric Chavez	+37	14	Chipper Jones	+6	24	Troy Glaus	-25
5	Morgan Ensberg	+26	15	Brandon Inge	+4	25	Eric Hinske	-25
6	Sean Burroughs	+22	16	Bill Mueller	+3	26	Wes Helms	-35
7	Alex Rodriguez	+19	17	Joe Randa	+2	27	Edgardo Alfonzo	-40
8	Hank Blalock	+18	18	Tony Batista	-5	28	Ty Wigginton	-48
9	Corey Koskie	+16	19	Melvin Mora	-9			
10	Casey Blake	+12	20	David Wright	-11			

2005 Plus/Minus Rankings

1	David Bell	+24	11	Melvin Mora	+6	21	Mike Lowell	-8
2	Pedro Feliz	+16	12	Bill Mueller	+6	22	Mike Cuddyer	-10
3	Eric Chavez	+15	13	Alex Rodriguez	+2	23	Edgardo Alfonzo	-10
4	Morgan Ensberg	+15	14	Joe Crede	+2	24	Troy Glaus	-12
5	Brandon Inge	+12	15	Aaron Boone	+1	25	David Wright	-17
6	Corey Koskie	+12	16	Aramis Ramirez	0	26	Hank Blalock	-21
7	Sean Burroughs	+12	17	Alex S. Gonzalez	0	27	Mark Teahen	-30
8	Adrian Beltre	+11	18	Chipper Jones	-2			
9	Garrett Atkins	+10	19	Vinny Castilla	-3			
10	Abraham Nunez	+9	20	Joe Randa	-6			

2004 Plus/Minus Rankings

1	Scott Rolen	+37	11	Kevin Youkilis	+7	21	Bill Mueller	-6
2	Adrian Beltre	+30	12	David Wright	+6	22	Scott Spiezio	-6
3	David Bell	+22	13	Hank Blalock	+5	23	Casey Blake	-7
4	Alex Rodriguez	+17	14	Corey Koskie	+3	24	Aramis Ramirez	-8
5	Chad Tracy	+17	15	Mark DeRosa	+2	25	Morgan Ensberg	-8
6	Sean Burroughs	+14	16	Chone Figgins	+1	26	Brandon Inge	-8
7	Eric Chavez	+13	17	Aubrey Huff	0	27	Joe Crede	-11
8	Joe Randa	+10	18	Mike Lowell	-1	28	Eric Munson	-13
9	Chipper Jones	+8	19	Tony Batista	-3	29	Melvin Mora	-15
10	Vinny Castilla	+7	20	Ty Wigginton	-4	30	Edgardo Alfonzo	-17
						31	Eric Hinske	-20
						32	Wes Helms	-24

2003 Plus/Minus Rankings

1	Hank Blalock	+34	11	Damian Rolls	+6	21	Sean Burroughs	-4
2	Adrian Beltre	+30	12	Geoff Blum	+6	22	Eric Munson	-4
3	Morgan Ensberg	+19	13	Vinny Castilla	+3	23	Eric Hinske	-5
4	Casey Blake	+18	14	Bill Mueller	+3	24	Jeff Cirillo	-6
5	Joe Crede	+16	15	Jose Hernandez	+3	25	Scott Rolen	-7
6	Eric Chavez	+9	16	Corey Koskie	+1	26	Wes Helms	-11
7	Aaron Boone	+9	17	Shea Hillenbrand	0	27	Mike Lowell	-12
8	Chris Stynes	+8	18	Tony Batista	-2	28	Troy Glaus	-12
9	David Bell	+6	19	Joe Randa	-2	29	Edgardo Alfonzo	-13
10	Robin Ventura	+6	20	Aramis Ramirez	-4	30	Ty Wigginton	-26

3-Year Bunt Rankings

1	Mike Lowell	.647	11	Hank Blalock	.534	21	Eric Hinske	.481
2	Adrian Beltre	.570	12	David Wright	.530	22	Troy Glaus	.479
3	Aaron Boone	.561	13	Chipper Jones	.526	23	Aramis Ramirez	.470
4	Sean Burroughs	.559	14	Joe Randa	.518	24	Joe Crede	.462
5	Eric Chavez	.556	15	Ty Wigginton	.514	25	Tony Batista	.451
6	Edgardo Alfonzo	.554	16	Brandon Inge	.501	26	Melvin Mora	.407
7	Bill Mueller	.540	17	Morgan Ensberg	.495	27	Casey Blake	.400
8	Scott Rolen	.539	18	Eric Munson	.495	28	Alex Rodriguez	.325
9	David Bell	.538	19	Vinny Castilla	.488			
10	Wes Helms	.536	20	Corey Koskie	.488			

2005 Bunt Rankings

1	Pedro Feliz	.731	11	David Bell	.519	21	Alex S. Gonzalez	.437
2	Eric Chavez	.671	12	Hank Blalock	.509	22	Morgan Ensberg	.433
3	Mike Lowell	.656	13	Vinny Castilla	.498	23	Garrett Atkins	.425
4	Aaron Boone	.633	14	Joe Randa	.494	24	Aramis Ramirez	.417
5	Bill Mueller	.578	15	Abraham Nunez	.492	25	Sean Burroughs	.407
6	Mike Cuddyer	.577	16	Joe Crede	.484	26	Melvin Mora	.356
7	David Wright	.542	17	Brandon Inge	.477	27	Alex Rodriguez	.312
8	Chipper Jones	.538	18	Troy Glaus	.467			
9	Adrian Beltre	.536	19	Edgardo Alfonzo	.467			
10	Mark Teahen	.521	20	Corey Koskie	.446			

2004 Bunt Rankings

1	Wes Helms	.975	11	David Bell	.534	21	David Wright	.481
2	Mike Lowell	.619	12	Eric Hinske	.527	22	Joe Crede	.470
3	Chone Figgins	.615	13	Eric Chavez	.511	23	Chad Tracy	.467
4	Bill Mueller	.613	14	Chipper Jones	.511	24	Melvin Mora	.450
5	Edgardo Alfonzo	.568	15	Morgan Ensberg	.510	25	Corey Koskie	.443
6	Hank Blalock	.563	16	Sean Burroughs	.504	26	Tony Batista	.430
7	Joe Randa	.560	17	Eric Munson	.497	27	Ty Wigginton	.420
8	Kevin Youkilis	.550	18	Vinny Castilla	.496	28	Scott Spiezio	.414
9	Scott Rolen	.544	19	Aramis Ramirez	.496	29	Casey Blake	.390
10	Brandon Inge	.539	20	Adrian Beltre	.496	30	Aubrey Huff	.382
						31	Alex Rodriguez	.336
						32	Mark DeRosa	.320

2003 Bunt Rankings

1	Adrian Beltre	.734	11	Morgan Ensberg	.553	21	Aaron Boone	.488
2	Chris Stynes	.675	12	Damian Rolls	.540	22	Tony Batista	.473
3	Mike Lowell	.670	13	Jose Hernandez	.539	23	Vinny Castilla	.470
4	Sean Burroughs	.633	14	Scott Rolen	.529	24	Wes Helms	.466
5	Ty Wigginton	.629	15	Eric Chavez	.528	25	Bill Mueller	.463
6	Robin Ventura	.619	16	Troy Glaus	.528	26	Eric Hinske	.434
7	Edgardo Alfonzo	.600	17	Hank Blalock	.526	27	Joe Crede	.433
8	David Bell	.588	18	Joe Randa	.505	28	Geoff Blum	.411
9	Shea Hillenbrand	.578	19	Eric Munson	.493	29	Casey Blake	.406
10	Corey Koskie	.560	20	Aramis Ramirez	.490	30	Jeff Cirillo	.386

Third Basemen

Adrian Beltre

3-Yr Plus/Minus: +71 in 4012 inn.

Plays to his right:	+5	2005 Enhanced P/M: +11 in 1326 inn.	
Straight on:	-3	2005 Basic P/M: +8	
To his left:	+5	Home: -2 in 657 inn.	RHP: +6 in 985 inn.
Plays in the air:	+1	Road: +10 in 657 inn.	LHP: +2 in 341 inn.

Beltre is one of the very best fielding third basemen in the game. He has fantastic range, particularly to his right. He charges well on soft hits and has a strong arm. He makes routine plays look easy and also throws in the occasional dazzling play for extra credit.

However, Beltre slumped in Seattle. He wasn't terrible, mind you. He was still +11 in enhanced plays, eighth in the majors. But he was +30 in each of the two previous years, ranking second both times. Perhaps it was a year of adjustment for Beltre; the home/road splits indicate that he had some difficulty adjusting to his new park, at least in the field.

Beltre retroactively wins our National League Gold Glove That Should Have Been in 2003 over Scott Rolen. His +30 that year far exceeds Rolen's -7, a rare poor year for Rolen.

David Bell

3-Yr Plus/Minus: +52 in 3241 inn.

Plays to his right:	-6	2005 Enhanced P/M: +24 in 1297 inn.	
Straight on:	+25	2005 Basic P/M: +26	
To his left:	+7	Home: +19 in 639 inn.	RHP: +24 in 1017 inn.
Plays in the air:	0	Road: +7 in 639 inn.	LHP: +2 in 280 inn.

Bell has overcome injuries that affected his play in the field, particularly in 2003, to re-establish himself as one of the top fielders at third base. He has very good range with good hands and footwork. Although he doesn't have a very strong arm for a third baseman, he has a quick release and good accuracy with his throws.

Given Mike Lowell's problems with balls hit straight on or to his left (see below) and given David Bell's major league leading +24 in 2005, Bell wins the National League Gold Glove That Should Have Been for 2005.

Scott Rolen

3-Yr Plus/Minus: +46 in 3053 inn.

Plays to his right:	+3	2005 Enhanced P/M: +16 in 486 inn.	
Straight on:	+3	2005 Basic P/M: +15	
To his left:	+9	Home: +4 in 306 inn.	RHP: +12 in 365 inn.
Plays in the air:	0	Road: +11 in 306 inn.	LHP: +3 in 121 inn.

Rolen was on pace to better his 2004 stats (+37 enhanced plays made, the best single year of any third baseman in this book), when he succumbed to a shoulder injury. Regardless, Rolen is probably the best fielding third baseman in the game. He has great range, hands and reactions, plus a very strong, accurate arm. In fact, he's made only two throwing errors in the past two years.

Eric Chavez

3-Yr Plus/Minus: +37 in 3810 inn.

Plays to his right:	+16	2005 Enhanced P/M: +15 in 1348 inn.	
Straight on:	-5	2005 Basic P/M: +10	
To his left:	-1	Home: +11 in 685 inn.	RHP: +8 in 1032 inn.
Plays in the air:	0	Road: -1 in 685 inn.	LHP: +2 in 316 inn.

Next to Rolen, Chavez is probably the best third base fielder in the game. He can make all the plays at third, from the proverbial hot smash down the line (+27 to his right) to charging in on a slow roller or short hop. His home/road splits indicate that he finds Oakland's McAfee Coliseum to his liking.

Pedro Feliz

3-Yr Plus/Minus: +36 in 1224 inn.

Plays to his right:	+2	2005 Enhanced P/M: +16 in 592 inn.	
Straight on:	+7	2005 Basic P/M: +16	
To his left:	+5	Home: +10 in 269 inn.	RHP: +7 in 386 inn.
Plays in the air:	+2	Road: +6 in 269 inn.	LHP: +9 in 206 inn.

Feliz has played many positions for the Giants, but he is a natural third baseman. Despite playing only 79 games at third in 2005, he was second in the majors in enhanced plays made (+16). He even scored an A+ for his handling of bunts. For a third baseman, he has good range (enough to have played shortstop in the past) and a strong arm. Feliz will likely take over as the everyday third baseman in 2006 with Bonds returning to left field.

Morgan Ensberg

3-Yr Plus/Minus: +26 in 3025 inn.

Plays to his right:	+3	2005 Enhanced P/M: +15 in 1286 inn.	
Straight on:	+6	2005 Basic P/M: +15	
To his left:	+7	Home: +5 in 650 inn.	RHP: +6 in 944 inn.
Plays in the air:	-1	Road: +10 in 650 inn.	LHP: +9 in 342 inn.

Ensberg is a decent defender with a strong throwing arm. An elbow injury in 2004 led to below-average defense but he has recovered from that and is back to normal. He doesn't have great range but can move well to both his left and to his right. He equates playing third base to being a goalie in hockey, saying that it's all about reactions and having the right angle to block the ball from getting by you.

Sean Burroughs

3-Yr Plus/Minus: +22 in 2862 inn.

Plays to his right:	-2	2005 Enhanced P/M: +12 in 657 inn.	
Straight on:	+7	2005 Basic P/M: +12	
To his left:	+7	Home: +9 in 396 inn.	RHP: +12 in 569 inn.
Plays in the air:	0	Road: +3 in 396 inn.	LHP: 0 in 88 inn.

Burroughs may not hit like a third baseman, but he fields like one. He's got good range to both sides and a strong arm, and he managed to rank seventh in the majors in enhanced plays made (+12) despite starting in less than half of the Padres' games. At this point in time, it looks like he'll be flashing the third base leather in Tampa Bay in 2006.

Third Basemen

Alex Rodriguez

3-Yr Plus/Minus: +19 in 2748 inn.

Plays to his right: -7	2005 Enhanced P/M: +2 in 1384 inn.
Straight on: +13	2005 Basic P/M: +6
To his left: -3	Home: -1 in 721 inn. RHP: -2 in 1023 inn.
Plays in the air: +4	Road: +7 in 721 inn. LHP: +8 in 361 inn.

Who takes a Gold Glove shortstop and moves him to third base? The Yankees, of course. If you've read our shortstop ratings, you can probably guess what we think of that. Still, A-Rod is a fine third baseman, with natural instincts and a very strong arm. In 2004, he ranked fourth among all third basemen. After a shaky start in 2005, with 11 errors through June, he settled down and only made one error the rest of the year.

Surprisingly, A-Rod's stats indicate a lack of range and a definite weakness on bunts (for which he gets an F). For the past two years, A-Rod is -1 play to his left and -8 plays up the line. His strength is with balls hit in his "zone," where he is +32 plays. In the field, his most similar player is Hank Blalock.

Hank Blalock

3-Yr Plus/Minus: +18 in 3919 inn.

Plays to his right: -6	2005 Enhanced P/M: -21 in 1374 inn.
Straight on: -4	2005 Basic P/M: -17
To his left: -6	Home: -7 in 702 inn. RHP: -2 in 1008 inn.
Plays in the air: -1	Road: -10 in 702 inn. LHP: -15 in 366 inn.

There's 2003 Hank Blalock and there's 2005 Hank Blalock. In 2003, Blalock had an .872 OPS at bat and was the top-ranked fielding third baseman (+34 enhanced plays) by our reckoning. His performance slid a bit in 2004 and then fell all the way to .749 OPS and -21 enhanced plays last year (26th in the majors). Skill-wise, he looks like a good young third baseman, with range, instincts and an above-average arm. But which Hank Blalock will show up in 2006? Best guess: the 2004 version.

Corey Koskie

3-Yr Plus/Minus: +16 in 2806 inn.

Plays to his right: -3	2005 Enhanced P/M: +12 in 674 inn.
Straight on: +12	2005 Basic P/M: +12
To his left: +6	Home: +5 in 366 inn. RHP: +6 in 467 inn.
Plays in the air: -2	Road: +7 in 366 inn. LHP: +6 in 207 inn.

Koskie is an above-average third baseman with real good reactions and instincts at the hot corner. He has good hands, a strong arm and gets rid of the ball quickly. After ranking in the middle of the pack in 2003 and 2004, he ranked sixth in 2005 despite starting less than half of Toronto's games at third.

Aaron Boone

3-Yr Plus/Minus: +10 in 2428 inn.

Plays to his right: +1	2005 Enhanced P/M: +1 in 1250 inn.
Straight on: -3	2005 Basic P/M: -1
To his left: +1	Home: -2 in 573 inn. RHP: -2 in 833 inn.
Plays in the air: 0	Road: +1 in 573 inn. LHP: +1 in 417 inn.

Boone is a fine third baseman, but he showed some rust after missing all of 2004 with a torn knee, particularly with his range. He still played well; his natural instincts and accurate arm landed him in the middle of our 2005 rankings.

Abraham O. Nunez

3-Yr Plus/Minus: +8 in 743 inn.

Plays to his right: +6	2005 Enhanced P/M: +9 in 721 inn.
Straight on: +1	2005 Basic P/M: +7
To his left: -2	Home: +2 in 308 inn. RHP: +10 in 565 inn.
Plays in the air: +1	Road: +5 in 308 inn. LHP: -3 in 156 inn.

Abraham Nunez had played only seven major league games at third base before taking over third on a full-time basis when Scott Rolen went down with a shoulder injury. Nunez more than held his own, as his years as a backup middle infielder served him well. However, don't look for him to match his 2005 offensive output any time soon.

Garrett Atkins

3-Yr Plus/Minus: +7 in 1323 inn.

Plays to his right: +6	2005 Enhanced P/M: +10 in 1162 inn.
Straight on: +1	2005 Basic P/M: +6
To his left: -1	Home: +8 in 580 inn. RHP: +9 in 855 inn.
Plays in the air: 0	Road: -2 in 580 inn. LHP: -3 in 307 inn.

Atkins is supposed to be a stopgap while the Rockies wait for prospect Ian Stewart but he has proved to be so much more. He has delivered offensively and his defense, which was a worry, has proven to be adequate. The former first baseman has worked hard in his conversion to third and improved his defensive play. He has gotten in better shape to improve his quickness and agility. He will never be elite defensively but he has a strong arm, can go to his right well (+6 right rating) and is working on his ability to go to his left and also start double plays. His defense may have been one of the season's biggest surprises.

Joe Crede

3-Yr Plus/Minus: +7 in 3661 inn.

Plays to his right: -14	2005 Enhanced P/M: +2 in 1120 inn.
Straight on: +16	2005 Basic P/M: +11
To his left: +11	Home: +9 in 578 inn. RHP: +5 in 856 inn.
Plays in the air: -1	Road: +2 in 578 inn. LHP: +6 in 264 inn.

Crede turned heads in the World Series with several great reaction plays. Overall, he is a solid, above-average third baseman. He has good instincts and reactions, moves well and has a good arm. He has also managed to lower his error rate each of the past three years. His rankings jumped up and down between 2003 and 2005, but his overall ranking (13th, +7 enhanced plays made) probably says it best.

It appears that in 2005 he may have been positioning himself a step farther to his left than necessary. This had two effects. 1) His plus/minus figures of +11 to his left and +16 on balls hit straight on are superb, but the -14 to his right is quite poor. He can make that play to his right, but if he's too far away to start with he can't get there. 2) Because many of the plays that he misses to his right go for doubles, his enhanced plus/minus figure drops down to +2 overall, a very average performance.

Vinny Castilla
3-Yr Plus/Minus: +7 in 3724 inn.

Plays to his right:	-4	2005 Enhanced P/M: -3 in 1171 inn.	
Straight on:	+2	2005 Basic P/M: -5	
To his left:	-2	Home: -4 in 582 inn.	RHP: -3 in 1104 inn.
Plays in the air:	-1	Road: -1 in 582 inn.	LHP: -2 in 67 inn.

At 38, Vinny Castilla is still a good defender but on the downside of his career. He no longer has speed or range but he does not make mistakes. He has good positioning and reactions, good hands and an extremely accurate arm.

Chipper Jones
3-Yr Plus/Minus: +6 in 1632 inn.

Plays to his right:	+1	2005 Enhanced P/M: -2 in 830 inn.	
Straight on:	+1	2005 Basic P/M: -1	
To his left:	-3	Home: -1 in 441 inn.	RHP: -1 in 625 inn.
Plays in the air:	0	Road: 0 in 441 inn.	LHP: 0 in 205 inn.

After a few seasons in left field, Chipper returned to third base during the 2004 season. Never a great defender, he has played better since returning to third base last season but is no better than average. He has OK range with a good throwing arm which seems to be more accurate than it was years ago.

Chone Figgins
3-Yr Plus/Minus: +5 in 1143 inn.

Plays to his right:	+3	2005 Enhanced P/M: +4 in 438 inn.	
Straight on:	+6	2005 Basic P/M: +2	
To his left:	-5	Home: 0 in 197 inn.	RHP: -3 in 371 inn.
Plays in the air:	-1	Road: +2 in 197 inn.	LHP: +5 in 67 inn.

If there was a Gold Glove award for utility players Figgins would win it hands down. He plays very good defense at many positions and third base, his most common position, is no exception. He also filled in well for Adam Kennedy at second and Steve Finley in center field this season. Some scouts feel that the Angels like to move him around because he can be exposed defensively by just playing one position every day.

Brandon Inge
3-Yr Plus/Minus: +4 in 1925 inn.

Plays to his right:	+16	2005 Enhanced P/M: +12 in 1400 inn.	
Straight on:	-6	2005 Basic P/M: +5	
To his left:	-3	Home: -3 in 729 inn.	RHP: +3 in 857 inn.
Plays in the air:	-2	Road: +8 in 729 inn.	LHP: +2 in 543 inn.

Inge is an athletic and gifted defensive player wherever he plays. In his first full season at third base he showed good footwork, a great throwing arm (former catcher) and good range. He has made a number of errors while learning the position but his range has allowed him to cover everywhere between the line and the shortstop's territory in the hole.

Bill Mueller
3-Yr Plus/Minus: +3 in 3155 inn.

Plays to his right:	+7	2005 Enhanced P/M: +6 in 1209 inn.	
Straight on:	0	2005 Basic P/M: +4	
To his left:	-3	Home: +8 in 642 inn.	RHP: -3 in 923 inn.
Plays in the air:	+1	Road: -4 in 642 inn.	LHP: +7 in 286 inn.

Mueller is a textbook player who does everything fundamentally well. His good range may not be elite but he makes all the plays he should. He also has a solid, accurate arm, great reflexes and is one of the best in the game at snaring hard-hit balls down the line. Mueller played better defense in 2005 than he had the previous two years. He was outstanding.

Joe Randa
3-Yr Plus/Minus: +2 in 3305 inn.

Plays to his right:	+1	2005 Enhanced P/M: -6 in 1210 inn.	
Straight on:	-6	2005 Basic P/M: -5	
To his left:	-1	Home: +1 in 682 inn.	RHP: -1 in 979 inn.
Plays in the air:	+1	Road: -6 in 682 inn.	LHP: -4 in 231 inn.

Randa is a fine defender, in the same general grade as Aaron Boone. He has very sure hands and a strong, accurate arm, and his error rate is one of the lowest at the hot corner. He has consistently shown better range up the line than to his left. The Reds traded Randa to the Padres midseason when they decided top prospect Edwin Encarnacion was ready.

Alex S. Gonzalez
3-Yr Plus/Minus: 0 in 780 inn.

Plays to his right:	+4	2005 Enhanced P/M: 0 in 780 inn.	
Straight on:	-4	2005 Basic P/M: -6	
To his left:	-5	Home: -3 in 400 inn.	RHP: -4 in 450 inn.
Plays in the air:	-1	Road: -3 in 400 inn.	LHP: -2 in 330 inn.

For years, Gonzalez was one of the better defensive shortstops in baseball. He made a nice conversion to third base in 2005, kind of similar to A-Rod's switch in 2004. Gonzalez showed good instincts and reactions in his first season at the hot corner and has a strong and accurate arm to help him with the longer throws from third.

Tony Batista
3-Yr Plus/Minus: -5 in 2690 inn.

Plays to his right:	+7	2004 Enhanced P/M: -3 in 1326 inn.	
Straight on:	+1	2004 Basic P/M: -6	
To his left:	-14	Home: 0 in 665 inn.	RHP: -6 in 1193 inn.
Plays in the air:	0	Road: -6 in 661 inn.	LHP: 0 in 133 inn.

After a one-year hiatus in Japan, Batista returns with a shot to win a starting job in Minnesota. Although he was a former shortstop, his range is now rather limited. His arm isn't completely reliable, as he doesn't get much on his throws, making plays down the line a challenge for

Third Basemen

him to handle. The Twins will take his plus power and hope he can be a close to an average defender.

Melvin Mora

3-Yr Plus/Minus: -9 in 2500 inn.

Plays to his right:	+2	2005 Enhanced P/M: +6 in 1290 inn.	
Straight on:	+4	2005 Basic P/M: +5	
To his left:	-2	Home: +3 in 669 inn.	RHP: +8 in 783 inn.
Plays in the air:	+1	Road: +2 in 669 inn.	LHP: -3 in 507 inn.

The versatile Mora has played third for the past two years, and he showed striking improvement in 2005. He has made a lot of adjustments and worked hard on his footwork. A student of the position, Mora likes to emulate the techniques of top third basemen like Rolen, Chavez, and former teammate Robin Ventura.

David Wright

3-Yr Plus/Minus: -11 in 2008 inn.

Plays to his right:	-14	2005 Enhanced P/M: -17 in 1404 inn.	
Straight on:	+2	2005 Basic P/M: -14	
To his left:	0	Home: -11 in 726 inn.	RHP: -16 in 1059 inn.
Plays in the air:	-2	Road: -3 in 726 inn.	LHP: +2 in 345 inn.

Wright came to the major leagues with a reputation as a good defensive third baseman, but he didn't play the part early in the year. Instead, he displayed bad range and poor footwork, and made a number of throwing errors. However, he really turned the corner and was much better in the second half.

2006 will be a telling year for the youngster. One thing to watch: how well he handles balls in the air (at -5 plays over the last two years, he ranks last among third basemen).

Aramis Ramirez

3-Yr Plus/Minus: -12 in 3663 inn.

Plays to his right:	-2	2005 Enhanced P/M: 0 in 1020 inn.	
Straight on:	0	2005 Basic P/M: +1	
To his left:	+3	Home: -5 in 510 inn.	RHP: +4 in 818 inn.
Plays in the air:	0	Road: +6 in 510 inn.	LHP: -3 in 202 inn.

Ramirez had been a below-average defender before coming to the Cubs in 2003. After joining the Cubs he worked hard to improve his footwork and reduced his errors dramatically. However, groin injuries late in 2004 and 2005 seemed to cause a relapse in his defensive play. He does not have very good range but the injuries may have thrown off all the progress he made with his footwork and throwing. If he can get healthy again in 2006 it will be interesting to see if he can resume the previous progress he was making defensively.

Mike Lowell

3-Yr Plus/Minus: -21 in 3563 inn.

Plays to his right:	+16	2005 Enhanced P/M: -8 in 1127 inn.	
Straight on:	-19	2005 Basic P/M: -13	
To his left:	-7	Home: -8 in 680 inn.	RHP: -11 in 732 inn.
Plays in the air:	-3	Road: -5 in 680 inn.	LHP: -2 in 395 inn.

If handling bunts and guarding the line were the only two skill requirements for a third baseman, Mike Lowell would stand head and shoulders above all others defensively. He is outstanding at charging balls and making barehanded plays, and is the only player with an "A" rating at handling bunts over three years. He's had that "A" rating in each of those years showing tremendous consistency. He also has the best plus/minus figure (+30) on balls hit to his right in that time. He is sure-handed as well, having made only 22 errors in the past three years, two less than David Wright's (and Troy Glaus') total in 2005 alone.

Yet he ranks 23rd overall in our book. The reason? He is -45 plays made on balls hit to him (by far the worst three-year count), and -15 on plays to his left (also the worst). Yeah, numbers sometimes lie, but on the whole, Mike Lowell doesn't appear to deserve his glowing reputation, nor his glowing Gold Glove from 2005.

Mike Cuddyer

3-Yr Plus/Minus: -24 in 1206 inn.

Plays to his right:	+4	2005 Enhanced P/M: -10 in 816 inn.	
Straight on:	-6	2005 Basic P/M: -12	
To his left:	-8	Home: -2 in 443 inn.	RHP: -6 in 620 inn.
Plays in the air:	-1	Road: -10 in 443 inn.	LHP: -6 in 196 inn.

Cuddyer did not look comfortable at third base. Though he has a strong arm, he may be better positioned at second base. The Twins thought he was ready to take over as the everyday third baseman in 2005 but a utility role may be his future where he can play second, third and even some outfield.

Troy Glaus

3-Yr Plus/Minus: -25 in 2161 inn.

Plays to his right:	-2	2005 Enhanced P/M: -12 in 1264 inn.	
Straight on:	-1	2005 Basic P/M: -12	
To his left:	-11	Home: -14 in 628 inn.	RHP: -17 in 943 inn.
Plays in the air:	+2	Road: +2 in 628 inn.	LHP: +5 in 321 inn.

Glaus was once an excellent third baseman but injuries to both his knees and shoulder have taken their toll. He still has good instincts and makes plays but his range has decreased over the years and a once powerful throwing arm has weakened. He made more throwing errors (15) than any major league player in 2005.

Mark Teahen

3-Yr Plus/Minus: -30 in 1068 inn.

Plays to his right:	-9	2005 Enhanced P/M: -30 in 1068 inn.	
Straight on:	-6	2005 Basic P/M: -24	
To his left:	-11	Home: -15 in 533 inn.	RHP: -20 in 835 inn.
Plays in the air:	+1	Road: -9 in 533 inn.	LHP: -4 in 233 inn.

He was ghastly. It would be unfair to judge him prematurely based on a season when he should have been at AAA, but. . .he was ghastly. He is tall for a third baseman, and he was a tangle of arms and legs, playing third base with great energy but little grace. Balls hit right at him would tie him up; balls hit to his left or right would get away before he did. He was very good at chasing down popups. His arm is certainly strong enough to play third, but his throws often sailed high and wide, and, when he attempted to compensate for this, you can guess what happened. My honest opinion is that he is not quick enough or agile enough to play third base in the major leagues, but, as I said, it would be premature to reach that conclusion yet.

Edgardo Alfonzo

3-Yr Plus/Minus: -40 in 3037 inn.		
Plays to his right: -2	2005 Enhanced P/M: -10 in 813 inn.	
Straight on: -10	2005 Basic P/M: -12	
To his left: 0	Home: +1 in 450 inn.	RHP: -10 in 500 inn.
Plays in the air: 0	Road: -13 in 450 inn.	LHP: -2 in 313 inn.

It's hard to believe, but Alfonzo played shortstop in the minors and almost won Gold Gloves at second and third with the Mets in the last '90s. Back problems have robbed this once-fine player of his bat and glove, and the Giants finally gave up and traded him to the Angels during the offseason.

Shortstops Evaluations

Year	League	Gold Glove Winners	Should Have Been
2003	AL	Alex Rodriguez	Alex Rodriguez
	NL	Edgar Renteria	Adam Everett
2004	AL	Derek Jeter	Miguel Tejada
	NL	Cesar Izturis	Cesar Izturis
2005	AL	Derek Jeter	Juan Uribe
	NL	Omar Vizquel	Adam Everett

My Personal Ratings

Top Ten

1 Adam Everett, Hou
2 Jack Wilson, Pit
3 Jimmy Rollins, Phi
4 Rafael Furcal, LAD
5 Juan Uribe, CWS
6 Neifi Perez, ChC
7 Orlando Cabrera, LAA
8 Cesar Izturis, LAD
9 Miguel Tejada, Bal
10 David Eckstein, StL

Bottom Five

26 Felipe Lopez, Cin
27 Cristian Guzman, Was
28 Russ Adams, Tor
29 Angel Berroa, KC
30 Michael Young, Tex

Player teams based on transactions through February 5, 2006

Shortstops Rankings

3-Year Plus/Minus Rankings

1	Adam Everett	+76	11	Miguel Tejada	+15	21 Edgar Renteria -4
2	Jack Wilson	+50	12	Bobby Crosby	+11	22 Rich Aurilia -5
3	Jimmy Rollins	+40	13	Julio Lugo	+5	23 Khalil Greene -12
4	Rafael Furcal	+38	14	Alex Cintron	+4	24 Royce Clayton -14
5	Neifi Perez	+36	15	David Eckstein	+3	25 Jhonny Peralta -15
6	Cesar Izturis	+33	16	Alex Gonzalez	-1	26 Felipe Lopez -15
7	Orlando Cabrera	+25	17	Nomar Garciaparra	-1	27 Carlos Guillen -19
8	Juan Uribe	+25	18	Jose Reyes	-2	28 Cristian Guzman -22
9	Omar Vizquel	+20	19	Alex Gonzalez	-2	29 Angel Berroa -59
10	Jose Valentin	+16	20	J.J. Hardy	-3	30 Derek Jeter -64
						31 Michael Young -73

2005 Plus/Minus Rankings

1	Adam Everett	+33	11	Bobby Crosby	+8	22 Royce Clayton -6
2	Jack Wilson	+31	12	Orlando Cabrera	+7	23 Cristian Guzman -6
3	Rafael Furcal	+26	13	Miguel Tejada	+5	24 Marcos Scutaro -8
4	Jimmy Rollins	+23	14	Omar Vizquel	+4	25 Jose Reyes -10
5	Neifi Perez	+20	15	Cesar Izturis	+4	26 Edgar Renteria -11
6	Clint Barmes	+17	16	Bill Hall	+4	27 Jhonny Peralta -14
7	Jason Bartlett	+14	17	Carlos Guillen	+3	28 Khalil Greene -16
8	J.J. Hardy	+10	18	Felipe Lopez	0	29 Russ Adams -17
9	Juan Uribe	+9	19	Alex Gonzalez	-1	30 Angel Berroa -26
10	Juan Castro	+9	20	David Eckstein	-2	31 Derek Jeter -34
			21	Julio Lugo	-2	32 Michael Young -39

2004 Plus/Minus Rankings

1	Adam Everett	+22	11	Neifi Perez	+6	23 Cristian Guzman 0
2	Cesar Izturis	+19	12	Bobby Crosby	+5	24 Chris Gomez 0
3	Pokey Reese	+16	13	Julio Lugo	+5	25 Ramon Martinez -3
4	Miguel Tejada	+14	14	Jimmy Rollins	+5	26 Alex S. Gonzalez -3
5	Orlando Cabrera	+13	15	Jose Valentin	+4	27 Kazuo Matsui -6
6	Jack Wilson	+11	16	Khalil Greene	+4	28 Deivi Cruz -9
7	Alex Gonzalez	+9	17	Alex Cintron	+3	29 Nomar Garciaparra -12
8	Edgar Renteria	+9	18	Rafael Furcal	+2	30 Barry Larkin -13
9	Omar Vizquel	+6	19	Rich Aurilia	+2	31 Derek Jeter -16
10	Craig Counsell	+6	20	David Eckstein	+1	32 Carlos Guillen -18
			21	Chris Woodward	+1	33 Angel Berroa -20
			22	Royce Clayton	0	34 Michael Young -34

2003 Plus/Minus Rankings

1	Adam Everett	+21	11	Juan Uribe	+7	23 Edgar Renteria -2
2	Nomar Garciaparra	+13	12	Deivi Cruz	+5	24 Chris Woodward -2
3	Jimmy Rollins	+12	13	Orlando Cabrera	+5	25 Miguel Tejada -4
4	Jose Valentin	+12	14	David Eckstein	+4	26 Tony Womack -4
5	Alex Rodriguez	+11	15	Rey Sanchez	+4	27 Carlos Guillen -4
6	Rafael Furcal	+10	16	Mike Bordick	+4	28 Rich Aurilia -7
7	Cesar Izturis	+10	17	Julio Lugo	+2	29 Ramon Santiago -7
8	Jose Reyes	+10	18	Alex S. Gonzalez	0	30 Royce Clayton -8
9	Omar Vizquel	+10	19	Ramon Vazquez	0	31 Alex Gonzalez -9
10	Jack Wilson	+8	20	Jhonny Peralta	0	32 Jose Hernandez -11
			21	Alex Cintron	-1	33 Angel Berroa -13
			22	Omar Infante	-1	34 Derek Jeter -14
						35 Cristian Guzman -16

3-Year GDP Rankings

1	Jhonny Peralta	.660	11	Juan Uribe	.608	21	Julio Lugo	.568
2	Alex Gonzalez	.652	12	Bobby Crosby	.605	22	Orlando Cabrera	.568
3	Jack Wilson	.640	13	Jose Valentin	.604	23	Edgar Renteria	.567
4	Angel Berroa	.626	14	David Eckstein	.592	24	Omar Vizquel	.562
5	Jimmy Rollins	.622	15	Alex Gonzalez	.592	25	Miguel Tejada	.561
6	Deivi Cruz	.618	16	Neifi Perez	.591	26	Michael Young	.555
7	Jose Reyes	.613	17	Adam Everett	.591	27	Rich Aurilia	.554
8	Carlos Guillen	.611	18	Cesar Izturis	.589	28	Derek Jeter	.551
9	Cristian Guzman	.610	19	Khalil Greene	.582	29	Felipe Lopez	.511
10	Rafael Furcal	.609	20	Royce Clayton	.569	30	Alex Cintron	.508
						31	Nomar Garciaparra	.488

2005 GDP Rankings

1	Jhonny Peralta	.712	11	David Eckstein	.628	22	Clint Barmes	.562
2	Juan Castro	.688	12	Marcos Scutaro	.605	23	Michael Young	.561
3	Jason Bartlett	.677	13	Neifi Perez	.603	24	Cesar Izturis	.557
4	Bobby Crosby	.671	14	Jimmy Rollins	.598	25	Carlos Guillen	.553
5	Jose Reyes	.655	15	Juan Uribe	.597	26	Felipe Lopez	.543
6	Jack Wilson	.652	16	J.J. Hardy	.590	27	Khalil Greene	.541
7	Alex Gonzalez	.652	17	Royce Clayton	.588	28	Julio Lugo	.539
8	Cristian Guzman	.650	18	Adam Everett	.587	29	Derek Jeter	.538
9	Rafael Furcal	.640	19	Orlando Cabrera	.586	30	Edgar Renteria	.532
10	Angel Berroa	.634	20	Russ Adams	.586	31	Bill Hall	.528
			21	Miguel Tejada	.572	32	Omar Vizquel	.528

2004 GDP Rankings

1	Jack Wilson	.667	11	Carlos Guillen	.609	23	Michael Young	.551
2	Angel Berroa	.632	12	Jose Valentin	.597	24	Miguel Tejada	.550
3	Jimmy Rollins	.631	13	Rafael Furcal	.594	25	Royce Clayton	.547
4	Julio Lugo	.623	14	Kazuo Matsui	.593	26	Alex S. Gonzalez	.547
5	Deivi Cruz	.620	15	Bobby Crosby	.592	27	Orlando Cabrera	.546
6	Cesar Izturis	.618	16	Chris Woodward	.587	28	David Eckstein	.544
7	Khalil Greene	.618	17	Derek Jeter	.582	29	Rich Aurilia	.542
8	Adam Everett	.614	18	Ramon Martinez	.571	30	Omar Vizquel	.529
9	Cristian Guzman	.614	19	Craig Counsell	.569	31	Neifi Perez	.515
10	Alex Gonzalez	.611	20	Edgar Renteria	.565	32	Barry Larkin	.500
			21	Pokey Reese	.559	33	Alex Cintron	.479
			22	Chris Gomez	.558	34	Nomar Garciaparra	.413

2003 GDP Rankings

1	Alex Gonzalez	.692	11	Deivi Cruz	.613	23	Royce Clayton	.571
2	Omar Vizquel	.684	12	Jose Valentin	.607	24	Jhonny Peralta	.567
3	Carlos Guillen	.682	13	Jack Wilson	.596	25	Chris Woodward	.566
4	Alex S. Gonzalez	.636	14	Rafael Furcal	.592	26	Omar Infante	.565
5	Jimmy Rollins	.636	15	Juan Uribe	.589	27	Miguel Tejada	.563
6	Ramon Santiago	.635	16	Alex Rodriguez	.586	28	Cristian Guzman	.560
7	Mike Bordick	.625	17	David Eckstein	.584	29	Ramon Vazquez	.557
8	Rey Sanchez	.624	18	Cesar Izturis	.584	30	Julio Lugo	.545
9	Angel Berroa	.614	19	Jose Hernandez	.582	31	Jose Reyes	.534
10	Edgar Renteria	.613	20	Adam Everett	.578	32	Alex Cintron	.526
			21	Rich Aurilia	.577	33	Derek Jeter	.523
			22	Orlando Cabrera	.573	34	Nomar Garciaparra	.503
						35	Tony Womack	.444

Shortstops

Adam Everett
3-Yr Plus/Minus: +76 in 3135 inn.

Plays to his right: +15
Straight on: +4
To his left: +14
Plays in the air: -1

2005 Plus/Minus: +33 in 1292 inn.

Home: +17 in 663 inn.   RHP: +18 in 923 inn.
Road: +16 in 663 inn.   LHP: +15 in 369 inn.

Quite simply the best shortstop in baseball. He has ranked number one in plus/minus in each of the last three years. See Bill James' essay on page 3.

Jack Wilson
3-Yr Plus/Minus: +50 in 4011 inn.

Plays to his right: +27
Straight on: +8
To his left: -9
Plays in the air: +5

2005 Plus/Minus: +31 in 1360 inn.

Home: +8 in 729 inn.   RHP: +17 in 738 inn.
Road: +23 in 729 inn.   LHP: +14 in 622 inn.

Wilson arrived in the majors with a strong defensive reputation, and he's improved enough to now rank among the best in the game. His range is excellent, handling more balls in the hole over the last three years than any other shortstop. His stats indicate that he may be shading in that direction, with talented Jose Castillo playing second and I Don't Know-Third Base.

Jimmy Rollins
3-Yr Plus/Minus: +40 in 4091 inn.

Plays to his right: +3
Straight on: -2
To his left: +17
Plays in the air: +4

2005 Plus/Minus: +23 in 1356 inn.

Home: +7 in 693 inn.   RHP: +22 in 1086 inn.
Road: +16 in 693 inn.   LHP: +1 in 270 inn.

Rollins is an outstanding fielder, with excellent feet, range and a strong, accurate arm. Thanks to his arm, he's particularly good with balls hit in the shortstop hole. In 2005 he also handled grounders up the middle (to his left) extremely well (+17, the highest total of the past three years).

Rafael Furcal
3-Yr Plus/Minus: +38 in 3790 inn.

Plays to his right: +14
Straight on: 0
To his left: +8
Plays in the air: +4

2005 Plus/Minus: +26 in 1306 inn.

Home: +10 in 696 inn.   RHP: +14 in 1014 inn.
Road: +16 in 696 inn.   LHP: +12 in 292 inn.

Furcal is one of the most gifted shortstops in baseball. He is blessed with great speed, range and a cannon right arm which is among the best infield arms in baseball. 2005 was his best year in the field, thanks partially to a reduction in throwing errors from 13 in 2004 to 7 in 2005.

Neifi Perez
3-Yr Plus/Minus: +36 in 1934 inn.

Plays to his right: +10
Straight on: +8
To his left: +2
Plays in the air: 0

2005 Plus/Minus: +20 in 1063 inn.

Home: +15 in 557 inn.   RHP: +13 in 840 inn.
Road: +5 in 557 inn.   LHP: +7 in 223 inn.

After a few years of inconsistent play, the former Gold Glove winner thrived in 2005 defensively as he returned to playing every day. Perez has great range, especially to his right, and a good arm and it looks like he

has returned to his high level of defensive play.

Cesar Izturis
3-Yr Plus/Minus: +33 in 3669 inn.

Plays to his right: +5
Straight on: +3
To his left: -2
Plays in the air: -1

2005 Plus/Minus: +4 in 918 inn.

Home: +5 in 466 inn.   RHP: +2 in 772 inn.
Road: -1 in 466 inn.   LHP: +2 in 146 inn.

Izturis is an exceptional defensive shortstop, a smooth fielder with a strong arm and the ability to make off-balance throws. He models himself after his idol and fellow Venezuelan Omar Vizquel. Izturis won a Gold Glove in 2004, but 2005 was an injury-filled season for Izturis, and his fielding stats reflect that. An elbow injury (and subsequent Tommy John surgery) ended his season and could hamper his throwing in the future. He is not expected to play this year (2006) before the All-Star break.

Juan Uribe
3-Yr Plus/Minus: +25 in 2178 inn.

Plays to his right: +12
Straight on: -2
To his left: -7
Plays in the air: +6

2005 Plus/Minus: +9 in 1293 inn.

Home: +13 in 636 inn.   RHP: +13 in 982 inn.
Road: -4 in 636 inn.   LHP: -4 in 311 inn.

Uribe probably has the most unique style of any major league shortstop. Manager Ozzie Guillen said that "he seems to play the ball sideways" while calling him "the best shortstop to ever play the game." He doesn't rank quite that highly here, but he does have fine range and a strong arm. He's particularly strong on balls in the hole, where his arm allows him to take deep angles to the ball. He is also one of the best at handling popups and liners. Look no further than the last two plays of the World Series to see just how good Uribe can be.

Orlando Cabrera
3-Yr Plus/Minus: +25 in 3986 inn.

Plays to his right: -8
Straight on: 0
To his left: +16
Plays in the air: 0

2005 Plus/Minus: +7 in 1241 inn.

Home: +2 in 639 inn.   RHP: +3 in 1071 inn.
Road: +5 in 639 inn.   LHP: +4 in 170 inn.

Cabrera is one of the most reliable shortstops in the game. He has great range, a quick release and a strong arm. Most people don't realize that he won a Gold Glove with the Expos a few years ago. Not real flashy but very, very consistent. After the year Edgar Renteria had, the Red Sox must be kicking themselves for letting Cabrera go.

Omar Vizquel
3-Yr Plus/Minus: +20 in 3088 inn.

Plays to his right: -7
Straight on: +16
To his left: -5
Plays in the air: 0

2005 Plus/Minus: +4 in 1292 inn.

Home: +8 in 670 inn.   RHP: -1 in 809 inn.
Road: -4 in 670 inn.   LHP: +5 in 483 inn.

Vizquel is widely considered one of the best fielding shortstops of all time, but he hasn't ranked that highly in the last three years. In particular, Vizquel seemed to lose

Shortstops

range this year, but he kept his errors down and handled balls hit in his range extremely well. He may be one of the all-time best, but let's give the Gold Glove to *he who truly deserves it* (that's Latin for "Adam Everett").

Vizquel turned or fed only 75 double plays last year in 142 opportunities, the lowest percentage of any regular shortstop in baseball. In terms of range, we have Vizquel last year at +16 (16 plays better than an average shortstop) on balls hit more or less right at the shortstop, but -7 on balls hit to his right, and -5 on balls hit to his left. This is what you would expect from an all-time great shortstop at age 38, isn't it? If the ball is hit near him, he's still wonderful—the best in baseball. But if he has to go to his left or go to his right, he just isn't as quick as the guys who are ten or fifteen years younger.

Clint Barmes

	3-Yr Plus/Minus: +15 in 833 inn.	
Plays to his right: +12	2005 Plus/Minus: +17 in 682 inn.	
Straight on: -5		
To his left: +10	Home: +7 in 362 inn.	RHP: +15 in 509 inn.
Plays in the air: 0	Road: +10 in 362 inn.	LHP: +2 in 173 inn.

Barmes garnered a lot of attention with his hot start at bat, but he also had a surprisingly good year in the field. Considering that he only played half the year, his +17 plays made is outstanding. A former center fielder, he has a good arm, positions himself well and makes all of the routine plays. He has been compared defensively to a larger version of David Eckstein. Although his range statistics were surprisingly good in 2005, he needs to cut down on his errors (.958 fielding percentage). Note: Rookie of the Year slipped through his grasp after a freak accident in June where he broke his collarbone falling down the stairs carrying some venison. He was hitting .329 at the time.

Jason Bartlett

	3-Yr Plus/Minus: +15 in 608 inn.	
Plays to his right: +1	2005 Plus/Minus: +14 in 586 inn.	
Straight on: +3		
To his left: +9	Home: +7 in 301 inn.	RHP: +14 in 440 inn.
Plays in the air: +2	Road: +7 in 301 inn.	LHP: 0 in 146 inn.

Although Bartlett's steady defense needs a little more polish, he will likely be the shortstop of the future in Minnesota. He does not have any overwhelming tools but he does have good range to both sides and an arm that can handle all the throws.

Juan Castro

	3-Yr Plus/Minus: +15 in 913 inn.	
Plays to his right: 0	2005 Plus/Minus: +9 in 569 inn.	
Straight on: +3		
To his left: +5	Home: +12 in 308 inn.	RHP: +6 in 428 inn.
Plays in the air: +1	Road: -3 in 308 inn.	LHP: +3 in 141 inn.

Castro is a smooth fielder and has the skills to play anywhere in the infield. However, he is more of a utility guy and just does not hit enough to earn an everyday job.

Castro is very good defensively wherever you play him though short may be his best position.

Miguel Tejada

	3-Yr Plus/Minus: +15 in 4235 inn.	
Plays to his right: +25	2005 Plus/Minus: +5 in 1395 inn.	
Straight on: -4		
To his left: -17	Home: +2 in 727 inn.	RHP: -4 in 872 inn.
Plays in the air: +1	Road: +3 in 727 inn.	LHP: +9 in 523 inn.

Tejada excels on balls hit into the hole (note the +25 right rating), thanks in no small part to his arm. He has one of the strongest arms of any infielder in the game, not just among shortstops. While there have been complaints about the number of errors he makes (21, 24 and 22 over the last three seasons), his fielding percentage of .971 in that time frame is just a shade below the 2005 league average of .974 for shortstops.

Bobby Crosby

	3-Yr Plus/Minus: +11 in 2119 inn.	
Plays to his right: +3	2005 Plus/Minus: +8 in 743 inn.	
Straight on: +4		
To his left: 0	Home: +4 in 462 inn.	RHP: +2 in 568 inn.
Plays in the air: 0	Road: +4 in 462 inn.	LHP: +6 in 175 inn.

Crosby plays very good defense with a strong arm. He has great range and can go into the hole and make strong throws to get runners in time. He is sometimes very flashy and acrobatic in the field.

J.J. Hardy

	3-Yr Plus/Minus: +10 in 938 inn.	
Plays to his right: +13	2005 Plus/Minus: +10 in 938 inn.	
Straight on: 0		
To his left: -4	Home: +15 in 504 inn.	RHP: +11 in 561 inn.
Plays in the air: +1	Road: -5 in 504 inn.	LHP: -1 in 377 inn.

Hardy is a good defensive shortstop with the potential to become better. He has good range, hands and a fine throwing arm. He struggled tremendously early in the year at the plate but was able to maintain his defensive play throughout his slump. He makes excellent adjustments in the field, especially on bad hops, which helps reduce his error totals. Hardy hit fairly well the second half of the year, which could be a sign of things to come for the youngster.

Bill Hall

	3-Yr Plus/Minus: +5 in 957 inn.	
Plays to his right: 0	2005 Plus/Minus: +4 in 500 inn.	
Straight on: +1		
To his left: +4	Home: +5 in 228 inn.	RHP: +5 in 338 inn.
Plays in the air: -1	Road: -1 in 228 inn.	LHP: -1 in 162 inn.

When rookie J.J. Hardy slumped at the beginning of the year, Bill Hall took over at shortstop. Although short isn't his best position, Hall held his own. He's fast and has good range, but he's an inconsistent defender. He could be the Brewers' everyday third baseman in 2006, though he might have too much value as a utility infielder. Second and third are probably his best positions.

Shortstops

Julio Lugo

3-Yr Plus/Minus: +5 in 3775 inn.

Plays to his right:	-4	2005 Plus/Minus: -2 in 1339 inn.	
Straight on:	-5		
To his left:	+6	Home: +1 in 674 inn.	RHP: -1 in 776 inn.
Plays in the air:	+1	Road: -3 in 674 inn.	LHP: -1 in 563 inn.

Lugo shows good range and is a very athletic defender with a strong arm. However, he is very erratic and inconsistent. He does not have the best instincts in the field. One minute he can make a great play and then boot a routine grounder in his next chance. A lot of his problems seem to come from issues with his footwork and throwing mechanics.

Lugo in 2005 had 311 putouts, which was the most putouts by a shortstop since 1986, and was 49 more than any other major league shortstop. This puzzled us for some time, since our study did not show Lugo to be exceptional at catching balls in the air.

If a team has many opposing runners on first base—that is, if they walk people and give up lots of singles—then that does cause the shortstop and second baseman to have more putouts, as there are more forceouts at second base. The D Rays did put a lot of runners on base, and this did increase Lugo's putouts—but only to a minor extent; Lugo still has about 50 putouts more than you would expect him to have.

We believe that the reason this happened was that the D Rays were playing two inexperienced players at second base (Green and Cantu), at least one of whom is not even really a second baseman. We think that the very high putout total for Lugo is largely caused by the lack of confidence in the second basemen, which led the D Rays to have Lugo take pop outs and plays at second which would be ordinarily handled by a second baseman.

David Eckstein

3-Yr Plus/Minus: +3 in 3518 inn.

Plays to his right:	-6	2005 Plus/Minus: -2 in 1341 inn.	
Straight on:	+7		
To his left:	-1	Home: -2 in 688 inn.	RHP: -1 in 1062 inn.
Plays in the air:	-2	Road: 0 in 688 inn.	LHP: -1 in 279 inn.

Eckstein is a guy who is much better than the sum of his tools. He has a notoriously weak arm for a shortstop and doesn't have great range, so he has particular difficulties in the shortstop hole (-6 to his right). But he does have good hands and a very quick release which allow him to compensate for his weak arm. He's also very good at turning the double play.

Alex Gonzalez

3-Yr Plus/Minus: -1 in 3755 inn.

Plays to his right:	+2	2005 Plus/Minus: -1 in 1087 inn.	
Straight on:	0		
To his left:	-1	Home: +5 in 576 inn.	RHP: +4 in 721 inn.
Plays in the air:	-2	Road: -6 in 576 inn.	LHP: -5 in 366 inn.

Gonzalez is an underrated defender. His range and

athleticism are top-notch, he has a powerful arm and can make throws from deep in the hole from his knees. He is excellent on the double play. Over the past few years, he and Luis Castillo have formed one of the most dynamic double play tandems in baseball.

Nomar Garciaparra

3-Yr Plus/Minus: -1 in 2247 inn.

Plays to his right:	-4	2005 Plus/Minus: -2 in 206 inn.	
Straight on:	+1		
To his left:	0	Home: +2 in 102 inn.	RHP: 0 in 171 inn.
Plays in the air:	+1	Road: -4 in 102 inn.	LHP: -2 in 35 inn.

Although Nomar will be making a move across the diamond to first base in 2006, he gets grouped here with the shortstops one final time. Injuries have limited his range and he's been horrible on the double play in recent years (for more on this, see the section GDP Rankings on page 168). He still has good hands and a strong arm. He had limited overall success but showed flashes of brilliance for the Cubs at the hot corner last year. He will have to learn a new position. Nomar prides himself on his work ethic, and that coupled with his athleticism should make him at least a slightly above average defender at first base.

Jose Reyes

3-Yr Plus/Minus: -2 in 2067 inn.

Plays to his right:	-14	2005 Plus/Minus: -10 in 1398 inn.	
Straight on:	-1		
To his left:	+3	Home: -13 in 721 inn.	RHP: -13 in 1064 inn.
Plays in the air:	+3	Road: +3 in 721 inn.	LHP: +3 in 334 inn.

Reyes returned to shortstop after a year away playing second base, though he didn't play the position as well as he did in his 2003 debut. He has all the tools: great range and a rocket throwing arm. With his quickness, he can get to popups beyond the foul line that others can't reach. If he can play with more consistency, Reyes will be one of the premier shortstops in the game. He needs to make routine plays as well as the spectacular ones. The fielding splits indicate he may have some positioning issues with a right-handed pitcher on the mound (-13 vs. +3 with lefties).

Edgar Renteria

3-Yr Plus/Minus: -4 in 3967 inn.

Plays to his right:	+3	2005 Plus/Minus: -11 in 1293 inn.	
Straight on:	-14		
To his left:	+2	Home: +9 in 663 inn.	RHP: -12 in 1016 inn.
Plays in the air:	-2	Road: -20 in 663 inn.	LHP: +1 in 277 inn.

Renteria joined the Red Sox with a reputation for defensive excellence, but had an extremely disappointing defensive season. Although he certainly was not fat he looked heavy, thick through the middle, bigger butt, thicker legs. He showed no quickness, and, beginning in spring training and carrying through to the end of September, he made constant mistakes—30 errors and also 41 Defensive Misplays. Balls went off his glove,

Shortstops

over his glove, under his glove, throws were off-line. . .there wasn't anything simple you could put your finger on. Very few players in baseball history have ever gone from 11 errors as a regular one year to 30 the next, and it is hard to know what to make of it. Orlando Cabrera a few years ago did go from 11 to 29, and he did snap back. John Schuerholz apparently believes that Edgar will as well, and John Schuerholz is a smart man.

Marco Scutaro

3-Yr Plus/Minus: -11 in 778 inn.			
Plays to his right:	-7	2005 Plus/Minus: -8 in 663 inn.	
Straight on:	+2		
To his left:	-2	Home: 0 in 253 inn.	RHP: -6 in 507 inn.
Plays in the air:	0	Road: -8 in 253 inn.	LHP: -2 in 156 inn.

Scutaro is basically a utility player. He is agile and has good range and he's an above-average defender, but he doesn't hit enough to warrant an everyday job. He has good middle infield skills but is better at second than at short. He has filled in significantly for the injured Mark Ellis at second in 2004 and Bobby Crosby at short in 2005 but he's not as good a defender as either of those starters.

Khalil Greene

3-Yr Plus/Minus: -12 in 2374 inn.			
Plays to his right:	-7	2005 Plus/Minus: -16 in 1029 inn.	
Straight on:	-2		
To his left:	-5	Home: -15 in 565 inn.	RHP: -9 in 910 inn.
Plays in the air:	-2	Road: -1 in 565 inn.	LHP: -7 in 119 inn.

Greene is a very good defender despite having only average range and arm for the position. He has superb instincts, always positions himself well and has a quick release that makes up for his lack of arm strength. He is also very smooth turning double plays. His 2004 rating (+4) is probably closer to his true talent level than 2005's. And take a look at that home/road split (-15 at home, +1 on the road). There may be park effects involved that we don't yet understand.

Royce Clayton

3-Yr Plus/Minus: -14 in 3636 inn.			
Plays to his right:	-13	2005 Plus/Minus: -6 in 1177 inn.	
Straight on:	0		
To his left:	+9	Home: +1 in 617 inn.	RHP: 0 in 906 inn.
Plays in the air:	-2	Road: -7 in 617 inn.	LHP: -6 in 271 inn.

Clayton is a solid defensive shortstop but may not be as good as he once was. He still has good range and a pretty accurate arm and has learned to position himself smartly to make up for any loss in range and throwing ability he has suffered. Over the past three years, with three different teams, he clearly has been better with balls up the middle than in the shortstop hole.

Felipe Lopez

3-Yr Plus/Minus: -15 in 1963 inn.			
Plays to his right:	-6	2005 Plus/Minus: 0 in 1175 inn.	
Straight on:	+4		
To his left:	+6	Home: +7 in 611 inn.	RHP: +2 in 757 inn.
Plays in the air:	-3	Road: -7 in 611 inn.	LHP: -2 in 418 inn.

When Rich Aurilia went down early in the year, Felipe Lopez took over the Reds' shortstop job on a full-time basis and wound up having one of the best offensive seasons of any shortstop in the league (.291 with 23 home runs). However, Lopez's defense isn't any better than Aurilia's—average at best.

Jhonny Peralta

3-Yr Plus/Minus: -15 in 1911 inn.			
Plays to his right:	-5	2005 Plus/Minus: -14 in 1232 inn.	
Straight on:	+3		
To his left:	-10	Home: -5 in 642 inn.	RHP: -10 in 832 inn.
Plays in the air:	-2	Road: -9 in 642 inn.	LHP: -4 in 400 inn.

The successor to the popular Omar Vizquel has big shoes to fill. Peralta is not the equal of Vizquel defensively, but after a very shaky start in 2005 he settled down to provide some solid defense and an accurate arm. Given his potent bat, the Indians will be happy to settle for the second-half Peralta in the field. Peralta turned 94 double plays in 132 double play situations, the highest percentage of any shortstop in baseball.

Carlos Guillen

3-Yr Plus/Minus: -19 in 2396 inn.			
Plays to his right:	+9	2005 Plus/Minus: +3 in 625 inn.	
Straight on:	-1		
To his left:	-2	Home: 0 in 334 inn.	RHP: +4 in 397 inn.
Plays in the air:	-2	Road: +3 in 334 inn.	LHP: -1 in 228 inn.

Guillen is a smooth fielder with fine range to his glove side up the middle and a true and accurate shortstop's arm. His range in the hole is not as good and his plus/minus figure of -21 to his right in 2004 is probably more indicative of his true skill than the +9 in 2005. Having Inge at third and Polanco/Infante at second might have helped him this past year.

Russ Adams

3-Yr Plus/Minus: -19 in 1259 inn.			
Plays to his right:	+2	2005 Plus/Minus: -17 in 1100 inn.	
Straight on:	-11		
To his left:	-2	Home: -11 in 596 inn.	RHP: -3 in 743 inn.
Plays in the air:	-6	Road: -6 in 596 inn.	LHP: -14 in 357 inn.

Adams has worked hard to improve his defense. The Blue Jays were concerned about his fielding coming into 2005 but overall he handled the position better than expected. He has good hands, range and middle infield instincts but an arm that is below average for the shortstop position. He will likely move to second base in the future.

Shortstops

Cristian Guzman

3-Yr Plus/Minus: -22 in 3698 inn.

Plays to his right:	-8	2005 Plus/Minus: -6 in 1161 inn.
Straight on:	+2	
To his left:	+4	Home: +6 in 581 inn. RHP: -7 in 1083 inn.
Plays in the air:	-4	Road: -12 in 581 inn. LHP: +1 in 78 inn.

You can make a case that Guzman was the most disappointing position player in baseball in 2005. He struggled mightily at bat all year long, and his defense deteriorated as the season progressed. However, Guzman has never been as good a defender as his reputation suggests—he ranks 28th among all major league shortstops over the past three years. There was a great quote from Frank Robinson late in the year complaining that a guy from "class Z ball" could make some of the plays he was not making.

Guzman was playing regularly on a grass field for the first time after six years on the turf at Minnesota. Our analysis shows him as +6 (six plays better than average) at home, but -12 on the road. This suggests that there may be something odd about the park. I don't know if you have ever seen a game at RFK stadium, but it's kind of like going to a major league baseball game in somebody's converted basement. It's not BAD; it's kind of fun, actually, but it is just really, really obvious that this place was never intended to be a major league baseball park, at least recently. So there could be some odd park factor there they we haven't figured out yet, or it could be that he just played bad defense on the road.

Angel Berroa

3-Yr Plus/Minus: -59 in 3885 inn.

Plays to his right:	-23	2005 Plus/Minus: -26 in 1360 inn.
Straight on:	-5	
To his left:	+4	Home: -13 in 731 inn. RHP: -20 in 1076 inn.
Plays in the air:	-2	Road: -13 in 731 inn. LHP: -6 in 284 inn.

Berroa is a marvelous athlete who will make very impressive defensive plays, and his fielding percentage will probably improve if he plays the season with Doug Mientkiewicz at first base. His basic problem is that he just has no judgment. He doesn't anticipate, he doesn't think through the play; he just reacts. His motto, as a player, is "Maybe I shouldn't have swung at that." OK, it isn't, but it ought to be. If he has an easy force play at second or a difficult throw to first, he'll throw to first—you hope. But he may not; he may start to throw to first, and wind up with no play anywhere. Hopefully experience will cure this, but it is certainly taking its own sweet time about it.

Derek Jeter

3-Yr Plus/Minus: -64 in 3728 inn.

Plays to his right:	-18	2005 Plus/Minus: -34 in 1352 inn.
Straight on:	+3	
To his left:	-25	Home: -22 in 717 inn. RHP: -22 in 993 inn.
Plays in the air:	+5	Road: -12 in 717 inn. LHP: -12 in 359 inn.

There is perception and there is reality. For the latter, see Bill James' essay on page 3.

There's one other element that we analyzed for Derek Jeter in the plus/minus system. We broke down all balls hit to the shortstop position with Jeter in the field based on how hard the ball was hit: slow, medium, and hard hit balls. Here's how his -39 plus/minus on groundballs in 2005 broke out. On slowly hit balls, Jeter was actually slightly above average with a +1. It's on medium and hard hit balls where he had trouble. On medium hit balls he was -23 and and hard hit balls -17.

Michael Young

3-Yr Plus/Minus: -73 in 2760 inn.

Plays to his right:	-15	2005 Plus/Minus: -39 in 1356 inn.
Straight on:	-2	
To his left:	-19	Home: -15 in 697 inn. RHP: -30 in 997 inn.
Plays in the air:	-3	Road: -24 in 697 inn. LHP: -9 in 359 inn.

Before switching over to shortstop, Young had a reputation as an excellent defensive second basemen. However, his 2003 plus/minus figure of -16 suggests otherwise. We reviewed videotape of many of his plays that year to try to figure out the discrepancy, because his basic tools are superb. The problem became apparent very quickly. He simply was playing too close to second base and missed hit after hit to his left. His plus/minus figure was -22 to his left that year and +10 to his right. Now, after having moved to shortstop in 2004, he continues to have problems to his left with a cumulative -46 over the last two seasons. He has a very strong arm and it seems pretty likely at this point that he shades too far to his right to try and take advantage of that arm.

In 2005 the average Major League team allowed 292 hits up the middle or in the shortstop hole. The Rangers allowed 374. That was the most in baseball. So, in only two years of work as a shortstop, Young claims last place in three-year plus/minus, three-year zone ratings, team hits allowed near the shortstop position in 2005, and he's second to last in Bill James' new relative range plus/minus. Not good.

Left Fielders Evaluations

Year	League	Gold Glove Winners	Should Have Been
2003	AL	none	none
	NL	none	none
2004	AL	none	none
	NL	none	none
2005	AL	none	almost: Carl Crawford
	NL	none	none

My Personal Ratings

Top Ten

1 Carl Crawford, TB
2 Coco Crisp, Bos
3 Scott Podsednik, CWS
4 Reed Johnson, Tor
5 Chris Burke, Hou
6 Kelly Johnson, Atl
7 Ryan Langerhans, Atl
8 Matt Holliday, Col
9 Terrence Long, FA
10 Carlos Lee, Mil

Bottom Five

26 Miguel Cabrera, Fla
27 Hideki Matsui, NYY
28 Ryan Klesko, SD
29 Adam Dunn, Cin
30 Manny Ramirez, Bos

Player teams based on transactions through February 5, 2006

Left Fielders Rankings

3-Year Plus/Minus Rankings

1	Carl Crawford	+45	11	Barry Bonds	+7	21	Jason Bay	-3
2	Coco Crisp	+39	12	Randy Winn	+5	22	Frank Catalanotto	-3
3	Carlos Lee	+18	13	Geoff Jenkins	+5	23	Lance Berkman	-4
4	Pat Burrell	+12	14	Moises Alou	+3	24	Garret Anderson	-5
5	Rondell White	+10	15	Larry Bigbie	+2	25	Kevin Mench	-5
6	Matt Holliday	+9	16	Shannon Stewart	+1	26	Ryan Klesko	-21
7	Raul Ibanez	+8	17	Craig Monroe	-1	27	Matt Lawton	-26
8	Eric Byrnes	+8	18	Jay Payton	-2	28	Miguel Cabrera	-27
9	Terrence Long	+8	19	Chipper Jones	-2	29	Hideki Matsui	-33
10	Luis Gonzalez	+7	20	Cliff Floyd	-3	30	Adam Dunn	-38
						31	Manny Ramirez	-69

2005 Plus/Minus Rankings

1	Coco Crisp	+26	11	Hideki Matsui	+3	21	Ryan Klesko	-3
2	Carl Crawford	+20	12	Moises Alou	+2	22	Terrence Long	-3
3	Scott Podsednik	+20	13	Cliff Floyd	+1	23	Carlos Lee	-4
4	Reed Johnson	+17	14	Craig Monroe	0	24	Jason Bay	-4
5	Kelly Johnson	+10	15	Kevin Mench	0	25	Frank Catalanotto	-5
6	Matt Holliday	+9	16	Shannon Stewart	-1	26	Rondell White	-5
7	Chris Burke	+8	17	Pedro Feliz	-2	27	Garret Anderson	-7
8	Luis Gonzalez	+7	18	Reggie Sanders	-2	28	Adam Dunn	-16
9	Eric Byrnes	+6	19	Todd Hollandsworth	-2	29	Miguel Cabrera	-28
10	Pat Burrell	+3	20	Randy Winn	-3	30	Manny Ramirez	-31

2004 Plus/Minus Rankings

1	Larry Bigbie	+17	11	Moises Alou	+3	21	Cliff Floyd	-4
2	Carl Crawford	+14	12	Luis Gonzalez	+3	22	Lance Berkman	-5
3	Jayson Werth	+11	13	Charles Thomas	+2	23	David Dellucci	-6
4	Lew Ford	+9	14	Jason Bay	+1	24	Craig Biggio	-6
5	Carlos Lee	+8	15	Eric Byrnes	+1	25	Jose Guillen	-9
6	Geoff Jenkins	+7	16	Matt Holliday	0	26	Adam Dunn	-18
7	Raul Ibanez	+7	17	Shannon Stewart	0	27	Manny Ramirez	-18
8	Rondell White	+7	18	Barry Bonds	-2	28	Ryan Klesko	-18
9	Miguel Cabrera	+6	19	Pat Burrell	-2	29	Matt Lawton	-22
10	Terrmel Sledge	+5	20	Jeff Conine	-3	30	Hideki Matsui	-24

2003 Plus/Minus Rankings

1	Carlos Lee	+14	11	Terrence Long	+1	21	Raul Ibanez	-5
2	Carl Crawford	+11	12	Jacque Jones	0	22	Albert Pujols	-6
3	Pat Burrell	+11	13	Cliff Floyd	0	23	Matt Lawton	-8
4	Randy Winn	+10	14	Lance Berkman	-1	24	Brian Giles	-9
5	Rondell White	+8	15	Geoff Jenkins	-2	25	Larry Bigbie	-10
6	Brad Wilkerson	+8	16	Moises Alou	-2	26	Hideki Matsui	-12
7	Barry Bonds	+6	17	Luis Gonzalez	-3	27	Dmitri Young	-14
8	Garret Anderson	+2	18	Adam Dunn	-4	28	Manny Ramirez	-20
9	Shannon Stewart	+2	19	Craig Monroe	-4			
10	Chipper Jones	+1	20	Jay Payton	-5			

3-Year Outfield Arms Rankings

1	Jay Payton	.276	11	Randy Winn	.374	21	Rondell White	.417
2	Frank Catalanotto	.309	12	Coco Crisp	.380	22	Carlos Lee	.417
3	Carl Crawford	.312	13	Shannon Stewart	.381	23	Barry Bonds	.418
4	Miguel Cabrera	.328	14	Manny Ramirez	.384	24	Garret Anderson	.419
5	Pat Burrell	.338	15	Geoff Jenkins	.388	25	Moises Alou	.419
6	Adam Dunn	.347	16	Terrence Long	.395	26	Chipper Jones	.421
7	Lance Berkman	.348	17	Kevin Mench	.399	27	Luis Gonzalez	.423
8	Raul Ibanez	.352	18	Larry Bigbie	.407	28	Craig Monroe	.429
9	Hideki Matsui	.354	19	Matt Holliday	.408	29	Matt Lawton	.441
10	Eric Byrnes	.365	20	Cliff Floyd	.411	30	Jason Bay	.442
						31	Ryan Klesko	.503

2005 Outfield Arms Rankings

1	Frank Catalanotto	.241	11	Shannon Stewart	.346	21	Garret Anderson	.400
2	Carl Crawford	.258	12	Cliff Floyd	.354	22	Matt Holliday	.402
3	Pedro Feliz	.303	13	Pat Burrell	.354	23	Terrence Long	.403
4	Reggie Sanders	.308	14	Hideki Matsui	.363	24	Luis Gonzalez	.405
5	Kelly Johnson	.310	15	Adam Dunn	.363	25	Craig Monroe	.407
6	Reed Johnson	.326	16	Scott Podsednik	.365	26	Ryan Klesko	.419
7	Chris Burke	.333	17	Carlos Lee	.366	27	Kevin Mench	.426
8	Moises Alou	.333	18	Rondell White	.366	28	Jason Bay	.438
9	Miguel Cabrera	.340	19	Coco Crisp	.373	29	Todd Hollandsworth	.442
10	Randy Winn	.345	20	Manny Ramirez	.381	30	Eric Byrnes	.459

2004 Outfield Arms Rankings

1	Charles Thomas	.250	11	Lew Ford	.345	21	Luis Gonzalez	.422
2	Hideki Matsui	.282	12	Raul Ibanez	.362	22	Manny Ramirez	.423
3	Terrmel Sledge	.283	13	Jose Guillen	.384	23	Jason Bay	.447
4	Pat Burrell	.286	14	Geoff Jenkins	.395	24	Larry Bigbie	.457
5	Adam Dunn	.297	15	Moises Alou	.396	25	Craig Biggio	.476
6	Miguel Cabrera	.300	16	Matt Lawton	.403	26	Rondell White	.476
7	Carl Crawford	.300	17	Carlos Lee	.407	27	Barry Bonds	.486
8	Jayson Werth	.310	18	Matt Holliday	.414	28	David Dellucci	.508
9	Eric Byrnes	.315	19	Lance Berkman	.418	29	Cliff Floyd	.516
10	Jeff Conine	.329	20	Shannon Stewart	.421	30	Ryan Klesko	.618

2003 Outfield Arms Rankings

1	Jay Payton	.272	11	Rondell White	.391	21	Craig Monroe	.438
2	Lance Berkman	.305	12	Terrence Long	.391	22	Chipper Jones	.441
3	Barry Bonds	.341	13	Cliff Floyd	.392	23	Luis Gonzalez	.447
4	Manny Ramirez	.347	14	Adam Dunn	.394	24	Jacque Jones	.452
5	Raul Ibanez	.353	15	Shannon Stewart	.396	25	Matt Lawton	.466
6	Pat Burrell	.364	16	Larry Bigbie	.403	26	Carlos Lee	.478
7	Brad Wilkerson	.370	17	Randy Winn	.408	27	Moises Alou	.491
8	Brian Giles	.372	18	Hideki Matsui	.425	28	Albert Pujols	.511
9	Geoff Jenkins	.380	19	Garret Anderson	.430			
10	Carl Crawford	.382	20	Dmitri Young	.433			

Left Fielders

Crisp replaces Johnny Damon for 2006.

Carl Crawford

3-Yr Plus/Minus: +45 in 3416 inn.

2005 Basic P/M: +16

2005 Enhanced P/M: +20 in 1247 inn.
Home: +8 in 661 inn.   RHP: +9 in 725 inn.
Road: +8 in 586 inn.   LHP: +7 in 522 inn.

Carl Crawford is the best defensive left fielder in baseball today. He possesses world-class speed and routinely turns gap hits into outs. He ranks first in enhanced plays made the past three years and has never ranked lower than second in any one season. What's more, his throwing comes in third best in the game. Crawford has been compared defensively to a young Barry Bonds but with a much stronger arm and the ability to get to the left field line more quickly.

Crawford is the first left fielder in years who warrants strong consideration for a Gold Glove. Bonds' win in 1998 was the last one for a left fielder. We debated long and hard about giving a Gold Glove That Should Have Been to Crawford for his great defensive performance in 2005. He was second in enhanced plays (+20) and second in throwing (.258). The problem is that, after having given Aaron Rowand a Gold Glove That Should Have Been, we'd have to look to either Ichiro Suzuki or Torii Hunter for Crawford to replace. While Suzuki and Hunter each had somewhat down years at their positions, they are considered by many, including us, to be the best players at their positions. And their down years weren't all that down. What we have here then is: Crawford, the best left fielder in baseball, Hunter, the best center fielder in baseball, and Suzuki, the best right fielder in baseball. In the end, we have to stay with Hunter and Suzuki. Center and right field are more demanding positions. Plus, the competition is higher at those positions making the three-year ratings for Hunter and Suzuki even more impressive.

Coco Crisp

3-Yr Plus/Minus: +39 in 1840 inn.

2005 Basic P/M: +15

2005 Enhanced P/M: +26 in 1200 inn.
Home: +4 in 642 inn.   RHP: +8 in 802 inn.
Road: +11 in 558 inn.   LHP: +7 in 398 inn.

The former center fielder had a great year in left for the Indians, leading all left fielders in enhanced plays made (+26) in 2005. Like Chicago's Scott Podsednik, Crisp moved over and has proven to be a better left fielder than center fielder. Over the last three years, in about 200 games in left field he's +39. In about 150 games in center, he's about average with an enhanced plus/minus total of -1. Crisp has a weak arm that plays out close to average in our rankings for left field. But he's only had a total a four baserunner kills in the last three years, three in left and one in center. That's a very low total and very indicative of a very poor arm. Boston is used to having a center fielder who can't throw as

Reed Johnson

3-Yr Plus/Minus: +29 in 1379 inn.

2005 Basic P/M: +10

2005 Enhanced P/M: +17 in 591 inn.
Home: +6 in 302 inn.   RHP: +6 in 400 inn.
Road: +4 in 289 inn.   LHP: +4 in 191 inn.

Johnson is a leadoff batter whose speed serves him very well in left field (+17 enhanced plays made last year). He also has a good arm for a left fielder. Over the past three years he has seen considerable action at all three outfield positions. Johnson was Frank Catalanotto's defensive caddy in 2005. He entered a game as a late inning defensive replacement 18 time, the most in the majors.

Scott Podsednik

3-Yr Plus/Minus: +20 in 1070 inn.

2005 Basic P/M: +12

2005 Enhanced P/M: +20 in 1062 inn.
Home: +2 in 572 inn.   RHP: +8 in 817 inn.
Road: +10 in 490 inn.   LHP: +4 in 245 inn.

Podsednik is another former center fielder playing in left. He has above-average range in left but a below-average arm. Some groin problems hampered him for a short time during the 2005 season but for the most part his defense was above average.

Our plus/minus system shows what a defensive asset it is to have a center fielder in left. Podsednik, Coco Crisp, and Reed Johnson are all natural center fielders playing left. Based on their performance in 2005 a rule of thumb might be that a center fielder will gain you about 15-20 enhanced plays over the course of a season playing left field.

Carlos Lee

3-Yr Plus/Minus: +18 in 4011 inn.

2005 Basic P/M: -5

2005 Enhanced P/M: -4 in 1404 inn.
Home: +2 in 712 inn.   RHP: +2 in 872 inn.
Road: -7 in 692 inn.   LHP: -7 in 532 inn.

Lee has a reputation as a poor defensive player, but that isn't deserved. He has worked hard to improve his fielding and he ranks third overall in enhanced plays made over the last three years. He even managed to top the list in 2003. His arm is serviceable for left field and his 17 baserunner kills over the last three years is quite good, tied for sixth among major league left fielders.

Pat Burrell

3-Yr Plus/Minus: +12 in 3544 inn.

2005 Basic P/M: +4

2005 Enhanced P/M: +3 in 1297 inn.
Home: -2 in 709 inn.   RHP: -1 in 1042 inn.
Road: +6 in 588 inn.   LHP: +5 in 255 inn.

Burrell doesn't have great speed or range, but his ranking (fourth in enhanced plays made at +12) suggests that he holds his own in left field. Twelve plays above average is a good total, but not great, and we think there could be a park illusion that is helping his numbers. He has a good arm and a quick release.

Left Fielders

Ryan Langerhans
3-Yr Plus/Minus: +10 in 384 inn.

2005 Basic P/M: +6

2005 Enhanced P/M: +10 in 379 inn.
Home: +5 in 209 inn.   RHP: +6 in 297 inn.
Road: +1 in 170 inn.   LHP: 0 in 82 inn.

Langerhans was an excellent defender for the Braves last season. He has the ability to play all three outfield positions and play them well, as evidenced by his +11 enhanced plays in right field, +10 in left, and +3 in center when he spelled Andruw Jones. He covers a fair amount of ground, and uses excellent instincts to get good jumps. He is particularly adept at going back on balls hit over his head. His arm is above average, as he gets rid of the ball quickly and has decent throwing strength. Langerhans fits in nicely in Atlanta, and if he can show some of his power potential on a more consistent basis the Braves will have a well-rounded player, at a cheap price, for several years to come.

Kelly Johnson
3-Yr Plus/Minus: +10 in 648 inn.

2005 Basic P/M: +5

2005 Enhanced P/M: +10 in 648 inn.
Home: +2 in 331 inn.   RHP: +4 in 524 inn.
Road: +3 in 317 inn.   LHP: +1 in 124 inn.

Johnson came out of nowhere to team with Andruw Jones, Jeff Francoeur and Ryan Langerhans to form the best defensive outfield in the majors. He's a converted minor league shortstop who made a relatively seamless switch to the outfield in 2004. He has displayed great range and good arm strength, and as he learns the nuances of playing the outfield he will become an even better defender.

Reggie Sanders
3-Yr Plus/Minus: +10 in 1245 inn.

2005 Basic P/M: -3

2005 Enhanced P/M: -2 in 636 inn.
Home: 0 in 334 inn.   RHP: -2 in 495 inn.
Road: -3 in 302 inn.   LHP: -1 in 141 inn.

At 38, Sanders can still cover enough ground in left to be an average defender. He has good range and speed. His arm is average but he has a very quick release which helps deceive runners who try to run on him. Sanders broke his leg in July and missed the second half of the season, but he returned in time for his postseason heroics.

Rondell White
3-Yr Plus/Minus: +10 in 2119 inn.

2005 Basic P/M: -4

2005 Enhanced P/M: -5 in 535 inn.
Home: -3 in 231 inn.   RHP: -2 in 328 inn.
Road: -1 in 304 inn.   LHP: -2 in 207 inn.

A history of knee problems and a very weak arm have limited White in the field. He often serves as a designated hitter to rest his body. He had good range earlier in his career but has lost most of it. Teams will run on him at will.

Matt Holliday
3-Yr Plus/Minus: +9 in 1967 inn.

2005 Basic P/M: +7

2005 Enhanced P/M: +9 in 1050 inn.
Home: +6 in 536 inn.   RHP: +8 in 779 inn.
Road: +1 in 514 inn.   LHP: -1 in 271 inn.

Holliday is a converted third baseman and he's struggled at times in the outfield. In the off-season he lost some weight which helped his mobility, and he is learning to get better jumps on the ball. He has a decent arm for left field (he was a high school All-America quarterback), but it's lacking for the other outfield positions. Holliday has the potential to become a good outfielder and his defensive skills will blossom with experience.

Chris Burke
3-Yr Plus/Minus: +8 in 634 inn.

2005 Basic P/M: +6

2005 Enhanced P/M: +8 in 634 inn.
Home: +3 in 300 inn.   RHP: +4 in 435 inn.
Road: +3 in 334 inn.   LHP: +2 in 199 inn.

Burke is a converted second baseman who was blocked by the return of Craig Biggio to second. His natural athleticism helped him transition to left field, where he ranked well last year (seventh in both enhanced plays made and throwing). He has good speed, which helps him cover ground and also cover some of his growing pains in a new position.

Raul Ibanez
3-Yr Plus/Minus: +8 in 2455 inn.

2005 Basic P/M: +2

2005 Enhanced P/M: +6 in 464 inn.
Home: +2 in 200 inn.   RHP: +2 in 350 inn.
Road: 0 in 264 inn.   LHP: 0 in 114 inn.

Ibanez is a solid outfielder. Early in his career he had some trouble reading the ball off the bat but he has learned to take better routes and angles to the ball and has acceptable speed. He was originally drafted as a catcher though is arm is just average.

Eric Byrnes
3-Yr Plus/Minus: +8 in 1957 inn.

2005 Basic P/M: +2

2005 Enhanced P/M: +6 in 803 inn.
Home: -2 in 367 inn.   RHP: -1 in 532 inn.
Road: +3 in 403 inn.   LHP: +3 in 271 inn.

Despite Byrnes being on the positive side in the plus/minus system, he is not a very good outfielder. He gets bad jumps and runs bad routes, and has to make up for it by using his speed to make circus catches. He just doesn't look coordinated out there, and the D'Backs may wind up regretting their plan to play him in center. His arm may be a liability in center as well.

Terrence Long
3-Yr Plus/Minus: +8 in 1693 inn.

2005 Basic P/M: 0

2005 Enhanced P/M: -3 in 794 inn.
Home: -1 in 449 inn.   RHP: -2 in 620 inn.
Road: +1 in 345 inn.   LHP: +2 in 174 inn.

Long can play all three outfield positions but his arm

Left Fielders

isn't strong enough for right and his range isn't good enough for center. That leaves left. Long doesn't get good reads or breaks on balls, and he's historically had some trouble with sun and vision during day games. As a result, his range is pretty average despite his good speed. The Royals management late in the season tried to claim that Long was a Gold Glove outfielder, which was greeted by the local media with derision and amusement.

Luis Gonzalez
3-Yr Plus/Minus: +7 in 3578 inn.
2005 Basic P/M: +4

2005 Enhanced P/M: +7 in 1318 inn.
Home: +6 in 662 inn. RHP: +8 in 987 inn.
Road: -2 in 656 inn. LHP: -4 in 331 inn.

Gonzalez plays deep, much deeper than most outfielders, so he can get better angles on balls and reach those hit close to the wall. However, he lets a lot of balls drop in front of him. The 120 hits allowed in front of left field against the Diamondbacks last year were the most in baseball. But it turns out that it was only fourteen hits above the league average. There were eight hits over the left fielders head against the D'Backs, six below average. Based on these numbers Gonzalez traded fourteen singles for six extra base hits. All things being equal, six extra-base hits is probably worth less than the fourteen singles, but it's really pretty close. Overall, his seven enhanced plays above average is the key. His throwing arm was weak even before elbow surgery in 2004; thankfully, the surgery didn't weaken it any further.

Barry Bonds
3-Yr Plus/Minus: +7 in 2270 inn.
2005 Basic P/M: +1

2005 Enhanced P/M: +3 in 95 inn.
Home: +1 in 37 inn. RHP: 0 in 64 inn.
Road: 0 in 58 inn. LHP: +1 in 31 inn.

While Bonds is still the best hitter on the planet, his defensive skills have severely diminished since his younger days. An eight-time Gold Glove winner, Bonds must now rely on good instincts to have any defensive value. His arm is still rather accurate and his quick release makes up for some of what he has lost in arm strength. Obviously, various knee surgeries and the added weight have slowed Bonds down a good deal. At times, Bonds appears to be loafing as he is hesitant to go hard after balls, and a lot of hits land in front of him.

Randy Winn
3-Yr Plus/Minus: +5 in 2272 inn.
2005 Basic P/M: 0

2005 Enhanced P/M: -3 in 796 inn.
Home: +4 in 437 inn. RHP: -1 in 572 inn.
Road: -4 in 359 inn. LHP: +1 in 224 inn.

Winn struggles in center field but he's a good left fielder. He sometimes runs bad angles and has trouble picking up flyballs, and then he has to rely on his speed to save himself. He's also got a pretty weak arm.

Moises Alou
3-Yr Plus/Minus: +3 in 3133 inn.
2005 Basic P/M: +1

2005 Enhanced P/M: +2 in 576 inn.
Home: +3 in 265 inn. RHP: 0 in 370 inn.
Road: -2 in 311 inn. LHP: +1 in 206 inn.

Alou is merely an adequate defender. A history of nagging injuries has really hurt his speed and range over the years but he handles balls he can get to. He also has a pretty weak arm. When Alou takes his fielding position, waiting for the pitch, it seems that he spreads his legs as wide as he possibly can without permanently injuring himself. How he manages to reach any ball at all from that position is a minor miracle.

Larry Bigbie
3-Yr Plus/Minus: +2 in 2043 inn.
2005 Basic P/M: -4

2005 Enhanced P/M: -5 in 480 inn.
Home: +1 in 305 inn. RHP: -4 in 322 inn.
Road: -5 in 175 inn. LHP: 0 in 158 inn.

Bigbie is a speedy, sound corner outfielder who has played center field in the past. He does not always get great jumps or reads on the ball which can affect his range but he rarely, if ever, makes a mistake when he gets to the ball. He has made only three errors in his five-year career.

Shannon Stewart
3-Yr Plus/Minus: +1 in 2732 inn.
2005 Basic P/M: 0

2005 Enhanced P/M: -1 in 1107 inn.
Home: +5 in 603 inn. RHP: +3 in 858 inn.
Road: -5 in 504 inn. LHP: -3 in 249 inn.

Stewart can hustle and covers enough ground to make plays in the outfield but sometimes takes poor routes to balls. His arm is relatively weak but he makes it work for left field, where he ranks in the middle of the pack in our throwing rankings. He is pretty much an average defensive left fielder.

Pedro Feliz
3-Yr Plus/Minus: 0 in 711 inn.
2005 Basic P/M: +2

2005 Enhanced P/M: -2 in 616 inn.
Home: +4 in 370 inn. RHP: +6 in 368 inn.
Road: -2 in 246 inn. LHP: -4 in 248 inn.

His best position is third base but Feliz is not too shabby in left, either. He has average range and a strong arm out there. He split time between third base and left field in 2006 and has played center, right, second and short for the Giants over the years. That Bonds guy may want his spot back, so look for Feliz to settle in at third in 2006. His third base commentary is on page 162.

Craig Monroe
3-Yr Plus/Minus: -1 in 1551 inn.
2005 Basic P/M: 0

2005 Enhanced P/M: 0 in 502 inn.
Home: -2 in 282 inn. RHP: +2 in 341 inn.
Road: +2 in 220 inn. LHP: -2 in 161 inn.

See his right field commentary on page 198.

Left Fielders

Jay Payton

3-Yr Plus/Minus: -2 in 1743 inn.

2005 Basic P/M: +2

2005 Enhanced P/M: +1 in 465 inn.
Home: +1 in 244 inn.   RHP: +4 in 338 inn.
Road: +1 in 221 inn.   LHP: -1 in 127 inn.

Payton is a good outfielder who can man all three outfield spots. He has good speed and range which he sometimes will use to overcome not always taking the best routes to balls. He has a strong and accurate arm; he owns the best Outfield Advance percentage (.276) among all left fielders in the last three years. Payton is a bit above average at the corner positions and decent in center.

Cliff Floyd

3-Yr Plus/Minus: -3 in 2857 inn.

2005 Basic P/M: -3

2005 Enhanced P/M: +1 in 1264 inn.
Home: +3 in 631 inn.   RHP: +1 in 968 inn.
Road: -6 in 633 inn.   LHP: -4 in 296 inn.

At the beginning of the season, Floyd publicly rejoiced that there would be no more artificial turf in the National League torturing his knees. Coincidence or not, Floyd stayed free of serious injuries and displayed mobility that had been missing for years. He also takes great pride in his throwing, and his total of 23 baserunner kills is the highest of any left fielder in the past three years.

Jason Bay

3-Yr Plus/Minus: -3 in 2329 inn.

2005 Basic P/M: -3

2005 Enhanced P/M: -4 in 1186 inn.
Home: -3 in 639 inn.   RHP: -4 in 649 inn.
Road: 0 in 547 inn.   LHP: +1 in 537 inn.

Bay is one of the finest young hitters in baseball, and his glove ain't bad either. He has good range, enough to play center field if needed. He had a strong arm before shoulder surgery in November 2003 set him back. Since then baserunners have taken the extra base quite often on Bay as he ranks second to last in our throwing rankings.

Frank Catalanotto

3-Yr Plus/Minus: -3 in 1531 inn.

2005 Basic P/M: -1

2005 Enhanced P/M: -5 in 761 inn.
Home: +1 in 396 inn.   RHP: +2 in 503 inn.
Road: -2 in 365 inn.   LHP: -3 in 258 inn.

Catalanotto is an offensive player. He can play in both the infield and the outfield but is below average wherever he goes. He doesn't have good speed, range or arm strength. But in left field his arm was an asset for him last year. Only 24% of baserunners took an extra base on him last year, the best percentage among all left fielders in baseball. Catalanotto is very similar to Tony Phillips late in his career; he can play everywhere but not very well.

Kevin Mench

3-Yr Plus/Minus: -5 in 1608 inn.

2005 Basic P/M: +4

2005 Enhanced P/M: 0 in 978 inn.
Home: +2 in 519 inn.   RHP: +2 in 712 inn.
Road: +2 459 inn.   LHP: +2 in 266 inn.

Mench moves better than you would think for a guy his size (6-0, 225) and offers enough range to be an above-average defender. In fact, the Rangers will put him in center field when the need arises. He also has a fine arm, which makes right field a good position for him as well.

Garret Anderson

3-Yr Plus/Minus: -5 in 2161 inn.

2005 Basic P/M: -6

2005 Enhanced P/M: -7 in 920 inn.
Home: -6 in 468 inn.   RHP: -5 in 801 inn.
Road: 0 in 452 inn.   LHP: -1 in 119 inn.

Anderson was once a great outfielder but a multitude of injuries have sapped his range and speed. He is still a very smart player with an accurate arm but he now is a below-average defender.

David Dellucci

3-Yr Plus/Minus: -9 in 1049 inn.

2005 Basic P/M: -2

2005 Enhanced P/M: -4 in 379 inn.
Home: -2 in 199 inn.   RHP: -1 in 303 inn.
Road: 0 in 180 inn.   LHP: -1 in 76 inn.

Dellucci plays without fear in the outfield, will go to any length, even physical harm, to make a catch. He can play all three outfield positions but he profiles best in left field because of his poor throwing arm. He doesn't cover enough ground for center and his arm is too weak for right.

Todd Hollandsworth

3-Yr Plus/Minus: -10 in 1119 inn.

2005 Basic P/M: -2

2005 Enhanced P/M: -2 in 599 inn.
Home: 0 in 295 inn.   RHP: -1 in 492 inn.
Road: -2 in 304 inn.   LHP: 0 in 107 inn.

Hollandsworth is at best an average defender in the outfield. He does not have good range or quickness and his defense can be inconsistent.

Ryan Klesko

3-Yr Plus/Minus: -21 in 1651 inn.

2005 Basic P/M: -1

2005 Enhanced P/M: -3 in 927 inn.
Home: 0 in 487 inn.   RHP: +2 in 810 inn.
Road: -1 in 440 inn.   LHP: -3 in 117 inn.

Klesko is not a good defender. His speed is okay, but he takes bad routes to the ball and doesn't get good jumps. While his arm is reasonably strong, it's totally ineffective. He is the only qualifying left fielder in baseball to allow baserunners to advance an extra base over 50% of the time over the last three years. He's had only two baserunner kills in that time period. The Padres would like to move him back to first base to "speed up" their outfield but back problems in 2005 prevented Klesko from returning to the infield. He struggled to

Left Fielders

bend over for grounders.

The Padres were well aware of Klesko's deficiencies in the field last year. They replaced him for defense 24 times, the most in the majors.

Miguel Cabrera
3-Yr Plus/Minus: -27 in 2091 inn.

2005 Basic P/M: -16

2005 Enhanced P/M: -28 in 1106 inn.
Home: -10 in 617 inn.   RHP: -6 in 743 inn.
Road: -6 in 489 inn.   LHP: -10 in 363 inn.

Cabrera played third base for years, so he prefers playing left field instead of right because of the angle at which the ball comes off the bat. Nevertheless his performance is lacking at both outfield positions. He scored a -8 in enhanced plays in right field over 100 games in 2004 and a -28 in 134 games playing left in 2005. His best defensive tool is his strong, accurate arm, probably the best among all left fielders in baseball. He does not always look comfortable in the outfield and often shows lapses in concentration.

Hideki Matsui
3-Yr Plus/Minus: -33 in 3362 inn.

2005 Basic P/M: -2

2005 Enhanced P/M: +3 in 977 inn.
Home: -2 in 489 inn.   RHP: +3 in 707 inn.
Road: 0 in 488 inn.   LHP: -5 in 270 inn.

Matsui ranks near the bottom in enhanced plays made over three years. This is a bit of a surprise, because he played center field in Japan (and some for the Yankees last year) and has great fundamentals. But he's inconsistent and struggles with his routes to the ball. Plus, his arm is weak and runners like to test him. Don't be fooled by his numeric improvement in 2005.

Adam Dunn
3-Yr Plus/Minus: -38 in 3247 inn.

2005 Basic P/M: -4

2005 Enhanced P/M: -16 in 1091 inn.
Home: -5 in 551 inn.   RHP: -2 in 712 inn.
Road: +1 in 540 inn.   LHP: -2 in 379 inn.

The past three years, Dunn has been a first baseman playing left. He really is a sub-par outfielder who was forced to play the outfield until first base opened up. With the Reds moving Sean Casey to Pittsburgh, it appears that time has come.

Manny Ramirez
3-Yr Plus/Minus: -69 in 3386 inn.

2005 Basic P/M: -14

2005 Enhanced P/M: -31 in 1225 inn.
Home: -13 in 598 inn.   RHP: -9 in 964 inn.
Road: -1 in 627 inn.   LHP: -5 in 261 inn.

As lethal as his offense is, Ramirez' defense can at times be toxic, and there are differences of opinion about the cost of this. At times he doesn't read the ball well. He often does not hustle, and as a result sometimes gets burned. But he is a very cagey player who will surprise the opposition by making a big play when you try to take advantage of him. His arm is quite good, generally accurate, and he reads the ball extremely well off the Green Monster. He led the American League in baserunner kills in 2005, with 13.

By the way, no left field position is more influenced by its park than Fenway's. Manny's home/road splits are wider than any other left fielder's in 2005, but over three years the gap between his home and road basic plus/minus figures narrows significantly (-19 at home and -12 on the road).

Center Fielders Evaluations

Year	League	Gold Glove Winners	Should Have Been
2003	AL	Mike Cameron Torii Hunter	Mike Cameron Torii Hunter
	NL	Andruw Jones Jim Edmonds	Andruw Jones Jim Edmonds
2004	AL	Torii Hunter Vernon Wells	Torii Hunter Vernon Wells
	NL	Andruw Jones Steve Finley Jim Edmonds	Andruw Jones Steve Finley
2005	AL	Torii Hunter Vernon Wells	Torii Hunter Aaron Rowand
	NL	Andruw Jones Jim Edmonds	Andruw Jones Willy Taveras

My Personal Ratings

Top Ten

1 Torii Hunter, Min
2 Andruw Jones, Atl
3 Aaron Rowand, Phi
4 Mark Kotsay, Oak
5 Vernon Wells, Tor
6 Willy Taveras, Hou
7 Carlos Beltran, NYM
8 Grady Sizemore, Cle
9 Jeremy Reed, Sea
10 Nook Logan, Det

Bottom Five

26 Dave Roberts, SD
27 Damon Hollins, TB
28 Preston Wilson, Hou
29 Ken Griffey Jr., Cin
30 Bernie Williams, NYY

Player teams based on transactions through February 5, 2006

Center Fielders Rankings

3-Year Plus/Minus Rankings

1 Torii Hunter	+44	11 Randy Winn	+7	22 Milton Bradley	-5
2 Aaron Rowand	+34	12 Vernon Wells	+6	23 Marquis Grissom	-6
3 Andruw Jones	+26	13 Mike Cameron	+3	24 Rocco Baldelli	-9
4 Gary Matthews Jr.	+19	14 Corey Patterson	+2	25 Marlon Byrd	-10
5 Carlos Beltran	+14	15 Endy Chavez	+2	26 Dave Roberts	-10
6 Luis Matos	+13	16 Juan Pierre	0	27 Scott Podsednik	-14
7 Mark Kotsay	+12	17 Kenny Lofton	0	28 Jim Edmonds	-15
8 Grady Sizemore	+12	18 Laynce Nix	0	29 Craig Biggio	-15
9 Steve Finley	+11	19 Alex Sanchez	-1	30 Preston Wilson	-47
10 David DeJesus	+11	20 Tike Redman	-2	31 Ken Griffey Jr.	-58
		21 Johnny Damon	-3	32 Bernie Williams	-78

2005 Plus/Minus Rankings

1 Aaron Rowand	+30	11 Torii Hunter	+5	23 Johnny Damon	-2
2 Jeremy Reed	+28	12 Vernon Wells	+4	24 Corey Patterson	-2
3 Joey Gathright	+23	13 Luis Matos	+4	25 Jim Edmonds	-6
4 Nook Logan	+19	14 Jason Michaels	+4	26 Milton Bradley	-6
5 Lew Ford	+11	15 Jason Ellison	+3	27 Steve Finley	-7
6 Grady Sizemore	+10	16 Tike Redman	+3	28 Juan Pierre	-9
7 Willy Taveras	+9	17 Laynce Nix	+2	29 Brad Wilkerson	-9
8 Carlos Beltran	+7	18 Brady Clark	+1	30 Dave Roberts	-10
9 Andruw Jones	+7	19 David DeJesus	+1	31 Randy Winn	-10
10 Gary Matthews Jr.	+5	20 Mark Kotsay	+1	32 Damon Hollins	-13
		21 Kenny Lofton	+1	33 Ken Griffey Jr.	-27
		22 Cory Sullivan	+1	34 Preston Wilson	-28
				35 Bernie Williams	-37

2004 Plus/Minus Rankings

1 Steve Finley	+22	11 Aaron Rowand	+5	22 Scott Podsednik	-5
2 Torii Hunter	+17	12 Corey Patterson	+3	23 Laynce Nix	-6
3 Vernon Wells	+12	13 Marquis Grissom	+1	24 Tike Redman	-8
4 Randy Winn	+11	14 Milton Bradley	0	25 Garret Anderson	-8
5 David DeJesus	+10	15 Jay Payton	-1	26 Mike Cameron	-11
6 Carlos Beltran	+9	16 Rocco Baldelli	-2	27 Jim Edmonds	-12
7 Endy Chavez	+9	17 Coco Crisp	-2	28 Jeromy Burnitz	-13
8 Mark Kotsay	+7	18 Craig Biggio	-2	29 Marlon Byrd	-15
9 Andruw Jones	+6	19 Juan Pierre	-3	30 Johnny Damon	-16
10 Alex Sanchez	+6	20 Luis Matos	-3	31 Bernie Williams	-21
		21 Kenny Lofton	-3	32 Ken Griffey Jr.	-25

2003 Plus/Minus Rankings

1 Torii Hunter	+22	11 Gary Matthews Jr.	+6	21 Rocco Baldelli	-7
2 Mike Cameron	+15	12 Mark Kotsay	+4	22 Eric Byrnes	-7
3 Johnny Damon	+15	13 Jim Edmonds	+3	23 Endy Chavez	-8
4 Andruw Jones	+13	14 Dave Roberts	+3	24 Vernon Wells	-10
5 Juan Pierre	+12	15 Kenny Lofton	+2	25 Chris Singleton	-10
6 Luis Matos	+12	16 Milton Bradley	+1	26 Scott Podsednik	-11
7 Darin Erstad	+9	17 Corey Patterson	+1	27 Craig Biggio	-13
8 Carl Everett	+8	18 Carlos Beltran	-2	28 Preston Wilson	-15
9 Marquis Grissom	+7	19 Alex Sanchez	-3	29 Bernie Williams	-20
10 Marlon Byrd	+7	20 Steve Finley	-4		

3-Year Outfield Arms Rankings

1	Jim Edmonds	.464	11	Laynce Nix	.556	22	Preston Wilson	.611
2	Grady Sizemore	.490	12	Torii Hunter	.565	23	Dave Roberts	.615
3	Endy Chavez	.510	13	Ken Griffey Jr.	.566	24	Carlos Beltran	.617
4	Rocco Baldelli	.527	14	Marlon Byrd	.583	25	Craig Biggio	.619
5	Aaron Rowand	.535	15	Mike Cameron	.594	26	Vernon Wells	.631
6	Steve Finley	.537	16	Gary Matthews Jr.	.595	27	Marquis Grissom	.635
7	Andruw Jones	.538	17	Milton Bradley	.600	28	Luis Matos	.639
8	Mark Kotsay	.545	18	David DeJesus	.604	29	Tike Redman	.646
9	Scott Podsednik	.548	19	Corey Patterson	.605	30	Juan Pierre	.656
10	Randy Winn	.553	20	Johnny Damon	.606	31	Alex Sanchez	.697
			21	Kenny Lofton	.610	32	Bernie Williams	.703

2005 Outfield Arms Rankings

1	Jim Edmonds	.410	11	Randy Winn	.531	23	Luis Matos	.610
2	Jason Michaels	.442	12	Ken Griffey Jr.	.544	24	Vernon Wells	.611
3	Mark Kotsay	.485	13	Brad Wilkerson	.547	25	Joey Gathright	.611
4	Aaron Rowand	.496	14	Cory Sullivan	.547	26	Torii Hunter	.617
5	Steve Finley	.500	15	David DeJesus	.549	27	Jeremy Reed	.617
6	Grady Sizemore	.508	16	Willy Taveras	.560	28	Tike Redman	.620
7	Kenny Lofton	.510	17	Milton Bradley	.569	29	Dave Roberts	.630
8	Laynce Nix	.517	18	Johnny Damon	.575	30	Juan Pierre	.635
9	Lew Ford	.526	19	Nook Logan	.586	31	Preston Wilson	.648
10	Andruw Jones	.529	20	Gary Matthews Jr.	.590	32	Carlos Beltran	.659
			21	Brady Clark	.603	33	Bernie Williams	.677
			22	Corey Patterson	.608	34	Damon Hollins	.681
						35	Jason Ellison	.700

2004 Outfield Arms Rankings

1	Jim Edmonds	.444	11	Randy Winn	.570	22	Garret Anderson	.611
2	Jay Payton	.463	12	Endy Chavez	.579	23	Vernon Wells	.612
3	Torii Hunter	.515	13	Laynce Nix	.588	24	Marlon Byrd	.615
4	Corey Patterson	.523	14	Steve Finley	.588	25	Jeromy Burnitz	.644
5	Mike Cameron	.531	15	Scott Podsednik	.589	26	David DeJesus	.653
6	Andruw Jones	.540	16	Carlos Beltran	.591	27	Marquis Grissom	.656
7	Ken Griffey Jr.	.554	17	Craig Biggio	.594	28	Juan Pierre	.707
8	Aaron Rowand	.558	18	Johnny Damon	.595	29	Bernie Williams	.716
9	Mark Kotsay	.558	19	Tike Redman	.606	30	Alex Sanchez	.730
10	Rocco Baldelli	.561	20	Coco Crisp	.607	31	Kenny Lofton	.731
			21	Milton Bradley	.609	32	Luis Matos	.765

2003 Outfield Arms Rankings

1	Endy Chavez	.430	11	Preston Wilson	.577	21	Craig Biggio	.632
2	Steve Finley	.500	12	Luis Matos	.577	22	Juan Pierre	.633
3	Rocco Baldelli	.500	13	Mark Kotsay	.577	23	Johnny Damon	.644
4	Scott Podsednik	.500	14	Torii Hunter	.578	24	Mike Cameron	.654
5	Darin Erstad	.524	15	Gary Matthews Jr.	.588	25	Carl Everett	.655
6	Jim Edmonds	.540	16	Kenny Lofton	.598	26	Vernon Wells	.667
7	Andruw Jones	.545	17	Carlos Beltran	.600	27	Alex Sanchez	.702
8	Marlon Byrd	.559	18	Dave Roberts	.600	28	Bernie Williams	.714
9	Chris Singleton	.568	19	Marquis Grissom	.605	29	Corey Patterson	.726
10	Eric Byrnes	.571	20	Milton Bradley	.615			

Center Fielders

Torii Hunter

3-Yr Plus/Minus: +44 in 3212 inn.

2005 Basic P/M: +1   2005 Enhanced P/M: +5 in 813 inn.

    Home: +1 in 420 inn.   RHP: +1 in 591 inn.
    Road: 0 in 393 inn.   LHP: 0 in 222 inn.

Hunter is the cream of the crop in center field. He gets excellent jumps on balls and his range is exceptional. Add to that a strong and accurate throwing arm and a fearless willingness to dive, crash into and leap above fences to take away a hit and he may be the tops in the game in center. They don't call him "Spiderman" for nothing. The great play he made to rob Barry Bonds in the All Star game a few years ago is almost routine for Hunter.

Aaron Rowand

3-Yr Plus/Minus: +34 in 2766 inn.

2005 Basic P/M: +15   2005 Enhanced P/M: +30 in 1368 inn.

    Home: +7 in 731 inn.   RHP: +15 in 1038 inn.
    Road: +8 in 637 inn.   LHP: 0 in 330 inn.

Not always the fastest or smoothest defensive center fielder, Rowand more than gets the job done nonetheless. He shows excellent play in center utilizing great reads and good jumps. Rowand plays with reckless abandon. He reminds many of Darin Erstad in center field in that he would run through a wall to make a play.

His +30 enhanced plays made last year led all major league outfielders. His throwing arm rates well also as he ranked fourth in Outfield Advance percentage. His awesome performance garners him the Gold Glove That Should Have Been over Vernon Wells for 2005.

Jeremy Reed

3-Yr Plus/Minus: +31 in 1273 inn.

2005 Basic P/M: +13   2005 Enhanced P/M: +28 in 1150 inn.

    Home: +8 in 609 inn.   RHP: +10 in 863 inn.
    Road: +5 in 541 inn.   LHP: +3 in 287 inn.

Reed is an up-and-coming elite defensive center fielder. He has a knack for picking up the ball off the bat and running a precise route to make the play. A great first step and jump on the ball helps him overcome a lack of a classic center fielder's blazing speed. If Reed can come close to his +28 showing of 2005, the words Gold Glove may begin to surface.

Andruw Jones

3-Yr Plus/Minus: +26 in 4042 inn.

2005 Basic P/M: +4   2005 Enhanced P/M: +7 in 1366 inn.

    Home: +4 in 698 inn.   RHP: +5 in 1059 inn.
    Road: 0 in 668 inn.   LHP: -1 in 307 inn.

Jones has won eight straight Gold Gloves and is an all-time great defender in center field. He has bulked up in recent years to help his offense, which has affected his range slightly. Jones is still one of the top defenders today at the position. He gets amazing jumps on the ball, which can overcome any slight loss of range in recent years. His throwing arm is top notch.

Joey Gathright

3-Yr Plus/Minus: +22 in 602 inn.

2005 Basic P/M: +11   2005 Enhanced P/M: +23 in 506 inn.

    Home: +6 in 259 inn.   RHP: +8 in 291 inn.
    Road: +5 in 247 inn.   LHP: +3 in 215 inn.

Gathright may be the fastest man in baseball, even faster than teammate Carl Crawford. Gathright's speed makes great range almost an automatic. He is learning how to use his angles better which could eventually make him one of the finest center fielders in the major leagues.

Nook Logan

3-Yr Plus/Minus: +20 in 1234 inn.

2005 Basic P/M: +8   2005 Enhanced P/M: +19 in 874 inn.

    Home: 0 in 427 inn.   RHP: +4 in 531 inn.
    Road: +8 in 447 inn.   LHP: +4 in 343 inn.

One of the fastest players in the league, Logan is consequently a very good center fielder. His outstanding speed enhances his defense, enabling him to run down balls that would elude a slower center fielder. His +19 enhanced plays last year ranked him fourth among center fielders.

Lew Ford

3-Yr Plus/Minus: +20 in 963 inn.

2005 Basic P/M: +6   2005 Enhanced P/M: +11 in 548 inn.

    Home: +4 in 288 inn.   RHP: +5 in 427 inn.
    Road: +2 in 260 inn.   LHP: +1 in 121 inn.

Ford is a good outfielder who is versatile enough to play all three positions. He gets a good jump on the ball, though he can sometimes take a bad route or angle. As a corner outfielder he is excellent, but he is still good in center.

Gary Matthews Jr.

3-Yr Plus/Minus: +19 in 1662 inn.

2005 Basic P/M: +1   2005 Enhanced P/M: +5 in 846 inn.

    Home: -1 in 419 inn.   RHP: -2 in 624 inn.
    Road: +2 in 427 inn.   LHP: +3 in 222 inn.

Matthews runs well, has good range and is versatile enough to play all three outfield spots. He combines a center fielder's range with a right fielder's arm. Matthews has had trouble shaking the "extra outfielder" label and will continue to be a fill-in until he can produce with consistency on offense.

Carlos Beltran

3-Yr Plus/Minus: +14 in 3781 inn.

2005 Basic P/M: +1   2005 Enhanced P/M: +7 in 1289 inn.

    Home: 0 in 699 inn.   RHP: +1 in 980 inn.
    Road: +1 in 590 inn.   LHP: 0 in 309 inn.

Beltran played most of his first season in New York with a leg injury, and that may have affected his often-stellar defense. Problems stemming from this leg injury seemed to hinder not only his range but also his aggressive nature; he did not have his usual explosive burst in 2005, though he certainly remains an above average center fielder. He is known for a good arm, but runners ran on him more often than ever in 2005. His Outfield Advance percentage was among the worst of all regular center fielders in baseball as runners took an extra base on him 66% of the time while he could muster only four baserunner kills.

Luis Matos
3-Yr Plus/Minus: +13 in 2691 inn.

2005 Basic P/M: +1   2005 Enhanced P/M: +4 in 990 inn.
Home: -2 in 519 inn.   RHP: +3 in 590 inn.
Road: +3 in 471 inn.   LHP: -2 in 400 inn.

Matos is a speedy center fielder who covers lots of ground. However, some within the Orioles organization do not consider him much more than an average fielder for some reason. Could this be a reflection of his disappointing offensive production? Still, he ranks sixth among all center fielders in the last three years with +13 enhanced plays made in center field. Matos also has a good, accurate arm, especially for a center fielder.

Grady Sizemore
3-Yr Plus/Minus: +12 in 1718 inn.

2005 Basic P/M: +3   2005 Enhanced P/M: +10 in 1370 inn.
Home: +5 in 728 inn.   RHP: 0 in 901 inn.
Road: -2 in 642 inn.   LHP: +3 in 469 inn.

A great athlete, Sizemore was recruited to play quarterback at the University of Washington. His great speed and daredevil style allow him to track down balls most outfielders cannot reach. His range is well above average. While Sizemore's throwing arm doesn't look strong, baserunners have not yet been able to take a lot of extra bases on him. His .490 Outfield Advance percentage in center field over the first season-and-a-third of his career is excellent.

Mark Kotsay
3-Yr Plus/Minus: +12 in 3494 inn.

2005 Basic P/M: 0   2005 Enhanced P/M: +1 in 1184 inn.
Home: -2 in 581 inn.   RHP: +3 in 914 inn.
Road: +2 in 603 inn.   LHP: -3 in 270 inn.

Kotsay covers a good amount of ground in center field. He combines good range with good reads on the ball, good routes and a strong, accurate arm. His 18 baserunner kills over the last three years is second only to Jim Edmonds in center field in that time period.

David DeJesus
3-Yr Plus/Minus: +11 in 1758 inn.

2005 Basic P/M: +5   2005 Enhanced P/M: +1 in 1005 inn.
Home: 0 in 505 inn.   RHP: 0 in 812 inn.
Road: +5 in 500 inn.   LHP: +5 in 193 inn.

DeJesus is a very smart player, and he runs OK when he gets going. But he has a square body, doesn't accelerate at all well, and he just really is not fast enough to be a good center fielder. His arm is average. It's not Jose Guillen, but there's nothing wrong with his arm.

Steve Finley
3-Yr Plus/Minus: +11 in 3446 inn.

2005 Basic P/M: -7   2005 Enhanced P/M: -7 in 896 inn.
Home: -4 in 434 inn.   RHP: -8 in 751 inn.
Road: -3 in 462 inn.   LHP: +1 in 145 inn.

Now past 40, Finley suffered a sharp decline defensively in 2005. The perennial Gold Glove center fielder is still solid, but he no longer shows the elite range that he has had in the past. Finley has a good throwing arm, better than most in center field.

Willy Taveras
3-Yr Plus/Minus: +7 in 1260 inn.

2005 Basic P/M: +3   2005 Enhanced P/M: +9 in 1254 inn.
Home: +5 in 656 inn.   RHP: +3 in 914 inn.
Road: -2 in 598 inn.   LHP: 0 in 340 inn.

Taveras has outstanding speed and range in center field as well as a good, strong throwing arm. That speed and range allow him to run down balls in the gaps and also help him overcome his mistakes.

Taveras had +9 enhanced plays in 2005 and a major-league leading eight baserunner kills. Jim Edmonds was -6 and had only two kills, though he did lead in Outfield Advance percentage for center fielders. On the strength of these numbers the National League Gold Glove That Should Have Been goes to Willy Taveras over Jim Edmonds for 2005.

Randy Winn
3-Yr Plus/Minus: +7 in 1757 inn.

2005 Basic P/M: -1   2005 Enhanced P/M: -10 in 533 inn.
Home: -1 in 253 inn.   RHP: -1 in 389 inn.
Road: -1 in 233 inn.   LHP: 0 in 144 inn.

Winn struggled in center field last year and his -10 enhanced plus/minus figure shows it. He causes trouble for himself by running bad angles to track down flyballs. He does not get great jumps and relies too much on his speed to bail himself out. His weak arm entices runners to test him. Normally Winn is more dependable than he was last year and if he could move to his best position, left field, he would be a plus defensively. But it looks like the Giants are going to give him another try in center.

Vernon Wells
3-Yr Plus/Minus: +6 in 3909 inn.

2005 Basic P/M: +1   2005 Enhanced P/M: +4 in 1358 inn.
Home: +5 in 708 inn.   RHP: 0 in 896 inn.
Road: -4 in 650 inn.   LHP: +1 in 462 inn.

Wells is a superb defensive center fielder. He is very smooth in the field, has good instincts and is particularly adept at going back on the ball. Wells has been an American League Gold Glove outfielder the past two seasons. He's made only one error in the last two seasons combined. The next closest center fielder who played in 2000 or more innings during the same time period is Andruw Jones, who had five.

Center Fielders

We gave our Gold Glove That Should Have Been to Aaron Rowand over Wells for 2005. That's doesn't mean Wells performed poorly. While it was clear that Rowand deserved the Gold Glove, it was a tough choice between Wells and Torii Hunter as to whom Rowand should replace. We went with Rowand replacing Wells even though Hunter missed some time. That was partly based on Hunter's overall three-year best showing among centerfielders with a +44 plus/minus. But it was also based on the fact that despite missing that playing time he had a +5 in 2005 compared to +4 for Wells. Hunter and Wells tied for the American League lead with seven baserunner kills apiece.

Jason Ellison
3-Yr Plus/Minus: +4 in 603 inn.

2005 Basic P/M: +4

2005 Enhanced P/M: +3 in 592 inn.
Home: -2 in 293 inn.   RHP: -1 in 345 inn.
Road: +6 in 299 inn.   LHP: +5 in 247 inn.

Ellison is a speedy, versatile outfielder who flashes good range at all three outfield positions. He is a risk taker who can sometimes get too aggressive. Thus far in his young career, baserunners have run amok on his arm.

Jason Michaels
3-Yr Plus/Minus: +2 in 888 inn.

2005 Basic P/M: +5

2005 Enhanced P/M: +4 in 536 inn.
Home: +2 in 260 inn.   RHP: +5 in 408 inn.
Road: +3 in 276 inn.   LHP: 0 in 128 inn.

Michaels is a solid defensive outfielder who can play all three outfield positions. He has good range but is probably best suited for a corner position. Michaels may have been the best defender the Phillies had in the outfield in 2005.

Brady Clark
3-Yr Plus/Minus: +2 in 1387 inn.

2005 Basic P/M: +1

2005 Enhanced P/M: +1 in 1275 inn.
Home: 0 in 660 inn.   RHP: +4 in 799 inn.
Road: +1 in 615 inn.   LHP: -3 in 476 inn.

Clark is a capable defensive outfielder who, like Michaels, is best suited to play a corner outfield spot. What he lacks in range, he partially makes up for with great effort and hustle.

Corey Patterson
3-Yr Plus/Minus: +2 in 3065 inn.

2005 Basic P/M: -3

2005 Enhanced P/M: -2 in 987 inn.
Home: 0 in 496 inn.   RHP: -1 in 782 inn.
Road: -3 in 491 inn.   LHP: -2 in 205 inn.

In terms of defense, Corey Patterson is the definition of average. He has very good speed but his defense is only average. His plus/minus totals have been the model of consistency going +1, +3, and -2 over the last three years. His arm is strong but once again the results are average.

Cory Sullivan
3-Yr Plus/Minus: +1 in 618 inn.

2005 Basic P/M: 0

2005 Enhanced P/M: +1 in 618 inn.
Home: +2 in 258 inn.   RHP: +1 in 459 inn.
Road: -2 in 360 inn.   LHP: -1 in 159 inn.

Sullivan provides good speed, range and solid fundamentals in the outfield. He is an above-average center fielder who had never played above Double-A until 2005. If Sullivan fails in a full-time role, he would make a great fourth outfielder, providing speed and defense in the late innings.

Laynce Nix
3-Yr Plus/Minus: 0 in 1547 inn.

2005 Basic P/M: +1

2005 Enhanced P/M: +2 in 526 inn.
Home: -1 in 288 inn.   RHP: +1 in 392 inn.
Road: +2 in 238 inn.   LHP: 0 in 134 inn.

Although Nix has been asked to play center field almost exclusively the past couple of seasons, he may be better off eventually settling in at a corner outfield spot. His range is lacking in center, although his arm is good.

Kenny Lofton
3-Yr Plus/Minus: 0 in 2450 inn.

2005 Basic P/M: +2

2005 Enhanced P/M: +1 in 741 inn.
Home: -3 in 399 inn.   RHP: +5 in 606 inn.
Road: +5 in 342 inn.   LHP: -3 in 135 inn.

Lofton is still a decent defender. However, he has lost a step over the years and can no longer always rely on his speed to make up for mistakes he makes getting bad jumps or taking bad angles to the ball. Still, Lofton can make the occasional highlight-film play.

Juan Pierre
3-Yr Plus/Minus: 0 in 4255 inn.

2005 Basic P/M: -2

2005 Enhanced P/M: -9 in 1383 inn.
Home: +4 in 704 inn.   RHP: -3 in 923 inn.
Road: -6 in 679 inn.   LHP: +1 in 460 inn.

Pierre's good early-career range has slipped recently. Leg injuries seem to have sapped a good deal of his speed. Pierre's arm is well below average and most runners won't hesitate to challenge him.

Pierre's plus/minus progression over the last three years: +12, -3, -9. Not a good trend for the new Cub center fielder and leadoff man.

Tike Redman
3-Yr Plus/Minus: -2 in 2180 inn.

2005 Basic P/M: +3

2005 Enhanced P/M: +3 in 523 inn.
Home: +1 in 239 inn.   RHP: +1 in 294 inn.
Road: +2 in 284 inn.   LHP: +2 in 229 inn.

Redman has great speed and good range but his improving defense is still erratic. He does not always get a good jump on the ball and sometimes takes a bad route or angle to the ball.

Center Fielders

Johnny Damon
3-Yr Plus/Minus: -3 in 3746 inn.

2005 Basic P/M: -2

2005 Enhanced P/M: -2 in 1225 inn.
Home: -2 in 634 inn. RHP: +3 in 944 inn.
Road: 0 in 591 inn. LHP: -5 in 281 inn.

Damon is a very fast outfielder with a lot of experience in center field. He does not have the instincts of an Andruw Jones or a Torii Hunter, and at times he will run bad routes, although this usually just results in his catching the ball in an awkward way. His arm, of course, is a joke.

Milton Bradley
3-Yr Plus/Minus: -5 in 2260 inn.

2005 Basic P/M: -1

2005 Enhanced P/M: -6 in 628 inn.
Home: +1 in 300 inn. RHP: -3 in 514 inn.
Road: -2 in 328 inn. LHP: +2 in 114 inn.

Bradley is a good, versatile defensive player. He can play all three outfield spots. He prefers to remain in center field, but he'll play right field with the A's. He has good range and an arm strong enough for right. Bradley has worked hard in recent years to improve his jump on the ball, something he struggled with early in his career.

Brad Wilkerson
3-Yr Plus/Minus: -7 in 1202 inn.

2005 Basic P/M: -5

2005 Enhanced P/M: -9 in 759 inn.
Home: -1 in 363 inn. RHP: -5 in 733 inn.
Road: -4 in 396 inn. LHP: 0 in 26 inn.

The 2005 season was Wilkerson's first playing predominantly center field since his first full year back in 2002. As one might expect, it was a bit of a stretch. While he can handle center field, Wilkerson's best positions are left field and first base. In the outfield, he gets good breaks on the ball, takes good routes and angles and has a strong and accurate arm. If he has any weakness, it is that he sometimes has difficulties getting to line drives hit in front of him.

Dave Roberts
3-Yr Plus/Minus: -10 in 1977 inn.

2005 Basic P/M: -5

2005 Enhanced P/M: -10 in 901 inn.
Home: 0 in 444 inn. RHP: -6 in 788 inn.
Road: -5 in 457 inn. LHP: +1 in 113 inn.

Roberts' history prior to 2005 is that of a good defensive center fielder. He has the speed and range to man the position, but his throwing arm is weak. Perhaps the spaciousness of Petco Park and some injury troubles were responsible for Roberts' sub-par defensive performance in 2005.

Damon Hollins
3-Yr Plus/Minus: -13 in 619 inn.

2005 Basic P/M: -8

2005 Enhanced P/M: -13 in 619 inn.
Home: -5 in 354 inn. RHP: -5 in 359 inn.
Road: -3 in 265 inn. LHP: -3 in 260 inn.

Hollins had some difficulties in the outfield in 2005. He turned around a number of early-season gaffs to play some competent defense later in the year. At the corner outfield spots, he is an average defender, but isn't quite good enough for center field.

Jim Edmonds
3-Yr Plus/Minus: -15 in 3412 inn.

2005 Basic P/M: 0

2005 Enhanced P/M: -6 in 1153 inn.
Home: +1 in 623 inn. RHP: -4 in 898 inn.
Road: -1 in 530 inn. LHP: +4 in 255 inn.

Edmonds was once a human highlight reel, but has now lost a step. Although his once-outstanding range has diminished, he still has a knack for making flashy and spectacular plays. He goes back on a ball as well as any center fielder in the game. His arm is the absolute best. He led all center fielders in both baserunner hold percentage (.464) and baserunner kills (19) over the last three years.

Edmonds has won eight consecutive Gold Gloves. The last two are questionable. He's had enhanced plus/minus figures of -12 and -6 in 2004 and 2005. Due to his decline, we've given the two Gold Gloves That Should Have Been for the last two years to Richard Hidalgo (2004) and Willy Taveras (2005).

Preston Wilson
3-Yr Plus/Minus: -47 in 2812 inn.

2005 Basic P/M: -15

2005 Enhanced P/M: -28 in 1069 inn.
Home: -7 in 611 inn. RHP: -9 in 818 inn.
Road: -8 in 458 inn. LHP: -6 in 251 inn.

Knee injuries over the last few seasons have sapped Wilson's speed and range. He is now well below average as a center fielder. In 2005 he began to play some at the corner positions. While his arm is strong, it's erratic and both coaches and baserunners know it. He's only had seven baserunner kills in the last three years, the second lowest total of any center fielder with 300 or more opportunities. Keep reading to learn about the player with the lowest.

Ken Griffey Jr.
3-Yr Plus/Minus: -58 in 2078 inn.

2005 Basic P/M: -13

2005 Enhanced P/M: -27 in 1066 inn.
Home: -7 in 563 inn. RHP: -12 in 709 inn.
Road: -6 in 503 inn. LHP: -1 in 357 inn.

Griffey won an American League Gold Glove for ten straight years, 1990 to 1999. For ten straight years, when we did our zone ratings at STATS, Inc. we wondered why. While his throwing arm was intimidating his ability to cover ground in center field certainly appeared to be lacking. At least that's what the numbers said. Here's how Griffey stacked up, as published in *The Baseball Scoreboard* for ten years.

Griffey's rank among American League center fielders in his Gold Glove years:

Year	Zone Rating	Outfield Advance
1990	9	1
1991	14 (last)	4
1992	11	3
1993	14 (last)	4
1994	14 (last)	4
1995	14 (last)	7
1996	6	2
1997	7	2
1998	6 of 8 qualifiers	2
1999	6 of 7 qualifiers	2

Griffey was last or near the bottom of zone ratings almost every year, though his throwing arm ranked with the best. One year, after the 1994 season and five consecutive Gold Gloves, we broke down batted balls hit to center field while Griffey was there into every possible breakdown we could think of: how hard the ball was hit, the edge of the zone, outside of the zone, type of batted ball, etc. Griffey was last or near the bottom in every single breakdown. We concluded back then that he was a great finisher with a flair for the dramatic, but didn't get a good jump and simply fielded fewer balls hit to center than other center fielders. He had a gold arm, for sure, but not a gold glove. And we disagreed with his Gold Glove reputation.

Amazingly enough, in his first year in the National League with the Reds in 2000, Griffey had the highest zone rating in the league for the first time ever and *didn't* win the Gold Glove. His throwing arm ranking slid to tenth that year, however. Since then he's been wracked by injuries. In the plus/minus system, he's the worst center fielder in the National League with a total of -58 enhanced plays in the past three years, despite all the time off due to injury.

Bernie Williams

3-Yr Plus/Minus: -78 in 2693 inn.

2005 Basic P/M: -21

2005 Enhanced P/M: -37 in 862 inn.
Home: -9 in 463 inn.   RHP: -16 in 614 inn.
Road: -12 in 399 inn.   LHP: -5 in 248 inn.

Williams has been on a steady decline defensively for years. In 2005, he hit rock bottom. He was always a bit overrated defensively, even in his Gold Glove heyday, but he is now a definite liability in center field. His range is very limited and he can no longer cover the ground needed in center, especially in the spacious outfield of Yankee Stadium. On top of that, baserunners run wild on his arm. He only had one baserunner kill last year and only four over the last three.

Right Fielders Evaluations

Year	League	Gold Glove Winners	Should Have Been
2003	AL	Ichiro Suzuki	Ichiro Suzuki
	NL	Jose Cruz	Richard Hidalgo
2004	AL	Ichiro Suzuki	Ichiro Suzuki
	NL	none	Richard Hidalgo
2005	AL	Ichiro Suzuki	Ichiro Suzuki
	NL	Bobby Abreu	Geoff Jenkins

My Personal Ratings

Top Ten

1 Ichiro Suzuki, Sea
2 Richard Hidalgo, FA
3 Trot Nixon, Bos
4 Geoff Jenkins, Mil
5 Austin Kearns, Cin
6 J.D. Drew, LAD
7 Alexis Rios, Tor
8 Jeff Francoeur, Atl
9 Jose Guillen, Was
10 Jose Cruz, LAD

Bottom Five

26 Emil Brown, KC
27 Jeromy Burnitz, Pit
28 Sammy Sosa, FA
29 Matt Lawton, Sea
30 Gary Sheffield, NYY

Player teams based on transactions through February 5, 2006

Right Fielders Rankings

3-Year Plus/Minus Rankings

1	Ichiro Suzuki	+48	11	Raul Mondesi	+2	21	Vladimir Guerrero	-14
2	Trot Nixon	+26	12	Jose Cruz	+1	22	Sammy Sosa	-14
3	J.D. Drew	+25	13	Shawn Green	+1	23	Jody Gerut	-15
4	Richard Hidalgo	+21	14	Brian Giles	-2	24	Jacque Jones	-16
5	Jose Guillen	+21	15	Larry Walker	-5	25	Juan Encarnacion	-20
6	Austin Kearns	+13	16	Aubrey Huff	-6	26	Michael Tucker	-20
7	Alexis Rios	+12	17	Jermaine Dye	-7	27	Gary Sheffield	-38
8	Bobby Higginson	+12	18	Jeromy Burnitz	-7			
9	Magglio Ordonez	+10	19	Danny Bautista	-10			
10	Jay Gibbons	+3	20	Bobby Abreu	-12			

2005 Plus/Minus Rankings

1	Trot Nixon	+18	11	Magglio Ordonez	+3	21	Jermaine Dye	-6
2	Casey Blake	+14	12	Mike Cameron	+2	22	Jacque Jones	-8
3	Geoff Jenkins	+13	13	Alexis Rios	+1	23	Victor Diaz	-8
4	Jose Guillen	+10	14	Nick Swisher	-1	24	Sammy Sosa	-8
5	Vladimir Guerrero	+10	15	Brad Hawpe	-3	25	Larry Walker	-8
6	Jay Gibbons	+10	16	Jeromy Burnitz	-4	26	Emil Brown	-9
7	Jeff Francoeur	+10	17	Shawn Green	-4	27	Juan Encarnacion	-12
8	Richard Hidalgo	+8	18	Jason Lane	-4	28	Bobby Abreu	-13
9	Ichiro Suzuki	+7	19	Aubrey Huff	-4	29	Matt Lawton	-17
10	Austin Kearns	+7	20	Brian Giles	-5	30	Craig Monroe	-18
						31	Gary Sheffield	-25

2004 Plus/Minus Rankings

1	Ichiro Suzuki	+30	11	Abraham Nunez	+4	21	Bobby Abreu	-6
2	J.D. Drew	+21	12	Brian Giles	+3	22	Jacque Jones	-7
3	Brady Clark	+20	13	Jay Gibbons	+2	23	Jose Cruz	-8
4	Alexis Rios	+11	14	Juan Encarnacion	+1	24	Danny Bautista	-8
5	Richard Hidalgo	+9	15	Larry Walker	0	25	Michael Tucker	-8
6	Bobby Higginson	+8	16	Jermaine Dye	-1	26	Miguel Cabrera	-8
7	Gabe Kapler	+8	17	Sammy Sosa	-2	27	Gary Sheffield	-11
8	Kevin Mench	+5	18	Jeromy Burnitz	-3	28	Craig Wilson	-14
9	Austin Kearns	+5	19	Reggie Sanders	-4	29	Jody Gerut	-15
10	Juan Rivera	+4	20	Lance Berkman	-5	30	Vladimir Guerrero	-18

2003 Plus/Minus Rankings

1	Ichiro Suzuki	+11	11	Bobby Higginson	+3	21	John Vander Wal	-2
2	Jose Guillen	+11	12	Larry Walker	+3	22	Aaron Guiel	-3
3	Jeff DaVanon	+11	13	Jose Cruz	0	23	Sammy Sosa	-4
4	Magglio Ordonez	+10	14	Jermaine Dye	0	24	Bobby Kielty	-4
5	Bobby Abreu	+7	15	Dustan Mohr	-1	25	Reed Johnson	-4
6	Trot Nixon	+7	16	Reggie Sanders	-1	26	Vladimir Guerrero	-6
7	Xavier Nady	+6	17	Terrence Long	-1	27	Tim Salmon	-6
8	Raul Mondesi	+5	18	Gary Sheffield	-2	28	Roger Cedeno	-7
9	Richard Hidalgo	+4	19	Shawn Green	-2	29	Juan Encarnacion	-9
10	Jody Gerut	+4	20	Aubrey Huff	-2	30	Jay Gibbons	-9

3-Year Outfield Arms Rankings

1	Richard Hidalgo	.427	11	Gary Sheffield	.528	21	Juan Encarnacion	.575
2	Alexis Rios	.432	12	Vladimir Guerrero	.532	22	Sammy Sosa	.585
3	Jacque Jones	.471	13	Jay Gibbons	.543	23	J.D. Drew	.586
4	Larry Walker	.472	14	Magglio Ordonez	.544	24	Michael Tucker	.592
5	Ichiro Suzuki	.477	15	Jose Guillen	.555	25	Jody Gerut	.593
6	Jose Cruz	.491	16	Trot Nixon	.557	26	Bobby Higginson	.595
7	Raul Mondesi	.500	17	Jermaine Dye	.563	27	Danny Bautista	.611
8	Bobby Abreu	.507	18	Brian Giles	.564			
9	Austin Kearns	.511	19	Jeromy Burnitz	.572			
10	Aubrey Huff	.519	20	Shawn Green	.574			

2005 Outfield Arms Rankings

1	Victor Diaz	.379	11	Bobby Abreu	.492	21	Jay Gibbons	.545
2	Alexis Rios	.424	12	Jeff Francoeur	.493	22	Brad Hawpe	.551
3	Jason Lane	.432	13	Richard Hidalgo	.494	23	Nick Swisher	.561
4	Matt Lawton	.447	14	Aubrey Huff	.510	24	Trot Nixon	.564
5	Gary Sheffield	.449	15	Jermaine Dye	.513	25	Geoff Jenkins	.567
6	Vladimir Guerrero	.458	16	Juan Encarnacion	.524	26	Ichiro Suzuki	.572
7	Larry Walker	.464	17	Craig Monroe	.531	27	Magglio Ordonez	.573
8	Jacque Jones	.475	18	Jose Guillen	.537	28	Sammy Sosa	.574
9	Austin Kearns	.485	19	Shawn Green	.544	29	Casey Blake	.594
10	Mike Cameron	.491	20	Brian Giles	.545	30	Emil Brown	.617
						31	Jeromy Burnitz	.629

2004 Outfield Arms Rankings

1	Richard Hidalgo	.421	11	Abraham Nunez	.500	21	Jermaine Dye	.597
2	Ichiro Suzuki	.434	12	Jeromy Burnitz	.516	22	Bobby Abreu	.597
3	Alexis Rios	.441	13	Bobby Higginson	.535	23	Jody Gerut	.600
4	Kevin Mench	.453	14	Austin Kearns	.540	24	Miguel Cabrera	.614
5	Jay Gibbons	.462	15	Vladimir Guerrero	.547	25	Gabe Kapler	.619
6	Jacque Jones	.462	16	Gary Sheffield	.557	26	Michael Tucker	.621
7	Juan Rivera	.468	17	Juan Encarnacion	.573	27	Larry Walker	.625
8	Lance Berkman	.484	18	Brian Giles	.580	28	Craig Wilson	.625
9	Reggie Sanders	.493	19	Danny Bautista	.586	29	Sammy Sosa	.656
10	Jose Cruz	.493	20	J.D. Drew	.594	30	Brady Clark	.736

2003 Outfield Arms Rankings

1	Richard Hidalgo	.383	11	Raul Mondesi	.522	21	Jose Guillen	.583
2	Jeff DaVanon	.396	12	Aubrey Huff	.529	22	Jay Gibbons	.584
3	Larry Walker	.398	13	Sammy Sosa	.530	23	Jermaine Dye	.596
4	Ichiro Suzuki	.400	14	Bobby Kielty	.533	24	Tim Salmon	.597
5	Bobby Abreu	.421	15	Reed Johnson	.564	25	Reggie Sanders	.598
6	Jose Cruz	.465	16	Xavier Nady	.570	26	Shawn Green	.610
7	Dustan Mohr	.475	17	John Vander Wal	.571	27	Roger Cedeno	.611
8	Trot Nixon	.492	18	Gary Sheffield	.574	28	Juan Encarnacion	.627
9	Aaron Guiel	.495	19	Vladimir Guerrero	.576	29	Bobby Higginson	.657
10	Magglio Ordonez	.500	20	Jody Gerut	.582	30	Terrence Long	.683

Right Fielders

Ichiro Suzuki

3-Yr Plus/Minus: +48 in 4160 inn.

2005 Basic P/M: +6

2005 Enhanced P/M: +7 in 1388 inn.
Home: +1 in 743 inn.   RHP: +5 in 1017 inn.
Road: +5 in 645 inn.   LHP: +1 in 371 inn.

Ichiro is probably the finest defensive player in the game. He combines tremendous speed and range with the most feared throwing arm in the game. However, his game showed some decline in 2005. After two years of ranking first in enhanced plays made, he fell to ninth. And his arm rating slipped even further, from fourth and second in 2003 and 2004, to 26th in 2005. 2006 will be a pivotal year for one of the most unique players in the game: will he rebound to his past greatness or are we witnessing the beginning of his sunset years?

Trot Nixon

3-Yr Plus/Minus: +26 in 2320 inn.

2005 Basic P/M: +12

2005 Enhanced P/M: +18 in 935 inn.
Home: +1 in 481 inn.   RHP: +9 in 725 inn.
Road: +11 in 454 inn.   LHP: +3 in 210 inn.

Nixon is a solid outfielder with good outfield instincts. He gets good jumps on balls and has a strong, above-average arm. He covers the gap in right-center exceptionally well, particularly in Fenway, where the absence of foul territory enables him to shade toward center. He led all right fielders last year with +18 enhanced plays.

J.D. Drew

3-Yr Plus/Minus: +25 in 1966 inn.

2005 Basic P/M: -1

2005 Enhanced P/M: +1 in 382 inn.
Home: -2 in 198 inn.   RHP: -1 in 315 inn.
Road: +1 in 184 inn.   LHP: 0 in 67 inn.

Drew is the total package; he can hit, run and play defense. His only problem is that he cannot stay on the field for a full season. He is a very good right fielder displaying great range. He ranks third in enhanced plays (+25) over the last three years. While his arm is strong, it hasn't been as intimidating as he would like in keeping runners from taking the extra base. He also can play center field, well enough to be as good as most teams' regular center fielder.

Jose Guillen

3-Yr Plus/Minus: +21 in 2015 inn.

2005 Basic P/M: +2

2005 Enhanced P/M: +10 in 1190 inn.
Home: +1 in 598 inn.   RHP: 0 in 1119 inn.
Road: +1 in 592 inn.   LHP: +2 in 71 inn.

Guillen is known for one defensive tool, his arm. His throwing arm is a rocket, although his intimidation factor in terms of how often runners take an extra base is only average. His Outfield Advance percentage of .555 ranks him 15th over the last three years. Although his range doesn't typically get the highest marks, our enhanced play rankings (fifth overall) place him on the major league honor roll.

Richard Hidalgo

3-Yr Plus/Minus: +21 in 3060 inn.

2005 Basic P/M: +6

2005 Enhanced P/M: +8 in 700 inn.
Home: +3 in 332 inn.   RHP: +4 in 495 inn.
Road: +3 in 368 inn.   LHP: +2 in 205 inn.

It's time to expose Richard Hidalgo. Ichiro Suzuki gets all the notoriety for his overall play and his throwing arm in right field, but Richard Hidalgo is not far behind. He doesn't have Ichiro's speed and quickness but he covers ground and the results speak for themselves. When it comes to throwing, Hidalgo surpasses even Suzuki and the results also speak for themselves.

What are those results?

Two years ago, in 2003, Hidalgo successfully threw out 19 runners trying to take an extra base on him. We call them baserunner kills. We don't count the relays. These are throws made by Hidalgo directly to the base to nail the runner. That's the best single performance we have over the three years this book covers. By a wide margin. The second best performance? Richard Hidalgo, 2004. He had 13 baserunner kills (tied with Jose Cruz who had 13 kills for the Giants in 2003). Ichiro's biggest year in the last three: eight kills in 2003, which still is a very good single season total for a right fielder. How about intimidation? Runners have tested Hidalgo's arm and succeeded in taking the extra base only 43% of the time over the last three years. That's the best Outfield Advance percentage in baseball. Ichiro's 48% is also a very good number but it's a full five percent higher than Hidalgo's.

When it comes to covering ground in right field no one does it better than Ichiro. His +48 enhanced plays lead all right fielders over the last three years by a wide margin. He's also first in zone rating with a .709 figure and the 95 plays he made outside his zone is first as well. But Hidalgo ranks high on the lists as well. He's fourth in enhanced plus/minus with +21, fifth in zone rating (.676) and second to Ichiro in plays made (66) outside the right field zone—very good for a guy not blessed with speed like Suzuki.

Hidalgo wins our Gold Glove That Should Have Been for both 2003 and 2004. He supplants Jose Cruz in 2003 and Jim Edmonds in 2004. As mentioned above, Cruz's 13 kills in right field in 2003 were second to Hidalgo's 19 and his exactly average zero enhanced plays were less than Hidalgo's +4. Edmonds, who is also known for his cannon arm, had nine kills in 2004 to Hidalgo's 13 while enhanced plus/minus strongly favored Hidalgo, +9 to -12.

Right Fielders

Casey Blake
3-Yr Plus/Minus: +14 in 1189 inn.

2005 Basic P/M: +3

2005 Enhanced P/M: +14 in 1189 inn.
Home: +9 in 574 inn.   RHP: 0 in 798 inn.
Road: -6 in 615 inn.   LHP: +3 in 391 inn.

The former third baseman moved to right field with the acquisition of Aaron Boone in 2005. Talk about successful transitions. . .Blake teamed with Grady Sizemore and Coco Crisp to provide outstanding outfield defense for Cleveland pitchers. His range was above average and his third-base arm should eventually adapt to outfield throwing. However, he'll likely be just a versatile role player unless his bat improves.

Geoff Jenkins
3-Yr Plus/Minus: +13 in 1241 inn.

2005 Basic P/M: +7

2005 Enhanced P/M: +13 in 1241 inn.
Home: +3 in 627 inn.   RHP: +3 in 767 inn.
Road: +4 in 614 inn.   LHP: +4 in 474 inn.

Jenkins was a career left fielder until 2005 when he moved over to right due to the acquisition of Carlos Lee. Jenkins is a very good defensive outfielder with a solid throwing arm strong enough for right field. He had no problems with the transition and remains a very good defender.

Geoff Jenkins wins our National League Gold Glove That Should Have Been for 2005 over Bobby Abreu. Jenkins' enhanced plus/minus figure of +13 was best in the National League in 2005 among right fielders. He also had the best zone rating in the National League. His 10 baserunner kills tied him for top honors among all major league right fielders with Atlanta's Jeff Francouer. Compare that to Bobby Abreu's -13 enhanced plays and four baserunner kills.

Austin Kearns
3-Yr Plus/Minus: +13 in 1763 inn.

2005 Basic P/M: +6

2005 Enhanced P/M: +7 in 890 inn.
Home: +1 in 430 inn.   RHP: +3 in 605 inn.
Road: +5 in 460 inn.   LHP: +3 in 285 inn.

Kearns is an excellent defender and the best defensive outfielder on the Reds. He has very good range, takes good routes on the ball and has a strong arm. He has enough range to play center field if necessary and his arm is good enough to play in right.

Alexis Rios
3-Yr Plus/Minus: +12 in 2001 inn.

2005 Basic P/M: +2

2005 Enhanced P/M: +1 in 1057 inn.
Home: +3 in 531 inn.   RHP: +6 in 700 inn.
Road: -1 in 526 inn.   LHP: -4 in 357 inn.

Rios is an excellent young defender, a five-tool player with outstanding range and speed and a strong, accurate arm suited for right field. Over his first two seasons his throwing arm ranked second best with a .432 Outfield Advance percentage on the three-year chart. The Jays would love to switch him to center field where he is a better offensive fit, but they have a Gold Glover in Vernon Wells entrenched there.

Jeff Francoeur
3-Yr Plus/Minus: +10 in 589 inn.

2005 Basic P/M: +5

2005 Enhanced P/M: +10 in 589 inn.
Home: +2 in 354 inn.   RHP: +6 in 472 inn.
Road: +3 in 235 inn.   LHP: -1 in 117 inn.

The Braves have a lot of youngsters, but Francoeur is the one who gets most of the press. He is a very good defender with the speed and range to play center and the strong arm needed to play right. In less than half a season, he tied Geoff Jenkins for the major league lead among right fielders in baserunner kills with 10. Impressive. His arm is also extremely accurate; he rarely overthrows the cutoff man. He has great baseball instincts and gets really good jumps on balls hit his way. Francouer is an excellent athlete who turned down a football scholarship at Clemson (defensive back) to play baseball instead.

Magglio Ordonez
3-Yr Plus/Minus: +10 in 2361 inn.

2005 Basic P/M: +1

2005 Enhanced P/M: +3 in 672 inn.
Home: 0 in 357 inn.   RHP: +2 in 443 inn.
Road: +1 in 315 inn.   LHP: -1 in 229 inn.

Ordonez was a solid and skilled outfielder, but he has been slowed by recent knee injuries and hasn't played a full season in two years. He had a solid, very accurate arm and good range, but those skills have probably been diminished by injuries and lack of playing time.

Xavier Nady
3-Yr Plus/Minus: +5 in 943 inn.

2005 Basic P/M: 0

2005 Enhanced P/M: 0 in 82 inn.
Home: 0 in 39 inn.   RHP: 0 in 70 inn.
Road: 0 in 43 inn.   LHP: 0 in 12 inn.

Nady is a jack of all trades. He can play many positions but is not really great defensively anywhere. He can play first base, third base and all three outfield spots. Nady is athletic and has surprising speed for a bigger guy. He has some range—he played 30 games in center field—and could probably be an average defender if he just stayed at one position. His best position is first base (+5 in 44 games at first in 2005), but he'll patrol right field for the Mets this season.

Jay Gibbons
3-Yr Plus/Minus: +3 in 2390 inn.

2005 Basic P/M: +5

2005 Enhanced P/M: +10 in 559 inn.
Home: +2 in 257 inn.   RHP: +2 in 348 inn.
Road: +3 in 302 inn.   LHP: +3 in 211 inn.

Gibbons does not have much speed but he has improved as a fielder and put together a nice year in 2005 with +10 enhanced plays. His range and arm are limited in the outfield. Gibbons' future likely lies at first base.

Right Fielders

Mike Cameron
3-Yr Plus/Minus: +2 in 593 inn.

2005 Basic P/M: 0 | 2005 Enhanced P/M: +2 in 593 inn.
Home: 0 in 371 inn. | RHP: -2 in 436 inn.
Road: 0 in 222 inn. | LHP: +2 in 157 inn.

Cameron was a Gold Glove center fielder who reluctantly slid over to right after the signing of Carlos Beltran. He had some troubles adjusting to right at first (early season injuries may have played a role) but he quickly began to master his new position until a terrible collision with Beltran finished him for the year. Cameron has a good throwing arm which made the position switch work. He will return to his natural center field position with the Padres in 2006.

Shawn Green
3-Yr Plus/Minus: +1 in 2856 inn.

2005 Basic P/M: 0 | 2005 Enhanced P/M: -4 in 1031 inn.
Home: 0 in 530 inn. | RHP: +1 in 753 inn.
Road: 0 in 501 inn. | LHP: -1 in 278 inn.

With the 2004 first base experiment behind him, Green returned to his natural right field position. He even saw some time in center field, which is more of a commentary on Arizona's needs than his skills. He has lost a bit of speed and range over the years and seems stiffer in the field now. His arm is strong, but the results haven't been great over the past three years as he ranks 20th in Outfield Advance percentage and had only five baserunner kills. He was the only qualifying right fielder with zero kills last year. Green was not a good fit at first base and was glad to be back exclusively in the outfield last year.

Nick Swisher
3-Yr Plus/Minus: -2 in 1055 inn.

2005 Basic P/M: +5 | 2005 Enhanced P/M: -1 in 1027 inn.
Home: 0 in 523 inn. | RHP: +3 in 797 inn.
Road: +5 in 504 inn. | LHP: +2 in 230 inn.

Swisher came up through the minors as a center fielder but doesn't have the speed to stick there, so he's relegated to a corner outfield slot. He plays solid defense with excellent effort no matter where he plays. Swisher's best position probably isn't in the outfield, however, but at first base. Scouts say he could be a Gold Glove first baseman if he were to make the switch.

Brian Giles
3-Yr Plus/Minus: -2 in 2603 inn.

2005 Basic P/M: -2 | 2005 Enhanced P/M: -5 in 1220 inn.
Home: -3 in 598 inn. | RHP: -1 in 1063 inn.
Road: +1 in 622 inn. | LHP: -1 in 157 inn.

Giles is a solid defender who makes up for average range and speed by getting good jumps and excellent reads. He doesn't have a strong arm, especially for right field, so he enhances it by charging balls hard and throwing with a quick release. The Yankees briefly considered signing him to play center field this offseason, but his center fielding days are long behind him.

Brad Hawpe
3-Yr Plus/Minus: -5 in 926 inn.

2005 Basic P/M: -2 | 2005 Enhanced P/M: -3 in 693 inn.
Home: -1 in 367 inn. | RHP: 0 in 482 inn.
Road: -1 in 326 inn. | LHP: -2 in 211 inn.

Hawpe played first base in the minors, but as sure as you can say "Todd Helton" he was moved to the outfield in the majors. He has worked hard to learn the outfield, and moving to a position on the same side of the field helped him pick up the ball off the bat easily. He has decent range and his arm is good enough to play right.

Jason Lane
3-Yr Plus/Minus: -5 in 1263 inn.

2005 Basic P/M: -1 | 2005 Enhanced P/M: -4 in 1116 inn.
Home: 0 in 571 inn. | RHP: -3 in 797 inn.
Road: -1 in 545 inn. | LHP: +2 in 319 inn.

Lane is a good outfielder with good speed; he can run down most balls and has a good throwing arm, which plays well in right field. His .432 Outfield Advance percentage ranked him third last year. He's versatile and can play all three outfield slots, but right field is his best fit.

Larry Walker
3-Yr Plus/Minus: -5 in 2356 inn.

2005 Basic P/M: -5 | 2005 Enhanced P/M: -8 in 649 inn.
Home: -7 in 380 inn. | RHP: -4 in 506 inn.
Road: +2 in 269 inn. | LHP: -1 in 143 inn.

The great Larry Walker announced his retirement at the end of the year. Over the past few years, Walker's speed and range had eroded and he had become an average fielder at best. In his prime, however, he had great range, a great arm, great instincts and won seven Gold Gloves.

Aubrey Huff
3-Yr Plus/Minus: -6 in 1638 inn.

2005 Basic P/M: -1 | 2005 Enhanced P/M: -4 in 787 inn.
Home: -1 in 403 inn. | RHP: -4 in 461 inn.
Road: 0 in 384 inn. | LHP: +3 in 326 inn.

The Devil Rays need to either trade Huff or settle on a position for him. He has bounced around from third to first to right field in the last few seasons. He is not very athletic but he can make the routine plays. Huff has limited range in the outfield and while third base may be his best position don't expect much

Jeromy Burnitz
3-Yr Plus/Minus: -7 in 2229 inn.

2005 Basic P/M: -8 | 2005 Enhanced P/M: -4 in 1360 inn.
Home: -1 in 699 inn. | RHP: -4 in 1093 inn.
Road: -7 in 661 inn. | LHP: -4 in 267 inn.

Burnitz was once an above-average fielder but these days is no better than average. He still has a little bit of speed and can play all three outfield positions if needed, but right field is his best position. He plays aggressively at all times and can get worn down and injured. Runners ran easily on him last year as he finished last in baseball with a .629 Outfield Advance percentage against him with only one baserunner kill.

Jermaine Dye
3-Yr Plus/Minus: -7 in 2913 inn.
2005 Basic P/M: -6
2005 Enhanced P/M: -6 in 1235 inn.
Home: 0 in 608 inn.   RHP: -6 in 922 inn.
Road: -6 in 627 inn.   LHP: 0 in 313 inn.

Dye is no longer the elite Gold Glove level right fielder he was a few years ago. He still shows good range, a strong arm and plays above-average defense, but he never completely recovered from the horrible broken leg injury he suffered in the 2001 ALCS.

Emil Brown
3-Yr Plus/Minus: -9 in 1097 inn.
2005 Basic P/M: -5
2005 Enhanced P/M: -9 in 1097 inn.
Home: -2 in 634 inn.   RHP: -5 in 881 inn.
Road: -3 in 463 inn.   LHP: 0 in 216 inn.

Brown has above-average speed, but that doesn't mean he has good range. He is an erratic fielder who plays balls in front of his body well but has trouble going back on the ball. Likewise, he has a strong arm but was last in the American League in throwing in 2005. The Royals moved him to left field at the end of the year.

Bobby Abreu
3-Yr Plus/Minus: -12 in 4132 inn.
2005 Basic P/M: -5
2005 Enhanced P/M: -13 in 1364 inn.
Home: -1 in 710 inn.   RHP: -4 in 1084 inn.
Road: -4 in 654 inn.   LHP: -1 in 280 inn.

Abreu won a Gold Glove in 2005. Wow. Where do we start with this one? The Balls Sticks & Stuff blog (www.ballssticksstuff.com) announced "No, Seriously, They're Giving Him an Award." A reader replied "Did you read that in the Onion?" Another said "That must be why it's so difficult for him to hustle out there—freakin' gold gloves are heavy."

Look, Abreu is a great offensive player who does have good speed, range and a strong throwing arm. However, he is a very conservative defender. He has been accused of having lapses in concentration, fear of diving for balls or running into walls on the warning track, and just not giving a maximum effort in the field. He often gets bad jumps on the ball and in the past has let a lot of balls fall in front of him.

Great batter? Yup. Great fielder? Nope.

Vladimir Guerrero
3-Yr Plus/Minus: -14 in 3224 inn.
2005 Basic P/M: +7
2005 Enhanced P/M: +10 in 1040 inn.
Home: -1 in 593 inn.   RHP: +6 in 879 inn.
Road: +8 in 447 inn.   LHP: +1 in 161 inn.

Guerrero's tools are among the best in the game, but the results aren't always there. He has a cannon arm but he seems to think he can throw out every runner, and he often overthrows the cutoff man. Though opponents fear his arm they will run on him to force throwing errors. He really improved in this department last year as he kept runners in check and only had three errors for the season, his lowest single season total of his career. He's got real speed and above-average range, but he's -14 in enhanced plays made the last three years. After a difficult first year with the Angels in 2004 (-18 plus/minus), he settled in last year, handling seven plays more than the average right fielder (+7 basic plus/minus), saving a total of ten bases (+10 enhanced plus/minus).

Victor Diaz
3-Yr Plus/Minus: -14 in 760 inn.
2005 Basic P/M: -6
2005 Enhanced P/M: -8 in 652 inn.
Home: -5 in 303 inn.   RHP: -4 in 504 inn.
Road: -1 in 349 inn.   LHP: -2 in 148 inn.

Diaz is a converted infielder who switched to the outfield in 2004. He is still learning how to play right field; he has an average arm and can make the routine plays but not much more. He needs more outfield experience to improve his defensive skills, especially his ability to get good jumps and track the ball better. His poor defense could prevent him from becoming an everyday outfielder.

Sammy Sosa
3-Yr Plus/Minus: -14 in 2854 inn.
2005 Basic P/M: -5
2005 Enhanced P/M: -8 in 577 inn.
Home: -6 in 296 inn.   RHP: -4 in 380 inn.
Road: +1 in 281 inn.   LHP: -1 in 197 inn.

Sosa, never a good defensive player, has been in decline for years in the field. Foot and toe injuries in 2005 made Sammy's range even more limited than in the past. With his decline both at bat and in the field, it's just about closing time for Slammin' Sammy.

Matt Lawton
3-Yr Plus/Minus: -15 in 1232 inn.
2005 Basic P/M: -3
2005 Enhanced P/M: -17 in 954 inn.
Home: -3 in 482 inn.   RHP: +2 in 543 inn.
Road: 0 in 472 inn.   LHP: -5 in 411 inn.

Lawton was once a good outfielder with decent range and ability but knee injuries have shortened the ground he can cover. He is now a below-average defender in the outfield.

Jacque Jones
3-Yr Plus/Minus: -16 in 2398 inn.
2005 Basic P/M: -4
2005 Enhanced P/M: -8 in 1080 inn.
Home: -7 in 574 inn.   RHP: -5 in 815 inn.
Road: +3 in 506 inn.   LHP: +1 in 265 inn.

Jones has good speed and athleticism, but he doesn't always get good jumps on balls and ranks 24th in enhanced plays made. Ironically, his throwing has ranked in the top ten the past two years even though he doesn't have a typical right field arm.

Right Fielders

Juan Encarnacion
3-Yr Plus/Minus: -20 in 3540 inn.

2005 Basic P/M: -4

2005 Enhanced P/M: -12 in 1113 inn.
Home: 0 in 555 inn.   RHP: -6 in 763 inn.
Road: -4 in 558 inn.   LHP: +2 in 350 inn.

Encarnacion has the skills, but not the consistency. He has good speed and often makes spectacular catches, but then turns around and botches routine plays. He has a strong arm, but his throws are not always on target.

Craig Monroe
3-Yr Plus/Minus: -22 in 1298 inn.

2005 Basic P/M: -9

2005 Enhanced P/M: -18 in 632 inn.
Home: -8 in 328 inn.   RHP: -5 in 372 inn.
Road: -1 in 304 inn.   LHP: -4 in 260 inn.

Monroe is a versatile outfielder who played all three outfield positions in 2005. He saw the most action in right. He gets decent jumps on the ball and has good speed and range for a corner outfielder. He can handle center field in a pinch. But his -18 enhanced plays in right field last year were second worst to Gary Sheffield's -25. He did improve in the error department, dropping down to six errors after struggling with 11 in 2004.

Gary Sheffield
3-Yr Plus/Minus: -38 in 3566 inn.

2005 Basic P/M: -20

2005 Enhanced P/M: -25 in 1099 inn.
Home: -10 in 579 inn.   RHP: -18 in 803 inn.
Road: -10 in 520 inn.   LHP: -2 in 296 inn.

Sheffield's best defensive tool is his strong arm. He doesn't offer much range and plays very conservatively, which is why he is last among all right fielders in enhanced plays made. As one scout says, he "turns outs into outs."

Relative Range Factors

Bill James

One of the first published articles of my career was about Range Factors. It was in the March, 1976, edition of the Baseball Digest, and ran under the title of "Big League Fielding Statistics *Do* Make Sense". "What we should be looking at," I wrote, "is not the number of plays the fielder *doesn't* make but the number he *does*."

Range Factors, for those of you who skipped the first thirty years of the discussion, are simply the number of plays per game made by a fielder—putouts, plus assists, divided by games played. There are no range factors for catchers or first basemen, but I think that the number of plays made by players at the other positions gives some indication of their defensive range. I think. I'm not too optimistic about it.

In the 1976 article, I was too optimistic about it, but then I didn't have time for subtlety. Of course it is intuitively obvious that a good fielder should make more plays per game than a lousy fielder, a fence post, a gravestone or Emil Brown, but there are numerous problems with the category. The problems include:

1) It doesn't adjust for defensive innings. Deivi Cruz played 147 games at shortstop in 2002, and 147 in 2003—but he played a hundred more innings in 2003 than he had in 2002. Not surprisingly, Cruz made far more plays in 2003 than he had in 2002, which doesn't necessarily prove that he was a better shortstop in 2003 than he was in 2002.

2) It doesn't adjust for strikeouts. Chicago Cub pitchers last year struck out 1,256 batters; Detroit Tiger pitchers struck out 907. Not surprisingly, the Tigers' second basemen, third basemen and shortstops made more plays than the Cub players at the same positions. Again, there is a serious outside influence which affects the legitimacy of the statistic.

3) It doesn't adjust for the groundball tendency of the pitching staff. Arizona Diamondback pitchers had more strikeouts in 2005 than Washington Nationals' pitchers—but they also threw more than 200 more groundballs than Nationals' pitchers.

Obviously, this has an impact on the range factors of the infielders and the outfielders who play behind these men.

4) It doesn't adjust for the left/right tendencies of the pitching staff. When a team puts a left-handed pitcher on the mound, the other team responds by using more right-handed hitters. This results in more groundballs being hit to third base, which has a significant impact on the range factors of the third basemen, and, to a lesser extent, the other infielders.

5) It doesn't adjust for team defense. Every team makes 27 putouts a game, whether they field like a team of Adam Everetts or a team of Jason Giambis. The overall range factor of a bad team is the same as the overall range factor of a good team.

Over the years, I have made some tentative efforts to correct Range Factors for these biases. Here, since John Dewan is writing a whole book about fielding and fielding statistics, I thought perhaps it was time to take on the challenge of creating a "new" range factor which adjusts for all of these problems.

The question could be asked, "Since Range Factors are inherently flawed, since you are never going to be able to correct perfectly for the biases in the data, why figure them at all? Since we have now much better and more precise ways of looking at the question of defensive range, why try to update this outmoded approximation?"

There are two answers to this question. First, looking at an issue in multiple ways is usually better than looking at it in just one way. I have one way of figuring runs created; Pete Palmer has a vastly different approach, but it gets essentially the same answers 99% of the time. This is good. If you look at the issue two different ways and you get the same answer both times, you're more certain that you're right. If you look at the question a different way and you get a different answer, why? Does one of the methods not work as well as you thought it did?

Second, Relative Range Factors can be reconstructed back to 1876. Dewan's Plus/Minus System, as good as it is, only exists for modern players. Zone ratings date back only fifteen or twenty years. If we can develop a different method which gives results which are consistent with these newer and better methods, then we're in a better position to evaluate the defensive contribution of Rogers Hornsby and Honus Wagner and the other 10,000 guys who played before we had all this wondrous modern technology.

OK, how do we re-design Range Factors to remove these biases? The essential process is as follows:
1) Estimate for each player his *expected* Assists.
2) Estimate for each player his expected Putouts.
3) Add those together.
4) Divide his actual total by his expected total.
5) Multiply by his team's Defensive Efficiency Record (DER).
6) Divide by the league DER.

To walk you through the process, I'll use Ozzie Smith, with the 1982 Cardinals, and Wilfredo Cordero, with the 1995 Montreal Expos. This is going to get boring in a minute. . .sorry. I'll put in a sub-heading below, "The Math is Done", so that if your eyes start to glaze over you can just skip ahead to that point. The process I am outlining here is specifically for shortstops. The process for other positions is essentially the same, but the adjustments are somewhat different. And I don't know that I'm going to explain them all for every position, because there is just some realistic limit to how much math John can put in the book. Anyway:

Step One: Estimating the player's Expected Assists.
1. Start with the league assists total.
2. Subtract assists by outfielders and assists by catchers.
3. Figure what percentage of the remaining assists were recorded by shortstops.
4. Take the team assist total.
5. Subtract assists by the team's outfielders and catchers.
6. Multiply that by the league percentage (3 above).
7. Figure out how many innings of left-handed pitching the team had.
8. Figure the league average.
9. For each 25 innings that the team is above or below the league average, add one expected assist for the shortstop.
10. Multiply the total after (9) by the innings played or the estimated innings played by this shortstop.
11. Divide by the total innings played by the team.

Ozzie Smith, 1982. After going through steps 1-6 above, you would conclude that the Cardinal shortstops in 1982 had an expectation of 589 assists. The Cardinals that year, however, had only three left-handed pitchers, who pitched only 294 innings, against a league average of 383. (That's actually not the league *average*, exactly. . .it is the league percentage of innings pitched which were pitched by left-handers, multiplied by the Cardinals' innings pitched.) Anyway, the Cardinals had 89.47 fewer innings by left-handed pitchers than expected.

Divide that by 25; that's 3.58. . .yes, I know it's piddly-wash, but we have to do it because one time in a thousand it matters. This reduces the expected assists by St. Louis shortstops in 1982 to 585.

We know from Retrosheet that Ozzie Smith played 1,249 innings at shortstop for the Cardinals that year. The team total was 1,465.1 innings.

Multiplying by one and dividing by the other, we could have expected Ozzie Smith in 1982 to have recorded 499 assists. In fact, he recorded 535 assists—36 more than expected.

Wilfredo Cordero, 1995. The Expos in 1995, with a strike-shortened schedule and a flyball staff, could have been expected to have only 437 assists by shortstops. The Expos that year, however, had 573 innings pitched by left-handed pitchers, which was almost twice the league average, over the average by 241 innings. Dividing that by 25, that increases their expected assists by shortstops to 447.

The Expos that year played 1283.2 innings, of which Cordero played 928.2 at short. Cordero, then, could have been expected to record 309 assists as a shortstop—447, times 928.67, divided by 1283.67. In fact, he recorded 280 assists—29 fewer than expected.

A note about figuring these historically, if you're into that. Before 1914, teams platooned very little or not at all. . .thus, left-handed pitching is not really relevant. For all times prior to 1914, the "left-handed pitching" adjustment should be zero.

Step Two: Estimating the player's Expected Putouts.
1. Start with the league putouts total.
2. Subtract strikeouts (since strikeouts result in "phony putouts" by catchers).
3. Subtract putouts by outfielders (flyballs).
4. Subtract assists by third basemen and shortstops. We will call the result "remaining putouts". (We are trying to estimate the pool of putouts from which this shortstop claims his share. Since assists rarely go 5-6

and never go 6-6, assists by shortstops and third basemen create putouts which are not a part of the pool from which the shortstop draws.)

5. Figure the percentage of those remaining putouts which are recorded by shortstops.

6. Repeat points 1-4 for the player's team.

7. Multiply the league percentage (5) by the team remaining putouts (6).

8. For each 90 innings above or below the league average of left-handed innings, SUBTRACT one expected putout.

9. Figure the team's Estimated Runners on First Base, above or below the league average. (I'll explain later, when I walk through the Ozzie Smith/Wilfredo Cordero example.)

10. For each 25 estimated runners on first base above or below the league norm, add one expected putout for the shortstop.

11. Multiply the total after (10) by the innings played or the estimated innings played by this shortstop.

12. Divide by the total innings played by the team.

We'll walk through Ozzie Smith, 1982, and Wilfredo Cordero, 1995, to illustrate the process. There were 52,630 league putouts in 1982, 54,168 in 1995. From this, we will subtract league strikeouts, putouts by outfielders, assists by third basemen, and assists by shortstops.

	Ozzie, 1982	Cordero, 1995
League Putouts	52,630	54,168
Strikeouts	10,300	13,309
Putouts by Outfielders	12,725	12,529
Assists by Third Basemen	3,966	4,198
Assists by Shortstops	6,365	6,121
Remaining Putouts	19,274	18,011

In the NL in 1982, 17.6% of the "remaining putouts" were recorded by shortstops; in the NL in 1995, 16.2%.

We then repeat the steps above, but for each player's *team.*

	Ozzie, 1982	Cordero, 1995
Team Putouts	4,396	3,851
Strikeouts	689	950
Putouts by Outfielders	1,060	865
Assists by Third Basemen	380	330
Assists by Shortstops	627	404
Remaining Putouts	1,640	1,302

Ozzie is drawing putouts from a pool of 1,640 plays, of which the league norm suggests he should have 17.6%. This creates an initial expectation, for St. Louis Cardinal shortstops, 1982, of 289 putouts

The 1982 Cardinals, as noted above, were 89.47 innings below the league norm for left-handed innings. . .divide that by 90, and you have some number real close to one, so that increases their expected putouts by about one.

The Cardinals also had very slightly more opposition runners on first base than the league average, and more runners on first base means more putouts for shortstops and second basemen. We estimate the opposition runners on first base by this formula:

(H-HR)*.781 + BB + HBP - WP - BK - PB - SB - CS

Figure that number for the 1982 Cardinals, and it figures out to 7.83 runners on first per nine innings, as opposed to a league average of 7.82. They were over expectation by 1.32 baserunners for the season. Divide that by 25, and it figures out to. . .well, nothing, but we still have to do it because sometimes it might matter. The Cardinal shortstops in 1982 have an expectation of 290 putouts.

Cordero in '95 is drawing putouts from a pool of 1,302 plays, of which the league norm suggests he should have 16.2%. This creates an initial expectation, for Montreal shortstops, 1995, of 211.3 putouts.

The Expos had 241 more innings by left-handed pitchers than the league norm, which decreases their expected putouts by shortstops by about two and a half. The Expos pitchers that year had very good control, so the Expos had 7.84 runners on first base per nine innings as opposed to a league norm of 8.39. . .they were 78 opposition runners below average. Dividing that by 25, that takes away another 3+ expected putouts for Montreal shortstops. Making those adjustments, we have Montreal shortstops in 1995 with an expectation of 205.5 putouts.

Cardinal shortstops in 1982 had an expectation of 290 putouts, and Ozzie played 1,249 of the team's 1,465.1 defensive innings. Ozzie, then, could have been expected to record 247 putouts. He actually recorded 279 putouts—32 more than expected.

Montreal shortstops in 1995 had an expectation of 205.5 putouts, and Cordero played 928.2 of 1283.2 defensive innings. Wilfredo could have been expected to record 149 putouts. He actually recorded only 124 putouts—25 less than expected.

From here on the process is quick and easy:

3) Add the putouts and assists together.

4) Divide his actual total by his expected total.

5) Multiply by the team's Defensive Efficiency Record (DER).

6) Divide by the league DER.

There are slightly different versions of DER around, but the figures I have are .719 for the St. Louis Cardinals in 1982, against a league average of .708.

For Ozzie Smith, 1982, then, this creates:

$$\frac{(279 + 535) * .719}{(247.12 + 498.91) * .708} = 1.107 \text{ Relative Range Factor}$$

For Wilfredo Cordero, 1995, this creates:

$$\frac{(124 + 280) * .692}{(148.67 + 309.07) * .693} = .881 \text{ Relative Range Factor}$$

Ozzie Smith in 1982 was +80, meaning that he made an estimated 80 plays more than an average shortstop would have made—a very high number. Cordero in 1995 was -54. This is figured as follows:

(Relative Range - 1) * (Expected Putouts + Expected Assists)

I have been asked why we multiply the player's range factor by the team and divide by the league. The reason we have to do this is that, unless we do this, we might evaluate the players on a good defensive team as being the same as the players on a bad defensive team. We have figured so far the range for each player *relative to his team*, relative to the plays available. In 2005 the Philadelphia Phillies had a team mostly of players with good range; the New York Yankees had a team of players with very limited range. If we didn't make this DER adjustment, we might evaluate them as just the same, since we would be evaluating each player relative to the plays available on his own team.

What I worry about with the DER adjustment is that I may be doing it wrong. Let's say the best team in the league gets 72 outs out of 100 balls in play—a .720 DER—the average team 70 outs (.700), the weakest team 68 outs for a .680 DER. Measured the way I have constructed this adjustment, the best defensive team is 5.9% better than the weakest defensive team—.720 versus .680. But is that right? Measured by the hits

they will allow, you get a different answer: that the weakest defensive team is 14% worse than the best defensive team (.320 versus .280). Isn't that really the more relevant criteria, how many more hits they are allowing? Aren't the players on the "good" defensive team really 14% better than those on the bad defensive team, rather than 5.9%?

I kind of think they are, but I'm not exactly sure what the best way to handle the situation is, so I decided to use the more cautious approach. I suspect that the larger adjustment might be more accurate, but I'll wait and see what other people think when they see the method, I guess.

The Math is Done

Ozzie Smith in 1982 was +80, meaning that he made an estimated 80 plays more than an average shortstop would have made—a very impressive number. Cordero in 1995 was -54. He never played an inning at shortstop after that season.

At the start of the article I cited five problems with Range Factor:

1) It doesn't adjust for defensive innings.

2) It doesn't adjust for strikeouts.

3) It doesn't adjust for the groundball tendency of the pitching staff.

4) It doesn't adjust for the left/right tendencies of the pitching staff.

5) It doesn't adjust for team defense.

As recently as six years ago, in *Win Shares*, I argued against trying to estimate defensive innings, but the problem of defensive innings is nothing like it used to be, in large part because of Retrosheet. . .we have actual defensive innings going back to 1960, and we have learned to estimate defensive innings well enough now to minimize that problem when we don't have them.

We have dodged the problem with strikeouts by stating plays made relative to the team. If the team has more strikeouts, that creates lower expectations for the fielders.

We have adjusted for the groundball tendency of the pitching staff by using team assists to project expected assists. When a team records a groundball out, most of the time—90% of the time—there is an assist on that play. Conversely, most of a team's assists—90% of them, or something like that—result from groundballs. Thus, the team's assists total is so closely linked to the groundball tendency of the pitching staff that the team assists total may be used as a stand-in for the groundball tendency. This is essentially what we have done here.

We had adjusted for the left/right bias of the pitching staff, and we have adjusted for the overall quality of the defense by using DER. Thus, we have at least made a good faith effort to remove all of these biases from the statistic. We have also made an adjustment for another incidental bias, which is the tendency of shortstops to get more putouts if the other team has more runners on base. Thus, we believe that the relative range factor should be relatively free of the problems that limit the usefulness of the raw range factor.

But Does It Work?

Ah, there's the $64,000 question. . .does the damn thing actually work? Have we, by making all of these adjustments, made range factors into a reliable instrument for evaluating fielders, or have we simply removed five barriers to seeing the truth about fielders, while eight others stand unmoved in front of us?

It probably isn't appropriate for me to try to evaluate my own work; I might better leave that to others. For what it is worth, it seems to me that there are three essential tests of whether or not a fielding statistic "works", which are:

1) Does it deliver results consistent with the observations of informed observers?

2) Does it make assessments of defensive performance consistent with other statistical tools? And

3) Internal consistency. Do players who do well one year tend to do well the following season?

There are some other things. . .for example, does it correlate with winning? We usually test the validity of a statistic by whether or not it correlates with winning, but

a) The extent to which a team wins because their shortstop has good range is so limited that it would not be easy to detect even if you started with a perfect measure of shortstop's range, and

b) We may have polluted the environment by using DER, which does correlate with winning, as an element of our relative range formula—thus, our data might correlate with winning even if the method didn't actually measure range.

Also, one would expect that, for example, 25-year-old shortstops would have better range than 35-year-old shortstops, and we will test for that. On a certain level, I think there are some problems with fielding stats that aren't going to go away no matter what you do. Brooks

Robinson in 1966, winning the Gold Glove as he always did, had only 313 assists in 157 games. In 1967 he had 405 assists in 158 games. If you look at the data for his team, there is no apparent reason for the upward spike. . .*something* happened, but one can't really explain what it was. Evaluating his defense by the statistics, it seems impossible to avoid the conclusion that he was a very different fielder in 1967 than he had been in 1966. But why?

Perhaps we shouldn't worry about this. After all, if we look at his batting record, Brooksie had a great year in 1962 (.303 with 23 homers, 86 RBI) and an MVP year in 1964 (.317 with 28 and 118), but a very poor season the year in between (.251 with 11 homers, 67 RBI, playing every game.) There's no real explanation for it; batting statistics just bounce up and down, and sometimes they bounce big. Shouldn't we expect the same thing to happen in fielding statistics?

We should, but also, what reason is there to believe that the random factors in fielding stats are on the same scale as those in batting? Maybe they're larger; maybe they're smaller. My point is that there may be some randomness there that we're just not going to get away from. Only by presenting consistent metrics over a long period of time can fielding statistics acquire what batting and pitching statistics have long since acquired: the powers of language. The ability to *describe* the player's skills.

Anyway, as a first step toward nailing down the value of Relative Range Factors, I figured the Relative Range Factors for every season of their career for every shortstop who ever won a Gold Glove award. There have been 97 Gold Gloves for shortstops. . .two per season, 1958-2005, plus one in 1957. Those 97 awards have been won by 36 different shortstops, whose careers total 515 seasons with at least one inning at shortstop. . .actually, not 515 different seasons, because when a player plays for two teams in one season, that shows up in my data as two lines of data. It's actually 490 seasons or something.

Anyway, I thought that, as a first step to evaluating the data, I would look at Gold Glove seasons, and at the career performance of Gold Glove shortstops. If we found that the Gold Glove shortstops had relative range factors of 1.000 or less, this would strongly suggest that the method didn't work, since this would mean that the players perceived as the best in the league at the position had only average relative range factors.

Over the course of their careers, the 36 Gold Glove-winning shortstops have a Relative Range Factor of

1.015, making them 4,123 plays better than average. The Gold Glove shortstops had an average expectation, for every season of their careers, of 177 putouts, 325 assists. They actually produced 181 putouts, 329 assists, making them +8 in an average season, a figure which is increased slightly because the Defensive Efficiency of the teams on which they played was .709 against an average of .707.

Focusing strictly on the 97 Gold Glove seasons, the award-winning shortstops:

- Had a Relative Range Factor of 1.034.
- Exceeded expectation by 2,205 plays.
- Exceeded expectation by an average of 9 putouts and 10 assists per season.
- Played for teams with an average DER of .711, as opposed to .707, and
- Scored, on the average, at +23.

However, not all of the Gold Glove shortstops show in the stats as having good range. 68 of the 97 shortstops score as having better-than-league average range; 29 score as below average. The 29 awards to players with average or below-average range could be caused by any of the following:

1. The award was given to an undeserving fielder.

2. The award winner may have been outstanding in some area of defensive play other than range.

3. The Relative Range Factor may not have been an accurate statement of the fielder's actual range, either because of park effects, because of unknown and undocumented biases in the data, or because random perturbations in the data obscured the player's ability.

Ultimately, it will be up to you to decide how much stock you wish to put in each of those three explanations. I doubt that very many people believe that the Gold Glove voters *always* choose a good defensive player. I suspect that most people know that the voting system isn't all that well designed, and that sometimes the voters are just sort of playing Pin the Glove on the Donkey. At the same time, I doubt that the Relative Range Factor is an accurate analysis in 100% of the cases, either. It seems clear that there ARE random fluctuations in the data large enough to cause a player to look bad sometimes when he isn't, or to look good sometimes when he isn't.

In any case, we can safely assert that there is a very significant degree of agreement between Gold Glove selections and high Relative Range Factors at shortstop.

After doing this study, I realized that I should study as well some "ordinary" shortstops, some non-Gold Glove winners, to see how they compared to the Gold Glovers. Using the Sabermetric Encyclopedia, I drew up a list of the 100 players who had played the most games at shortstop in the years 1960-2005, and went down that list picking off the top ten players who never won a Gold Glove award, and then there were some other guys later on the list that I was wondering about, so that list grew to include 17 players, whose careers I then studied in the same way that I had studied the Gold Glovers.

But that list was mostly comprised of players who, while they didn't happen to win a Gold Glove, were nonetheless widely recognized as quality defensive players. . .they just happened to get stuck behind Ozzie Smith or Mark Belanger or somebody, and never quite got past them. That list included Garry Templeton, Greg Gagne, Tim Foli, Royce Clayton, Bucky Dent, Shawon Dunston, Dick Schofield, Spike Owen, Freddie Patek. . .guys who were certainly pretty good defensive players.

So then I went looking for another list of players. . .what I called "failed shortstops", who were guys who had careers of only 500-999 games although they hit pretty well for shortstops. I went looking for ten of those guys, and of course I wound up with twelve of them. . .this is how a simple little research project winds up consuming three days of your life.

Altogether, I wound up with Relative Range Factors for 889 shortstop seasons:

97 Gold Glove seasons,
418 other seasons by Gold Glove shortstops,
260 seasons by long-term shortstops who never won the award, and
114 seasons by short-term shortstops who hit pretty well.

These 889 seasons were turned in by 65 different players. The ten best shortstops in that group, in terms of career plus or minus plays, are:

Player (Years)	Innings	Rel RF	Plus Plays
Ozzie Smith (1978-1996)	21,785.2	1.052	+621
Dave Concepcion (1970-1988)	18,380.0	1.052	+508
Mark Belanger (1965-1982)	15,337.1	1.056	+505
Garry Templeton (1976-1991)	16,747.0	1.048	+465
Barry Larkin (1986-2004)	17,554.2	1.045	+414
Ozzie Guillen (1985-2000)	15,802.2	1.046	+375
Bud Harrelson (1965-1980)	11,509.2	1.059	+374
Tony Fernandez (1983-1997)	13.464.1	1.050	+354
Roy McMillan (1951-1966)	16,935.0	1.035	+338
Rick Burleson (1974-1986)	10,333.0	1.051	+275

I think that's a reasonable list of the greatest defensive shortstops of the last fifty years. Luis Aparicio would have made the list, but he was -125 over his last five seasons, and dropped off the list, and Dal Maxvill would have made the list if we had ranked players by Relative Range Factors, rather than the +/-, but Maxvill didn't have as many innings as these guys.

In terms of individual seasons, these are the best that we found:

Player	Year	Team	Range	Rel Range	+/-
Dave Concepcion	1976	Reds	5.56	1.171	+119
Bud Harrelson	1971	Mets	5.12	1.162	+99
Garry Templeton	1980	Cardinals	6.12	1.163	+95
Ozzie Guillen	1988	White Sox	5.58	1.122	+91
Walt Weiss	1988	A's	4.97	1.147	+89
Cal Ripken	1984	Orioles	5.50	1.107	+87
Barry Larkin	1991	Reds	5.22	1.166	+85
Ozzie Smith	1980	Padres	5.85	1.100	+83
Ozzie Guillen	1986	White Sox	4.90	1.125	+82
Ozzie Smith	1982	Cardinals	5.87	1.107	+80
Ozzie Guillen	1987	White Sox	5.17	1.118	+80
Maury Wills	1960	Dodgers	5.10	1.129	+80

If asked this question: Do you really believe that Dave Concepcion in 1976 made 119 plays that would otherwise have been hits for the opposition, my answer would be "absolutely not". There are three problems with assuming that to be true:

1) It ignores random surges in the data, when there is reason to believe that the number of balls which are hit to the shortstop is subject to significant random variation.

2) It is not likely that all of these plays made are plays which would otherwise be hits. It is more likely that some of them are plays which would otherwise be made by another fielder, and also, remember that we are counting putouts **and** assists, some of which might better be regarded as half-plays than whole plays.

3) There is no independent evidence that a shortstop can make 119 plays in a season which would otherwise

go unmade. It's a fairly remarkable assertion, and one is naturally reluctant to accept a remarkable assertion without independent verification.

One of the tests of a meaningful statistic is internal consistency. It is quite apparent—beyond needing proof—that the data does have a very high degree of internal consistency.

Barry Larkin, in his first six years as a regular shortstop, is +25, +52, +67, +72, +85 and +55. In his last five years, 2000-2004, he is -13, -7, -7, -11 and -13.

Bud Harrelson in five consecutive years is +29, +33, +71, +35 and +99. Then, after one bad year, he is +72.

Cal Ripken at ages 21 to 23 is +29, +48 and +87. In his last four years at shortstop he is -36, -39, -35 and -42.

Dal Maxvill in consecutive seasons is +46, +52, +29, +68 and +58.

Dave Concepcion, in consecutive seasons, is +37, +37, +50, +75, +119, +61, +34 and +69. Then, after one bad year, he is +45, +46 and +27.

Edgar Renteria, the last three seasons, has been -24, -31 and -49.

Another contemporary shortstop, whose name I won't bring up right now, has had consecutive seasons in which he was -34, -38, -71, -46, -61, -92 and -74.

Freddie Patek, in consecutive seasons, was +51, +53 and +54.

Garry Templeton, in three consecutive seasons as a young player, was +72, +71 and +95.

Greg Gagne, in consecutive seasons with two different teams, was +52, +38 and +31. Kurt Stillwell, in consecutive seasons, was -55, -74, -63 and -44. Those seasons were with the Royals, 1988-1991; Gagne's +38 and +31 were with the Royals in 1993-94.

Larry Bowa, despite a very good defensive reputation including two Gold Gloves, had negative numbers in every season of his career except one, and had a stretch of seasons late in his career in which he was -59, -57, -83 and -40.

Larvell Blanks, in consecutive seasons of limited playing time, was -37, -22 and -21.

Luis Aparicio, in consecutive seasons, was +75, +38, +56 and +18.

Mark Belanger, in six consecutive seasons, was +71, +35, +36, +48, +50 and +29. Then, after one so-so season, he had four consecutive seasons of +67, +35, +65 and +50.

Ozzie Guillen, his first six seasons as a regular, was +82, +80, +91, +63, +43 and +65. There are only twelve seasons in our data in which a shortstop was +80.

Guillen did it three straight seasons. After his injury in 1992 he played another eight seasons, but was never more than +4, and was usually in the red.

Ozzie Smith, in consecutive seasons, was +37, +31, +83, +54, +80, +42, +42 and +65. Even as an old player, he was great, but less consistent due to injuries. At ages 37 and 38 he was +59 and +58.

Rick Burleson, in his first seven seasons as a regular, was +42, +35, +23, +52, +51, +22 and +49. After his injury in '82 he was never better than -3.

Roy McMillan, the first Gold Glove winner at shortstop, had consecutive seasons in which he was +47, +38, +48, +52, +72, +32, +51 and +23.

Royce Clayton, as a young man, had consecutive seasons in which he was +46, +47, +42 and +37. In his last three seasons (2003-2005) he has been -27, -68 and -50.

Walt Weiss, after a couple of brilliant seasons early in his career, had consecutive seasons later in his career, playing for three different teams, in which he was -52, -11, -24, -70, -21, -29 and -17.

Overall, taking all the players in this study who were +50 or better in a season (there were 77 of them). . .those players averaged in the following season +32, and, in the season following that, +31. Taking all of the players who were +20 to +49 in a season, those players averaged +16 in the following season, and +16 again in the season after that.

On the other hand, taking the players who were MINUS 50 or more in one season. . .those players averaged -21 in the next season, and -14 in the season after that. The players who were -20 to -49 in any season averaged -7 the following season, and -3 the season after that (the numbers shrinking rapidly because the players tended to lose playing time.)

Internal consistency, by itself, does not prove accuracy. The data could be internally consistent because of persistant biases in the data which we have not yet identified or learned to correct for. But it is very clear that there is a high degree of internal consistency in the data.

A couple of other notes: the twelve players I identified who were fairly good hitters for shortstops but had short careers anyway were Eddie Bressoud, Wayne Causey, U L Washington, Andre Rodgers, Larvell Blanks, Dick Howser, Luis Aguayo, Bob Johnson, Kurt Stillwell, Bobby Valentine, Dave Anderson and Roberto Pena. All of these players scored as having below-average range (sub zero) for their careers except Causey; Causey came out +42 for his career.

Also, one argument which is frequently heard on behalf of Larry Bowa is, "couldn't Bowa's range numbers have been depressed by all of those years playing next to Mike Schmidt? Couldn't Schmidt's exceptional range have meant that there were fewer plays left for Bowa to make?"

This argument is clearly untrue, for several reasons:

1) There are many parallel situations on other teams. Mark Belanger played for twelve years beside Brooks Robinson. Both Robinson and Belanger compiled outstanding range numbers, side by side, throughout most of that period.

2) Bowa's negative numbers are larger than Schmidt's positive numbers. Add them together, they're in the red. That can't be explained as one great defensive player playing next to another.

3) Bowa had six seasons in his career when he was not Schmidt's teammate at all. Add in the 1972 season, when Schmidt played just 11 games at third as a late-season callup, and we have seven seasons in which Bowa was not next to Schmidt.

In his nine seasons in which he was next to Schmidt, 1973-1982, Bowa's plus/minus range total is -297, an average of -33. But in his seven seasons in which he was not next to Schmidt, his total is -169, an average of -24. Schmidt may have contributed to this score on some small level, but Mike Schmidt is not the reason that Bowa does not rate well as a shortstop.

For the sake of clarity, I am not saying that these numbers prove Bowa to have been a poor shortstop. Many people who saw him play thought that he was a superb shortstop; I am sure that what they saw was real and meaningful. But if his range was good or even adequate, then there is some glitch or bias in our data which we are as yet unable to remove.

Defensive Range by Age

I sorted the data so that I could compare shortstops by age. 63 of the 65 shortstops in the study were active at age 27. At age 27 the 63 shortstops were an aggregate +853 plays, an average of +13, had an average zone rating of 1.023, and 39 of the 63 were in the black. This was the best defensive performance at any one age.

Overall, the players began to lose range after age 30, and slowed down considerably after age 35:

Group	Relative Range	Average Plus/Minus
Up to Age 24	1.014	+6
Ages 25-29	1.014	+7
Ages 30-34	1.008	+3
Ages 35 and up	.985	-5

There's another pattern which is harder to show, which is that rookie seasons and seasons by very young players tend to have low numbers. If we could pull those out of the chart above, the highest Relative Range would be by the youngest group.

This last group includes a fluke season by Ozzie Smith in 1996, aged 41, his last year in the majors. Ozzie played only 53 games, 442 innings that year, but scores at +41! Obviously there is some sort of fluke there; even Ozzie isn't *that* good. It may be that Ozzie was being used by LaRussa mostly behind the Cardinals' groundball pitchers, or it may be that he played only a part of the season and that the Cardinal pitching staff was different in that portion of the season than it was the rest of the year, I don't know. At some point in the future, analysis of Retrosheet data will explain this phenomenon.

Relative Range by Playing Time

I sorted these 889 seasons by playing time, into four groups:

1300 or more innings (full time regulars)
1000 to 1299.2 innings (near regulars)
400 to 999.2 innings (part-time players)
Less than 400 innings (limited playing time)

The groups were defined to create about even numbers of players in each group. This study showed that these 65 players had dramatically better range in those seasons in which they played regularly than in those seasons in which they played less regularly:

Group	Relative Range	Average Plus/Minus
1300 or More Innings	1.016	+12
1000 - 1299.2 Innings	1.012	+8
400 - 999.2 innings	1.008	+3
Less than 400 Innings	.967	-2

Cautions and Conclusions

Based on these studies, I think we may safely state the following things:

1) That those shortstops commonly recognized as being defensively outstanding generally, but not universally, have good Relative Range Factors.

2) That Relative Range Factors have a good deal of internal consistency,

3) That players have better Relative Range Factors when they are young than when they are older.

4) That players have better Relative Range Factors in those seasons when they are regulars than in those seasons in which they are not regulars.

However, there is a great deal that remains unknown about these new numbers, these Relative Range Factors.

1) I have not yet studied systematically how Relative Range Factors match up against John Dewan's new and more sophisiticated range data.

2) We have, as yet, no ability to translate plus and minus plays into runs saved or runs allowed in any manner which is anything but wildly speculative.

3) Relative Range Factors can be meaningful in the aggregate without being very meaningful in specific cases. Suppose that there are two outstanding shortstops, equally outstanding, but that one scores at +80, the other at zero, and that there are two horrible shortstops, equally horrible, but that one scores at -80 and the other at zero. In the aggregate, the data is meaningful; the good shortstops average +40; the bad shortstops average -40. But in specific cases, the data is unreliable, because it fails in one case to see any distinction between an outstanding shortstop and a horrible one.

4) There is a good deal of internal consistency in the data, but there is also enough bouncing up and down to give us considerable pause to reflect. Let's look at a few examples:

Neifi Perez was +69 with the Colorado Rockies in 2000, and was +50 with the Cubs last year (2005). In the interim, however, he was +24, -1, +16 and +7. What happened?

This isn't an example that concerns us a lot, because it is consistent with other observations about Perez. . .he played great with Colorado at one time, he played great with the Cubs last year, and in between those seasons he didn't do squat. Still, as we have observed the internal consistency in our own data, we should take note of the inconsistency.

Alan Trammell was +35 in 1981, but -47 in 1980. He was +37 in 1986, +28 in 1988 and +29 in 1989, but he was -25 in 1985, -2 in 1984, when the Tigers won 108 games, and -5 in 1987, when many people believe that he should have been the American League's Most Valuable Player. Why?

There may be some reasonable explanation for this. Trammell did have periodic shoulder problems throughout his career, which could explain some ups and downs. Still, this seems somewhat puzzling.

Alfredo Griffin was +45 with the Dodgers in 1990 and +47 in 1991, but -6 in 1989. Why?

Bert Campaneris was +55 with the A's in 1972, +56 in 1973 and +30 in 1974. In '75 and '76, however, he was +2 and +/-0. Moving to the Rangers in 1977, he rebounded to +69. Why? How can he have been that good in '72, '73, '74, and '77, but average in '75 and '76? There may be an explanation for it, but I don't know what it is.

Bill Russell, who was negative for most of the rest of his career, was +47 in 1978. Why?

Bucky Dent was +48 with the Yankees in 1978, and was always in the black with the Yankees except in 1981, when he was -10. On joining the Rangers in 1982, he was -27 and -71 his first two seasons in Texas. Why?

Again, this example does not especially concern me, as it does tell a story consistent with Dent's career. He was older in Texas than in New York, he had been slipping at the end of his New York career, and his career did end quickly after his very low relative range factors in Texas. Still, there is a lack of consistency in this data.

Chris Speier was +36 with the Expos in 1978, +36 again in 1979—but he was -43 with the Giants in 1976. Why? It seems to me that there may have been an injury there, but a swing of almost 80 plays does call for some sort of explanation.

Dave Anderson, a limited-range player the rest of his career, was +26 with the Dodgers in 1988.

Dick Howser was -54 with the Kansas City A's in 1961, but +38 with Cleveland in 1964. He was a rookie in 1961, and there is a "rookie effect" apparent in the data, but still, a swing of 92 plays seems fairly remarkable.

Dick Schofield was +56 with the Angels in 1986, -13 in 1987.

Eddie Bressoud was +49 with the Red Sox in 1962, but -42 in 1964.

Freddie Patek was -60 with the Pirates in 1969, but +18 with them as a part-time player in 1970, and +50 or more the next three seasons with the Royals.

These sort of large swings in the data—80, 90, 100 plays between seasons—have to give us great concern in relying too much upon the data. There appear to be random "waves" in the data which are easily large enough to make a good defensive player look bad or a bad defensive player look good for at least a couple of years.

Further, while it is *generally* true that those players regarded as outstanding defensively have good Relative Range Factors, it is not always true. Don Kessinger, the National League's Gold Glove shortstop in 1970 and 1971, is -251 in his career, including -64 in 1966 and -71 in 1975. Granted, he was just breaking in in 1966, and the Cubs did move him out after 1975, but still, we would certainly have expected him to do better.

There actually are four highly-regarded shortstops in the Gold Glove era who score as having below average range: Kessinger, Bowa, and the two Gold Glove winners of 2005. . .also, to a lesser extent, Alan Trammell, Renteria, A-Rod, Roger Metzger and Jim Fregosi, but the ones that really bother me are Bowa and Omar Vizquel.

Vizquel is not Bowa; he doesn't come out as being hundreds of plays below average in career range. He's +63 in 1991, +29 in 2003, +22 in 2005, and above water in some other seasons. Still, for his career, he shows as -106, with a career Relative Range Factor of .990.

There are a lot of people whose opinions I respect who will tell you that Vizquel is the greatest shortstop who ever lived. I respect the data; I respect the facts— but I respect the opinions of professional baseball men, too. Vizquel does *something* awfully well that we're just not picking up. I don't think we're in any position, at this point, to reach the conclusion that the numbers are right and the observations of professionals are baseless.

Another situation that really bothers me is the Pirate shortstops of the 1960s. Gene Alley was the National League's Gold Glove shortstop in 1966 and 1967, and. . . I am old enough to remember this. . .was widely thought to be an outstanding defensive shortstop before he got a chance to play. People would say about him that he was an outstanding shortstop who might not hit enough to play every day.

Gene Alley was +37 in 1970, +29 for his career— but in his Gold Glove seasons of 1966 and 1967, he was -16 and -31. And it's not just him; we have data for other Pirate shortstops in that era. Andre Rodgers was -6 in 1965. Maury Wills, playing just 10 games at short in 1968, is -10, while Freddie Patek is -8 in 1968 and -60 in 1969, while Alley was hurt.

Then in 1970 the Pirates moved into Three Rivers, and Patek goes to +19, Alley to +37. Maury Wills, back playing shortstop with the Dodgers in '69, was +24. Something is wrong here. There is some sort of park illusion, or some sort of Bill Mazeroski effect or something. There is something in the data that we don't understand that we need to get a better handle on before we rush to any judgments based strictly on these numbers.

Fielding Bunts

Whenever a major league player attempts to bunt the ball, our scorers, scoring the games by satellite and other wondrous modern technologies from a spider hole in Malaysia or Pennsylvania or someplace, record the fact that the batter has attempted to bunt. Following through logically, they then record *where* the batter has bunted the ball—toward third base, or toward first base, or toward Singapore, whatever is appropriate; this is done by vectors and other wondrous modern technologies.

One of the things that we can study about a fielder, then, is how good a job he has done of converting bunts into good results for the team in the field. We score them in this way:

1. If the bunt try results in a double play, we give the fielder 2 points.

2. If the bunt try results in a pure out, with no base advancement, we give the fielder 1 point.

3. If the bunt try results in a sacrifice bunt, we give the fielder 6/10 of one point.

4. If the bunt try results in a base hit, no out recorded, we give the fielder one-quarter of a point.

5. If the fielder makes an error on the play, we give him no points.

The average score for an average third baseman on an average bunt is .500. . .actually, it is .500 or some number very close to that. It is intended to be .500. If the fielder turns bunts into double plays or if he gets outs with no advancement, his average will be higher than .50; if he makes errors or people bunt for a hit in front of him, it will be less than .50.

Since the statistic is new, we made up a chart to convert the stat into a letter grade, in case this would help you interpret the performance. . . .58 to .61 is a "B+", .61 to .64 is an "A-", .33 to .36 is a "D-", etc.

In the data that follows, then, there is a category for first and third basemen called "bunts", which gives this data:

- The number of bunts the fielder has been challenged to field (Opps),
- The average score we have assigned him for the results of these bunts (Score), and
- A letter grade corresponding to the score.

The best third baseman in the majors at fielding bunts, it turns out, is Mike Lowell. Over the last three years he has graded out at A+, A- and A, and also at A+ in 2002, although we don't include that data in the chart. He won't do as well in 2006, probably, because there is a little league bias in the data, since National Leaguers sacrifice more. The worst at fielding bunts is A-Rod, who has graded out at D- and F. I know, I know; A-Rod is supposed to be the best third baseman since Tacitus or Plutarch or somebody, but. . .all I know is, they bunted 17 times against him last year and the results were 14 hits and three sac bunts, and they bunted on him 21 times in 2004 and the results then included 17 hits. Maybe he plays too deep; maybe the Yankee pitchers are too easy to bunt on, maybe he lacks experience at third, maybe it's a random fluke based on limited trials. All I know is, when A-Rod gets better outcomes, we'll give him a better grade.

We also have bunt data for first basemen. . .for middle infielders turning the double play, for corner infielders fielding bunts. The scale for first basemen is a little different, since the numbers are different. . .the average first baseman scores at .58, rather than .50.

This was kind of a surprise at first, because. . .well, we all know that first basemen are not better at fielding bunts than third basemen. But when you think about it, where do batters *usually* try to bunt? They most often try to bunt toward third base. Why? Because it's a tougher play for a third baseman than it is a first baseman. So it makes sense that the numbers are higher for first basemen. The best first baseman at handling bunts, ten or more tries, was Albert Pujols, and the worst was Daryle Ward.

First Basemen - 3-Year Bunt Defense

Player	Opps	Bunt DP	Pure Outs	Sac Hits	Bunt Hits	Errors	Score	Grade
Pujols,Albert	30	1	8	12	9	0	.648	B
Lee,Derrek	83	2	13	55	13	2	.642	B
Mientkiewicz,Doug	39	1	11	15	12	0	.641	B
Morneau,Justin	18	0	7	5	6	0	.639	B
Giambi,Jason	18	0	6	7	5	1	.636	B
Helton,Todd	90	5	7	59	19	0	.635	B
Choi,Hee Seop	36	1	5	22	8	0	.617	B-
Lee,Travis	22	0	6	10	6	0	.614	B-
Olerud,John	29	1	7	10	11	0	.612	B-
Palmeiro,Rafael	14	0	3	8	3	0	.611	B-
Conine,Jeff	27	0	6	14	7	1	.598	C+
Bagwell,Jeff	60	0	11	35	14	2	.592	C+
Casey,Sean	71	0	19	28	24	0	.589	C+
Overbay,Lyle	61	1	12	28	20	0	.587	C+
Thome,Jim	51	0	13	21	17	0	.585	C+
Johnson,Nick	35	2	2	19	12	0	.583	C+
Snow,J.T.	43	1	7	20	15	1	.576	C+
Konerko,Paul	54	0	14	20	20	0	.574	C+
Broussard,Ben	43	0	11	16	16	1	.572	C+
Hatteberg,Scott	37	1	8	11	17	0	.564	C+
Hillenbrand,Shea	39	1	5	19	14	0	.562	C+
Martinez,Tino	28	0	3	17	8	0	.543	C
Clark,Tony	22	0	2	14	6	0	.541	C
LaRoche,Adam	23	0	3	12	8	0	.530	C
Millar,Kevin	26	0	5	10	11	1	.529	C-
Sexson,Richie	61	0	8	31	22	3	.526	C-
Nevin,Phil	47	0	7	21	19	0	.518	C-
Erstad,Darin	30	0	6	9	15	0	.505	C-
Pena,Carlos	34	0	7	9	18	4	.497	D+
Delgado,Carlos	44	0	5	20	19	0	.494	D+
Teixeira,Mark	48	0	6	19	23	0	.482	D+
Ward,Daryle	25	0	0	13	12	0	.432	D-

First Basemen - 2005 Bunt Defense

Player	Tm	Opps	Bunt DP	Pure Outs	Sac Hits	Bunt Hits	Errors	Score	Grade
Morneau,Justin	Min	12	0	6	4	2	0	.742	A
Pujols,Albert	StL	14	1	5	3	5	0	.718	A-
Berkman,Lance	Hou	11	0	4	6	1	0	.714	A-
Hinske,Eric	Tor	4	0	1	3	0	0	.700	A-
Shelton,Chris	Det	6	0	3	1	2	0	.683	B+
Lee,Derrek	ChC	29	1	5	20	3	0	.681	B+
Mientkiewicz,Doug	NYM	16	0	4	10	2	0	.656	B
Tracy,Chad	Ari	9	0	3	4	2	0	.656	B
Johnson,Nick	Was	22	2	1	13	6	0	.650	B
Giambi,Jason	NYY	7	0	2	3	2	0	.614	B-
Casey,Sean	Cin	29	0	8	13	8	0	.614	B-
Martinez,Tino	NYY	4	0	1	2	1	0	.613	B-
Helton,Todd	Col	21	1	1	14	5	0	.602	B-
Konerko,Paul	CWS	19	0	4	9	6	0	.574	C+
Teixeira,Mark	Tex	16	0	4	6	6	0	.569	C+
Nevin,Phil	SD-Tex	12	0	2	6	4	0	.550	C
Choi,Hee Seop	LAD	12	0	1	8	3	0	.546	C
Snow,J.T.	SF	15	0	3	6	6	0	.540	C
Hillenbrand,Shea	Tor	5	0	1	2	2	0	.540	C
Sexson,Richie	Sea	19	0	3	9	7	0	.534	C
LaRoche,Adam	Atl	14	0	2	7	5	0	.532	C
Palmeiro,Rafael	Bal	4	0	1	1	2	0	.525	C-
Overbay,Lyle	Mil	26	0	4	11	11	0	.513	C-
Stairs,Matt	KC	4	0	0	3	1	0	.513	C-
Delgado,Carlos	Fla	25	0	2	14	9	0	.506	C-
Erstad,Darin	LAA	20	0	4	6	10	0	.505	C-
Clark,Tony	Ari	7	0	0	5	2	0	.500	C-
Howard,Ryan	Phi	7	0	0	5	2	1	.500	C-
Lee,Travis	TB	9	0	1	4	4	0	.489	D+
Johnson,Dan	Oak	6	0	0	4	2	0	.483	D+
Broussard,Ben	Cle	11	0	2	3	6	0	.482	D+
Millar,Kevin	Bos	8	0	1	3	4	1	.475	D+
Niekro,Lance	SF	4	0	1	0	3	0	.438	D-
Ward,Daryle	Pit	13	0	0	6	7	0	.412	D-

First Basemen - 2004 Bunt Defense

Player	Tm	Opps	Bunt DP	Pure Outs	Sac Hits	Bunt Hits	Errors	Score	Grade
Millar,Kevin	Bos	4	0	2	2	0	0	.800	A+
Wilkerson,Brad	Mon	20	1	6	10	3	0	.738	A
Palmeiro,Rafael	Bal	8	0	2	6	0	0	.700	A-
Green,Shawn	LA	13	1	2	6	4	0	.662	B+
Choi,Hee Seop	Fla-LA	16	1	3	7	5	0	.653	B
Mientkiewicz,Doug	Min-Bos	13	0	5	4	4	0	.646	B
Helton,Todd	Col	39	2	3	27	7	0	.640	B
Lee,Derrek	ChC	32	1	4	21	6	2	.628	B-
Overbay,Lyle	Mil	25	0	7	12	6	0	.628	B-
Broussard,Ben	Cle	6	0	2	2	2	1	.617	B-
Pujols,Albert	StL	13	0	3	7	3	0	.612	B-
Franco,Julio	Atl	10	0	2	6	2	0	.610	B-
Hillenbrand,Shea	Ari	21	1	3	10	7	0	.607	B-
Clark,Tony	NYY	3	0	0	3	0	0	.600	B-
Harvey,Ken	KC	10	0	4	1	5	0	.585	C+
Hatteberg,Scott	Oak	10	0	2	5	3	0	.575	C+
Bagwell,Jeff	Hou	33	0	4	22	7	1	.574	C+
Thome,Jim	Phi	16	0	3	8	5	0	.566	C+
Olerud,John	Sea-NYY	13	0	4	3	6	0	.562	C+
Pena,Carlos	Det	12	0	3	4	5	1	.554	C
Feliz,Pedro	SF	12	0	2	6	4	0	.550	C
Piazza,Mike	NYM	16	0	2	9	5	0	.541	C
Konerko,Paul	CWS	18	0	5	4	9	0	.536	C
LaRoche,Adam	Atl	9	0	1	5	3	0	.528	C-
Erstad,Darin	Ana	10	0	2	3	5	0	.505	C-
Delgado,Carlos	Tor	9	0	1	4	4	0	.489	D+
Nevin,Phil	SD	30	0	3	14	13	0	.488	D+
Casey,Sean	Cin	23	0	4	7	12	0	.487	D+
Teixeira,Mark	Tex	15	0	1	8	6	0	.487	D+
Snow,J.T.	SF	11	0	1	5	5	0	.477	D+
Ward,Daryle	Pit	10	0	0	6	4	0	.460	D
Johnson,Nick	Mon	5	0	0	3	2	0	.460	D
Martinez,Tino	TB	6	0	0	2	4	0	.367	F
Morneau,Justin	Min	5	0	0	1	4	0	.320	F

First Basemen - 2003 Bunt Defense

Player	Tm	Opps	Bunt DP	Pure Outs	Sac Hits	Bunt Hits	Errors	Score	Grade
McGriff,Fred	LA	9	1	3	3	2	1	.811	A+
Klesko,Ryan	SD	12	0	5	5	2	0	.708	A-
Spiezio,Scott	Ana	9	0	5	1	3	0	.706	A-
Lee,Travis	TB	13	0	5	6	2	0	.700	A-
Giambi,Jason	NYY	5	0	2	2	1	1	.690	A-
Overbay,Lyle	Ari	10	1	1	5	3	0	.675	B+
Casey,Sean	Cin	19	0	7	8	4	0	.674	B+
Snow,J.T.	SF	17	1	3	9	4	1	.671	B+
Olerud,John	Sea	12	1	1	7	3	0	.663	B+
Helton,Todd	Col	30	2	3	18	7	0	.652	B
Choi,Hee Seop	ChC	8	0	1	7	0	0	.650	B
Bagwell,Jeff	Hou	22	0	7	9	6	1	.632	B
Thome,Jim	Phi	27	0	8	12	7	0	.628	B-
Konerko,Paul	CWS	17	0	5	7	5	0	.615	B-
Mientkiewicz,Doug	Min	10	1	2	1	6	0	.610	B-
Lee,Derrek	Fla	22	0	4	14	4	0	.609	B-
Broussard,Ben	Cle	26	0	7	11	8	0	.600	B-
Martinez,Tino	StL	18	0	2	13	3	0	.586	C+
Conine,Jeff	Bal-Fla	13	0	3	6	4	0	.585	C+
Phillips,Jason	NYM	9	0	3	2	4	1	.578	C+
Simon,Randall	Pit-ChC	18	0	1	13	4	0	.544	C
Sexson,Richie	Mil	35	0	4	17	14	3	.506	C-
Fick,Robert	Atl	11	0	0	8	3	0	.505	C-
Hillenbrand,Shea	Bos-Ari	13	0	1	7	5	0	.496	D+
Galarraga,Andres	SF	9	0	2	2	5	1	.494	D+
Karros,Eric	ChC	15	0	2	6	7	0	.490	D+
Harvey,Ken	KC	20	0	4	5	11	1	.488	D+
Pena,Carlos	Det	14	0	3	3	8	2	.486	D+
Millar,Kevin	Bos	14	0	2	5	7	0	.482	D+
Johnson,Nick	NYY	8	0	1	3	4	0	.475	D+
Delgado,Carlos	Tor	10	0	2	2	6	0	.470	D
Hatteberg,Scott	Oak	22	0	4	5	13	0	.466	D
Cordero,Wil	Mon	13	0	0	6	7	0	.412	D-
Teixeira,Mark	Tex	17	0	1	5	11	0	.397	F

Third Basemen - 3-Year Bunt Defense

Player	Opps	Bunt DP	Pure Outs	Sac Hits	Bunt Hits	Errors	Score	Grade
Lowell,Mike	86	4	18	39	25	0	.647	A
Beltre,Adrian	71	2	16	22	29	2	.570	B
Boone,Aaron	42	0	9	18	15	0	.561	B
Burroughs,Sean	44	1	11	11	20	1	.559	B
Chavez,Eric	59	2	9	23	24	1	.556	B
Alfonzo,Edgardo	69	0	13	32	24	0	.554	B
Mueller,Bill	29	0	7	9	13	0	.540	B-
Rolen,Scott	38	1	3	20	14	0	.539	B-
Bell,David	64	0	16	19	28	1	.538	B-
Helms,Wes	44	2	8	11	20	3	.536	B-
Blalock,Hank	53	0	12	18	22	1	.534	B-
Wright,David	40	1	7	12	20	0	.530	B-
Jones,Chipper	39	1	5	15	18	0	.526	B-
Randa,Joe	65	0	13	22	30	0	.518	C+
Wigginton,Ty	59	1	10	18	30	0	.514	C+
Inge,Brandon	36	0	6	13	17	0	.501	C+
Ensberg,Morgan	53	0	6	25	21	1	.495	C+
Munson,Eric	31	0	5	11	15	0	.495	C+
Castilla,Vinny	69	0	8	32	26	3	.488	C+
Koskie,Corey	56	0	7	23	26	0	.488	C+
Hinske,Eric	44	0	7	14	23	0	.481	C+
Glaus,Troy	45	0	8	13	23	1	.479	C
Ramirez,Aramis	70	0	7	29	34	0	.470	C
Crede,Joe	69	0	8	26	33	2	.462	C
Batista,Tony	44	0	7	11	25	1	.451	C
Mora,Melvin	37	0	4	8	25	0	.407	D+
Blake,Casey	39	0	3	11	24	1	.400	D+
Rodriguez,Alex	38	0	1	6	31	0	.325	F

Third Basemen - 2005 Bunt Defense

Player	Tm	Opps	Bunt DP	Pure Outs	Sac Hits	Bunt Hits	Errors	Score	Grade
Feliz,Pedro	SF	13	1	4	5	2	1	.731	A+
Chavez,Eric	Oak	14	1	4	4	4	1	.671	A+
Lowell,Mike	Fla	24	1	6	10	7	0	.656	A
Boone,Aaron	Cle	21	0	7	8	6	0	.633	A-
Mueller,Bill	Bos	9	0	3	2	4	0	.578	B
Cuddyer,Mike	Min	11	0	2	6	3	0	.577	B
Wright,David	NYM	32	1	5	11	15	0	.542	B-
Jones,Chipper	Atl	21	1	2	8	10	0	.538	B-
Beltre,Adrian	Sea	18	0	5	4	9	0	.536	B-
Teahen,Mark	KC	19	0	5	4	10	0	.521	B-
Bell,David	Phi	27	0	5	10	12	0	.519	C+
Blalock,Hank	Tex	17	0	4	4	9	0	.509	C+
Castilla,Vinny	Was	22	0	4	7	11	0	.498	C+
Randa,Joe	Cin-SD	24	0	5	6	13	0	.494	C+
Nunez,Abraham O	StL	12	0	2	4	6	0	.492	C+
Crede,Joe	CWS	22	0	3	9	9	1	.484	C+
Inge,Brandon	Det	22	0	2	10	10	0	.477	C
Glaus,Troy	Ari	27	0	3	11	12	1	.467	C
Alfonzo,Edgardo	SF	18	0	1	9	8	0	.467	C
Koskie,Corey	Tor	13	0	2	3	8	0	.446	C-
Gonzalez,Alex S	TB	15	0	0	8	7	0	.437	C-
Ensberg,Morgan	Hou	20	0	1	9	9	1	.433	C-
Atkins,Garrett	Col	26	0	3	8	13	2	.425	C-
Ramirez,Aramis	ChC	21	0	0	10	11	0	.417	D+
Burroughs,Sean	SD	7	0	1	1	5	0	.407	D+
Mora,Melvin	Bal	17	0	1	3	13	0	.356	D-
Rodriguez,Alex	NYY	17	0	0	3	14	0	.312	F

Third Basemen - 2004 Bunt Defense

Player	Tm	Opps	Bunt DP	Pure Outs	Sac Hits	Bunt Hits	Errors	Score	Grade
Helms,Wes	Mil	6	2	1	1	1	1	.975	A+
Lowell,Mike	Fla	32	2	5	13	12	0	.619	A-
Figgins,Chone	Ana	13	0	4	5	4	0	.615	A-
Mueller,Bill	Bos	8	0	2	4	2	0	.613	A-
Alfonzo,Edgardo	SF	25	0	5	12	8	0	.568	B
Blalock,Hank	Tex	19	0	5	7	6	1	.563	B
Randa,Joe	KC	21	0	4	10	7	0	.560	B
Youkilis,Kevin	Bos	6	0	1	3	2	0	.550	B
Rolen,Scott	StL	18	1	1	8	8	0	.544	B-
Inge,Brandon	Det	14	0	4	3	7	0	.539	B-
Bell,David	Phi	25	0	7	6	11	1	.534	B-
Hinske,Eric	Tor	22	0	3	11	8	0	.527	B-
Chavez,Eric	Oak	22	0	3	10	9	0	.511	C+
Jones,Chipper	Atl	18	0	3	7	8	0	.511	C+
Ensberg,Morgan	Hou	15	0	1	9	5	0	.510	C+
Burroughs,Sean	SD	13	0	3	3	7	0	.504	C+
Munson,Eric	Det	16	0	2	7	7	0	.497	C+
Castilla,Vinny	Col	25	0	2	14	8	1	.496	C+
Ramirez,Aramis	ChC	25	0	4	9	12	0	.496	C+
Beltre,Adrian	LA	34	0	4	16	13	1	.496	C+
Wright,David	NYM	8	0	2	1	5	0	.481	C+
Crede,Joe	CWS	23	0	3	8	12	0	.470	C
Tracy,Chad	Ari	15	0	2	5	8	0	.467	C
Mora,Melvin	Bal	20	0	3	5	12	0	.450	C
Koskie,Corey	Min	22	0	1	10	11	0	.443	C-
Batista,Tony	Mon	22	0	2	7	13	0	.430	C-
Wigginton,Ty	NYM-Pit	25	0	1	10	14	0	.420	C-
Spiezio,Scott	Sea	7	0	0	4	2	1	.414	D+
Blake,Casey	Cle	15	0	0	6	9	0	.390	D+
Huff,Aubrey	TB	11	0	1	2	8	0	.382	D
Rodriguez,Alex	NYY	21	0	1	3	17	0	.336	D-
DeRosa,Mark	Atl	5	0	0	1	4	0	.320	F

Third Basemen - 2003 Bunt Defense

Player	Tm	Opps	Bunt DP	Pure Outs	Sac Hits	Bunt Hits	Errors	Score	Grade
Beltre,Adrian	LA	19	2	7	2	7	1	.734	A+
Stynes,Chris	Col	12	0	4	6	2	0	.675	A+
Lowell,Mike	Fla	30	1	7	16	6	0	.670	A+
Burroughs,Sean	SD	24	1	7	7	8	1	.633	A-
Wigginton,Ty	NYM	28	1	9	6	12	0	.629	A-
Ventura,Robin	NYY-LA	13	0	5	3	5	0	.619	A-
Alfonzo,Edgardo	SF	26	0	7	11	8	0	.600	B+
Bell,David	Phi	12	0	4	3	5	0	.588	B+
Hillenbrand,Shea	Bos-Ari	9	0	3	2	4	0	.578	B
Koskie,Corey	Min	21	0	4	10	7	0	.560	B
Ensberg,Morgan	Hou	18	0	4	7	7	0	.553	B
Rolls,Damian	TB	5	0	1	2	2	0	.540	B-
Hernandez,Jose	3 teams	14	0	4	3	7	0	.539	B-
Rolen,Scott	StL	14	0	1	9	4	0	.529	B-
Chavez,Eric	Oak	23	1	2	9	11	0	.528	B-
Glaus,Troy	Ana	16	0	5	2	9	0	.528	B-
Blalock,Hank	Tex	17	0	3	7	7	0	.526	B-
Randa,Joe	KC	20	0	4	6	10	0	.505	C+
Munson,Eric	Det	15	0	3	4	8	0	.493	C+
Ramirez,Aramis	Pit-ChC	24	0	3	10	11	0	.490	C+
Boone,Aaron	Cin-NYY	21	0	2	10	9	0	.488	C+
Batista,Tony	Bal	22	0	5	4	12	1	.473	C
Castilla,Vinny	Atl	22	0	2	11	7	2	.470	C
Helms,Wes	Mil	35	0	7	8	18	2	.466	C
Mueller,Bill	Bos	12	0	2	3	7	0	.463	C
Hinske,Eric	Tor	22	0	4	3	15	0	.434	C-
Crede,Joe	CWS	24	0	2	9	12	1	.433	C-
Blum,Geoff	Hou	9	0	1	2	6	0	.411	D+
Blake,Casey	Cle	24	0	3	5	15	1	.406	D+
Cirillo,Jeff	Sea	14	0	1	4	8	1	.386	D

Groundball Double Plays and Pivots

For middle infielders, the Plus/Minus System looks at how many plays each player makes above what the average player would do. But it does not look at how well each player handles the double play. That's where our GDP and Pivot ratings come into play. Here is what we're tracking:

GDPs: How many times the player was involved in a groundball double play,

GDP Opps: How many times the player was involved in a fielding play on a groundball in a double play situation (man on first with less than two outs). This includes DPs, forceouts, errors, etc.

Pivots: How many times the player made the double play pivot (6-4-3 DP or 5-4-3 DP or 1-4-3 or 3-4-3, not that there are actually any 3-4-3 double plays),

Pivot Opps: How many times the player accepted a force out at second in a situation that could have been a double play (6-4, 5-4, 1-4 or 3-4).

We measure Pivots and Pivot Opps as a separate skill even though they are included in GDPs and GDP Opps. Making the pivot on a double play requires a different set of talents than fielding a grounder to start the double play. The word "pivot" applies more to a second baseman who has to accept a throw and then pivot to make his own throw to first. But we also use the term for shortstops as well for convenience, even though there's not much of an actual pivot that the shortstop has to make on a double play attempt.

Here are some observations from the charts that follow:

- Over the last three years, second basemen Jose Castillo (Pittsburgh) and Alex Cora (mostly with the Dodgers but now with Boston) were head-and-shoulders the best second basemen on the double play. They rank one and two in both GDP percentage and Pivot percentage.
- Cleveland's Jhonny Peralta was the first player to accomplish the feat of leading the league in both GDP and Pivot percentage the same year when he led the American League at shortstop in 2005 with a .712 GDP percentage and a .791 Pivot percentage.
- Nomar Garciaparra is at the other end of the spectrum. Over three years he finished last (31st) in GDP percentage and second to last in Pivot percentage at shortstop. He is also one of two players to finish last in both categories in one season, accomplishing this feat in 2004 as he split his time between Boston and the Chicago Cubs. Amazingly, Nomar finished second to last in both GDP and Pivot percentage the year before (2003) to Tony Womack. Womack was the other player to accomplish the dubious Double Play Double, finishing 35th and last in both categories. Womack also spread out the pain as he actually played for three different teams that season. A change will do them good. Garciaparra is slated to handle first base chores for the Dodgers this season while Womack handles second base for Cincinnati. The dreadful 2003 season marked the end of the three-year experiment at shortstop for Womack.

Second Basemen - 3-Year GDPs & Pivots

Player	GDP Opps	GDP	GDP Pct	Rank	Pivot Opps	Pivots	Pivot Pct	Rank
Castillo,Jose	277	156	.563	1	144	108	.750	1
Cora,Alex	383	215	.561	2	198	148	.747	2
Cairo,Miguel	221	122	.552	3	115	71	.617	16
Grudzielanek,Mark	402	220	.547	4	212	153	.722	3
Boone,Bret	428	231	.540	5	223	135	.605	20
Roberts,Brian	439	236	.538	6	222	149	.671	8
Belliard,Ronnie	433	230	.531	7	231	154	.667	10
Kennedy,Adam	374	197	.527	8	193	114	.591	23
Polanco,Placido	426	224	.526	9	234	156	.667	9
Ellis,Mark	308	161	.523	10	171	100	.585	24
Rivas,Luis	278	145	.522	11	141	95	.674	7
Hudson,Orlando	485	249	.513	12	254	164	.646	12
Loretta,Mark	447	227	.508	13	232	160	.690	6
Bellhorn,Mark	233	117	.502	14	123	76	.618	15
Castillo,Luis	520	259	.498	15	222	160	.721	4
Soriano,Alfonso	558	275	.493	16	314	192	.611	19
Utley,Chase	245	119	.486	17	116	76	.655	11
Spivey,Junior	254	122	.480	18	122	77	.631	14
Giles,Marcus	494	237	.480	19	216	155	.718	5
Vidro,Jose	336	161	.479	20	160	95	.594	22
Jimenez,D'Angelo	359	168	.468	21	194	119	.613	18
Durham,Ray	422	190	.450	22	200	121	.605	21
Kent,Jeff	536	230	.429	23	260	160	.615	17
Walker,Todd	339	141	.416	24	153	80	.523	25
Miles,Aaron	269	108	.401	25	117	74	.632	13

Second Basemen - 2005 GDPs & Pivots

Player	Tm	GDP Opps	GDP	GDP Pct	Rank	Pivot Opps	Pivots	Pivot Pct	Rank
Grudzielanek,Mark	StL	166	104	.627	1	103	76	.738	4
Castillo,Jose	Pit	131	82	.626	2	72	54	.750	1
Punto,Nick	Min	70	42	.600	3	43	26	.605	29
Kennedy,Adam	LAA	110	65	.591	4	67	44	.657	17
Belliard,Ronnie	Cle	146	86	.589	5	85	55	.647	20
Polanco,Placido	Phi-Det	158	90	.570	6	90	58	.644	21
Cairo,Miguel	NYM	88	50	.568	7	41	30	.732	6
Iguchi,Tadahito	CWS	141	79	.560	8	72	49	.681	12
Roberts,Brian	Bal	152	84	.553	9	79	54	.684	11
Ellis,Mark	Oak	134	74	.552	10	77	46	.597	30
Bellhorn,Mark	Bos-NYY	102	55	.539	11	55	36	.655	18
Hudson,Orlando	Tor	143	77	.538	12	77	51	.662	14
Infante,Omar	Det	88	47	.534	13	57	35	.614	26
Gotay,Ruben	KC	87	46	.529	14	38	25	.658	16
Loretta,Mark	SD	109	57	.523	15	58	41	.707	8
Counsell,Craig	Ari	185	95	.514	16	97	69	.711	7
Aurilia,Rich	Cin	74	38	.514	17	40	30	.750	2
Green,Nick	TB	76	39	.513	18	33	20	.606	28
Graffanino,Tony	KC-Bos	63	32	.508	19	32	20	.625	25
Spivey,Junior	Mil-Was	73	37	.507	20	36	22	.611	27
Boone,Bret	Sea-Min	103	50	.485	21	52	28	.538	35
Matsui,Kazuo	NYM	64	31	.484	22	31	16	.516	36
Giles,Marcus	Atl	190	92	.484	23	73	54	.740	3
Biggio,Craig	Hou	152	73	.480	24	82	52	.634	23
Weeks,Rickie	Mil	109	52	.477	25	52	36	.692	9
Cantu,Jorge	TB	78	37	.474	26	38	22	.579	32
Soriano,Alfonso	Tex	198	93	.470	27	107	63	.589	31
Gonzalez,Luis A	Col	81	38	.469	28	40	22	.550	34
Cano,Robinson	NYY	152	70	.461	29	77	43	.558	33
Vidro,Jose	Was	76	35	.461	30	28	19	.679	13
Castillo,Luis	Fla	172	79	.459	31	71	52	.732	5
Miles,Aaron	Col	100	45	.450	32	49	32	.653	19
Durham,Ray	SF	148	66	.446	33	74	49	.662	15
Utley,Chase	Phi	144	64	.444	34	69	44	.638	22
Kent,Jeff	LAD	177	78	.441	35	84	58	.690	10
Walker,Todd	ChC	101	40	.396	36	40	25	.625	24

Second Basemen - 2004 GDPs & Pivots

Player	Tm	GDP Opps	GDP	GDP Pct	Rank	Pivot Opps	Pivots	Pivot Pct	Rank
Infante,Omar	Det	124	71	.573	1	71	45	.634	17
Graffanino,Tony	KC	109	62	.569	2	63	44	.698	7
Boone,Bret	Sea	148	81	.547	3	77	46	.597	22
Rivas,Luis	Min	121	65	.537	4	57	39	.684	8
Roberts,Brian	Bal	167	89	.533	5	85	55	.647	15
Cora,Alex	LA	166	88	.530	6	77	59	.766	1
Scutaro,Marco	Oak	136	72	.529	7	80	52	.650	13
Cairo,Miguel	NYY	104	55	.529	8	56	32	.571	27
Sanchez,Rey	TB	93	49	.527	9	54	34	.630	19
Castillo,Luis	Fla	164	86	.524	10	73	51	.699	6
Uribe,Juan	CWS	88	46	.523	11	54	32	.593	24
Loretta,Mark	SD	178	93	.522	12	85	63	.741	3
Spivey,Junior	Mil	70	36	.514	13	35	25	.714	4
Castillo,Jose	Pit	146	74	.507	14	72	54	.750	2
Soriano,Alfonso	Tex	198	100	.505	15	109	69	.633	18
Vidro,Jose	Mon	119	60	.504	16	62	40	.645	16
Belliard,Ronnie	Cle	144	72	.500	17	77	50	.649	14
Hudson,Orlando	Tor	162	79	.488	18	84	56	.667	9
Polanco,Placido	Phi	138	67	.486	19	76	54	.711	5
Giles,Marcus	Atl	136	66	.485	20	67	44	.657	11
Bellhorn,Mark	Bos	117	56	.479	21	62	37	.597	23
Kennedy,Adam	Ana	133	62	.466	22	67	36	.537	30
Harris,Willie	CWS	94	43	.457	23	52	34	.654	12
Womack,Tony	StL	160	72	.450	24	71	39	.549	28
Green,Nick	Atl	99	41	.414	25	39	24	.615	21
Jimenez,D'Angelo	Cin	157	65	.414	26	81	47	.580	26
Durham,Ray	SF	158	64	.405	27	74	40	.541	29
Kent,Jeff	Hou	185	71	.384	28	83	49	.590	25
Hairston,Scott	Ari	117	44	.376	29	57	27	.474	31
Miles,Aaron	Col	169	63	.373	30	68	42	.618	20
Grudzielanek,Mark	ChC	78	28	.359	31	33	22	.667	10
Wilson,Enrique	NYY	64	21	.328	32	43	13	.302	33
Walker,Todd	ChC	93	30	.323	33	41	14	.341	32

Second Basemen - 2003 GDPs & Pivots

Player	Tm	GDP Opps	GDP	GDP Pct	Rank	Pivot Opps	Pivots	Pivot Pct	Rank
Morris,Warren	Det	123	75	.610	1	61	44	.721	6
Reboulet,Jeff	Pit	82	47	.573	2	49	37	.755	1
Anderson,Marlon	TB	145	82	.566	3	64	43	.672	10
Boone,Bret	Sea	177	100	.565	4	94	61	.649	14
Grudzielanek,Mark	ChC	158	88	.557	5	76	55	.724	5
Cora,Alex	LA	178	99	.556	6	99	74	.747	3
Young,Michael	Tex	196	109	.556	7	114	75	.658	13
Kennedy,Adam	Ana	131	70	.534	8	59	34	.576	28
Roberts,Brian	Bal	120	63	.525	9	58	40	.690	9
Febles,Carlos	KC	61	32	.525	10	30	19	.633	16
Durham,Ray	SF	116	60	.517	11	52	32	.615	21
Hudson,Orlando	Tor	180	93	.517	12	93	57	.613	22
Polanco,Placido	Phi	130	67	.515	13	68	44	.647	15
Castillo,Luis	Fla	184	94	.511	14	78	57	.731	4
Phillips,Brandon	Cle	144	73	.507	15	86	57	.663	11
Vina,Fernando	StL	75	38	.507	16	38	27	.711	7
Soriano,Alfonso	NYY	162	82	.506	17	98	60	.612	23
Belliard,Ronnie	Col	143	72	.503	18	69	49	.710	8
Jimenez,D'Angelo	CWS-Cin	173	87	.503	19	95	60	.632	17
Ellis,Mark	Oak	174	87	.500	20	94	54	.574	29
Walker,Todd	Bos	145	71	.490	21	72	41	.569	31
Alomar,Roberto	NYM-CWS	160	78	.488	22	84	52	.619	19
Nunez,Abraham O	Pit	83	40	.482	23	41	27	.659	12
Loretta,Mark	SD	160	77	.481	24	89	56	.629	18
Rivas,Luis	Min	121	58	.479	25	61	37	.607	24
Relaford,Desi	KC	93	44	.473	26	54	32	.593	25
Giles,Marcus	Atl	168	79	.470	27	76	57	.750	2
Vidro,Jose	Mon	141	66	.468	28	70	36	.514	32
Kent,Jeff	Hou	174	81	.466	29	93	53	.570	30
Hart,Bo	StL	72	33	.458	30	34	21	.618	20
Spivey,Junior	Ari	111	49	.441	31	51	30	.588	26
Young,Eric	Mil-SF	140	60	.429	32	65	38	.585	27

Shortstops - 3-Year GDPs & Pivots

Player	GDP Opps	GDP	GDP Pct	Rank	Pivot Opps	Pivots	Pivot Pct	Rank
Peralta,Jhonny	203	134	.660	1	100	73	.730	2
Gonzalez,Alex	425	277	.652	2	254	169	.665	5
Wilson,Jack	522	334	.640	3	282	179	.635	12
Berroa,Angel	452	283	.626	4	233	154	.661	6
Rollins,Jimmy	397	247	.622	5	214	146	.682	4
Cruz,Deivi	254	157	.618	6	148	94	.635	11
Reyes,Jose	230	141	.613	7	122	87	.713	3
Guillen,Carlos	280	171	.611	8	135	99	.733	1
Guzman,Cristian	387	236	.610	9	225	144	.640	9
Furcal,Rafael	506	308	.609	10	310	191	.616	16
Uribe,Juan	283	172	.608	11	177	116	.655	7
Crosby,Bobby	263	159	.605	12	121	71	.587	23
Valentin,Jose	275	166	.604	13	144	93	.646	8
Eckstein,David	414	245	.592	14	240	145	.604	19
Gonzalez,Alex S	213	126	.592	15	130	82	.631	13
Perez,Neifi	235	139	.591	16	140	86	.614	17
Everett,Adam	342	202	.591	17	192	116	.604	20
Izturis,Cesar	399	235	.589	18	205	115	.561	26
Greene,Khalil	251	146	.582	19	136	78	.574	25
Clayton,Royce	429	244	.569	20	235	131	.557	27
Lugo,Julio	424	241	.568	21	251	157	.625	15
Cabrera,Orlando	437	248	.568	22	242	139	.574	24
Renteria,Edgar	425	241	.567	23	249	151	.606	18
Vizquel,Omar	361	203	.562	24	182	107	.588	22
Tejada,Miguel	508	285	.561	25	283	169	.597	21
Young,Michael	326	181	.555	26	178	99	.556	29
Aurilia,Rich	224	124	.554	27	108	69	.639	10
Jeter,Derek	390	215	.551	28	222	140	.631	14
Lopez,Felipe	219	112	.511	29	118	55	.466	31
Cintron,Alex	246	125	.508	30	131	73	.557	28
Garciaparra,Nomar	254	124	.488	31	153	79	.516	30

Shortstops - 2005 GDPs & Pivots

Player	Tm	GDP Opps	GDP	GDP Pct	Rank	Pivot Opps	Pivots	Pivot Pct	Rank
Peralta,Jhonny	Cle	132	94	.712	1	67	53	.791	1
Castro,Juan	Min	64	44	.688	2	35	27	.771	3
Bartlett,Jason	Min	62	42	.677	3	28	22	.786	2
Crosby,Bobby	Oak	85	57	.671	4	41	27	.659	11
Reyes,Jose	NYM	148	97	.655	5	87	63	.724	4
Wilson,Jack	Pit	184	120	.652	6	103	68	.660	10
Gonzalez,Alex	Fla	138	90	.652	7	87	53	.609	17
Guzman,Cristian	Was	120	78	.650	8	77	53	.688	6
Furcal,Rafael	Atl	172	110	.640	9	111	68	.613	16
Berroa,Angel	KC	161	102	.634	10	87	58	.667	9
Eckstein,David	StL	188	118	.628	11	107	67	.626	14
Scutaro,Marco	Oak	76	46	.605	12	43	30	.698	5
Perez,Neifi	ChC	121	73	.603	13	73	43	.589	22
Rollins,Jimmy	Phi	127	76	.598	14	75	49	.653	12
Uribe,Juan	CWS	149	89	.597	15	97	65	.670	8
Hardy,J.J.	Mil	78	46	.590	16	38	21	.553	27
Clayton,Royce	Ari	153	90	.588	17	79	46	.582	24
Everett,Adam	Hou	150	88	.587	18	82	49	.598	20
Cabrera,Orlando	LAA	128	75	.586	19	71	38	.535	30
Adams,Russ	Tor	111	65	.586	20	74	42	.568	26
Tejada,Miguel	Bal	166	95	.572	21	95	57	.600	18
Barmes,Clint	Col	105	59	.562	22	57	36	.632	13
Young,Michael	Tex	157	88	.561	23	93	51	.548	28
Izturis,Cesar	LAD	106	59	.557	24	61	35	.574	25
Guillen,Carlos	Det	76	42	.553	25	37	25	.676	7
Lopez,Felipe	Cin	127	69	.543	26	63	29	.460	32
Greene,Khalil	SD	111	60	.541	27	58	30	.517	31
Lugo,Julio	TB	154	83	.539	28	95	57	.600	18
Jeter,Derek	NYY	156	84	.538	29	95	56	.589	21
Renteria,Edgar	Bos	154	82	.532	30	91	53	.582	23
Hall,Bill	Mil	53	28	.528	31	32	20	.625	15
Vizquel,Omar	SF	142	75	.528	32	72	39	.542	29

Shortstops - 2004 GDPs & Pivots

Player	Tm	GDP Opps	GDP	GDP Pct	Rank	Pivot Opps	Pivots	Pivot Pct	Rank
Wilson,Jack	Pit	177	118	.667	1	94	64	.681	5
Berroa,Angel	KC	133	84	.632	2	62	42	.677	6
Rollins,Jimmy	Phi	130	82	.631	3	63	41	.651	10
Lugo,Julio	TB	138	86	.623	4	79	54	.684	4
Cruz,Deivi	SF	92	57	.620	5	49	32	.653	9
Izturis,Cesar	LA	144	89	.618	6	77	41	.532	30
Greene,Khalil	SD	123	76	.618	7	64	40	.625	12
Everett,Adam	Hou	83	51	.614	8	50	31	.620	15
Guzman,Cristian	Min	158	97	.614	9	86	57	.663	8
Gonzalez,Alex	Fla	144	88	.611	10	79	55	.696	2
Guillen,Carlos	Det	138	84	.609	11	68	49	.721	1
Valentin,Jose	CWS	129	77	.597	12	59	37	.627	11
Furcal,Rafael	Atl	160	95	.594	13	91	56	.615	18
Matsui,Kazuo	NYM	108	64	.593	14	63	39	.619	16
Crosby,Bobby	Oak	169	100	.592	15	76	43	.566	27
Woodward,Chris	Tor	63	37	.587	16	29	18	.621	14
Jeter,Derek	NYY	146	85	.582	17	89	60	.674	7
Martinez,Ramon	ChC	56	32	.571	18	31	18	.581	22
Counsell,Craig	Mil	109	62	.569	19	60	37	.617	17
Renteria,Edgar	StL	147	83	.565	20	91	53	.582	21
Reese,Pokey	Bos	59	33	.559	21	32	20	.625	13
Gomez,Chris	Tor	77	43	.558	22	41	21	.512	32
Young,Michael	Tex	167	92	.551	23	84	48	.571	24
Tejada,Miguel	Bal	191	105	.550	24	105	62	.590	19
Clayton,Royce	Col	150	82	.547	25	87	46	.529	31
Gonzalez,Alex S	3 teams	75	41	.547	26	53	31	.585	20
Cabrera,Orlando	Mon-Bos	152	83	.546	27	84	48	.571	24
Eckstein,David	Ana	125	68	.544	28	74	41	.554	29
Aurilia,Rich	Sea-SD	72	39	.542	29	38	26	.684	3
Vizquel,Omar	Cle	140	74	.529	30	73	41	.562	28
Perez,Neifi	SF-ChC	66	34	.515	31	37	21	.568	26
Larkin,Barry	Cin	60	30	.500	32	26	11	.423	33
Cintron,Alex	Ari	119	57	.479	33	57	33	.579	23
Garciaparra,Nomar	Bos-ChC	75	31	.413	34	45	19	.422	34

Shortstops - 2003 GDPs & Pivots

Player	Tm	GDP Opps	GDP	GDP Pct	Rank	Pivot Opps	Pivots	Pivot Pct	Rank
Gonzalez,Alex	Fla	143	99	.692	1	88	61	.693	5
Vizquel,Omar	Cle	79	54	.684	2	37	27	.730	3
Guillen,Carlos	Sea	66	45	.682	3	30	25	.833	1
Gonzalez,Alex S	ChC	132	84	.636	4	73	51	.699	4
Rollins,Jimmy	Phi	140	89	.636	5	76	56	.737	2
Santiago,Ramon	Det	104	66	.635	6	64	41	.641	12
Bordick,Mike	Tor	80	50	.625	7	47	27	.574	27
Sanchez,Rey	NYM-Sea	85	53	.624	8	45	29	.644	9
Berroa,Angel	KC	158	97	.614	9	84	54	.643	11
Renteria,Edgar	StL	124	76	.613	10	67	45	.672	7
Cruz,Deivi	Bal	142	87	.613	11	89	57	.640	13
Valentin,Jose	CWS	145	88	.607	12	85	56	.659	8
Wilson,Jack	Pit	161	96	.596	13	85	47	.553	30
Furcal,Rafael	Atl	174	103	.592	14	108	67	.620	17
Uribe,Juan	Col	90	53	.589	15	57	35	.614	18
Rodriguez,Alex	Tex	169	99	.586	16	93	56	.602	21
Eckstein,David	Ana	101	59	.584	17	59	37	.627	15
Izturis,Cesar	LA	149	87	.584	18	67	39	.582	26
Hernandez,Jose	3 teams	79	46	.582	19	40	22	.550	31
Everett,Adam	Hou	109	63	.578	20	60	36	.600	22
Aurilia,Rich	SF	123	71	.577	21	60	36	.600	22
Cabrera,Orlando	Mon	157	90	.573	22	87	53	.609	19
Clayton,Royce	Mil	126	72	.571	23	69	39	.565	28
Peralta,Jhonny	Cle	67	38	.567	24	32	20	.625	16
Woodward,Chris	Tor	113	64	.566	25	59	38	.644	10
Infante,Omar	Det	85	48	.565	26	48	28	.583	25
Tejada,Miguel	Oak	151	85	.563	27	83	50	.602	20
Guzman,Cristian	Min	109	61	.560	28	62	34	.548	32
Vazquez,Ramon	SD	97	54	.557	29	50	26	.520	33
Lugo,Julio	Hou-TB	132	72	.545	30	77	46	.597	24
Reyes,Jose	NYM	73	39	.534	31	29	20	.690	6
Cintron,Alex	Ari	97	51	.526	32	59	33	.559	29
Jeter,Derek	NYY	88	46	.523	33	38	24	.632	14
Garciaparra,Nomar	Bos	155	78	.503	34	92	47	.511	34
Womack,Tony	3 teams	63	28	.444	35	29	11	.379	35

221

Outfielder Throwing Arms

A base hit to center. The man on second rounds third. The center fielder charges the ball and guns the runner out at the plate.

Or.

A base hit to center. The man on second rounds third. The center fielder charges the ball. The runner scoots back to third as the first baseman cuts the throw near the pitcher's mound.

In the first outcome, it's clear that the strength and accuracy of the center fielder's arm will determine how often he's able to "kill" that runner at the plate. But the second outcome is also dependant on the arm of the center fielder. The strength and accuracy of the center fielder's arm comes into play by reputation. The third base coach, and usually the runner as well, have a good idea about who they can run on and who they can't. They know that if it's Jim Edmonds or Ichiro Suzuki, they need to hold up more often than not.

Our mission is to track both outcomes and measure them for every outfielder in the game. We've developed two statistics. The first one is called Baserunner Kills. This is one step beyond the traditional statistic, Assists, for outfielders. An outfielder will get an assist on any throw that eventually turns into an out. A ball hit into the gap that is relayed on to the shortstop who then throws out the runner at the plate is an Assist, but not a Baserunner Kill, for the outfielder. The arm of the outfielder comes into play on that relay play, but the arm of the infielder is at least as important as the outfielder's in determining the outcome. A Baserunner Kill is a pure measure for outfielders.

The second statistic we have is Outfield Advance Percentage. It's a measure of the intimidation factor for outfielders. For those of you who were fans of our Baseball Scoreboard series at my old company STATS, Inc., this is the same thing that we did every year in that book. If a base hit is hit to the center fielder with a man on second, that's an Opportunity to Advance an extra base against the center fielder. If the runner scores on the hit, that's an Extra Base taken. We do the same thing for base hits with a man on first. In this case it only counts as an Opportunity if second base is open. The Extra Base gets tallied if the runner goes from first to third on the hit. Finally, we have our third situation where we tally an

Opportunity when a double is hit to an outfielder with a man on first with second base open. If he comes around to score, that's an Extra Base. Add up all the Extra Bases against each outfielder, divide by the Opportunities, and we get Outfield Advance Percentage.

Looking at the charts that follow here are some of the things we find:

- The two best throwing outfielders over the last three seasons are center fielder Jim Edmonds and right fielder Richard Hidalgo. Both had the lowest Outfield Advance Percentage and the most Kills at their positions over that time period. Hidalgo's 34 kills were far and away more than anyone else's total. Edmonds led center fielders with 19.

- Ichiro Suzuki tied Vladimir Guerrero for third most kills in right field during the three years with 21. Jose Cruz Jr. was second (25). Ichiro "slumped" in 2005 to only six kills, but before you think that must be because they were running less often, they weren't. He also slumped in Outfield Advance Percentage to .572, near the bottom of the league. Over three years, however, he still remains near the top, ranked fifth in baseball with a .477 percentage.

- The strongest arm in left field? Probably Miguel Cabrera. His hold percentage of .328 is fourth over three years in left field while his 20 kills is tied for second.

- Ryan Klesko was the easiest left fielder among regulars to run on with a .503 percentage over the last three years. That was a wide margin over the next worst percentage, Jason Bay at .442. Klesko also had the fewest Kills among regulars in left. Given that he plays left field, the position that you play the fielder with the weakest arm, you can probably give him the title of Easiest Outfielder To Run On overall. Despite the generally longer throw from right field, there were eight right fielders with better percentages than Klesko.

- Bernie Williams gives Klesko a run for his money, but at the center field spot, with a .703 Outfield Advance Percentage. Alex Sanchez is close behind Bernie at .697.

- The single most impressive season: Richard Hidalgo had 19 Kills with the best Advance Percentage in right field of .383 in 2003.

Left Fielders - 3-Year Throwing

Player	Opps	Extra Bases	Pct	Kills
Payton,Jay	185	51	.276	4
Catalanotto,Frank	136	42	.309	7
Crawford,Carl	391	122	.312	11
Cabrera,Miguel	198	65	.328	20
Burrell,Pat	355	120	.338	20
Dunn,Adam	340	118	.347	12
Berkman,Lance	184	64	.348	9
Ibanez,Raul	256	90	.352	17
Matsui,Hideki	364	129	.354	13
Byrnes,Eric	192	70	.365	8
Winn,Randy	219	82	.374	3
Crisp,Coco	166	63	.380	3
Stewart,Shannon	257	98	.381	8
Ramirez,Manny	388	149	.384	20
Jenkins,Geoff	245	95	.388	18
Long,Terrence	205	81	.395	8
Mench,Kevin	188	75	.399	7
Bigbie,Larry	231	94	.407	5
Holliday,Matt	228	93	.408	4
Floyd,Cliff	314	129	.411	23
White,Rondell	235	98	.417	6
Lee,Carlos	381	159	.417	17
Bonds,Barry	201	84	.418	8
Anderson,Garret	215	90	.419	10
Alou,Moises	260	109	.419	9
Jones,Chipper	140	59	.421	7
Gonzalez,Luis	350	148	.423	4
Monroe,Craig	175	75	.429	8
Lawton,Matt	202	89	.441	5
Bay,Jason	231	102	.442	5
Klesko,Ryan	161	81	.503	2

Left Fielders - 2004 Throwing

Player	Tm	Opps	Extra Bases	Pct	Kills
Thomas,Charles	Atl	52	13	.250	3
Matsui,Hideki	NYY	131	37	.282	5
Sledge,Terrmel	Mon	53	15	.283	3
Burrell,Pat	Phi	98	28	.286	7
Dunn,Adam	Cin	128	38	.297	7
Cabrera,Miguel	Fla	40	12	.300	5
Crawford,Carl	TB	100	30	.300	3
Werth,Jayson	LA	42	13	.310	4
Byrnes,Eric	Oak	89	28	.315	3
Conine,Jeff	Fla	70	23	.329	4
Ford,Lew	Min	58	20	.345	3
Ibanez,Raul	Sea	94	34	.362	6
Guillen,Jose	Ana	112	43	.384	7
Jenkins,Geoff	Mil	124	49	.395	10
Alou,Moises	ChC	91	36	.396	4
Lawton,Matt	Cle	129	52	.403	4
Lee,Carlos	CWS	113	46	.407	8
Holliday,Matt	Col	111	46	.414	1
Berkman,Lance	Hou	55	23	.418	2
Stewart,Shannon	Min	57	24	.421	0
Gonzalez,Luis	Ari	83	35	.422	2
Ramirez,Manny	Bos	123	52	.423	2
Bay,Jason	Pit	94	42	.447	2
Bigbie,Larry	Bal	116	53	.457	1
White,Rondell	Det	84	40	.476	1
Biggio,Craig	Hou	63	30	.476	1
Bonds,Barry	SF	111	54	.486	5
Dellucci,David	Tex	61	31	.508	0
Floyd,Cliff	NYM	93	48	.516	3
Klesko,Ryan	SD	68	42	.618	0

Left Fielders - 2005 Throwing

Player	Tm	Opps	Extra Bases	Pct	Kills
Catalanotto,Frank	Tor	54	13	.241	3
Crawford,Carl	TB	155	40	.258	3
Feliz,Pedro	SF	66	20	.303	0
Sanders,Reggie	StL	52	16	.308	2
Johnson,Kelly	Atl	71	22	.310	5
Johnson,Reed	Tor	46	15	.326	2
Burke,Chris	Hou	45	15	.333	2
Alou,Moises	SF	63	21	.333	1
Cabrera,Miguel	Fla	106	36	.340	10
Winn,Randy	Sea-SF	84	29	.345	2
Stewart,Shannon	Min	104	36	.346	3
Floyd,Cliff	NYM	147	52	.354	14
Burrell,Pat	Phi	147	52	.354	9
Matsui,Hideki	NYY	113	41	.363	4
Dunn,Adam	Cin	113	41	.363	2
Podsednik,Scott	CWS	96	35	.365	3
Lee,Carlos	Mil	134	49	.366	5
White,Rondell	Det	41	15	.366	0
Crisp,Coco	Cle	110	41	.373	1
Ramirez,Manny	Bos	147	56	.381	13
Anderson,Garret	LAA	80	32	.400	3
Holliday,Matt	Col	117	47	.402	3
Long,Terrence	KC	129	52	.403	6
Gonzalez,Luis	Ari	153	62	.405	0
Monroe,Craig	Det	54	22	.407	3
Klesko,Ryan	SD	93	39	.419	2
Mench,Kevin	Tex	122	52	.426	7
Bay,Jason	Pit	121	53	.438	3
Hollandsworth,Todd	ChC-Atl	77	34	.442	2
Byrnes,Eric	3 teams	74	34	.459	4

Left Fielders - 2003 Throwing

Player	Tm	Opps	Extra Bases	Pct	Kills
Payton,Jay	Col	147	40	.272	3
Berkman,Lance	Hou	105	32	.305	6
Bonds,Barry	SF	82	28	.341	3
Ramirez,Manny	Bos	118	41	.347	5
Ibanez,Raul	KC	102	36	.353	6
Burrell,Pat	Phi	110	40	.364	4
Wilkerson,Brad	Mon	73	27	.370	7
Giles,Brian	Pit-SD	113	42	.372	2
Jenkins,Geoff	Mil	121	46	.380	8
Crawford,Carl	TB	136	52	.382	5
White,Rondell	SD-KC	110	43	.391	5
Long,Terrence	Oak	46	18	.391	1
Floyd,Cliff	NYM	74	29	.392	6
Dunn,Adam	Cin	99	39	.394	3
Stewart,Shannon	Tor-Min	96	38	.396	5
Bigbie,Larry	Bal	67	27	.403	2
Winn,Randy	Sea	98	40	.408	1
Matsui,Hideki	NYY	120	51	.425	4
Anderson,Garret	Ana	135	58	.430	7
Young,Dmitri	Det	67	29	.433	2
Monroe,Craig	Det	73	32	.438	5
Jones,Chipper	Atl	127	56	.441	6
Gonzalez,Luis	Ari	114	51	.447	2
Jones,Jacque	Min	62	28	.452	2
Lawton,Matt	Cle	58	27	.466	1
Lee,Carlos	CWS	134	64	.478	4
Alou,Moises	ChC	106	52	.491	4
Pujols,Albert	StL	90	46	.511	5

Center Fielders - 3-Year Throwing

Player	Opps	Extra Bases	Pct	Kills
Edmonds,Jim	347	161	.464	19
Sizemore,Grady	155	76	.490	2
Chavez,Endy	200	102	.510	13
Baldelli,Rocco	264	139	.527	14
Rowand,Aaron	256	137	.535	10
Finley,Steve	361	194	.537	13
Jones,Andruw	457	246	.538	15
Kotsay,Mark	374	204	.545	18
Podsednik,Scott	230	126	.548	6
Winn,Randy	190	105	.553	3
Nix,Laynce	169	94	.556	3
Hunter,Torii	384	217	.565	16
Griffey Jr.,Ken	249	141	.566	7
Byrd,Marlon	168	98	.583	4
Cameron,Mike	278	165	.594	2
Matthews Jr.,Gary	227	135	.595	7
Bradley,Milton	230	138	.600	8
DeJesus,David	222	134	.604	10
Patterson,Corey	281	170	.605	12
Damon,Johnny	373	226	.606	11
Lofton,Kenny	210	128	.610	15
Wilson,Preston	337	206	.611	7
Roberts,Dave	161	99	.615	4
Beltran,Carlos	412	254	.617	17
Biggio,Craig	189	117	.619	5
Wells,Vernon	412	260	.631	14
Grissom,Marquis	274	174	.635	4
Matos,Luis	313	200	.639	9
Redman,Tike	243	157	.646	2
Pierre,Juan	421	276	.656	11
Sanchez,Alex	251	175	.697	5
Williams,Bernie	300	211	.703	4

Center Fielders - 2004 Throwing

Player	Tm	Opps	Extra Bases	Pct	Kills
Edmonds,Jim	StL	117	52	.444	9
Payton,Jay	SD	95	44	.463	7
Hunter,Torii	Min	136	70	.515	5
Patterson,Corey	ChC	111	58	.523	6
Cameron,Mike	NYM	143	76	.531	0
Jones,Andruw	Atl	163	88	.540	6
Griffey Jr.,Ken	Cin	74	41	.554	1
Rowand,Aaron	CWS	104	58	.558	6
Kotsay,Mark	Oak	129	72	.558	6
Baldelli,Rocco	TB	114	64	.561	9
Winn,Randy	Sea	121	69	.570	2
Chavez,Endy	Mon	107	62	.579	6
Nix,Laynce	Tex	97	57	.588	1
Finley,Steve	Ari-LA	153	90	.588	2
Podsednik,Scott	Mil	124	73	.589	3
Beltran,Carlos	KC-Hou	154	91	.591	7
Biggio,Craig	Hou	64	38	.594	1
Damon,Johnny	Bos	121	72	.595	4
Redman,Tike	Pit	127	77	.606	2
Crisp,Coco	Cle	89	54	.607	0
Bradley,Milton	LA	69	42	.609	1
Anderson,Garret	Ana	95	58	.611	2
Wells,Vernon	Tor	116	71	.612	4
Byrd,Marlon	Phi	65	40	.615	1
Burnitz,Jeromy	Col	59	38	.644	2
DeJesus,David	KC	95	62	.653	3
Grissom,Marquis	SF	122	80	.656	2
Pierre,Juan	Fla	123	87	.707	1
Williams,Bernie	NYY	88	63	.716	2
Sanchez,Alex	Det	74	54	.730	1
Lofton,Kenny	NYY	52	38	.731	3
Matos,Luis	Bal	85	65	.765	2

Center Fielders - 2005 Throwing

Player	Tm	Opps	Extra Bases	Pct	Kills
Edmonds,Jim	StL	117	48	.410	2
Michaels,Jason	Phi	43	19	.442	1
Kotsay,Mark	Oak	103	50	.485	6
Rowand,Aaron	CWS	117	58	.496	1
Finley,Steve	LAA	88	44	.500	3
Sizemore,Grady	Cle	118	60	.508	2
Lofton,Kenny	Phi	51	26	.510	6
Nix,Laynce	Tex	60	31	.517	2
Ford,Lew	Min	76	40	.526	1
Jones,Andruw	Atl	138	73	.529	6
Winn,Randy	Sea-SF	49	26	.531	1
Griffey Jr.,Ken	Cin	136	74	.544	4
Wilkerson,Brad	Was	75	41	.547	4
Sullivan,Cory	Col	64	35	.547	3
DeJesus,David	KC	122	67	.549	7
Taveras,Willy	Hou	100	56	.560	8
Bradley,Milton	LAD	65	37	.569	4
Damon,Johnny	Bos	120	69	.575	4
Logan,Nook	Det	87	51	.586	1
Matthews Jr.,Gary	Tex	134	79	.590	3
Clark,Brady	Mil	131	79	.603	5
Patterson,Corey	ChC	97	59	.608	5
Matos,Luis	Bal	105	64	.610	3
Wells,Vernon	Tor	149	91	.611	7
Gathright,Joey	TB	54	33	.611	3
Hunter,Torii	Min	94	58	.617	7
Reed,Jeremy	Sea	128	79	.617	4
Redman,Tike	Pit	50	31	.620	0
Roberts,Dave	SD	81	51	.630	2
Pierre,Juan	Fla	148	94	.635	5
Wilson,Preston	Col-Was	122	79	.648	3
Beltran,Carlos	NYM	138	91	.659	4
Williams,Bernie	NYY	93	63	.677	1
Hollins,Damon	TB	91	62	.681	3
Ellison,Jason	SF	70	49	.700	3

Center Fielders - 2003 Throwing

Player	Tm	Opps	Extra Bases	Pct	Kills
Chavez,Endy	Mon	86	37	.430	6
Finley,Steve	Ari	120	60	.500	8
Baldelli,Rocco	TB	150	75	.500	5
Podsednik,Scott	Mil	104	52	.500	3
Erstad,Darin	Ana	63	33	.524	1
Edmonds,Jim	StL	113	61	.540	8
Jones,Andruw	Atl	156	85	.545	3
Byrd,Marlon	Phi	102	57	.559	3
Singleton,Chris	Oak	74	42	.568	1
Byrnes,Eric	Oak	63	36	.571	2
Wilson,Preston	Col	163	94	.577	4
Matos,Luis	Bal	123	71	.577	4
Kotsay,Mark	SD	142	82	.577	6
Hunter,Torii	Min	154	89	.578	4
Matthews Jr.,Gary	Bal-SD	68	40	.588	1
Lofton,Kenny	Pit-ChC	107	64	.598	6
Beltran,Carlos	KC	120	72	.600	6
Roberts,Dave	LA	70	42	.600	1
Grissom,Marquis	SF	119	72	.605	2
Bradley,Milton	Cle	96	59	.615	4
Biggio,Craig	Hou	125	79	.632	4
Pierre,Juan	Fla	150	95	.633	5
Damon,Johnny	Bos	132	85	.644	3
Cameron,Mike	Sea	127	83	.654	2
Everett,Carl	Tex-CWS	55	36	.655	0
Wells,Vernon	Tor	147	98	.667	3
Sanchez,Alex	Mil-Det	151	106	.702	4
Williams,Bernie	NYY	119	85	.714	1
Patterson,Corey	ChC	73	53	.726	1

Right Fielders - 3-Year Throwing

Player	Opps	Extra Bases	Pct	Kills
Hidalgo,Richard	316	135	.427	34
Rios,Alexis	229	99	.432	12
Jones,Jacque	240	113	.471	8
Walker,Larry	248	117	.472	9
Suzuki,Ichiro	465	222	.477	21
Cruz,Jose	322	158	.491	25
Mondesi,Raul	172	86	.500	10
Abreu,Bobby	383	194	.507	16
Kearns,Austin	186	95	.511	11
Huff,Aubrey	181	94	.519	8
Sheffield,Gary	373	197	.528	16
Guerrero,Vladimir	310	165	.532	21
Gibbons,Jay	267	145	.543	13
Ordonez,Magglio	252	137	.544	9
Guillen,Jose	209	116	.555	14
Nixon,Trot	264	147	.557	7
Dye,Jermaine	295	166	.563	8
Giles,Brian	305	172	.564	9
Burnitz,Jeromy	222	127	.572	4
Green,Shawn	244	140	.574	5
Encarnacion,Juan	334	192	.575	9
Sosa,Sammy	258	151	.585	5
Drew,J.D.	227	133	.586	10
Tucker,Michael	174	103	.592	7
Gerut,Jody	194	115	.593	11
Higginson,Bobby	195	116	.595	12
Bautista,Danny	162	99	.611	4

Right Fielders - 2004 Throwing

Player	Tm	Opps	Extra Bases	Pct	Kills
Hidalgo,Richard	Hou-NYM	114	48	.421	13
Suzuki,Ichiro	Sea	145	63	.434	7
Rios,Alexis	Tor	111	49	.441	8
Mench,Kevin	Tex	53	24	.453	4
Gibbons,Jay	Bal	65	30	.462	6
Jones,Jacque	Min	132	61	.462	1
Rivera,Juan	Mon	79	37	.468	12
Berkman,Lance	Hou	64	31	.484	7
Sanders,Reggie	StL	73	36	.493	3
Cruz,Jose	TB	148	73	.493	8
Nunez,Abraham	Fla-KC	66	33	.500	1
Burnitz,Jeromy	Col	64	33	.516	2
Higginson,Bobby	Det	86	46	.535	8
Kearns,Austin	Cin	50	27	.540	1
Guerrero,Vladimir	Ana	128	70	.547	8
Sheffield,Gary	NYY	140	78	.557	8
Encarnacion,Juan	LA-Fla	82	47	.573	2
Giles,Brian	SD	162	94	.580	5
Bautista,Danny	Ari	116	68	.586	4
Drew,J.D.	Atl	133	79	.594	5
Dye,Jermaine	Oak	119	71	.597	3
Abreu,Bobby	Phi	139	83	.597	9
Gerut,Jody	Cle	115	69	.600	6
Cabrera,Miguel	Fla	88	54	.614	4
Kapler,Gabe	Bos	42	26	.619	3
Tucker,Michael	SF	87	54	.621	1
Walker,Larry	Col-StL	64	40	.625	2
Wilson,Craig	Pit	64	40	.625	0
Sosa,Sammy	ChC	96	63	.656	3
Clark,Brady	Mil	87	64	.736	1

Right Fielders - 2005 Throwing

Player	Tm	Opps	Extra Bases	Pct	Kills
Diaz,Victor	NYM	66	25	.379	2
Rios,Alexis	Tor	118	50	.424	4
Lane,Jason	Hou	111	48	.432	3
Lawton,Matt	3 teams	94	42	.447	3
Sheffield,Gary	NYY	118	53	.449	3
Guerrero,Vladimir	LAA	83	38	.458	6
Walker,Larry	StL	56	26	.464	1
Jones,Jacque	Min	101	48	.475	7
Kearns,Austin	Cin	97	47	.485	8
Cameron,Mike	NYM	55	27	.491	2
Abreu,Bobby	Phi	118	58	.492	4
Francoeur,Jeff	Atl	69	34	.493	10
Hidalgo,Richard	Tex	87	43	.494	2
Huff,Aubrey	TB	96	49	.510	4
Dye,Jermaine	CWS	119	61	.513	5
Encarnacion,Juan	Fla	126	66	.524	2
Monroe,Craig	Det	49	26	.531	2
Guillen,Jose	Was	136	73	.537	7
Green,Shawn	Ari	103	56	.544	0
Giles,Brian	SD	143	78	.545	4
Gibbons,Jay	Bal	77	42	.545	1
Hawpe,Brad	Col	107	59	.551	6
Swisher,Nick	Oak	82	46	.561	4
Nixon,Trot	Bos	110	62	.564	5
Jenkins,Geoff	Mil	127	72	.567	10
Suzuki,Ichiro	Sea	180	103	.572	6
Ordonez,Magglio	Det	82	47	.573	2
Sosa,Sammy	Bal	47	27	.574	1
Blake,Casey	Cle	128	76	.594	2
Brown,Emil	KC	154	95	.617	1
Burnitz,Jeromy	ChC	124	78	.629	1

Right Fielders - 2003 Throwing

Player	Tm	Opps	Extra Bases	Pct	Kills
Hidalgo,Richard	Hou	115	44	.383	19
DaVanon,Jeff	Ana	48	19	.396	1
Walker,Larry	Col	128	51	.398	6
Suzuki,Ichiro	Sea	140	56	.400	8
Abreu,Bobby	Phi	126	53	.421	3
Cruz,Jose	SF	129	60	.465	13
Mohr,Dustan	Min	59	28	.475	1
Nixon,Trot	Bos	120	59	.492	2
Guiel,Aaron	KC	107	53	.495	5
Ordonez,Magglio	CWS	130	65	.500	7
Mondesi,Raul	NYY-Ari	115	60	.522	6
Huff,Aubrey	TB	85	45	.529	4
Sosa,Sammy	ChC	115	61	.530	1
Kielty,Bobby	Min-Tor	60	32	.533	0
Johnson,Reed	Tor	55	31	.564	4
Nady,Xavier	SD	79	45	.570	8
Vander Wal,John	Mil	70	40	.571	2
Sheffield,Gary	Atl	115	66	.574	5
Guerrero,Vladimir	Mon	99	57	.576	7
Gerut,Jody	Cle	55	32	.582	5
Guillen,Jose	Cin-Oak	72	42	.583	7
Gibbons,Jay	Bal	125	73	.584	6
Dye,Jermaine	Oak	57	34	.596	0
Salmon,Tim	Ana	62	37	.597	2
Sanders,Reggie	Pit	82	49	.598	3
Green,Shawn	LA	105	64	.610	3
Cedeno,Roger	NYM	72	44	.611	1
Encarnacion,Juan	Fla	126	79	.627	5
Higginson,Bobby	Det	105	69	.657	4
Long,Terrence	Oak	41	28	.683	1

Revised Zone Ratings

I developed the Zone Rating system back in the 80's—no, not the 1880's, I'm not quite that old—while at my old company, STATS Inc.

The basic concept was straightforward. Figure out an area around each fielder that we call his zone. This is an area where he should be expected to make plays. Specifically, it's any area where fielders as a whole successfully handle at least 50% of the batted balls in that area. Count all the batted balls that are hit into a player's zone. Count all the balls that he successfully fields. Divide the number that he successfully fields by the number in his zone and that's his zone rating.

The zone rating number is supposed to be like a fielding percentage. Fielding percentage also divides the number of successfully fielded balls by the number of total batted balls. But the number of batted balls excludes a huge element: hits allowed in the fielder's area. With fielding percentage you get numbers like .978, Adam Everett's fielding percentage in 2005. With zone rating you get numbers like .860, Adam Everett's zone rating in 2005.

When I originally developed zone ratings I was looking for a one-number system to include as many fielding elements as possible. The two elements that I then included were balls hit outside the zone and double plays. To handle balls hit outside the zone I simply added them in as a both an opportunity and a success. This would have the effect of raising a guy's zone rating for handling balls hit outside his zone. Let's use Adam Everett as an example again. He successfully fielded 296 out of 344 batted balls in the shortstop zone for the Astros last year. He also had 78 balls successfully fielded outside his zone. My old zone rating system added the 78 balls as both a success and an opportunity giving him a zone rating of $(296+78)/(344+78) = .896$. But then I went one step further. I gave double credit for groundballs hit to the player that became a double play. Everett started 39 double plays last year. That 39 simply got added in as additional successfully fielded balls making the calculation $(296+78+39)/(344+78)$ for a zone rating of .979.

You may notice that his zone rating now looks a lot like his fielding percentage (.979 .vs .978). Everett's two numbers are remarkably close, more so than you'll find with most players. But my intention was that the zone rating number looks like a fielding percentage, albeit by

definition not identical, so I felt comfortable with the process.

However, this is where Bill James and I began our debates. I contended that the system went one step beyond range factors in that it removed several biases. One bias is that a groundball pitching staff inflates range factors for infielders and deflates them for outfielders. Another bias is that a pitching staff with a lot of left-handed pitching innings faces more right-handed batters and subsequently more groundballs to the left side of the infield. That inflates the range factors for shortstops and especially for third basemen. In the zone rating system it didn't matter what kind of pitcher was pitching. We just looked at balls hit into a fielder's zone. If the third baseman got fewer opportunities it didn't matter, because the zone rating number was a "rate" calculation. At what rate was he making the plays?

While Bill was comfortable with that argument, he felt there was too much mixing of apples and oranges in the calculation. Namely, he thought the two adjustments mentioned above for balls hit outside the zone and double plays were arbitrary and therefore confusing the issue. The end result of that debate is this book, *The Fielding Bible*.

Bill has come up with Relative Range Factors (see "Relative Range Factors" on page 199) to address the biases in range factors. I've come up with the Plus/Minus System and, in this article, Revised Zone Ratings. These revised zone ratings remove the two adjustments for balls hit outside the zone and double plays. So instead of a zone rating of .979 for Everett, we're going with the .860 and then telling you he made 78 plays outside his zone. You can compare that to Omar Vizquel's numbers directly, for example. Vizquel had a zone rating based on the new calculation of .856 with 43 plays outside the zone. The sure-handed Vizquel did about the same as Everett in the zone (.856 to .860) but he had just over half of Everett's total of balls handled outside the zone (43 to 78). Thus, zone rating is another number that suggests Everett as the Gold Glover That Should Have Been at shortstop in 2005 over the actual winner, Omar Vizquel.

In terms of results there are a lot of consistencies between the zone rating system and the Plus/Minus System. That makes sense. They both have batted ball location as their foundation. However, the Plus/Minus

System goes a few steps further. Instead of a black and white separation of zones into those that are above 50% successful for fielders and those that are below 50%, we break each zone into smaller sectors and each sector's success percentage itself is factored into the Plus/Minus System. The Plus/Minus System then even takes each sector and breaks it down by additional factors such as the speed and type of batted ball. We believe that the Plus/Minus System advances the analysis of fielding range. But the revised zone rating system, and the older zone rating system, are still useful to provide another perspective.

The charts that follow provide revised zone ratings for all regulars during the past three years. Here are some highlights:

- Zone Ratings for 2005 concur, for the most part, with the following Gold Glove winners: Mark Teixeira, Luis Castillo, Orlando Hudson, Eric Chavez, Torii Hunter and Ichiro Suzuki. Castillo and Suzuki both performed significantly better in zone ratings than they did in the Plus/Minus System.
- These 2005 Gold Glovers performed poorly in the new zone rating system: Derrek Lee, Mike Lowell, Derek Jeter, Bobby Abreu. These are the exact same guys that the Plus/Minus System was unhappy about.
- Let's put together an all-star team for the last three years. Remember, when you are looking at the charts to evaluate a player, also factor in plays made on balls outside the zone.

Mark Teixeira, 1B
Orlando Hudson, 2B
Adrian Beltre, 3B
Adam Everett, SS
Carl Crawford, LF
Aaron Rowand, CF
Ichiro Suzuki, RF

That's a very respectable list. You could win a lot of games with that lineup!

First Basemen - 3-Year Zone Ratings

Player	Balls In Zone	Plays Made	Zone Rating	Plays Out Of Zone
Justin Morneau	198	170	.859	64
Mark Teixeira	490	400	.816	214
Albert Pujols	458	368	.803	146
Doug Mientkiewicz	332	265	.798	124
Daryle Ward	172	135	.785	54
John Olerud	389	305	.784	108
Travis Lee	337	264	.783	71
J.T. Snow	301	235	.781	101
Nick Johnson	300	233	.777	85
Scott Hatteberg	353	274	.776	65
Darin Erstad	287	222	.774	132
Jeff Bagwell	329	254	.772	97
Tony Clark	213	164	.770	51
Sean Casey	483	371	.768	100
Hee Seop Choi	263	202	.768	80
Kevin Millar	378	287	.759	102
Ben Broussard	380	287	.755	110
Jeff Conine	284	214	.754	77
Paul Konerko	415	312	.752	135
Todd Helton	568	427	.752	182
Lyle Overbay	424	318	.750	127
Shea Hillenbrand	342	256	.749	66
Tino Martinez	357	266	.745	136
Phil Nevin	262	195	.744	111
Carlos Pena	333	245	.736	94
Derrek Lee	508	372	.732	138
Jason Giambi	210	153	.729	49
Rafael Palmeiro	312	227	.728	104
Richie Sexson	389	280	.720	105
Carlos Delgado	605	434	.717	126
Jim Thome	371	260	.701	115
Adam LaRoche	233	162	.695	82

First Basemen - 2004 Zone Ratings

Player	Tm	Balls In Zone	Plays Made	Zone Rating	Plays Out Of Zone
Tony Clark	NYY	78	65	.833	28
Albert Pujols	StL	206	166	.806	61
Ben Broussard	Cle	117	94	.803	44
Mark Teixeira	Tex	204	163	.799	61
Pedro Feliz	SF	57	45	.789	25
Brad Wilkerson	Mon	90	71	.789	34
Kevin Millar	Bos	75	59	.787	27
Daryle Ward	Pit	56	44	.786	16
Julio Franco	Atl	65	51	.785	29
Sean Casey	Cin	140	109	.779	40
Scott Hatteberg	Oak	152	118	.776	34
Tino Martinez	TB	133	103	.774	39
Doug Mientkiewicz	2 tms	124	96	.774	44
Shawn Green	LA	87	67	.770	24
John Olerud	2 tms	134	103	.769	45
Jeff Bagwell	Hou	155	119	.768	39
Justin Morneau	Min	60	46	.767	20
Shea Hillenbrand	Ari	149	114	.765	29
Carlos Pena	Det	116	88	.759	41
Nick Johnson	Mon	69	52	.754	24
Todd Helton	Col	173	129	.746	62
J.T. Snow	SF	95	70	.737	33
Phil Nevin	SD	147	108	.735	55
Darin Erstad	Ana	138	101	.732	60
Carlos Delgado	Tor	193	141	.731	44
Jim Thome	Phi	115	83	.722	65
Paul Konerko	CWS	128	92	.719	38
Derrek Lee	ChC	182	130	.714	55
Ken Harvey	KC	62	44	.710	21
Adam LaRoche	Atl	80	56	.700	31
Rafael Palmeiro	Bal	162	112	.691	44
Lyle Overbay	Mil	158	107	.677	55
Hee Seop Choi	2 tms	91	60	.659	32
Mike Piazza	NYM	56	36	.643	23

First Basemen - 2005 Zone Ratings

Player	Tm	Balls In Zone	Plays Made	Zone Rating	Plays Out Of Zone
Doug Mientkiewicz	NYM	56	51	.911	38
Justin Morneau	Min	132	120	.909	42
Chad Tracy	Ari	74	64	.865	33
Tony Clark	Ari	72	61	.847	16
J.T. Snow	SF	103	87	.845	35
Eric Hinske	Tor	131	110	.840	34
Nick Johnson	Was	156	130	.833	45
Hee Seop Choi	LAD	109	90	.826	31
Lance Niekro	SF	63	52	.825	33
Mark Teixeira	Tex	178	145	.815	96
Darin Erstad	LAA	149	121	.812	72
Albert Pujols	StL	203	164	.808	68
Daryle Ward	Pit	104	84	.808	31
Shea Hillenbrand	Tor	88	71	.807	24
Dan Johnson	Oak	99	79	.798	37
Matt Stairs	KC	69	55	.797	22
Lyle Overbay	Mil	136	108	.794	49
Chris Shelton	Det	97	77	.794	29
Richie Sexson	Sea	174	138	.793	49
Kevin Millar	Bos	142	112	.789	42
Paul Konerko	CWS	144	113	.785	59
Ben Broussard	Cle	124	97	.782	41
Todd Helton	Col	179	140	.782	59
Derrek Lee	ChC	149	116	.779	59
Rafael Palmeiro	Bal	92	71	.772	25
Sean Casey	Cin	157	121	.771	32
Phil Nevin	2 tms	74	57	.770	41
Travis Lee	TB	129	99	.767	32
Tino Martinez	NYY	83	61	.735	64
Lance Berkman	Hou	86	63	.733	36
Ryan Howard	Phi	72	52	.722	49
Jason Giambi	NYY	54	39	.722	22
Adam LaRoche	Atl	153	106	.693	51
Carlos Delgado	Fla	166	114	.687	47

First Basemen - 2003 Zone Ratings

Player	Tm	Balls In Zone	Plays Made	Zone Rating	Plays Out Of Zone
Mark Teixeira	Tex	108	92	.852	57
Scott Spiezio	Ana	103	86	.835	26
Hee Seop Choi	ChC	63	52	.825	17
Robert Fick	Atl	113	92	.814	35
Fred McGriff	LA	65	52	.800	17
Travis Lee	TB	199	158	.794	37
Lyle Overbay	Ari	130	103	.792	23
Jason Phillips	NYM	70	55	.786	19
Doug Mientkiewicz	Min	152	118	.776	42
John Olerud	Sea	200	155	.775	39
Jeff Bagwell	Hou	150	114	.760	45
Sean Casey	Cin	186	141	.758	28
J.T. Snow	SF	103	78	.757	33
Scott Hatteberg	Oak	130	98	.754	20
Ken Harvey	KC	124	93	.750	29
Paul Konerko	CWS	143	107	.748	38
Andres Galarraga	SF	61	45	.738	13
Todd Helton	Col	216	158	.731	61
Jeff Conine	2 tms	185	135	.730	32
Carlos Delgado	Tor	246	179	.728	35
Tino Martinez	StL	141	102	.723	33
Kevin Millar	Bos	161	116	.720	33
Randall Simon	2 tms	117	84	.718	26
Derrek Lee	Fla	177	126	.712	24
Jason Giambi	NYY	112	78	.696	15
Carlos Pena	Det	158	110	.696	39
Ryan Klesko	SD	133	92	.692	25
Ben Broussard	Cle	139	96	.691	25
Nick Johnson	NYY	75	51	.680	16
Shea Hillenbrand	2 tms	105	71	.676	13
Jim Thome	Phi	214	144	.673	28
Wil Cordero	Mon	130	87	.669	26
Richie Sexson	Mil	186	121	.651	44
Eric Karros	ChC	73	47	.644	27

Second Basemen - 3-Year Zone Ratings

Player	Balls In Zone	Plays Made	Zone Rating	Plays Out Of Zone
Mark Ellis	653	587	.899	81
Luis Castillo	968	837	.865	130
Orlando Hudson	1095	944	.862	166
D'Angelo Jimenez	678	580	.855	90
Marcus Giles	1068	913	.855	135
Ray Durham	844	720	.853	88
Mark Grudzielanek	816	696	.853	97
Adam Kennedy	958	817	.853	131
Junior Spivey	523	446	.853	89
Placido Polanco	737	627	.851	104
Chase Utley	523	444	.849	64
Jeff Kent	969	818	.844	115
Alex Cora	653	549	.841	94
Mark Loretta	992	834	.841	99
Brian Roberts	997	836	.839	143
Jose Vidro	755	633	.838	67
Ronnie Belliard	979	818	.836	132
Aaron Miles	465	384	.826	67
Todd Walker	803	663	.826	87
Mark Bellhorn	595	491	.825	69
Alfonso Soriano	1160	957	.825	138
Luis Rivas	634	512	.808	80
Bret Boone	940	752	.800	90
Miguel Cairo	551	430	.780	46
Jose Castillo	486	379	.780	44

Second Basemen - 2004 Zone Ratings

Player	Tm	Balls In Zone	Plays Made	Zone Rating	Plays Out Of Zone
Rey Sanchez	TB	194	172	.887	20
D'Angelo Jimenez	Cin	309	264	.854	39
Aaron Miles	Col	266	227	.853	45
Junior Spivey	Mil	145	122	.841	19
Jeff Kent	Hou	296	249	.841	42
Luis Castillo	Fla	340	286	.841	33
Orlando Hudson	Tor	384	323	.841	47
Mark Bellhorn	Bos	306	257	.840	41
Tony Womack	StL	340	285	.838	44
Marcus Giles	Atl	254	211	.831	26
Mark Loretta	SD	408	336	.824	29
Scott Hairston	Ari	181	149	.823	20
Adam Kennedy	Ana	346	284	.821	36
Todd Walker	ChC	222	181	.815	16
Willie Harris	CWS	198	161	.813	20
Mark Grudzielanek	ChC	171	139	.813	16
Alfonso Soriano	Tex	379	308	.813	26
Ray Durham	SF	292	237	.812	21
Nick Green	Atl	180	146	.811	22
Alex Cora	LA	296	240	.811	24
Ronnie Belliard	Cle	373	301	.807	39
Omar Infante	Det	223	179	.803	17
Juan Uribe	CWS	183	146	.798	18
Tony Graffanino	KC	153	121	.791	16
Brian Roberts	Bal	393	310	.789	45
Luis Rivas	Min	246	194	.789	35
Marco Scutaro	Oak	269	212	.788	20
Jose Castillo	Pit	235	185	.787	27
Jose Vidro	Mon	225	175	.778	10
Bret Boone	Sea	336	260	.774	27
Enrique Wilson	NYY	194	150	.773	9
Placido Polanco	Phi	261	201	.770	23
Miguel Cairo	NYY	274	201	.734	19

Second Basemen - 2005 Zone Ratings

Player	Tm	Balls In Zone	Plays Made	Zone Rating	Plays Out Of Zone
Rich Aurilia	Cin	142	124	.873	23
Tony Graffanino	2 tms	152	132	.868	25
Mark Ellis	Oak	292	252	.863	22
Mark Grudzielanek	StL	367	313	.853	51
Orlando Hudson	Tor	326	278	.853	52
Chase Utley	Phi	338	287	.849	38
Ronnie Belliard	Cle	371	315	.849	38
Brian Roberts	Bal	347	294	.847	58
Nick Punto	Min	170	144	.847	25
Adam Kennedy	LAA	305	257	.843	45
Ray Durham	SF	293	245	.836	37
Placido Polanco	2 tms	256	214	.836	41
Luis Castillo	Fla	296	245	.828	47
Marcus Giles	Atl	433	356	.822	43
Craig Counsell	Ari	371	305	.822	64
Luis A Gonzalez	Col	188	154	.819	20
Jeff Kent	LAD	389	318	.817	33
Tadahito Iguchi	CWS	327	267	.817	44
Jose Vidro	Was	196	160	.816	9
Kazuo Matsui	NYM	184	150	.815	9
Miguel Cairo	NYM	199	160	.804	17
Mark Bellhorn	2 tms	255	205	.804	22
Alfonso Soriano	Tex	436	349	.800	33
Ruben Gotay	KC	220	176	.800	24
Nick Green	TB	179	143	.799	26
Junior Spivey	2 tms	154	123	.799	33
Craig Biggio	Hou	374	297	.794	30
Aaron Miles	Col	192	151	.786	22
Mark Loretta	SD	254	199	.783	17
Omar Infante	Det	165	129	.782	21
Todd Walker	ChC	233	182	.781	31
Jose Castillo	Pit	251	194	.773	17
Jorge Cantu	TB	174	133	.764	19
Robinson Cano	NYY	410	313	.763	19
Bret Boone	2 tms	243	177	.728	20
Rickie Weeks	Mil	229	165	.721	35

Second Basemen - 2003 Zone Ratings

Player	Tm	Balls In Zone	Plays Made	Zone Rating	Plays Out Of Zone
Placido Polanco	Phi	220	212	.964	40
Jeff Reboulet	Pit	153	142	.928	29
Mark Ellis	Oak	361	335	.928	59
Luis Castillo	Fla	332	306	.922	50
Ray Durham	SF	259	238	.919	30
Marcus Giles	Atl	381	346	.908	66
Mark Loretta	SD	330	299	.906	53
Brandon Phillips	Cle	250	226	.904	37
Abraham O Nunez	Pit	156	141	.904	27
Brian Roberts	Bal	257	232	.903	40
Marlon Anderson	TB	281	253	.900	38
Adam Kennedy	Ana	307	276	.899	50
Junior Spivey	Ari	224	201	.897	37
Jose Vidro	Mon	334	298	.892	48
Orlando Hudson	Tor	385	343	.891	67
Eric Young	2 tms	254	226	.890	31
Jeff Kent	Hou	284	251	.884	40
Mark Grudzielanek	ChC	278	244	.878	30
Bret Boone	Sea	361	315	.873	43
Bo Hart	StL	148	129	.872	25
Alfonso Soriano	NYY	345	300	.870	79
Warren Morris	Det	219	190	.868	30
D'Angelo Jimenez	2 tms	311	269	.865	46
Roberto Alomar	2 tms	294	254	.864	28
Todd Walker	Bos	348	300	.862	40
Alex Cora	LA	278	239	.860	51
Ronnie Belliard	Col	235	202	.860	55
Desi Relaford	KC	186	157	.844	25
Michael Young	Tex	431	360	.835	20
Carlos Febles	KC	144	120	.833	16
Luis Rivas	Min	293	241	.823	34
Fernando Vina	StL	128	105	.820	17

Third Basemen - 3-Year Zone Ratings

Player	Balls In Zone	Plays Made	Zone Rating	Plays Out Of Zone
Adrian Beltre	838	632	.754	185
Alex Rodriguez	475	351	.739	179
Morgan Ensberg	638	471	.738	129
Eric Chavez	903	665	.736	160
Brandon Inge	486	356	.733	122
Scott Rolen	739	541	.732	150
David Wright	456	333	.730	114
Joe Randa	705	513	.728	124
David Bell	733	533	.727	177
Chipper Jones	302	219	.725	99
Tony Batista	595	431	.724	66
Hank Blalock	820	589	.718	178
Bill Mueller	718	513	.714	131
Vinny Castilla	859	612	.712	148
Corey Koskie	580	411	.709	111
Aaron Boone	587	415	.707	118
Melvin Mora	585	411	.703	124
Aramis Ramirez	831	581	.699	135
Sean Burroughs	577	402	.697	153
Joe Crede	774	539	.696	166
Casey Blake	644	446	.693	81
Troy Glaus	526	357	.679	74
Mike Lowell	824	559	.678	111
Edgardo Alfonzo	643	434	.675	126
Eric Hinske	522	342	.655	60
Wes Helms	426	276	.648	56
Ty Wigginton	664	423	.637	86
Eric Munson	363	230	.634	58

Third Basemen - 2004 Zone Ratings

Player	Tm	Balls In Zone	Plays Made	Zone Rating	Plays Out Of Zone
Adrian Beltre	LA	267	214	.801	68
Joe Randa	KC	207	161	.778	36
Scott Rolen	StL	285	216	.758	86
David Wright	NYM	130	97	.746	35
Alex Rodriguez	NYY	220	164	.745	80
Chad Tracy	Ari	254	188	.740	49
Tony Batista	Mon	259	191	.737	47
Kevin Youkilis	Bos	102	75	.735	33
Hank Blalock	Tex	259	186	.718	76
Eric Chavez	Oak	259	186	.718	57
David Bell	Phi	272	195	.717	73
Edgardo Alfonzo	SF	235	168	.715	52
Aubrey Huff	TB	133	95	.714	32
Sean Burroughs	SD	175	122	.697	72
Chipper Jones	Atl	163	113	.693	52
Vinny Castilla	Col	295	202	.685	72
Aramis Ramirez	ChC	232	158	.681	47
Ty Wigginton	2 tms	221	149	.674	37
Bill Mueller	Bos	167	112	.671	39
Scott Spiezio	Sea	136	91	.669	25
Corey Koskie	Min	195	129	.662	43
Eric Hinske	Tor	258	170	.659	42
Joe Crede	CWS	252	165	.655	54
Mike Lowell	Fla	269	176	.654	52
Chone Figgins	Ana	118	77	.653	37
Morgan Ensberg	Hou	177	114	.644	34
Melvin Mora	Bal	275	177	.644	63
Casey Blake	Cle	312	200	.641	51
Eric Munson	Det	175	111	.634	41
Brandon Inge	Det	118	74	.627	40
Mark DeRosa	Atl	118	73	.619	43
Wes Helms	Mil	128	75	.586	15

Third Basemen - 2005 Zone Ratings

Player	Tm	Balls In Zone	Plays Made	Zone Rating	Plays Out Of Zone
Corey Koskie	Tor	137	109	.796	45
Eric Chavez	Oak	289	228	.789	62
Pedro Feliz	SF	116	90	.776	42
Bill Mueller	Bos	254	196	.772	65
Morgan Ensberg	Hou	268	206	.769	79
Brandon Inge	Det	368	282	.766	82
Abraham O Nunez	StL	188	144	.766	50
Chipper Jones	Atl	139	106	.763	47
David Bell	Phi	272	206	.757	80
Melvin Mora	Bal	310	234	.755	61
Garrett Atkins	Col	238	178	.748	72
Vinny Castilla	Was	206	153	.743	45
Joe Crede	CWS	213	157	.737	79
Aaron Boone	Cle	271	199	.734	79
Alex Rodriguez	NYY	255	187	.733	99
Aramis Ramirez	ChC	207	151	.729	54
Mike Lowell	Fla	254	185	.728	39
Mark Teahen	KC	239	174	.728	54
Sean Burroughs	SD	124	90	.726	52
David Wright	NYM	326	236	.724	79
Adrian Beltre	Sea	262	189	.721	76
Mike Cuddyer	Min	187	134	.717	49
Alex S Gonzalez	TB	178	127	.713	35
Troy Glaus	Ari	328	234	.713	63
Joe Randa	2 tms	223	158	.709	64
Hank Blalock	Tex	310	217	.700	72
Edgardo Alfonzo	SF	156	104	.667	41

Third Basemen - 2003 Zone Ratings

Player	Tm	Balls In Zone	Plays Made	Zone Rating	Plays Out Of Zone
Morgan Ensberg	Hou	193	151	.782	16
Geoff Blum	Hou	141	106	.752	17
Adrian Beltre	LA	309	229	.741	41
Hank Blalock	Tex	251	186	.741	30
Casey Blake	Cle	326	241	.739	26
Damian Rolls	TB	145	107	.738	16
Chris Stynes	Col	225	163	.724	26
Vinny Castilla	Atl	358	257	.718	31
Tony Batista	Bal	336	240	.714	19
Eric Chavez	Oak	355	251	.707	41
Joe Randa	KC	275	194	.705	24
Joe Crede	CWS	309	217	.702	33
David Bell	Phi	189	132	.698	24
Corey Koskie	Min	248	173	.698	23
Aramis Ramirez	2 tms	392	272	.694	34
Bill Mueller	Bos	297	205	.690	27
Jose Hernandez	3 tms	154	106	.688	15
Scott Rolen	StL	323	221	.684	28
Aaron Boone	2 tms	316	216	.684	39
Sean Burroughs	SD	278	190	.683	29
Shea Hillenbrand	2 tms	106	71	.670	14
Wes Helms	Mil	262	175	.668	28
Jeff Cirillo	Sea	132	87	.659	11
Mike Lowell	Fla	301	198	.658	20
Robin Ventura	2 tms	177	116	.655	19
Eric Hinske	Tor	264	172	.652	18
Edgardo Alfonzo	SF	252	162	.643	33
Ty Wigginton	NYM	372	236	.634	35
Eric Munson	Det	187	118	.631	17
Troy Glaus	Ana	164	97	.591	11

Shortstops - 3-Year Zone Ratings

Player	Balls In Zone	Plays Made	Zone Rating	Plays Out Of Zone
Jose Valentin	623	553	.888	109
Rich Aurilia	465	409	.880	87
Adam Everett	845	742	.878	179
Jack Wilson	1111	963	.867	216
Neifi Perez	578	500	.865	105
Cesar Izturis	988	854	.864	197
Alex S Gonzalez	486	419	.862	99
Bobby Crosby	655	562	.858	90
Alex Cintron	588	502	.854	103
Alex Gonzalez	984	840	.854	192
Omar Vizquel	887	757	.853	136
Juan Uribe	622	527	.847	126
David Eckstein	978	825	.844	144
Deivi Cruz	590	497	.842	129
Nomar Garciaparra	572	481	.841	123
Edgar Renteria	994	835	.840	202
Orlando Cabrera	924	776	.840	180
Jimmy Rollins	1062	889	.837	201
Cristian Guzman	891	745	.836	172
Royce Clayton	1010	842	.834	171
Jhonny Peralta	541	451	.834	89
Miguel Tejada	1185	986	.832	251
Julio Lugo	1051	870	.828	192
Rafael Furcal	1149	950	.827	249
Jose Reyes	565	467	.827	104
Khalil Greene	662	544	.822	92
Derek Jeter	1065	871	.818	91
Angel Berroa	1076	869	.808	188
Felipe Lopez	547	441	.806	88
Carlos Guillen	642	513	.799	130
Michael Young	821	654	.797	82

Shortstops - 2004 Zone Ratings

Player	Tm	Balls In Zone	Plays Made	Zone Rating	Plays Out Of Zone
Adam Everett	Hou	236	207	.877	35
Chris Woodward	Tor	139	120	.863	19
Cesar Izturis	LA	356	307	.862	69
Rich Aurilia	2 tms	168	144	.857	26
Jose Valentin	CWS	335	286	.854	36
Pokey Reese	Bos	149	127	.852	38
Bobby Crosby	Oak	419	357	.852	63
Jack Wilson	Pit	370	315	.851	73
Jimmy Rollins	Phi	321	270	.841	52
Khalil Greene	SD	322	270	.839	46
Cristian Guzman	Min	320	268	.838	73
Ramon Martinez	ChC	160	134	.838	22
Alex Cintron	Ari	338	282	.834	52
Julio Lugo	TB	368	307	.834	53
Edgar Renteria	StL	343	286	.834	61
Miguel Tejada	Bal	427	355	.831	93
Neifi Perez	2 tms	159	132	.830	34
Omar Vizquel	Cle	345	284	.823	52
Royce Clayton	Col	356	293	.823	52
Orlando Cabrera	2 tms	330	270	.818	55
Alex Gonzalez	Fla	346	283	.818	74
Barry Larkin	Cin	207	169	.816	26
David Eckstein	Ana	277	226	.816	44
Alex S Gonzalez	3 tms	150	121	.807	24
Deivi Cruz	SF	242	195	.806	37
Craig Counsell	Mil	284	228	.803	54
Michael Young	Tex	399	320	.802	39
Derek Jeter	NYY	372	298	.801	29
Kazuo Matsui	NYM	288	230	.799	36
Carlos Guillen	Det	323	257	.796	52
Chris Gomez	Tor	180	143	.794	39
Rafael Furcal	Atl	356	282	.792	61
Nomar Garciaparra	2 tms	163	125	.767	30
Angel Berroa	KC	329	252	.766	42

Shortstops - 2005 Zone Ratings

Player	Tm	Balls In Zone	Plays Made	Zone Rating	Plays Out Of Zone
Bobby Crosby	Oak	224	196	.875	26
Neifi Perez	ChC	330	285	.864	54
Jack Wilson	Pit	438	377	.861	63
Adam Everett	Hou	344	296	.860	78
Omar Vizquel	SF	397	340	.856	43
Jason Bartlett	Min	195	167	.856	38
Alex Gonzalez	Fla	324	276	.852	41
Cesar Izturis	LAD	278	235	.845	47
David Eckstein	StL	468	395	.844	59
Rafael Furcal	Atl	429	359	.837	78
Juan Castro	Min	204	170	.833	34
Juan Uribe	CWS	368	303	.823	61
Clint Barmes	Col	183	150	.820	62
J.J. Hardy	Mil	242	198	.818	42
Jhonny Peralta	Cle	377	308	.817	44
Felipe Lopez	Cin	337	273	.810	49
Orlando Cabrera	LAA	324	262	.809	52
Russ Adams	Tor	291	235	.808	46
Royce Clayton	Ari	366	295	.806	58
Cristian Guzman	Was	288	232	.806	47
Miguel Tejada	Bal	427	343	.803	74
Edgar Renteria	Bos	349	280	.802	63
Jose Reyes	NYM	386	309	.801	50
Khalil Greene	SD	304	243	.799	37
Derek Jeter	NYY	472	374	.792	26
Julio Lugo	TB	380	301	.792	70
Marco Scutaro	Oak	216	171	.792	19
Michael Young	Tex	416	328	.788	43
Angel Berroa	KC	391	308	.788	71
Jimmy Rollins	Phi	384	301	.784	64
Bill Hall	Mil	141	110	.780	28
Carlos Guillen	Det	193	149	.772	53

Shortstops - 2003 Zone Ratings

Player	Tm	Balls In Zone	Plays Made	Zone Rating	Plays Out Of Zone
Jose Valentin	CWS	286	265	.927	73
Rey Sanchez	2 tms	177	164	.927	35
Omar Vizquel	Cle	145	133	.917	41
Rich Aurilia	SF	222	202	.910	50
Orlando Cabrera	Mon	270	244	.904	73
Adam Everett	Hou	265	239	.902	66
Alex Rodriguez	Tex	377	340	.902	45
Omar Infante	Det	151	136	.901	30
Derek Jeter	NYY	221	199	.900	36
Juan Uribe	Col	159	143	.899	48
Jhonny Peralta	Cle	148	133	.899	43
Alex Gonzalez	Fla	314	281	.895	77
Jack Wilson	Pit	303	271	.894	80
Alex Cintron	Ari	160	143	.894	39
Jimmy Rollins	Phi	357	318	.891	85
Edgar Renteria	StL	302	269	.891	78
Jose Reyes	NYM	155	138	.890	51
Alex S Gonzalez	ChC	317	282	.890	73
Nomar Garciaparra	Bos	361	321	.889	86
Tony Womack	3 tms	128	113	.883	25
Royce Clayton	Mil	288	254	.882	61
Cesar Izturis	LA	354	312	.881	81
Chris Woodward	Tor	211	185	.877	54
David Eckstein	Ana	233	204	.876	41
Deivi Cruz	Bal	295	258	.875	80
Jose Hernandez	3 tms	142	124	.873	27
Ramon Vazquez	SD	212	185	.873	42
Miguel Tejada	Oak	331	288	.870	84
Angel Berroa	KC	356	309	.868	75
Cristian Guzman	Min	283	245	.866	52
Julio Lugo	2 tms	303	262	.865	69
Mike Bordick	Tor	128	109	.852	23
Carlos Guillen	Sea	126	107	.849	25
Rafael Furcal	Atl	364	309	.849	110
Ramon Santiago	Det	172	145	.843	49

Left Fielders - 3-Year Zone Ratings

Player	Balls In Zone	Plays Made	Zone Rating	Plays Out Of Zone
Coco Crisp	575	404	.703	47
Randy Winn	766	531	.693	55
Carl Crawford	1195	803	.672	102
Eric Byrnes	563	370	.657	44
Jay Payton	525	345	.657	43
Kevin Mench	492	322	.654	36
Barry Bonds	601	393	.654	42
Garret Anderson	710	464	.654	39
Raul Ibanez	747	487	.652	50
Cliff Floyd	884	569	.644	35
Larry Bigbie	645	415	.643	40
Carlos Lee	1253	806	.643	81
Rondell White	606	388	.640	50
Moises Alou	831	529	.637	38
Jason Bay	695	442	.636	32
Pat Burrell	994	626	.630	46
Matt Holliday	580	364	.628	40
Hideki Matsui	1041	652	.626	66
Geoff Jenkins	631	394	.624	46
Lance Berkman	548	342	.624	48
Shannon Stewart	818	510	.623	68
Frank Catalanotto	452	280	.619	29
Ryan Klesko	491	303	.617	29
Terrence Long	485	299	.616	39
Craig Monroe	452	278	.615	39
Matt Lawton	579	356	.615	22
Adam Dunn	991	609	.615	46
Luis Gonzalez	980	593	.605	69
Chipper Jones	361	214	.593	21
Miguel Cabrera	571	333	.583	41
Manny Ramirez	1051	585	.557	62

Left Fielders - 2004 Zone Ratings

Player	Tm	Balls In Zone	Plays Made	Zone Rating	Plays Out Of Zone
Lew Ford	Min	176	123	.699	12
Jeff Conine	Fla	222	152	.685	14
Larry Bigbie	Bal	271	184	.679	23
Carl Crawford	TB	355	240	.676	30
Raul Ibanez	Sea	292	197	.675	19
Charles Thomas	Atl	179	120	.670	11
Jose Guillen	Ana	343	226	.659	30
Barry Bonds	SF	296	193	.652	15
Eric Byrnes	Oak	231	150	.649	15
Jayson Werth	LA	145	94	.648	16
Hideki Matsui	NYY	409	264	.645	25
David Dellucci	Tex	208	134	.644	13
Terrmel Sledge	Mon	157	101	.643	15
Moises Alou	ChC	350	223	.637	13
Jason Bay	Pit	259	165	.637	14
Pat Burrell	Phi	305	193	.633	14
Carlos Lee	CWS	392	248	.633	29
Matt Lawton	Cle	336	212	.631	10
Miguel Cabrera	Fla	119	75	.630	12
Geoff Jenkins	Mil	337	212	.629	27
Ryan Klesko	SD	191	120	.628	8
Matt Holliday	Col	235	145	.617	23
Cliff Floyd	NYM	243	149	.613	13
Rondell White	Det	152	93	.612	17
Adam Dunn	Cin	356	207	.581	18
Manny Ramirez	Bos	303	175	.578	22
Shannon Stewart	Min	142	82	.577	14
Luis Gonzalez	Ari	247	139	.563	18
Lance Berkman	Hou	151	84	.556	8
Craig Biggio	Hou	162	90	.556	9

Left Fielders - 2005 Zone Ratings

Player	Tm	Balls In Zone	Plays Made	Zone Rating	Plays Out Of Zone
Reed Johnson	Tor	172	126	.733	8
Randy Winn	2 tms	293	206	.703	20
Coco Crisp	Cle	379	266	.702	28
Carl Crawford	TB	445	309	.694	32
Kevin Mench	Tex	306	210	.686	21
Eric Byrnes	3 tms	269	184	.684	25
Scott Podsednik	CWS	353	241	.683	19
Kelly Johnson	Atl	232	158	.681	8
Rondell White	Det	161	109	.677	10
Chris Burke	Hou	164	110	.671	10
Moises Alou	SF	182	122	.670	10
Pedro Feliz	SF	197	130	.660	8
Cliff Floyd	NYM	411	268	.652	15
Todd Hollandsworth	2 tms	153	98	.641	5
Carlos Lee	Mil	451	288	.639	19
Frank Catalanotto	Tor	240	153	.638	10
Matt Holliday	Col	345	219	.635	17
Hideki Matsui	NYY	308	194	.630	25
Shannon Stewart	Min	362	228	.630	21
Garret Anderson	LAA	293	184	.628	17
Jason Bay	Pit	398	249	.626	17
Luis Gonzalez	Ari	409	250	.611	20
Ryan Klesko	SD	300	183	.610	21
Pat Burrell	Phi	364	222	.610	14
Adam Dunn	Cin	377	228	.605	18
Craig Monroe	Det	150	90	.600	9
Terrence Long	KC	260	151	.581	15
Reggie Sanders	StL	174	101	.580	7
Miguel Cabrera	Fla	301	172	.571	16
Manny Ramirez	Bos	420	225	.536	18

Left Fielders - 2003 Zone Ratings

Player	Tm	Balls In Zone	Plays Made	Zone Rating	Plays Out Of Zone
Randy Winn	Sea	377	259	.687	31
Adam Dunn	Cin	258	174	.674	10
Garret Anderson	Ana	417	280	.671	22
Cliff Floyd	NYM	230	152	.661	7
Carlos Lee	CWS	410	270	.659	33
Brad Wilkerson	Mon	172	113	.657	15
Brian Giles	2 tms	326	214	.656	12
Barry Bonds	SF	281	184	.655	25
Lance Berkman	Hou	326	213	.653	35
Pat Burrell	Phi	325	211	.649	18
Albert Pujols	StL	242	157	.649	9
Jay Payton	Col	365	236	.647	37
Carl Crawford	TB	395	254	.643	40
Jacque Jones	Min	237	152	.641	16
Raul Ibanez	KC	302	193	.639	22
Shannon Stewart	2 tms	314	200	.637	33
Rondell White	2 tms	293	186	.635	23
Luis Gonzalez	Ari	324	204	.630	31
Terrence Long	Oak	121	75	.620	17
Geoff Jenkins	Mil	294	182	.619	19
Moises Alou	ChC	299	184	.615	15
Larry Bigbie	Bal	223	136	.610	14
Hideki Matsui	NYY	324	194	.599	16
Craig Monroe	Det	203	120	.591	18
Matt Lawton	Cle	185	109	.589	7
Chipper Jones	Atl	312	183	.587	17
Dmitri Young	Det	169	97	.574	16
Manny Ramirez	Bos	328	185	.564	22

Center Fielders - 3-Year Zone Ratings

Player	Balls In Zone	Plays Made	Zone Rating	Plays Out Of Zone
Aaron Rowand	760	627	.825	148
Randy Winn	599	493	.823	81
Grady Sizemore	515	421	.817	47
David DeJesus	504	412	.817	102
Tike Redman	567	462	.815	109
Laynce Nix	457	371	.812	59
Torii Hunter	932	752	.807	157
Mike Cameron	886	710	.801	129
Mark Kotsay	978	783	.801	163
Gary Matthews Jr.	513	409	.797	76
Carlos Beltran	1128	894	.793	154
Kenny Lofton	721	571	.792	88
Jim Edmonds	956	757	.792	172
Endy Chavez	520	411	.790	93
Corey Patterson	719	568	.790	143
Vernon Wells	1089	860	.790	155
Juan Pierre	1128	890	.789	178
Milton Bradley	685	539	.787	107
Johnny Damon	1191	936	.786	169
Marlon Byrd	495	385	.778	104
Dave Roberts	494	384	.777	97
Andruw Jones	1181	916	.776	218
Steve Finley	942	729	.774	133
Scott Podsednik	688	531	.772	143
Rocco Baldelli	804	619	.770	123
Alex Sanchez	609	462	.759	110
Marquis Grissom	781	589	.754	128
Luis Matos	915	681	.744	122
Preston Wilson	751	556	.740	121
Craig Biggio	454	333	.733	107
Bernie Williams	866	620	.716	104
Ken Griffey Jr.	635	454	.715	87

Center Fielders - 2004 Zone Ratings

Player	Tm	Balls In Zone	Plays Made	Zone Rating	Plays Out Of Zone
Endy Chavez	Mon	252	210	.833	48
Jay Payton	SD	311	257	.826	61
Laynce Nix	Tex	236	194	.822	24
Aaron Rowand	CWS	301	247	.821	42
Carlos Beltran	2 tms	349	286	.819	46
Tike Redman	Pit	298	243	.815	62
Juan Pierre	Fla	358	291	.813	54
Milton Bradley	LA	245	199	.812	31
Mark Kotsay	Oak	338	274	.811	57
Torii Hunter	Min	296	239	.807	62
Randy Winn	Sea	354	285	.805	45
Vernon Wells	Tor	328	262	.799	51
Kenny Lofton	NYY	181	144	.796	11
Coco Crisp	Cle	199	158	.794	41
Jim Edmonds	StL	310	246	.794	59
Scott Podsednik	Mil	367	290	.790	77
Rocco Baldelli	TB	339	267	.788	60
David DeJesus	KC	205	160	.780	46
Corey Patterson	ChC	320	248	.775	73
Garret Anderson	Ana	234	181	.774	25
Marlon Byrd	Phi	181	140	.773	41
Mike Cameron	NYM	370	285	.770	64
Steve Finley	2 tms	369	284	.770	67
Johnny Damon	Bos	389	297	.763	49
Andruw Jones	Atl	405	309	.763	73
Craig Biggio	Hou	122	92	.754	39
Alex Sanchez	Det	161	121	.752	34
Marquis Grissom	SF	362	271	.749	52
Ken Griffey Jr.	Cin	184	137	.745	31
Luis Matos	Bal	249	184	.739	35
Jeromy Burnitz	Col	110	78	.709	27
Bernie Williams	NYY	260	180	.692	27

Center Fielders - 2005 Zone Ratings

Player	Tm	Balls In Zone	Plays Made	Zone Rating	Plays Out Of Zone
Joey Gathright	TB	175	158	.903	23
Nook Logan	Det	255	223	.875	59
Jeremy Reed	Sea	380	331	.871	53
David DeJesus	KC	294	250	.850	56
Aaron Rowand	CWS	366	305	.833	83
Randy Winn	2 tms	189	157	.831	27
Corey Patterson	ChC	246	204	.829	36
Torii Hunter	Min	229	189	.825	29
Willy Taveras	Hou	330	271	.821	61
Jason Michaels	Phi	161	132	.820	29
Lew Ford	Min	143	117	.818	23
Steve Finley	LAA	290	237	.817	29
Tike Redman	Pit	158	129	.816	29
Johnny Damon	Bos	415	338	.814	58
Andruw Jones	Atl	381	308	.808	57
Vernon Wells	Tor	381	307	.806	44
Grady Sizemore	Cle	422	340	.806	33
Brady Clark	Mil	431	347	.805	52
Cory Sullivan	Col	182	146	.802	26
Jim Edmonds	StL	338	271	.802	48
Gary Matthews Jr.	Tex	272	218	.801	40
Kenny Lofton	Phi	210	168	.800	33
Laynce Nix	Tex	171	135	.789	25
Carlos Beltran	NYM	418	329	.787	49
Damon Hollins	TB	223	175	.785	23
Brad Wilkerson	Was	264	207	.784	27
Preston Wilson	2 tms	285	223	.782	43
Jason Ellison	SF	204	159	.779	38
Dave Roberts	SD	235	183	.779	51
Juan Pierre	Fla	355	276	.777	56
Luis Matos	Bal	342	262	.766	37
Milton Bradley	LAD	198	151	.763	30
Mark Kotsay	Oak	333	253	.760	47
Ken Griffey Jr.	Cin	345	245	.710	41
Bernie Williams	NYY	280	197	.704	29

Center Fielders - 2003 Zone Ratings

Player	Tm	Balls In Zone	Plays Made	Zone Rating	Plays Out Of Zone
Mark Kotsay	SD	307	256	.834	59
Mike Cameron	Sea	500	413	.826	62
Darin Erstad	Ana	186	153	.823	35
Torii Hunter	Min	407	324	.796	66
Carl Everett	2 tms	168	133	.792	25
Kenny Lofton	2 tms	330	259	.785	44
Milton Bradley	Cle	242	189	.781	46
Jim Edmonds	StL	308	240	.779	65
Marlon Byrd	Phi	294	229	.779	59
Juan Pierre	Fla	415	323	.778	68
Johnny Damon	Bos	387	301	.778	62
Carlos Beltran	KC	361	279	.773	59
Marquis Grissom	SF	337	259	.769	67
Gary Matthews Jr.	2 tms	171	131	.766	27
Chris Singleton	Oak	171	131	.766	24
Vernon Wells	Tor	380	291	.766	60
Dave Roberts	LA	200	153	.765	38
Corey Patterson	ChC	153	116	.758	34
Alex Sanchez	2 tms	387	293	.757	65
Rocco Baldelli	TB	465	352	.757	63
Andruw Jones	Atl	395	299	.757	88
Endy Chavez	Mon	236	178	.754	36
Scott Podsednik	Mil	314	236	.752	57
Bernie Williams	NYY	326	243	.745	48
Steve Finley	Ari	283	208	.735	37
Eric Byrnes	Oak	164	120	.732	27
Craig Biggio	Hou	332	241	.726	68
Luis Matos	Bal	324	235	.725	50
Preston Wilson	Col	340	239	.703	58

Right Fielders - 3-Year Zone Ratings

Player	Balls In Zone	Plays Made	Zone Rating	Plays Out Of Zone
Ichiro Suzuki	1394	988	.709	95
Jose Cruz	935	662	.708	62
Austin Kearns	598	410	.686	27
Alexis Rios	638	433	.679	22
Richard Hidalgo	938	634	.676	66
Jeromy Burnitz	673	450	.669	28
Trot Nixon	719	480	.668	54
Sammy Sosa	794	527	.664	38
Jacque Jones	779	516	.662	49
Vladimir Guerrero	1006	664	.660	50
Magglio Ordonez	769	506	.658	38
Raul Mondesi	497	327	.658	32
Juan Encarnacion	1090	714	.655	65
Jermaine Dye	836	546	.653	38
Bobby Abreu	1238	806	.651	58
Jay Gibbons	735	478	.650	39
Aubrey Huff	523	340	.650	33
J.D. Drew	622	401	.645	44
Brian Giles	891	567	.636	42
Jose Guillen	652	414	.635	50
Gary Sheffield	1136	717	.631	64
Bobby Higginson	622	392	.630	39
Shawn Green	820	514	.627	38
Danny Bautista	487	304	.624	27
Jody Gerut	548	340	.620	34
Michael Tucker	542	336	.620	31
Larry Walker	684	424	.620	26

Right Fielders - 2004 Zone Ratings

Player	Tm	Balls In Zone	Plays Made	Zone Rating	Plays Out Of Zone
Abraham Nunez	2 tms	161	116	.720	8
Ichiro Suzuki	Sea	466	335	.719	32
Austin Kearns	Cin	148	103	.696	3
Jermaine Dye	Oak	310	215	.694	19
Jose Cruz	TB	404	280	.693	27
Brady Clark	Mil	259	179	.691	20
Richard Hidalgo	2 tms	345	238	.690	21
Sammy Sosa	ChC	324	223	.688	10
Vladimir Guerrero	Ana	403	277	.687	22
Juan Encarnacion	2 tms	328	224	.683	21
Alexis Rios	Tor	295	200	.678	9
Bobby Higginson	Det	267	180	.674	21
Jacque Jones	Min	387	260	.672	25
Bobby Abreu	Phi	405	272	.672	23
Jeromy Burnitz	Col	132	88	.667	6
Kevin Mench	Tex	174	114	.655	9
J.D. Drew	Atl	373	244	.654	28
Larry Walker	2 tms	174	113	.649	8
Reggie Sanders	StL	188	121	.644	11
Miguel Cabrera	Fla	227	146	.643	15
Jay Gibbons	Bal	157	100	.637	14
Gabe Kapler	Bos	190	120	.632	13
Juan Rivera	Mon	198	125	.631	12
Brian Giles	SD	471	296	.628	18
Danny Bautista	Ari	373	234	.627	17
Jody Gerut	Cle	333	207	.622	19
Lance Berkman	Hou	192	119	.620	8
Gary Sheffield	NYY	379	234	.617	27
Michael Tucker	SF	294	181	.616	24
Craig Wilson	Pit	210	125	.595	6

Right Fielders - 2005 Zone Ratings

Player	Tm	Balls In Zone	Plays Made	Zone Rating	Plays Out Of Zone
Ichiro Suzuki	Sea	495	357	.721	26
Jay Gibbons	Bal	178	125	.702	8
Geoff Jenkins	Mil	416	289	.695	18
Austin Kearns	Cin	322	223	.693	15
Casey Blake	Cle	392	271	.691	16
Trot Nixon	Bos	315	216	.686	24
Alexis Rios	Tor	343	233	.679	13
Victor Diaz	NYM	218	148	.679	5
Richard Hidalgo	Tex	239	160	.669	14
Jeromy Burnitz	ChC	432	288	.667	15
Aubrey Huff	TB	277	184	.664	20
Vladimir Guerrero	LAA	351	232	.661	13
Jacque Jones	Min	365	240	.658	22
Craig Monroe	Det	192	126	.656	6
Matt Lawton	3 tms	333	218	.655	12
Emil Brown	KC	350	227	.649	16
Brian Giles	SD	420	271	.645	24
Jose Guillen	Was	421	270	.641	29
Bobby Abreu	Phi	399	255	.639	12
Sammy Sosa	Bal	177	113	.638	8
Jeff Francoeur	Atl	196	125	.638	6
Shawn Green	Ari	349	222	.636	10
Magglio Ordonez	Det	214	136	.636	3
Mike Cameron	NYM	197	123	.624	14
Jason Lane	Hou	342	213	.623	12
Nick Swisher	Oak	291	181	.622	16
Jermaine Dye	CWS	397	244	.615	15
Juan Encarnacion	Fla	320	196	.613	20
Gary Sheffield	NYY	372	226	.608	14
Larry Walker	StL	169	101	.598	6
Brad Hawpe	Col	238	135	.567	13

Right Fielders - 2003 Zone Ratings

Player	Tm	Balls In Zone	Plays Made	Zone Rating	Plays Out Of Zone
Jose Cruz	SF	389	284	.730	23
Roger Cedeno	NYM	259	185	.714	12
Terrence Long	Oak	153	108	.706	6
Jeff DaVanon	Ana	173	121	.699	14
Raul Mondesi	2 tms	359	247	.688	22
Ichiro Suzuki	Sea	433	296	.684	37
Jermaine Dye	Oak	129	87	.674	4
Gary Sheffield	Atl	385	257	.668	23
Richard Hidalgo	Hou	354	236	.667	31
Juan Encarnacion	Fla	442	294	.665	24
Dustan Mohr	Min	202	134	.663	16
Magglio Ordonez	CWS	424	279	.658	32
John Vander Wal	Mil	194	127	.655	12
Sammy Sosa	ChC	293	191	.652	20
Xavier Nady	SD	230	149	.648	10
Bobby Abreu	Phi	434	279	.643	23
Trot Nixon	Bos	322	206	.640	25
Aubrey Huff	TB	246	156	.634	13
Jay Gibbons	Bal	400	253	.633	17
Reggie Sanders	Pit	204	129	.632	11
Jose Guillen	2 tms	226	142	.628	19
Bobby Kielty	2 tms	188	118	.628	10
Shawn Green	LA	347	217	.625	22
Aaron Guiel	KC	246	153	.622	19
Larry Walker	Col	341	210	.616	12
Vladimir Guerrero	Mon	252	155	.615	15
Tim Salmon	Ana	178	107	.601	11
Jody Gerut	Cle	159	95	.597	13
Bobby Higginson	Det	348	206	.592	18
Reed Johnson	Tor	133	72	.541	14

Defensive Replacements

Ramon Castro was used as a defensive substitute 15 times last year, and was never removed from the game for another catcher. Mike Piazza, on the other hand, was substituted for on defense 16 times, and was never used as a defensive substitute.

Tino Martinez was used as a defensive substitute 15 times; Jason Giambi no times. Martinez was never removed for a defensive substitute; Giambi was removed 18 times.

Frank Catalanotto and his strange eyes were removed from the game for defense 20 times, while Catalanotto was put in on defense only once. His teammate Reed Johnson, on the other hand, was used as a defensive sub 18 times, and was removed only once.

What does this data tell you? Sure; Castro, Martinez and Reed Johnson were good defensive players; Piazza, Giambi and Catalanotto were not so good—or, at least, this is what their managers believed. One way of getting factual information about a player's defense, then, is simply to look at how many times he was put into the game for defense, and how many times he was taken out of the game for defense.

The chart below gives all players who were used as defensive substitutes five or more times in 2005, or who were removed for substitutes five or more times.

Team	Position	Player	Def In	Def Out
Arizona Diamondbacks	Shortstop	Royce Clayton	7	0
		Alex Cintron	0	7
	Center Field	Quinton McCracken	5	0
		Luis Terrero	5	3
	Right Field	Shawn Green	9	1
		Chad Tracy	0	9
Baltimore Orioles	Catcher	Geronimo Gil	5	0
		Javy Lopez	0	8
	Left Field	David Newhan	0	5
	Right Field	David Newhan	6	0
		Jay Gibbons	0	7
Boston Red Sox	First Base	John Olerud	8	1
		Kevin Millar	1	10
Chicago Cubs	Second Base	Todd Walker	0	5
	Shortstop	Ronny Cedeno	5	3
		Neifi Perez	5	6
	Left Field	Todd Hollandsworth	7	5
		Jason Dubois	1	7
	Center Field	Jerry Hairston Jr.	1	5
Cincinnati Reds	Second Base	Ray Olmedo	6	0
Cleveland Indians	First Base	Ben Broussard	7	0
Colorado Rockies	Catcher	Danny Ardoin	10	0
		JD Closser	1	7
	Second Base	Luis A Gonzalez	9	1
		Aaron Miles	1	6
	Third Base	Garrett Atkins	0	6
	Center Field	Cory Sullivan	5	0
	Right Field	Dustan Mohr	6	2
Detroit Tigers	Left Field	Curtis Granderson	7	1
		Craig Monroe	4	7
	Center Field	Nook Logan	7	0

Team	Position	Player	Def In	Def Out
Florida Marlins	First Base	Jeff Conine	6	0
		Carlos Delgado	0	6
	Left Field	Jeff Conine	1	7
Houston Astros	First Base	Lance Berkman	9	3
		Mike Lamb	4	9
	Second Base	Eric Bruntlett	7	1
		Craig Biggio	0	10
	Left Field	Orlando Palmeiro	7	2
		Lance Berkman	3	8
		Luke Scott	2	5
		Chris Burke	2	5
	Right Field	Jason Lane	5	3
Los Angeles Angels	Third Base	Maicer Izturis	8	0
		Robb Quinlan	0	5
Los Angeles Dodgers	Left Field	Jayson Werth	12	3
		Ricky Ledee	3	6
	Right Field	Jason Repko	5	0
Milwaukee Brewers	Third Base	Wes Helms	6	0
		Bill Hall	3	5
	Shortstop	J.J. Hardy	6	2
		Bill Hall	2	6
	Right Field	Chris Magruder	5	0
		Geoff Jenkins	0	7
Minnesota Twins	Second Base	Luis Rodriguez	8	2
		Nick Punto	2	5
		Brent Abernathy	1	5
New York Mets	Catcher	Ramon Castro	15	0
		Mike Piazza	0	16
	First Base	Chris Woodward	5	0
	Right Field	Gerald Williams	5	0
New York Yankees	First Base	Tino Martinez	15	0
		Jason Giambi	0	18
	Center Field	Bubba Crosby	9	0
		Bernie Williams	0	6
Pittsburgh Pirates	Catcher	Humberto Cota	7	2
		Ryan Doumit	0	6
	Second Base	Freddy Sanchez	5	3
		Rob Mackowiak	0	5
	Third Base	Rob Mackowiak	5	3
		Ty Wigginton	1	5
San Diego Padres	Left Field	Damian Jackson	12	0
		Adam Hyzdu	8	1
		Xavier Nady	6	0
		Ryan Klesko	1	24
San Francisco Giants	Second Base	Ray Durham	2	5
	Left Field	Moises Alou	5	2
		Pedro Feliz	1	8
	Center Field	Jason Ellison	5	0
St Louis Cardinals	Third Base	Abraham O Nunez	7	1
	Left Field	So Taguchi	8	3
	Right Field	John Mabry	8	1
		Larry Walker	1	7
Tampa Bay Devil Rays	Third Base	Alex S Gonzalez	5	0
		Jorge Cantu	0	5
	Left Field	Jonny Gomes	0	5
	Center Field	Joey Gathright	5	0
		Damon Hollins	2	6
	Right Field	Damon Hollins	13	0
		Aubrey Huff	0	12
Toronto Blue Jays	Left Field	Reed Johnson	18	1
		Frank Catalanotto	1	20
	Right Field	Alexis Rios	6	0
		Reed Johnson	0	6
Washington Nationals	Left Field	Marlon Byrd	6	1

Note: Includes players who were used as defensive substitutes 5 or more times in 2005, or who were removed for substitutes 5 or more times

Defensive Misplays

Coming Soon to a Theater Near Somebody Else

Bill James

This is the first publicly available edition of *The Fielding Bible*, and the only thing we can tell you for certain is that if there is a second edition, it will be even better than this one. We've worked hard on this sucker, but. . .it's a new thing, and we'll learn from experience.

One thing that isn't here is Defensive Misplays. I've been hawking Defensive Misplays for several years now, and we've made some progress. Baseball Info Solutions is in the process of reviewing 2005 videotapes as I write this, compiling a complete record of Defensive Misplays, but we are unable to share the data with you, because BIS has sold the output to several major league teams who would not be pleased to learn that they could have gotten the same stuff for the price of this book.

What is a Defensive Misplay, you ask? A defensive misplay is:

Any play which is not an error (or a passed ball), on which the fielder surrenders a base advance or the opportunity to make an out when a better play or a different play would have or might have gotten the out or prevented the advance.

Two things are required for a defensive misplay. First, it has to be clear that the fielder did not complete the play in the optimal manner. Second, there has to be a cost to his team of the failure.

You might fear that we are trying to inject subjective judgments into the record of the game. I want to assure you that we are not. We have gone to great lengths to ensure that there is no subjective judgment involved. A Defensive Misplay is a specific observation of a specific event.

Suppose that there is a runner on second base, for example, and a single is hit to center, and the center fielder throws home. The runner scores, but the batter moves to second on the throw. That's a Defensive Misplay. The throw home has no benefit to the team, since no out is recorded, and there is a cost to the fielder's team, which is the loss of a base. That's a defensive misplay. It is ALWAYS a defensive misplay,

without any room for judgment, because it is always clear that the action of the fielder resulted in a cost to his team.

If the shortstop throws wide to first, drawing the first baseman off base, the press box may say it's an infield hit—but it's a defensive misplay. We don't make any judgment as to whether the batter would have been out or safe if the throw was on line; we just record the facts. It's a fact that the throw was off line; it's a fact that the runner was safe. That's a Defensive Misplay—period.

If an outfielder breaks back and the ball lands in front of him, that's a Defensive Misplay.

If two infielders run into each other trying to catch a popup and the ball drops for a hit, that's a Defensive Misplay.

If an outfielder chases a ball to the wall and the ball comes off the wall over his head, rocketing back to the infield and allowing the runners to move up, that's a Defensive Misplay.

If the second baseman drops the ball after recording the out at second, but before he can make the relay throw to attempt to complete the double play, that's a Defensive Misplay. We don't make any judgment about whether he could have completed the double play or whether he couldn't. If he drops the ball before he has a chance to try, that's a Defensive Misplay, period.

If an outfielder loses a ball in the sun, that's a Defensive Misplay.

If the third baseman double-clutches or double-pumps before throwing to second to start the double play, that's a Defensive Misplay.

If the right fielder falls down chasing a flyball, the official scorer may call that a triple, but we call it a Defensive Misplay.

What is and what is not a Defensive Misplay is very carefully spelled out to avoid confusion. Of course we are not able to reach the goal of entirely eliminating the need for subjective judgments, but we did our best.

Look, anybody who watches major league baseball games knows that these kind of plays are common.

They are more than twice as common as errors—but they don't get counted. That was fine in 1950, when they didn't have computers and videotape, but there's no reason for it now. We are in the business of documenting the game of baseball, and this is a very important part of the game of baseball. It should be studied.

So far, we have identified 54 different types of Defensive Misplays. Part of the idea is not merely to count Defensive Misplays, but to identify them by type, so that we can understand what it is that the fielder has done that he shouldn't have done.

For the 2005 season, the data will exist, but it won't be public, at least not yet. It's expensive to count this stuff; it's not something you can do in your spare time. We'll make available what information about it we can, when we can. I would like for the information to be public, but we'll just have to take it one step at a time.

While counting Defensive Misplays, we will also count all kinds of other things, only one of which I will bother with here. The other thing I will try to explain is "Good Fielding Plays".

A Good Fielding Play is the counterpoint to a Defensive Misplay. It is a play that a fielder makes when you don't know whether he can make it or not. The main reason to count Good Fielding Plays, honestly, is fairness. If I were a major league player and somebody was going to go to this much trouble to identify every time I did something wrong, the first thing I would ask was whether he was also going to keep track of the things I did right. It is simple fairness.

As with Defensive Misplays, we have tried as hard as we could to make the definitions purely objective. Unfortunately, it's very hard to do. I'm not sure that I can explain why, but it is much harder to make a purely objective definition of a Good Fielding Play than it is a purely objective definition of a Defensive Misplay. I am afraid that much more subjective judgment will leak into the logbook of GFPs, and I suspect that the data will be less interesting because of that. But we'll do the best we can with it.

Doing research for this book—or any book about baseball anymore—I spent considerable time with Retrosheet. Retrosheet hyperlinks these "Dailies", which are day by day logs of a player's performance.

Seeing those hyperlinks to Fielder's Dailies, it occurred to me how uninteresting those would be, and this reminded me again of the essential failure of defensive statistics, which is the failure to create a portrait of the game or of the player's skills. The batter's daily logs are interesting, because you can find the games you remember, and you can find the games where a hitter did something extraordinary. I remember a game in which Brett gave the Royals the lead four times with four extra-base hits. . .you look at a log of his season, you can find that game.

Fielding dailies don't have that; it's just. . .this game the guy had 4 assists and a putout, that game he had 2 putouts and 2 assists. It has no descriptive power, so it doesn't connect to anything in our minds. John Dewan's Plus/Minus Rating System, as good a system as that is, won't make that connection for us.

But Defensive Misplays and Good Fielding Plays, if added to the daily logs, *would* make that connection. I remember a game that Frank White killed rally after rally after rally with brilliant defensive plays. . .I think seven of them. Don't you remember a game like that, with Mark Belanger or Ozzie Guillen or Torii Hunter or whoever your guy is?

In 2003, when I figured Defensive Misplays for the Red Sox, there was an inning in which the Red Sox made six Defensive Misplays in one half-inning. . .unbelievable, but it happened. No errors, but they fouled up six plays in one inning. Needless to say, the other team scored a bunch of runs. A daily log of DMs and GFPs, if it could be added to the record, would make those things stick out in the statistics like they do in our memory.

Baseball Info Solutions

Before you can argue about baseball statistics, you have to have accurate, helpful and innovative baseball statistics to argue about. Baseball Info Solutions (BIS) has been collecting, analyzing and supplying high quality, timely and in-depth baseball data to its customers since 2002.

BIS collects a statistical snapshot of every important moment of every Major League Baseball game with the most advanced technology, resulting in a database that includes traditional data, pitch-by-pitch data, and spray-chart hit location data. The company also has the highest quality pitch charting data available anywhere, including pitch type, location and velocity.

BIS provides comprehensive services to a dozen or so Major League Baseball teams, as well as many sports agents, media, fantasy services, game companies, and private individuals.

John Dewan, the principal owner of BIS, has been on the cutting edge of baseball analysis for over 20 years.

President Steve Moyer brings 15 years of baseball industry experience to BIS. His hands-on, can-do business attitude helps set BIS apart from its competition.

The rest of the BIS team includes former professional and collegiate baseball players as well as programming and database management experts. Over the last three seasons, BIS has more than tripled its full-time staff.

BIS publishes *The Bill James Handbook*, containing all the stats for the previous major league season, by November 1 of each year. They also publish an update of the batter and pitcher projections from the Handbook on March 1 called the *Bill James Handbook Projections Update*, available only as a downloadable file. *The Fielding Bible* is the newest BIS offering.

To contact BIS:

Baseball Info Solutions
528 North New Street
Bethlehem, PA 18018-5752
610-814-0107
www.baseballinfosolutions.com
info@baseballinfosolutions.com

BEHIND-THE-SCENES BASEBALL
Real-Life Applications of Statistical Analysis
Actually Used by Major League Teams… and Other Stories
DOUG DECATUR

DOUG DECATUR lives in Williamsburg, Ohio, with his wife Caitlin and their two sons, Stephen and Joseph. Decatur has worked as a statistical consultant for the Cincinnati Reds, Milwaukee Brewers, Chicago Cubs, Manager Phil Garner of the Houston Astros, and player agent Myles Shoda. He has an MBA from Xavier University.

For the baseball fan wondering why, when and how analytical managers and GMs make key decisions in a game and over a season, this insider's book explains the practical applications of statistics in baseball. Written in three parts, *Behind-the-Scenes Baseball* begins with stories from Doug Decatur's long career as a statistical consultant. He details how teams have successfully used statistical analyses when building a team, making key decisions in a game, and preparing for the postseason. He also details the ignominious failures of teams that have ignored what the numbers have told them.

Part two is the GM IQ Test—what every major league manager and GM should know… but doesn't. Match your wits against some of the smartest baseball gurus out there. There's one manager who will be tough to beat — Houston Astros' manager Phil Garner only missed one question! Questions are multiple choice, true/false, and essay format.

The third part is a concise look at the Houston Astros 2004 run for the pennant, Decatur's relationship with Manager Phil Garner, and the Astro's amazing 36-10 run and their first-ever postseason series win.

While many baseball fans may have ambiguous feelings about the role statistical analysis plays in the game, this book shows how statistics and "sabermetrics" don't detract from the passion of the game, but rather contribute to an understanding of and love for baseball.

Sample GM IQ Test questions:

1) The correlation between winning a division title and leading the league in which category is the weakest:

    (A) home runs   (C) stolen bases

    (B) batting average   (D) walks

2) True or False — No team last in the league in walks has ever won a World Championship.

ANSWERS: 1) C; 2) True

256 pages, paperback
ISBN: 0-87946-300-7, $14.95

www.actasports.com

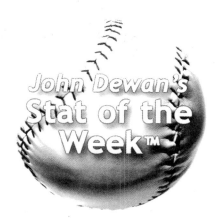